A EUROPA E OS DESAFIOS
DO SÉCULO XXI

INSTITUTO EUROPEU DA FACULDADE DE DIREITO DE LISBOA
AREP – ASSOCIAÇÃO INTERUNIVERSITÁRIA DE ESTUDOS EUROPEUS
PÓLO EUROPEU DA UNIVERSIDADE DE LISBOA

A EUROPA E OS DESAFIOS DO SÉCULO XXI

CONFERÊNCIA INTERNACIONAL

Organizadores:
PAULO DE PITTA E CUNHA
LUÍS SILVA MORAIS

ALMEDINA
2008

A EUROPA E OS DESAFIOS DO SÉCULO XXI

ORGANIZADORES
PAULO DE PITTA E CUNHA
LUÍS SILVA MORAIS

EDITOR
EDIÇÕES ALMEDINA, SA
Av. Fernão Magalhães, n.º 584, 5.º Andar
3000-174 Coimbra
Tel.: 239 851 904
Fax: 239 851 901
www.almedina.net
editora@almedina.net

PRÉ-IMPRESSÃO | IMPRESSÃO | ACABAMENTO
G.C. GRÁFICA DE COIMBRA, LDA.
Palheira – Assafarge
3001-453 Coimbra
producao@graficadecoimbra.pt

Abril, 2008

DEPÓSITO LEGAL
274333/08

Os dados e as opiniões inseridos na presente publicação
são da exclusiva responsabilidade do(s) seu(s) autor(es).

Toda a reprodução desta obra, por fotocópia ou outro qualquer
processo, sem prévia autorização escrita do Editor, é ilícita
e passível de procedimento judicial contra o infractor.

Biblioteca Nacional de Portugal - Catalogação na Publicação

CONFERÊNCIA INTERNACIONAL A EUROPA E OS DESAFIOS
DO SÉCULO XXI, Lisboa, 2007

A Europa e os Desafios do Século XXI : [actas] / Conferência Internacional
A Europa... ; [org.] Instituto Europeu da Faculdade de Direito de Lisboa,
Associação Interuniversitária de Estudos Europeus ; org. Paulo de Pitta e
Cunha, Luís Silva Morais
ISBN 978-972-40-3491-1

I – UNIVERSIDADE DE LISBOA. Faculdade de Direito. Instituto Europeu
II – ASSOCIAÇÂO INTERUNIVERSITÁRIA DE ESTUDOS EUROPEUS
III – CUNHA, Paulo de Pita e, 1937-
IV – MORAIS, Luís

CDU 342

APRESENTAÇÃO

A presente edição reúne os textos que correspondem às intervenções dos oradores que se ocuparam dos diferentes temas previstos no programa da Conferência Internacional sobre "A Europa e os Desafios do Século XXI".

A todos se agradece a disponibilidade que tiveram para elaborar a versão escrita das respectivas intervenções, ou para rever os extractos das gravações das sessões da Conferência.

Os organizadores exprimem o seu apreço pela excelente colaboração dos Mestres Sónia Donário, Olívio Mota Amador e Nuno Cunha Rodrigues, e manifestam o seu agradecimento pelas colaborações das entidades patrocinadoras referidas em outra página deste livro, sem as quais a Conferência Internacional não teria tido a amplitude que alcançou, com a participação de alguns dos maiores especialistas mundiais na temática da integração. Tratou-se, sem dúvida, de um acontecimento ímpar no quadro das iniciativas desta índole.

Lisboa, Março de 2008

PAULO DE PITTA E CUNHA
LUÍS DA SILVA MORAIS

A EUROPA E OS DESAFIOS DO SÉCULO XXI
– No Limiar da Presidência Portuguesa da União Europeia

CONFERÊNCIA INTERNACIONAL

Quarta-feira, dia 27 de Junho de 2007

9h30m – Abertura da Conferência
Introdução
PAULO DE PITTA E CUNHA, Presidente da Direcção do Instituto Europeu da Faculdade de Direito de Lisboa

9h45m – 1ª Sessão
50 anos de integração europeia: Do Plano Schuman ao período de reflexão sobre o futuro Tratado Constitucional
ETIENNE CEREXHE (Universidade de Lovaina)

Política de Integração Europeia: Uma utopia realista?
GLYN MORGAN (Universidade de Harvard)

A Integração Europeia num mundo globalizado
LOUKAS TSOUKALIS (Universidade de Atenas)
11h15m – Debate

12h00m – 2ª Sessão
A evolução do sistema judiciário da União Europeia
KOEN LENAERTS (Juiz do Tribunal de Justiça da Comunidade Europeia)

O modelo social europeu e a Estratégia de Lisboa
ANTÓNIO VITORINO (Universidade de Lisboa)
13h00m – Debate

14h30m – 3ª Sessão
Os alargamentos e os limites da União Europeia
JEAN-CLAUDE GAUTRON (Universidade de Bordéus)

Democracia e integração europeia: Um legado de tensões e um potencial construtivo
CHRISTIAN JOERGES (Universidade de Bremen)

Os referendos no processo de ratificação dos Tratados Europeus
PHILIPPE MOREAU DEFARGES (Institut Français des Relations Internationales)
16h30m – Debate

17h00m – 4ª Sessão
A cooperação externa da União Europeia
EDUARDO PAZ FERREIRA (Universidade de Lisboa)

Constituição Europeia – Melhoria do processo comunitário de decisão?
SIMON HIX (London School of Economics)

O futuro da Constituição Europeia
JOSEPH H. WEILER (Universidade de Nova Iorque)

Constituição Europeia e Constituição da República Portuguesa
RUI MOURA RAMOS (Universidade de Coimbra e Presidente do Tribunal Constitucional)

As Presidências portuguesas de 1992 e 2000
FERNANDO NEVES (Secretario-Geral do Ministério dos Negócios Estrangeiros)

Quinta-feira, dia 28 de Junho de 2007

9h15m – 5ª Sessão
A coordenação das políticas económicas nacionais na integração europeia
JACQUES BOURRINET (Universidade de Aix-Marseille)

A hipótese de um referendo europeu
MARTIN SEIDEL (Universidade de Bonn)

A União Europeia e outros sistemas de integração
LUIZ OLAVO BAPTISTA (Universidade de São Paulo)
11h15m – Debate

11h45m – 6ª Sessão
O Pacto de Estabilidade e sua revisão
VITO TANZI (Universidade de George Washington).
A União Europeia – A caminho de um orçamento federal?
JOSÉ DA SILVA LOPES (Presidente do Montepio Geral)
13h15m – Debate

14h30m – 7ª Sessão
Política de concorrência e nacionalismo económico na UE e nos EUA
DOUG ROSENTHAL (Universidade de Yale)

A função de redistribuição da União Europeia
WILLEM MOLLE (Universidade Erasmus de Roterdão)

Europa e Estados Unidos no Século XXI – A visão americana da política externa
e de defesa da UE
JOAQUIN ROY (Universidade de Miami)

Função reguladora e estruturas de regulação na UE
LUÍS SILVA MORAIS (Universidade de Lisboa)
16h30m – Debate

17h15m – 8ª Sessão
A União Europeia nas negociações comerciais internacionais
TERESA MOREIRA (Universidade de Lisboa)

A reacção europeia às alterações climáticas
DIMITRI ZENGHELIS (Membro da Comissão Stern)

A Europa e a dependência energética – Que caminhos para o mercado único da
energia?
PIET JAN SLOT (Universidade de Leiden)

As diferentes visões da integração europeia
PAULO DE PITTA E CUNHA (Universidade de Lisboa)
19h15m – Debate

Sexta-feira, dia 29 de Junho de 2007

Portugal e a integração europeia

9h15m – 9ª Sessão
Portugal e a Europa – o Passado
EDUARDO VERA-CRUZ PINTO (Universidade de Lisboa)

Aspectos históricos da integração de Portugal na Europa comunitária
MANUEL LOPES PORTO (Universidade de Coimbra)
11h00m – Debate

11h45m – 10ª Sessão
O envolvimento na integração económica e na integração política
JOÃO SALGUEIRO (Presidente da Associação Portuguesa de Bancos)

O modelo económico comunitário e a constituição económica portuguesa
MIGUEL POIARES MADURO (Advogado-Geral do Tribunal de Justiça das Comunidades Europeias)

O euro e a economia portuguesa
JOÃO FERREIRA DO AMARAL (Instituto Superior de Economia e Gestão)
13h15m – Debate

15h00m – 11ª Sessão
Portugal na Europa e no mundo
 Rui Machete (Presidente da Fundação Luso-Americana para o Desenvolvimento)
A política cultural europeia
 Emílio Rui Vilar (Presidente da Fundação Calouste Gulbenkian)
O programa da presidência portuguesa de 2007
 Luís Amado (Ministro dos Negócios Estrangeiros)

16h30m – 12ª Sessão

Mesa Redonda
A Presidência Portuguesa das Comunidades Europeias em 2007
e a situação da União Europeia

• Mário Soares
• José Pacheco Pereira
• António Goucha Soares
• José Medeiros Ferreira
• Marcelo Rebelo de Sousa
• Carlos Blanco de Morais

Moderaram as sessões da Conferências os Senhores Prof. Doutor Adriano Moreira (Universidade Técnica de Lisboa), Prof. Doutor André Gonçalves Pereira (Universidade de Lisboa), Prof. Doutor António de Sousa (Universidade Nova de Lisboa), Prof. Doutor Eduardo Paz Ferreira (Universidade de Lisboa), Conselheiro Guilherme d'Oliveira Martins (Presidente do Tribunal de Contas), Prof. Doutor Jorge Miranda (Universidade de Lisboa), Doutor Jorge Sampaio, Prof. Doutor José da Cruz Villaça (Universidade Nova de Lisboa), Conselheiro José Cunha Rodrigues (Juiz do Tribunal de Justiça das Comunidades Europeias) e Prof. Doutor Luís Silva Morais (Universidade de Lisboa).

A conferência realizou-se no Auditório 2 da Fundação Calouste Gulbenkian, na Avenida de Berna em Lisboa.

A Conferência contou com o patrocínio da Fundação Calouste Gulbenkian e da Fundação Luso-Americana para o Desenvolvimento, e o apoio da Embaixada de França, do Goethe Institut Lissabon, do British Council, do Ministério dos Negócios Estrangeiros, da Caixa Geral de Depósitos, do Banco de Portugal, do Banco Espírito Santo, do Millennium BCP, do Banco BPI e da Representação da Comissão Europeia em Portugal.

INTRODUÇÃO

Palavras proferidas na abertura da Conferência Internacional sobre "A Europa e os Desafios do Século XXI", na Fundação Gulbenkian, em 27 de Junho de 2007.

No final de 2006, o Instituto Europeu da Faculdade de Direito de Lisboa, em conjugação com a AREP – Associação Interuniversitária de Estudos Europeus, concebeu um projecto de um grande encontro internacional para debate, entre académicos, dos grandes desafios que se põem à integração europeia no Século XXI.

Previu-se fazer confluir este debate com a iminência da presidência portuguesa da União Europeia e com a celebração do meio centenário do Tratado de Roma, ao mesmo tempo que se comemorava a passagem do 20º aniversário do Instituto. Deveria estar então no auge a discussão das questões institucionais – como efectivamente aconteceu.

A ideia frutificou, tendo sido possível congregar numerosos especialistas no programa versado, quer oriundos de Universidades estrangeiras, quer provenientes de Instituições homólogas portuguesas.

Os dois primeiros dias da conferência foram reservados à problemática dos desafios postos, em geral, à União Europeia, quer no plano das relações externas, quer no da problemática interna da integração.

Entre os principais desafios contam-se o do enfrentamento da globalização, o da preservação do modelo social europeu (e desenvolvimento da estratégia de Lisboa que lhe está associada), os novos alargamentos, a questão institucional e o futuro do Tratado constitucional, a coordenação das políticas económicas, o Pacto de Estabilidade e a hipótese do orçamento federal, o nacionalismo económico no quadro da política de concorrência, as questões recentes da regulação, dos efeitos das alterações climáticas e da dependência energética, as relações entre a União e o mundo exterior.

O terceiro e último dia da conferência (29 de Junho) foi consagrado à temática de Portugal na Europa, nele se examinando o programa da presidência portuguesa de 2007 (após rememoração das duas anteriores presidências), e finalizando com uma mesa redonda sobre a situação da União Europeia e a Presidência portuguesa.

Cremos que dificilmente será possível juntar de novo um tão categorizado escol de especialistas internacionais, provenientes, entre outras, das Universidades de Harvard, Lovaina, Atenas, Bremen, Nova York, Londres (London School of Economics), Aix-en-Marseille, Bordéus, São Paulo, Yale, Roterdão, Leiden, incluindo ainda um dos membros da Comissão Stern, e também Juízes do Tribunal de Justiça das Comunidades Europeias, além de reputados cultores portugueses destas matérias.

Em nome das entidades organizadoras, formulo os melhores votos pelo êxito da Conferência.

Muito obrigado.

PAULO DE PITTA E CUNHA
Presidente da Direcção do Instituto Europeu da
Faculdade de Direito de Lisboa e do Conselho Directivo da AREP
– Associação Interuniversitária de Estudos Europeus

INTRODUCTION

Words delivered at the opening of the International Conference on "Europe and the Challenges of the 21st Century", at Gulbenkian Foundation, 27 June 2007.

By the ends of 2006, the European Institute of the Faculty of Law of Lisbon, in co-ordination with the AREP – Inter-University Association for European Studies, conceived the Project of a great international meeting to discuss among scholars the great challenges faced by the European integration in the 21st Century.

This debate was intended to coincide with the forthcoming Portuguese presidency of the European Union, celebration of the half century of the European Economic Community, commemorating at the same time the 20th anniversary of the Institute. The discussion of the institutional issues should by then be at its height (as it effectively happened to be).

The idea borne fruit and it was possible to congregate a considerable number of experts on the chosen topics, either from foreign universities or from homologous Portuguese institutions.

The first two days of the Conference were reserved to the problematic of challenges met by the European Union in general both at the level of external relations and of the internal integration issues.

Among such major challenges reference should be made to: the globalisation confront/defy; the maintenance of the European social model (and the development of the Lisbon Strategy connected thereto); the new enlargements; the institutional question and the future of the Constitutional Treaty; the coordination of the economic policies; the Stability and Growth Pact and the hypothesis of a federal budget; the economic nationalism in the framework of a competitiveness policy; the recent questions on regulation, impact of climate changes and energy dependence; the relations between the Union and the outside world.

The third and last day of the Conference (29 June) was consecrated to the theme of Portugal in Europe, during which the programme of the 2007 Portuguese presidency was analysed (after remembering the two previous presidencies), and concluding with a round-table on the situation of the European Union and the Portuguese Presidency.

We believe that it will be hard to join again such a distinguished cast of international experts, coming, among others, from Harvard, Louvain, Athens, Bremen, New York, London (London School of Economics), Aix--en-Marseille, Bordeaux, San Paulo, Yale, Rotterdam, Leiden Universities, including a member of the Stern Commission, and also Judges from the Court of Justice of the European Communities, besides some renowned Portuguese authorities on these subject matters.

On behalf of the organising entities, I am pleased to express our best wishes for the success of this Conference.

Thank you very much.

PAULO DE PITTA E CUNHA
President of the Board of the European Institute of
Faculty of Law of Lisbon and of the Board of AREP
– European Studies Interuniversities Association

50 ANS D'INTEGRATION EUROPEENNE: DU PLAN SCHUMAN A LA PERIODE DE REFLEXION SUR LA CONSTITUTION EUROPEENNE

ETIENNE CEREXHE[*]

On m'a demandé quelque chose qui est à peu près surhumain, c'est--à-dire de vous donner les éléments importants de la construction européenne pendant les cinquante dernières années. J'aurais pu passer en revue un certain nombre de dates. J'ai préféré choisir un certain nombre de thèmes et vous les présenter sous forme de tableau.

Premier tableau: l'objet de la construction européenne.

Que voulait-on en 1957 et que veut-on encore aujourd'hui? En 1957, nous voulions deux choses: la création d'un marché unique et un rapprochement des politiques des Etats membres.

1) Ce marché unique à l'origine, c'était une union douanière, la libre circulation des services, des personnes et des capitaux, le tout dominé par un principe unique de libre concurrence.

Petit à petit, la création de ce marché va évoluer dans l'Acte Unique Européen en 1986, dans lequel apparaît l'idée d'un marché intérieur qui doit être réalisé pour fin 1992. Ce marché intérieur va plus loin que le marché originaire, puisqu'il implique la suppression de toutes les frontières quelles qu'elles soient, de toutes les entraves à la libre circulation des marchandises, des personnes, des services et des capitaux.

---

[*] Juge à la Cour d'Arbitrage
Professeur à l'Université Catholique de Louvain et à la Faculté de Droit de Namur
Consul honoraire du Burkina Faso

Nous allons faire un pas de plus dans le Traité de Maastricht, (Traité sur l'Union Européenne). Nous allons réaliser la libre circulation des personnes indépendamment de toute activité économique. Ainsi apparaît l'idée de la citoyenneté européenne qui va être reprise dans le Traité d'Amsterdam et confirmée dans le Traité de Nice.

2) Le deuxième objet, c'est le rapprochement des politiques des Etats. A l'origine, nous avons été très audacieux, car nous avions envisagé des politiques communautaires et des politiques coordonnées: des politiques communautaires, c'est-à-dire de véritables politiques communes, dans les domaines de la politique agricole, de la politique de concurrence et de la politique commerciale; dans un certain nombre d'autres domaines simplement des politiques coordonnées.

Dans quelle mesure avons-nous évolué? Je ne crois pas que nous ayons évolué d'une manière très positive, car s'il est vrai que nous avons étendu les domaines de rapprochement des politiques, dans l'Acte Unique Européen et dans le Traité de Maastricht, notamment dans les domaines de la culture, de l'audiovisuel, de la protection du consommateur, de la santé, de l'éducation, ce sont des politiques coordonnées que l'on a mises en place, et non des politiques communes.

Dans le Traité sur l'Union Européenne, il y a lieu en outre de mettre en évidence:

a) L'extension du champ des compétences de la Communauté européenne;

b) Le renforcement de la cohésion économique et sociale;

c) L'enclenchement d'un processus irréversible vers l'Union économique et monétaire;

d) L'affirmation du principe de subsidiarité et de proportionnalité.

Enfin, le Traité d'Amsterdam va renforcer les moyens d'action de la Communauté dans certaines politiques qui touchent à la libre circulation des personnes (asile, immigration).

Deuxième tableau: le cadre géographique.

Le cadre géographique a évolué dans une mesure considérable. Nous étions six en 1957 et puis nous avons eu toute une série d'adhésions. L'adhésion difficile, hésitante, de la Grande Bretagne, du Danemark et de l'Irlande, qui se rendaient compte qu'ils ne pouvaient pas laisser de côté la naissance d'une intégration dont ils ne seraient pas parties. Et puis nous avons eu l'adhésion de la Grèce, en grande partie pour consolider la démocratie qui s'était installée dans le pays. Ensuite, l'adhésion de l'Espagne et du Portugal, un peu pour la même raison. A partir du moment où ces pays avaient vu naître la démocratie, nous devions assurer, consolider et fortifier cette démocratie naissante. Ce fut en 1995 l'adhésion de l'Autriche, de la Finlande et de la Suède, mais pour des raisons différentes: ce sont des pays industrialisés où la démocratie existait depuis longtemps, mais qui se rendaient compte qu'ils ne pouvaient pas rester à l'entour d'un système d'intégration. Enfin, en 2004 l'ensemble des pays de l'est adhéraient à l'Union Européenne et la Roumanie ainsi que la Bulgarie en 2007.

En réalité, l'Europe a profondément changé avec toutes ces adhésions, et ce à de nombreux points de vue. D'abord, du point de vue de la superficie et du nombre des habitants, mais elle a changé également du point de vue de sa configuration économique. Plusieurs pays ont un PIB qui est de 40% celui de la moyenne du PIB de l'Europe intégrée. Nous avons également une Europe qui est, du point de vue de ces membres, beaucoup plus hétérogène: 6 grands pays à côté de 21 ou 22 pays moyens et petits, des cultures et des langues différentes, des traditions diverses. Ensuite, nous avons des pays qui viennent de voir reconnaître leur souveraineté et qui ne sont pas prêts à l'abandonner rapidement. Enfin, il y a des pays qui sont plus atlantiques qu'européens, convaincus qu'ils seront mieux protégés dans le cadre de l'atlantisme que dans le cadre de l'Union Européenne.

Je voudrais tout de même encore vous dire un mot sur les limites. Sommes-nous au terme des élargissements? Est-ce que demain nous n'allons pas être confrontés à un problème important qui est celui de l'adhésion de la Turquie. Je ne ferais que poser le problème, car on ne m'a pas demandé de prendre position sur la question. Il est certain que l'adhésion de la Turquie présente des atouts: c'est l'ouverture à un grand marché; ensuite, la Turquie peut être un trait d'union entre l'Europe et le Moyen Orient; enfin, le multiculturalisme est finalement source de bénéfices et d'enrichissement pour tout le monde. Mais, il y a tout de même trois éléments qui nous forcent à réfléchir. D'abord, n'oublions pas que certains droits fondamentaux, comme le droit à l'égalité, n'ont pas la même consistance en Turquie que dans nos pays; je songe à l'égalité de l'homme et de la femme, à l'égalité des religions et à l'égalité des ethnies. Deuxièmement, il y a en Turquie un rôle politique non négligeable joué par le Conseil de Sécurité, dans lequel siègent les militaires. Enfin, troisième question qui nous interpelle, c'est le problème de la reconnaissance de Chypre. En conclusion, l'extension géographique de l'Europe vers la Turquie pose des questions.

Troisième tableau: le système institutionnel.

A l'origine, nous avions en 1957 deux organes, la Commission, qui était porteuse de la volonté européenne et le Conseil, qui était l'expression de la volonté des Etats. En réalité, la prise de décisions résultait d'un dialogue entre le Conseil et la Commission. Le Parlement était un organe parallèle, purement consultatif. Ce n'était qu'une assemblée composée de représentants des Etats. En 1976, la décision est prise d'élire le Parlement au suffrage universel direct. A partir du moment où, après les premières élections de 1979, on a un Parlement doté d'une nouvelle légitimité, il va être associé plus étroitement à la prise de décision. Et, contrairement à ce que nous avions à l'origine, une prise de décision fondée sur des rapports Conseil/Commission, nous allons avoir, à partir de 1979, une prise de décision fondée sur une relation Conseil/Commission/Parlement, qui va se traduire dans l'Acte Unique Européen, par la procédure de coopération et celle de l'avis conforme.

Dans le Traité de Maastricht on fait un pas de plus: c'est la procédure de codécision. En même temps, on voit apparaître deux nouveaux organes: le Comité des Régions, dont il ne faut pas dénier l'importance – et dans le débat toute à l'heure, je suis prêt à intervenir sur les problèmes du Comité des Régions, car certains sont aujourd'hui encore convaincus que l'Europe des régions est la voie dans laquelle nous devons nous engager – et, deuxièmement, le système des banques centrales.

Dans le Traité d'Amsterdam, la procédure de codécision et les pouvoirs du Parlement vont être élargis et simplifiés. Ensuite, on va en arriver à désigner, d'un commun accord entre le Parlement et le Conseil, le Président de la Commission et à faire confirmer le choix des Commissaires par le Parlement. Petit à petit, le Parlement est ainsi en train de prendre sa place dans le processus de décision, ce qui confère au système institutionnel un caractère plus démocratique.

Quatre réformes importantes sont introduites par le Traité de Nice: la pondération des voix au Conseil est modifiée; la répartition des sièges au niveau du Parlement est également revue pour ne pas avoir un Parlement pléthorique; il n'y a plus qu'un Commissaire par Etat membre, une rotation étant envisagée pour l'avenir; le système des concertations renforcées est simplifié.

Quatrième tableau: le système de financement.

A l'origine le système de financement était entièrement dépendant des contributions des Etats membres, sauf au niveau de la CECA. C'était une véritable allégeance de l'Europe à l'égard des Etats en ce qui concerne son financement. En 1970, on voit apparaître la notion de ressources propres. L'Europe va avoir son propre financement. Les ressources propres sont constituées par: 1) les droits du tarif douanier extérieur; 2) le prélèvement sur les échanges dans les relations avec les pays tiers dans le cadre de la PAC; 3) les recettes provenant de l'application d'un taux de 1% sur l'assiette de la TVA; et, enfin, les recettes provenant de l'application d'un taux, à fixer dans le cadre de la procédure budgétaire, au PNB des Etats membres. Cette quatrième recette m'apparaît avoir une certaine importance, car elle atténue la notion de ressources propres. Quant à la procédure budgétaire, je n'en parlerais pas. Elle s'articule sur la distinction entre dépenses obligatoires et dépenses non obligatoires; c'est encore aujourd'hui la procédure qui continue à s'appliquer.

Cinquième tableau: les droits fondamentaux.

Dès le début de la CEE, la Cour de Justice a très clairement affirmé que (l'arrêt du 15 juillet 1960) les droits fondamentaux font intégralement partie des principes généraux du droit, dont elle assure le respect et la sauvegarde, dans le cadre communautaire. Par la suite, il y eut toute une série d'arrêts qui font des références à ces droits fondamentaux.

En 1977 une déclaration commune du Parlement, du Conseil et de la Commission souligne l'importance fondamentale qu'il y a lieu d'attacher au respect des droits fondamentaux et indique que, dans l'exercice de leur pouvoir et en poursuivant les objectifs des Communautés, les trois institutions respecteront les droits fondamentaux tels qu'ils résultent, des Constitutions des Etats membres ainsi que de la Convention Européenne de Sauvegarde des Droits de l'Homme et des Libertés Fondamentales.

Après cette déclaration commune, c'est le Traité de Maastricht qui à l'article F.2 affirme que l'Union respecte les droits fondamentaux tels qu'ils sont garantis par la Convention Européenne de Sauvegarde des Droits de l'Homme et des Libertés Fondamentales et tels qu'ils résultent des traditions constitutionnelles communes aux Etats membres.

Etant donné que la Cour de Justice n'assurait pas le contrôle de cet article F.2 du Traité de Maastricht, le Traité d'Amsterdam fait un pas supplémentaire en reconnaissant la compétence à la Cour.

Enfin, il y a le Traité de Nice. En réalité, c'est le Conseil Européen de Biarritz qui a accepté et avalisé la Charte des Droits Fondamentaux, qui n'est malheureusement pas intégrée dans le Traité de Nice et qui n'a pas de force contraignante.

Dernier tableau: l'union politique.

Quand on parle de l'union politique, n'oublions pas que toute politique quelle qu'elle soit, économique, de concurrence, agricole, a une dimension politique. Lorsque l'on parle d'union politique, ce que l'on vise surtout c'est la politique étrangère, c'est-à-dire le comportement de l'Union à l'égard des pays tiers et son comportement dans les relations internationales. A l'origine, la Déclaration Schuman parlait d'une fédération européenne, ce qui avait un accent politique.

Après la signature du Traité CECA, nous signons le traité instituant la Communauté Européenne de défense, mais dès lors qu'on intégrait les armées on s'est rendu compte qu'on portait atteinte à la souveraineté des Etats. On sent donc le besoin d'une communauté politique européenne. Cette communauté politique européenne, en fait, nous la voulions, comme nous avons voulu la défense, parce que nous avions peur. C'était l'époque de la guerre froide. Mais lorsqu'il s'est agi de ratifier le Traité de la CED, Staline était mort et le Parlement français refusa la ratification. Nous n'avions plus peur. C'est le glas du Traité CED, c'est le glas de la construction de l'Europe politique.

Par la suite, nous avons eu en 1961 le Plan Fouchet qui prévoyait l'instauration d'une union indissoluble à laquelle était assignée l'élaboration en commun de la politique étrangère et de la politique de défense. Ce Plan là échoua, parce qu'il était trop marqué du sceau de l'intergouvernemental, dans le cadre duquel on voulait intégrer les Communautés européennes.

En 1969, c'est le Sommet de La Haye, où les ministres des affaires étrangères furent chargés d'étudier «la meilleure manière de réaliser des progrès dans le domaine de l'unification politique» et qui déboucha sur le rapport Davignon, qui prévoyait une concertation en matière de politique étrangère, en marge du système communautaire.

En 1974, l'idée s'imposa d'institutionnaliser les Sommets qui devaient se réunir trois fois par an, à la fois comme organe de la coopération politique et comme une formation du Conseil des Communautés.

L'Acte Unique Européen de 1987 consacra formellement l'existence du Conseil européen. Il a en outre prévu un certain nombre de dispositions sur «la coopération européenne en matière de politique étrangère».

Le Traité de Maastricht va lui, dans le deuxième pilier, aller plus loin et définir la politique étrangère et de sécurité commune. Mais, reconnaissons-le les modes d'action sont limités: la coordination, la coopération, la définition de stratégie commune et ce à l'unanimité.

Le Traité de Amsterdam a peut-être fait un pas de plus en sorte qu'il atténue la règle de l'unanimité par ce que l'on a appelé les abstentions constructives et dans le Traité de Nice, la coopération est renforcée dans les trois piliers, c'est-à-dire que la coopération partielle entre un certain nombre d'Etats, qui à l'origine n'était possible que dans le cas du Traité CEE, est aujourd'hui étendue aux trois piliers.

Conclusions

Lorsqu'en 1950 l'idée de la construction européenne est née, elle était inspirée d'une part par la peur, d'autre part par une certaine rationalité. Il en est résulté une espèce d'enthousiasme pour l'Europe dans les années 52, 53, 57. Je me rappelle avoir entendu un grand européen, Pierre-Henri Teitgen, venant parler à l'Université de Louvain devant des centaines d'étudiants enthousiastes pour l'Europe. Cela aujourd'hui nous ne le connaissons plus. C'est vrai que notre monde a changé, de bipolaire qu'il était à l'origine, les Etats-Unis et l'URSS, il est devenu multipolaire. Nous voyons l'émergence de pays comme l'Inde, la Chine, le

Japon. Malgré cette dimension mondiale de la planète, que constatons-nous chez nous? Des relents de souveraineté, des relents d'égoïsme, des relents de nationalisme. Nous devons surmonter ces «vers» dans la construction européenne. Il faut retrouver la foi en l'Europe, une foi fondée sur la raison. Il faut avoir confiance et foi dans l'Europe, mais il faut rationnellement aussi comprendre, comme le disait le Premier Ministre Belge qui avait été chargé par le Conseil Européen de rédiger le rapport sur l'Union européenne, que la voix d'un seul Etat aujourd'hui est inaudible. Seuls, isolés, le Etats perdent consistance. Il faut une Europe forte et solide, sinon nous serons dans une ou deux générations un continent sous-développé.

EUROPEAN INTEGRATION AS A REALISTIC UTOPIA[*]

GLYN MORGAN[1]

The title of my talk today derives from the work of John Rawls, perhaps the most influential twentieth century political philosopher. In his later work, Rawls argued that a central task of political philosophy is to propose, what he terms, "realistic utopias."[2] In other words, a conception of justice put forward to regulate any "utopia" must also be "realistic" – it must respect the inescapable conditions of our social and political world. In his own work, Rawls identifies and defends two different "realistic utopias:" one, a domestic society that protects individual liberties and organizes its institutions in accordance with the interests of the least well-off (what Rawls terms "justice as fairness"); and two, an international society that consists of independent "peoples," and which allows liberal and decent societies a robust right of non-intervention ("the law of peoples"). For Rawls – if not for his critics – these two "realistic utopias" are compatible and complementary.[3]

---

[*] Paper (Revised January 2008) Prepared for the International Conference, "A Europa e os Desafios do Seculo XXI," Lisbon, Portugal, June 27-9, 2007.

[1] Associate Professor of Government and Social Studies. Harvard University. glynmorgan@aol.com

[2] For Rawls's account of a "realistic utopia," see John Rawls, *Law of Peoples* (Cambridge: Harvard University Press, 1999), 4-7, 124; *Justice as Fairness: A Restatement* (Cambridge: Harvard University Press, 2000), 4, 13. There are earlier anticipations of this concept in such passages as: "We strive for the best we can attain within the scope the world allows," *Political Liberalism*, (New York: Columbia University Press, 1993), 88.

[3] For a powerful criticism that questions the compatibility of Rawls's domestic and international political theories, see Thomas W. Pogge, "The Law of Peoples: The Incoherence Between Rawls's Theories of Justice," *Fordham Law Review* 72 (2004), 1739-1754.

Given this quintessentially liberal perspective on domestic and international society, it might have been expected that Rawls would have endorsed the project of European integration. Surprisingly, he did not. In a series of posthumously published letters, Rawls reveals himself to be something of a Eurosceptic.[4] Interestingly, Rawls's Euroscepticism reflects a line of argument that was popular on the left in Britain in the 1970s and which re-emerged (albeit in a slightly different form) on the left in France at the time of the Constitutional Referendum in 2005: namely, that European integration works to the advantages of businessmen and disadvantages the least well off in Europe. (In the French terminology, European integration is a stalking horse for neo-liberalism, delocalization, and globalization.)[5]

Rawls's argument against European integration deserves further consideration, not least because it raises some difficult questions about social justice and European integration. In my talk today, I want to draw upon Rawls's work on justice to say something, admittedly preliminary and doubtless inadequate, about an important aspect of European political integration – namely European Enlargement. My argument proceeds in three parts. Part One argues that European Enlargement can be viewed as a form of "managed globalization." In this section, I argue that many of the ethical debates over globalization – including debates over "fair trade" – apply *a fortiori* in the case of European Enlargement. Part Two examines John Rawls's skeptical position on European political integration. And Part Three argues that despite Rawls's own skepticism, a case can be made that European Enlargement constitutes, what he could endorse as, "a realistic utopia."

---

[4] John Rawls and Philippe Van Parijs. "Three letters on *The Law of Peoples* and the European Union," *Revue de philosophie économique*, 7, 2003, pp. 7-20 (available at http://www.uclouvain.be/cps/ucl/doc/etes/documents/RawlsVanParijs1.Rev.phil.Econ.pdf)

[5] Thus in a post-referendum poll in France, the most common reason mentioned for voting "no" was: "It will have negative effects on the employment situation in France/relocation of French enterprises/loss of jobs," see "The European Constitution: Post Referendum Survey in France," *Eurobarometer* 2005 (available at http://ec.europa.eu/public_opinion/flash/fl171_en.pdf)

I – European Enlargement as Managed Globalization

In some respects, European Enlargement has been the most successful feature of the postwar process of European integration. The admission of Portugal, Spain, and Greece in 1986 to the then European Community is now widely seen as one of the shining moments of postwar Europe. The admission of ten new countries in May 2004 (and two further ones in January 2007) might be seen in the same favorable light. And yet, European Enlargement is an issue mired in controversy. Part of the controversy concerns the prospective admission of Turkey – a country much larger and much poorer than any other country recently admitted. But some of the controversy attaches to the European Enlargement that took place in 2004 and 2007. Simply stated, this Enlargement has initiated a form of labor and capital mobility that came as a surprise to many Europeans. Some examples:

(i) By the end of 2007, it was estimated that there were nearly 500,000 Romanians living or working in Italy. In the face of a rising tide of anti-immigration sentiment, Prime Minister Prodi conceded, "Nobody was expecting the outflow from Romania... [P]sychologically and socially, the speed, the impact is incredible... [F]or necessity Italy is prepared. And businessmen they press for more immigration. In psychological terms it is an enormous change."[6]

(ii) Two years after enlargement, it was estimated that about 600,000 Poles were working in Britain. The overall economic impact of these Polish workers is hard to assess. But on one view, these workers depress wages in some sectors of the British economy – the building trades, for instance – and they make it less likely that companies will train unskilled British workers when they can hire skilled Polish workers. The joint effect of this is to produce "a benefit trap" – unskilled British workers find their skills insufficient to earn in the labor markets any more than they can receive in state benefits.[7]

---

[6] "Prodi expands on EU migration," *Financial Times*, Nov 06, 2007.

[7] "Outline of the Problem." *MigrationWatch* 2007 (available at http://www.migrationwatchuk.com/outline_of_the_problem.asp).

(iii) The Polish Ministry of Labor estimates that between 600,000 and 1 million workers have left Poland for Western Europe. This out-migration of workers, mostly younger and more qualified, has caused labor shortages in key sectors of the Polish economy. For instance, nearly 20 per cent of Poland's anesthesiologists have gone abroad to work. In an effort to fill labor shortages, Poland is employing increasing numbers of Ukrainian workers.[8]

(iv) The Western European car industry has long been a source of high paid manufacturing jobs. The car industry in Germany, for example, still provides one in seven of its manufacturing jobs. Hourly labor costs in Germany remain, however, more than triple those in the Czech Republic and Slovakia; and more than seven times those in Romania. Not surprisingly, the car industry is building more car plants in Eastern and Central Europe. Volkswagen now assembles cars in Slovakia; and Peugeot and Citroen assemble cars in Kolin in the Czech Republic. The movement of the car industry from west to east is likely to continue.

The types of changes described in the four examples are neither exclusive to Europe, nor attributable entirely to European Enlargement. In some respects, such changes go on all over the world, both within and between different countries. Thus in the United States, the shoe industry, once concentrated in the Northeastern states, moved, first, to the southern states of the USA, and, more recently, to China. In recent years, a consensus appears to be emerging that global labor and capital mobility – "globalization," in short – while generally desirable, can nonetheless hurt certain groups of workers in developed countries, particularly the unskilled, who face job losses and declining relative wages.[9] In the United States, much of the debate over globalization has focused on the rise of Chinese manufacturing exports and the outsourcing of service jobs to India. In Europe, the debate has focused on European Enlargement, which, at

---

[8] "Gone West: Why eastern Europe is laboring under an abundance of jobs," *Financial Times*, January 18 2008.

[9]. Paul Krugman, "Trade and Inequality, Revisited," available at http://www.voxeu.org/index.php?q=node/261.

least in the short run, promises to have a greater impact on people's lives than the rise of China and India. A French or German car worker is more likely to see his or her job go to Slovakia than go to China or India.

To describe the economic changes initiated by European Enlargement as a form of globalization is, however, somewhat misleading. European Enlargement is different from globalization as we normally think of it, because of the following five factors:

(i) The European Union defines a common regulatory regime that seeks to remove national obstacles to European-wide economic activity. Moreover, this is a regulatory regime with teeth. The European Court has the authority to penalize national states and corporations whose actions violate EU law.

(ii) The European Union is legally committed – through its founding Treaty of Rome and its later formative treaties – to "four freedoms" of movement (goods, capital, services, and people).

(iii) The European Union calls into question the ethical and political significance of national boundaries within the EU. Indeed, the preamble to the Treaty of Rome sets the EU's member states on the road to "an ever closer union."

(iv) The European Union provides something of a democratic forum – which include the EU Council and EU Parliament – where those disadvantaged by the "four freedoms" can, through their elected representatives, air their grievances, and seek redress.

(v) The European Union is committed to some form of a social market. In its founding treaties, it acknowledges as one of the Union's objectives "a highly competitive social market economy, aiming at full employment and social progress."[10]

These five factors bear on the process of globalization in different ways. Factors (i) and (ii) and (iii) work to speed up and intensify the processes of labor and capital mobility. While (iv) and (v) seek, however inadequately, to ensure that the European Union is something other than a pure market order. In short, (iv) and (v) aim to temper globalization – to modify its effects in accordance with the will of Europe's citizens and with a conception of social justice. Needless to say, there is considerable

---

[10] Treaty Article 1:3.

disagreement within European concerning the appropriate balance between these two forms of globalization. Part of the difficulty here is that globalization affects different groups of people in different ways. Thus while it might hurt the highly paid German car worker; it might benefit the no less highly paid German software engineer and, through eventually lowering the price of cars, it might benefit German consumers.

To confine attention to the effects of globalization on the members of any single nation is, however, to ignore one of the distinctive features of European Enlargement as a form of globalization – namely (iii) above – the establishment of an overarching European legal and political community that entails a conception of European membership that, in certain instances, takes priority over national membership. To give an illustration of the importance of this dimension of the European Union, another example would be helpful.

In January 2008, one year after the entry of Bulgaria and Romania into the EU, the Finnish Company Nokia announced that it was closing its factory in Bochum, Germany and moving its production to a new factory in Cluj, Romania. This plan involved 2300 workers in Bochum losing their jobs, while 4300 Romanians gained new jobs. The management of Nokia justified their decision, on the basis of the lower wage costs in Romania. Initially, it was thought that the Bochum workers would be helped by the EU globalization fund, which is intended to compensate workers who lose their jobs from globalization. But then it became apparent that this globalization fund could be used only when firms relocated outside the EU. If Nokia had relocated their factory to China, the workers might have received assistance, but since the firm relocated within Europe, they received nothing from this fund. In other words, Europe – a Europe that includes Romania and Bulgaria – is now the relevant boundary when it comes to compensating workers for jobs lost to globalization.[11]

The Nokia plant closing helps focus the question of whether it makes any difference whether a worker loses a job to a firm that: (a) relocates from one area in a nation to another in the same nation (moving, say, from Bochum, Germany to Stuttgart, Germany); (b) relocates from one nation in the EU to another in the EU (moving, as in case of Nokia,

---

[11] "German protests grow over Nokia relocation." *Financial Times*, January 19/20; "EU bietet Nokia-Mitarbeitern Hilfe an," *Der Spiegel*, January 19 2008.

from Germany to Romania); or (c) relocates from somewhere in Europe to somewhere outside of Europe (moving say from Germany to China). From the perspective of the workers who lose their jobs, it is difficult to see what the difference is between (a), (b), and (c). Perhaps, it could be argued that in case (a), the workers laid off in one place could move to the other – something not possible in cases (b) and (c) – but absent this possibility, the three cases, when seen from the perspective of the job-losers, seem identical.

Clearly, the difference between (a), (b), and (c) emerges only when we consider the beneficiaries of the relocation. There are a number of different ways of characterizing these beneficiaries. Typically, in debates about trade, factory relocation, and outsourcing – globalization, in short – the focus is on the group that benefits. Domestic supporters of globalization commonly say that while trade, relocation, and outsourcing might hurt some specific workers in country X, it is nonetheless the case that country X as a whole benefits.[12] It is also possible to distinguish a more hard-nosed utilitarian position that denies the relevance of particular national (or sub-national) boundaries. Following this utilitarian logic, trade agreements, factory relocation, and outsourcing are all desirable, insofar as they improve the aggregate welfare of all those affected, regardless of national boundaries. From this utilitarian perspective, the distribution of benefits (between, say, Germany, Romania, and China) is unimportant, so long as it leads to an aggregate gain in benefits. In other words, if a trade agreement produced gains in benefits to those outside Germany that exceeded the losses in benefits to those inside Germany, then the utilitarian would consider the trade agreement justified.

There remain some obvious difficulties with this crude utilitarian perspective. For one thing, it is politically unrealistic. Imagine the German politician who supported a trade agreement that was bad for his constituents, bad (at least in the short term) for Germany, but good on some aggregative measure that took in a broader section of humanity.

---

[12] Thus consider, for example, the following comment from a neo-classical economist: "All economists know that when American jobs are outsourced, Americans as a group are net winners. What we lose through lower wages is more than offset by what we gain through lower prices." Steven Landsburg, "What to expect when you are free trading," *New York Times*, January 16 2008.

Such a politician would soon be out of office. This is not to suggest that one has to be a nationalist to oppose utilitarian approaches to globalization. Indeed, it is possible to identify a fairness-based objection to utilitarianism in general and globalization in particular. It is here that John Rawls's moral and political philosophy is so important.

II – Rawls, Van Parijs, and Euroscepticism

There are many reasons why John Rawls is celebrated as the most influential twentieth century political philosopher. Perhaps the most obvious reason is that his writings provided a philosophical justification for elevating distributive considerations – considerations of fairness, in other words – above the purely aggregative considerations favored by utilitarians. No less importantly, Rawls's political philosophy is of practical importance, because it focuses on the merits of different institutional arrangements. Thus Rawls invites us, to put it very simply, to consider how different domestic and international institutional arrangements contribute to the well-being of two representative citizens: (i) the free and equal citizen; and (ii) the citizen who is the least well-off in material terms.[13]

John Rawls never mentions European integration in any of his written works. His position emerges only in a series of letters (published posthumously) exchanged with the Belgian political philosopher Philippe van Parijs. The context of the exchange concerns the compatibility of the position that Rawls takes on distributive justice in the domestic and international realms. For the domestic realm – i.e. within the state – Rawls defends a robust form of redistribution. More specifically, he favors a conception of justice that requires societal institutions to maximize the social and economic position of the least well-off (the so called "difference principle"). Yet for the international realm, Rawls defends a much less demanding conception of justice. When it comes to the redistribution of material goods, rich states (and their members) owe poor states (and their members) only duties of charity.

In their exchange of letters, Van Parijs presses Rawls on the criteria that distinguish the domestic from the international realms, particularly

---

[13] This summary account is, to be sure, a crude simplification of Rawls's argument in his *Theory of Justice* (Cambridge: Harvard University Press, 1971).

because Rawls refers to his international political theory as "the law of peoples" not "the law of states." Yet if "peoples" are the relevant category, as Van Parijs points out, then why is it not the case that, say, Flems owe Walloons only duties of charity not the duty to distribute according to Rawls's more demanding difference principle? And what happens, Van Parijs asks, in the case of the European Union? Do the members of the EU owe each other duties of charity or duties of social solidarity?

In his answer, Rawls appears to be skeptical of whether the duties of social solidarity will survive the abolition of Europe's nation-states and the creation of a more integrated polity. This leads him to make the following remark:

> One question the Europeans should ask themselves, if I may hazard a suggestion, is how far–reaching they want their union of be. It seems to me that *much would be lost if the European union became a federal union like the United States....* The large open market including all of Europe is the aim of the large banks and the capitalist business class whose main goal is simply larger profit. The idea of economic growth, onwards and upwards, with no specific end in sight, fits this class perfectly. If they speak about distribution, it is [al]most always in terms of trickle-down. The long–term result of this – which we already have in the United States – is a civil society awash in a meaningless consumerism of some kind. I can't believe that that is what you want (emphasis added).[14]

While Rawls's remarks on the EU are made only in a personal letter and cannot be taken as a considered position, these remarks are worth taking seriously because they coincide with a line of criticism developed by a number of European social democrats who share Rawls's commitment to redistribution. The criticism can be put very simply: the European Union establishes a European-wide market anchored by the four freedoms of movement (goods, capital, services, and people), but it does not establish a European-wide welfare regime that can adequately compensate losers in the European market. Indeed, under present rules, the EU limits compensation to cases where companies move outside EU borders; and it constrains the types of financial assistance that a region or nation can give to their companies to persuade them to remain put.

---

[14] Rawls, "Three Letters," 5.

Scholars have identified a number of different explanations for the asymmetrical development of Europe's market and Europe's welfare regime. For present purposes, we can distinguish two different explanations for this asymmetry: (i) an institutional explanation; and (ii) a socio-psychological explanation. According to the institutional explanation – developed most fully by Fritz Scharpf – EU policies and institutions make it easier to strike down national obstacles to economic integration – negative integration, as it has been called – than it is to develop new European-wide welfare institutions – positive integration.[15] None of this would matter, if national welfare regimes could coexist with a European-wide market. But the graver institutional worry is that European economic integration will contribute to the erosion of national welfare regimes. Due to increased capital mobility, European nation-states that fund generous welfare regimes through high personal and company taxation find themselves losing out to nation-states with less generous welfare regimes and lower taxation. The EU, in short, facilitates a race to the bottom.

The social-psychological explanation for Europe's asymmetrical development points to the absence of a European-wide sense of common nationality or "we-feeling." The premise of this argument is that human beings can share a sense of solidarity only with those with whom they share a sense of commonality. In the modern world, the widest body capable of engendering such a sense of commonality is the nation. People who share a common nationality are uniquely willing, so it is claimed, to make sustained sacrifices on each others' behalf. Such sacrifices are necessary, if a modern polity is to establish a welfare state. The fact that Europe lacks a welfare state – and from this perspective will always lack a welfare state – can be explained solely on the basis of Europe's lack of a common nationality.

At first glance, it seems that Rawls's hostility to European integration is based upon the social-psychological explanation. He does not think that a European wide polity would possess the sense of solidarity necessary to support distributive justice – particularly the demanding form of distributive justice envisaged by Rawls's so-called "difference

---

[15] Fritz Scharpf, *Government in Europe: Effective and Democratic* (Oxford: Oxford University Press, 1999).

principle."[16] In the *Law of Peoples*, Rawls certainly says a number of things that appear to support this line of argument. "[T]he affinity among peoples," he writes, "is naturally weaker (as a matter of human psychology) as society wide institutions include a larger area and cultural distances increase."[17] Furthermore, his point of departure when considering international society is a Westphalian society of nation-states. He sometimes seems to think that our commitment to a *realistic* utopia – a commitment to taking the world as it is – requires us to acknowledge the centrality of the nation-state and the international state system. And yet, he qualifies this inherent institutional conservatism in a number of important ways. Thus having appeared to endorse the sentiment of nationality "as a matter of human psychology," he goes on to endorse this very different thesis:

> The relatively narrow circle of mutually caring peoples in the world today may expand over time and must never be viewed as fixed. Gradually peoples...come to endorse their liberal and decent civilization and culture, until eventually they become ready to act on the ideals and principles their civilization specifies.[18]

Furthermore, a commitment to taking the political world as it is hardly leads to an endorsement of the nation-state and the Westphalian international state system, because the world as it is includes both nation-states and the European Union, which in its present form is anything but a nation-state. If Rawls is going to make good on his misgivings about the European Union, he needs a firmer peg to support his argument. I want to suggest that Rawls can support his argument against a federal Europe on the basis of two further interrelated arguments: (i) an argument concerning the least well-off; and (ii) an argument concerning national legal personality.

---

[16] According to Rawls's difference principle, social and political institutions ought to be arranged so that they benefit the least well-off. For the details, see Rawls, *Theory of Justice*.

[17] Rawls, *Law of Peoples*, 112.

[18] Rawls, *Law of Peoples*, 113.

(i) The Least Well-Off

Rawls's political theory has a great deal to say about the way to choose between alternative basic structures.[19] Simply stated, Rawls proposes a standard of justice – justice as fairness – as the criterion of evaluation. According to this conception of justice, a basic structure (i.e. political and social institutions) ought to guarantee a set of basic liberties for all individuals and ensure that the least well off have as much wealth and income (or what Rawls calls "social primary goods") as possible. For the moment, let's assume that basic liberties are equally well-protected in a Federal Europe as in a Europe of nation-states (or intergovernmental Europe). This being the case, we need only inquire into the situation of the least well-off.[20] Applied to the European situation, we need to ask whether the least well-off will fare better in a federal European Union than in a Europe of nation-states. If they fare better in a Europe of nation-states, then Rawls is right to criticize (as he does in the letter to Van Parijs) progress towards a federal European Union.

Given the fact that Rawls's argument rests upon a counterfactual – how the least well-off would fare in a federal European Union – his argument (or the one being imputed to him here at least) is difficult to evaluate. There are two ambiguities, in particular, that have to be resolved: *the least well-off where* – i.e. what geographical boundaries are relevant in identifying the least well-off? – and *the least well-off when* – i.e. what time frame is relevant in calculating the position of the least well-off? The importance of these questions can be illustrated by way of a couple of simplifying scenarios.

Imagine a Europe that consists of two sovereign nation-states. One nation-state is very rich – call it Germany – the other is very poor – call it Romania. Imagine further that each nation state has a population of

---

[19] The task of evaluating different basic structures can mean two rather different things: (i) how a basic structure ought to be designed – i.e. as if there were any number of options: and (ii) how, given a choice between a limited number of options, a basic structure should be chosen.

[20] The intricacies of Rawls's argument here need not concern us. For a helpful discussion, see Philippe Van Parijs, "Difference Principles," in Samuel Freeman ed., *The Cambridge Companion to Rawls* (Cambridge: Cambridge University Press, 2003).

European Integration as a Realistic Utopia

three thousand people; and the income distribution within and between both countries is as follows:

Table One

Germany	Income (thousands)	Romania	Income (thousands)
Top Third	100 Euros	Top Third	20 Euros
Middle Third	50 Euros	Middle Third	10 Euros
Bottom Third	20 Euros	Bottom Third	5 Euros
Gross Personal Income	170,000	Gross Personal Income	35,000

Given this income distribution (and assuming the income reflects purchasing power parity), then the least well off in Romania are much worse off than the least well-off in Germany. And Germans as a whole are much better off – nearly five times better off – than Romanians. Now imagine that Germany and Romania formed one country of six thousand people – call it a Federal Europe – with the following distribution of incomes. (Here it would be useful to distinguish two different scenarios: (i) an economically stagnant Europe; and (ii) an economically vibrant Europe.)

Table Two

Stagnant Europe	Income (thousands)	Vibrant Europe	Income (thousands)
Top Third	60 Euros	Top Third	120 Euros
Middle Third	30 Euros	Middle Third	60 Euros
Bottom Third	12.5 Euros	Bottom Third	24 Euros
Gross Personal Income	205,000	Gross Personal Income	408,000

The important point to recognize in Table Two is the position of the least well-off. In Stagnant Europe, which has a Gross Personal Income of Germany and Romania combined, the least well-off have an income of 12,500 Euros. This represents a huge gain for the *ex post* least well-off in Romania, when measured against the *ex ante* least well-off in Romania, but a huge loss for the *ex post* least well-off, when measured against the *ex ante* least well-off in Germany. In such a situation, it would seem that Romanians who cared about *their* own least well-off would support a federal Europe, because *their* least well-off fare better in both Stagnant Europe and Vibrant Europe. The situation facing the Germans is more complicated. On the face of it, Germans ought to embrace a Federal Europe only insofar as it leads to Vibrant Europe. From the German perspective, a Stagnant Europe diminishes the well-being of *their* least well-off.

This scenario provides qualified support for Rawls's rejection of a Federal Europe. His argument, on this interpretation, boils down to the claim that a Federal Europe must be rejected if it entails any lowering of the material welfare of the least well-off of one's co-nationals. I say qualified support, only because it suggests that Romanians who care about *their* least well-off ought to support a Federal Europe whether Stagnant or Vibrant. Furthermore, even Germans ought to support a Federal Europe if it were likely to become Vibrant. This last point raises the further question of the time frame relevant for assessing the emergence of Stagnant and Vibrant Europe. In *Theory of Justice*, Rawls makes it quite clear that we are to assess alternative basic structures in terms of the minimum representative lifetime share of social primary goods. This suggests that we must consider developments over, say, a 30 year time period. This being the case, the relevant comparison is the projected *ex post* positions of the least well-off in Germany and the least well-off in Vibrant Europe over a 30 year time period. In short, we must decide between alternative basic structures – and thus between a Federal Europe and a Europe of Nation-States – on the basis of counterfactual judgments about economic growth over the next thirty years.

On the basis of these scenarios, we are now in a position to provide an argument that might support Rawls's rejection of a Federal Europe. The argument rests on the claim that a Federal Europe fails to improve the condition of one's least well-off co-nationals. This argument is, however, rather weak. For one thing, it offers, what philosophers call, an *agent-relative* rather than an *agent neutral* reason to oppose a Federal Europe. (In other words, it offers a reason not for all people, but only for people whose least well-off co-nationals would fare worse in a Federal Europe than in their own nation-state.) Furthermore, it begs the question why "least well-off co-nationals" is the relevant reference group, rather than "least well-off Europeans in general" or "least well-off members of my sub-national group." Such questions about the relevant reference group cut to the heart of Van Parijs's challenge to Rawls in their exchange of letters. For Rawls's argument to be persuasive, he must justify prioritizing the welfare of co-nationals – and co-nationals in the sense of people who share a common state rather than co-nationals who share a common language or ethnicity.

(ii) National Legal Personality

One of the most striking – and to critics, most disappointing – features of Rawls's international political theory is the central place it allots to the nation-state and the priority it gives to our obligations to co-nationals. We mentioned an aspect of this argument earlier in discussing Rawls's socio-psychological assumptions concerning moral motivation. There we saw how Rawls thinks that we are predisposed towards people who are culturally similar. As a justification for limiting the scope of our duties to these least well-off, this line of argument is, however, deeply problematic. For one thing, it seems to allow wealthy suburbanites to argue that they will fund schools for the children of those in their wealthy suburb, but not for children in the city with whom they share no affinity. For another thing, it allows Van Parijs to suggest that the boundaries of affinity in a multinational state like Belgium might connect Flem to Flem and Walloon to Walloon, but not Belgian to Belgian. If Rawls is to justify limiting our duties of distributive justice to co-nationals, he needs a stronger justification than his claims about our psychological motivations.

One suggestion – advanced recently by Thomas Nagel and others – is that our duties to co-nationals are different, because we share with our co-nationals a common coercive authority. On this view, mutual coercion establishes a necessary condition for duties of distributive justice. "Socioeconomic justice," argues Nagel,

> depends on positive rights that we do not have against all other persons or groups, rights that arise only because we are joined together with certain others in a political society under strong centralized control. It is only from such a system, and from our fellow

members through its institutions, that we can claim a right to democracy, equal citizenship, nondiscrimination, equality of opportunity, and the amelioration through public policy of unfairness in the distribution of social and economic goods.[21]

Nagel's argument offers little support, however, for Rawls's rejection of a Federal Europe, because his argument could be embraced by both a proponent of a Federal Europe and a proponent of a Europe of Nation--States. "Yes," they both might argue, "strong centralized control is a precondition of duties of distributive justice." But they will disagree where centralized control ought to be located. Nagel himself has nothing to say either for or against a Federal Europe. He merely acknowledges that Europeans do not currently favor such an entity, partly because they are aware of the far-reaching consequences for socioeconomic justice. As Nagel puts this point:

> [I]f there came into being a genuine European federation with some form of democratically elected representative government, politics would eventually develop on a European scale to compete for control of this centralized power. The real problem is that any such government would be subject to claims of legitimacy and justice that are more than the several European populations are willing to submit themselves to. That reflects in part a conviction that they are not morally obliged to expand their moral vulnerabilities in this way.

If Nagel's argument about coercion cannot provide a justification for Rawls's rejection of a federal Europe, then what other options are available? Although Rawls does not make the argument explicit, his position in the *Law of Peoples* does appear to rest upon an argument from, what might be termed, *national legal personality*. It is worth recalling here Van Parijs's puzzle over Rawls's usage of "law of peoples" rather than "law of states." If "peoples," Van Parijs asks, why not consider Flems, Walloons, and Europe's many other stateless peoples (the Welsh, for instance). The answer to this question lies in Rawls's implicit view of

---

[21] Thomas Nagel, "The Problem of Global Justice," *Philosophy and Public Affairs,* 33(2), 2005, 113-147.

the state as an embodiment of a national legal personality. Consider, for example, the two following passages from the *Law of Peoples*:

> I believe that the causes of the wealth of a people and the forms it takes lie in their political culture and in the religious, philosophical, and moral traditions that support the basic structure of their political and social institutions.[22]

And:

> The members of a single domestic society share a common central government and political culture...the moral learning of political concepts and principles works most effectively in the context of society wide political and social institutions that are part of their shared daily life.[23]

We see in such passages the suggestion that a culture-state nexus acts as a repository of a people's historical memory and, in particular, their record of political successes and failures. Through familiarity with this culture-state nexus, people acquire a sense of who they are and how they have developed. To lose their particular anchor to a political tradition is to lose something of great importance – it is to lose the opportunity for practical political wisdom. Put differently, Rawls suggests that a national-legal personality – another term for a culture-state nexus – is a precondition for democratic self-government. His answer to Van Parijs can thus be reformulated along the following lines. "The peoples I have in mind are peoples with a culture embodied in laws and institutions. These laws and institutions transform a culture from a mere language or assemblage of folk customs into a more impersonal, but nonetheless quite specific, political culture. I am opposed to a federal Europe, because I fear that it signals the end of such specific political cultures, which are embodied in Europe's nation-states."

---

[22] Rawls, *Law of Peoples*, 108.
[23] Rawls, *Law of Peoples*, 112.

III – Two Arguments for a Federal Europe

The preceding section offered an interpretation of the Eurosceptic position that Rawls expresses in his exchange of letters with Philippe Van Parijs. In this concluding part of my talk, I want to suggest that Rawls is wrong to reject a federal Europe. It is possible, I believe, to share much of Rawls's political philosophy and come to the conclusion that a federal Europe is "a realistic utopia." Here I want to sketch out two possible lines of argument that lead from "Rawlsian" premises to a federal Europe: one, an argument from security; and two, an argument from liberal political incorporation.

(i) An Argument from Security.

Rawls takes as a point of departure the idea of a free and equal person. Quite plausibly, Rawls maintains that the members of a modern democratic society must be thought of, first and foremost, as free and equal citizens. Thus whatever else is true of these people – that they practice one religion, rather than another, or no religion; that they are rich, middling, or poor – their freedom and equality are basic. Rawls rightly points out that this conception of the free and equal person belongs to the public culture of a democratic society, by which he means that it is an historical achievement that is rightly prized. All plausible political arguments in a democratic society must acknowledge the centrality of this idea of the person.

Elsewhere I have suggested that we think of this idea of the person in terms of a conception of, what might be termed, bare citizenship.[24] Following Rawls, we can distinguish certain basic goods ("social primary goods," as he terms them) that are necessary for the bare citizen to flourish. Such goods include personal liberty, (including the rights of personhood), political liberty, and certain socio-economic goods. Faced with a choice of different social and political arrangements – different "basic structures," in Rawls terminology – we ought to choose those

---

[24] For a more extended discussion, see Glyn Morgan, *Public Justification and European Integration* (Princeton: Princeton University Press, 2005), Chapter 1, esp. pp. 34-5.

arrangements that provide the highest level of these basic goods. Presented with the choice that Europeans today face between social and political arrangements that "deepen" and/or "widen" Europe – i.e. give more power to Brussels and/or expand the political boundaries of the European Union – we ought to weigh their impact on these basic goods.

In a further step in his argument, Rawls distinguishes two different types of social primary goods – basic liberties and socioeconomic goods. Rawls maintains that the basic liberties occupy a higher status, such that a bare citizen would never willingly trade off such liberties for socioeconomic goods. For present purposes, Rawls's argument for the priority of basic liberties can be taken as given. We are more interested here in the practical implication of this argument for a deeper and/or wider European basic structure. On the face of it, there would seem to be no route from these basic liberties to a federal Europe. Certainly, from the perspective of a citizen of one of the EU15 countries, there seems no compelling reason to think that basic liberties would be better protected in an enlarged, federal Europe than in a smaller, intergovernmental Europe or even in a nation-state that was not part of the European Union (such as current day Norway or Switzerland). Perhaps a stronger argument is available, however, from the perspective of a member of one of the newly-admitted EU countries. A Romanian, for instance, might argue that her basic liberties would be better protected by the European Union than by her own only very recently liberal democratic country.

There is, however, another route from primary goods to a federal Europe. This route starts from the assumption that security is a primary good – i.e. security is an essential condition for the bare citizen to flourish. Rawls himself has very little to say about security. But he does acknowledge the importance of security of life, liberty, and property. Yet once this point is acknowledged, the obvious question arises: what are the principal threats to security in a modern society? Clearly, the answer leads us to consider not merely domestic threats – other individuals and an arbitrary state – but international threats – whether in the form of terrorists or foreign wars. No individual can be secure unless he or she inhabits a state that protects against these threats.

Typically modern states aim to keep themselves secure partly through diplomacy and partly, if diplomacy fails, through collective

---

[25] Morgan, *Idea of a European Superstate.*

security arrangements (NATO, UN, etc). In Europe we have outgrown (or nearly so) the era of history when states would resort to war to resolve international disagreements. But we have not outgrown an era when domestic security requires an international society with laws and norms that reward and sustain cooperative transactions. Elsewhere I have argued that the security of individual Europeans is threatened by a normless, egoistic, international society.[25] I have also argued that no single European state is itself powerful enough to create such an international society; and it is dangerous to become dependent on a powerful ally. If Europeans are to play a role here, they need the power that a federal Europe can alone provide. Doubtless, this security-based justification for a Federal Europe is controversial and open to criticism.[26] Nonetheless, it provides one line of argument in support of a federal Europe that can be developed from Rawlsian premises.

(ii) An Argument from Liberal Political Incorporation

The argument from security takes as its point of departure Rawls's account of the free and equal person ("the bare citizen," as I termed him) in a domestic society. An alternative argument in support of a federal Europe might draw upon the account Rawls provides in the *Law of Peoples* concerning the relations between, what he terms, "liberal societies," and "burdened societies." Perhaps the most controversial element of Rawls's *Law of Peoples* is the open disavowal of any duties of distributive justice between wealthy liberal societies and poorer "burdened societies." In Rawls's words, such burdened societies "lack the political and cultural traditions, the human capital and know how, and, often, the material and technological resources needed to be well-ordered."[27] Rawls places particular emphasis upon the cultural determinants of political and economic backwardness. (His argument here is quite consonant with his understanding of the role played by, what I termed earlier, a national legal personality.) Since people are, in an important way, responsible for their own

---

[26] For a trenchant criticism, Rainer Schmalz-Bruns, "*The Idea of a European Superstate: Public Justification and European Integration* by Glyn Morgan," *Constellations* 14 (2007): 664-668.

[27] Rawls. *Law of Peoples*, 106.

national legal personality, which itself determines their material well-being, they cannot expect much assistance from wealthy liberal societies. Furthermore, if culture is the root of their problem, then financial assistance from outside will not make much of a difference.

Despite the fact that Rawls rejects the idea of international distributive justice, Rawls believes that wealthy liberal societies do have some duties of assistance towards burdened societies. Ideally, liberal societies ought to assist burdened societies in establishing liberal democratic regimes – i.e. assist in the transformation of the political culture of the burdened society. However, as Rawls concedes, "there is no...easy recipe...to help a burdened society to change its political and social culture."[28]

Noticeably absent from this account of "burdened societies" is any discussion of the type of liberal political incorporation that the process of European Enlargement exemplifies. States such as Romania and Bulgaria are classic examples of societies burdened by their political culture. European Enlargement might be viewed as a mechanism for changing a burdened society by way of financial inducements and political cultural transplantation. In order for a state to gain admittance to the European Union, it has to show that it is willing and able to absorb the so-called *acquis communautaire*. To the extent that the process of European Enlargement proves successful, it seems that a recipe has been found for peacefully and effectively transforming a "burdened" political culture. In short, a federal Europe provides a way that liberal wealthy states can fulfill their duties of assistance to the burdened societies in their region.

The two arguments identified here – the argument from security and the argument from liberal political accommodation – are merely meant to illustrate possible lines of argument that might lead a Rawlsian to accept European Integration as "a realistic utopia." Clearly, more work needs to be done to fill out and strengthen such arguments. A key unresolved issue concerns the nature and importance of a national legal personality. Is it plausible to think that a European legal personality can take over the role played by Europe's different national legal personalities? I think so. Rawls thinks not. Ultimately, this disagreement can be settled only by the accomplishments of the European Union. There lies the greatest challenge facing Europe in the twenty-first century.

---

[28] Rawls. *Law of Peoples*, 108.

THE EUROPEAN INTEGRATION IN A GLOBAL WORLD

LOUKAS TSOUKALIS*

Thank you very much, Mr Chairman. Thank you also to the organisers for their very kind invitation. I have been asked to talk about European integration in a global world and, although there was no coordination, what I have to say will be complementary to what Prof. Morgan has just said. I am not a philosopher; I have more humble origins. I started as an economist and gradually developed into a political economist. Surely, nobody is perfect in this world.

I shall start with a historical observation: European integration started basically as an inward looking venture. Europeans began to lay the foundations for peace and reconciliation of the continent, while taking global order as a given and shaped by external actors. That was the beginning.

The external dimension of European integration came later via trade. And I think it is fair to say, nowadays, that through the common commercial policy, the Europeans have helped to shape pretty decisively the world trading order – and, I think, for the better. But the experience with external trade has proved difficult to transplant to other areas of policy. The result has been that Europe's influence in international affairs, be it in finance or services, not to mention high politics, has never been commensurate with its collective size. In simple words, Europe is less than the sum of its parts as far as its role and influence in

---

* Professor, University of Athens; President, Hellenic Foundation for European and Foreign Policy (ELIAMEP).

international affairs. And this, of course, has to do with the lack of unity in Europe. I believe that the biggest challenge facing Europeans nowadays is to define and effectively defend common interests and values in a rapidly changing world in which the asymmetry of power persists. Europe's relative weight, as measured in terms of population, income or trade has been declining steadily for years; it is likely to continue doing so in the foreseeable future. The reasons are obvious and well known: one is demography, another is the rise of new powers in what we used to call the Third World.

In a rapidly changing world, in which size matters, Europe's relative weight is bound to continue declining. The same will be even more true of individual European countries and their relative influence or power in international affairs, although, admittedly, illusions of great power die hard. The basic question to ask is whether and when Europeans decide to invest in their unity as a means of maximising their collective global influence, assuming of course that the commonality of interests vis-à-vis the rest of the world prevails over diversity. Until now, some Europeans have invested in unity, others have tried to reap extra benefits by following the leader, while a third group has played the free rider. Whether we all reach the conclusion that our common interests are more important than our differences remains an open question.

What is it all about? First of all, it is about defending common interests and values in a globalising world, interests and values that extend much beyond external trade. It is also about defending global public goods, such as the environment, an area in which Europeans have been pioneers, despite the gap between rhetoric and action. Last but not least, it is about exporting their own experience of jointly managing interdependence through common rules and institutions, an experience painfully accumulated over the years. This would be a worthwhile European contribution to the construction of an effective system of multilateral governance through common rules and institutions in a world which is becoming increasingly multipolar.

Take globalisation, for example. With the risk of oversimplifying, I think there are two big opposing camps in Europe. One pretends that Europeans can protect themselves from externally induced change simply by erecting high walls separating us from the rest of the world. The other camp argues that globalisation is externally determined and that all we can do is to lie back and enjoy it – at least, those of us who can afford to enjoy the benefits of globalisation, I honestly believe there is a third option, and that this third option should be about adjustment but also about concerted efforts to influence and shape the forces of globalisation. To do that, you need collective European action. Individual countries have little other choice but simply to adjust as best as they can. Together, we can make a difference in the world.

We need effective forms of governance at the European level that go beyond simple intergovernmental structures operating on the basis of unanimity. Intergovernmental structures or fuzzy shapes of international systems do not deliver effective policies. Let us be clear about it. In other words, if we want to influence the world around us, we first need to invest in our own unity and in institutional structures that operate on the basis of majority voting (even super qualified-majority voting, if and when necessary), And we also need joint representation vis-à-vis the rest of the world. The experience of the common commercial policy is very clear: we need to draw some lessons and gradually apply them to other areas of policy.

Let us now turn to high politics. Europe has invested in different forms of soft power; it is after all the international soft power par excellence. Cynics would say that Europeans have only tried to make virtue out of necessity. Virtue or necessity, I think it is unavoidable that soft power will remain the main manifestation of European influence in the rest of the world for a long time to come, although hopefully complemented with a few hard elements. The attempt to define a European common foreign policy depends largely on the ability to define a common policy vis-à-vis the United States. Of course, a common policy vis--à-vis the United States is not the same as a policy against the United States – far from it. It is not about building a counterweight. It is about creating a credible partner who works closely with America, but whose interests and policies may sometimes legitimately differ. We need to agree on that among Europeans. Otherwise, a common foreign policy will be a snare and an illusion – and nothing more than that.

Let me now add a few words about our neighbours. After all, foreign policy begins with the neighbours. Many people have argued – and I think they are right – that enlargement has been so far the most successful foreign policy of the European Union. Successive rounds of enlargement have helped to export Pax Europeae to formerly unstable and less developed parts of the European periphery, including countries like mine, namely Greece, and also Portugal, which is hosting us today. The process of extending Pax Europeae to the geographical periphery of Europe has so far been an extremely successful affair, and one that Europe should be proud of. Portugal and Greece are very different (and better) countries from what they were twenty-five years ago. Much of that difference – of course, not all of it – is due to their participation in the European Union. Whether the experience of Portugal, Greece or Spain is repeated with the more recent arrivals from central and eastern Europe still remains to be seen. Some of the road has already been covered successfully. But we also know that their integration is likely to prove more difficult in many ways compared with that of previous entrants. It has to do with numbers, with lower starting points in terms of economic development and also with the traumas caused by long periods of communist rule.

If enlargement has been such a successful policy, why not continue? Why not continue enlarging towards the rest of the Western Balkans and also towards Turkey? There are certainly many arguments in favour of doing so. But there is also a basic and rather awkward question that needs answering: how much diversity can a political system take before it implodes? It is a basic question to which the answer is not at all easy or obvious. We know that in the Europe of 27 the lowest common denominator in some policy areas is very low indeed. Continuing with enlargement carries a price in terms of internal cohesion. And there is also a price in terms of both money and institutions. It is not yet clear who are ready to pay; some pretend it is for free.

At best, further enlargement is likely to move slowly in the foreseeable future. People talk of enlargement fatigue in the EU, which is clearly registered in Eurobarometer surveys. Enlargement has become politicised, and there is no way back. On the other hand, candidate countries do not presently fulfil the political and economic criteria for membership, and they are not expected to do so for some time, with the possible exception of Croatia.

This is where we are now. At this stage, I believe it is important that we do not shut completely the door on the face of the candidates. There will be candidates in the waiting room for some years to come, and several others keen on joining them there. Since the waiting room will remain crowded, it would make sense to try and make the waiting more comfortable, if not enjoyable. In other words, we may need to narrow the distance between membership and non-membership by offering better access to the European market and programmes to those who are not already members. And this should be done without prejudice to eventual full membership. We have an interest in doing that, because the European perspective has already acted as a catalyst for change in the candidate countries.

And then comes the wider neighbourhood: it consists of countries that are not eligible for membership, at least in the foreseeable future. There are several countries, which belong to that category, lying to the east and the south of Europe – there are only polar bears in the north and fish in the west. Almost all of our immediate neighbours are poor economically and fragile (or unstable) politically. Can the European Union export Pax Europeae to the wider neighbourhood without being able to use the instrument of membership? This is a hundred billion euro question. We know from experience, such as the one drawn from Mediterranean policy, that the mix of carrots and sticks we have tried to use in the past has been of little effect. Europe has had little success in promoting political and economic reform in its neighbouring countries – and without it, there is little hope of economic development and political stability. How effective can be EU conditionality when dealing with weak and potentially unstable neighbours? Unfortunately, we know that instability easily crosses borders. We have learned that in the Balkans and elsewhere.

There are many sources of instability in the wider neighbourhood of the European Union, including of course the long unresolved conflict between Israel and the Arabs. Europeans understand, clearly better than the current US Administration, that the creation of a viable Palestinian state that co-exists peacefully with Israel is a necessary, albeit not sufficient, condition for stability and peace in the wider Middle East. Europeans understand this, but so far they have shown limited capacity to act or influence. Such may be the limitations and frustrations of a civilian or post-modern power, like the European Union, in a world with many pre-modern characteristics.

THE EVOLUTION OF THE JUDICIAL SYSTEM
OF THE EUROPEAN UNION

KOEN LENAERTS[*]

INTRODUCTION

A fundamental component underlying the system of judicial protection in the European Union is the relationship between the Court of Justice of the European Communities ("Court of Justice") and the national courts. As is well-known, the system of legal protection laid down in the Treaties does not provide for the creation of "Community courts" in the different Member States. Rather, it starts from the premise that the national courts are the bodies to which individuals may turn whenever action or failure to act on the part of Member State authorities or other private parties infringes rights conferred upon them by Community law. This means that the national court is the "normal" Community court to hear and decide all cases involving Community law that do not fall within the jurisdiction of the Court of Justice under the Treaties.[1] In other words, national courts are the true bridgehead of the Community legal order and strive to secure the enforcement of Community law through the crucial dialogue with the Court of Justice.

---

[*] President of Chamber at the Court of Justice of the European Communities and Professor of European Law at Leuven University. All views expressed are personal.

[1] This is underscored by Art. 240 EC which provides: "Save where jurisdiction is conferred on the Court of Justice by this Treaty, disputes to which the Community is a party shall not on that ground be excluded from the jurisdiction of the courts or tribunals of the Member States."

It is for this reason that the evolution of the judicial system of the European Union cannot be restricted to examining the Union judicial architecture *stricto sensu* as seen through the various reforms put forward to address, *inter alia*, the increasing workload of cases handled by the Court of Justice. Instead, it must be viewed in a wider perspective because it hinges on the interlocking relationship between the Community courts[2] and the national courts in which both work together, as envisaged by the Treaties, to ensure the full enforcement and effectiveness of Community law and thus to uphold the principle of the "rule of law" in the Community legal order. As the Court of Justice proclaimed in its landmark judgment in *Les Verts*[3]: "[T]he European [then Economic] Community is a Community based on the rule of law, inasmuch as neither its Member States nor its institutions can avoid a review of the question whether the measures adopted by them are in conformity with the basic constitutional charter, the Treaty."[4] In this way, the Community courts and the national courts each carry out their respective tasks in relation to Community law guided by this core principle.

In view of these remarks, the purpose of this article is to explore, through recent case law of the Court of Justice and ongoing reforms of the European judicial architecture, how the interlocking relationship of the Community courts and the national courts contributes to the evolution of the judicial system of the European Union. This will be done in three main parts. Part One examines the judicial review of the legality of the acts of the institutions. Part Two then considers the judicial review of the compatibility of acts of the Member States with Community law. Taken together, these parts therefore address the twofold components of the "rule of law" enshrined in *Les Verts*. Finally, Part Three delves into several reforms of the Union judicature, thereby demonstrating how some of these reforms will further strengthen the contribution of the Community courts in their role alongside the national courts to guarantee effective judicial protection and the "rule of law" in the Union legal order.

---

[2] Although this text deals with the judicial system of the European Union, thereby extending to the non-Community pillars of the Union, the traditional expression, "Community courts", will nevertheless be used.

[3] Case 294/83, *Parti écologiste 'Les Verts' v. European Parliament*, [1986] ECR 1339.

[4] Ibid., para. 23.

I. JUDICIAL REVIEW OF ACTS OF THE INSTITUTIONS

The central focus here is the interlocking relationship between the Community courts and the national courts in relation to the progressive establishment of a complete and coherent system of judicial protection vis-à-vis the institutions of the European Union. The system is "complete" in the sense that several legal remedies and procedures operate before the Community courts and the national courts to ensure the review of the legality of the acts of the institutions. The system is "coherent" in the sense that there exist both direct and indirect routes for the review of such acts in relation to the respective tasks attributed to the Community courts and the national courts under the Treaties.

A. The "complete" system of judicial protection

To recall, the "complete" system of judicial protection means that sufficient legal remedies and procedures exist before the Community courts and the national courts so as to ensure judicial review of the legality of the acts of the institutions. The result is that when the review of the legality of a Community act cannot be carried out directly by the Community courts for reasons of inadmissibility, it must somehow be possible to be brought before the national courts which will then make a reference for a preliminary ruling on the validity of such act.

As the European Court of Justice ("ECJ") held in *Les Verts*, by virtue of Articles 230 EC and 241 EC, on the one hand, and Article 234 EC, on the other, "the Treaty established a complete system of legal remedies and procedures" designed to permit the Court of Justice to review the legality of acts adopted by the institutions.[5] Specifically, the Court envisaged:

Where the Community institutions are responsible for the administrative implementation of such measures, natural or legal persons may bring a direct action before the Court against implementing measures which are addressed to them or which are of direct and individual concern to them and, in support of such action, plead the illegality of the

---

[5] Ibid.

general measure on which they are based. Where implementation is a matter for the national authorities, such persons may plead the invalidity of general measures before the national courts and cause the latter to request the Court of Justice for a preliminary ruling.[6]

However, the allegedly "complete" Community system of judicial protection affirmed in *Les Verts* has become controversial in view of subsequent case law highlighting certain gaps in that system.

The quintessential examples were the cases of *Unión de Pequeños Agricultores*[7] and *Jégo-Quéré*[8], in which the ECJ deemed inadmissible two actions for the annulment of Community regulations because the respective applicants did not satisfy the condition of individual concern under Article 230 EC. This was because it became evident that the objection of illegality under Article 241 EC and the preliminary ruling procedure under Article 234 EC provide a sufficient legal remedy for natural or legal persons contesting the legality of a Community act of general application *only* when there exists a Community or a national implementing measure that will permit such persons to challenge the Community act before the Community court or the national court in an action brought against the implementing measure. Accordingly, in circumstances where a Community act of general application requires no implementing measures at Community level or at national level and national law affords no declaratory relief[9], gaps in the Community system of judicial protection may remain even though such an act directly imposes obligations on natural or legal persons or deprives them of some rights.[10]

---

[6] Ibid.

[7] Case C-50/00 P, *Unión de Pequeños Agricultores v. Council*, [2002] ECR I-6677, affirming Case T-173/98, *Unión de Pequeños Agricultores v. Council*, [1999] ECR II-3357.

[8] Case C-263/02 P, *Commission v. Jégo-Quéré & Cie SA*, [2004] ECR I-3425, setting aside Case T-177/01, *Jégo-Quéré & Cie SA v. Commission*, [2002] ECR II-2365.

[9] Compare, e.g., Case C-491/01, *British American Tobacco (Investments) Ltd and Imperial Tobacco Ltd ("BAT")*, [2002] ECR I-11453. This case is further discussed *infra* at note 18 and accompanying text.

[10] Moreover, it would be difficult to argue that there are no gaps in the system if the sole form of legal remedy for challenging the compatibility of a Community act with superior Community law was to be subject to administrative or criminal proceedings and to any penalties that may result from having infringed the Community act whose legality is being contested. Such legal remedy would undoubtedly not be sufficient to secure effective judicial protection for the natural or legal person concerned. *Compare* Case

Taken together, *Unión de Pequeños Agricultores* and *Jégo-Quéré* demonstrate that there are three possible solutions to address such gaps. The first solution lies in the Court of Justice's more relaxed interpretation of the notion of individual concern in order to permit standing for natural or legal persons seeking to challenge Community acts of general application. However, this approach was rejected by the ECJ despite the attempts made by Advocate General Jacobs in his Opinion in *Unión de Pequeños Agricultores*[11] and by the Court of First Instance ("CFI") in its judgment in *Jégo-Quéré* to put forward flexible constructions of individual concern.[12] The ECJ's affirmation of the CFI's dismissal in *Unión de Pequeños Agricultores*[13] and its setting aside of the CFI's judgment in *Jégo-Quéré*[14] indeed evidence that the Court considers the matter beyond its jurisdiction, thereby leaving it to the Member States to amend the Treaty in this regard.[15]

The second solution places central focus on the role of the national courts to fill the gaps. As the Court emphasised in both *Unión de Pequeños Agricultores* and *Jégo-Quéré*, "it is for the Member States to establish a system of legal remedies and procedures which ensure respect for the right to effective judicial protection."[16] Yet, this solution still leaves open the risk of some gaps in the system of judicial protection, since the degree of judicial protection available to natural and legal persons is made dependent on the ability of the national courts to provide an appropriate legal remedy. Furthermore, the emphasis placed on the national courts appears to constitute only an obligation to make best endeavours, rather than an obligation to declare an action admissible where the procedural law of the particular Member State does not provide for any form of "declaratory relief".[17] Nevertheless, as evidenced by cases such

---

C-432/05, *Unibet (London) Ltd and Unibet (International) Ltd ("Unibet")*, judgment of 13 March 2007, nyr, para. 64.

[11] See Opinion of Advocate General Jacobs in Case C-50/00 P, *Unión de Pequeños Agricultores v. Council*, [2002] ECR I-6677, paras 59-60, 103.

[12] See Case T-177/01, *Jégo-Quéré v. Commission*, paras 50-51.

[13] Case C-50/00 P, *Unión de Pequeños Agricultores v. Council*, paras 46-47.

[14] Case C-263/02 P, *Commission v Jégo-Quéré*, paras 39, 50.

[15] Case C-50/00 P, *Unión de Pequeños Agricultores v. Council*, paras 43-45.

[16] Case C-50/00 P, *Unión de Pequeños Agricultores v. Council*, para. 41; Case C-263/02 P, *Commission v. Jégo-Quéré*, para. 31.

[17] Case C-50/00 P, *Unión de Pequeños Agricultores v. Council*, para. 42; Case C-263/02 P, *Commission v. Jégo-Quéré*, para. 32.

as *BAT*[18] and *Omega Air*[19], for those national legal systems that do provide for such declaratory relief, the Court has sought to ensure that this route should be taken advantage of to the full.

The third solution consists of amending the Treaty pursuant to Article 48 EU, as suggested by the Court in *Unión de Pequeños Agricultores*.[20] The Draft Treaty amending the Treaty on European Union and the Treaty establishing the European Community ("Draft Reform Treaty")[21] would introduce two important changes in this regard. First, it would amend the fourth paragraph of Article 230 EC so as to widen the conditions for standing of a natural or legal person in relation to the review of "a regulatory act which is of direct concern to him or her and does not entail implementing measures".[22] Second, it would introduce a new provision, Article 9f, which states: "Member States shall provide remedies sufficient to ensure effective legal protection in the fields covered by Union law."[23] This latter provision might have far-reaching implications in terms of possibly prompting the Court to transform the above-mentioned obligation for the national courts to make best endeavours into an obligation for the Member States to achieve a particular result, i.e., to provide an appropriate legal remedy so as to allow the national courts to request a preliminary ruling on the validity of Community acts. This is all the more apparent when the said Article 9f is read against the background of Article 47 of the Charter of Fundamental

---

[18] Case C-491/01, *BAT*, [2002] ECR I-11453, paras 39-41.

[19] Joined Cases C-27/00 & C-122/00, *Omega Air Ltd and Others*, [2002] ECR I-2569. Here, the Court did not even consider the issue of admissibility of the reference for a preliminary ruling, which was triggered by way of a request for declaratory relief in the English and Irish courts: see ibid., para. 39.

[20] See Case C-50/00 P, *Unión de Pequeños Agricultores v. Council*, para. 45.

[21] Draft Treaty amending the Treaty on European Union and the Treaty establishing the European Community, CIG 1/1/07 REV 1, dated 5 October 2007 [hereinafter Draft Reform Treaty], *available at* the website of the Council of the European Union, http://www.consilium.europa.eu/showPage.asp?id=1317&lang=en&mode=g.

[22] Draft Reform Treaty, point 214(c), at 121. This had already been included in Art. III-365(4) of the Treaty establishing a Constitution for Europe, [2004] O.J. C 310/1 [hereinafter Constitutional Treaty]. See further Lenaerts, Arts and Maselis, *Procedural Law of the European Union* 2nd ed. (Sweet & Maxwell, 2006) paras 7-186 to 7-188, at 327-328.

[23] Draft Reform Treaty Art. 9(f)(1), second para., point 20, at 16. This provision is identical to Art. I-29(1), second para. of the Constitutional Treaty.

Rights of the European Union[24] and the relevant case law of the European Court of Human Rights.[25] In fact, recent case law of the Court of Justice has already made full sense of the principle underlying Article 9f in the context of the judicial review of the compatibility of acts of the Member States with Community law.[26]

Proceeding to the EU Treaty, as far as the third pillar of police and judicial cooperation in criminal matters is concerned[27], the question of the "complete" system of judicial protection outlined by *Les Verts* has also attracted controversy. In the recent cases of *Gestoras Pro-Amnistía* and *Segi*[28], for example, the ECJ confirmed that it had no jurisdiction to

---

[24] The first para. of Art. 47 of the Charter of Fundamental Rights of the European Union, proclaimed in Nice on 7 December 2000, [2000] O.J. C 364/1, provides: "Everyone whose rights and freedoms guaranteed by the law of the Union are violated has the right to an effective remedy before a tribunal in compliance with the conditions laid down in this Article." The legally binding force of the Charter would be recognised in the Draft Reform Treaty. See Draft Reform Treaty Art. 6(1), point 8, at 6.

[25] In its judgment of 24 September 2002 in Case 27824/95, *Posti and Rahko v. Finland*, [2002] ECHR 634, the European Court of Human Rights ruled that the European Convention on Human Rights had been violated on account of the fact that no remedy was available against a Finnish decree which curtailed the applicants' rights. The idea that one could obtain judicial review by first breaching the contested act was rejected by the European Court of Human Rights in the following terms: "no one can be required to breach the law so as to be able to have a 'civil right' determined in accordance with Article 6 § 1." Ibid., para. 64.

[26] See Case C-432/05, *Unibet*, judgment of 13 March 2007, nyr. This has also inspired the Court of Justice in relation to the duties of the national courts in the third pillar: see Case C-354/04 P, *Gestoras Pro Amnistía and Others v. Council*, judgment of 27 February 2007, nyr; Case C-355/04 P *Segi and Others v. Council*, judgment of 27 February 2007, nyr. These cases are discussed *infra* at notes 29-34 and accompanying text.

[27] As regards the second pillar concerning the common foreign and security policy in relation to this issue, see further Lenaerts, "The Basic Constitutional Charter of a Community based on the Rule of Law – Case 294/83 *Parti écologiste 'Les Verts' v European Parliament* [1986] ECR 1339", in Poiares Maduro and Azoulai (eds), *The Past and Future of EU Law; The Classics of EU Law Revisited on the 50th Anniversary of the Rome Treaty* (Hart Publishing, forthcoming 2007).

[28] Case C-354/04 P, *Gestoras Pro Amnistía and Others v. Council*, judgment of 27 February 2007, nyr; Case C-355/04 P *Segi and Others v. Council*, judgment of 27 February 2007, nyr. Since the relevant part of the Court's findings in the two cases is practically identical, reference will be made only to the former judgment. For recent discussion of the cases and their implications, see Peers, "Salvation outside the Church: Judicial protection in the third Pillar after the *Pupino* and *Segi* judgments", 44 *Common*

entertain an action for damages in the third pillar.[29] This was so, despite the applicants' alleged damages resulting from being placed on a list of terrorist organisations by virtue of certain common positions adopted by the Council.[30] That being said, the Court rejected the applicants' argument that they had been deprived of all judicial protection.[31] This was because although its jurisdiction relating to preliminary rulings and actions for annulment under Article 35 EU did not, in principle, include judicial review of common positions, the Court reasoned that since the preliminary ruling procedure was "designed to guarantee observance of the law in the interpretation and application of the Treaty, it would run counter to that objective to interpret Article 35(1) EU narrowly."[32] As a result, the right to make a preliminary reference must exist "in respect of all measures adopted by the Council, whatever their nature or form, which are intended to have legal effects in relation to third parties."[33] Importantly, the outcome of these two cases would be different under the Draft Reform Treaty, since the Court of Justice would have jurisdiction to review the legality of acts adopted by Union institutions and bodies in the former third pillar by way of actions for annulment[34] and actions for

---

Market Law Review 883 (2007); Garbagnati Ketvel, "Almost but not quite: The Court of Justice and Judicial Protection of Individuals in the Third Pillar", *European Law Reporter* 223 (2007); Nettesheim, "U.N. sanctions against individuals – A challenge to the architecture of European Union governance", 44 *Common Market Law Review* 567 (2007).

[29] Case C-354/04 P, *Gestoras Pro Amnistía and Others v. Council*, paras 46-48.

[30] See ibid., para. 1.

[31] Ibid., para. 51.

[32] Ibid., paras 52-53.

[33] Ibid., para. 53. The Court also pointed out that it had jurisdiction to review the lawfulness of such acts under circumstances where either a Member State or the Commission brought an action pursuant to Art. 35(6) EU, and importantly, it called attention to the national court's role in interpreting and applying national procedural rules so as to enable natural and legal persons to challenge before such court the lawfulness of national measures relating to Union acts and to seek damanges where appropriate. Ibid., paras 55-56.

[34] In view of the proposed amendments of Article 230 EC by the Draft Reform Treaty, the Court would be given jurisdiction to "review the legality of acts of bodies, offices or agencies of the Union intended to produce legal effects vis-à-vis third parties." See Draft Reform Treaty, point 214(a), at 121. The Draft Reform Treaty would also provide for specific arrangements to be made in this regard: see ibid., point 214(d), at

The Evolution of the Judicial System of the European Union 59

damages[35], even if certain limitations would remain in relation to the Court's jurisdiction in this field.[36]

B. The "coherent" system of judicial protection

The "coherent" system of judicial protection means that there exist both direct and indirect routes as far as the review of the legality of the acts of the institutions is concerned, each of which implicates important, albeit differing, tasks for the Community courts and the national courts as laid down in the Treaties. The coherence of the system of judicial protection has been ventilated through three series of cases concerning: first, the power to declare a Community act invalid; second, the inadmissibility of the indirect route of a preliminary ruling on the validity of a Community act where the direct route of the action for annulment is available; and third, illegality resulting from the failure to act on the part of the institutions.

The first series of cases concerning the power to declare a Community act invalid was clearly marked by *Foto-Frost*[37], the seminal judgment in which the ECJ established that a national court does not have the power to declare an act of the institutions invalid. Since Article 230 EC gives the Court exclusive jurisdiction to declare a Community act void, the Court concluded that "the coherence of the system requires that where the validity of a Community act is challenged before a national court the power to declare the act invalid must also be reserved to the Court of Justice."[38]

---

121. The Constitutional Treaty contained virtually identical provisions: see Art. III-361(1) and Art. III-365(5), respectively.

[35] In this regard, the amendments brought by the Draft Reform Treaty would not substantively change the present Art. 235 EC and Art. 288, second para. EC save with regard to paying specific heed to the European Central Bank: see Draft Reform Treaty, point 219, at 122 and point 282, at 147 (this had also been the case for the Constitutional Treaty: see Art. III-370 and Art. III-431, second para.).

[36] See Draft Reform Treaty Art. 66, point 64, at 59 and Art. 240b, point 223, at 123 (which are virtually the same as Constitutional Treaty Art. III-262 and Art. III-377, respectively).

[37] Case 314/85, *Foto-Frost*, [1987] ECR 4199.

[38] Ibid., para. 17.

Recently, in the *IATA*[39] case, the Court clarified that "the fact that the validity of a Community act is contested before a national court is not in itself sufficient to warrant referral of a question to the Court for a preliminary ruling."[40] Where a lower national court considers that the arguments challenging the validity of a Community act are unfounded, it may reject such arguments and conclude that the act is valid, since under those circumstances it is "not calling into question the existence of the Community act."[41] In contrast, where such a court considers that the arguments challenging the validity of a Community act are well-founded, then it must make a preliminary reference to the Court on the act's validity.[42]

There are two fields in which the Court of Justice's preliminary ruling jurisdiction is restricted as compared to Article 234 EC: Title IV of the EC Treaty concerning visas, asylum, immigration and other policies related to the free movement of persons and the third pillar concerning police and judicial cooperation in criminal matters. As for Title IV, the Court's preliminary ruling jurisdiction is limited to the highest courts of the Member States under Article 68 EC.[43] Yet, this matter may soon be resolved in accordance with Article 67(2) EC[44], given the Commission's recent proposal to align this area with Article 234 EC.[45] In any event, these present limitations under Article 68 EC would be eliminated by the Draft Reform Treaty.[46] As for the third pillar, Article 35 EU provides that for the Court to have preliminary ruling jurisdiction, each

---

[39] Case C-344/04, *International Air Transport Association and European Low Fares Airline Association ("IATA")*, [2006] ECR I-403. Certainly, this was not the only issue raised in the case: see St Clair Bradley, Case note, 43 *Common Market Law Review* 1101 (2006).

[40] Ibid., para. 28.

[41] Ibid., para. 29.

[42] Ibid., paras 30, 32. See also, with particular emphasis on the obligations of the highest national courts under the third para. of Art. 234 EC in this regard, Case C-461/03, *Gaston Schul Douane-expediteur BV*, [2005] ECR I-10513, paras 17-25.

[43] See Art. 68(1) EC.

[44] See Art. 67(2), second indent EC.

[45] See Commission Communication, "Adaptation of the provisions of Title IV of the Treaty establishing the European Community relating to the jurisdiction of the Court of Justice with a view to ensuring more effective judicial protection", COM (2006) 346 final, 28 June 2006. For further discussion, see Editorial, "Preliminary rulings and the area of freedom, security and justice", 44 *Common Market Law Review* 1, 2-5 (2007).

[46] See Draft Reform Treaty, points 63-66, at 58-65 and point 68, at 70-71.

Member State is to make a declaration either accepting the Court's jurisdiction for all national courts or for only the highest. To date, many Member States have submitted declarations allowing their lower courts to make references, but several others have either opted for the more restrictive approach or else have refrained from submitting a declaration altogether.[47] However, with the entry into force of the Draft Reform Treaty, these restrictions would also be eliminated.[48]

The second series of cases concerns the interplay between the direct route of an action for annulment under Article 230 EC and the indirect route of a preliminary ruling on the validity of Community acts under Article 234 EC. Here, the coherence requirement operates so as to preclude an applicant from arguing before a national court that a Community act is invalid for the purposes of a preliminary ruling under Article 234 EC under circumstances where the applicant could have directly challenged such act before the Community courts under Article 230 EC. The Court's case law in this context was paved by *TWD Textilwerke Deggendorf*[49], in which the Court held that an applicant who could "without any doubt" have challenged a Commission decision and who allowed the mandatory time-limit laid down by the Treaty to expire was precluded from calling into question the lawfulness of that decision before the national courts in an action brought against the measures taken by the national authorities to implement that decision.[50] To rule otherwise "would in effect enable the person concerned to overcome the definitive nature which the decision assumes as against that person once the time-limit for bringing an action has expired."[51]

---

[47] According to the 2005 Notice issued by the Council ([2005] O.J. L 327/19; [2005] O.J. C 318/1), only 14 Member States have made declarations accepting the Court's preliminary ruling jurisdiction. Spain and Hungary submitted declarations allowing only the highest courts to make references, whereas the remaining 12 Member States (Austria, Belgium, the Czech Republic, Finland, France, Germany, Greece, Italy, Luxembourg, the Netherlands, Portugal and Sweden) submitted declarations allowing both the lower and the highest courts to make such references. Since then, Slovenia has decided to make a declaration opting for the latter, more extensive category. To date, the remaining 12 Member States have not submitted any declaration.

[48] See Draft Reform Treaty, point 50, at 34; points 63-64, at 58-60; and points 67-68, at 65-71.

[49] Case C-188/92, *TWD Textilwerke Deggendorf GmbH*, [1997] ECR I-833.

[50] Ibid., paras 17, 24.

[51] Ibid., para. 18.

Conversely, the Court's case law makes clear that if there remains doubt on the admissibility of the action for annulment, then access to the indirect route of a preliminary ruling must be left open. The case of *Roquette Frères*[52] recently underscored this requirement. There, by way of national proceedings, the applicant sought to challenge several Community regulations concerning the common organisation of the markets in the sugar sector.[53] In its ruling, the Court considered that the disputed regulations put in place a scheme for basic production quantities of isoglucose allocated to the Member States, which gave the Member States "some room for manoeuvre" as regards the redistribution of such quotas particularly so as to enable new entrants in the market to start up isoglucose production.[54] Under these circumstances, the Court found that a producer could not in principle satisfy the requirement of direct concern for the purposes of the fourth paragraph of Article 230 EC.[55] This meant that it could not be argued that the applicant could "undoubtedly" have brought an admissible action for annulment against the Community regulations, and therefore, it was allowed to plead the illegality of the relevant provisions of these regulations before the national court.[56]

The third series of cases implicates the coherence of the system of judicial protection where the alleged illegality results from a failure to act on the part of the institutions. In *T. Port*[57], the question arose as to whether a national court was authorised to order interim measures for a trader of third-country bananas in a situation involving a failure to act by the Commission. The Court held that "[t]he Treaty makes no provision

---

[52] Case C-441/05, *Roquette Frères*, judgment of 8 March 2007, nyr.

[53] Ibid., paras 1, 26-33.

[54] Ibid., paras 42-44.

[55] Ibid., para. 45. As the Court found the requirement of "direct concern" lacking in relation to the applicant, this could explain why it did not proceed further as regards the assessment of the requirement of "individual concern" for the purposes of the fourth paragraph of Article 230 EC. Compare Opinion of Advocate General Kokott in Case C-441/05, *Roquette Frères*, judgment of 8 March 2007, nyr, paras 44-53 (concluding that the applicant was not individually concerned by the contested provisions of the Community regulations).

[56] Ibid., paras 47-48 of the judgment. The fact that the applicant was the only isoglucose producer in France and had been assigned the entire basic production quantity allocated under the relevant Community measures did "nothing to change that finding": ibid., para. 46.

[57] Case C-68/95, *T. Port GmbH & Co KG*, [1996] ECR I-6065.

for a reference for a preliminary ruling by which a national court asks the Court of Justice to rule that an institution has failed to act."[58] With that said, the Court posited various avenues so as to ensure judicial protection for the persons concerned, contemplating that the Member State or the particular trader could bring an action for failure to act before the Community courts under Article 232 EC.[59] Specifically, the Court pointed out that such a trader would be able to take the direct route by bringing this type of action, since it would be the addressee of the contested measure which the Commission allegedly failed to adopt or at the very least directly and individually concerned by it.[60]

T. Port can be considered the "mirror image" of the Court's more recent judgment in *Ten Kate*[61]. This case involved the possible liability of a Member State arising from the fact that it had refrained from bringing either an action for failure to act or an action for annulment against the Commission in a situation where the parties themselves were unable to do so because – contrary to what seemed to have been the case in *T. Port* – they were not individually concerned.[62] The Court ruled that Community law did not impose any such obligation on a Member State under these circumstances.[63] At the same time, however, it found that just as a natural or legal person should be able to challenge before a national court the legality of any decision or other national measure relative to the application to him or her of a Community act of general application by pleading the invalidity of such an act, "[t]he same holds true where a natural or legal person invokes a failure to take a decision, within the meaning of Article 232 EC, which it considers to be contrary to Community law."[64] As such, the Court ensured that the indirect route of a preliminary ruling on the validity of a failure to act was open to such persons since the direct route of an action for failure to act was not available.

---

[58] Ibid., para. 53.

[59] Ibid., paras 58-61.

[60] Ibid., para. 58.

[61] Case C-511/03, *Ten Kate Holding Musselkanaal BV and Others*, [2005] ECR I-8979.

[62] Ibid., paras 17, 20. Moreover, an action for damages against the Community would not have been of use to the applicants in this case: see ibid., para. 17.

[63] Ibid., para. 32.

[64] Ibid., para. 29.

II. JUDICIAL REVIEW OF ACTS OF THE MEMBER STATES IN RELATION TO COMMUNITY LAW

As underscored in *Les Verts*, the complete and coherent system of judicial review of acts of the Member States is just as much an essential component of "a Community based on the rule of law".[65] By virtue of the interlocking relationship between the Community courts and the national courts, the "complete" review of the acts of the Member States ensures thorough examination of the compatibility of such acts with Community law. As far as the "coherent" component is concerned, this highlights the operation of both direct and indirect routes of legality control in relation to the compatibility of national acts with Community law. First, there is the direct route of the action for a Member State's failure to fulfil its obligations under the Treaty (the infringement action) under Articles 226-228 EC, which allows the European Commission (or a Member State) to bring a Member State before the Court of Justice in relation to a national measure that is allegedly contrary to Community law. Second, there is the indirect route of the preliminary ruling procedure whereby a national court may make a reference to the Court of Justice concerning the interpretation of Community law under Article 234 EC, which will lead, albeit indirectly, to the assessment of the compatibility of a national measure with Community law.

A. Infringement actions

The action for infringement is for the purpose of obtaining a declaration from the Court of Justice that the conduct of a Member State infringes Community law, leading to the obligation for the Member State concerned to terminate that conduct. Notably, it is the only action in which the Court engages in the direct assessment of the compatibility of national measures (as well as other types of national conduct and practices[66]) with Community law. As a general matter, it is most often the

---

[65] Case 294/83, *Parti écologiste 'Les Verts' v. European Parliament*, [1986] ECR 1339, para. 23. For the complete passage, see *supra* note 4 and accompanying text.

[66] See, e.g., Case C-129/00, *Commission v. Italy*, [2003] ECR I-14637 (concerning the practices of the national courts and administrative authorities).

Commission, in accordance with its task as "guardian of the Treaty"[67], which brings an infringement action against a Member State under Article 226 EC.[68] That being said, a Member State can also institute an infringement action against another Member State under Article 227 EC although this occurs on a more infrequent basis.[69]

Either way, a special characteristic of the infringement action is the two-stage pre-litigation procedure requiring both the submission of a letter of formal notice and a reasoned opinion. This affords the Member State concerned with the opportunity both to remedy the infringement before the matter is brought before the Court of Justice and to put forward its defense to the Commission's allegations. In essence, part of the rationale underlying the pre-litigation stage is the attempt to reach an amicable settlement of the dispute so as to bring the Member State's infringement of Community law to an immediate end.

Under Article 228 EC, the Member State which has been found by the Court of Justice to have failed to fulfil its obligations under the Treaty is under a firm obligation to take all "the necessary measures" in order to comply with the Court's judgment.[70] This duty entails a prohibition having the full force of law against applying a national rule held to be incompatible with Community law as well as the obligation placed on national authorities to take every measure to enable Community law to be fully applied. This means that legislative and executive authorities have to bring the infringing provisions of national law in conformity with Community law and that the national courts must disregard those provisions when deciding cases.

---

[67] See Art. 211, first indent EC.

[68] Recently, the Court confirmed in Case C-494/01, *Commission v. Ireland* ("*Irish waste case*"), [2005] ECR I-3331, that the Commission can bring an action not only in relation to individual incidents of infringements, but also as regards a Member State's "general and persistent" breach of Community law, which has been considered to greatly augment the Commission's enforcement powers in this regard. See further Wennerås, "A new dawn for Commission enforcement under Articles 226 and 228 EC: General and persistent (gap) infringements, lump sums and penalty payments", 43 *Common Market Law Review* 31 (2006); Schrauwen, "Fishery, Waste Management and Persistent and General Failure to Fulfil Control Obligations: The Role of Lump Sums and Penalty Payments in Enforcement Actions Under Community Law", 18 *Journal of Environmental Law* 289 (2006).

[69] See, e.g., Case C-145/04, *Spain v. United Kingdom*, [2006] ECR I-7917 (concerning European elections in Gibraltar).

[70] Art. 228(1) EC.

In the event of a Member State's non-compliance with the Court's judgment finding the infringement, the Court is empowered to impose "a lump sum or penalty payment" on the Member State concerned pursuant to Article 228(2) EC.[71] In *Commission v. France*[72], despite the explicit reference to "lump sum *or* penalty payment" inscribed in the Treaty[73], the Court confirmed that it may impose both a lump sum *and* a penalty payment on the infringing Member State, finding that "recourse to both types of penalty provided for in Article 228(2) EC is not precluded, in particular where the breach of obligations both has continued for a long period and is inclined to persist."[74] In this way, the Court has sought to increase the effectiveness of the infringement proceedings for the Community system.

Nonetheless, the procedure under Article 228 EC is somewhat inefficient. This is because as the law stands at present, it is only when a Member State fails to comply with the Court's judgment that the Commission can bring new proceedings before the ECJ – after having completed another two-stage pre-litigation procedure (i.e., a letter of formal notice and a reasoned opinion)[75] – in which it asks the Court for a declaration that the Member State concerned failed to comply with the first infringement judgment and for the imposition of a pecuniary sanction. The Draft Reform Treaty would introduce two changes in an effort to remedy this inefficiency. First, it would amend Art. 228(2) EC so that where the Commission considers that a Member State has failed to comply with a judgment of the Court finding an infringement, it would be able to bring an action before the Court in which it asks for the imposition of a pecuniary sanction after having invited the Member State concerned to submit its observations.[76] This would make the second

---

[71] Art. 228(2), third para. EC.

[72] Case C-304/02, *Commission v. France*, [2005] ECR I-6263.

[73] See Art. 228(2), second and third paras EC (emphasis added).

[74] Case C-304/02, *Commission v. France*, paras 82-83. The Court also affirmed that it could impose a sanction different from that proposed by the Commisson, thereby departing from its request: see ibid., paras 89-97. For detailed discussion of the case, see further Wennerås, *supra* note 68, at 50-61; Kilbey, "Financial penalties under Article 228(2) EC: Excessive complexity?", 44 *Common Market Law Review* 743 (2007); Schrauwen, *supra* note 68.

[75] See Art. 228(2), first and second paras EC.

[76] Draft Reform Treaty, point 212(a), at 120. This amendment appeared in almost identical terms in Constitutional Treaty Art. III-362(2), first para.

action less onerous because it eliminates the requirement of a reasoned opinion in the pre-litigation stage.

Second, the Draft Reform Treaty would introduce a new third paragraph to Article 228 EC. Under circumstances where a Member State has failed to fulfil its obligation to notify measures transposing a directive adopted under a legislative procedure[77], the Commission would be able to bring a case before the ECJ, asking it to find an infringement *and* to impose a pecuniary sanction.[78] This would mean that in cases where a Member State has not taken any transposition measures, at the same time that the Commission brings an infringement action against the Member State concerned under Article 226 EC, it could also ask the Court to impose a pecuniary sanction.[79] This new enforcement mechanism might in turn have an impact on the distribution of the Court's workload. Generally, infringement cases concerning Member States' non-transposition of directives are decided by a Chamber of three Judges of the Court of Justice, since the infringing Member State usually does not challenge such proceedings. But with the possibility to impose a pecuniary sanction on the infringing Member State right away, this would most likely warrant a full hearing on the matter and a detailed assessment as regards the amount of the sanction to be imposed, thereby requiring in many instances a bench composed of a larger number of Judges, normally a Chamber of five Judges. In any event, the changes envisaged by the Draft Reform Treaty in this regard can be considered to improve the

---

[77] In light of the proposed changes to Art. 249 EC by the Draft Reform Treaty, this is essentially meant to denote directives that are legislative, as opposed to non-legislative, acts. See Draft Reform Treaty Art. 249a, point 236, at 126-127.

[78] Draft Reform Treaty, point 212(b), at 120. Moreover, this provision specifies that where the Court finds that there is an infringement, "it may impose a lump sum or penalty payment on the Member State concerned *not exceeding the amount specified by the Commission.*" Ibid. (emphasis added). Both of these proposed changes had already been taken up in Art. III-362(3) of the Constitutional Treaty, as highlighted by Advocate General Geelhoed's (second) Opinion in Case C-304/02, *Commission v. France*, [2005] ECR I-6263, para. 27.

[79] However, as for all other types of infringements, such as a Member State's incorrect implementation of directives (as opposed to the failure to take any implementing measures), the "normal" procedure would still stand, whereby the imposition of a pecuniary sanction would be conditional upon a first judgment of the Court finding against the Member State and non-compliance with the judgment by the Member State concerned.

effectiveness of infringement proceedings so as to assure the utmost review of the compatibility of national acts with Community law.

Moreover, the Draft Reform Treaty would remedy the gap in the current framework whereby the Treaty makes no provision for actions for infringement in the third pillar. The practical effects of the absence of infringement actions in this field can be illustrated by the Member States' heterogeneous application of the Framework Decision on the European arrest warrant.[80] Following the 2005 judgment by the German Constitutional Court[81] setting aside German legislation transposing the Framework Decision, certain courts of the other Member States chose not to apply their national measures implementing the Framework Decision in relation to Germany due to the lack of reciprocity.[82] This situation was resolved when Germany adopted new implementing legislation the following year.[83] Thus, in order to overcome these disparities, the Draft Reform Treaty would extend the Community method to the third pillar.[84] In fact, the Commission is already considering the use of the *passerelle* (or bridging) clause laid down in Article 42 EU[85] in order to remedy this

---

[80] Council Framework Decision 2002/584/JHA of 13 June 2002 on the European arrest warrant and the surrender procedures between Member States, [2002] O.J. L 190/1.

[81] Judgment of the Bundesverfassungsgericht of 18 July 2005, 2 BvR 2236/04, Deutsches Verwaltungsblatt 2005, at 1119-1128, which has been reprinted in [2006] 1 *Common Market Law Reports* 16.

[82] For general discussion of the problems encountered by certain constitutional courts of the Member States in relation to the transposition of the Framework Decision on the European arrest warrant and the broader implications, see Komárek, "European constitutionalism and the European arrest warrant: In search of the limits of 'contrapunctual principles'", 44 *Common Market Law Review* 9 (2007).

[83] See Commission Report on the implementation since 2005 of the Council Framework Decision of 13 June 2002 on the European arrest warrant and the surrender procedures between Member States, COM (2007) 407 final, 11 July 2007, point 2.1.2, at 5. See also Böhm, "Das neue Europäische Haftbefehlsgesetz", *Neue Juristische Wochenschrift* 2592 (2006).

[84] This had already been the case in relation to the Constitutional Treaty: see Lenaerts and Van Nuffel, *Constitutional Law of the European Union* 2nd ed. (Sweet & Maxwell, 2005) para. 6-014, at 336; Lenaerts and Van Nuffel, "La Constitution pour l'Europe et l'Union comme entité politique et ordre juridique", 41 *Cahiers de droit européen* paras 38-39, at 51-53 (2005).

[85] Art. 42 EU provides for a right of initiative of either the Commission or a Member State to propose that action in areas referred to in Art. 29 EU concerning police and judicial cooperation in criminal matters should fall within Title IV of the EC Treaty.

The Evolution of the Judicial System of the European Union 69

and other deficiencies in the third pillar.[86] Although the Commission currently cannot bring a Member State before the ECJ for an infringement of European Union law governed by the third pillar, this does not preclude the national courts from interpreting national law in conformity with provisions adopted in the context of the third pillar as seen further below.[87]

Notwithstanding these shortcomings in relation to the third pillar, it should not be overlooked that the real "bite" of infringement actions is grounded in its link to the principle of State liability. The Court's judgment finding an infringement may form the basis for an action against the Member State in damages for breach of Community law in accordance with the requisite conditions for State liability set down in the Court's case law.[88] Recently, following in the footsteps of *Köbler*[89], the Court confirmed in *Traghetti del Mediterraneo*[90] the application of this principle when the infringement of Community law is attributable to a national court adjudicating at last instance. The Court ruled that Community law precluded national legislation which excluded State liability, in a general manner, for damage caused to individuals by an infringement of Community law attributable to a court adjudicating at last instance by reason of the fact that the infringement in question resulted from an interpretation of provisions of law or an assessment of facts and evidence carried out by that court.[91] It also emphasised that Community law precluded national rules which limited State liability solely to cases of

---

However, the decision on the use of Art. 42 EU is subject to unanimity in the Council, after consultation with the European Parliament, and it must be adopted in accordance with the Member States' constitutional requirements.

[86] See Commission Communication, "Implementing The Hague Programme: the way forward", COM (2006) 331 final, 28 June 2006, para. 3.2.

[87] See *infra* notes 103-107 and accompanying text.

[88] See Lenaerts and Van Nuffel, *supra* note 84, paras 17-012 to 17-014, at 674-678.

[89] Case C-224/01, *Köbler v. Austria*, [2003] ECR I-10239.

[90] Case C-173/03, *Traghetti del Mediterraneo SpA in Liquidation v. Italy*, [2006] ECR I-5177. See further Ruffert, Case note, 44 *Common Market Law Review* 479 (2007); D'Sa, "Limits on suing an EU Member State for non-contractual damages for judicial errors made by a national court of last instance", *European Current Law* xi (2006); Remy-Corlay, Case note, *Revue trimestrielle de droit civil* 728 (2006).

[91] Case C-173/03, *Traghetti del Mediterraneo SpA in Liquidation v. Italy*, paras 24, 32-41.

intentional fault and serious misconduct on the part of such a court, if such a limitation were to lead to the exclusion of State liability in cases where a manifest infringement of the applicable Community law was committed.[92]

Although the Court's judgment finding an infringement is not a prerequisite for State liability, the Court affirmed in *Brasserie du Pêcheur and Factortame IV*[93] that if the Member State's breach continued after the judgment finding an infringement is delivered, then such non-compliance is in and of itself considered to constitute a "sufficiently serious" breach for the purposes of satisfying the conditions of State liability.[94] In this way, the effective enforcement of the Court's judgments is secured not only through direct enforcement by the Commission (or a Member State), but also through indirect enforcement with a role for national courts and individuals to play. Indeed, it should not be missed that the effectiveness of the principle of State liability largely depends on the national courts which are charged – in their role as the "normal" Community courts – to adjudicate the cases brought by such individuals concerning a Member State's liability.

All of the above notwithstanding, the infringement action is not watertight. One particular difficulty stems from the fact that the commencement of proceedings under Article 226 EC depends on the Commission. It may be the case that the Commission is sometimes not aware of certain infringements committed by the Member States, and it may not even want to act in certain cases in line with the broad discretion it holds in this area. Thus, there is a complementary mechanism set down in the Treaty: preliminary rulings on the interpretation of Community law.

---

[92] Ibid., paras 42-46.

[93] Joined Cases C-46/93 & C-48/93, *Brasserie du Pêcheur SA v. Germany and The Queen v. Secretary of State for Transport, ex parte: Factortame Ltd and Others ("Brasserie du Pêcheur and Factortame IV")*, [1996] ECR I-1029.

[94] See ibid., para. 57, in which the Court held: "On any view, a breach of Community law will clearly be sufficiently serious if it has persisted despite a judgment finding the infringement in question to be established, or a preliminary ruling or settled case-law of the Court on the matter from which it is clear that the conduct in question constituted an infringement."

B. Preliminary rulings on the interpretation of Community (and Union) law

Like infringement actions, preliminary rulings on the interpretation of Community law are a means of ensuring the judicial review of the compatibility of acts of Member States with Community law, even though they constitute an indirect, rather than direct, route for doing so. In principle, "it is not for the Court to rule on the compatibility of national rules with provisions of Community law", since "the Court is competent [only] to give a ruling on the interpretation of Community law in order to enable the national court to assess the compatibility of those rules with the Community provisions."[95] However, from a practical standpoint, the Court's rulings can prove to be determinative of the outcome of such assessment.

In this regard, it should be noted that the Court's interpretation of Community law is binding not only on the national court that made the reference, but also on all national courts outside the specific dispute, subject to their right to make further references on interpretation to the Court of Justice, i.e., it has *"erga omnes"* effects. Moreover, since the Court's interpretation simply expresses what was contained *ab initio* in the Community law provisions, generally such an interpretation is effective as from their entry into force or *"ex tunc"*. The ECJ's recent judgment in *Meilicke*[96] concerning the *"ex tunc"* effects of preliminary rulings in fact serves to bolster the rationale concerning their *"erga omnes"* effects. There, the Court held that "there must necessarily be a single occasion when a decision is made on the temporal effects of the requested interpretation" such that "the principle that a restriction may be allowed only in the actual judgment ruling upon that interpretation guarantees the equal treatment of the Member States and of other persons subject to Community law, under that law, fulfilling, at the same time, the requirements arising from the principle of legal certainty."[97] The Court's reasoning was premised on the fact that its ruling must be viewed as applicable to all those within its purview, including the Member States and private parties. In this way, the Court's preliminary rulings on the

---

[95] Case C-130/93, *Lamaire NV*, [1994] ECR I-3215, para. 10.
[96] Case C-292/04, *Meilicke and Others*, judgment of 6 March 2007, nyr.
[97] Ibid., para. 37.

interpretation of Community law can be of use to national courts, beyond just the referring court, in relation to the (indirect) assessment of national measures vis-à-vis Community law.

Furthermore, in the preliminary ruling context, there are important duties not just for the Court of Justice in relation to its interpretation of the relevant provisions of Community law, but also for the national courts, particularly in relation to the principle of "consistent interpretation". *Pfeiffer*[98] is a notable example. In this case, the Court ruled that the relevant provision of the Working Time Directive[99] could not be invoked in proceedings between private parties[100]. Yet, it proceeded to underscore the obligation placed on the referring court to interpret national law "so far as possible" in light of the wording and the purpose of the Directive.[101] Although in the instant case the principle of "consistent interpretation" chiefly concerned domestic provisions enacted in order to implement the Directive, the Court stressed that this principle required the national court to consider national law "as a whole" in order to assess to what extent the said provisions may be applied so as not to produce a result contrary to that sought by the Directive and to take account of all interpretative methods available in pursuance of this task.[102]

Going one step further, in *Pupino*[103], the Court established that the principle of "consistent interpretation" was applicable to acts adopted in

---

[98] Joined Cases C-397-403/01, *Pfeiffer and Others*, [2004] ECR I-8835, with a case note by Prechal, 42 *Common Market Law Review* 1445 (2005). While the literature involving this case is quite voluminous, for a recent selection (with further citations therein), see Dougan, "When worlds collide! Competing visions of the relationship between direct effect and supremacy", 44 *Common Market Law Review* 931 (2007); Lenaerts and Corthaut, "Towards an internally consistent doctrine on invoking norms of EU law", in Prechal et al. (ed.), *The Coherence of EU Law* (OUP, forthcoming 2007).

[99] Council Directive 93/104/EC of 23 November 1993 concerning certain aspects of the organisation of working time, [1993] O.J. L 307/18.

[100] Joined Cases C-397-403/01, *Pfeiffer and Others*, paras 107-109.

[101] Ibid., para. 113.

[102] Ibid., paras 115-116.

[103] Case C-105/03, *Pupino*, [2005] ECR I-5285. For recent discussion of this case and its implications, see Peers, *supra* note 28, at 909-924; Lebeck, "Sliding Towards Supranationalism? The Constitutional Status of EU Framework Decisions after *Pupino*", 8 *German Law Journal* 501 (2007); Magno, "The *Pupino* Case: Background in Italian Law and Consequences for the National Judge", 8 *ERA Forum* 215 (2007); Spaventa, "Opening Pandora's Box: Some Reflections on the Constitutional Effects of the Decision in *Pupino*", 3 *European Constitutional Law Review* 5 (2007).

the third pillar. Here, an Italian court asked the Court of Justice whether, in view of the Framework Decision on the standing of victims in criminal proceedings[104], it must allow several children claiming to be the victims of maltreatment by Ms. Pupino to give their testimony under special arrangements outside the confines of the trial proceedings even though the relevant Italian legislation greatly restricted the use of such arrangements.[105] In response, the Court held that, in applying national law, the national court was required to interpret it as far as possible in the light of the wording and the purpose of a framework decision in order to attain the result envisaged, adding that, where necessary, the national court must consider "the whole of national law" in this regard.[106] Consequently, even though the Framework Decision at issue did not define the concept of a victim's vulnerability, the Court found that the children concerned could be considered particularly vulnerable so that recourse to special arrangements could be made.[107]

It should not be overlooked that it was an Italian lower court that submitted the reference for a preliminary ruling in *Pupino* by virtue of Italy's declaration under Article 35 EU allowing all national courts to make such references in relation to the third pillar.[108] Thus, for the Member States which have submitted declarations restricting references to the highest courts or have failed to submit any such declaration altogether, this has detrimental effects for the dialogue between the national courts and the Court of Justice and for the effectiveness of Union law.

III. REFORMS OF THE UNION JUDICATURE

Building on the discussion above concerning the interlocking relationship between the Community courts and the national courts in the

---

[104] Council Framework Decision 2001/220/JHA of 15 March 2001 on the standing of victims in criminal proceedings, [2001] O.J. L 82/1.

[105] See Case C-105/03, *Pupino*, paras 12-18.

[106] Ibid., paras 43-47.

[107] Ibid., paras 53-56, 61. At the same time, however, the Court ruled that the special arrangements at issue must be applied so as to ensure protection of Ms. Pupino's fundamental rights, particularly the right to a fair trial under Art. 6 of the European Convention on Human Rights: see ibid., paras 57-60.

[108] See *supra* note 47.

context of the judicial review of acts of the institutions and the Member States, attention can now be directed at the Community courts *stricto sensu* and certain reforms that have been decided or are envisaged with a view to strengthening the judicial system of the European Union as a whole. For the present purposes, this means that the discussion will be organised around the central question whether the Community courts are suited, in terms of their division of work and the procedural tools at their disposal, to cope with the tasks conferred upon them by the Treaties in the most qualitative, efficient and effective way possible. As such, it is not just a matter of delving into ways to combat the Court of Justice's increasing workload (although this is certainly an important consideration)[109], but also of addressing other core values and ideas underlying the structure of the Union judicature. In particular, these include the proximity of the Union judicature to the various litigants (whether it be the Union citizens, the institutions or the Member States) seeking to claim their Community and Union law rights and the theoretical framework underpinning the different nature of the tasks conferred on the ECJ and the CFI, which in turn directly implicates the ECJ's basic function as the constitutional and supreme court of the Union.

Under the framework of national constitutional law, the notion of a constitutional court is typically attached to the notion of a formal constitution expressing the identity of a *demos*. In contrast, the Treaties upon which the European Union is founded operate as a substantive constitution, meaning that they contain all the "rules of play" in order to make the legal order work, but they are instituted on the basis of a compact between States and peoples. Such a compact contains all that it takes to agree, without distinguishing between rules concerning the political decision-making process and fundamental rights protection, on the one hand, and other basic rules, such as those relating to the various policies of the Community, on the other. This means that the Treaties contain

---

[109] For detailed reflection on the Court of Justice's workload in relation to preliminary rulings, see Lenaerts, "The Unity of European Law and the Overload of the ECJ – The System of Preliminary Rulings Revisited", *in* Pernice, Kokott and Saunders (eds), *The Future of the European Judicial System in a Comparative Perspective*, 6 European Constitutional Law Network Series 211 (Nomos, 2006) (also published in 1 *The Global Community. Yearbook of International Law and Jurisprudence 2005* 173 (Oceana Publications, 2006)).

elements that are not generally found in national constitutions, but are necessary for the balance of the Union legal order taken as a whole and therefore included in the compact between States and peoples.[110] That also explains why the ECJ is charged with the function of both a constitutional and a supreme court since it has been given the task to have the last word on the interpretation of elements that are not traditionally included in national constitutions, yet are of foundational significance to the European Union.

Be that as it may, the ECJ will undoubtedly continue to carry out its role as the Union's constitutional court, that is to say, as the guardian of the objectives and rules of law laid down in the Treaties. This is evidenced by the Court's adjudication of cases relating to the horizontal division of powers between the Union institutions, the vertical division of powers between the Union and the Member States and the protection of fundamental rights.[111] At the same time, the ECJ carries out the function of a supreme court when, by way of a national court's request for a preliminary ruling, it ensures the uniform application of Community (and Union) law. There are constitutional aspects to this function as well, inasmuch as the divergent application of Community law in the Member States would run counter to the achievement of the objectives set down in the Treaties.[112] While this does not mean that constitutional issues of Community and Union law do not invariably arise in the CFI or in the national courts as well, this still marks an important line in the fundamental division of tasks in the Community courts: the mainstay of the CFI's tasks can be considered that of a "judicial review" court whose core function involves assessing the facts and scrutinising the evidence, whereas the core tasks

---

[110] This corresponds to the Court's proclamation in *Les Verts* that the Community has a "basic constitutional charter, the Treaty": Case 294/83, *Parti écologiste 'Les Verts' v. European Parliament*, [1986] ECR 1339, para. 23. It also bears mentioning that this would continue to be the case in light of the Draft Reform Treaty.

[111] See further Lenaerts, "La constitutionnalisation de l'ordre juridique de l'Union européenne", *in Mélanges en l'honneur du Professeur Francis Delpérée. Itinéraires d'un constitutionnaliste* (Bruylant, forthcoming 2007).

[112] See Skouris, "The Position of the European Court of Justice in the EU Legal Order and its Relationship with National Constitutional Courts", 60 *Zeitschrift für öffentliches Recht* 323, 327 (2005) (noting that "the most accurate characterisation of the ECJ is that of a very specific court performing both the functions of a supreme and a constitutional court.").

attributed to the ECJ revolve around its functions as the constitutional and supreme court of the Union legal order.

In view of this division of tasks, many types of reforms of the structure of the Union judicature have been contemplated. While all of the various proposals cannot be taken up here, some recent and much discussed reforms instigated by the Nice Treaty and the Court itself will be considered in order to find the best match for the Union judicature in line with the objectives and values mentioned above. First, as for reforms relating to the Court of Justice, the urgent preliminary ruling procedure in the area of freedom, security and justice is of utmost importance, as are other procedural reforms concerning the functioning of the Court in chambers and the contribution of the Advocates General. Second, as for reforms instigated by the Nice Treaty, the prospect of conferring jurisdiction on the CFI to handle preliminary rulings and infringement cases will be evaluated with a view to providing reflection on how best to put these proposals to use so as to fortify, rather than to undercut, the ideal division of tasks between the ECJ and the CFI and their relationship with the national courts.

A. *Reforms relating to the Court of Justice*

To begin with, the Court of Justice has recently drawn up a proposal for an urgent preliminary ruling procedure in the area of freedom, security and justice. The purpose of this procedure is to allow the ECJ to give preliminary rulings more speedily on questions arising in both the fields of Title IV of the EC Treaty concerning visas, asylum, immigration and other policies related to the free movement of persons and Title VI of the EU Treaty concerning police and judicial cooperation in criminal matters. The idea emanated from the Presidency Conclusions of the Brussels European Council of 4-5 November 2004[113], which had made reference to Article III-369 of the Constitutional Treaty requiring the Court, in the context of its preliminary ruling jurisdiction, to "act with the minimum of delay" in relation to cases pending before national courts

---

[113] See Presidency Conclusions of the Brussels European Council of 4-5 November 2004, point 3.1.

The Evolution of the Judicial System of the European Union 77

involving persons in custody[114] – a provision which has been taken up in virtually identical terms by the Draft Reform Treaty.[115] Yet, the need for such a procedure is already warranted under the present Treaty framework, since as the result of Community and national rules, cases decided by the national courts concerning the area of freedom, security and justice often require decisions to be delivered within a short period of time.[116] For example, Article 11(3) of the "Brussels II*bis*" Regulation concerning the jurisdiction and the recognition and enforcement of judgments in matrimonial matters and the matters of parental responsibility[117] lays down a time limit of "no later than six weeks" for giving a ruling where proceedings are brought before a national court seeking the return of a child who has been wrongfully removed.[118]

Notably, the Rules of Procedure of the Court of Justice already provide for an accelerated procedure for dealing with preliminary rulings of exceptional urgency.[119] However, this accelerated procedure has been considered insufficient for the present purposes because, among other things, it has not been found to cut down sufficiently on the duration of the proceedings and its acceleration is achieved at the expense of all the other cases pending before the Court, thereby explaining why it has been used only on an exceptional basis.[120]

---

[114] Constitutional Treaty Art. III-369, fourth para.

[115] See Draft Reform Treaty, point 218, at 122.

[116] For further discussion of the urgent preliminary ruling procedure, see Editorial, *supra* note 45, at 5-7.

[117] Council Regulation (EC) No 2201/2003 of 27 November 2003 concerning jurisdiction and the recognition and enforcement of judgments in matrimonial matters and the matters of parental responsibility, repealing Regulation (EC) No 1347/2000, [2003] O.J. L 338/1.

[118] Ibid., Art. 11(3), second para.; see also ibid., Arts 11(6), 15(5) and 31(1). For further examples of Community and national rules in this regard, see Court of Justice Discussion Paper dated 25 September 2006, at 2-3, *available at* the website of the Court of Justice, http://www.curia.europa.eu.

[119] See Art. 104a of the Rules of Procedure of the Court of Justice. This should be distinguished from the expedited procedure that may be used in connection with direct actions of particular urgency before the ECJ and the CFI: see Art. 62a of the Rules of Procedure of the Court of Justice; Art. 76a of the Rules of Procedure of the Court of First Instance. See further Barbier de la Serre, "Accelerated and expedited procedures before the EC courts: A review of the practice", 43 *Common Market Law Review* 783 (2006).

[120] See Court of Justice Discussion Paper dated 25 September 2006, at 4; Court of Justice Discussion Paper dated 21 December 2006, at 2, *available at* the website of the Court of Justice, http://www.curia.europa.eu.

Following further discussion between the Court and the Council, the Court of Justice recently put forward its proposed amendments to the Statute and the Rules of Procedure with a view to establishing this new procedure.[121] Under the proposal, recourse to the urgent procedure will be made either on the request of the national court making the reference or of the Court of Justice's own motion. A Chamber of five Judges will be designated for the purpose of handling the references for preliminary rulings in this area, and it will decide whether a reference should be dealt with under the urgent procedure, in which case it will be entrusted with giving a ruling (although it may decide to sit in a formation of three Judges). Where the Chamber finds that a case would not be suitable for the urgent procedure, it will be reassigned through the normal channels. The Chamber can also decide to refer the case back to the Court of Justice in order for it to be assigned to a formation composed of a greater number of Judges (namely, the Grand Chamber) where, for example, it involves issues of great complexity or importance, which serves to safeguard the unity and consistency of European law.

As regards the substance of the procedure, it allows for all the Member States to participate in a manner close to what currently applies in normal preliminary ruling proceedings, particularly as regards the availability of translations, but it limits the procedure for most Member States (as well as other parties listed in Article 23 of the Statute) to the oral part. Save for exceptional cases, there is also a written part, but in order to be as speedy as possible, that part is confined to the parties to the main proceedings before the national court, the Member State to which that court or tribunal belongs, the Commission and, where relevant, the institution(s) whose measure is at issue. This procedure therefore serves both to allay the concerns of the Member States and institutions that they are able to participate in preliminary rulings involving new and often very sensitive areas of Community and Union law and to allow for a full debate on the matter. At the same time, it guarantees that the proceedings are handled very swiftly so that the national court can decide the case before it as soon as possible.

---

[121] See Draft Amendments to the Statute of the Court of Justice and Draft Amendments to the Rules of Procedure of the Court of Justice, *available at* http://www.curia.europa.eu/en/instit/txtdocfr/index.htm, both dated 21 June 2007 and transmitted to the Council on 5 July 2007.

---

[122] The Draft Reform Treaty would in any case do away with the present limits on

Despite the importance of the urgent procedure, it does not stand alone. The priority of remedying the present restrictions on the Court of Justice's preliminary ruling jurisdiction in the area of freedom, security and justice under Article 68 EC and Article 35 EU by recourse to Article 67(2) EC and Article 42 EU, respectively, should not be neglected. Indeed, aligning these areas with the preliminary ruling procedure under Article 234 EC goes hand-in-hand with the urgent procedure, thereby greatly enhancing the dialogue between the ECJ and the national courts.[122]

Moreover, the urgent procedure should be seen against the background of other procedural reforms of the Court of Justice which are designed to improve the quality and the quantity of its output. For one thing, by virtue of Article 20 of the Statute of the Court of Justice, the Court can render judgments without an opinion of an Advocate General in certain cases.[123] On a similar note, in the context of preliminary rulings, the ECJ can deliver a ruling by "reasoned order" in certain cases pursuant to Article 104(3) of the Rules of Procedure of the Court of Justice.[124] For another thing, since the Nice Treaty's introduction of the formation of the Grand Chamber composed of thirteen judges, the Court has been able to streamline the cases of constitutional importance for the unity and consistency of European law to the Grand Chamber, while relegating others to the Chambers of either five or three Judges.[125] Lastly, it should be mentioned that in the context of the negotiations surrounding the Draft Reform Treaty, provision has been made to allow the Court of Justice to increase the number of Advocates General from eight to eleven[126], which could considerably increase the Court's productivity.

---

the Court of Justice's preliminary ruling jurisdiction under Art. 68 EC and Art. 35 EU: see *supra* notes 46 and 48 and accompanying text, respectively.

[123] See Art. 20, fifth para. of the Statute of the Court of Justice.

[124] Generally speaking, the Court of Justice can give a preliminary ruling by "reasoned order" where: (1) the question referred to the Court is identical to a question on which it has already ruled; (2) the answer to such a question may be "clearly deduced" from the existing case law; and (3) the answer to the question admits of "no reasonable doubt". See further Article 104(3) of the Rules of Procedure of the Court of Justice.

[125] For further discussion of these procedural reforms, see Lenaerts, *supra* note 109, at 236-238.

[126] It has been foreseen that Poland would have a permanent Advocate General (as do Germany, France, Italy, Spain and the UK already) and that the rotation system would

B. Reforms relating to the Nice Treaty

Taken together, these reforms manifest ways of improving the efficiency and the effectiveness of the Community courts without putting at risk either their functional division of tasks or the uniform application of Community law.

B. Reforms relating to the Nice Treaty

As mentioned above, two notable reforms heralded by the Nice Treaty stand out. These concern the possibility of conferring jurisdiction on the CFI to deliver preliminary rulings and to decide infringement actions, both of which would have a considerable impact on the relationship between the Community courts and the national courts and the routes for assessing the compatibility of acts of the Member States with Community law.

The prospect of the CFI delivering preliminary rulings, this has been the center of much debate since the insertion of Article 225(3) EC which envisaged the conferral of preliminary ruling jurisdiction on the CFI "in *specific areas* laid down by the Statute."[127] Yet, at present, this possibility has not been put into action. This can be explained by the tremendous difficulties in delineating the "specific areas" ripe for transfer without harming the unity and the consistency of Community law. In other words, there does not seem to be too many areas of Community law that constitute a separate body of law that can effectively be carved out without affecting the other areas of Community law.

Nevertheless, there do exist some areas in which the unity of European law would probably not stand in the way of a partial transfer

---

therefore involve the rotation of five, not three, Advocates General. See Draft Declaration ad Article 222 of the Treaty on the Functioning of the European Union on the number of Advocates-General in the Court of Justice, DS 866/07, dated 18 October 2007, *available at* http://www.consilium.europa.eu/showPage.asp?id=1317&lang=en&mode=g.

[127] Art. 225(3), first para. EC (emphasis added). It should be noted from the outset that aside from certain proposed changes in relation to renaming the CFI "the General Court" and the judicial panels "specialised courts" and prescribing the latter's establishment by way of the co-decision procedure involving the Council and the European Parliament, the Draft Reform Treaty would not substantively change the relevant provisions of Arts 225 and 225a EC as discussed herein. See Draft Reform Treaty, point 20, at 16-17 and points 210-211, at 119-120.

[128] Case C-338/95, *Wiener S.I. GmbH*, [1997] ECR I-6495.

The Evolution of the Judicial System of the European Union

of preliminary ruling jurisdiction to the CFI. First, customs matters seem a viable field, since it is one inviting the Court of Justice to assume the CFI's role of assessing the facts within the context of the classification of a certain product under the Combined Nomenclature. This was aptly illustrated by the *Wiener* case[128], which expended the Court's time in deciding whether women's clothing should be classified as nightwear (pyjamas) or beachwear. These cases may be easily severable from general European law, especially when only those cases exclusively involving the classification issue are transferred to the CFI, as opposed to those simultaneously involving other issues.

Second, for matters in which the CFI acts as an appellate court, *not* as a first instance court, and the preliminary reference pertains to the same subject as that on appeal, the CFI's preliminary ruling jurisdiction would not be likely to harm the unity of Community law. With the proliferation of intellectual property cases gradually occupying the place formerly reserved to staff cases in the CFI's docket before the creation of the EU Civil Service Tribunal, the creation of a Community intellectual property court could be envisaged.[129] Then, since the CFI would act as a court of appeals in relation to such cases, as provided by the first paragraph of Article 225(2) EC[130], the Court of Justice's exceptional review jurisdiction would equally exist for direct actions and preliminary rulings in this field in case of transfer of the jurisdiction to give such rulings to the CFI.[131]

---

[129] Such a court would at present essentially deal with the rising number of trademark cases pending in the CFI. Moreover, the Commission has already submitted a Proposal for a Council Decision establishing the Community Patent Court and concerning appeals before the Court of First Instance, COM (2003) 828 final, 23 December 2003; see also its Proposal for a Council Decision conferring jurisdiction on the Court of Justice in disputes relating to the Community patent, COM (2003) 827 final, 23 December 2003. This is so even though the instrument providing for the Community patent has not yet been adopted, although there have been recent developments in this regard: see Commission Communication, "Enhancing the patent system in Europe", COM (2007) 165 final, 3 April 2007, with comments by the Editorial, "Patent failure?", 32 *European Law Review* 293 (2007).

[130] See also Art. 225a, third para. EC.

[131] Art. 225(2), second para. EC provides for the Court of Justice's exceptional review of the CFI's judgments concerning appeals from the judicial panels, whereas Art. 225(3), third para. EC concerns the Court of Justice's exceptional review of the CFI's preliminary rulings. In both cases, under Art. 62 of the Statute of the Court of Justice,

Importantly, this shows why the transfer of preliminary ruling jurisdiction to the CFI in matters for which the CFI acts as a first instance court would not work. It would leave the Court of Justice with only exceptional review jurisdiction in relation to the CFI's preliminary rulings in these matters, while it would have full appeal jurisdiction on points of law in relation to the CFI's direct action jurisdiction in the very same matters. As a result, the parallelism between direct actions and preliminary rulings in relation to these matters would be broken; this would upset in an unacceptable manner the coherence of the judicial system of the Union.

As far as proposals advocating the transfer of not just partial but general preliminary ruling jurisdiction to the CFI are concerned, two points should be kept in mind. First, this would require a Treaty amendment, since Article 225(3) EC explicitly provides for such a transfer only in "specific areas". Second, care should be taken to distinguish the CFI's *general jurisdiction over most direct actions* – as provided by the Nice Treaty[132] and further implemented by the Council[133] – from the prospect of the CFI's *general preliminary ruling jurisdiction*, which would lead to the problem linked to the absence of procedural parallelism between direct actions and preliminary rulings mentioned above, i.e., the CFI would effectively be delivering quasi-final preliminary rulings in areas of law in which as to direct actions it would be acting as a true first instance court on points of law. It should be added that even if attempts were made to ensure that certain cases of particular importance or complexity or those that could seriously affect the unity and consistency of European law were to be referred to the ECJ by the CFI, in line with the second paragraph of Article 225(3) EC, problems of demarcation still abound, not only as regards the detachability of constitutional issues from general European law, but also given the fact that the constitutional significance of a reference may not become apparent until much later in

---

the First Advocate General may propose that the Court of Justice review the CFI's decision where he or she "considers that there is a serious risk of the unity or consistency of Community law being affected".

[132] See Art. 225(1), first para. EC.

[133] See Council Decision 2004/407/EC, Euratom of 26 April 2004 amending Articles 51 and 54 of the Protocol on the Statute of the Court of Justice, [2004] O.J. L 132/5; *corrigendum*, [2004] O.J. L 194/3.

The Evolution of the Judicial System of the European Union

the proceedings. Therefore, attention should concentrate on other procedural reforms set down by the Nice Treaty and the Court itself, and only when these reforms have been exhausted should the CFI's preliminary ruling jurisdiction in the specific areas identified above then be firmly considered.

As a result of the problems just mentioned, it has been advocated that the ECJ should keep the monopoly over preliminary rulings, and instead, the CFI's jurisdiction over direct actions should be extended, namely to infringement actions. In fact, this would not even require a Treaty amendment, since the last sentence of Article 225(1) EC expressly states that the Statute of the Court of Justice "may provide for the Court of First Instance to have jurisdiction for other classes of action or proceeding."[134] Even so, this issue warrants close consideration. On the one hand, it could be posited that infringement actions often require the appraisal of facts, thereby making the CFI the natural forum for such cases. On the other hand, infringement cases are often of great importance for the development of European law and, in any event, are always important for the uniform application of European law in the Member States, as seen above in terms of ensuring the compatibility of national measures with Community law. In contrast to other types of direct actions, it seems extremely difficult to elaborate a sufficient criterion for the division of jurisdiction between the ECJ and the CFI that would direct the infringement actions raising constitutional issues immediately to the former Community court. Thus, if one day, the increasing workload of the ECJ would make the transfer of infringement actions to the CFI unavoidable, a provision could be inserted into the Statute of the Court of Justice by which the CFI – acting on its own motion or at the request of the parties – could refer an infringement case to the ECJ under circumstances where it required a decision likely to affect the unity or consistency of Community law.[135]

---

[134] Art. 225(1), first para. EC.

[135] This is somewhat analogous to Art. 225(3), second para. EC, which would allow the CFI to refer a preliminary ruling to the Court of Justice where the case requires "a decision of principle likely to affect the unity or consistency of Community law."

CONCLUSION

In view of the foregoing discussion, it becomes clear that the evolution of the judicial system of the European Union does not rest solely on the Community courts, but rather on the interlocking relationship between the Community courts and the national courts. As evidenced by the examination of the judicial review of acts of the institutions and of acts of the Member States in relation to Community law, each set of courts does its part in line with the division of tasks set down by the Treaties to uphold the system of judicial protection and the "rule of law" in the European Union. It is in this light that the structural reforms of the Union judicature must be seen, since it is paramount that such reforms serve to fortify the contribution of the Community courts in their role alongside the national courts to ensure the full enforcement and effectiveness of Community and Union law for the years to come.

O MODELO SOCIAL EUROPEU
E A ESTRATÉGIA DE LISBOA

ANTÓNIO VITORINO[*]

Muito obrigado Sr. Conselheiro Cunha Rodrigues. Muito obrigado ao Instituto Europeu da Faculdade de Direito de Lisboa pelo convite, em especial ao Senhor Professor Doutor Pitta e Cunha, de quem fui aluno. Queria dizer que tenho muito gosto em estar aqui com o Presidente Koen Lenaerts, com quem partilhei muitos debates sobre os temas que ele tão brilhantemente acabou de abordar.

Esta sessão é uma sessão um bocadinho heterogénea porque agora saltamos da dignidade das questões judiciárias para a dura realidade do mundo social.

Para começo de conversa gostaria de sublinhar que creio que depois do referendo francês se reforçou na Europa a ideia de que a dimensão social da construção europeia é o "parente pobre" do projecto europeu. De alguma forma esta ideia é uma ideia parcial e até injusta! Na verdade, se virmos as quatro liberdades fundadoras – liberdade de circulação de mercadorias, de serviços, de capitais e de pessoas – é forçoso reconhecer que a liberdade de circulação de pessoas foi aquela que teve, ao longo destes cinquenta anos de integração europeia, um desenvolvimento menos dinâmico e menos aprofundado. Os números mais recentes que conheço indicavam que exerceram o direito de circular livremente e, portanto, de se fixarem e trabalharem num outro Estado-membro, cerca de 4 milhões a 5 milhões de europeus. Se adicionarmos os membros das famílias, alguns deles também com acesso ao mercado de trabalho, teremos um

---

[*] Instituto Europeu da Faculdade de Direito de Lisboa.

universo de 7 milhões de pessoas no conjunto da União Europeia a quinze, na medida em que, como se sabe, esta liberdade ainda não é hoje plenamente garantida aos doze Estados-membros que aderiram depois de 2004.

Curiosamente, um inquérito recente do Eurobarómetro indicava, por contraste, que cerca de 15% dos pensionistas dos países do norte da Europa tencionavam gozar a sua aposentação num país da Europa do Sul. E sem querer ser demasiado irónico, quase que se diria que, com esta tendência, a liberdade de circulação de trabalhadores vai ser em breve ultrapassada pela liberdade de circulação dos pensionistas.

Mas esta visão parcial e injusta da dimensão social esquece, em larga medida, que por impulso essencialmente do Tribunal de Justiça, assistimos, ao longo destes cinquenta anos, a um esforço meritório de densificação de direitos laborais importantes. Nós, portugueses, estamos particularmente bem posicionados para recordar que um conjunto de regras sobre higiene e segurança no trabalho, sobre duração do horário de trabalho, o próprio rendimento social de inserção, inclusive a dinâmica da coordenação das políticas de emprego (de que comemoramos este ano o 10º aniversário da denominada Estratégia do Luxemburgo), foram introduzidas no nosso ordenamento jurídico nacional por impulso do projecto europeu e das decisões tomadas a nível europeu. O mesmo se pode dizer do activo que representa, para o projecto europeu, o diálogo social europeu, seja nas cimeiras tripartidas, seja inclusivamente na formação de organizações transnacionais representativas dos trabalhadores ou do patronato, a nível sócio-profissional, a nível de sectores de actividade económica ou, mesmo até, a nível das próprias empresas.

Não é possível esquecer que valores estruturantes daquilo que nós consideramos a civilização europeia tiveram sempre, no projecto europeu, uma alavanca de promoção relevante: por exemplo, a igualdade entre homens e mulheres, designadamente no plano do acesso ao mercado de trabalho, ou as medidas anti-discriminação, contra a discriminação em função da nacionalidade, em função do território de origem ou mesmo, em função da raça ou do credo religioso, que foram incentivadas pelos planos de acção anti-discriminação adoptados a nível europeu.

Finalmente, para fazer a defesa de que a dimensão social europeia não é o tal "parente pobre" do projecto europeu, não podemos esquecer que políticas estruturantes do projecto europeu, como a política ambiental ou a política de defesa do consumidor, são dois pilares importantes de uma interpretação ampla do que é a dimensão social europeia em termos de qualidade de vida dos cidadãos.

O *Modelo Social Europeu e a Estratégia de Lisboa*

Poderá então perguntar-se: perante estes activos, porquê então este sentimento tão difundido de que há um défice social no projecto europeu?! É verdade que esse défice social existe, não o vou negar! O meu ponto é que ele não é tão grave quanto muitos dos críticos assinalam, mas existe por uma razão básica quanto às vulnerabilidades da dimensão social do projecto de integração europeia: é que não podemos falar num sólido acordo político de princípio, entre os Estados-membros, sobre o papel a atribuir à dimensão social no projecto europeu. A que acresce que o processo de alargamento da União, ao ampliar a diversidade social europeia e ao aprofundar os desníveis sociais entre os países que pertencem à União, tornou mais difícil obter esse consenso sobre as políticas sociais a desenvolver no plano europeu.

A "Convenção sobre o futuro da Europa", de que aqui já foi apresentado um relato positivo no que diz respeito à matéria judiciária, não pode ser vista à luz de uma idêntico balanço positivo no que diz respeito às questões sociais. Neste capítulo, a Convenção ficou aquém de muitas das expectativas que foram criadas, designadamente quando se optou por um referencial constitucional. Convém recordar que na Convenção, que se atribuía uma vocação refundadora da própria União, não foi possível lograr um acordo substantivo entre os membros do grupo de trabalho que foi por ela criado sobre a Europa social, grupo esse que visava debater e adoptar as possíveis linhas de desenvolvimento da dimensão social em sede de reforma dos Tratados. Mesmo assim, foi possível acordar em alguns contributos que, tendo alcance limitado e escassa visibilidade no debate público, representam contudo alguma evolução positiva que espero que não seja deixada para trás na transposição do conteúdo do Tratado Constitucional para o futuro Tratado Reformador.

O primeiro aspecto inovatório do Tratado Constitucional no capítulo das políticas sociais, relevante por ser acolhido pela primeira vez explicitamente em sede dos próprios Tratados, diz respeito à consagração da interacção ou implicação recíproca das chamadas linhas de orientação da política económica ("Broad Economic Policy Guidelines") e das linhas de orientação da política do emprego ("Employment Guidelines"). Levou anos o debate entre as instituições e os Estados-membros até se chegar à decisão de fazer coincidir no tempo a adopção dos instrumentos de política económica propostos pela Comissão ao Conselho, e a adopção das linhas de acção prioritárias em matéria de política de emprego. Levou anos a que as instituições tivessem que analisar conjuntamente as *Economic Policy Guidelines* e as *Employment Guidelines* e consequentemente curarem da sua coerência recíproca. Mesmo assim, quando estes dois instrumentos de programação política macro-económica e macro-social estão simultaneamente em cima da mesa, é manifesto que a corrente dominante aponta no sentido de considerar que o instrumento nobre e determinante é o do planeamento económico e que o instrumento subsidiário ou auxiliar é o das linhas do emprego.

Sobre este tema importa reconhecer que o Tratado Constitucional (e agora provavelmente o futuro Tratado Reformador), encerra uma contradição em potência, ou, no mínimo, uma certa tensão quanto ao estatuto que confere à questão do emprego no conjunto da retórica constitucional europeia, na medida em que ficou consagrado como objectivo da União o "pleno emprego", isto no artigo correspondente aos objectivos da União Europeia mas, por contraste, já no artigo que tem a ver com a União Económica e Monetária não figura o tal objectivo do pleno emprego, mas antes mantém-se inalterada a fórmula adoptada no Tratado de Maastricht, que refere como objectivo um "elevado nível de emprego".

Ora, esta tensão entre as políticas de emprego e a política económica é, em meu entender, um dos factores que provoca alguma desconfiança em relação à capacidade de afirmação da dimensão social europeia.

Permitam-me que refira neste momento algo que sucedeu há dois dias no Conselho Europeu sobre as regras aplicáveis à política da concorrência no futuro Tratado Reformador. A circunstância de se ter eliminado a "concorrência livre e não distorcida" do elenco dos objectivos da União Europeia, para além da sua relevância própria no quadro daquela política europeia, tem também que ser lida à luz da escassa relevância que tem sido dada à dimensão social no elenco dos critérios que têm sido reiteradamente chamados à colação para analisar quer os casos de fusão entre empresas com dimensão europeia quer no âmbito da avaliação das ajudas de Estado concedidas pelos Estados-membros quando submetidas a autorização da Comissão Europeia. Não se pode deixar de reconhecer que tem sido flagrante que as detalhadas análises do impacto económico global e sobre os mercados em concreto levadas a cabo sobre uma fusão entre duas empresas, análises que incidem sobretudo no número de *stakeholders* no mercado, na sustentabilidade das linhas de produtos que seriam afectadas pela fusão ou na repercussão sobre os seus preços na óptica do consumidor, raramente mostram sensibilidade para contemplarem ao mesmo título o concreto impacto social dessas fusões ou mesmo das próprias medidas de ajudas de Estado concedidas, designadamente no plano do emprego. Isso criou, naturalmente, a ideia de que esta Europa era uma Europa demasiado liberal, era uma Europa onde a concorrência prevalecia em excesso, quando todos sabemos que há ainda hoje inúmeros entraves a uma concorrência livre e não distorcida no contexto europeu. E digamos que o efeito negativo desta leitura demasiado estreita dos critérios a chamar à colação na definição das orientações fundamentais da política de concorrência levou agora a este resultado que acabámos de assistir e que é, na minha opinião, um resultado negativo para o desenvolvimento do projecto europeu. Sem embargo, devemos reconhecer que subsistem, nos Tratados, algumas garantias, do ponto de vista jurídico, de que a eliminação da referência à política da concorrência no elenco dos objectivos da União não impede o recurso ao artigo 308.º, à cláusula de flexibilidade, para adopção de regras em matéria de política da concorrência e que as bases legais específicas não serão afectadas por aquela eliminação no preceito atinente aos objectivos.

Mas não podemos ignorar o relevo político que tal eliminação obviamente apresenta para o futuro da política de concorrência europeia...

Onde reside então a questão fundamental da dimensão social não ser sentida como uma efectiva prioridade da União Europeia?

Na minha opinião, a questão fundamental reside num desfasamento entre as prioridades que os cidadãos atribuem às políticas sociais e aquilo que são os instrumentos efectivos ao dispor da União Europeia nesses mesmos domínios. Para quem lê atentamente o Eurobarómetro, verifica que, em sede de políticas sociais, os cidadãos exprimem três preocupações centrais: emprego, sustentabilidade da segurança social e cuidados de saúde. Nestes três domínios a capacidade autónoma de intervenção da União Europeia é particularmente limitada. Talvez menos no domínio do emprego mas, sobretudo e decididamente, no domínio da segurança social e no domínio da saúde. Basta ler, no mandato da Conferência Intergovernamental que vai ser convocada pela presidência portuguesa, aprovado no fim-de-semana passado em Bruxelas, a redacção verdadeiramente esdrúxula do artigo sobre a portabilidade dos direitos de segurança social dos trabalhadores que exercem a liberdade de circulação – cheio de reservas, cheio de salvaguardas, com a ressalva de integridade orgânica, da sustentabilidade financeira dos sistemas de segurança social nacionais – para perceber que, no domínio da segurança social, a palavra de ordem a nível europeu é a mais profunda desconfiança quanto a qualquer nível de aproximação conjunta europeia.

Ora, este tipo de reservas, cautelas, salvaguardas e precauções tem impacto directo na percepção por parte dos cidadãos quanto ao estatuto das políticas sociais. Ninguém pode ignorar, por exemplo, que no referendo dinamarquês sobre a possível adesão daquele país à União Económica e Monetária, onde estava em causa a adopção do Euro, o receio mais profundo dos dinamarqueses apurado pelas sondagens levadas a cabo antes e depois do referendo dizia precisamente respeito ao medo de que a existência de uma zona monetária única levasse a um nivelamento por baixo dos sistemas de segurança social nacionais, designadamente do sistema de segurança social dinamarquês que é, manifestamente, um sistema enraizado na sociedade e que os cidadãos daquele país consideram oferecer regalias confortáveis. Ou seja, não estando em causa, pelo menos directamente, o estatuto da segurança social, a opinião pública dinamarquesa entendeu que a moeda única representava uma ameaça a esse mesmo sistema de solidariedade social, tendo rejeitado a adopção do Euro.

Portanto, quando se fala de segurança social na Europa, o norte tende, de facto, a olhar para as tentativas de aproximação europeia como uma "race to the bottom", isto é, uma corrida para o nivelamento por baixo, enquanto que os países do sul tendem a ver, na ideia de aproximação dos mecanismos de segurança social, uma alavancagem da promoção dos seus próprios sistemas de protecção e de segurança social. Estas perspectivas conflituantes reflectem-se, depois, na margem de manobra dos respectivos governos em sede europeia quando são chamados a tratar das questões sociais.

O mesmo se diga da questão da saúde. Será interessantíssimo ver como é que o Conselho vai gerir a jurisprudência, cada vez mais relevante, do Tribunal de Justiça sobre a liberdade de circulação dos doentes no espaço europeu. E é manifesto que houve, quer na Constituição, quer agora no Tratado Reformador, uma preocupação do legislador de tentar limitar as "asas" do Tribunal no "voo" sobre a consagração desta liberdade de circulação dos doentes, mais uma vez em nome da sustentabilidade dos respectivos sistemas de saúde nacionais.

Isto significa, no meu entender, que é obvio que há um desfasamento entre as expectativas dos cidadãos no domínio social e aquilo que já foi hoje, no primeiro painel, identificado como "the capacity to deliver" da União Europeia, a capacidade de gerar resultados a nível europeu nestes domínios de matérias.

O *Modelo Social Europeu e a Estratégia de Lisboa* 91

Sendo assim, a questão essencial que se coloca, em meu entender, não é tanto uma questão de alteração dos Tratados na medida em que, como acabei de vos descrever com alguns exemplos concretos, não me parece que seja previsível que, no curto prazo, seja possível introduzir nos Tratados as competências, os instrumentos necessários para responder mais efectivamente a estas expectativas dos cidadãos. Sem embargo, parece-me óbvio que o conjunto das políticas europeias – a começar pela política económica e monetária – não poderão deixar de ser convocadas para dar resposta às transformações das sociedades europeias que põem mais claramente em causa o sucesso do próprio projecto de integração económica e que têm a ver com a sustentabilidade do modelo de coesão e de solidariedade social.

Tentando explicar esta ideia de outra forma: em vez de tentar fazer da política social um instrumento *a se* no plano europeu, ou seja, a criação de uma "política social europeia" abrangente e compreensiva, no que, sinceramente, não acredito por entender que não existe nem o consenso nem a vontade política dos Estados-membros para assim proceder, vai ser necessário, pelo contrário, identificar quais são aquelas transformações das sociedades europeias que põem mais directamente em causa a sustentabilidade do próprio projecto de integração económica e, por essa via, tentar responder a algumas das expectativas sociais dos cidadãos europeus.

Recentemente a Comissão Europeia publicou um documento para debate, da responsabilidade do grupo de conselheiros políticos, sobre a realidade social europeia, e é em torno das quatro grandes transformações das sociedades europeias identificadas nesse documento que, em meu entender, haverá que retirar as ilações necessárias, não apenas para a política social em sentido estrito, com as limitações que já lhe assinalei, mas para um conjunto horizontal de outras políticas europeias – a política económica, a política de concorrência, a política comercial mas, também, a política de imigração por exemplo – que serão fundamentais para o futuro do próprio projecto económico.

Não vou entrar agora em detalhes de um estudo muito interessante e complexo, mas para este efeito releva identificar essas quatro transformações fundamentais a que haverá que encontrar uma resposta integrada e envolvendo as várias políticas da União.

Em primeiro lugar, temos o panorama demográfico europeu e o impacto que a evolução demográfica previsível vai ter na mão-de-obra activa nos próximos vinte a vinte e cinco anos na União Europeia, onde se prevê que, no conjunto da população mundial, os europeus, que hoje são 8% da população mundial, daqui a cerca de vinte e cinco anos serão apenas cerca de 6% daquela população mundial. Quando se fala no papel dominante da Europa na regulação à escala global não se pode esquecer a base de partida e esta reporta-se a um continente demograficamente decadente e em perda de peso relativo em relação aos outros continentes, talvez com excepção da Rússia que tem um problema de envelhecimento ainda mais grave do que o problema europeu.

Portanto, primeiro bloco de questões essencial: a demografia, o impacto da demografia na mão-de-obra activa, o impacto da demografia na sustentabilidade dos sistemas de segurança social, isto é, no tal modelo de coesão e de solidariedade que foi fundamental para o sucesso da prosperidade do projecto europeu, a quebra da fecundidade que, na Europa a vinte e cinco, hoje está cifrada em 1.48, quando na realidade a taxa de reposição da população activa andaria à volta dos 2.1.

O problema demográfico liga-se com um segundo problema intimamente conexionado mas que apela a uma política distinta: refiro--me à necessidade de sabermos gerir a diversidade étnica e cultural da Europa, não apenas da Europa alargada mas também de uma Europa que, por estas razões, se tornará, cada vez mais, pólo de atracção de fluxos migratórios e, portanto, um continente para onde convergirão pessoas oriundas de outros continentes, que decerto continuarão a colocar complexas questões de integração nas sociedades europeias de acolhimento.

Terceira grande transformação: aquilo que o estudo a que me estou a referir identifica como a individualização dos valores. Isto é, há nas sociedades europeias uma perda do sentido colectivo e essa perda do sentido colectivo e da solidariedade colectiva tem impactos na predisposição dos cidadãos à participação na vida pública (inclusive no plano da própria participação eleitoral), mas também num conjunto de outros planos fundamentais que historicamente contribuíram para o aprofundamento do modelo de coesão e solidariedade europeu. Refiro-me, por exemplo, à evolução da taxa de divórcios na Europa, que numa geração aumentou em 50%, sendo que hoje em dia 25% das crianças europeias nascem fora de casamentos. As famílias não tradicionais têm vindo a conhecer uma evolução progressiva em todos os Estados, cuja realidade tem que ser compreendida e integrada de pleno nos mecanismos de solidariedade social que foram originariamente pensados em função de um outro paradigma que deixou de ser único ou mesmo, em alguns casos, dominante. Ora, curiosamente, uma das questões mais difíceis da negociação do mandato para o Tratado Reformador, que decorreu nestes últimos dois dias em Bruxelas, evidenciou exactamente a desconfiança que alguns Estados manifestaram em que pudesse haver, a nível europeu, qualquer tipo de regras que pudessem pôr em causa as legislações nacionais em matéria de direito da família ou de tratamento social das famílias. Esta questão dos valores das estruturas organizativas da própria sociedade é uma questão central e particularmente difícil com que se confronta hoje e cada vez mais no futuro o projecto europeu.

Quarta e última nota: a questão da sociedade dual de vencedores e vencidos no contexto global em que vivemos. Na minha maneira de ver, o essencial da desconfiança dos europeus sobre o projecto de integração europeia é o de que, nestes cinquenta anos, a avaliação que fazem da história da integração é globalmente positiva. Com efeito, foi um caso de sucesso na garantia da paz e da estabilidade, uma história de igualdade de oportunidades, de combate às desigualdades sociais e de aproximação dos níveis de rendimento. Só que, hoje em dia, perante a globalização económica, os desafios da sociedade do conhecimento, a concorrência global acrescida e social e ambientalmente desigual, os europeus vão tendo cada vez mais a percepção de que, diferentemente do que sucedeu no passado, o fosso entre os vencedores e os vencidos se vai agravando e que o modelo económico que sustenta um quadro de referência de coesão e de solidariedade europeu já não é suficientemente eficaz para garantir essa coesão básica das nossas sociedades. Logo, o défice social, neste aspecto, resulta da desconfiança em relação à própria base económica que sustenta as nossas sociedades baseadas na redistribuição fiscal e na solidariedade social.

É ao essencial destas questões, angústias e desconfianças que a União Europeia pretendeu responder através da chamada "Estratégia de Lisboa". Mas essa resposta defrontou-se com três problemas fundamentais que me vou limitar a enunciar.

Primeiro: a "Estratégia de Lisboa" não tem, aos olhos do comum dos cidadãos, um perfil político claro para responder a estes desafios. As dificuldades de compreensão e de assumpção desta Agenda de reformas resulta de ela ser muito dispersiva, já houve quem lhe chamasse uma estratégia "catch-all parties", e embora tenha havido uma tentativa de prioritarizar objectivos em torno do emprego e da competitividade (na revisão a meio percurso na Primavera de 2005), a verdade é que a acção com base na "Estratégia de Lisboa" não aparece aos europeus como "a" resposta necessária perante aquelas quatro grandes transformações das sociedades europeias.

O segundo problema da "Estratégia de Lisboa" prende-se com as insuficiências do método de coordenação aberta. Há pouco, o Presidente Lenaerts referiu que o mercado interno foi construído com base num centro difusor de objectivos, que adoptava legislação cuja aplicação cabia à periferia, aos Estados-membros, mas, se estes não cumprissem as suas obrigações de transposição daquela legislação, ser-lhes-iam aplicadas sanções correspondentes. Ora, na lógica do método de coordenação aberta que inspira a "Estratégia de Lisboa", os objectivos definidos centralmente, em conjunto pela própria União, são, à partida, mais difusos e diluídos, muito mais indicativos do que obrigatórios. O que faz com que os resultados do conjunto dependam sobretudo do ritmo das reformas aplicadas por cada uma das periferias, por cada um dos Estados-membros, ou seja, o produto global (e a sua percepção pelo conjunto dos europeus) é muito mais assimétrico na medida em que está muito mais dependente do ritmo das reformas adoptadas pelos Estados-membros individualmente considerados, em função das suas específicas condições políticas, económicas e sociais. Em resumo, a vantagem da flexibilidade e da adaptabilidade e um universo de destinatários diferenciados entre si do ponto de vista do desenvolvimento económico e social acaba por tornar menos premente a obtenção dos resultados e paradoxalmente menos claro o valor acrescentado da "Estratégia de Lisboa".

Terceira insuficiência da "Estratégia de Lisboa: além dos problemas de *governance* típicos do método de coordenação aberta, é difícil aceitar que não haja nenhuma forma de articulação entre a lógica da gestão dos objectivos da "Estratégia de Lisboa" e um modelo de coordenação das políticas económicas dos Estados-membros, pelo menos na zona Euro. Ou seja, a magnitude dos desafios torna indissociável o aprofundamento da União Económica e Monetária através de uma mais consistente coordenação das políticas económicas nacionais da zona Euro, com os próprios objectivos da Agenda de Lisboa. Não escapa de modo algum aos cidadãos europeus que este "casamento" entre estes dois objectivos ainda não foi alcançado.

Já excedi o meu tempo e concluo apenas, com uma nota num tom provavelmente menos crítico. Para sublinhar que nem tudo são dificuldades, claro está! Nestes dois últimos dias, no Conselho Europeu de Bruxelas, foi possível garantir que a Carta dos Direitos Fundamentais da União Europeia terá valor jurídico com a mesma dignidade dos próprios Tratados da União. O preço a pagar por esta decisão foi a inclusão de um Protocolo sobre o estatuto especial do Reino Unido, protocolo esse que decerto suscitará muitas interpretações no Tribunal a que pertencem os meus dois ilustres parceiros deste painel. Não lhes antevejo tarefa fácil.

Mas tirando a especificidade da situação do Reino Unido, a boa notícia é a de que os Estados-membros reconheceram que a Carta devia ter valor jurídico e nessa Carta contem-se uma declaração de direitos que não só retoma os direito civis e políticos clássicos, mas coloca em pé de igualdade com estes e com a mesma dimensão jurídica os direitos económicos, sociais e culturais, que estão e terão que estar no centro da dimensão social da União Europeia. Por isso haverá que dizer aos europeus aquilo que um dia o Ronald Dworkin escreveu como título de um seu célebre livro: "Taking Rights Serioulsy"!

Também espero que o projecto europeu tome os direitos sociais que a Carta consagra muito a sério!

LES ELARGISSEMENTS ET LES LIMITES DE L'UNION EUROPEENNE

JEAN-CLAUDE GAUTRON[*]

Je tiens à exprimer l'honneur et le plaisir de me retrouver à Lisbonne, où j'ai l'occasion de venir depuis un certain nombre d'années, et dire tout l'intérêt que je porte à l'organisation de ce Colloque. Il nous faut rendre hommage, bien sûr, au Professeur Pitta e Cunha. Nous l'avons déjà fait, mais je le refais en termes très sincères et très amicaux.

La question qu'il m'a été demandé de traiter est celle des élargissements et des limites de l'Union Européenne. D'une certaine manière, on pourrait dire que les deux choses vont ensemble, puisque tout élargissement détermine par lui-même les nouvelles frontières, les limites réelles de l'Union Européenne. Mais, pourtant, à ce bon sens apparent, j'opposerais une réflexion d'ordre théorique à savoir que l'élargissement, en tant que processus juridique et politique, est maintenant, depuis les cinquième et sixième élargissements, assez bien connu. Les processus d'élargissement sont bien maîtrisés instrumentalement, et pourtant les limites de l'Union Européenne demeurent toujours assez mystérieuses, elles relèvent du futur et sont, en l'état actuel des choses, très largement indéterminées. C'est autour de ce contraste que je voudrais bâtir mon exposé en rappelant l'énoncé de l'article 49 du Traité de l'Union Européenne: tout Etat européen qui respecte les principes énoncés à l'article 6, paragraphe 1, peut demander à devenir membre de l'Union. «Peut demander», «tout Etat européen», il n'y a là aucun automatisme.

---

[*] Professeur émérite de l'Université Montesquieu-Bordeaux IV

Je reviendrai sur ce point en disant qu'il existe à l'heure actuelle une certaine tendance à confondre les limites de l'Europe, qui sont une reconstruction culturelle et historique de notre continent, avec les limites de l'Union Européenne. Or, il ne s'agit pas de la même chose.

I – Des processus d'élargissement identifiés

Le schéma classique initial qui a prévalu pendant une trentaine d'années était limpide.

Il reposait implicitement sur une dialectique entre élargissement et approfondissement. Dans tous les cas, l'élargissement exigeait la réunion de trois points fondamentaux: l'acceptation de l'acquis communautaire, une modification des institutions et le recours à des mesures transitoires. Or, les successifs élargissements, dans le passé, ont en outre impliqué des révisions, soit préalables, soit collatérales. Exemple de réglementation/ révision préalable: avant l'entrée du Royaume-Uni dans la Communauté, il a fallu arrêter un règlement financier définitif; il fallait y procéder avant son entrée, afin de lui imposer les obligations de la politique agricole commune, dont on savait qu'elles seront largement contestées dès son entrée. Avant l'entrée de l'Espagne dans la Communauté, en 1983, fût arrêté un règlement pêche, qui n'avait jamais été arrêté jusqu'alors, et c'est évidement l'imminence de l'élargissement qui provoqua alors l'institutionnalisation d'une politique encore indéfinie. Avec l'Espagne et le Portugal, en 1985, il fût procédé à une révision du marché vini-viticole dans un sens, on le sait, plus sévère, c'est-à-dire que les soutiens publics à la viticulture ont perdu le caractère automatique qu'ils avaient au début. On peut dire aussi que l'arrivée de l'Espagne, du Portugal, de la Grèce a revivifié collatéralement les processus de cohésion économique et so-ciale. Les fonds structurels ont été une réponse aux attentes des nouveaux Etats et aux insatisfactions de quelques anciens Etats, tels le Royaume- -Uni et l'Italie face à la politique agricole commune.

Malheureusement, la révision des institutions a été ajournée face au quatrième élargissement, Finlande, Suède et Autriche. Il a donc fallu y procéder dans des conditions plutôt médiocres avec le Traité de Nice, en l'an 2000, dans les conditions que nous savons. Puis, on a cherché à dépasser cela avec le projet de révision constitutionnelle, le projet de

Constitution européenne dont l'échec a fait émerger l'urgence d'une reforme institutionnelle. Désormais, elle est en cours dans des conditions que l'on suppose satisfaisantes par le jeu du Traité de Lisbonne.

A / L'expérience des 5ème et 6ème élargissements

On doit d'abord tirer, dans un premier point, les conséquences de ce qui s'est passé pour le cinquième et le sixième élargissements très différents de tous les précédents, vu la nature des Etats candidats, pour l'essentiel des Etats postcommunistes, dix sur douze. L'Union Européenne à cet égard a tiré les conséquences de l'effacement de l'empire soviétique et de l'effondrement du mur de Berlin. On peut dire que ce choix balance entre l'enthousiasme réel pour un élargissement à l'Est et la nécessité historique et politique, parce que les faits sont têtus, de prendre immédiatement en charge les Etats postcommunistes issus de cette rupture. Ces cinquième et sixième élargissements se sont traduits par une double adaptation, une adaptation d'abord des Etats candidats et en même temps une adaptation de l'Union Européenne. C'est sans doute une idée intéressante. Il faut à la fois adapter les Etats futurs membres et, en même temps, adapter l'Union Européenne à ce qu'elle va devenir, c'est-à-dire une entité comportant un plus grand nombre d'Etats. Ce qui rappelle le principe de Hegel pour qui un changement de dimension implique toujours un changement de nature.

1) L'adaptation des candidats est intervenue dans de bonnes conditions, en jouant sur la succession des accords, accords de plus en plus précis, qui conduisaient vers l'adhésion, accords de commerce, puis de coopération, puis accords européens d'association, auxquels ce sont surajoutés très vite les fameux critères de Copenhague, critères politiques, mais aussi critères économiques. Les critères politiques sont connus, il en a été question ce matin. Les critères économiques sont au nombre de deux: une économie de marché viable, mais aussi la capacité de résister à la pression concurrentielle. Nous ne pensons pas que la disparition du mot «concurrence libre et non faussée» à la suite des travaux du Conseil européen d'avant-hier, sous la pression du Président de la République française et compte tenu de la nécessité pour lui de faire adopter cette révision par une partie de son opposition, donc du parti socialiste, constitue un quelconque changement puisqu'il faut en chercher les véritables motifs dans la logique interne de l'Etat. Critères de Copenhague auxquels s'ajoutait le critère de la réception de l'acquis communautaire. Donc, pour ce qui est de l'acquis communautaire, on a procédé à une ventilation de cet acquis en trente et un chapitres, qui faisaient l'objet successivement de négociation, négociation ouverte, négociation suspendue s'il y a lieu, négociation close ou refermée dès lors que l'on ne revenait pas sur le chapitre. De trente et un chapitres, on est passé aujourd'hui à trente cinq chapitres, c'est une indication du durcissement des critères, d'un infléchissement des critères sur lesquels je reviendrai.

2) Quant à l'adaptation de l'Union Européenne, elle s'est faite au moyen de quelques grandes révisions sur les valeurs communes et les droits fondamentaux, on en a parlé beaucoup, et une révision des institutions en trois temps: dans un premier temps, le Traité de Nice, avec ses imperfections; dans un deuxième temps, l'émergence d'une constitution européenne; et dans un troisième temps, un retour vers un traité institutionnel, mais qui, comme l'ensemble du droit communautaire, emporte avec lui une constitution matérielle. On n'a pas attendu les constitutionnalistes pour observer la prévoyance d'une constitution matérielle. Beaucoup de nos collègues ont travaillé très tôt sur la question puisque cette constitution matérielle a commencé avec les premiers jours de la CECA, en 1951. Peu d'entités politiques, aujourd'hui souveraines, peuvent se vanter d'avoir connu une période d'incubation, de maturation sur le plan juridique et politique de plus de cinquante ans. Si l'on se réfère aux travaux de l'école historique allemande du droit, on s'aperçoit que dans ces facteurs historiques il y a une richesse réelle.

En même temps, sur les politiques il fallait adopter des compromis. Ils ont été adoptés en ce qui concerne la circulation des personnes, la politique agricole commune, la cohésion, le cadre financier pluriannuel et aussi le saupoudrage dans les instruments d'adhésion de clauses de sauvegarde. Il y a à cet égard, en Bulgarie, une clause de sauvegarde importante dans le troisième pilier, coopération en matière de justice et d'affaires intérieures, devenu coopération judiciaire et policière.

B / L'infléchissement actuel des critères

1) Aujourd'hui on assiste, toujours sous le couvert de l'élargissement, à un infléchissement de ces critères. Un nouveau critère a émergé que l'on l'appelle la capacité de l'Union à intégrer de nouveaux membres. Est-ce véritablement un nouveau critère? Pas tout à fait. Il était déjà sous-jacent dès le début. Il était présent aussi à Copenhague. Il a été repris par la Commission et par le Conseil Européen en 2006. Il s'agit d'un critère défensif, qui consiste à veiller à ce que l'arrivée de nouveaux membres ne contrevienne pas aux objectifs des traités, à l'équilibre et au bon fonctionnement de l'Union Européenne.

La Commission précise que l'Union doit rester capable de «conserver l'élan» de l'intégration européenne d'où il découle que l'appréciation doit porter sur l'aménagement et le fonctionnement des institutions (c'est l'idée de réforme institutionnelle), ainsi que sur l'étude des incidences budgétaires de tout élargissement; en outre il convient de procéder à une étude de l'impact de l'élargissement sur les politiques de l'Union.

Symétriquement, les nouveaux membres doivent, donc, être évalués selon des critères de conditionnalité plus stricts qu'auparavant et disons le, de plus en plus stricts.

On assiste de ce fait à un durcissement des critères de conditionnalité. Ainsi, existe-t-il désormais des critères de référence propres à chaque Etat candidat à l'adhésion, qui s'appliquent à l'ouverture et à la clôture des différents chapitres.

Donc, le système est le même mais il se durcit, il devient plus sévère. Ainsi, il y a trois jours, le gouvernement français s'est opposé à l'ouverture de la négociation sur l'Union économique et monétaire avec la Turquie et c'est peut-être un signe, une anticipation probable de la position finale, sauf changement qui interviendrait plus tard, de la France face à l'adhésion de la Turquie.

Une troisième idée, qui est aujourd'hui largement développée, c'est l'idée de légitimer les élargissements. Je crois que par là on a bien tiré les conséquences des referendums négatifs intervenus en France et en Hollande. L'élargissement n'a pas été légitimé, il n'a pas été très bien compris, il a été confondu avec une endogénéisation de la mondialisation. Il a donc provoqué des réactions de rejet. Cela ne saurait être contesté. On observe d'ailleurs qu'en matière européenne l'opinion des gouvernements et l'opinion publique ne sont pas toujours en parfaite concordance. Lorsque M. Tsoukalis dit que la Grèce est favorable à l'adhésion de la Turquie, oui. Les hommes politiques grecs ont fait ce choix et l'on peut comprendre pourquoi. Ils l'ont fait parce que la Grèce aspire à jouer un rôle beaucoup plus important dans sa sphère, ce qu'on appelle les Balkans. On l'a classée dans les Balkans orientaux, de surcroît. Elle veut donc que le trou soit comblé et que les Balkans occidentaux rentrent à leur tour dans l'Union et il est clair qu'elle entend mieux régler ses contentieux bilatéraux avec la Turquie dans le cadre de l'Union, même sur Chypre, que dans le cadre bilatéral international.

Alors, ce nouveaux critère est-il vraiment satisfaisant? Il l'est, mais en vérité cette capacité de l'Union à subir, à supporter l'intégration de nouveaux membres fait l'objet d'une lecture subjective selon les Etats. Ce n'est pas un critère objectif. C'est sous la plume de la Commission un critère objectif, parce qu'il faut bien faire un document qui ne heurte personne, mais, en vérité, si je viens de citer la Grèce, on peut prendre le cas du Royaume-Uni ; le Royaume-Uni est favorable à une extension du grand marché intérieur, aussi large que possible, non assortie d'ailleurs nécessairement, d'un développement de la puissance politique. Le Royaume-Uni se situera, donc, dans cette affaire de la Turquie, sur une position qui ne sera pas celle de la France ou de tel ou tel Etat. Si l'on observe l'Autriche on voit que l'Autriche, pour des raisons historico-culturelles est évidement ouverte à l'arrivée des Balkans et plutôt réservée en ce qui concerne l'arrivée de la Turquie, etc. Ces variations se retrouvent même à l'intérieur des Etats et au sein des partis politiques nationaux.

2) L'infléchissement des critères apparaît clairement dans les phases de pré-négociation et de négociation.

Le renforcement technique des conditionnalités est manifeste. Les domaines de la conditionnalité sont élargis. Aux domaines politiques (démocratie, Etat de droit, droits fondamentaux et protection des minorités) et économiques s'ajoutent une appréciation de la capacité administrative et judiciaire des Etats candidats à l'adhésion et une évaluation de leurs aptitudes en matière de gestion des visas, du droit d'asile ou de surveillance des frontières. L'échelle de la qualité normative des Etats est évidemment surveillée (marché, concurrence, marchés publics). Un autre aspect de la conditionnalité s'attache aux modalités et au degré du respect de leurs obligations internationales.

Il revient à la Commission d'élaborer des rapports sur l'ensemble de ces points. Elle y procède régulièrement mais souvent les rapports qu'elle produit demeurent en partie elliptiques. En effet pour des raisons politiques et diplomatiques, d'ordre externe et d'ordre interne, elle pratique une certaine autocensure et se garde d'appuyer trop à fond ses réserves ou ses critiques.

Deux secteurs géopolitiques sont impliqués aujourd'hui par ces processus: les Balkans «occidentaux» et la Turquie.

Les Balkans «occidentaux» sont engagés, ou susceptibles de s'engager, dans une stratégie de pré-adhésion. La Croatie est l'Etat le plus avancé puisque des négociations d'adhésion ont été ouvertes à la fin de l'année 2005. Chaque chapitre de la négociation comporte des critères de référence dont l'application se fait jour à l'ouverture et à la clôture des négociations thématiques par chapitres. Depuis 2007 l'aide à la pré-adhésion passe par l'Instrument d'Aide de Pré-Adhésion (IAD) qui remplace de façon progressive les programmes Phare, Ispa, Sapard. Une dimension multilatérale est incluse dans la négociation sous la forme d'un soutien à la signature d'un accord régional de libre-échange pour l'Europe du Sud-Est. L'émergence d'une candidature éventuelle passe désormais par la négociation préalable d'accords de stabilisation et d'association. Les pays concernés sont l'Albanie, la Bosnie, le Monténégro, la Serbie.

L'équation turque est encore plus délicate. En effet les négociations d'adhésion sont corrélées à une conditionnalité spécifique, l'application du protocole additionnel à l'accord d'Ankara (juillet 2005) qui implique l'élimination des obstacles à la libre circulation des marchandises et aux transports. C'est le problème de Chypre. Or, à la date actuelle, la situation est toujours bloquée. La Turquie nous incite à passer du problème de l'élargissement à celui, plus crucial encore, des limites de l'Union européenne.

II – Des limites indéterminées

Il convient de distinguer les frontières de l'Europe et les frontières de l'Union européenne. Les frontières de l'Europe relèvent d'une approche historique et culturelle très englobante et laissent place à des incertitudes ou des interrogations récurrentes, issues des controverses qu'entretiennent les historiens. La seule certitude est qu'il n'existe aucun déterminisme géographique car la géographie physique et la géographie politique ne coïncident pas de manière mécanique. L'Europe à la fois réelle et réinterprétée sert de toile de fond à l'Union européenne en ce sens que l'Union européenne ne saurait excéder les limites de l'Europe quelles que soient les implantations externes durables engendrées par les Européens à travers le monde. La question des limites de l'Union européenne ne s'est vraiment posée qu'après la chute des régimes communistes en Europe centrale, en Europe orientale et dans l'Europe septentrionale. De même l'insertion des pays ibériques dans la Communauté européenne ne pouvait être envisagée avant la fin des régimes autoritaires en Espagne et au Portugal. Les frontières de l'Union européenne sont celles d'une organisation politique et économique qui doit conserver une cohérence optimale quant à ses objectifs et ses mécanismes internes. Elles se situent donc nécessairement en deçà des frontières de l'Europe. Les incertitudes de cette double évaluation ont provoqué une série d'initiatives qui autorisent autant d'alternatives à l'obligation de fixer des limites. Il s'agit de substituer à la nature classique de frontière-ligne une notion plus souple, et d'ailleurs plus ancienne, de frontière-zone. Ces initiatives sont la politique de voisinage (article I-57 du projet de Constitution européenne) ou le partenariat privilégié, notion théoriquement distincte de la précédente mais assez proche sur plusieurs points. Ces alternatives, dont le projet du Président français Sarkozy pour une Union méditerranéenne est un avatar récent, ne parviendront pas à évacuer la question des frontières. Or la question des frontières ne relève pas d'un traitement unique, en quelque sorte objectif: elle fait l'objet d'approches idéologiques et conceptuelles plurales car elle est le siège de stratégies étatiques et politiques diversifiées. À chacun sa vérité quant aux frontières de l'Union?

A / Sur quelques alternatives

Les deux alternatives se situent en continuité. La politique de voisinage est plutôt zonale, le partenariat privilégié est plutôt ciblé vers un grand partenaire.

1) La politique de voisinage
Cf. art. I-57 du projet de Constitution. On peut lire aussi la communication de la Commission en 2003 «stratégie en 2004». La politique

européenne de voisinage est-elle un instrument dynamique ou un substitut à l'adhésion? Ou encore vise-t-elle à préserver une pause dans les adhésions? Initialement elle fut élaborée en direction de l'Est (Ukraine, Moldavie – tirée par la Roumanie – Biélorussie et Russie puis Géorgie). La formule initiée par Romano Prodi, «tout sauf les institutions» est plutôt brillante mais assez peu convaincante quant au fond. La PEV a été mise en oeuvre d'une certaine manière par l'Acte de Barcelone (1995) et le partenariat euro méditerranéen qui visaient à un projet multilatéral de création d'une zone de libre-échange mais, dans les faits, ont prévalu les accords bilatéraux d'association et de partenariat. On y retrouve largement la même idée, à savoir une volonté d'équilibre entre l'Est et le Sud. Les instruments de la politique européenne de voisinage sont divers. On soulignera les plans d'action (sur la base des rapports «Pays») proposés aux Etats et l'Instrument financier de voisinage (en voie de création); on note une influence manifeste de la politique de cohésion économique et sociale. L'idée est de reconnaître des zones : Est, Caucase du Sud, Méditerranée.

- Est (Ukraine, priorité de la Pologne) (Baltes, priorité au dossier russe)
- Méditerranée (intérêt de la France d'où proposition Sarkozy d'une «union méditerranéenne»).

La politique européenne de voisinage fait émerger une zone grise: plus que l'association, moins que l'adhésion:

- plus que l'association dès lors qu'elle recouvre les accords d'association (Sud) et de partenariat (Est) et comporte des programmes communautaires et une mise en convergence des législations économiques
- moins que l'adhésion mais pour certains partenaires (Ukraine par exemple) ce serait une étape vers l'adhésion.

La politique européenne de voisinage comporte une dimension «sécurité et gestion des crises» (terrorisme) largement présente dans les plans d'action (Maroc par exemple).

Reste les poids lourds qui impliquent de toutes façons pour des raisons évidentes des relations particulières d'où l'idée de partenariat privilégié. Le partenariat privilégié peut être soit un élément (géopolitique) de la PEV, soit un élément autonome. Pour l'heure les concepts sont encore assez peu différenciés.

2) Le partenariat privilégié

On ne peut désigner pour l'heure lesdits partenaires saufs que la Russie ne demande rien (et entend conserver sa prééminence énergétique), et que la Turquie en refuse la perspective. En fait c'est la Turquie qui a poussé certains européens à proposer ce nouveau statut (notamment en France). Le schéma s'inscrit dans une nouvelle théorie des cercles concentriques allant du plus étroit, pour l'heure encore virtuel (la coopération renforcée) au plus large. L'idée a été théorisée par Karl zu Guttenberg et reprise dans un ouvrage collectif de la Fondation R. Schuman.

Le modèle EEE est-il envisageable? Il ajouterait assez peu à l'actuelle union douanière, il conviendrait donc de l'étendre sur le plan institutionnel à partir des organes de l'association et dans le champ des politiques sous certaines limites (produits agricoles, circulation des personnes). Un problème particulier (la PESC et PESD) pourrait faire émerger une association plus poussée mais dans ce cas l'Union européenne serait tenue de mieux définir ses orientations qu'elle ne le fait aujourd'hui.

B / La question des frontières de l'Union

C'est une question cruciale qui pour l'heure n'appelle pas une réponse tranchée. La seule certitude est que, d'ores et déjà, il n'existe pas de consensus a priori sur la question.

La première précaution à prendre concerne, comme cela a été dit plus haut, la distinction entre l'Europe (les frontières de l'Europe) et l'Union européenne (les frontières de l'Union). Les premières sont basées sur des facteurs historiques, politiques et culturels. C'est dire qu'elles impliquent des interprétations historiques souvent singulièrement divergentes et toujours sujettes à des débats entre historiens. À l'Est l'émergence de l'Asie et de grands pays comme l'Inde et surtout la Chine incite les pays de la zone intermédiaire à décliner plus fortement encore leurs caractères européens. On rappellera la formule célèbre du général De Gaulle « l'Europe de l'Atlantique à l'Oural ». Or l'Oural traversait l'Union soviétique de part en part et séparait la Russie en une partie européenne et une partie asiatique. L'invocation de l'Oural consistait, pour son auteur, à réintroduire la Russie dans le champ européen afin d'y trouver un contrepoids à l'influence prédominante des États-Unis d'Amérique. S'il est clair que l'Ukraine ou la Géorgie entendent affirmer leur européanité afin de mieux se distancer de la Russie, la Russie elle-même pourrait, si ses dirigeants le souhaitaient – tel n'est pas le cas – faire valoir ses caractères européens sur la base de ses origines ou de ses orientations passées de Pierre le Grand à Catherine II.

La deuxième remarque à trait à une autre distinction en ce sens que les critères politiques applicables au Conseil de l'Europe et les critères propres à l'Union européenne ne sauraient être de la même nature. Certains des arguments présentés en faveur de l'adhésion à l'Union sont en adéquation avec une candidature au Conseil de l'Europe, du moins dans les cas où l'Etat de référence n'en serait pas encore membre. Pour participer au Conseil de l'Europe, la Russie a accepté d'instaurer un moratoire sur la peine de mort. Pour parvenir aux mêmes fins, la Croatie a dû s'engager à respecter les accords de Dayton dont les imperfections et les ambiguïtés sont notoires. Avant d'adhérer au Conseil de l'Europe, l'Ukraine a procédé à une révision de sa constitution. Ces critères d'honorabilité politique sont importants, ils sont dignes du Conseil de l'Europe mais ils doivent être perçus comme insuffisants pour étayer une demande d'adhésion à l'Union européenne. Ainsi, il ne paraît pas acceptable que le fait pour un Etat de livrer des criminels de guerre à la justice internationale puisse lui ouvrir de ce seul fait la voie à une adhésion à l'Union. C'est sans doute méconnaître les exigences et aussi la vraie nature de l'Union. Pourtant de nombreux hommes politiques européens semblent disposés à considérer que le retour à la paix civile ou le rétablissement d'une stabilité politique méritent d'être en quelque sorte récompensés par le ticket d'entrée dans l'Union européenne.

Une nouvelle remarque peut être faite, très proche de la précédente. Contrairement à ce que suggère avec brio le professeur Tsoukalis, il n'est pas certain que l'adhésion ou la promesse d'adhésion fassent partie des meilleurs instruments de la politique extérieure de l'Union. S'il est vrai que toute politique extérieure est très largement la continuation de la politique intérieure, quelle que soit l'entité politique concernée, l'ambivalence ne saurait être portée jusqu'à un point extrême où la recherche de la stabilité à la périphérie de l'Union implique une endogénéisation des entités externes réputées instables, au risque d'intérioriser les conflits ou les sources de tension. À l'issue de la seconde guerre mondiale, certains dirigeants communistes avaient songé à faire des Etats de l'Europe centrale des Républiques fédérées de l'URSS, poursuivant ainsi la «marche en avant» de la patrie du socialisme. Mais le pragmatisme l'a emporté et la direction soviétique a préféré la prudence. Bien que les situations ne soient heureusement en rien comparables, il convient de rappeler que la confusion entre l'interne et l'externe comporte des risques. En effet l'extension de l'espace de l'Union européenne, en provoquant sa dilution, peut contredire son aspiration à former une entité politique internationalement reconnue et donc l'orienter exclusivement vers le seul marché. Il est patent que le projet de repousser encore plus loin les frontières est souvent stimulé par l'euroscepticisme et tend à ramener l'Union européenne vers la catégorie des organisations internationales ouvertes. Paradoxalement la quête des frontières élargies peut équivaloir à la négation de la nature de l'Union. A contrario la réalisation effective – et non purement mythique – de coopérations renforcées au sein de l'Union pourrait favoriser l'élargissement de ses frontières.

La question actuelle porte sur la Turquie et plusieurs des intervenants y ont fait référence au cours de la présente Conférence internationale. Nous avons indiqué plus haut que l'adhésion implique pour la Turquie la reconnaissance de Chypre et l'application du Protocole additionnel à l'accord d'association. De plus, la stricte application des conditions instituées par le traité concerne principalement en Turquie la liberté de la presse, la liberté religieuse, le respect des droits des femmes, les droits de la minorité kurde. Ces conditions pourraient être jugées satisfaites à un moment donné et donc les préalables à l'adhésion levés. Le débat sur le fond n'en subsiste pas moins quant aux frontières de l'Union européenne. Les dirigeants et les peuples de l'Union sont-ils disposés à entretenir un voisinage physique avec les puissances moyen-orientales telles que la Syrie, l'Iran, voire l'Irak de demain? Ou les entités issues d'un démembrement de l'Irak? Accepteront-ils d'intérioriser le conflit sur le problème kurde et accepter les risques d'instabilité qui s'y attachent? Peuvent-ils comprendre que la fraction politique la plus nettement pro-européenne (AKP) soit issue d'un parti islamiste alors que le parti de la laïcité issue du kémalisme affiche, au nom de la défense de valeurs pourtant largement répandues en Europe, une méfiance persistante vis-à-vis de l'Union européenne? Et surtout, les dirigeants et les peuples européens sont-ils prêts à penser que l'adhésion d'une population de religion musulmane abaissera de plusieurs degrés la tension (le «choc des civilisations») entre le monde musulman et l'Occident, comme le suggèrent de nombreux commentateurs, attendu que les musulmans n'éprouvent pas un sentiment de réelle communauté avec la Turquie et que la Turquie est de surcroît un membre clé sur le plan stratégique de l'alliance Atlantique et qu'elle a par ailleurs conclu un accord de coopération militaire avec Israël? À beaucoup d'égards la question turque se pose «à fronts renversés»; il est symptomatique que les États-Unis appuient fermement l'adhésion turque à l'Union européenne.

Reste la question existentielle des rapports entre l'Union et les Etats qui la composent. L'Union européenne exige de l'Etat entrant un haut degré de maturité: modernisation économique, administration efficace, respect des droits de l'homme, caractère libéral des structures politiques partisanes, capacité d'appliquer des normes exigeantes... Cet acquis doit être vérifié avant l'adhésion. Sur la base de cet acquis les Etats qui s'engagent dans l'Union consentent à des limitations de souveraineté ou plus exactement à un exercice collectif de leurs compétences souveraines. L'Union européenne contribue alors à poursuivre leur modernisation et donc la réhabilitation de l'Etat membre. Si elle ne peut créer l'Etat membre ex nihilo, il lui revient de l'améliorer par le jeu des disciplines collectives, disciplines consenties après négociations mutuelles et appliquées sous contrôle réciproque. Tel est le coeur du pacte d'Etats. La détermination des frontières de l'Union ne devrait en aucun cas porter atteinte à l'essence du pacte.

DEMOCRACY AND EUROPEAN INTEGRATION: A LEGACY OF TENSIONS, A RE-CONCEPTUALISATION AND RECENT TRUE CONFLICTS[*]

CHRISTIAN JOERGES[**]

A) Introductory Remarks

'Democracy and European integration' is an unavoidable assignment in an event which addresses European challenges in the present century. It is also an extremely wide, and, in this sense, an indeterminate one. In the sub-heading, I have taken the liberty of substantiating my assignment in a manageable way – the wording inevitably reflects specific interpretation of these challenges. This interpretation may, at the outset, be summarised in three theses or problems: The first concerns the original construction of the European Community. According to a widely-held view, this construction suffers from a democracy deficit; this view, it is submitted, is too simplistic; Europe's so-called democracy deficit requires responses to a "social deficit", which is deeply engraved into the institutional structure of the European polity. The second thesis concerns the

---

[*] Contribution to the conference on 'Europe and the Challenges of the 21st Century on the Eve of the Portuguese Presidency of the EU', organised by AREP – European Studies Interuniversity Association/European Institute, School of Law, University of Lisbon in collaboration with the Calouste Gulbenkian Foundation and the Luso-American Foundation, 27-29 June 2007, Lisbon.

[**] University of Bremen
European University Institute, Florence.

responses on which policy-makers and academics place so much hope: Europe's institutional *impasses* have led to a gradual substitution of the traditional Community method by new modes of governance. However, the turn to governance, although unavoidable and successful in many policy fields, will not cure Europe's social deficit. This failure, we argue, threatens the legitimacy of the integration project as a whole. There are now ready-made recipes available for these queries. Europe should – this is the third thesis – first of all understand the conflicts that it is confronted with, and re-design its objectives accordingly.

These three concerns will be substantiated in three steps. In the first (Part B), we will substantiate the thesis that tensions exist between democratic principles and the integration project, by first outlining our understanding of constitutional democracy (B.I) and then confronting this understanding with integration strategies pursued in the formative era of the European Community and thereafter (B.II-III). The second step (Part C) will be dedicated to the most recent of these strategies, namely, the turn to governance. It will first explain why this turn occurred and why it seems irreversible (C.I). It will then point to the risks that this turn involves, in particular, its tensions with the European commitment to the rule of law. The third step of the argument (Part D) is a response to this dilemma. The tensions between the original design of the European Community and the irrefutable needs of the EU can be overcome by a re--conceptualisation of European law as a new type of supranational conflict of laws. This law seeks to achieve what the Constitutional Treaty had called the "motto of the Union", namely, a reconciliation of "unity and diversity". It is submitted that such a move would not only help to rescue the rule of law, but would also increase our capacity to cope with the unresolved substantive tensions within the European polity. This, however, is only a potential; the Epilogue (E) of this essay will point to two current controversies in which Europe's capability to cope with the tensions between democracy and integration is at stake.

B) Tensions

I. Principles of Constitutional Democracy

Professional constitutionalists tend to start their deliberations with a sketch of the extremely rich theoretical debate on democratic constitutionalism both in our disciplines and in political philosophy. On the basis of such exercises they will reflect upon the specifics of the European constellation and focus upon three issues:[1] (1) Is it adequate to call the legal framework in place in Europe a constitution in the formal sense, and/or, indeed, in a material sense? (2) Is the constitutional frame democratic, or can it claim some other type of authority? (3) If this frame is not fully democratic and alternative claims to authority cannot meet with general acceptance, how can Europe's democratic deficit be cured?

I have to refrain, however, from such an exercise and restrict myself to revealing the two most important among my own theoretical premises.

- Constitutionalism and democracy are not just academic artefacts but socially and historically embedded products. The recent striving for a European Constitution has disregarded this insight.
- One particularly sensitive legacy of Europe's constitutionalism is the promise of social justice, which is neither a uniform heritage nor an innocent one, but is one to which European constitutionalism must find a response.

It must suffice here to elucidate these points with references to the German case. Germany's post-war constitutionalism needs to be understood as a response to the experiences of the Weimar Republic and its *Staatsrechtslehre*. It was Hermann Heller, building upon the ideas of *Wirtschaftsdemokratie* (economic democracy) and *Sozialverfassung* (social constitution) as promoted by Franz Neumann, Hugo Sinzheimer and Ernst Fraenkel, who presented a constitutional theory of a *social Rechtsstaat*. The "bitter experiences" of the Weimar Republic were present in the minds of the drafters of Germany's basic law.[2] What did this mean

---

[1] See, for a particularly well structured legal analysis, M. Kumm, 'Beyond Golf Clubs and the Judicialization of Politics: Why Europe has a Constitution Properly So Called', (2006) 54 *American Journal of Comparative Law* 505 *et seq.*, and, for a recent summary of the democracy debate in social theory and political science, C. Offe & U.K. Preuß. 'The Problem of legitimacy in the European Polity. Is Democratization the Answer?' in: C. Crouch & W. Streeck (eds.), *The Diversity of Democracy. Corporatism, Social Order and political Conflict*, (Cheltenham, UK: Edward Elgar), available also at: www.qub.ac.uk/schools/SchoolofPoliticsInternationalStudiesandPhilosophy/Research/PaperSeries/ConWEBPapers/.

[2] P.C. Caldwell, 'Is a Social *Rechtsstaat* Possible? The Weimar Roots of a Bonn Controversy', in: P.C. Caldwell & W. Scheuerman (eds.), *From Liberal Democracy to Fascism: Legal and Political Thought in the Weimar Republic*, (Boston: Humanities Press, 2000), 136 *et seq.*

in 1948? The constitution, in order to foster legitimacy of the new political order, had to distance itself from the past, and, in addition, had to strive for social justice. This is not just a German *Sonderweg*. Certainly, there is no particular common social model in Europe.[3] What Europeans have in common, however, is a broad social consensus on nationally specific variants of welfarism.[4] The constitutional status of these commitments varies and the strength and design of social policy is never written in stone. What is quite firmly established, however, is the understanding that the citizens of a constitutional democracy are entitled to vote in favour of welfare policies.[5] This is, legally speaking, by no means a trivial principle, certainly not at European level, as we will see in the next Sections, but not even at national level. Friedrich August von Hayek was the most outspoken proponent of this thesis, namely, that the turn to welfare policies means taking "The Road to Serfdom".[6] A legendary debate in the young German Federal Republic between Wolfgang Abendroth and Ernst Forsthoff concerned precisely that *problématique*,[7] and these debates are going on even today.[8] Not in European constitutionalism, however – and this is a failure with significant consequences.

---

[3] The use of the term is nevertheless widespread; see, with many references, B. Bercusson, 'The Institutional Architecture of the European Social Model', in: T. Tridimas & P. Nebbia (eds.), *European Union Law for the Twenty-First Century: Rethinking the New Legal Order*. Vol. 2 (Oxford: Hart Publishing, 2004), 311-331. That may be explained by the wish to underline differences to the US, but does not provide us with a positive definition.

[4] See, for example, recently St. Leibfried & M. Zürn, 'Reconfiguring the national constellation', in: St. Leibfried & Michael Zürn (eds.) *Transformation of the State*, (Cambridge: Cambridge UP, 2005), 93-117. [= European Review, Volume 13, Supplement S1, available at: http://0journals.cambridge.org.].

[5] The possibility of a change between government and opposition is, according to Niklas Luhmann, a constitutive feature of democracies (see, for example, his 'Meinungsfreiheit, öffentliche Meinung, Demokratie", in: E.-J. Lampe (ed.), *Meinungsfreiheit als Menschenrecht*, (Baden-Baden: Nomos, 1998), 99 *et seq.*, 106 *et seq.* One need not subscribe to systems theory, however, to come to that conclusion (see, for example, Offe & Preuß, note 1, at 9 *et seq.*). I prefer to substantiate that formula because it seems to me that European constitutionalism has lost of sight that constitutions are supposed to reach out into *Wirtschaft und Gesellschaft* (economy and society).

[6] (London: Routledge, 1944).

[7] See A. Fischer-Lescano & O. Eberl, 'Der Kampf um ein soziales und demokratisches Recht. Zum 100. Geburtstag von Wolfgang Abendroth', (2006) 51 *Blätter für deutsche und internationale Politik*, 577-585.

[8] See, the Special Issue on 'Social Democracy' of the (2004) 17 *Canadian Journal of Law and Jurisprudence on Social Democracy*, (Guest Editor: Colin Harvey); to cite just

To rephrase this point and to prepare for the next step: the integration project was designed as an economic project that would leave competences for social policy in the hands of the Member States. Fritz Scharpf has called this division the decoupling of the social sphere from the economic sphere.[9] As the integration project has progressed, this decoupling has produced a "social deficit".[10] The European "economic constitution"

---

one contributor, namely, R. Burchill, 'The EU and European Democracy – Social Democracy or Democracy with a Social Dimension?', 185 *et seq*, who argues: "In addressing the 'wider issues' of democracy, we are taken beyond the political sphere to engage with the social and economic organisation of society. Once we move in this direction, agreement about the nature, scope and content of democracy becomes very contentious. If the overall purpose of democracy is to provide the conditions for the full and free development of the essential human capacities of all the members of the society ... [D]emocracy needs to be something more than the existence of a few basic political procedures. By bringing the idea of 'social' into the frame, we then begin to address the wider issues by incorporating the social and economic aspects of society into our understanding of democracy. However, as this involves making normative claims in relation to democracy, it is widely felt that this stretches the understanding of democracy too far" (*ibid.*, at 186).

[9] F.W. Scharpf, 'The European Social Model: Coping with the Challenges of Diversity', (2002) 40 *Journal of Common Market Studies*, 645-670. – It deserves to be underlined that the founding fathers of Ordo-liberalism to whom we owe the theory of the economic constitution have insisted on the interdependence of both spheres (the *Interdependenz der Ordnungen*; see, famously, W. Eucken, *Grundzüge der Wirtschaftspolitik*, (Tübingen: Mohr/Siebeck, 1952), 6th ed. 1990, 180 *et seq.*); out of the rich literature on the interdependence theorem, see, for an extremely subtle reconstruction, M. Wegmann, *Früher Neoliberalismus und europäische Integration: Interdependenz der nationalen, supranationalen und internationalen Ordnung von Wirtschaft und Gesellschaft (1932-1965)*, (Baden-Baden: Nomos, 2002), in particular at 369 *et seq.* This may look like a tiny detail, but it is one which reveals, that the drafters of the Constitutional Treaty did not really know what they were referring to when they inserted the notion "*soziale Marktwirtschaft*" (social market economy) in the Constitutional Treaty; see Section E.I below.

[10] The use of the term is by no means uniform. For example, according to M. Poiares Maduro, 'Striking the Elusive Balance Between Economic Freedom and Social Rights in the EU', in P. Alston (ed.), *The EU and Human Rights* (Oxford, Oxford U.P., 1999), 449-472, at 464 *et seq.*, the European social deficit can be defined by the sytematic bias of the inegration process for econonmic freedoms as opposed to social rights. His analysis is based upon the distinction between competition within markets (the domain of economic freedoms) and competition among states (the process of regulatory competition which affects the balance achieved within States between social values and economic freedoms). Social rights concern the latter. In the integration process they to "guarantee participation and representation in market decisions" (470). The premises of the argument

has been completed. It has affected the room for manoeuvre for social policy at national level while failing to compensate this erosion by establishing European competences of equivalent weight in the field of social policy. Assuming that this description is fairly adequate, do we have to conclude that Europe's social deficit is of constitutional importance? The dominance of economic policies would mean that European integration is a partisan project. Its in-built bias is not exposed to the cycles of government and opposition which characterise democracies. There is an additional risk involved. If it should turn out to be true that the design of the integration project is politically-biased, Europe is likely to lose support from a significant part of its population.[11] Since the people cannot direct their protest against the dichotomy of government or opposition, they will oppose the European project itself. There are many reasons to believe that this mechanism was at work in the French referendum, and it is certainly useful to take a closer look at the dynamics which resulted from the decoupling of the social from the economic constitution, since the formative era of the European Economic Community.

II. Tensions between Integration and Democracy

The observation that the integration project stands in a tense relationship with democratic constitutionalism may be understood to be only one exemplar of a more general problem, namely that of the social integration of capitalist societies; an issue which the German Ordo-liberal tradition characterises as the necessary interdependence of societal and the economic "orders" (*Ordnungen/Verfassungen*[12]). The following

---

are explained in: M. Poares Maduro, *We the Court – The European Court of Justice and the European Economic Constitution*, (Oxford: Hart, 1998), esp. at 103-149.

[11] A political science version of this thesis is Fritz Scharpf's well-known contention that democracies that prove to be unable to resolve problems of economic and social stability risk the loss of social legitimacy, ['Democratic Policy in Europe', (1996) 2 *European Law Journal*, 136-155, a thesis closely linked to Scharpf's seminal analysis of Europe's "political deficit"; see 'The Joint-Decision Trap: Lessons from German Federalism and European Integration', (1988) 66 *Public Administration,* 239-278.

[12] *Verfassung* in German has a double meaning. It can be a legal constitution and a social structure or pattern. The notion of *Ordnung* (order) too, comprises this twofold meaning. This clarification is necessary to convey our idea of a constitutionalisation of

section will examine it in the specific context of the integration project. This project, we submit, has decoupled the European economic "constitution" *(Wirtschaftsverfassung)* from the national social "constitutions" *(Sozialverfassungen)*. How was this intervention into national orders perceived and reflected in Europe's *"Wandelverfassung"*?[13] In our discussion of the issues, we will distinguish between three conceptualisations of the European polity, each of which has relied upon different mechanisms as the bases of its institutional suggestions.[14] These three concepts of paradigmatic importance are law, economic efficiency, and, most recently, governance.

II.1 Integration through Law

This is the paradigm associated with the formative era of the European Community.[15] Generations of scholars have built upon it and tried to decipher it,[16]. The analytical strength of the paradigm becomes again apparent when we look at social and economic policy through its lenses.

---

the economy, of other societal spheres or parts of the legal system. Such constitutionalisation can either claim the dignity of constitutional law (e.g. supremacy within the legal system) or be an integral part of the constitutional order (in this sense, Jürgen Habermas talks of the co-originality of private and public law; see his *Faktizität und Geltung*, (Frankfurt aM: Suhrkamp, 1992), 112 *et seq.*

[13] H.P. Ipsen, 'Die Verfassungsrolle des Europäischen Gerichtshofs für die Integration', in: J. Schwarze (ed.), *Der Europäische Gerichtshof als Verfassungsgericht und Rechtsschutzinstanz*, (Baden-Baden: Nomos, 1982), 29 *et seq.*

[14] This approach is inspired by M.R. Lepsius, 'Die Europäische Gemeinschaft: Rationalitätskrterien der Regimebildung', in: W. Zapf (ed.), *Die Modernisierung moderner Gesellschaften.Verhandlungen des 25. Deutschen Soziologentages in Frankfurt am Main 1990*, Frankfurt a.M./New York: Campus 1991, 309-317. On the categorioes used here see, in more detail, Ch. Joerges & M. Everson, 'Law, economics and politics in the constitutionalization of Europe', in: E.O. Eriksen, J.E. Fossum & A.J. Menéndez (eds.), *Developing a Constitution for Europe*, (London/ew York: Routledge, 2004), 162-179; Ch. Joerges, 'What is left of the European economic constitution? A melancholic eulogy', (2005) 30 *European Law Review,* 461-489 (O que resta da Constituição Econômica Européia? Uma elegia melancólica, forthcoming).

[15] See, path breaking, J.H.H. Weiler, 'The Community system: the dual character of supranationalism'. (1981) 1 *Yearbook of European Law* 257-306.

[16] See most recently, A. Vauchez, "Integration through law. A Sociohistory of EU Political Commonsense", EUI WP Law 2008 (forthcoming).

118   *Christian Joerges*

Only the European economic system was juridified through supranational law, whereas social policy at European level could at best be said to have been handled through intergovernmental bargaining processes. This is why the integration through law paradigm combines so well with the theory of the European economic constitution promoted by Germany's Ordo-liberals.

Let me repeat this much here: the affinities between Ordo-liberalism and the construction of the European Economic Community of 1958 were manifold – for a series of reasons. As a concept, *Ordo*-liberalism appeared particularly appropriate in terms of both the legitimisation and the orientation of the integration project. The freedoms guaranteed in the EEC Treaty, the opening up of national economies, and anti-discrimination rules and the commitment to a system of undistorted competition were interpreted as a "decision" that supported an economic constitution, and which also matched the Ordo-liberal conceptions of the framework conditions for a market economic system (at least to the degree that the many departures from the system might be classified as exceptions, and a blind eye could be – had to be! – turned to the specific case of the Common Agricultural Policy). The fact that Europe had started out on its integrationist path as a mere economic community lent plausibility to Ordo-liberal arguments – and even required them: in the Ordo-liberal account, the Community acquired a legitimacy of its own by interpreting its pertinent provisions as prescribing a law-based order committed to guaranteeing economic freedoms and protecting competition by supranational institutions. This legitimacy was independent of the state's democratic constitutional institutions. By the same token, it imposed limits upon the Community: thus, discretionary economic policies seemed illegitimate and unlawful.[17]

---

[17] Significant, here, is A. Müller-Armack, 'Die Wirtschaftsordnung des Gemeinsamen Marktes', in: *idem, Wirtschaftsordnung und Wirtschaftspolitik*, (Freiburg i.Br: Rombach, 1966), 401 *et seq*. Ordo-liberalism continued to be the leading school of Economic and private law in the Federal Republic. Its outstanding intellectual head is Ernst-Joachim Mestmäcker is the uncontested and of the ordo-liberal tradition. He has recently published his most important essays on the constitutionalisation of the economy in the EU: *Wirtschaft und Verfassung in der Europäischen Union. Beiträge zu Recht, Theorie und Politik der europäischen Integration*, (Baden-Baden: Nomos, 2003). The time span ranges from 1965 to 2001. All the stages of the integration process are considered and all grand issues discussed. Less impressive in terms of theoretical grounding, however, is the new edition

Regardless of one's affinity for the argument, it is coherent and compatible with the institutional order of the European Economic Community as it was originally conceived. The Ordo-liberal European polity has a twofold structure: at supranational level, it is committed to economic rationality and a system of undistorted competition, while, at national level, re-distributive (social) policies may be pursued and developed further.

To summarise: Europe was constituted as a dual polity. Its "economic constitution" was non-political in the sense that it was not subject to political interventions. This was its constitutional-supranational *raison d'être*. Social policy was treated as a categorically-distinct subject. It belonged to the domain of political legislation and, as such, had to remain national. The social embeddedness of the market could, and, indeed, should, be accomplished by the Member States in differentiated ways – and, for a decade or so, the balance seemed stable.[18]

II.2 Jacques Delors' Internal Market Programme and the Erosion of Europe's Economic Constitution

The Delors Commission's 1985 *White Paper on Completion of the Internal Market*[19] is widely perceived as a turning point and a breakthrough in the integration process. Jacques Delors' initiative promised to overcome a long phase of stagnation; the means to this end was the strengthening Europe's competitiveness. Economic rationality, rather than "law", was from now on understood as Europe's orienting maxim, its first commitment and regulative idea. In this sense, it seems justified to characterise Delors' programme as a deliberate move towards an institutionalisation of economic rationality. This seems even more plausible

---

of his *Europäisches Wettbewerbsrecht* (Munich: Beck, 1974): E.-J. Mestmäcker & H. Schweitzer, *Europäisches Wettbewerbsrecht*, 2nd ed. (Munich: Beck, 2004).

[18] This all fits well into the analysis of "the national configuration of the state in the Golden Age" by St. Leibfried & M. Zürn (note 4, above) at 4 *et seq.*; it seems worth noting that the ordo-liberal construct has structural affinities, or is at least compatible, with J.H.H. Weiler's analysis of the co-existence of, and interdependence between, legal supranationalism and political intergovernmentalism in the EEC (see note 14 above).

[19] Commission of the EC, 'Commission White Paper to the European Council on Completion of the Internal Market', COM(85) 310 final of 14 June 1985.

when we consider the two complementary institutional innovations accomplished through and subsequent to the Maastricht Treaty, namely, monetary Union and the stability pact. Europe looked like a market-embedded polity governed by an economic constitution, rather than by political rule.

The praise of the Internal Market Programme was not to last long.[20] What had started out as a collective effort to strengthen Europe's competitiveness and to accomplish this objective through new (de-regulatory) strategies soon led to the entanglement of the EU in ever more policy fields and the development of sophisticated regulatory machinery. It was, in particular, the concern of the European legislation and the Commission with "social regulation" (health and safety of consumers and workers, and environmental protection) which served as irrefutable proof. The weight and dynamics of these policy fields had been thoroughly under-estimated by the proponents of the "economic constitution". Equally important and equally unsurprising was the fact that the integration process deepened with the completion of the Internal Market and affected ever more policy fields. This was significant not so much in terms of its factual weight, but, in view of Europe's "social deficit", in terms of the new efforts to strengthen Europe's presence in the spheres of labour and social policy.

These tendencies became mainstream during the preparation of the Maastricht Treaty which was adopted in 1992. This is why that Treaty, officially presented as both a deepening and a consolidation of the integration project, met with fierce criticism. The most outspoken critique came not from the left, but from the proponents of the new economic philosophy and in particular from German's Ordo-liberal school.[21] And, indeed, the Maastricht Treaty of 1992 can be read as a break with the Ordo-liberal economic constitution. After the explicit recognition and strengthening of new policy competences, it seemed no longer plausible to assign a constitutive function to the "system of undistorted competition" because this very "system" had been now downgraded to one among many others. It seemed obvious that, from now on, the relative weight of the competing political objectives was to be determined in political

---

[20] See, on the following, in some detail, Ch. Joerges, 'Economic Law, the Nation-State and the Maastricht Treaty", in: R. Dehousse (ed.), *Europe after Maastricht: an Ever Closer Union?* (Munich: C.H. Beck, 1994), 29-62.

[21] See M. Streit & W. Mussler, 'The Economic Constitution of the European Community. From "Rome" to "Maastricht",' (1995) 1 *European Law Journal* 5 -30.

processes.[22] The Ordo-liberal belief in competition as *the* discovery procedure in economic affairs was, in particular, irreconcilable with the acknowledgement of industrial policy as a constitutionally-legitimated concern. In addition, the expansion of competences in labour law by the Social Protocol and Agreement on Social Policy of the Treaty blurred the formerly clear lines between Europe's (unpolitical) economic constitution and the political responsibility Member States had for social and labour policies.

II.3 An Interim Conclusion

The efforts to institutionalise economic rationality, we have to conclude, were only partly successful. Competing policy objectives, even elements of a social policy, were established at European level. Why did all this happen? Was it the resistance of vested interests? The lobbying of environmentalists? The parochialism of national policy-makers? A bit of each of these? These are queries of fundamental importance. We cannot explore them empirically, but it seems useful to rephrase them with the help of the competing views of two master thinkers, namely, Michel Foucault and Karl Polanyi. In his lectures on the *Birth of Biopolitics* delivered at the *Collège de France* in the 1970s, Foucault discussed the Ordo-liberal philosophy quite extensively[23] – and he captured their messages well:

> "[A]u lieu d'accepter une liberté du marché, définie par l'État et maintenue en quelque sorte sur surveillance étatique... eh bien, disent les ordolibéraux, il faut entièrement retourner la formule et se donner la liberté du marché comme principe organisateur et régulateur de l'État ... Autrement dit, un État sur surveillance du marché plutôt qu'un marché sous surveillance de l'État."[24]

---

[22] See Article 2 ad 3 (g) of the Treaty as amended by G (2) and (3) TEU.

[23] M. Foucault, *Naissance de la biopolitique. Cours au Collège de France*, (Paris: Seuil/Gallimard 2004), in particular the lecture of 7 February 1979, 105-134 and the lecture of 14 February 1979, 135-164. Foucault's analysis of Ordoliberalism was long unnoticed by the proponents of Michel tradition; but see now N. Goldschmidt & H. Rauchenschwandtner: *The Philosophy of Social Market Economy: Michel Foucault's analysis of Ordoliberalism*, Freiburger Diskussionspapiere zur Ordnungsökonomik 07/4, available at http://www.wipo.uni-freiburg.de/Abeilungen/Vanberg/Forschung/discpap-2007.

[24] *Biopolitique* (previous note), Lecture 5, 120.

"That may be all right in theory, but does not do in practice", Polanyi might object. The message of his "Great Transformation", published back in 1944, questions the Ordo-liberal philosophy – and hence also the practical relevance of Foucault's argument – on sociological grounds: markets are "always socially embedded", he had insisted.[25] Polanyi had not spelled out the political and normative implications of his sociological observation, but they were, in principle, irrefutable. Once it was recognised that markets could not be understood simply as being mechanisms that functioned perfectly and automatically to adjust supply and demand, but, instead, were understood to be quite fragile, morally, socially and politically embedded institutions, then it also became necessary to consider how to ensure that they functioned in a way that was socially responsible.

> "[T]he critical question is no longer the quantitative issue of how much state or how much market, but rather the qualitative issue of how and for what ends should markets and states be combined and what are the structures and practices in civil society that will sustain a productive synergy of states and markets".[26]

It is unsurprising that the European policy process accompanying the completion of the internal market became both more important and more burdensome – and the European regulatory machinery more sophisticated and more dependent upon the support of governmental and non-governmental actors. This is the background against which Europe took another turn, the turn to governance. This turn, however, seems to have led the EU into a new dilemma.

C) The Turn to Governance

Our discussion of the turn to governance in this section will be primarily descriptive. We will start with some remarks on its officious beginning at the turn of the millennium and then briefly outline the main

---

[25] K. Polanyi, *The Great Transformation: The Political and Economic Origins of Our Time (1944)*, (Boston: Bacon Press, 1992), esp. at 45-58, 71-80.

[26] See F. Block, 'Towards a New Understanding of Economic Modernity,' in: Ch. Joerges, B. Stråth & P. Wagner (eds.), *The economy as a polity. The political construction of modern capitalism – an interdisciplinary perspective*, (London: UCL Press, 2005), 3.

modes of governance. They all depart, albeit with very different intensity, from the Community method. This is not – in itself – disquieting. Our real query is with the compatibility of governance practices with the EU's commitment to the rule of law. It is to this query that Section C will seek to respond.

I. The New Message

As the preceding remarks in Section B.II.3 should indicate, the turn to governance is, in my view, an irresistible development. This thesis implies that the turn cannot be so new, but must have had precursors, which is, indeed, the case. It is equally true, however, that the turn to governance became widely visible as an official Community strategy only at the turn of millennium, with a speech by the President of the Commission delivered on 15 February 2000 to the European Parliament. On this occasion, Romano Prodi announced far-reaching and ambitious reforms. This was a message spoken in a new vocabulary, announcing a fresh agenda and a novel working method. The Commission's – then – new president envisaged a new division of labour between political actors and civil society, and a more democratic form of partnership between the layers of governance in Europe. This was a package of innovation, openly admitting the need to embed the European market in European society better, that was launched strategically into the legally-undefined space located somewhere between administrative[27] and constitutional reform.[28] The Commission followed up on the rhetoric of the speech, and a "Governance Team" was entrusted with the task of elaborating the reform agenda.[29] Following intense debate both within and outside the Commission, a White

---

[27] See, Reforming the Commission – A White Paper, COM(2000) 200 final of 1 March 2000; See, http://europa.eu.int/comm/reform/index_en.htm.

[28] Which was set in motion by the EU Charter of Fundamental Rights, (OJ 2000, C 346/1 of 18 Dec. 2000), followed by the Laeken Conference of 14-15 Dec. 2001 with its concluding declaration on the future of the Union and the setting up of a constitutional convention, which took up its work in March 2002. (http://europeanconvention.eu.int/plen_sess.asp?lang=EN).

[29] 'Enhancing democracy in the European Union. Working Programme', SEC(2000) 1547, 7 final of 11.10.2000; http://europa.eu.int/comm/governance/work/en.pdf.

Paper was published in July of 2001.[30] While the first responses in academic circles were quite reserved and critical,[31] the new concept was to become an enormously popular object of academic endeavours, especially once the Commission decided to support the "Network of Excellence" (CONNEX, based in Mannheim) and one "Integrated Project" (NewGov, based at the EUI) dedicated to governance research. The CONNEX bibliography collecting the relevant literature now contains (May 2007)[32] 3.345 entries.

Political scientists dominate this literature. Indeed, the turn to governance is wonderfully compatible with what political-science integration research has been telling us for some years now: the EU must be understood as a "multi-level system of governance", a heterarchy, rather than a hierarchy, an only partially-integrated polity without a government, which needs to ensure the co-operation of semi-autonomous political and administrative bodies. Though a far broader term, governance can also, and in the specific terms of the "always socially-embedded market", be understood as an effort to structure civil society and market relations beyond our traditional understandings of state-market dichotomies.

II. Some New and not so New Modes of Governance

The language is new, the concepts employed are non-legal, but a good deal of the practices that these concepts describe have long been there and the law has observed them more or less attentively.

The European committee system is the oldest form of the "new" modes of governance. It emerged where complex European governance incorporating national actors first became indispensable, namely, in agricultural policy.[33] "Comitology" is by now legally well-defined. It is

---

[30] 'European Governance. A White Paper', COM(2001) 428.

[31] See, Ch. Joerges, Y. Mény & J.H.H. Weiler 'Mountain or Molehill? A Critical Appraisal of the Commission White Paper on Governance', European University Institute-Robert Schuman Centre/NYU School of Law-Jean Monnet Center 2002, www.jeanmonnetprogram.org/papers/01/010601.html.

[32] www.connex-network.org/govlit.

[33] See J. Falke, 'Komitologie – Entwicklung, Rechtsgrundlagen und erste empirische Annäherung', in: Ch. Joerges & J. Falke (eds.), Das Ausschuâwesen der Europäischen Union. Praxis der Risikoregulierung im Binnenmarkt und ihre rechtliche Verfassung, (Baden-Baden: Nomos, 2000), 43-159.

the term used for the committees entrusted with the "implementation" of Community law framework provisions.[34]

The principle of mutual recognition is widely perceived as a legal principle, not as a governance practice. The principle has been used sensitively and subtly by the ECJ, often so as to "regulate" regulatory competition. Political scientists Kalypso Nikolaïdes and Susanne Schmidt use the term "managed mutual recognition",[35] which designates the discretionary dimensions of the concept better. An adequate *legal* conceptualisation of mutual recognition requires – in my view – a conflict-of-laws methodology. This thesis will be explained in Section D below.

The "New Approach to technical harmonisation and standards" is, strangely enough, hardly ever mentioned in the new governance literature. This may be because the "new approach" is by now more than 20 years old. The features that one refers to when characterising "new governance" are, however, all present: a circumvention of the Community

---

[34] Through these committees, made up of representatives of the member states and experts appointed by them, the Commission organises a "Community" (*i.e.*, overarching and co-operative) "administration" of the internal market in such policy areas as food safety, safety of technical products and safety at work. The committee system has to compensate for the Community's lack of genuine administrative powers and guarantees. It ensures the accountability of the Commission-driven European administrative machinery to the Member States – not to the European Parliament, which for decades has striven for a strengthening of its institutional powers. By incorporating national bodies, however, it also promotes acceptance of European rules in Member States. The committees do the detailed work on reducing the functional and structural tensions of the internal market project. Even though, for the most part, the issues at stake seem purely technical, they may have important economic implications and politically sensitive dimensions. Thus comitology can be characterized as a mediator of functional requirements and normative concerns. The changing composition of the committees follows from the task of balancing differing sorts of technical knowledge and regulatory concerns and bringing them into a sort of synthesis. It also, however, reflects the multiplicity of interests and political differences that have to be coped with in the implementation process. The committees often act like "mini-Councils"; they act as venues for mediation between market integration and member states' concerns and reliable indications suggest that their discussions take place objectively and deliberatively [Ch. Joerges & J. Neyer, 'From Intergovernmental Bargaining to Deliberative Political Processes: The Constitutionalisation of Comitology', (1997) 3 *European Law Journal*, 273-299].

[35] K. Nikolaïdes & S.K. Schmidt, 'Mutual Recognition on Trial: The Long Road to Services Liberalisation", (2007) 18 *Journal of European Public Policy*, 667-681.

method, the involvement of non-governmental actors, resort to expertise, and European-wide networking.[36]

Independent agencies were the institutional core of Giandomenico Majone's conceptualisation of the EU as a "regulatory state".[37] However, while Europe took over the vocabulary that Majone had brought from the US and also created an impressive number of institutions that were termed agencies, it is not disputed that new European agencies share only nomenclature with their American namesakes. The new European agencies meet the need for market-correcting, sector-specific regulations, either indirectly or as executive organs working under the Commission's supervision. Despite their formal subordination and the fact that the representatives of national authorities sit on their management bodies, the agencies seem, thanks to their founding charters, their organisational stability, the relative autonomy of their budgets (taking different shapes in individual cases), and their networking with national administrations, to be fairly well-protected against direct, explicit political influences.

III. The Paradigmatic Case of the Open Method of Co-ordination

The so-called Open Method of Co-ordination (OMC) deserves particular attention in the present context for three interdependent reasons. Firstly, since the introduction of the new Title VIII on employment in the Amsterdam Treaty, and after the Lisbon European Council's recommendation to apply the OMC in areas of social policy, the OMC was

---

[36] The cunning in the "New Approach" was concealed in a package of interrelated measures: European law-making had a large burden taken away from it, essentially by henceforth contenting itself with laying down "essential safety requirements". Fleshing these out was delegated to experts from European and national standardisation organisations well-used to dealing with each other. In practice, the inclusion of non-state actors meant "a delegation" of legislative powers that obviously could not be admitted openly. The protagonists of the new approach had to paper over it with the fiction that the "essential safety requirements" adequately programmed the work of the standardisation organisations. "Private Transnationalism" is the adequate characterisation of this mode of governance; see H. Schepel, *The Constitution of Private Governance. Product Standards in the Regulation of Integrating Markets*, (Oxford: Hart, 2005).

[37] G. Majone, 'The Rise of the Regulatory State in Europe', (1994) 17 *West European Politics*, 77-101.

widely presented as the best cure to Europe's "social deficit" as described above.[38] Secondly, and somewhat irritatingly, the Method's proponents praise as a virtue what lawyers used to perceive as a weakness: the OMC is recommended and used in areas where political actors feel considerable pressure to act, but where the Treaty offers them no legislative powers. The mode of action is essentially one of multilateral supervision, in which, on the basis of guidelines or benchmarks laid down by the European Council, the Council and the Commission, governance occurs through mutual systematic monitoring (multilateral surveillance) and through assessment of the performance of the individual governments in peer review processes. In short, the method has moved social policy "from Bismarck to benchmark" (Gunnar F. Schuppert). No judicial protection is provided against this sort of governance, still less some constitutional review thereof. Similar measures would, after all, appear downright dysfunctional if political action were to be exercised outside the powers provided for by law. It is surprising to observe how lightly the legacy of the rule of law is taken. A related third query concerns the notion of law itself. David and Louise Trubek, in a recent analysis of the relationship between the Community method and new governance, differentiate between complementarity, rivalry and hybridity, arguing that all three should be understood as new modes of law.[39] Other prominent authors, such as Graínne de Búrca and Neil Walker, criticise the "conceptual imperialism of law", which they seek to overcome with a vision of "law as a distinctive *medium* of social activity" which would cover "both law and new governance, like all forms of normative order".[40]

All of the three concerns are related. Their interdependence becomes apparent when we contrast the new learning with the, by now, old efforts to come to terms with the deficiencies of legal formalism, political interventionism, command and control regulation in the 1980s.[41] These deficiencies were *cum grano salis* identical with those that the critique of the traditional Community Method has identified and the practices now

---

[38] Section A.I.

[39] D.M. Trubek & L.G. Trubek, 'Hard and Soft Law in the Construction of the Social Europe: the Role of the Open Method of Co-ordination', (2005) 11 *European Law Journal*, 343-364.

[40] G. de Búrca & N. Walker, 'Reconceiving Law and New Governance', EUI Working Paüper Law No. 2007/10 (San Domenico di Fiesole, 2007), at 13 ff, available at: www.iue.it/LAW/Publications.shtml.

named "governance" which were then called "post-interventionism" – the one and only important difference being that the debates of the 1980s focused on national, rather than post-national, constellations. It was characteristic of these efforts[42] that they sought to link legal theory to social theory (*Gesellschaftstheorie*), to define the functions of law, and to reflect the schisms between sociological studies of the legal system, normative theories and doctrinal arguments. When contrasted with these efforts to define the embeddedness of legal theory, the promotion of a new transformation of the category of law seems under-theorized and in that sense premature.[43]

European governance comes, as even this very brief outline has documented, in many forms. What these forms have in common is that they organise policies and decision-making processes outside the legal frameworks foreseen in the original Treaty and its successive amendments. But this is nothing unusual. All legal systems are continuously confronted with social change, new claims and the need to give answers to questions not yet decided. Each of the modes of governance is challenging in some distinct way. And it is precisely because the turn to governance is irreversible that it seems preferable to ask how the rule of law may survive that development. The answer to this question will have to operate at two levels. It will have to (re-) conceptualise Europe's post-national constellation – this will be done through a conflict-of-laws

---

[41] See, on the following, Ch. Joerges, 'Compliance research in legal perspectives', in: Ch. Joerges & M. Zürn (eds.), *Law and Governance in Postnational Europe. Compliance Beyond the Nation-State*, (Cambridge: Cambridge UP, 2005), 218-261 (Section 7.3) and Ch. Joerges, 'Integration through de-legislation? An irritated heckler', European Governance Papers (EUROGOV) No. N-07-03, 2007, available at: www.connex-network.org/eurogov/pdf/egp-newgov-N-07-03.pdf (Section 2).

[42] Mentioned just in passing by G. de Búrca & N. Walker (note 40), at 8, note 13.

[43] This critique neglects the links of the suggestions cited to the much more comprehensive and ambitious project of democratic experimentalism as developed in particular by Charles F. Sabel and Jonathan Zeitlin (see, recently, their 'Learning from Difference: The New Architecture of Experimentalist Governance in the European Union', EUROGOV Working Paper No. C-07-02, available at www.connex-network.org/eurogov/pdf/egp-connex-C-07-02.pdf.network.org/eurogov with many references). I cannot see, however, that this type of theorising would do justice to the historical weight of European diversity, the complex legacy of European welfarism; for these reasons, democratic experimentaliam cannot adequately address the political and social conflicts which Europe is currently facing. See the examples discussed in Section E below.

approach to European law – and it will have, at the same time, to explain its theoretical credentials – this will be done with the help of the discourse theory of law.

D) Constitutionalising Europe through a Supranational Conflict of Laws

The idea of re-conceptualising European law as a new type of conflict of laws is less idiosyncratic than it may appear at first sight. The argument rests upon two basic premises.

The first concerns the democracy deficit and suggests that we turn the pertinent debates on their head: European constitutionalism should not be fixated on curing the democracy deficits of the European Union. The law of the European Union should instead be understood as a potential cure for the democratic failure of its Member States and should derive its legitimacy out of that function. These democracy failures are structural. They stem from the inevitable extra-territorial effects that nation states impose – by all of their decisions of some weight – on other states and on their citizens. European law needs to address the gap between the empowerment to take decisions and the effect that those decisions have upon non-nationals – this is the task which should be assigned to a "first order conflict of laws".

The second suggestion builds upon the first. European law has to organise responses to the ever more apparent inability of the Member States of the European Union to deal with the concerns of their citizens autonomously at national level. Such responses require the institutionalisation of co-operative modes of problem-solving – "a second order conflict of laws".

I. First Order Conflict of Laws – the Legitimacy of European Suprantionalism

Back in 1997, Jürgen Neyer and I presented the first explicit argument under the heading of "deliberative suprantionalism".[44] The primary

---

[44] Ch. Joerges & J. Neyer, 'From Intergovernmental Bargaining to Deliberative Political Processes' (note 34, above).

objective of our essay was to explain the surprisingly sensible operation of the comitology system,[45] but the normative basis of our argument concerned the democracy failure of nation states:

"The legitimacy of governance within constitutional states is flawed insofar as it remains inevitably one-sided and parochial or selfish. The taming of the nation-state through democratic constitutions has its limits. [If and, indeed, because] democracies pre-suppose and represent collective identities, they have very few mechanisms [through which] to ensure that 'foreign' identities and their interests are taken into account within their decision-making processes."[46]

If the legitimacy of supranational institutions can be designed to cure these deficiencies – as a correction of "nation-state failures", as it were – they may then derive their legitimacy from this compensatory function. To quote my recent restatement:

"We must conceptualise supranational constitutionalism as an alternative to the model of the constitutional nation-state which respects that state's constitutional legitimacy but, at the same time, clarifies and sanctions the commitments arising from its interdependence with equally democratically legitimised states and with the supranational prerogatives that an institutionalisation of this interdependence requires."[47]

This, of course, is not the way in which the supranational validity of European law was originally understood and justified. Fortunately enough, however, the methodologically and theoretically bold and practically successful ECJ decision in favour of a European legal constitution[48] can be rationalised in this way. The European "federation" thus found a legal constitution that did not have to aim at Europe's becoming a state, but was able to derive its legitimacy from the fact that it compensates for

---

[45] See Section B.II (1) above.

[46] *Ibid.*, at 293.

[47] Ch. Joerges "'Deliberative Political Processes' Revisited: What Have we Learnt About the Legitimacy of Supranational Decision-Making', (2006) 44:*Journal of Common Market Studies*, 779-802, at 790.

[48] Case 26/62, [1963] ECR 1 – *Van Gend en Loos* v. *Nederlandse Administratie der Belastingen.*

the democratic deficits of the nation states. This is precisely the point of Deliberative Supranationalism. Existing European law had, we argued, validated principles and rules that meet with and deserve supranational recognition because they constitute a palpable community project. All one has to do is look: community members cannot implement their interests or laws without restraint, but are obliged to respect the European freedoms; they are not allowed to discriminate and can pursue only legitimate regulatory policies which have been blessed by the Community; they must, in relation to the objectives that they wish to pursue through regulation, harmonise with each other, and they must shape their national systems in the most community-friendly way possible. Why should this type of law be called a new type of conflict of law? Conflict of laws in all its sub-disciplines – private international law and public international law – has traditionally denied the application of foreign "public" law; each state unilaterally determines the international scope of public law. Traditional international administrative law is a paradigm example of "methodological nationalism".[49]

But conflict of laws thinking has a further potential: it is helpful wherever legal principles differing in content and objectives come up against each other. It needs to guide the search for responses to conflicting claims where no higher law is available for decision-makers to refer to. In the European case: to give voice to "foreign" concerns means, first of all, that Member States mutually "recognise" their laws (that they are prepared to "apply" foreign law), that they tolerate legal differences and refrain from insisting on their *lex fori* and domestic interests. This is the principle. The discipline imposed on a Member State's political autonomy must be limited. The principle and its limitations can be discovered and best studied in the jurisprudence of the ECJ pertaining to Article 28 [ex 30]. This jurisprudence has repeatedly documented how mediation between differences in regulatory policies and the diverse interests of the concerned jurisdictions can be accomplished. These examples, we submit,[50]

---

[49] M. Zürn, 'The State in the Post-national Constellation – Societal Denationalization and Multi-Level Governance', Oslo: ARENA Working Paper No. 35/1999.

[50] See references in notes 44, 47, and Ch. Joerges, 'Rethinking European Law's Supremacy: A Plea for a Supranational Conflict of Laws', in: B. Kohler-Koch & B. Rittberger (eds.), *Debating the Democratic Legitimacy of the European Union*, (Lanham MD: Rowman & Littlefield, 2007), 311-327).

represent a truly European law of conflict of laws. It is 'deliberative' in that it does not content itself with appealing to the supremacy of European law; it is 'European' because it seeks to identify principles and rules that make different laws within the EU compatible with one another.

Once it is recognised and acknowledged that legal responses to conflicting claims of democratically legitimised legal systems need to be conceptualised as conflict of laws problems, the methodological dimension and implication of this insight should become equally clear: European conflict of laws requires a proceduralisation of the category of law. It has to be understood as a "law of law-making",[51] a *Rechtfertigungs-Recht*.[52] This conflict of laws viewpoint retains the supranationality of European law, but gives it a different meaning. It takes away from European law those practical and legitimatory expectations that it cannot reasonably hope to fulfil. At the same time, it opens a window on the manifold vertical, horizontal, and diagonal[53] conflict situations in the European multilevel system. It promotes the insight that the Europeanisation process should seek flexible, varied solutions to conflicts, rather than striving to perfect an ever more comprehensive body of law.[54]

II. Second Order Conflict of Laws – The Juridification of Transnational Governance

"The EU can currently be understood as a decentralised, territorially differentiated, transnational negotiation system dominated by élites" – this

---

[51] F.I. Michelman, *Brennan and Democracy*, (Princeton NJ: Princeton UP, 1999), 34.

[52] 'Just-ifications of a Law of Society', in: O. Perez & G. Teubner (eds.), *Paradoxes and Inconsistencies in the Law*, (Oxford: Hart, 2005), 65-77, available at: www.jura.uni-frankfurt.de/ifawz1/teubner/RW.html.

[53] These conflicts arise out of the allocation of powers needed for problem-solving and therefore objectively connected to different levels of government. It follows from the principle of limited individual empowerment that the primacy rule can find no application here.

[54] This is readily compatible with the existence of European secondary law and does not in any way in principle call its legitimacy into question. There are important problem areas in which "second order" law of conflict is insufficient and the "federation" has to develop supranational substantive law. This question cannot be dealt with systematically here.

generalising description of the Union by Ulrich Beck and Edgar Grande[55] rephrases the multi-level analysis, and documents well how far political scientists and sociologists have moved away from the "integration-through--law" paradigm. "Deliberative supranationalism" remains faithful to this tradition. Comitology, as Jürgen Neyer and I argued a decade ago, needs to be "constitutionalised". The comitology procedures were developed in the course of the completion of the internal market in order to keep the internal market project compatible with concerns of social regulation (safety at work, consumer and environmental protection, etc.). The framework regulations to be implemented here typically employ general clause type formulae which do not seek to programme this co-ordination in detail, but leave the elaboration of individual solutions to the implementation process. Typically, the problem situations concerned are ones in which expert knowledge has to be taken into account. It is the involvement of the Member States – through their representatives on the regulatory committees combined with discussion by a plural expert community – that should guarantee both political legitimacy and the objective viability of the regulations developed. Safeguard clause procedures employed when new knowledge is acquired or a regulation proves to be insufficient serve to strengthen their normative and procedural qualities. A conflict of laws interpretation of this form of governance is appropriate because the co-ordination effort aims to achieve a solution that is acceptable to a Union of relatively autonomous states that have to manage without any hierarchically ordered, or, at least, any uniformly structured, administrative apparatus. Admittedly, a "constitutionalisation" of this machinery, then has to find answers to a series of further questions, such as: the appointment and function of the experts to be included in the decision--making process; the ties with parliamentary bodies on the one hand, and with civil society on the other; and the reversibility of decisions taken in the light of new knowledge or changes in social preferences. What needs to be understood is the status of these efforts. The constitutionalisation of European governance arrangements is no direct substitute for democratic rule; its objective, rather, is to define the procedures through which democratic polities organise their responses to common problems under conditions of mutual interdependence. There is no guarantee that such a

---

[55] U. Beck & E. Grande, *Cosmopolitan Europe*, (Cambridge: Polity, 2007), 53 (italics in the original).

solution will be discovered, but this is a price that we should be prepared to pay. In any event, it is not a sound enough reason to forget about the rule of law and the idea of law-mediated legitimation of governance practices.

E) Epilogue: "Judgment Day"?[56]

Would the conflict-of-laws approach help to cure Europe's social deficit? It is, of course, impossible to defend its potential through a comparative evaluation of the plethora of suggestions which have been developed in the broad debates on "social Europe" in this paper. We will restrict ourselves to some critical comments on the options which have gained prominence thanks to their inclusion in the Draft Constitutional Treaty as revised by the June 2004 IGC[57] (Section E.I). It is still difficult to predict whether these suggestions will one day form the pillars of a European social constitution in a new Treaty. Nevertheless, they remain on the agenda of both political actors and academics. This is but one reason to remain aware of their fallacies. Their weaknesses have become even more apparent in the light of two pending cases, which may prove to be acid tests for the potential of European law to further Europe's social integration. In these two cases – *Viking*[58] and *Laval*[59] – the new *problématique* of social Europe after the accession of the new Member States came to the for. We will not claim that the conflict-of-laws approach offers a convenient solution to these conflicts. What we submit, instead, is that this approach is helpful, at least to the extent that it provides a proper definition of the challenges we are confronted with (Section E.II).

---

[56] The term is a reference to B. Bercusson, 'The Trade Union Movement and the European Union: Judgment Day', (2007) 13 *European Law Journal*, 279-308.

[57] Final text in OJ 2004 C 310,1.

[58] Case C-438/05 *Viking Line Abp OU Viking Line Eesti* v. *The International Transport Workers' Federation, The Finnish Seamen's Union.*

[59] Case C-341/05, *Laval un Partneri Ltd* v. *Svenska Byggnadsarbetareforbundet, Svenska Byggnadsarbetareforbundet, Avdelning 1, Svenska Elektrikerforbundet.*

I. The Failures of the Draft Constitutional Treaty

Europe's "social deficit" came on the agenda of the Convention somewhat belatedly, but, given the strength of welfare state tradition in Europe, this was not surprising. The ambition of the Convention to design a document of constitutional dignity left no real choice. "Social Europe" was to rest, in particular, on three[60] corner stones: the commitment to a "competitive social market economy",[61] the recognition of "social rights",[62] and "soft law" techniques for the co-ordination of social policies.[63] This architecture was neither conceptually nor politically solid. Joschka Fischer and Dominique Villepin, to whom we owe the assignment of constitutional dignity to the concept of the "social market economy", were giving a political signal. But they were hardly aware of the interdependence of the economic and the social constitution in the theory of the "*soziale Marktwirtschaft*". This legacy would have required what was not yet an imperative in the formative era of the European Economic Community, namely, a compensation for the decoupling of both spheres in the European Treaty.[64] Thus, the new social rights and the new

---

[60] And, in addition, the defence of the *services publiques*/services of general economic interest, *Daseinsvorsorge* in Article II-36; this is an important signal, because it confirms the right of Member States to pursue distributional objectives. The compatibility of such policies with the opening of national or regional markets to "foreign" competitors is a complex issue Article II-36; this is an important signal, because it confirms the right of Member States to pursue distributional objectives. The compatibility of such policies with the opening of national or regional markets to "foreign" competitors is an issue, which can in my view productively be resolved within the conflict-of-laws approach; see, for an exemplary discussion of the *Altmark Trans* case, Ch. Joerges, 'The Challenges of Europeanization in the Realm of Private Law: A Plea for a New Legal Discipline', (2005) 24 *Duke Journal of Comparative and International Law*, pp. 149-196, at 187 *et seq.*

[61] Article 3 Section 3. –'Les tenants d'une Europe sociale se félicitent de quelques avancées – la référence à "l'économie sociale de marché", au plein-emploi, aux services publics', noted *Le Monde* on 10 November 2003.

[62] See Title IV of the Draft Constitutional Treaty (OJ C310/1, 16/12/2004).

[63] See, especially, Article I-14 (4) of the DCT; the assignment of a *competence* 'to promote and co-ordinate the economic and employment policies of the Member States' has been repealed. Article I-11(3) as amended on 22 June 2004.

[64] See Section B.I *supra*, and, in more detail, Ch. Joerges & F. Rödl, 'The 'Social Market Economy' as Europe's Social Model?', in: L. Magnusson & B. Stråth (eds.), *A European Social Citizenship? Preconditions for Future Policies in Historical Light*, (Brussels: Lang, 2005), 125-158.

co-ordination competences were presented as elements of precisely this type of cure.

In the case of social rights, a threefold difficulty has to be considered. One is their "political content", which has led social philosophers such as Jürgen Habermas to suggest that the content of such rights needs to substantiated through deliberative democratic political processes.[65] This seems to be too rigid a position for many people.[66] But should we, the citizens, really entrust the Court with the shaping of a "social Europe". Should the Court take over where the citizens' representatives in the Convention and elsewhere have failed to produce clear constitutional guidance? In the concrete case of the Constitutional Treaty, we could not even be confident that this text could have served as a sufficiently stable basis for some daring judicial activism.[67] To be sure, the social rights agenda will survive the Draft Constitutional Treaty in some form, and the view that their legitimate concretisation pre-supposes a legitimising framework is widely shared.[68] It is nevertheless difficult to believe that there is a sufficiently strong social basis for a proactive social rights policy which could be promoted, and could, therefore, be dependant upon the co-operation of all those involved.[69] And even assuming that this could

---

[65] J. Habermas, *Between Facts and Norms. Contributions to a Discourse Theory of law and Democracy*, (Cambridge MA: MIT Press, 1999), 82-132, 401-409, 503-507. "Social rights signify, from a *functionalist* viewpoint, the installation of welfare bureaucracies, whereas from a *normative* viewpoint, they grant compensatory claims to a just share of social wealth", *ibid.*, at 504); see, for a lucid interpretation, Baynes, 'Rights as Critique and the Critique of Rights. Karl Marx, Wendy Brown and the Social Function of Rights', (2000) 28 *Political Theory*, 451-468.

[66] See the contributions to G. de Búrca & B. de Witte (eds.), *Social Rights in Europe*, (Oxford: Hart, 2005).

[67] Article II-52 (5) which provided: "The provisions of this Charter which contain principles may be implemented by legislative and executive acts taken by Institutions and bodies of the Union, and by acts of Member States when they are implementing Union law, in the exercise of their respective powers. They shall be judicially cognisable only in the interpretation of such acts and in the ruling on their legality".

[68] Such as a European labour constitution (*Arbeitsverfassung*) guaranteeing the exercise of collective rights and the validity of collective agreements; see F. Rödl, 'Constitutional Integration of Labour Constitutions', in: E.O. Eriksen, Ch. Joerges & F. Rödl (eds.), *Law, Democracy, and Solidarity in Europe's Post-National Constellation*, (London: Routledge, forthcoming), Ch. 8.

[69] See S. Fredman, 'Transformation or Dilution: Fundamental Rights in the EU Social Space', (2006) 12 *European Law Journal*, 41-60, at 49; see, also, G. Ruffer, 'Can

happen, we should not be too sure that the ECJ will be ready to face the foreseeable fierce opposition against what would be perceived as imposing taxes on the Member States which would have to finance the new social rights. Last, but not least, would a European social rights strategy be a normatively attractive option in an economically and socially still very diverse Union?

This last question leads us back to the conflict-of-laws perspective and to the Open Method of Co-ordination. The conceptual difference between them is primarily about the need to subject the exercise of public power, hard or soft, to legal constraints and the function of law as a mediator of legitimacy.[70] However, the uncertainty about the practical impact of the Method[71] is not, in itself, a normative issue – unless the OMC is presented without proper caution as an effective cure for Europe's social deficit. The two approaches converge in that they both defend the autonomy of national societies/nation states in the search for their social policies, and in that a proceduralisation of the processes of co-ordination in the form of a "second order conflict of laws"[72] seems conceivable.[73] Last, but not least, the two approaches are likely to agree about the difficulty to respond to the new dimension of Europe's "social deficit", as it has come to the fore in *Laval*[74] and *Viking*.[75]

European Courts Cure the Social Deficit? *Justiciability* of Fundamental Social Rights of Non-EU Migrant Workers', contribution to the International Conference and Joint Annual Meetings of the Law and Society Association and the Research Committee on Sociology of Humboldt University, Berlin, Germany, July 25-28, 2007 (on file with author).

[70] See B.II above and Ch. Joerges, 'Integration through de-legislation?' (note 41, above).

[71] See, most recently, M. Lodge, 'Comparing Non-Hierarchical Governance in Action: the Open Method of Co-ordination in Pensions and Information Society", (2006) 45 *Journal of Common Market Studies*, 343-365.

[72] See C.II *supra*.

[73] B. Braams, 'Co-ordination as a Category of Competence? – New Modes of Governance and the Search for Legitimacy", Typescript Jena 2007 (on file with author).

[74] Case C-341/05, *Laval un Partneri Ltd* v *Svenska Byggnadsarbetareforbundet, Svenska Byggnadsarbetareforbundet, Avdelning 1, Svenska Elektrikerforbundet*

[75] Case C-438/05 *Viking Line Abp OU Viking Line Eesti* v *The International Transport Workers' Federation, The Finnish Seamen's Union.*

II. "True Conflicts"[76]

These two cases are about the tensions between economic freedoms guaranteed by the Treaty, and the potential of national labour law to limit the exercise of these freedoms.[77]

The plaintiffs in the *Viking* case[78] are a Finnish shipping company (Viking) and her Estonian subsidiary (OÜ Viking Line Eesti). Viking was the owner and operator of the ferry *Rosella*, registered under the Finnish flag. The crew was predominantly Finnish; a collective agreement negotiated by the Finnish Seamen's Union regulated the terms and conditions of employment. Viking decided to re-flag the ferry to Estonia with a view to replacing the Finnish crew with less costly Estonian seamen. Both the Finnish and the Estonian Union were affiliates to the The International Transport Workers' Federation. Both Unions sought to defend the principle that employment conditions should be negotiated by the Union of the country in which the ferry was owned.

The plaintiff in the *Laval* case (Laval Un Partneri)[79] is a company incorporated under Latvian law, whose registered office is in Riga. Its subsidiary L & P Baltic Bygg AB had won the tender for a school building on the outskirts of Stockholm. Laval posted several dozen workers from Latvia to work on the Swedish building sites. In obtaining the tender, Bygg (Laval's Swedish subsidiary) had profited from the wage level in Latvia, which was considerably below that of Sweden (and remained considerably lower even under the terms of a two collective agreements that Laval had signed with the buildings sector's trade unions in Latvia). Under Swedish law, the wage level agreed upon in collective bargaining is not binding upon outsiders. But the trade unions can take

---

[76] For an explanation of the term, see Section 3, *infra*.

[77] The following deliberations are preliminary. They owe much to discussions with Florian Rödl (Bremen/Florence). For more detailed analyses, see B. Bercusson, note 56. above; N. Reich, 'Gemeinschaftliche Verkehrsfreiheiten versus Nationales Arbeitskampfrecht', (2007) 18 *Europäische Zeitschriift für Wirtschaftsrecht*, 391-396; M. Weiss, 'Europa im Spannungsfeld zwischen Marktfreiheiten und Arbeitnehmerschutz', Manuscript Frankfurt a.M.. 2007 (on file with author).

[78] Case C-438/05, *Viking Line Abp OU Viking Line Eesti* v *The International Transport Workers' Federation, The Finnish Seamen's Union.*

[79] Case C-341/05, *Laval un Partneri Ltd* v. *Svenska Byggnadsarbetareforbundet, Svenska Byggnadsarbetareforbundet, Avdelning 1, Svenska Elektrikerforbundet.*

actions which aim at the imposition of Swedish wages. This they did with such determination that Laval gave up.

The debate on the two cases has already reached European-wide dimensions. "It is a bracing reminder to EU lawyers of the power of political and economic context to influence legal doctrine," notes Brian Bercusson,[80] "that the new Member States making submissions were unanimous on one side of the arguments on issues of fundamental legal doctrine (horizontal direct effect, discrimination, proportionality) and the old Member States virtually unanimous on the other." The conflict is bitter indeed. To understand the normatively sensitive economic and social implications of the two cases, it is sufficient to rephrase the freedom of establishment as the right to dislocate enterprises to low-cost countries and the freedom to provide services in high-cost markets at the conditions of low-cost jurisdictions. Such practices impose burdens on the workforce in the high-cost countries and offer new opportunities to the workforce in low-cost countries. Is not this exactly what a common market is all about, many commentators ask? What should be specific about services and labour? How can Old Europe talk about "social dumping" in services and labour, while it is profiting from the open boarders of Eastern Europe for the export of its products. Is it fair to impose European-wide high standards of product safety, safety at work and environmental protection and then foreclose market access where service providers could profit from the competitive advantages of the lower wage levels in Eastern Europe?

There is more at stake in these cases, most importantly, constitutional issues at both European and nation state level which cannot be addressed adequately in terms of fairness between the parties of the present conflicts or the treatment of the accession countries in generals. It is these issues from which the following analysis will depart (1). These constitutional deliberations will then serve as a framework for a series of comments on the opinions delivered by Advocate Generals Maduro and Mengozzi (2). Through both steps of the argument, it should become apparent that European law, is unable to provide normatively valid answers to the problems with which it is confronted. The ECJ cannot refuse to respond. But the Court could exercise judicial self restraint (3).

---

[80] Note 56, above, at 305.

1. The decoupling of the social from the economic constitution and the co-originality thesis

Back to the beginnings of this essay: Democratic governance, modern European *Sozialstaatlichkeit*, we have argued,[81] reaches out into "Economy and Society"; it comprises the promise that citizens can understand themselves as the authors of the economic and social order they live in, that they are therefore entitled to take a meaningful vote on competing political programmes and to authorise politically accountable bodies to act accordingly. These expectations have deep historical roots, in Western Europe at least,[82] and they define the core sociological feature of democratic political systems.[83] One way of rephrasing this observation in terms of constitutional theory and social philosophy is the co-originality thesis of Jürgen Habermas' constitutional theory:[84] The law of constitutional democracies enables private autonomy by shielding and protecting decentralised decisions "of self-interested individuals in morally neutralised spheres of action".[85] On the other hand, and beyond this functional dimension, modern law has to fulfil an additional requirement: "it must also satisfy the precarious conditions of a social integration that ultimately takes place through the achievements of mutual understanding on the part of communicatively acting subjects, that is, through the acceptability of validity claims."[86] When elaborating these ideals, Habermas clearly presupposed a constitutional state, in which private and public autonomy co-exist. The European constellation in which we find ourselves has, with the progress of the integration project, gradually led to a decoupling of both spheres and a destruction of their interdependence, which this theory did not foresee and which was factually not problematical during the "golden age" of the European welfare states.[87] By now,

---

[81] *Ibid.*

[82] Section B.I.

[83] See note 3, *supra.*

[84] *Between Facts and Norms* (note 55), at 82 et seq.; see, for an elaboration, R. Nickel, 'Private and Public Autonomy Revisited: Habermas' Concept of Co-Originality in Times of Globalization and the Militant Security State," (Ms. EUI Florence 2006, on file with author).

[85] *Between Facts and Norms* (previous note), at 83.

[86] *Ibid.*

[87] See Leibfried & Zürn, note 4, *supra.*

however, the tensions between Europeanisation and democratic *Sozialstaatlichkeit* have become obvious and Europe is facing difficult choices. (1) The option to re-establish some fully-fledged *Sozialstaatlichkeit* at European level is not really available. The historical, sociological and political obstacle to such a vision is the diversity and complexity of European *Sozialstaatlichkeit*;[88] its legal obstacle is the lack of pertinent European competences which is, in the case of a European labour constitution, plainly visible in Article 137 (5) TEU, which provides that "the provisions of this article shall not apply to pay, the right of association, the right to strike or the right to impose lock-outs". (2) The most drastic alternative is to complete the European economic constitution, to assign supranational validity to it, and thus forget about *Sozialstaatlichkeit* as Europe's constitutional vocation. This, however, is *not* about to happen,[89] and would, if openly promoted, destroy Europe's legitimacy. (3) Europe cannot but search for a Third Way. The reconceptualisation of European law in conflict-of-laws perspectives is such an alternative. We do, of course, not claim that this alternative would orient – somewhat clandestinely – the praxis in Europe. We do, however, claim that it is instructive to look at arguments like those submitted by AGs Maduro and Mengozzi in *Viking* and *Laval* from such a perspective.

2. Responses to Viking and Laval

The need to search for a third way is becoming readily apparent when one looks at the traces of the two alternatives considered in the two opinions.

(1) Both AGs point to the emergence of a social policy at European level, but also underline its limits.[90] Only in AG Maduro's opinion can one find an effort to base the solution of the case on social policy commitments valid at both European and national level. The pertinent passage is worth citing in full:

---

[88] See F.W. Scharpf, 'The European Social Model: Coping with Diversity', (2002) 40 *Journal of Common Market Studies*, 645-670.

[89] See Ch. Joerges, 'What is left', note 14, *supra*.

[90] See Maduro, *Viking,* para 13 *et seq.*; Mengozzi, *Laval,* para. 51 *et seq.*

"Although the Treaty establishes the common market, it does not turn a blind eye to the workers who are adversely affected by its negative traits. On the contrary, the European economic order is firmly anchored in a social contract: workers throughout Europe must accept the recurring negative consequences that are inherent to the common market's creation of increasing prosperity, in exchange for which society must commit itself to the general improvement of their living and working conditions, and to the provision of economic support to those workers who, as a consequence of market forces, come into difficulties".[91]

What AG Maduro seems to promote here is nothing less than a framework of solidarity which would ensure compensation for the losers in the integration process. His observations seem normatively highly plausible.[92] They are, however, without a binding legal basis; they are also hardly compatible with AG Maduro's interpretation of Europe's commitment to a common market, to which we will turn in the next sub--section.

Further elements of a European labour constitution can be detected in the acknowledgement of "fundamental social rights" as the basis of the collective actions taken by the unions. The legal status of these rights remains, however, weak. They are not understood as ensuring the exercise of some "countervailing power" by the unions and their members, but are subjected to legal restraints. Here, the views of both AGs diverge. AG Mengozzi, having asserted "that the right to resort to collective action to defend trade union members' interests is a fundamental right [and] is therefore not merely a 'general principle of labour law'",[93] subjects the exercise of this right to a "proportionality" requirement.[94] This requirement does not preclude *a priori* that service providers from another Member State are compelled to pay the same wages as their Swedish competitors. AG Mengozzi explicitly acknowledges the guest state's

---

[91] See Maduro, *Viking,* para 13 *et seq.;* Mengozzi, *Laval,* para. 51 *et seq.*

[92] A parallel problematic are the distributive implications of product and process standards which are systematically neglected in the discussion of European social regulation; see K. Zurek, 'Social Implications of Europeanisation of Risk Regulation: Theoretical Framework for Analysis of the Problem in the Case of Food Safety, Manuscript Exeter/Florence 2007 (on file with author).

[93] Mengozzi, *Laval,* para. 78.

[94] Mengozzi, *Laval,* paras. 76, 253 et seq.

"objectives of protecting workers and combating social dumping".[95] Such defences are potentially disproportionate, however, where the host state's wage level serves to ensure a degree of protection which the guests do not need because they enjoy an equivalent or essentially similar protection "under legislation and/or collective agreements in the Member State where the service provider is established".[96] This suggestion cannot be interpreted as an element of a European social constitution, however. What AG Mengozzi seems to defend is the chance of foreign service providers to profit from the lower wage levels in their home country, *i.e.*, to profit from the same competitive advantage as the exporters of products. Such an equation of the export of services/labour and of products would, however, neglect the specific *social functions* of labour law, in particular, of collective labour law and the governance structures within which wage level and the social costs of production are determined. The importation of products affects these factors only indirectly, whereas an "importation" of foreign wage levels amounts to a direct intervention into the social fabric of the domestic society.

AG Maduro comes closer than his colleague to acknowledging the social functions of collective labour rights, where he characterises them as "essential instruments for workers to express their voice and to make governments and employers live up to their part of the social contract".[97] But he strictly differentiates when it comes to the exercise of such rights. The actions of trade unions remain compatible with Community law if they are taken *prior* to the relocation; *after* relocation, however, such actions become illegal where they "prevent an undertaking that has moved elsewhere from lawfully providing its services in the Member States in which it was previously established".[98] This is not simply some formalistic distinction, but based upon AG Maduro's understanding of the social and normative functions of the common market. The properly functioning common market, he argues, will attain the Community's social policy objectives; there is, therefore, no sound reason to exempt measures of social policy from the regular market building mechanisms.[99] In this view,

---

[95] Mengozzi, *Laval,* paras. 293, 281.

[96] Mengozzi, *Laval,* para. 264.

[97] Maduro, *Viking,* para. 60.

[98] Maduro, *Viking,* para. 67.

[99] Maduro, *Viking,* para. 23.

Scharpf's decoupling thesis is as unfounded as Habermas' distinction between private autonomy and political rights.[100] In AG Maduro's view, the national economies of the Member States of the European Union are by now, so-to-speak, "embedded" in one common market. On such a basis, one can conclude that a "collective action that has the effect of partitioning the labour market and that impedes the hiring of seafarers from certain Member States in order to protect the jobs of seafarers in other Member States would strike at the heart of the principle of non-discrimination on which the common market is founded".[101] To read this argument as a rejection of the views of Scharpf and Habermas is not to confirm its validity. If there is no transnational legal framework of collective labour law (*Arbeitskampfrecht*) in place,[102] we cannot – without further ado – conclude that the freedoms guaranteed by the Treaty would trump national labour law.

(2) It seems clear to me that such a position would *not* be defended by the founding fathers of German Ordo-liberalism. It was, after all, Walter Eucken himself who had underlined the interdependence of the economic, legal and political order.[103] Franz Böhm, his juristic companion over the decades, held the same views.[104] To be sure, one will hardly find explicit Ordo-liberal warnings against an erosion of the social dimension of the *soziale Marktwirtschaft* by the opening of national borders to free European and international trade simply because such risks were not visible in the formative phase of the *soziale Marktwirtschaft*, in the early years of the integration project, and not even in the era of "embedded liberalism".[105] Only the second generation of Ordo-liberals

---

[100] See Sections E.II.1 and B.I., above.

[101] Maduro, *Viking,* para. 62.

[102] Directive 96/71/EC concerning the posting of workers in the framework of the provision of services ((OJ 1997 L 18, 1) is not a substitute fopr such a European "labour constitution", that Directive and the principle it lays down — posted workers enjoy during their work abroad minimum standards that are in force, as well as minimum standards that have been achieved through universally applicable collective agreements, in the Member State to which they are posted — can be best understood in a conflict-of-laws; see (3) below.

[103] See note 9, above.

[104] See, for example, 'Der Rechtsstaat und der soziale Wohlfahrtsstaat' (1953), in: *id., Reden und Schriften,* (Karlsruhe, C.F. Müller, 1960), 82-156.

[105] See G. Ruggie, 'International regimes, Transactions, and Change: Embedded Liberalism in the Postwar Economic Order, (1982) 36 *International Organizations,* 379-415.

held different views; their Hayekian turn, however, had very limited practical impact.[106]

It is therefore not surprising that the both AGs subscribe to the idea of the supremacy of European freedoms over national labour law and social policy only half-heartedly. In AG Maduro's opinion, one can, however, find pertinent methodological and substantive considerations. Interestingly, the AG determines the meaning of the freedom of establishment (Article 43) and of the freedom of services (Article 49) on the basis of an interpretation of the function of these provisions:

"Together with the provisions on competition, the provisions on freedom of movement are part of a coherent set of rules, the purpose of which is ... to ensure, as between Member States, the free movement of goods, services, persons and capital under conditions of fair competition.

The rules on freedom of movement and the rules on competition achieve this purpose principally by granting rights to market participants. Essentially, they protect market participants by empowering them to challenge certain impediments to the opportunity to compete on equal terms in the common market. The existence of that opportunity is the crucial element in the pursuit of allocative efficiency in the Community as a whole. Without the rules on freedom of movement and competition, it would be impossible to achieve the Community's fundamental aim of having a functioning common market."[107]

The predominance of "functions" over "institutions" is the core idea of classical Ordo-liberalism.[108] Franz Böhm explained this thesis and its implications many times, most stringently, in my view, in his seminal 1948 critique of the German *Reichsgericht* for its legalisation of cartels in the late 19th century.[109] This use of the freedom of contract, Böhm explained, was illegal; it destroyed the competitive *ordo* within which commercial

---

[106] See Ch. Joerges, 'What is left?' (note 14, above), at 473 *et seq.*

[107] Maduro, *Viking,* para.s 32, 33.

[108] See Wegmann (note 9, above) at 374 *et seq.*

[109] F. Böhm, 'Das Reichsgericht und die Kartelle. Eine wirtschaftsverfassungsrechtliche Kritik an dem Urteil des RG. vom 4. Februar 1897, RGZ. 38/155'. (1948) 1 ORDO, 197-213. [reprinted in E.-J. Mestmäcker, (ed.), *Reden und Schriften über die Ordnung einer freien Gesellschaft, einer freien Wirtschaft und über die Wiedergutmachung,* (Karlsruhe: C.F. Müller. 1960), 69-81].

freedom and the freedom of contract are to fulfil their economic and social function. It seems worth noting that this type of reasoning has affinities with Habermas' interpretation of private autonomy as a fundamental right which is to enable citizens to govern their own affairs. To be sure, Habermas[110] relies on political rights where Böhm invokes antitrust policies to ensure a "good order". Neither of them would, however, resort to the famous *Drittwirkungs*-doctrine which the German *Bundesverfassungsgericht* pronounced in is *Lüth* judgment of 1958[111] AG Maduro is following what has become a strong development when he advocates transposing this doctrine to European level.[112] Such a move is questionable for three interdependent reasons: first, the doctrine was not meant to protect the realm of the private over the political; quite to the contrary, the doctrine destroys conventional formalism in private law and "politicises" formerly "private" relationships; second, it presupposes soon provides the basis of an "objective order of values", a poor theoretical basis in pluralist societies and even more so in the European Union; third, when understood as a control of labour and social law, it contributes to the decoupling of the economic and societal orders and exerts a socially disintegrative effect.

The AGs may not have seen these difficulties. But they do avoid them in important respects. AG Maduro's distinction between collective action before and after the relocation of undertakings is significant here. This distinction presupposes what the AG underlines several times, namely, the political autonomy of Member States in the social sphere:

> "Even in cases that fall within their scope, the provisions on freedom of movement do not replace domestic law as the relevant normative framework for the assessment of conflicts between private

---

[110] *Between Facts and Norms* (note 55), at 84 *et seq,* also 313 *et seq.*

[111] *Entscheidungen des Bundesverfassungsgerichts* 7, 198; see for a historical reconstruction Th. Henne, 'Von 0 auf Lüth in 6 1/2 Jahren', in: *id.* & A. Riedlinger (eds.), *Das Lüth-Urteil aus (rechts-)historischer Sicht. Die Konflikte um Veit Harlan und die Grundrechtsjudikatur des Bundesverfassungsgerichts*, (Berlin: Berliner Wissenschafts-Verlag, 2005), 199 *et seq.*; for the dominat view in German jurisprudence, see C.-W. Canaris, 'Grundrechte und Privatrecht', (1984) 184 *Archiv für die civilistische Praxis*, 201-246; *id., Grundrechte und Privatrecht: Eine Zwischenbilanz*, (Berlin/New York: W. de Gruyter, 1999), 30 *et seq.*

[112] Maduro, *Viking,* paras. 35 *et seq.*

actors. Instead, Member States are free to regulate private conduct as long as they respect the boundaries set by Community law."[113]

His proviso that this political autonomy notwithstanding, namely that collective action organised by trade unions must not have "the effect of partitioning the labour market" so as to impede "the hiring of seafarers from certain Member States in order to protect the jobs of seafarers in other Member States",[114] I am inclined to read this passage as an effort to reconcile national autonomy with Community objectives,[115] and even a step towards a conflict-of-laws perspective, as will be explained in the next paragraph (3).

AG Mengozzi seems, at first sight, even more respectful of national law. The proportionality principle which he suggests imposing on the exercise of the right to take collective action is a general principle of law; this he finds hardly problematical since "the Constitutions of the Member States examined above all recognise the possibility of imposing certain restrictions on the exercise of the right to take collective action"... "I do not see", AG Mengozzi adds, "why only restrictions of a solely national origin may be imposed on the exercise of the right to take collective action".[116] It is, however, exactly the equation between the two levels of governance which would need further justification. The same hold true for the consideration "that Laval's economic activity constitutes a provision of services within the meaning of Article 49 EC and Directive 96/71".[117] With this consideration, AG Mengozzi confirms what the national court suggested. Neither that court nor the AG seem to be aware of the far-reaching implications of their consideration. What is at stake here is the legal characterisation of the activities in Sweden. This operation is the most fundamental problem of private international law (conflict of laws). To characterise labour relation as the provision of a service amounts to a replacement of labour law by contract law (and *vice versa*!). to contractual relation (service). It is commonly held in private

---

[113] Maduro, *Viking,* para. 51.

[114] Maduro, *Viking,* para. 62.

[115] Similarly to the suggestions of F.W. Scharpf, 'Community and Autonomy, Multi--Level Policy-Making in the European Union', (1993) 1 *Journal of European Public Policy*, 219–242.

[116] Mengozzi, *Laval,* para.s 81, 82.

[117] Mengozzi, *Laval,* para 99.

international law (conflict of laws) that the qualification follows the *lex fori*. AG Mengozzi implicitly assumes that Community law has suspended this principle. This assumption is widespread among Community lawyers. I have characterised this position as an "orthodox suprantionalism" on many occasions[118] and find it irreconcilable with the Community's order of competences.

(3) Could a conflict-of-law approach provide more convincing responses. In this perspective, diversity is not only the "motto of the Union",[119] but also a *factum brutum*, to which there is no satisfactory solution. The legal differences in the cases under consideration are not so unusual. The boarder-lines between contract law and labour law are not uniform in Europe's jurisdictions; collective labour law differs in many respects. But these differences explain the intensity of the conflict only partially. The real problem stems from the economic and social implications of the legal regime that is to govern the outcome of these cases. The East European parties to the conflict have massive interest in obtaining access to the West European service and labour markets. The West Europeans who have not been ready to support the accession of new Member States by significant transfer payments and do not seem inclined – as AG Maduro suggests – to commit themselves to "the provision of economic support to those workers who, as a consequence of market forces, come into difficulties".[120] This is the *factum brutum*. Can the law compensate this type of failure?

As I have indicated, one can identify elements of a conflict-of-laws approach in both opinions. Both Advocate Generals seem to search for solutions which mitigate between the openness of national economies and legitimate regulatory concerns. But their suggestions have clear practical and normative weaknesses. There may be the possibility that the kind of pressure that AG Maduro suggests imposing on the West Europeans will trigger the kind of compensatory action that he feels is adequate. It is not unconceivable that national courts will find ways of interpreting the

---

[118] Cf., recently, 'Rethinking European Law's Supremacy: A Plea for a Supranational Conflict of Laws', in: B. Kohler-Koch & B. Rittberger (eds.), *Debating the Democratic Legitimacy of the European Union*, (Lanham, MD: Rowman & Littlefield, 2007), 311-327. at 316 *et seq.*

[119] Art. I-8 of the Treaty on a Constitution for Europe, OJ C310/1, 16/12/2004.

[120] Maduro, *Viking*, para. 59.

proportionality requirements that AG Mengozzi has proposed in socially acceptable way. What cannot be ruled out, however, is the use of Community law, which would destruct the accomplishments of *Sozialstaatlichkeit*. It seems inevitable that such consequences would further populist opposition against the European project – and there is no guarantee that the advantages in the accession states would compensate for such costs.

3. *"True conflicts" and the judicial function.*

Conflicts brought before a Court must be decided upon; the parties to the conflict are entitled to receive such a decision. This seems to be but a common place. But is this expectation really so unproblematical? The American conflict-of-laws scholar Brainerd Currie defended a different position. In cases of true conflicts, conflicts-of-laws decisions are, in the last instance, political exercises, he argued:[121]

> "[C]hoice between the competing interests of co-ordinate states is a political function of a high order, which ought not, in a democracy, to be committed to the judiciary: ... the court is not equipped to perform such a function; and the Constitution specifically confers that function upon Congress."[122]

Brainerd Currie was writing for a federal system. Even in such a system, he asserted, the "politicisation" of modern law (its social functions) has transformed the choice-of-law problem into a delicate task which courts are ill-equipped and not legitimated to perform in situations where the "governmental interests" of the concerned states are in conflict. This is not a suggestion that Europe could live with. Europe has to tolerate legal differences; it must not tolerate discriminating practices. But it also needs to remain aware of its diversity, of social, economic and cultural differences. In the present type of conflict, the judges of the Union need

---

[121] Conflicts cases are true "if the court finds that the forum state has an interest in the application of its policy, it should apply the law of the forum, even though the foreign state also has an interest in the application of its contrary policy..."; B. Currie, 'The Constitution and the Choice of Law: Governmental Interests and the Judicial Function', (1958), in *idem, Selected Essays*, (Durham NC: Duke U P, 1963), 188-282, at 272.

[122] B. Currie, *ibid.*

to consider that the European level of governance is "higher" only in limited fields. The ECJ is not a constitutional court with comprehensive competences. It is not legitimated to reorganise the interdependence of Europe's social and economic constitutions, let alone to replace the variety of European social models by a uniform Hayekian *Rechtsstaat*. It should refrain from "weighing" the values of *Sozialstaatlichkeit* against the value of free market access. The ultimate reason for such restraint would be judicial respect for the dignity of national constitutional compromises. The objectives of the integration project would not be jeopardised, and the pressure on the Member States of the EU to ensure the compatibility of their labour constitutions with their commitment to open markets would hardly be diminished significantly.

LES REFERENDA DANS LE PROCESSUS
DE RATIFICATION DES TRAITES EUROPEENS

PHILIPPE MOREAU DEFARGES[*]

Merci, M. le Président. Je suis très content d'être à Lisbonne. J'aime beaucoup cette ville qui a beaucoup de charme et j'aime aussi beaucoup la Fondation Gulbenkian. Je crois que le mérite de ce genre de conférences, c'est de voir que l'Europe reste l'Europe de la diversité. Nous venons d'entendre un exposé français, avec M. Gautron, nous avons entendu un exposé je dirais très allemand, très germanique, maintenant vous irez retrouver un exposé français.

Alors, quand on m'a proposé ce sujet, j'ai été un peu perplexe. Vous savez, les referenda, est-ce que c'est un sujet intéressant ? Je me suis rendu compte que c'est, en effet, un sujet passionnant. Je vais l'aborder par l'un des auteurs que je préfère. Ce n'est pas un philosophe, c'est un fabuliste, c'est Jean de la Fontaine. Chaque fois que je me pose une question internationale, je regarde toujours les fables de La Fontaine. Est-ce qu'il a une fable de La Fontaine qui peut nous aider ? Et la fable de La Fontaine dont je vais me servir, c'est les grenouilles qui voulaient un roi. C'est une fable merveilleuse. Les grenouilles un jour se réunissent et se disent: ce n'est pas bien, nous n'avons pas de roi, nous ne sommes pas comme tout le monde. Et ces braves grenouilles, furieuses de ne pas avoir de roi, se tournent vers Dieu et disent à Dieu, écoute tu te moques de nous, tous les autres peuples, toutes les espèces ont des rois, nous nous n'avons pas de roi. Nous voulons un roi. Et Dieu les écoute. Les grenouilles s'endorment. Le lendemain elles se réveillent et elles ont un roi, c'est--à-dire un bout de bois planté dans le champ. Dieu leur a donné ce roi,

---

[*] Institut Français des Relations Internationales.

avec une couronne sur le bout de bois. Bien sur, les grenouilles sont furieuses et disent à Dieu: tu te moques de nous, ce n'est pas un vrai roi ça, c'est un bout de bois que tu nous donnes. Nous voulons un vrai roi. Très bien. Les grenouilles s'endorment et, le lendemain matin, elles ont enfin leur roi. Dieu leur envoie un héron. Oui, ce grand oiseau qui mord les grenouilles. Tout d'un coup, elles ont un roi et ce roi va leur imposer la dure loi des rois, c'est-à-dire une loi assez difficile. Donc, les grenouilles ont obtenu ce qu'elles voulaient.

Bien, je trouve que l'histoire des referenda dans la construction européenne, c'est un peu ça. Au fond, c'est une machine infernale qu'on a mis sur pied sans s'en rendre compte. Mais avant d'en venir à l'histoire des referenda dans la construction européenne, il faut faire leur historique pour les comprendre. Je voudrais donc rappeler la problématique de la démocratie. Pourquoi, comment se pose la question des referenda dans la démocratie? Je vous rappelle que la démocratie vit sur une contradiction assez bizarre : la démocratie c'est l'origine du peuple. Quand on prend la définition de base de la démocratie, la démocratie c'est l'origine du peuple. Donc, le but de la démocratie est de disposer des meilleures techniques pour recueillir l'opinion du peuple. De ce point de vue là, le referendum serait l'une des techniques, peut-être la meilleure des techniques possibles, pour recueillir l'opinion des peuples, puisque la démocratie repose sur le consentement du peuple. Donc, le referendum est la pratique démocratique par excellence. C'est ce que nous montre la Suisse qui pratique le referendum toutes les semaines. Mais, le problème surgit, et là je vais faire un peu l'allemand, parce que le démocrate est obligé de faire du conceptuel et se dire mais qu'est ce que c'est un peuple? A partir de quel moment y a-t-il un peuple? Et quand vous regardez du côté de la philosophie grecque, la philosophie grecque a eu toujours le soin de dire, il y a le peuple et il y a la foule. Il y a le peuple et il y a la populace. Il y a le peuple et il y a la masse. Donc, on voit bien que la démocratie se trouve devant un problème très difficile : la démocratie est le régime du peuple fondé sur le consentement du peuple et, en même temps, la démocratie a besoin pour exister d'avoir un peuple. Or, le peuple ça n'existe pas dans la nature. Le peuple, c'est une espèce de construction compliquée. À partir de quel moment y a-t-il un peuple? Et là, d'ailleurs, je pense que je fais un échos très fort à l'histoire de l'Allemagne, qui a un rapport très particulier avec le referendum, parce qu'elle sait très bien que la démocratie n'existe pas sans le peuple, mais que le peuple est souvent très imprévisible. Vous savez que c'est un problème qui ne se pose pas seulement à l'Union Européenne, qui se pose au monde entier. Regardez ce qui s'est passe en Algérie, regardez ce qui se passe en Palestine. Nous les occidentaux, nous disons la démocratie c'est le peuple, mais quand le peuple s'exprime de façon un peu imprévisible ou désagréable, on dit non, non, ce n'est pas le bon peuple. Non, il faut un autre peuple. Comme disait Brecht, si le peuple n'est pas bon, il faut dissoudre le peuple et faire un autre peuple. Voilà, donc, la problématique. Et c'est cette problématique là qui est au cœur des referenda dans l'Union Européenne.

Maintenant, je vais revenir à l'Union Européenne elle-même et à l'histoire, parce que l'histoire est très intéressante. Quand est-ce que le referendum apparaît dans la construction européenne? Il apparaît dans la construction européenne en 1972. En 1972, le brave Georges Pompidou, Président de la France, se dit : quand même, l'Europe n'est pas populaire, nous devons rendre l'Europe populaire. Comment faire pour que l'Europe soit populaire? Comment faire pour que les braves citoyens européens se sentent concernés par l'Europe ? Et Georges Pompidou se dit, formidable, j'ai la recette : faisons un referendum. Et je vous rappelle que, au fond, le premier referendum sur les questions européennes a eu lieu en France, en 1972, à l'occasion de l'adhésion du Royaume-Uni, de l'Irelande et du Danemark aux Communautés Européennes. Et Georges Pompidou se dit je vais rendre l'Europe populaire, je vais faire un referendum. Patatras! Ça n'a pas été une réussite, parce que je vous rappelle que le referendum effectivement a donné une majorité de oui, mais les français se sont peu déplacés et on s'est rendu compte que cette technique du referendum n'était pas si bonne que ça. Mais la graine était semée. On avait semée une première graine, la première graine.

Très intéressant, peu de temps après, notre grand ami britannique, le Royaume-Uni, lui aussi, tout d'un coup découvre le referendum. Je vous rappelle que le gouvernement travailliste, élu en 1974, alors que la Grande Bretagne venait de rentrer dans la Communauté Européenne, dit je n'ai pas d'envie d'y rester, j'ai envie de quitter la Communauté Européenne. Et commence alors ce qu'on a appelé la fameuse renégociation où le gouvernement travailliste britannique a renégocié en 73-74 les conditions d'entrée du Royaume-Uni dans les Communautés Européennes. Puis, le premier Ministre de l'époque, Wilson, s'est rendu compte que là aussi il s'était un peu mis dans une situation bizarre, parce qu'au fond le

Royaume-Uni quitter les Communautés Européennes, ce n'était pas si simple que ça. La renégociation se passe cas à cas et à un moment donné Wilson se dit, il faut que je fasse accepter ce truc là par les britanniques. Donc, il faut que je demande une confirmation de notre adhésion. Et le Royaume-Uni, qui n'a pas du tout la tradition référendaire – les britanniques aiment bien le peuple mais avec prudence, ils aiment surtout l'individu –, fait un referendum. Le gouvernement travailliste va faire une consultation, en 1974-75, pour bien vérifier que les britanniques sont contents d'entrer dans les Communautés Européennes, et ce referendum sera politique. Notez bien, ce qui est très intéressant c'est ces deux moments assez lointains où la graine référendaire est mise dans la construction européenne, avec l'idée qu'au fond le referendum c'est le moyen de rendre l'Europe populaire. Et là, la machine infernale est en marche. La machine infernale va se développer puisque la graine, les graines sont semées et le temps passe.

Puis, nous arrivons au moment du Traité de Maastricht. C'est un Traité important puisque ce Traité de 1992 crée l'Union Européenne et fait faire un véritable saut qualitatif à la construction européenne. En France, on l'a présenté comme un Traité compliqué. C'est vrai que c'est un Traité compliqué, c'est surtout un Traité extrêmement important parce qu'il crée l'Union Européenne, c'est-à-dire qu'il crée pour la première fois une structure politique globale. Et à ce moment là, effectivement, compte tenu de l'importante du Traité, certains Etats se disent qu'il faut faire des referendums et le premier à se prononcer c'est le Danemark. Le Danemark, qui, comme vous savez, est un peu eurosceptique, se dit il faut que je demande au peuple danois et le peuple danois dit non. Là, c'est clairement l'emmerdement. Le peuple Danois a dit non, qu'est-ce qu'on fait ? C'est là que va commencer la fameuse idée, on va leur resservir la même soupe quelques mois plus tard. Et c'est vrai qu'on va de nouveau soumettre au peuple danois le Traité de Maastricht, avec quelques protocoles d'aménagement, un an et demi plus tard, et cette fois-ci il dira oui. Vous voyez, c'est bien une machine infernale qui est en marche. Comme les grenouilles qui voulaient un roi, on a une mécanique, puis cette mécanique produit des effets imprévisibles.

L'autre pays d'ailleurs qui vit dans le Traité de Maastricht la même difficulté, c'est la France. François Mitterrand très pro-européen, croyant dans l'Europe et s'étant beaucoup battu pour ce Traité, se dit, au fond, ce Traité de Maastricht, j'y crois. C'est très important, c'est la monnaie unique, c'est la citoyenneté européenne. Il faut faire un referendum. Et François Mitterrand décide de soumettre le Traité de Maastricht aux français par referendum. Comme vous le savez, ça a été très difficile, extrêmement difficile puisque François Mitterrand a mouillé sa chemise et s'est battu avec beaucoup de courage. Je pense que ça a été la grande bataille politique de sa vie, où le oui l'a emporté sur le fil du rasoir. Et là, on s'est bien rendu compte qu'on était face à une espèce de monstre, le referendum, qui était là, qu'on ne pourrait pas le remettre dans le placard comme Amédée de Ionesco. On ne pouvait pas s'en débarrasser. Et, désormais, un lien s'est établi, le referendum c'est la démocratie.

Et on arrive au projet du Traité Constitutionnel. Au fond, toujours la même idée, l'Europe n'est pas démocratique, l'Europe ne sait pas se faire aimer, l'Europe est loin des peuples, l'Europe ignore le peuple, l'Europe est une machine technocratique, etc. Il faut rendre l'Europe populaire et le referendum est la voie nécessaire pour rendre l'Europe populaire. Simplement, on se rend compte qu'on est devant un problème insoluble. Pourquoi? Parce que, n'oubliez pas que pour que le projet du Traité constitutionnel, ou même le projet du Traité Simplifié ou Réformateur soit adopté, il faut qu'il soit adopté par tous les Etats membres. Quand on dit que l'Europe n'est pas démocratique, je ne suis pas tout à fait d'accord. Je sens que l'Europe est quand même très démocratique, puisque, pour qu'on fasse une reforme institutionnelle dans l'Union Européenne, il faut que chaque Etat dise oui individuellement. Pour reformer la Charte des Nations Unies, on n'est pas aussi exigeant. On n'exige pas l'accord de tous les Etats pour reformer la Charte des Nations Unies. Donc, vous voyez, cette exigence de l'unanimité, cumulée avec la réalisation de referenda dans les 27 Etats, c'est clair qu'il n'y a plus de réforme constitutionnelle possible.

On voit bien l'espèce de contradiction terrible que montre bien l'opinion française, soit on poursuit dans la voie du referendum, en disant l'Europe ne sera populaire que par des referenda et c'est clair qu'on en ajoute, on rend encore plus compliqué toute réforme institutionnelle, puisque toute réforme institutionnelle c'est l'accord individuel de chaque Etat. Qu'est-ce que nous dit le premier Traité Constitutionnel? C'est vrai que la France et les Pays Bas ont dit non, mais d'autres ont dit oui. L'Espagne a dit oui par referendum, le Luxembourg également. Nicolas Sarkozy, qui est un personnage assez efficace et expéditif a dit très clairement, je ne ferais pas de referendum, je ne veux pas de referendum. D'un côté, on voit l'hurlement des grenouilles qui disent il trahit la démocratie, et de l'autre coté la réponse du Président de la République: moi, je veux que l'Europe avance. Qu'est-ce que ça veut dire? Deux choses très simples.

Premièrement, le referendum est devenu une espèce de totem. Il faut faire des referenda, parce que le referendum c'est le peuple. L'histoire nous montre que le referendum est un élément dans un système. Et je vous rappelle qu'il n'y a pas très longtemps en France, et ça reste vrai en Allemagne, le referendum c'était le contraire de la démocratie. Lorsque le Général De Gaulle a utilisé, à plusieurs reprises, les referenda au début des années 60, c'étaient des plébiscites. Donc, ce qu'est devenu aujourd'hui le symbole de la démocratie était, à une autre époque, le symbole de la manipulation démocratique. D'ailleurs, je pense que une des raisons pour laquelle je crois que la loi fondamentale allemande interdit le recours au referendum, c'est parce qu'elle a une mémoire historique très claire du plébiscite à une certaine époque.

Là aussi la notion de referendum doit donc être analysée par rapport à un contexte institutionnel général. A nouveau, les referenda suisses ne peuvent pas être comparés aux referenda français, parce que le referendum suisse c'est une autre réalité institutionnelle. C'est une pratique de la vie démocratique suisse qui est propre, comme le dirait Jean Jacques Rousseau, à un petit pays, à un pays où la démocratie directe va de soi. C'est vrai qu'aux Etats-Unis beaucoup d'Etats pratiquent les referenda, parce qu'on voit bien que la logique de la démocratie directe se comprend mieux dans un espace, une entité limitée ou peu nombreuse. Mais, qu'est-ce que ça veut dire? Ça veut dire qu'il faut essayer de regarder à la fois le referendum par rapport au contexte institutionnel général. Je crois que la question que l'on doit se poser pour l'Union Européenne, c'est effectivement comment rendre l'Europe populaire, comment rendre l'Europe démocratique.

Je vais répondre deux choses. Premièrement, l'Europe, l'Union Européenne est démocratique, est vraiment démocratique et je peux le démontrer. Prenez un exemple : quand on dit que la Commission Européenne est un organisme technocratique, je ne suis pas d'accord. La Commission Européenne est pour moi parfaitement démocratique. Pourquoi? Je rappelle que le président de la Commission Européenne est choisi par accord entre les gouvernements, ce qui est tout à fait normal. Il faut demander aux Etats leur accord, évidement, et ensuite, le président de la Commission Européenne est investi par le Parlement Européen. Ensuite, le Président de la Commission compose, en accord avec les gouvernements, la Commission, et le collège revient devant le Parlement Européen pour investiture. Pour moi, ça me parait parfaitement démocratique. Si on est un peu tatillon, on pourrait dire il faudra qu'elle aille devant les parlements nationaux. On peut pousser le jeu encore plus loin. Mais, je crois qu'on ne peut pas considérer, comme les britanniques, que la Commission Européenne est technocratique. Son mécanisme de mise en place et parfaitement démocratique et, comme tout gouvernement disons du type parlementaire, elle peut être renversée par une motion de censure. La Commission Santer d'ailleurs a démissionné, parce qu'elle était menacée par une motion de censure.

Donc, l'Europe, premier point, est démocratique. Mais figurez-vous qu'elle n'est pas perçue comme démocratique. Je m'arrête, je n'entrerais pas dans les détails parce que ça n'est pas le sujet de mon exposé. Mais, qu'est-ce qui fera que l'Europe est démocratique? Les referendums peuvent être un élément parmi d'autres.

Deuxième remarque que je voudrai faire, c'est qu'au fond ces referenda dans l'Union Européenne sont passionnants, parce qu'ils nous montrent que dans certains sujets il n'y a pas de bonnes solutions. On voit bien que le recours au referendum dans les processus de ratification est extrêmement aléatoire. Pourquoi est-il extrêmement aléatoire? Le cas français l'a bien montré. Dans un referendum, les citoyens s'en donnent à cœur joie. Pourquoi les français ont dit non? Oui, ils ont dit non parce qu'il y avait la troisième partie du projet de Traité Constitutionnel. Mais ils ont dit non parce que c'était aussi l'occasion de se payer Chirac, parce que le pays en avait marre du chômage, etc. Dans certains cas, le referendum est une occasion de défoulement, une occasion de s'exprimer.

Donc, on voit bien que la solution du referendum n'est pas la bonne. En même temps c'est vrai que la solution parlementaire ira déchaîner des critiques de tous côtés. Prenez le cas de la France, qui est un cas assez représentatif, le Président de la République a dit j'utiliserais la voie parlementaire. Il est clair que la voie parlementaire va déchaîner des critiques de tous côtés en disant le Président Sarzoky ne respecte pas la démocratie. Si vous voulez, ce que Sarkozy pourrait répondre c'est je respecte la démocratie, je l'ai dit. J'ai dit que je n'utiliserais pas le referendum, je trouve ça trop dangereux. Il l'a dit dans sa campagne électorale, il a été franc.

Pour terminer, c'est vrai que je trouve ça un sujet tout à fait passionnant parce qu'au delà de ces questions un peu techniques du referendum, il y a toute la question de la démocratie et toute la question du rapport entre la démocratie et le peuple. Et on voit bien que la démocratie, je suis désolé, c'est plein de contradictions. La démocratie ne peut être qu'un lieu de contradictions, notamment la démocratie suppose le peuple. Pour qu'il y ait démocratie, il faut qu'il y ait peuple et je pense que l'un des problèmes de l'Europe c'est qu'il n'y a pas de peuple européen. L'Europe a du mal à être démocratique, parce qu'il n'y a pas de peuple européen. C'est clair. Mais en même temps qu'est-ce que c'est que le peuple. C'est vrai que nous les démocrates occidentaux nous disons, il faut des bons peuples. Qu'est-ce que c'est qu'un bon peuple? C'est un peuple gentil, c'est un peuple qui vote comme on le souhaite. Mais, je suis désolé, ces peuples ne sont pas bons. Je vous rappelle l'Algérie en 92 et la Palestine récemment. On a dit, il faut demander au peuple de voter et le peuple n'a pas voté comme on le souhaitait. Alors, on dit on change de peuple. Mais, pour reprendre la phrase de Bertold Brecht, le grand auteur allemand, au moment des émeutes de Berlin en 1953, quand les chars soviétiques ont tiré sur les ouvriers allemands et les ouvriers est-allemands, Brecht a été très désabusé et a dit, si le peule ne convient pas, dissolvons le peuple, changeons de peuple. C'est ce qu'ont fait les soviétiques et les pays de l'est. Simplement, au bout de quarante ans, il n'y avait plus de peuple du tout, les peuples sont passé ailleurs et ont rejeté les communistes. C'est un jeu très compliqué.

A COOPERAÇÃO EXTERNA DA UNIÃO EUROPEIA

EDUARDO PAZ FERREIRA[*]

Convocam-nos os organizadores da conferência – que gostaria de felicitar – a reflectir sobre os desafios com que a União Europeia se confronta no século XXI. Naturalmente que não penso – e, seguramente, ainda menos o pensam os professores Pitta e Cunha e Luís Morais – que seja possível considerar os séculos como divisões estanques. Todos temos a percepção de que muita da problemática que aqui está a ser abordada corresponde ao prolongamento dos debates das últimas décadas ou, se quisermos aproximarmo-nos do título da nossa conferência, aos desafios não respondidos pela União Europeia no século XX.

As Comunidades Europeias, primeiro, a União Europeia, depois, resolveram, no entanto, problemas fundamentais. Asseguraram um longo período de paz dentro das suas fronteiras – ainda que, mesmo ao lado, os ânimos e as armas se incendiassem – garantiram um apreciável grau de protecção dos direitos humanos, mesmo ignorando o que, para lá da cortina ou para cá (Portugal, Espanha, Grécia), se passava e criaram um espaço de prosperidade, visto como um clube de ricos, idílica visão um tanto esbatida pelos alargamentos e pelo agravamento das disparidades económicas.

Por importantes que hoje se apresentem muitos dos desafios à União, trata-se de desafios internos – brilhantemente analisados nesta conferência – que se prendem essencialmente com o grau de integração desejável e os instrumentos para o alcançar, ao serviço de um projecto que já assegurou ou facilitou uma vida boa – ainda que acompanhada,

---

[*] Professor Catedrático da Faculdade de Direito da Universidade de Lisboa.

aqui e além, pelo incómodo espectáculo dos excluídos do mercado da prosperidade – a faixas largas da população europeia.

Se é certo que os desafios internos se revestem da maior importância para os cidadãos dos Estados membros da União Europeia, aos quais se pede cada vez mais a aceitação de níveis supra-estaduais de decisão, não é menos certo que da forma como a União responder aos desafios externos dependerá muito do seu sucesso futuro e da sua capacidade para continuar a ser olhada como um pólo de referência cultural, económico e político.

Entre os desafios externos, assume preponderância a cooperação para o desenvolvimento económico. São várias as razões que me levam a essa consideração. Prendem-se, por um lado, com a importância decisiva do tema na cena internacional e, por outro, com a própria experiência da União neste domínio. Sobre ela se irá, pois, concentrar a minha exposição.

Ao abordar o tema da cooperação para o desenvolvimento, creio ser útil recordar uma passagem da encíclica *Pacem in Terris*, onde se afirma que "...nenhuma comunidade política se encontra em condições de zelar convenientemente os seus próprios interesses, fechando-se em si mesma, porquanto o nível da sua prosperidade e do seu desenvolvimento é um reflexo e uma componente do nível de prosperidade e desenvolvimento de outras comunidades políticas".

No caso da União Europeia pode-se, aliás, com pertinência, afirmar, com Atlee, que "não podemos criar um céu no interior e um inferno no exterior". Num momento em que os mecanismos de integração se aprofundam, é especialmente importante garantir que a pertença a um Estado e a uma União não corresponda a uma negação dos laços que nos unem a pessoas residentes noutras áreas geográficas ou que vivem em diferentes estádios de desenvolvimento, ou que professam religiões diversas. Como lucidamente adverte Amartya Senn, num recente livro, esta é a via para exacerbar as tensões e conflitos.

É, em suma, uma solução que não favorece os valores e interesses da União Europeia.

A exigência de desenvolvimento económico e de criação de uma sociedade globalmente mais equilibrada é uma imposição ética que nem sempre conseguiu a sua transposição para o plano jurídico, uma vez que a justiça na distribuição foi predominantemente considerada um problema que se colocava no interior das fronteiras de cada Estado. Mesmo

John Rawls – responsável por uma das mais importantes reflexões teóricas sobre e necessidade da política de redestribuição – não hesitou em considerar a sua teoria da justiça como respeitando apenas aos cidadãos de um mesmo Estado.

Data, no entanto, do início dos modernos Estados capitalistas liberais o brutal desenvolvimento das desigualdades económicas que até aí não eram tão significativas, num contexto de economias generalizadamente pobres, o que convida à reflexão sobre as razões dessa evolução e à não rejeição liminar das teses que sustentam ter a colonização desempenhado um papel decisivo no modelo de desenvolvimento capitalista.

Recorde-se que, segundo os dados do PNUD, a diferença entre países ricos e pobres seria de 3 para 1 em 1820 e chegava, no final do século passado, a 72 para 1.

Se após a segunda guerra mundial se assistiu a um processo de inquietação das consciências e se o crescente acesso à independência das antigas colónias se traduziu numa maior capacidade reivindicativa dos países pobres, nem assim se logrou afirmar um direito internacional do desenvolvimento, afogado em infindáveis discussões nas Nações Unidas e no permanente veto dos Estados Unidos a qualquer avanço real da política de cooperação.

Poucos – para não dizer nenhuns – tiveram, então, a generosidade e a audácia da Comunidade Económica Europeia, ao aceitar cooperar na tarefa do desenvolvimento económico no quadro de instrumentos jurídicos vinculativos que atribuíam direitos aos países menos desenvolvidos.

No mundo bipolar de então, a Europa soube constituir-se como uma referência necessária daqueles países, apesar de todas as reservas que possamos colocar quanto aos interesses subjacentes, patentes em formas de auxílio que perpetuaram modelos de monoprodução, geradores de dependência, quanto à indiferença aos fenómenos de corrupção e de violação dos direitos humanos e à resignação face aos escassos resultados da cooperação externa.

No longo debate em torno do desenvolvimento económico, profundamente influenciado por opções ideológicas e considerações estratégicas e marcado por uma retórica pesada, foi-se decantando uma noção ampla de desenvolvimento, bem expressa na Declaração das Nações Unidas para o Desenvolvimento, ao considerá-lo como "um processo económico, cultural e político de larga envergadura, que visa a melhoria constante do bem estar em conjunto da população e de todo os indivíduos com base na sua participação activa, livre e significativa e na justa divisão dos benefícios que daí decorram".

A definição – elaborada ainda num período de preponderância dos direitos colectivos sobre os direitos individuais e de prioridade ao investimento fixo – abre caminho para superar esse estádio, no sentido que viria a ser decisivamente trabalhado pelo PNUD, com a criação do índice de desenvolvimento humano, que conjuga indicadores relacionados com o Produto per capita com a esperança de vida à nascença e o sucesso educacional.

Seria Amartya Senn a elaborar a melhor síntese, ao identificar desenvolvimento e liberdade, sustentando que desenvolver implica a remoção de todas os factores que impedem a liberdade: tanto a pobreza como a tirania política, a ausência de oportunidades económicas, como a privação dos direitos sociais.

Ou seja, a concretização do desenvolvimento exige liberdades políticas, facilidades económicas, oportunidades sociais, garantias de transparência e de segurança individual ou colectiva, em suma condições que, no nosso pequeno mundo, tendemos a dar por adquiridas, identificando-as como pressupostos do nosso modelo cultural.

Lucidamente, já em 1967, Paulo VI considerara o desenvolvimento como o novo nome da paz, numa premonitória encíclica em que se viriam a rever mais tarde os que ligaram o sucesso do terrorismo e a sua aceitação em vastas camadas às condições de vida e de opressão.

Mais pragmaticamente, a OCDE, num estudo da década passada, sintetizava as razões para uma política de apoio ao desenvolvimento, apelando a três ideias fundamentais: valores humanitários em face de uma situação intolerável para as consciências, interesse dos países desenvolvidos em criar condições para a expansão económica e consequente travagem da migração e vantagens da comunidade internacional em assentar num conjunto de padrões comuns, que assegurem um desenvolvimento sustentável.

Ouvindo a voz do papa e da doutrina social da Igreja Católica – como dirão os mais crentes – ou a da OCDE e outras instâncias financeiras – sustentarão os menos crentes – certo é que a comunidade internacional se foi orientando no sentido de atribuir maior importância ao tema, até porque a questão da emigração ganhara, entretanto, um peso decisivo.

Ao mesmo tempo, um renovado interesse do pensamento económico sobre a matéria – determinado, aliás, em muitos casos pela vontade

A *Cooperação Externa da União Europeia* 163

de questionar a existência de uma problemática económica autónoma – veio desfazer muitas certezas adquiridas e abrir novos caminhos, de tal forma que se pode razoavelmente dizer que existe um amplo consenso sobre o que se não deve fazer.

Não é, porventura, tão claro o consenso em torno do que há a fazer, ainda que seja possível identificar pontos relevantes, tais como a necessidade de formação de capital e de investimento em infra-estruturas e conhecimento, a liberalização do comércio no quadro de regras multinacionais claras, a prioridade na redução da pobreza e a defesa do ambiente.

Nesse caminho conciliar-se-iam a abordagem neo-clássica com o reconhecimento da necessidade de intervenção pública, ainda que seja nítido que o primeiro vector se foi tornando cada vez mais importante em detrimento do segundo. Mesmo as divergências entre o FMI e o Banco Mundial, tão enfatizadas por Stiglitiz, tendem a esbater-se num pano de fundo neo-liberal, de que o Consenso de Washington foi paradigmático.

De todo o modo, não se pode ignorar que, depois de um conjunto de documentos em que as Nações Unidas se aproximaram das novas concepções de desenvolvimento, abandonando as proclamações ideológicas, aquela organização internacional optaria, na declaração do milénio, por levar os responsáveis de todos os Estados a congregarem-se em torno de uma estratégia assente na hierarquização de objectivos e na sua quantificação. A declaração do milénio constitui o momento mais alto desta estratégia, ao apontar objectivos concretos e calendarizados.

Passados sete anos, as dúvidas quanto à exequibilidade dos modestos objectivos adensam-se, num ambiente de estagnação do volume de apoio que os Estados desenvolvidos estão dispostos a mobilizar, em tudo contrários à concretização das metas propostas. Recorde-se que apenas quatro Estados – significativamente, todos membros da União Europeia – Dinamarca, Suécia, Holanda, Suécia e Luxemburgo cumpriram o objectivo de afectar 0,7% do PIB à ajuda ao desenvolvimento.

Um enorme rolo compressor e unificador foi-se estendendo sobre a problemática. Os países menos desenvolvidos viram-se convidados a seguir um modelo universal. Perderam referências e peso alternativo. Aos poucos, instalou-se uma nova geração de dirigentes sem ligação directa às independências, o que tendo aspectos positivos, se traduz, muitas vezes, numa visão de deslumbramento com o progresso económico, tal como ele é hoje entendido, indiferente às questões fundamentais da distribuição da riqueza e da independência nacional.

A sombra de um passado pouco brilhante como nações independentes, a poeira da corrupção, a usura do argumento relacionado com as sequelas económicas, sociais e culturais da colonização – ainda quando os velhos líderes (Nyerere), as tentam renovar – facilitam esse processo.

Mas interessa-nos, especialmente, ver mais de perto como a União Europeia – já apresentada como um exemplo positivo de apoio ao desenvolvimento – se situou e como foram evoluindo o pensamento e a prática comunitárias, num ambiente de constante transformação.

Torna-se naturalmente necessário reconhecer que a opção por uma política activa e efectiva no apoio ao desenvolvimento não corresponde apenas a um reflexo altruísta dos órgãos comunitários de decisão, antes surgindo como uma resposta ao que eram, então, os interesses franceses em África, que determinaram uma orientação regionalista na política de cooperação, em oposição à versão universalista que outros Estados membros – aqueles sem passado nem presente colonial – teriam desejado.

Vai, de resto, ser uma situação do mesmo tipo a determinar, aquando do primeiro alargamento, uma diversificação das áreas apoiadas pela Comunidade e dos produtos beneficiados por mecanismos de sustentação, para corresponder às exigências inglesas.

A verificação da existência de interesses concretos de vários países na prossecução da política de cooperação não deve, no entanto, levar a esquecer aquilo que parece ser a raiz genuinamente empenhada no desenvolvimento africano que preside à sua génese. Robert Schuman, logo no discurso de 9 de Maio de 1950, situara entre os desafios da Europa o desenvolvimento do Continente Africano.

Viviam-se, então, tempos em que aquilo que hoje é visto com hostilidade por franjas importantes da população comunitária – a possibilidade de utilização de mão de obra africana – era apresentado, a par com os fornecimentos de matérias primas, como um dos fundamentos da Comunidade, pressupondo o fornecimento pela Europa de ajuda financeira e técnica.

A ideia manteria apoio, durante as primeiras décadas de existência da Comunidade, não só em círculos políticos como, também, nos meios económicos. O seu rasto ficaria como ainda está – no preâmbulo do Tratado de Roma onde, entre as motivações para a criação da Comunidade, figura a pretensão de "confirmar a solidariedade que liga a Europa e os países ultramarinos e desejando assegurar o desenvolvimento e a prosperidade destes, em conformidade com os princípios da carta das Nações Unidas".

A Cooperação Externa da União Europeia   165

Eram tempos em que a colonização entrava em crise e se adivinhavam as futuras independências. Ainda assim, os territórios incluídos nessa lista constituíam essencialmente colónias francesas que, depois da independência, viriam a abandonar esse estatuto, passando a integrar o grupo de países ACP.

É a pensar neles que é desenhado um modelo de apoio através da ajuda financeira, canalizada pelo Fundo Europeu de Desenvolvimento, e a concessão de benefícios nas trocas comerciais que permitissem o livre acesso de produtos desses países aos mercados comunitários.

Esse modelo vai transitar para a Primeira Convenção de Yaoundé, que substitui a decisão unilateral no apoio ao desenvolvimento por uma solução negociada e acordada entre a Comunidade e os seus Estados membros, por um lado, e um conjunto de Estados malgaches e africanos, por outro. A natureza contratual da solução viria a ser enfatizada pelo Tribunal de Justiça, ao sustentar o efeito directo das disposições da Convenção que obrigavam a Comunidade não só a suprimir os gravames aduaneiros, mas também qualquer medida de efeito equivalente.

Se, do ponto de vista das soluções de apoio ao desenvolvimento, se não encontram inovações significativas, será de atentar que a Convenção marca o início de um esforço de diálogo político, patente na criação de órgãos como a Conferência Parlamentar e o Conselho da Associação, bem como de um Tribunal Arbitral.

O sistema assim criado e que, na opinião dos mais críticos, constituiu uma forma de perpetuar os laços coloniais, representou, para outros, a forma mais adequada de preservar as ligações com estes países, evitando os melindres que, numa primeira fase, se poderiam colocar quanto ao diálogo político e económico com as antigas metrópoles.

A passagem para as Convenções de Lomé vai marcar um significativo reforço dos mecanismos de apoio, patente na consagração, em termos generosos, do princípio da não reciprocidade, tão vivamente reclamado na UNCTAD pelos países em desenvolvimento, bem como a criação dos mecanismos STABEX e, mais tarde, SYSMIN e ainda o suporte do açúcar, para a garantia dos preços de matérias primas, assim como um alargamento dos países beneficiários e um reforço da cooperação política.

Criou-se, assim, uma forma de relacionamento especialmente criativa, na medida em que se trata de um mercado comum, de uma área de comércio livre ou de uma associação política, ainda que se possam encontrar elementos de todos esses modelos.

Por muito que se possa detectar neste desenho a sombra dos interesses de alguns dos Estados membros da União, está-se perante uma solução que corresponde a um grande avanço no relacionamento Norte-Sul, tanto mais de saudar quanto se iniciou numa fase de recessão económica na Europa. Poderá, mesmo, dizer-se que a subordinação da política de cooperação aos valores e interesses da União – de que, um tanto impudicamente, falava o projecto de Constituição europeia – sempre esteve presente. Apenas variou o peso relativo dos interesses e dos valores.

No preâmbulo da primeira Convenção lia-se, aliás, que ela visava "estabelecer um novo modelo para as relações entre os países desenvolvidos e os países em desenvolvimento, compatível com as aspirações da comunidade internacional no sentido de uma ordem económica mais justa e equilibrada". Creio que assim era, de facto e aquilo que se avançou ou não avançou nas sucessivas Convenções não pode ser isolado do contexto histórico da época, sendo, por exemplo, evidente que o diálogo político pode hoje ser aprofundado com muito mais facilidade do que há algumas décadas atrás.

Mas não se poderá esquecer que, à medida que se aproximava o termo da vigência da Quarta Convenção e o final do século passado, se multiplicaram as críticas ao sistema das Convenções de Lomé e os documentos comunitários de reflexão, profundamente cépticos dos caminhos até então seguidos. Um deles intitulou-se Horizonte 2000, mas houve quem perguntasse 2000 ou 0?

A União Europeia entrou, de facto, num processo – seguramente difícil de compreender para um observador externo – de autocrítica severa da sua política de cooperação, que tem o expoente máximo no Livro Verde, pronto a apontar as deficiências da experiência anterior, mas avaro a reconhecer os seus benefícios. E, no entanto, se não fosse essa experiência a vida difícil de muitas populações teria sido ainda mais insuportável.

Pode-se pensar que a Comunidade não soube avançar com uma política suficientemente autónoma e alternativa à das instituições financeiras internacionais mas, ainda assim, não se pode negar a sua maior permeabilidade à vertente social do desenvolvimento, bem como a relevância da abertura comercial – ainda que não tão ampla como seria de desejar – aos países ACP.

A maior crítica que pode ser dirigida é aquela que, lapidar e premonitoriamente, formulou, em 1986, o intelectual e político cabo-verdiano

Renato Cardoso – que não fora o seu brutal assassinato seria seguramente um dos líderes de uma nova África: "muitas vezes a cooperação contribui para perpetuar os bloqueios estruturais ao desenvolvimento, quando reforça poderes ilegítimos, quando encoraja monoculturas, quando prejudica a reforma de mentalidades, quando dificulta a integração regional, quando engrossa os laços de dependência bilateral".

Certo é que, aquando da elaboração do livro verde que antecedeu a negociação que conduziria ao Acordo de Cotonu, a paisagem geo-estratégica e o pensamento económico dominante se tinham alterado radicalmente. A isso acresceu a divisão cada vez mais nítida entre os países ACP e, simultaneamente, a saída dos quadros comunitários que vinham acompanhando a cooperação desde o início, substituídos por novos elementos com uma diferente formação e uma visão económica de raiz neo-liberal. Tudo isso veio criar um horizonte de negociações difícil para os Estados ACP e adequado a viabilizar as pretensões europeias, quer as novas quer as antigas.

Nesse ambiente foi possível introduzir inovações importantes e positivas, do desenvolvimento sustentável à defesa dos valores da democracia e dos direito humanos, mas o que mais impressiona, em visão global, é a abdicação de qualquer pensamento autónomo por parte da União, confortada com a adesão às linhas gerais norteadoras das instituições financeiras internacionais.

Naturalmente que se essas linhas gerais e a sua aplicação prática tivessem resolvido os problemas do desenvolvimento, a União e todos nós, cidadãos dos Estados membros, apenas nos poderíamos regozijar com a contribuição dada para um objectivo central da humanidade. Assim não sendo, continuo a pensar que havia caminhos alternativos a explorar e para os quais era possível desafiar os Estados em desenvolvimento, últimos responsáveis, afinal, pelas suas políticas económicas.

Um tanto paradoxalmente, depois da política de cooperação ter ganho consagração no Tratado – em contraste, aliás, com a prática ausência de referências na generalidade dos textos constitucionais dos Estados membros – uma legitimação expressa, anteriormente tão aplicadamente buscada em diversas disposições do Tratado, a União parece ter-se desinteressado da política de cooperação ou encará-la, mesmo, como um fardo do passado.

A aceitação das regras da globalização e, em particular, dos normativos da Organização Mundial do Comércio levou, de resto, a que a União pusesse fim ao emblemático princípio da não reciprocidade aduaneira, substituído pela negociação de uma série de acordos de livre comércio, processo que se tem vindo a desenrolar penosamente.

A União Europeia parece partilhar da esperança, ou certeza internacionalista, de que o comércio livre estará na base de uma prosperidade universal para atingir uma terra sem pobres, em que Norte e Sul não signifiquem mais do que meras referências geográficas.

Mas, será que, em nome da utopia liberal, valerá a pena para não perder o Norte perder o Sul? Tanto mais quanto essa opção significa perder os nossos valores e não cuidar dos nossos interesses.

WILL THE CONSTITUTION MAKE EU DECISION-MAKING EASIER?

SIMON HIX[*]

Thank you very much. It's a great pleasure to have been invited here. Will the Reform Treaty make the EU decision making easier?

Well, firstly, why the title? Once you strip away the symbols of the Constitution, the name, the title EU Foreign Minister, some of the other constitutional elements of it, what is left? What is left to justify selling the reform treaty to the people? The main justification is that it will make the EU work better, it will make the EU more effective, more efficient and more able to cope with the policy problems and challenges it faces with 27 member States. So, what I thought I would do for you is give you my assessment of this. I should declare an interest: I chaired a working group for the British Cabinet Office preparing the British negotiation position during the Convention that negotiates the Constitution. Unfortunately they didn't listen to me, but we will get to that at the end!

I see five main areas of changes related to the question of how would the Reform Treaty, if ratified, affect the decision making processes of the EU. First, the single President of the European Council, I get frustrated by the British press and, no doubt, the press everywhere, who keep calling this the single EU President. There will not be an 'EU President'. We already have three EU Presidents. There will be a single President of the European Council, little more than that. Second, the new qualified-majority voting system, which is a complete mess. I will explain

---

[*] Professor of European and Comparative Politics, London School of Economics and Political Science.

why. Third, extension of qualified-majority voting. Fourth, extension of the co-decision procedure, the so-called ordinary legislative procedure as it was called in the Constitution. And, fifth, the role of national parliaments – the new role of national parliaments in the protocol of national parliaments and proportionality and subsidiarity. I will then give my overall assessment of the Reform Treaty in perspective vis-à-vis previous treaty reforms, and I will try to persuade you that this is the least significant treaty the EU has ever signed.

The Single European Council President.

What is in the Treaty? A single European Council President elected for two and a half years, by qualified-majority, renewable for one term. Hopefully, Tony Blair would have fixed the Middle East by the time it enters into force, so he can take it on, so he thinks. The main claim is that this would improve decision-making efficiency in the European Council. For example, there would no longer be the rotation between the member states – the fear for so long is that Latvia would be followed by Lithuania, would be followed by Luxembourg, followed by Malta. A series of small states running the affairs of the EU of 27 would be replaced by a single President – a figurehead with whom the public can identify. Giulliano Amato liked to compare this model with the French model of Government: you would have a President and the Commission President would become the equivalent of the Prime Minister. We kept reminding him, however, that the President in France can, at least, hire and fire the Prime Minister. The new European Council President cannot really do anything.

The European Council President would have very little formal power, unlike the Commission President. The Commission President would still maintain a monopoly on legislative initiative. The President of the Council would have no real agenda setting power, some prioritizing power, of issues that should be discussed in the European Council, but no former legislative authority or power of initiative. Another concern is that the President of the European Council would not have the same legitimacy as the other heads of government. You can already see this, for example, with Tony Blair, when he announced that he was going to stand down as Primer Minister and he went off to negotiate with Putin and Putin said

"Why should I listen to you? You are not really an elected leader, you have no mandate, and you don't represent the people of Britain anymore". This is a concern, as why should the EU heads of government, election by their people, listen to the EU Council President, who they appoint. He or she would basically be an agent of the EU heads of government rather than their leader. And so, this is why I think this will be a really marginal role, purely an honorific figurehead type of role that would have very little formal power.

A bigger concern is that this post will more than likely lead to some serious conflicts with the Commission President. I like to say that the Council President will have 'high prestige but no power' while the Commission President will have 'high power but low prestige'. The Council President would say "I am the boss" and the Commission President would say "but I have all the power, and I will not do what you want". We tried to explain this to the British Government who liked the idea of a single Council President. They said "but the Commission President always listens to the governments and so if the Council President asks the Commission President to initiate policy X, the Commission will initiate policy X". In response, we argued that this will not be the case if the Commission President increasingly gains his or her authority from the European Parliament. So, the EU will have one President, the President of the European Council, elected by a majority of governments, and the other President elected by a majority in the European Parliament. In other words, this would be institutionalised cohabitation. When there is institutionalised cohabitation in France, who is the boss? Not the President, but the Prime Minister. And this is exactly what will happen in the EU. The Commission President will have all the authority, all the power and will more than likely be from an opposite side of the political divided from the Council President.

So, not much real impact of the new EU Council President. Some potentially positive gains, but also some potentially negative consequences. A possible long-term solution to the problems would be to fuse the office of the EU Council President with the Commission President. This would be following the example of fusing the two offices of the High Representative for CFSP in the Council and the Commissioner for External Relations.

The New System of Qualified-Majority Voting

This is the trickiest issue to explain to a non-technical audience. The Reform Treaty will replace the Nice Treaty rules of a 'triple majority' with a new 'double majority'. It sounds simple: a triple majority will be reduced down to a double majority. This must be an improvement, surely? However, the double majority, of 55% of states and 65% of population, thanks to the power and persuasion of the polish negotiators, will be delayed until 2014 with a transition period until 2017. None of the people who negotiated this deal will still be in power in 2007, so this really is in breach of an accountable mandate.

But, how do we understand the likely impact this change? This is where it gets tricky. The question to think about is how much power does a member state have to influence policy under a voting system? How do we measure power? The important thing to understand is that power is the ability to influence policy, and this is not necessarily related to ones voting weight under a particular system. Consider the following scenario: imagine that there is a parliament where one party has 51% of the seats and the other party has 49% of the seats. What do you think the power is between the two parties? In fact, Party A would have 100% of the power and party B would have 0. So, with only 51% of the seats, Party A does not have 51% of the power, but has 100% of the power. Following the same logic, mathematicians across the world have calculated the power of each member state under the Nice rules and proposed new rules.

48 economists, political scientists, mathematicians, physicists, and engineers signed a letter during the Convention to try to explain to the negotiators why the double-majority system was ludicrous. The Swedish Government was the only government who listen to us. The Polish then decided they would listen too, when they realised what we had to say. What we had to say was the following: under the new system, in absolute power terms, Germany would be the main beneficiaries of the new system and Poland would be the main losers. This is absolute power.

What is more interesting, however, is relative power. This is the increase or decrease in the proportion of power a member state has relative to the Nice Treaty rules. The main winners in these terms are Germany and the very small member states. The double-majority system means that the small states are hugely over-represented by the one-state--one-vote part of the rules, while the population-based part of the rules means that the biggest state, Germany, is massively also over-represented. Everyone between Germany and the tiny states is largely under--represented. The two systems are about the same for the other three big states (the UK, France and Italy), however Poland, Spain, Portugal, the Netherlands and all the other states in the middle will be under-represented in the new voting system. I cannot, for the life of me, understand why the majority of member states negotiating the reforms were willing to accept a system which would make them significantly worse off than the Nice Treaty!

What would be ideal is a system of decision making in the Council, where every citizen of every member state has equal chance of being on the winning side. This is known as 'true equity' in decision making. The reformers could have designed a truly equitable system of voting in the Council relatively easily by having a weighted-voting system, where the voting-weight of each member state is a proportion of the square-root of that member state's population – this would in practice be very similar to the qualified-majority rules in the Rome Treaty, the Maastricht Treaty, the Amsterdam Treaty and the Nice Treaty. However, sadly, this was not the case this time.

So, what I'm showing you here is the power of each member state under the Nice Treaty and the Reform Treaty relative to a system of 'true equity'. When comparing the Nice Treaty to true equity, it is clear that Germany was a lot worse off under the Nice Treaty rules they should be. Meanwhile, the very small member states were already much better off, and Poland was significantly better off. When comparing the Reform Treaty to a truly equitable system, Germany would be 20% better off than it should be, and Malta would almost 60% better off than it should be, whereas Portugal and the Netherlands would be 20% worse off than they should be. I worry very much about the long-term effects of this double--majority voting system in the Council for public support for the EU in each of the 18 member state who would be under-represented in the Council under the new qualified-majority voting rules.

Extension of Qualified-Majority Voting

The Reform Treaty extends qualified-majority voting to a number of areas. This is just a few of the ones that are most obvious: coordination of economic policy; common transport policy; tasks and objectives of the structural funds; crime prevention and some of the other areas of police cooperation; immigration, asylum and border controls; creation of the European defence agency; appointment of the executive board members of the ECB; and some of the new competences, space, energy, tourism, sport, humanitarian aid. It sounds like an impressive list. But, it is not really.

These are relatively minor changes and relatively minor policy issues relative to major extensions of qualified-majority in the Single European Act, the Maastricht Treaty and the Amsterdam Treaty. The main extension, the main new innovation is in the area of police cooperation. One of the other areas that some people have claimed would be a major extension is in the area of asylum, immigration and border control. This is not, in fact, the case, because there was a passerelle clause in the Amsterdam Treaty, which the governments invoked in November 2004 and so passed almost all of these issues from unanimity to QMV already. So, the governments signed the Constitution and then thought, "if we all agree we should move these issues to QMV, why don't we do it right now?". But, soon as they did this, one of the major policy implications of the new Treaty suddenly became irrelevant.

Extension of the Co-Decision Procedure

Co-decision, or the ordinary legislative procedure, would not really be extended very much at all: to the common commercial policy; agriculture; police cooperation; and some other relatively minor issues. The likely impact, again, would be very minor relative to the changes in Amsterdam Treaty, which was the major extension of the co-decision procedure in previous treaties. The most significant area, however, is agriculture, partly because a lot of legislation is passed on agriculture (about 30% of all EU legislation). This could mean that the Common agricultural Policy would be reformed via the European Parliament.

The Role of National Parliaments

You can make an argument that the issue of the role of national parliaments relates to accountability, democracy, openness, and transparency. However, I am not going to talk about those issues. What I am more interested in is what would the new role of national parliaments mean for the decision-making process? The new rules say that national parliaments would have 8 weeks to examine legislative proposals, to police the two principles of subsidiarity and proportionality. This provision is instead of a new third chamber or a new quasi-judicial institution composed of representatives of national parliaments. Several governments, including the British, proposed a new European-level court to police subsidiarity, composed of senior judges appointed by each member state. Several people point out, however, that that such a court already exists: the European Court of Justice! In response, several governments then proposed a chamber of national parliaments. However, how could national governments control national parliaments in a new chamber in Brussels? Hence, the governments decided that they could control the process much more easily of scrutiny is done in the domestic arenas inside national parliaments. In other words, by giving power to national parliaments, national governments are actually giving themselves power. We do not have a separation of powers at the national level in Europe. In parliamentary systems, parliaments is not like the US Congress relative to US President. Governments in almost all EU member states have a majority in their parliaments and so it is very easy for governments to say, "let's give our national parliaments power in the EU".

There would be a moderate increase, I think, in media coverage of the EU as a result of these changes. However, if you have ever been to the European Affairs Committee of a national parliament you will realise that the quality of the average MP sitting in these committees is extremely low. Hence, I do not think that the media will suddenly start to cover EU legislation just because of this new mechanism.

And, the new procedure involving national parliaments has the potential to slow down the passage of EU legislation. And, since the governments actually control their national parliaments, what the new procedure would effectively do is give each of the governments an extra veto power in the legislative process, under the auspices of policing the subsidiarity and proportionality principles.

The Reform Treaty Compared to Previous Treaties

In sum, how do we understand the Treaty in comparative perspective vis-à-vis the others treaties? Imagine two dimensions of change in reforms to the EU: (1) how much policy integration is there as a result of a treaty, in terms of how many new policy competences are added to the EU; and (2) how much supranational decision making is there, in terms of how far has qualified-majority voting, the co-decision procedure, and the power of the Court of Justice been extended.

The main innovation in the Rome Treaty was a new set of policy competences with some supranational authority, but ultimately decisions via intergovernmental mechanism (after the Luxembourg compromise). The main jump in the supranational decision-making direction was the Single European Act. The massive extension of qualified-majority voting for the completion of the internal market, new policy competences on social policy, the extension of qualified-majority voting on environment, and so on. Maastricht was a jump on the other direction: adding Economical and Monetary Union, Common Foreign Security Policy, and justice and home affairs, but it was still a relatively intergovernmental treaty. Apart from the co-decision procedure, the main decision-making innovations of the Maastricht Treaty were the intergovernmental mechanisms in Economical Monetary Union, CFSP and justice and home affairs. Amsterdam was a modest change from Maastricht. The main innovations in this treaty were the extension of co-decision, reform of the co-decision procedure (to increase the power of the European Parliament) and the extension of qualified-majority voting and the power of the Commission as an agenda setter over justice and home affairs. So, a moderate change from Maastricht. Nice was an even smaller change: Defence cooperation and a moderate extension of qualified-majority voting.

The Reform Treaty, measured like this, really is the least significant Treaty the EU has ever signed. If the treaty does not pass, what is the big deal?

This is not really surprising. What this story of the treaty reforms tells us is that the basic policy and institutional architecture of the EU is very close to 'equilibrium'. And with 27 member States it is going to be even more difficult to reform the basic policy and institutional architecture. The basic policy architecture is a market created and regulated at the European level and taxing and spending policies at the national level.

That basic architecture would not have been challenged by the constitution and would not be challenged by the current treaties and almost nobody really wants to challenge this. Sarkozy wants to come back a little bit on the competition in the internal market, but no really fundamental challenge. The institutional architecture, meanwhile is essentially two modes of decision-making: intergovernmental decision-making predominantly on foreign policy and policing; and supranational decision-making (meaning qualified-majority voting, plus the co-decision procedure, plus a monopoly on legislative initiative for the Commission, plus judicial review by the Court) in all other areas. This basic architecture it is not really challenged by the Reform Treaty, as we already very close to a stable equilibrium.

Returning to my starting question, will the Reform Treaty make EU decision-making easier? Answer: not in any noticeable way. The EU will still face the policy challenges it faces now. If member state governments and the Commission really think that what the EU needs to do is undertake policy reform, liberalise the service sector, have common immigration policies, tackle the issue of climate change, I don't see anything in this treaty that would change the institutions in any way that would make it more likely that the EU would be able to do those things.

I think the likely marginal gains in effectiveness are out-weighed by two potentially quite costly developments: (1) the single Council President, which may well undermine the authority of, and end up in conflict with, the Commission President – I see this as potentially quite dangerous and destabilising, a battle for legitimacy perhaps; and (2) the new qualified-majority voting system in the Council, which is highly inequitable, particularly for medium-sized states like Portugal. On this last issue, ideally, the double-majority system could hopefully be replaced before 2014 by a single weighted-voting system similar to the one in the Rome Treaty.

Some final words. Something that has not really been discussed in this conference so far. Will the Treaty be ratified? As of now, I think the Treaty has a 50% chance at best. There will be a referendum in Ireland, and the Irish voted No to the Nice Treaty, although the Irish showed overwhelming support for the Nice Treaty. Why? The No campaign had a brilliant slogan: "If you don't know, vote No". I am sure they will be repeating the slogan and this is the most arcane set of institutional changes anyone could ever imagine trying to explain to the public. The Green

Party in Ireland is opposed to the Treaty and they are in government with Fianna Fáil. So, one of the governing parties is opposed already. In Denmark, there might be a referendum, if the Treaty cannot pass the by four--fifths of the Parliament. The Danish People's Party and the Left Socialists are opposed to the Treaty and they have more than 20% of the seats in the Parliament. So, I guess that there will be a Danish referendum, and who knows how the Danish people will vote? In the UK, I feel the Treaty has a 50% chance of passing in the House of Commons. Labour has a 67 seat majority, and at least 35 Labour MPs are already opposed to the Treaty. If the Liberal Democrats abstain, my guess is the Treaty will be defeated in the House of Commons, regardless whether we have a referendum. In the Netherlands, from what I understand, one of the two Dutch main government parties, the PvdA have already started to say that they think there should be a new referendum. If there is referendum in these states, who knows what will happen in Poland, the Czech Republic, Sweden, Estonia and so on. So, my best guess right now is that the Treaty has a 50% chance of being ratified. But, if it is not ratified, I don't really mind.

Thank you.

THE CONSTITUTION OF EUROPE:
RESQUIESCAT IN PACEM

JOSEPH WEILER[*]

Funeral orations are traditionally short and one is never to speak ill of the dead. I fear that in the case of the Constitution of Europe I will violate both customs.

Let me start with a famous example of Jewish humor:

Moishe and Chayim, two fur traders, meet at Warsaw Railway Station. 'Where are you going to?' ask Moishe. 'To Lodz' answers Chayim. 'Oy, you are so dishonest!' says Moishe. 'You tell me you are going to Lodz because you want me to think that you are going to Krakow. But actually you are really going to Lodz! So why are you fibbing?'

Begin to wrap your mind around the subtle and multiple layers of deception encapsulated in this little exchange. Now imagine a variant: Moishe says:

'You tell me you are going to Lodz because you want me to think that you want me to think that you are going to Krakow and that I will therefore think that you are actually going to Lodz but you are in fact going to Krakow.'

Reach to your bottle of aspirin. And now you are in the right frame of mind to uncover the multiple layers of deception in the European constitutional saga.

---

[*] University of New York.

The Original Sin was to confuse the Institutional with the Constitutional and to peddle the idea that Europe was in need of a Constitution. What it really need was a serious institutional face lift, updating its decisional processes to a Union of 27. Constitutionally Europe was doing just fine – notably in the critical area of the relationship between the European Union, the Member States and European citizens. Not only had this relationship followed for decades a constitutional rather than an international law sensibility and discipline, it was original and noble: The Member States accepted the supremacy of European Union law, individuals could rely on their European rights even against conflicting State norms, the European Court of Justice developed a robust doctrine of protection of fundamental human rights – long before anyone even thought about the Charter.

The second deception was to pretend that the legal mongrel produced by the Convention was a Constitution.

It does not look like a constitution: in its English version it weighs in at 154,183 words! For comparison sake, the American Constitution is 5,800 words long and the Charter of the United Nations 8,890. The actual weight of the official two-tome printed version of the so called European Constitution is just under one kilogram.

It does not read like a constitution: constitutional opening phrases are typically of a magisterial style and make reference to the ultimate constitutional authority undergriding the document – the People. Thus, e.g.:

'We the people of the United States, in order to form a more perfect union...'

'Le peuple français proclame solennellement son attachement aux Droits de l'Homme et aux principes de la souveraineté nationale tels qu'ils ont été définis par la Déclaration de 1789...'

'Im Bewußtsein seiner Verantwortung vor Gott und den Menschen, von dem Willen beseelt, als gleichberechtigtes Glied in einem vereinten Europa dem Frieden der Welt zu dienen, hat sich das Deutsche Volk kraft seiner verfassungsgebenden Gewalt dieses Grundgesetz gegeben...'

The opening phrase of the Document put before Europe's peoples is equally revealing. It is the very same used since the very first Treaty establishing the European Coal and Steel Community in 1951:

'His Majesty the King of the Belgians...!'

The Constitution of Europe: Resquiescat in Pacem

This is followed by the long list of Heads of State.

'The President of the Czech Republic [etc. who].... Have designated as their plenipotentiaries ... Guy Verhofstadt Prime Minister[,] Karel de Gucht Minister for Foreign Affairs [etc.]... Who, having exchanged their full powers, found in good and due form, have agreed as follows...'

The non-initiated reader would be forgiven if he believed that he was reading the standard opening of an international treaty. He would be forgiven if the same opinion were formed by going to the conclusion of the Document. He will first find this:

'This Treaty shall be ratified by the High Contracting Parties in accordance with their respective constitutional requirements. The instruments of ratification shall be deposited with the Government of the Italian Republic.'

Followed by:

'IN WITNESS WHEREOF, the undersigned plenipotentiaries have signed this Treaty....'

'Res Ipsa Loquitur!' (The thing speaks for itself).

What of the content of the document, its substance? It is for the most part, including the integration of the Charter of Fundamental Rights, the kind of content which one had hoped to see in the Treaty of Amsterdam and certainly in the Treaty of Nice in the countdown to Enlargement: A sensible though far from radical amendment of the Institutional architecture and decision-making processes of the Union; some meaningful but equally non-radical nods towards the further democratization of the above; the Charter (more about which below) and some sensible cleaning up of language. The Treaty revision procedures have been interestingly amended to provide a multi-tier process: Convention and Intergovernmental Process; Intergovernmental Process without Convention; decision of the European Council alone. But, significantly, from a constitutional point of view, all three processes are, in conventional thinking, not typical of constitutions but rather of Treaties. They all require unanimity among the Governments of the High Contracting Parties and ratification by national procedures in all Member States.

But Europe paid a heavy price by this double deception. Had it been presented for what it really was rather than the deception that it was a

Constitution (based on the earlier deception that one needed a consti-tution) the peoples of Europe in their wisdom would have welcomed it for what it really was: a Reform Treaty adapting the European Union to Enlargement. No one would have used any superlatives to describe its content, it would have attracted very limited public attention or debate in most Member States, it would certainly not have generated the numerous referenda which are now planned in the Union, and there would have been no talk of the need for a Constitution (except, perhaps, among the European federalist fringe). No Convention, no European Philadelphia, no Constitutionspeak. We would have been today, Summer of 2007, where we now so want to be, with a sensible Reform Treaty already in place.

Instead, once presented as a Constituiton, it was only natural that a totally different standard was applied to the document. A constitution after all is a document with far greater gravitas. In a constitution one wants to find not simply sensible reform but a statement of identity, of ideals, of the type of society and polity one not only is but one wants to believe one is. And against this appropriate standard, the mongrel document, the Treaty pretending to be a Constitution, which found favor with bureaucrats, Eurocrats and government Ministers, was found wanting, and rightly so, by the peoples of Europe, and rejected.

(And, make no mistake: it is not a rejection by a freak vote in two Member States. Are we meant to be impressed by the ratification with Ceausescu-type majorities in some of our national parliaments? Does anyone have any doubt that, for example, had the Dutch vote and French vote come at the beginning of the process, one would have had similar rejections in quite a few other Member States?)

Now, one takes that Treaty which masqueraded as a Constitution, which was officially described and hailed and advocated as The Cons-titution of Europe and one repackages it with a new name The Reform Treaty. The repackaging is pretty crude: Strip away the word constitution. Pretend the Charter of Fundamental Rights is not part of the Reform Treaty, but actually have a little legal provision which will integrate it through the back door. So legally it is included, but presentationally it is airbrushed out – all this whilst pontificating on the need for transparency.

So let us review: You had a Reform Treaty which you deceptively pretended was a Constitution. Now you strip away a word or two, leave the substance intact, and deceptively pretend that "The Constitution" is a Reform Treaty, whereas it is really the very same Constitution that was rejected last year which really was a Reform Treaty pretending to be a Constitution. Even Moishe now would need a bottle of aspirin.

The Italians have a wonderful word to describe what the manner the European public has been treated by its reigning mandarins: 'Meschinita'!

The future of the European Constitution is, thus, paradoxically, it's Past. But the belief, expressed now by many that with the adoption of the Simplified Treaty one can return to the constitutional *status quo ante* is naïve.

The damage created by this moment of *hubris* in the history of European integration is not negligible.

Let me list the many ways in which we were all damaged by this exercise.

The first damage is exactly the degradation of the political process and of the seriousness of civic discourse. Europe has officially adopted an Orwellian Eurospeak in what was meant to be an upgrading of its legitimacy and transparency.

Second, there is damage to the future – since the "Non Constitution" now defines the Promised Land of European Constitutionalism. Imagine in five or ten years reopening the debate on a European Constitution. Imagine a text such as the mongrel text now abandoned which still leaves an amending process which depends on the High Contracting Parties by unanimity. By all accounts it should be objected to as contrary to a real constitution. But, with the legacy now created we will hear that it is indeed constitutionally acceptable – after all, did not the European Constitution of 2003 provide exactly for that? At a more profound level, our constitutional vocabulary has been diminished – inflationized.

Third, there will also be damage to the present. It would be nice to think that with the new Mini-Treaty one could just revert to the constitutional *status quo ante*. It will not be easy. Totally unnecessarily the Mongrel Text included, for example, a supremacy clause. That may drop from the Mini Treaty. So, something that was firmly established in the European constitutional architecture has been undermined – politically, not legally – and will be challenged sooner or later. After all, all aspects of the *acquis constitutionnel* will henceforth invite the attack – is that not exactly what Europe rejected, when it rejected the Constitution. Let me make clear: Legally, we are where we were. But politically, the damage has been done. Indeed, the damage is more profound. The European

Court on more than one occasion referred to the Treaties as the Constitutional Charter of Europe. And the Member States and their constitutional organs, such as parliaments, courts, executive branches, were invited to submit to a "new legal order" constitutional in nature which defined the originality and nobility of the European Construct. That vocabulary and that conceptual world have also been damaged.

Finally, the irony of the recent Summit could not have escaped you: In the ambition and desire to make constitutional progress, Chancellor Merkel was quite happy to threaten the most unconstitutional of moves, the threat to ride roughshod over the requirement of unanimity for Treaty amendment. It is interesting that only Estonia and Finland protested – Are we back to the era of the Euro Mandarins? What confidence in constitutional integrity if the champion of the Constitution is willing to violate the most primordial of constitutional law when things do not go ones way? Am I alone in thinking that when it comes to Europe, our leaders have a deep mistrust of the People?

Be that as it may: The European Constitution **requiescat in pace!** I am not shedding too many tears.

What then of the future – trying to restore the past?

The real constitutional agenda remains the same, just more challenging. The democracy deficit and the political deficit have not been closed. A meaningful check on Competences of the Union has not been established. The deeper issues of identity, immigration, demographics have, as usual, been swept under the carpet. The politics of deception – that is the name of the game.

CONSTITUIÇÃO EUROPEIA
E CONSTITUIÇÃO DA REPÚBLICA PORTUGUESA

RUI MANUEL MOURA RAMOS[*]

1. O tema que me foi atribuído *(Constituição Europeia e Constituição da República Portuguesa)* pode perfeitamente ser tratado fora do contexto da reflexão que presentemente nos reúne. Ele é independente da evolução que se vive neste momento mas não deixa de ser importante revisitá-lo porque lança um olhar decisivo sobre o que está em causa no processo actual.

A ligação que se estabelece entre duas entidades, a Constituição Europeia e a Constituição da República Portuguesa, sugere um diálogo, uma ponte ou um compromisso, mas supõe, antes de mais, que se caracterizem os termos entre os quais esse diálogo ou essa ponte podem ser estabelecidos. O que implica pois, principalmente, um esforço de definição das realidades que aqui se encontram em causa.

Tal afigura-se aparentemente fácil quanto a uma delas, a indicada em segundo lugar no enunciado do tema que nos cabe tratar – a Constituição da República Portuguesa. É algo bem conhecido de todos nós, a opção constituinte de 1976 que viria a ser aperfeiçoada ao longo das sete revisões que se lhe seguiram. Temos, hoje, com efeito, um texto que, mantendo substancialmente a matriz inicial, se demarca em pontos relevantes de algumas escolhas originárias denotando uma nítida evolução face ao que nos seus primórdios se havia consagrado. Mas esse processo ocorreu sem rupturas, com a preservação ou até mesmo o reforço da

---

[*] Presidente do Tribunal Constitucional.
Faculdade de Direito da Universidade de Coimbra.

respectiva identidade, pelo que não se hesitará em reconhecer que estamos perante a mesma entidade.

A identificação dos termos em presença é porém mais difícil quando falamos da outra realidade, por sinal a enunciada em primeiro lugar no título da nossa intervenção: a Constituição Europeia. Aqui há uma primeira tomada de posição que se afigura imperiosa, e que se traduz em saber se quando utilizamos esta noção temos em vista uma realidade mais ou menos formal, mais ou menos historicizada, concretamente aquela vertida no texto que foi estabelecido pelo Tratado assinado em 28 de Outubro de 2004, posteriormente sujeito a um interrompido processo de ratificação, e que, pelo menos nos precisos termos em que se encontrava redigido, acaba de ser de algum modo posto de lado pelas decisões do último Conselho Europeu.

Parece-me manifestamente que não faz sentido utilizar este texto para densificar aqui e agora o conceito de "Constituição europeia". E isto independentemente das reservas que se possam ter quanto à utilização naquele contexto do termo Constituição, reservas que na altura não deixei pela minha parte de formular. Sem querer discutir se era ou não abusiva a utilização de tal termo, e se com ela se pretendeu tão só qualificar desta forma uma realidade de natureza diversa, o certo é que cremos que não faz sentido voltar agora a esse texto. Ele é hoje um documento histórico, do passado, ainda que possa não vir sempre a dever ser qualificado como tal, pois que o essencial do seu conteúdo pode vir a ser retomado. Mas por enquanto é um texto mais que se vai juntar a outros que marcaram a evolução do processo de construção europeia e que por qualquer razão não foram adoptados. Dir-se-á apenas que a razão pela qual ele é hoje apenas um texto histórico se reveste de uma natureza algo diversa (dir-se-ia até que mais poderosa, em certo sentido) que a que determinou o abandono de outros. Recordaremos a este propósito que o projecto de Tratado que criava em 1952 a Comunidade Política Europeia viu a sua rejeição ser determinada pelo inêxito de um processo de ratificação parlamentar, na ocasião por uma convergência de votos negativos no Parlamento francês; e que um pouco mais de cinquenta anos decorridos o "Tratado que estabelece uma Constituição para a Europa" tem a seu débito uma rejeição de peso quiçá mais significativo, na medida em que se verificou em dois Estados Membros e no seio de um processo de natureza referendária.

A circunstância de se não justificar assim partir deste texto como elemento da comparação sugerida pelo enunciado da nossa intervenção não põe no entanto em causa que aquela possa ser desenvolvida. É que existe um outro conceito operativo de "Constituição europeia", uma vez que é inegável a existência de uma realidade organizatória que foi constituída, que logrou a sua efectividade e que tem mais de cinquenta anos de existência. Referimo-nos à ordenação base de um corpo institucional, que indica quais os titulares que exercem um poder público no interior de uma organização, que estabelece os seus órgãos e as respectivas competências, que enuncia os fins e objectivos que a esta são assinalados e que estabelece quais as garantias dos particulares no interior desta nova entidade jurídico-institucional. A este propósito, e referindo-se aos Tratados, falou o Tribunal de Justiça, já em 1986, no acórdão *Les Verts contra Parlamento Europeu*, em "Carta Constitucional de base de uma comunidade de direito". E, de facto, este conceito de "Constituição europeia", que apela para o estatuto de que foi dotada uma dada realidade institucional, estatuto que permite gerir a forma como o poder se exerce no interior da organização e que contém as "regras sobre regras" que presidem à sua ordenação, é um conceito que tem sido operativo e que não vemos razões para não utilizar, com este conteúdo e alcance, em termos de ciência jurídica.

Diremos assim que a noção de "Constituição europeia" que nestes termos revelou a sua operatividade até agora não deverá deixar de ser utilizada pelo facto de vir a ser abandonado o texto que adoptou essa designação. É este o ponto que me parece decisivo e em relação ao qual me distancio de algum modo de um dos sentidos possíveis da intervenção do ilustre orador que me precedeu. É claro que eu subscrevo a ideia de que os insucessos verificados neste processo não são (ou não devem ser) neutros em relação ao futuro, mas não estou persuadido de que eles marquem de tal modo esse futuro em termos de aquilo que foi adquirido até agora vir a deixar necessariamente de o ser. E sobretudo porque a "Constituição europeia" que até agora conhecemos, o *acquis communautaire* traduzido nos Tratados, permitiu a coexistência dinâmica entre estes e as Constituições nacionais dos Estados-Membros, levando a que da simbiose destes elementos resultasse um diálogo sobre que se alicerça aquilo a que se chamou também um constitucionalismo de múltiplo nível (*multilevel constitucionalism*).

A questão que pode colocar-se, repetimos, é a de saber se este processo se deve ou não ter por interrompido pelos sucessos ora verificados. E parece-nos que não está necessariamente interrompido. É certo que as premissas em que ele de alguma forma se sustentava foram alteradas, mas há que não esquecer que num contexto muito menos rico o diálogo entre as entidades estaduais nacionais e a entidade comunitária pode estabelecer-se e desenvolver-se. Em razão do que não vemos que tenha de acontecer para o futuro algo de diferente.

2. Aqui chegados importa agora referir o caso português, que me foi proposto como objecto de reflexão. E o menos que se pode dizer é que, em relação à situação portuguesa, a interacção entre os dois sistemas não deixou de se verificar, o que nos leva a concluir que o modelo delineado de diálogo e aproximação sempre logrou concretização. O certo é que, no sistema até agora vigente, sem as concretizações que se quiseram introduzir no texto agora de algum modo posto de lado, foi efectivamente possível a adaptação progressiva do sistema jurídico português ao direito comunitário, permitindo o desenvolvimento do processo de construção europeia e levando a uma identificação crescente, decidida e *raisonnée* do ordenamento português com os princípios gerais do direito comunitário.

Esta crescente identificação foi-se fazendo de forma progressiva, consolidando-se ao longo de várias revisões constitucionais. É conveniente recordar que em Portugal, das sete revisões até agora verificadas, duas tiveram por objecto exclusivo a inserção do ordenamento jurídico português no sistema comunitário; falo naturalmente, a este propósito, da terceira e da sétima revisão (a última), mas o certo é que, em todos os outros processos de revisão, a adaptação da ordem jurídica portuguesa ao sistema comunitário não deixou de ser um objecto fundamental do percurso seguido pelo nosso legislador de revisão. Os dois casos que começámos por referir e em que essa constituiu a preocupação exclusiva do legislador são apenas os mais emblemáticos, não se devendo esquecer que um tal desiderato se manifestou logo em momento ainda anterior à própria adesão de Portugal às Comunidades Europeias. Há que salientar que o texto inicial da Constituição foi redigido em 1975 e aprovado em 1976, num momento e num clima em que tal adesão não era sequer perspectivada, e em que por isso não seria alvo de particulares referências no seio da Assembleia Constituinte. É certo que o pedido de adesão viria a ser formulado muito pouco tempo depois, iniciando-se as negociações em 1978, mas seria à primeira revisão constitucional, acordada em 1982, que viria a caber como uma das missões essenciais fixar as condições jurídicas que permitiriam a aplicação em Portugal do direito comunitário.

Na verdade, esta primeira revisão começaria por eliminar uma disposição constitucional que, ao vedar o acesso de sociedades estrangeiras à propriedade de empresas jornalísticas, claramente infringia os preceitos comunitários relativos ao direito de estabelecimento. Mas sobretudo seria com este texto que se dariam os passos necessários para garantir a aplicabilidade directa na ordem jurídica interna portuguesa de algumas disposições de direito comunitário, com o acrescento do novo n.º 3 do artigo 8.º da Constituição Portuguesa, que assim abria o nosso sistema ao diálogo com o sistema comunitário, facilitando a absorção da ordenação comunitária.

Simplesmente, os termos desta recepção não poderiam deixar de ser tidos como algo frustres e insuficientes, ao considerarem tão só a aplicação na ordem interna portuguesa das normas comunitárias que se reconheciam como directamente aplicáveis, o que apenas alcançava os "regulamentos" comunitários, deixando de lado outras fontes de direito derivado como as directivas e as decisões, a quem os tratados comunitários não reconheciam aquele atributo. O que levaria ao alargamento desta recepção na segunda revisão constitucional (de 1989), que supriria o advérbio de modo "expressamente" contido na formulação que acabámos de citar, para tornar claro que com ele se visava abranger todas as fontes do direito derivado que, à luz dos tratados respectivos, se encontrassem dotadas de efeito directo, ainda que um tal atributo lhes não fosse expressamente reconhecido. E note-se que este instrumento de revisão não deixaria de adoptar uma primeira cláusula de legitimação da participação portuguesa no processo europeu, ao dispor no novo n.º 5 do artigo 7.º, dedicado às relações internacionais, que "Portugal empenha-se no esforço da identidade europeia e no fortalecimento de acção dos Estados europeus a favor da paz, do progresso económico e da justiça nas relações entre os povos".

Seria contudo na terceira revisão constitucional (de 1992), levada a cabo com o Tratado de Maastricht já assinado e em ordem a facilitar a respectiva ratificação, que se dariam os passos mais significativos para o processo de adaptação que temos vindo a considerar. Assim, alteraram-se as regras constitucionais nacionais que, como a do então artigo 109.º que previa a favor do Banco de Portugal a função clássica de emissão de moeda, poderiam vir a dificultar o avanço para a União Económica e Monetária previsto naquele Tratado. Previram-se cláusulas expressamente dirigidas a possibilitar o exercício dos certos direitos de participação política que este último texto viria a incluir na "cidadania da União", ao dispor-se no n.º 5 do artigo 15.º, que "a lei pode ainda atribuir, em condições de reciprocidade, aos cidadãos dos Estados-membros da União Europeia residentes em Portugal o direito de elegerem e serem eleitos deputados ao Parlamento Europeu". Precisou-se a posição dos órgãos de soberania nacionais nos mecanismos de decisão da União, ao permitir ao Parlamento português "acompanhar e apreciar, nos termos da lei, a participação de Portugal no processo de construção da União Europeia" (alínea f) do artigo 163.º), impondo consequentemente ao Governo a prestação da informação para o efeito relevante (alínea i) do n.º 1 do então artigo 197). Mas sobretudo legitimar-se-ia de forma mais clara a participação do Estado-Português na União Europeia instituída pelo mesmo Tratado de Maastricht, ao dispor-se num novo n.º 6 do já referido artigo 7.º que "Portugal pode, em condições de reciprocidade, com respeito pelo princípio da subsidiariedade e tendo em vista a realização da coesão económica e social, convencionar o exercício em comum dos poderes necessários à construção da União Europeia".

Legitimada a participação portuguesa no processo de construção da União Europeia, o mecanismo da adaptação constitucional, ao direito comunitário prosseguiria com a quarta revisão constitucional em 1997. Aí esvaziar-se-ia o elenco de competências do Banco de Portugal, passando a dizer-se agora no artigo 102.º, que ele "exerce as suas funções nos termos da lei e das normas internacionais a que o Estado Português se vincule"; estabeleceu-se, no novo n.º 9 do artigo 112.º, que a transposição das directivas comunitárias para a ordem jurídica interna assume a forma de lei ou de decreto-lei, conforme os casos"; previu-se a competência parlamentar para emitir pronúncia, nos termos da lei, sobre as matérias pendentes de decisão em órgãos no âmbito da União Europeia que incidam na esfera da sua competência legislativa reservada (alínea d) do novo artigo 161.º) e para regular o regime de designação dos membros dos órgãos da União Europeia, com excepção da Comissão (nova alínea p) do novo artigo 161.º); e determinou-se que as Regiões Autónomas passariam a poder pronunciar-se, "em matéria do seu interesse específico, na definição das posições do Estado Português no âmbito do processo de construção europeia" (alínea v) do n.º 1 do novo artigo 227.º) assim como "participar no processo de construção europeia mediante representação nas respectivas instituições regionais e nas delegações envolvidas em processos de decisão comunitária quando estejam em causa matérias do seu interesse específico" (alínea x) do mesmo n.º 1).

Posteriormente à adopção, em 1997, do Tratado de Amesterdão, a quinta revisão constitucional viria rever os termos da cláusula europeia do n.º 6 do artigo 7.º, que passa a incluir nos objectivos da União a realização de um espaço de liberdade, de segurança e de justiça e a qualificar a actividade da União como envolvendo um exercício em comum ou em cooperação dos poderes necessários à construção da União Europeia; e o novo n.º 5 do artigo 33.º salvaguardaria expressamente das regras constitucionais relativas à expulsão, à extradição e ao direito de asilo, a aplicação das normas da cooperação judiciária penal estabelecidas no âmbito da União Europeia.

Mas o passo mais relevante viria a ser dado com a sexta revisão constitucional, em 2004, quando, na previsão de ratificação do já referido Tratado que estabelece uma Constituição para a Europa e do sistema de relações entre o direito da União e o direito dos Estados-Membros nele consagrado, o artigo 8.º da Constituição passaria a conter um novo número (o 4.º) nos termos do qual "as disposições dos tratados que regem a União Europeia e as normas emanadas das suas instituições, no exercício das respectivas competências, são aplicáveis na ordem interna, nos termos definidos pelo direito da União, com respeito pelos princípios fundamentais do Estado de direito democrático". Para além disso, a cláusula europeia do artigo 7.º, n.º 6, passa a referir expressamente que a participação portuguesa, que se faz não só no processo de construção como também no de aprofundamento da União Europeia, implica o respeito pelos princípios fundamentais do Estado de direito democrático, persegue, além dos objectivos até então referidos, também o da definição e execução de uma politica externa, de segurança e de defesa comuns e compreende também a possibilidade de atribuir às instituições da União o exercício dos poderes necessários ao seu desenvolvimento. E, ainda no mesmo acto de revisão, admitir-se-ia que a transposição de directivas comunitárias passasse a fazer-se por decreto legislativo regional (novo n.º 8 do artigo 112.º e alínea x) do n.º 1 do artigo 227.º).

Finalmente, a sétima revisão constitucional, em 2005, voltaria a ter como tema exclusivo o processo de criação e desenvolvimento da União Europeia, limitando-se o único preceito por ela acrescentado ao texto anterior a prever que a possibilidade de convocação e de efectivação de referendo sobre a aprovação de tratado que vise a construção e aprofundamento da União Europeia se não encontra excluída pelo sistema constitucional, e em particular pelo n.º 3 do artigo 115.º (artigo 295.º).

3. Das considerações precedentes pode concluir-se que, no que em particular respeita à relacionação entre a Constituição Portuguesa e a ordenação jurídica essencial da União Europeia, as dificuldades que um tal processo aparentemente poderia suscitar não podem ser sobrevalorizadas. E isto desde logo porque o legislador português insere hoje, na sua cláusula europeia do n.º 6 do artigo 7.º, um conjunto amplo de possibilidades (o exercício em comum, pelos Estados-Membros, em cooperação entre estes, ou pura e simplesmente pelas instituições da União) de levar a cabo a construção e aprofundamento da União Europeia. Esta cláusula é pois uma cláusula aberta, legitimando por isso em termos muito amplos o desenvolvimento do processo de edificação da União Europeia. E, para além disso, teve o cuidado de, em sede de relacionamento da ordem jurídica portuguesa com outros ordenamentos constituídos segundo os quadros do direito internacional, prever um preceito específico (o actual n.º 4 do artigo 8.º) pensado especialmente para aplanar os problemas que o processo de ratificação do Tratado ora posto de lado poderia vir a suscitar. Na verdade, não se esqueça que o artigo I – 6.º deste texto previa, a propósito do direito da União, que "A Constituição e o direito adoptado pelas instituições da União, no exercício das competências que lhe são atribuídas, primam sobre o direito dos Estados-Membros", assim reafirmando de forma inequívoca a supremacia do direito da União, em toda a sua amplitude, sobre o direito dos Estados-Membros, qualquer que seja o sector deste (constitucional ou ordinário) que para o efeito se considere. Ora os termos da resposta do ordenamento português à questão assim colocada ("As disposições dos tratados que regem a União Europeia e as normas emanadas das suas instituições, no exercício das respectivas competências, são aplicáveis na ordem interna, nos termos definidos pelo direito da União, com respeito pelos princípios fundamentais do Estado de direito democrático") são de modo a levantar qualquer ambiguidade que pudesse existir até ao presente. O Estado Português deu aqui, na sua Constituição, o último passo que poderia dar, ao assumir que a recepção na ordem interna do direito da União deixava de decorrer por força exclusiva dos preceitos da ordem constitucional portuguesa, passando antes a resultar dos termos definidos pelo próprio direito da União. Trata-se assim de uma cláusula aberta, implicando uma ampla e dinâmica remissão também para os termos em que o tema possa vir a ser futuramente considerado pelo direito da União no seu todo, com a única ressalva do respeito pelos princípios fundamentais do Estado de direito democrático, respeito que cremos não poder deixar de ser assegurado pelas competentes instâncias do sistema constitucional português. Mas há assim nesta evolução, levada a cabo pelo sistema português, uma total abertura face à evolução futura da construção da União, evolução que se afigura independente da existência de um sistema central que a determinasse, mas que se explica pela aceitação e assumpção da cultura constitucional precedente, vindo assim a permitir expressamente que a convivência dos dois ordenamentos jurídicos se venha a fazer nos termos em que um deles (o da União Europeia) a venha a definir.

E, por último, o legislador de revisão português veio ainda tornar claro, especificamente em relação aos tratados europeus, algo que aparentemente não seria absolutamente certo nos termos de uma interpretação constitucionalmente adequada do texto da nossa lei fundamental no seu conjunto. E assim sublinhou a ideia de que o regime da Constituição Portuguesa, em particular as regras relativas aos referendos, não prejudicava a possibilidade de convocação e efectivação de referendos sobre a aprovação de tratados que visassem a construção e aprofundamento da União Europeia.

Afigura-se assim que a preocupação do legislador de revisão, no contexto que presidiu ao debate, que o último Conselho Europeu viria a encerrar, e em que se encontrava em causa a possibilidade de recorrer ou não ao processo referendário para ratificar o tratado ora abandonado, foi a de tornar claro que esse procedimento de ratificação devia considerar-se em aberto.

O que nos permite concluir que, sendo a construção europeia uma realidade movente, que se foi desenvolvendo e alargando ao longo de um processo complexo cujo curso não seria interrompido, ela pôde coexistir perfeitamente com uma evolução adequada do direito dos Estados-Membros. A mútua adaptação assim exigida pode dar-se, como cremos que se demonstra pelo sucinto relato da experiência portuguesa a que acabamos de proceder, sem outra obrigação específica que não a que decorre das exigências do dever de cooperação leal inscrito nos tratados e que, de alguma forma, não é mais do que a concretização de uma obrigação geral de Direito Internacional que igualmente se verifica nas relações internacionais comuns entre os Estados.

Pode pois dizer-se que o direito português pôde adaptar-se ao direito das Comunidades Europeias, primeiro, e da União Europeia, em seguida, e a Constituição Portuguesa pôde evoluir, no seu texto como na aplicação que dela foi feita, num sentido que se revelou congruente com o desenvolvimento do direito comunitário e da União. Este processo fez-se no seio de uma Constituição cuja garantia esteve no diálogo entre o Tribunal de Justiça e os Tribunais Constitucionais nacionais e que creio poder dizer que deverá continuar a ser garantido por esse mesmo diálogo. Diálogo e relacionamento que, independentemente das concretizações logradas no texto do Tratado que ora como tal veio a ser afastado, foi possível estabelecer até ao presente entre os vectores essenciais da evolução constitucional da União Europeia, do lado das Instituições da União como do dos Estados-Membros, e que creio continuarão a poder garantir no futuro o seu desenvolvimento.

AS PRESIDÊNCIAS PORTUGUESAS DE 1992 E 2000

FERNANDO NEVES[*]

Muito obrigado. Queria agradecer o convite que me foi formulado para aqui vir hoje a esta Conferência.

O meu tema, as anteriores presidências portuguesas da União Europeia, é menos aliciante que o tema antecedente. Mas tem uma vantagem: talvez corra menos riscos de fazer algumas afirmações politicamente menos correctas! Apesar de tudo, talvez concordando com muito do que foi dito, muito embora não creia que vá dizer nada que não esteja em consonância com o que diz o Governo, o que vou dizer digo-o em nome pessoal e não da política oficial do Governo português.

Antes de abordar a questão que me foi pedido que aqui tratasse, não quero deixar de dizer que o Professor Weiler tocou num ponto que me parece da maior importância e sobre o qual, aliás, já tive oportunidade de escrever alguns artigos. O ponto da democraticidade do processo de decisão europeu, o problema de que não existe um sistema de representação e de *accountability* no processo europeu tão claro como o que existe ao nível nacional. É, aliás, um tema que julgo que verdadeiramente nunca foi abordado com profundidade em nenhuma Conferência Intergovernamental (CIG) ou na própria Convenção. Mas tal obriga a salientar o papel central que cabe ao Conselho de Ministros no processo de decisão. Porque o Conselho de Ministros, por nele estarem presentes os Estados-membros, cuja legitimidade democrática nas duas vertentes – representatividade e *accountability* – é inegável, acaba por ser o órgão da União que tem uma verdadeira legitimidade democrática.

---

[*] Secretário-Geral do Ministério dos Negócios Estrangeiros.

Fazendo agora o balanço das presidências portuguesas da União Europeia não se pode deixar de abordar o contexto e as condicionantes objectivas dessas presidências. Há que recordar que Portugal presidiu a uma das Instituições da União Europeia, e não a toda a União Europeia. E que, embora o Presidente da Comissão seja um português, as restantes Instituições da União não estão subordinadas à presidência portuguesa.

Por outro lado, julgo que vale também a pena recordar que uma presidência do Conselho da União Europeia constitui, sobretudo, um conjunto de obrigações decorrentes do Tratado que se impõem ao Estado-membro que a assume. Convocar e presidir às reuniões do Conselho de Ministros, do COREPER e dos diversos grupos do Conselho; estabelecer a agenda do Conselho Europeu, gerir a actividade do Conselho em todas as suas formações; organizar o calendário e a acção no semestre correspondente; conduzir as reuniões do Conselho de Ministros e dos grupos do Conselho. No respeito pelo enquadramento jurídico estabelecido cabe, ainda, à Presidência, assegurar as relações entre o Conselho e as restantes Instituições da União e assumir a representação política da União no exterior, designadamente em países terceiros.

O Estado-membro que detém a presidência deve exercê-la com imparcialidade, com espírito comunitário e não procurar usá-la como uma ocasião para protagonismos de cariz nacional que não se insiram no processo comunitário. Fazê-lo diminuiria a credibilidade desse Estado perante os seus parceiros, o que seria contraproducente e afectaria a sua capacidade negocial a longo prazo.

Foi esse enquadramento que caracterizou o desempenho por Portugal das duas presidências da União Europeia que até hoje exerceu. Em 1992 fui encarregado da organização da presidência em Portugal. Havia, por parte do Governo, uma consciência muito clara de que Portugal, como um país pequeno e que tinha entrado há relativamente pouco tempo na União Europeia, tinha de assegurar uma presidência com uma organização impecável para, assim, granjear e consolidar credibilidade no quadro da União Europeia.

Julgo que foi um objectivo inteiramente conseguido e, tendo estado presente no processo de integração europeia em várias qualidades antes e depois dessa presidência, julgo poder afirmar que a boa forma como foi conduzida a presidência em geral, e naturalmente não apenas a organização do que teve lugar em Portugal, contribuiu muito para reforçar a nossa capacidade negocial no quadro da União Europeia.

As Presidências Portuguesas de 1992 e 2000

Recordo, por outro lado, que a agenda da União Europeia, como aliás é óbvio quando pensamos qual vai ser o principal tema da nossa presidência – o Tratado –, não é determinada pelo Estado que a exerce. Tem de ser estabelecida pela vontade de todos os Estados-membros e o Estado que exerce a presidência tem que dar continuidade a essa agenda, preservando o ambiente consensual e respeitando um ritmo adequado ao desenvolvimento da União.

Foi o que Portugal fez em 1992 e em 2000. Geriu com rigor e eficácia os mandatos que lhe foram confiados, indo nalguns casos para além do que seria expectável e avançando no tratamento de questões que estavam na ordem do dia da União de forma a estabelecer mandatos claros para as presidências que nos sucederam. Espero que o mandato que vamos agora herdar seja tão claro como foram esses! A este propósito devo recordar, ao contrário do que aqui foi dito várias vezes, sobre "o Tratado que foi assinado", que o Tratado ainda não foi assinado, não foi sequer negociado, apenas temos o mandato para o negociar.

Matérias como o alargamento, a reforma das Instituições, o lançamento e reforço da Política Europeia Comum de Segurança e Defesa e a revisão da política económico-social geral da União foram prioridades das nossas presidências. Mas Portugal foi além disso, interpretando o que lhe pareceu corresponder a um sentimento generalizado no seio da União, tomou em mão, no plano da política económica e social em 2000, o futuro da integração europeia com iniciativas inovadoras que, pelo acolhimento que mereceram, se revelaram acertadas e oportunas: a Estratégia de Lisboa, que hoje marca a agenda da União Europeia.

Queria, por outro lado, sublinhar a expressão que tiveram nas nossas duas presidências anteriores, e que vão ter nesta, as relações externas da União Europeia. Para resumir já o que nesse campo de mais relevante fizemos nas nossas duas presidências:

Foi durante a presidência portuguesa da União Europeia, em 1992, que teve lugar a primeira reunião Ministerial União Europeia – Mercosul, em Guimarães;

Foi também durante essa presidência que foi assinado o Tratado do Espaço Económico Europeu, no qual Portugal, como anterior país da EFTA, esteve particularmente empenhado;

Em 2000, por iniciativa de Portugal, teve lugar a primeira, e até hoje julgo que única, reunião Ministerial União Europeia-Rússia-Estados Unidos, que permitiu um debate de questões de interesse comum às três entidades num ambiente extremamente positivo e sem tensões bilaterais;

Foi também sob a presidência portuguesa de 2000, e por iniciativa portuguesa, que teve lugar a primeira Cimeira União Europeia-Índia e a primeira Cimeira União Europeia-África. E é também por nossa iniciativa que, na próxima semana, terá lugar, aqui em Lisboa, a primeira Cimeira União Europeia-Brasil, que vem conferir ao Brasil, como único dos BRIC (Brasil, Rússia, Índia, China) que ainda não tinha uma parceria estratégica com a União Europeia, a projecção que ele merece na Europa, o que também se reflectirá na sua posição a nível regional e mundial. Vai ainda ter lugar em Dezembro, como sabem, a segunda Cimeira União Europeia-África. Se eu chamo a atenção para esta questão é porque creio que há uma marca diversificante do relacionamento externo da União Europeia muito acentuada após a adesão de Portugal e Espanha em 1986, marca que certamente tem persistido pelo nosso lado;

Registando alguns dos principais pontos da nossa presidência em 92, recordo que foi então assinado o Tratado de Maastricht, ou melhor, foi efectuada a finalização jurídica do acordo obtido no Tratado de Maastricht em 7 de Fevereiro. É verdade que depois foi necessário convocar um Conselho extraordinário porque houve um "não" no referendo a esse Tratado por parte da Dinamarca e, como aqui já foi assinalado, foi dada mais tarde oportunidade aos dinamarqueses de "votarem bem". Voltaram a votar e dessa vez saiu o "voto correcto". Foi a primeira vez que tal sucedeu, repetindo-se depois com o Tratado de Nice por parte da Irlanda. Houve um referendo negativo sobre o Tratado de Nice, que foi repetido, dando lugar a um referendo positivo;

Foi também durante a nossa presidência que: se intensificaram negociações de alargamento – desde logo, com dois dos países da EFTA, a Finlândia e a Noruega, que pediu a adesão mas não veio a aderir; se consolidou o diálogo com a Turquia, Chipre e Malta; e, como se disse já, se assinou o Tratado do Espaço Económico Europeu;

Também no plano do Mercado Interno foi uma presidência muito marcada pela aprovação e o avanço das medidas previstas no *Livro Branco*, indispensáveis para cumprir a calendarização da realização do Mercado Interno, cuja meta, como se recordarão, era justamente o fim do ano de 1992, registando-se avanços em todas as áreas, sobretudo ao nível da supressão de controlos fronteiriços e da harmonização técnica e legislativa, tendo sido adoptadas na nossa presidência 90% das medidas necessárias à realização do Mercado Único sem fronteiras internas;

Também durante a nossa presidência foi apresentado o que veio a ser conhecido pelo pacote *Delors II*, ou seja, as perspectivas financeiras, como se designou no último exercício para os anos 93-97. Iniciou-se o debate sobre essas propostas e foi criado, nesse contexto, o fundo de coesão, cuja importância e relevância não valerá a pena aqui agora salientar;

E, finalmente, concretizou-se um dos principais objectivos da presidência portuguesa, com a aprovação formal da reforma da PAC, que é, normalmente, citada como o mais emblemático resultado da presidência portuguesa de 92;

Em 2000 a presidência teve outras características e foi, talvez, a mais marcante das últimas presidências da União Europeia, pela importância que a partir daí a Agenda de Lisboa tem tido na definição da acção da União Europeia. Em 2000 a União tinha começado a mudar, embora nos mantivéssemos ainda com quinze Estados-membros, mas o número de reuniões a nível de Comités e de Conselhos já se tinha multiplicado consideravelmente em relação a 1992. Apesar de tudo, tivemos cerca de duas mil reuniões (sem contar as da ONU, quer em Nova Iorque, quer em Genebra, que somaram cerca de mil). Na próxima presidência, estamos a contar realizar entre três mil e duzentas e três mil e seiscentas reuniões, ou seja, quase que duplicou em sete anos, o número de reuniões em que vamos estar envolvidos.

Julgo que é óbvio que a marca mais saliente da presidência portuguesa de 2000 foi a aprovação da Estratégia de Lisboa, no Conselho Europeu de Março. Foi, em certa medida, uma revolução no método e no modelo de funcionamento da União Europeia, desde logo, com a adopção do método de coordenação aberta. Muito se tem falado sobre a Agenda de Lisboa, sobre a Estratégia de Lisboa... é um êxito? Não é um êxito? Eu diria que a Agenda de Lisboa é a resposta adequada aos desafios que se colocam ainda hoje à Europa; resposta antecipada até, apresentada antes desses desafios se nos começarem a impor com maior acutilância. Mas a sua aplicação enfrentou vários obstáculos, desde logo, o facto de ter havido uma inversão, ou uma alteração no sentido negativo, da evolução da economia europeia. Por outro lado, talvez fosse possível encontrar um método mais consistente para aplicação das medidas da agenda europeia e talvez esta tenha sido um pouco ambiciosa. Mas penso que desde então as diversas revisões da Agenda de Lisboa nos têm colocado num plano mais realista, ao mesmo tempo que a realidade tem vindo a impô-la aos Estados-membros. Porque a questão é que a aplicação da Agenda de Lisboa está mais nas mãos dos Estados-membros do que das Instituições Europeias.

Falei já dos eventos no plano externo da nossa presidência de 2000, gostaria também de realçar que no plano da Política Europeia Comum de Segurança e Defesa, instrumento essencial para o peso internacional da União, houve iniciativas que deixaram uma marca visível, sendo a primeira presidência a actuar neste âmbito. Deixámos um legado em duas áreas essenciais: por um lado, na área que diz respeito aos aspectos militares de gestão de crises – foi na nossa presidência que entrou em funcionamento a estrutura institucional provisória – e, por outro, no desenvolvimento da elaboração do documento sobre o "Objectivo Prioritário e objectivos em matéria de capacidades colectivas", cumprindo também alguns dos primeiros passos nele identificados como metodologia a seguir.

Este documento é uma base sólida para os trabalhos que, desde então, a União tem vindo a desenvolver e foram também, durante a nossa presidência, elaborados documentos que permitiram estabelecer arranjos sobre as modalidades de consulta entre a União Europeia e a NATO e a União Europeia e países terceiros.

Avançando também na área dos aspectos civis de gestão das crises, a presidência portuguesa criou o Comité para a Gestão Civil de Crises, que teve a sua primeira reunião nesse período.

Finalmente foi também durante a presidência portuguesa que se abriu a Conferência Intergovernamental (CIG) que veio depois dar origem ao Tratado de Nice.

Não vou agora fazer o enunciado das prioridades da presidência portuguesa. Tal foi hoje feito em Lisboa, no local adequado, ou seja, na Assembleia da República. Gostaria, contudo, de partilhar algumas ideias pessoais sobre o conteúdo do Tratado, que surge como a principal prioridade da presidência portuguesa:

Em primeiro lugar, o futuro das presidências rotativas. Não posso ainda dizer como é que esta questão será tratada no Tratado, cuja negociação se iniciará no próximo mês. Mas com a criação do Presidente Permanente do Conselho Europeu e com o reforço do papel do Alto Representante, esbate-se o papel político dos Estados-membros que assumem a presidência. Os quais, contudo, terão de continuar a desenvolver enormes esforços para o exercício da presidência, sem a correspondente projecção política internacional. A este propósito devo dizer que julgo que havia uma razão muito forte para que o Alto Representante se chamasse Ministro dos Negócios Estrangeiros, título que foi "deixado cair". A minha experiência de muitos anos de trabalho no quadro das Instituições

As Presidências Portuguesas de 1992 e 2000

Europeias e sobretudo de três anos no Secretariado Geral do Conselho na área da PESC, leva-me a concluir que é muito difícil conseguir que os Ministros dos Negócios Estrangeiros europeus estejam presentes em reuniões a nível ministerial com Estados terceiros. Se eu tivesse aqui a lista das reuniões que vamos ter no próximo semestre, era imediatamente compreensível porquê. O número de reuniões ultrapassa de longe a capacidade que os ministros têm para nelas participar, a menos que deixem de ser ministros ou que sejam ministros só para estarem presentes naquelas reuniões. Eu assisti, por exemplo, a uma reunião com o Mercosul, no Luxemburgo. Os Ministros dos Negócios Estrangeiros vieram da América Latina, viajaram até ao Luxemburgo, chegaram ao Luxemburgo às cinco da tarde, pediu-se-lhes para esperarem porque nós estávamos reunidos a discutir, julgo que a questão do nome da Antiga República Jugoslava da Macedónia, discussão que normalmente se prolongava por muito tempo. Às sete e meia da tarde os ministros latino-americanos foram finalmente chamados à sala e foi-lhes pedido que fizessem um só discurso em nome do Mercosul, muito rápido, para que se pudesse passar ao jantar de trabalho. No início do jantar estava presente o Ministro de Itália, que presidia, e os Ministros de Portugal e de Espanha. No fim do jantar só estavam dois ministros. O de Espanha teve de sair mais cedo porque tinha de apanhar o avião e o jantar começou muito tarde. Alguns Estados-membros estavam representados por Secretários de Embaixada. Isto já levou recentemente a que países terceiros, ou outras organizações, tenham cancelado reuniões ministeriais com a União Europeia, o que não é bom para a União. Leva muitas vezes a situações de grande melindre e embaraço. A União Europeia, que promove o diálogo político para se projectar no exterior, acaba por começar as reuniões numa situação de *demandeur*... de quem está a pedir desculpa, uma situação de inferioridade por não estar representada ao nível adequado, o que não é correcto para os países terceiros ou para as outras organizações. Era essa uma das razões pelas quais muita gente em Bruxelas pensou que se tivéssemos um Alto Representante com o título e funções de Ministro dos Negócios Estrangeiros da União Europeia este problema seria resolvido.

Penso, também, como foi aqui muito bem focado, quer na intervenção do Professor Simon Hix, quer do Professor Weiler, que no Conselho Europeu, nestes últimos meses, no debate em torno da questão da Constituição Europeia e agora do Tratado Reformador, se libertaram um pouco os "demónios da luta pelo poder" que dominaram a Europa em todos os séculos anteriores ao início do processo de integração europeia a seguir à II Guerra Mundial.

Assisti a muitos Conselhos Europeus, alguns muito controversos, onde houve polémicas muito acesas – por exemplo, quando em Estrasburgo a então R.F.A. pediu uma declaração em favor da unificação da Alemanha –, mas não me recordo de nenhum em que a luta pelo poder tenha estado tão ostensivamente aberta e tenha sido travada de forma tão pouco contida como nestes últimos tempos. É verdade que, como me dizia o meu colega francês às três da manhã num Conselho Europeu em Bruxelas que nunca mais acabava: "Sempre é melhor do que as trincheiras!". Mesmo assim é manifesto que estamos, desde Nice e com mais acutilância recentemente, a reabrir a questão do equilíbrio de poder no seio da União Europeia.

A chave do incomparável êxito do processo de integração europeia residiu, por um lado, no direito de iniciativa da Comissão e no papel que tal lhe confere no processo de decisão, por as suas propostas só poderem ser alteradas por unanimidade, e, por outro, no voto qualificado baseado numa ponderação não explícita, que equilibrava o princípio da igualdade entre os Estados e o peso real e relativo de cada um.

Penso que uma solução baseada nesse método, utilizado até ao Tratado de Nice, poderia ser provavelmente mais equitativo e seria para todos nós mais fácil de lidar com ele. De qualquer maneira, espero que o mandato saído deste Conselho Europeu e o êxito da Conferência Intergovernamental que a presidência portuguesa vai convocar nos permita pôr de lado o escolho político-institucional que o Tratado Constitucional tem constituído; escolho esse que, julgo que ficou provado aqui, é muito mais político do que institucional, mais mediático do que real.

Como referiu o Prof. Hix, o Tratado que permitiu dar um maior salto no sentido da integração e da supranacionalidade foi o Acto Único, até hoje o menos falado, o menos mediático, o mais fácil de conseguir e o mais relevante, porquê? Porque não partiu de cima para baixo, não foram os governantes que disseram "Vamos reforçar as Instituições, vamos chamar Constituição ao Tratado, vamos dizer que somos os fundadores da Europa", foi a necessidade de realizar o Mercado Único que levou às alterações institucionais necessárias no sentido da integração e no sentido da supranacionalidade.

Agora, nesta crise de crença no processo de integração europeu, e para contrariar alguns factores de diluição que derivam de todo este processo, seria prudente voltar aos princípios básicos da integração europeia: reforçar a iniciativa da Comissão; reforçar o método comunitário; acelerar a aplicação da Estratégia de Lisboa com métodos mais eficazes e mais comunitários; dotar a União das políticas necessárias para aproveitar a globalização e dos instrumentos necessários para fazer face aos novos desafios como o da energia e das alterações climatéricas e, sobretudo, completar o Mercado Único. Muitas vezes diz-se que a União Europeia não pode ser só o Mercado Único, que não é isso que desejamos para a União Europeia. Mas o problema é que o Mercado Único, que não está sequer concluído, é o verdadeiro cimento da União. É ele que poderá fazer convergir os interesses dos Estados-membros e permitirá dar os passos que todos nós desejamos para melhorar as condições de concorrência da União Europeia a nível mundial e preservar o estatuto económico e o modelo social de que todos temos vindo a usufruir ao longo destes últimos 60 anos, sem dúvida os melhores para todos os povos da Europa. Só assim poderemos transmitir aos nossos filhos aquilo que os nossos pais nos deram: a esperança de que poderão ter uma vida melhor que a nossa!

Muito obrigado.

L'EVOLUTION DE LA COORDINATION DES POLITIQUES ECONOMIQUES NATIONALES AUX DIFFERENTS STADES DE L'INTEGRATION EUROPEENNE

JACQUES BOURRINET[*]

Le thème de l'intervention qui m'a été confié porte sur la coordination des politiques économiques. C'est un sujet vaste et permanent, que l'on retrouve à tous les stades de l'intégration, depuis les premières lignes du Traité de Rome jusqu'aux dernières déclarations des responsables de la Commission Européenne, de l'Euro groupe ou de la Banque Centrale Européenne.

Pour tenter de préciser ce thème très vaste, je proposerais de le présenter comme étant un problème lancinant. Un problème lancinant, c'est un problème qui préoccupe, qui tourmente d'une façon continue, à toutes les étapes d'un processus et qui par cette pression constante peut même créer des obsessions auprès des sujets qui sont les plus fragiles et qui n'arriveraient plus à supporter cette pression. La coordination des politiques économiques dans l'histoire et dans l'évolution de l'intégration européenne me semble remplir assez précisément cette fonction.

La coordination des politiques économiques est, en effet, une contrainte récurrente à tous les stades de l'intégration. Mais la coordination des politiques économiques est, par ailleurs, une contrainte spécifique à l'intérieur de la zone euro, stade le plus avancé de l'intégration, a créé une monnaie unique pour 15 Etats membres sur les 27 Etats de l'Union Européenne.

---

[*] Professeur émérite de l'Université Paul Cézanne Aix-Marseille III.
Président honoraire de la CEDECE (Association française des européanistes).

I – La coordination des politiques économiques, contrainte récurrente dans le processus d'intégration

Prenons quelques points de repère dans l'intégration européenne. Le premier, c'est, évidemment, le Traité de Rome. En 1957, les rédacteurs du Traité de Rome écrivent qu'il faut organiser un rapprochement progressif des politiques économiques. C'est à la fois beaucoup et trop peu. C'est beaucoup puisque, dès le départ, le rapprochement progressif des politiques économiques est affirmé comme nécessaire, voir incontournable. Mais on ne va pas beaucoup plus loin que cette affirmation générale. On ne fixe ni le calendrier de réalisation, ni les étapes principales, ni la méthode. Le rapprochement progressif se limite à l'amorce d'un mouvement – qui est nécessaire et peut-être suffisant tant que les échanges ne sont pas entièrement libéralisés à l'intérieur du marché commun.

Pendant les dix années qui suivent le démarrage de la Communauté Économique Européenne, on ne parle pratiquement pas de ce rapprochement progressif des politiques économiques. C'est un document du 12 février 1969 de la Commission Européenne, qui a pour titre «Communication de la Commission sur la Coordination des Politiques Économiques et la Coopération Monétaire», mémorandum qui a souvent été appelé dans l'histoire européenne le Plan Barre, car il émanait des services de M. Raymond Barre, à l'époque Commissaire en charge des Affaires Économiques et Monétaires, qui va véritablement marquer le départ de la coordination des politiques économiques.

Ce document établit deux points essentiels. Il dresse un double constat et il dégage les trois premiers piliers de la coordination des politiques économiques.

Double constat, tout d'abord. La Commission affirme que la simple juxtaposition des politiques économiques nationales ne convient pas, le terme employé par la Commission est «n'est pas adéquat». Pourquoi cette simple juxtaposition des politiques économiques nationales ne convient-elle pas? Pour deux raisons: tout d'abord, parce que les divergences, les conflits entre politiques économiques nationales peuvent remettre en cause la libéralisation des échanges commerciaux, qui a été acquise depuis le 1er juillet 1968, à peine sept ou huit mois avant la publication du document. Ensuite, parce que la Commission explique très clairement que la coordination des politiques économiques est la condition sine qua non pour développer de nouveaux stades de l'intégration allant au delà du simple libre échange des marchandises. Le deuxième constat de la Commission, concerne la solution technique la plus parfaite qui serait l'unification des politiques économiques nationales au sein d'une politique économique européenne. La Commission souligne, au début de l'année 1969, que les conditions économiques, politiques et psychologiques pour la fusion des politiques économiques nationales dans une seule politique économique européenne ne sont pas, pour l'instant, remplies.

A partir de ce double constat, la Commission va amorcer la construction technique d'une coordination des politiques économiques. Elle propose, pour démarrer ce mouvement, trois piliers. Premier pilier, assurer une convergence des normes indicatives du moyen terme, c'est-à-dire des projections à plusieurs semestres ou à plusieurs années, que chaque Etat dans sa politique économique nationale est obligé de prévoir et de faire adopter par ses différentes instances économiques, politiques et sociales. Il faut, donc, selon la Commission, qu'il y ait une certaine convergence de ces normes indicatives de moyen terme. Deuxième pilier, assurer des actions de court terme, de quelques semaines ou de quelques mois, qui soient concertées et cohérentes au niveau des politiques économiques nationales. Enfin, troisième pilier annoncé par le document de la Commission, commencer à amorcer des formes de coopération en matière monétaire.

Sur la base de ces trois piliers, va s'instaurer un vaste débat pour savoir s'il convient, préalablement, d'assurer un degré effectif de coordination des politiques économiques – avant de passer à l'union monétaire, ou si l'on doit avoir une démarche inverse – qui placerait au premier stade la création de nouvelles institutions monétaires européennes, ces réalités monétaires européennes obligeant les Etats membres à un degré effectif de coordination des politiques économiques. C'est tout le débat du Plan Werner, tout le débat sur la méthode de l'union économique et monétaire, qui sera amorcé et développé tout au long des années 70.

On sait que les années 70 n'ont pas été très favorables à cette amorce de coopération économique, parce que la fin des trente glorieuses et le premier choc pétrolier ont changé radicalement la situation des économies nationales. Ces évènements imprévus ont cassé le rythme de croissance très fort que l'on connaissait depuis plus de trente ans et ont fait apparaître un chômage croissant et un chômage de masse, inconnu pendant la première décennie ou les quinze premières années de la Communauté Européenne, de telles circonstances ne sont pas favorables à la coordination. Chaque Etat membre devant les contraintes spécifiques qu'il a ressenti au niveau du choc pétrolier, au niveau des difficultés sectorielles et au niveau de la montée du chômage, a pensé pouvoir trouver plus directement dans sa propre politique économique des solutions adaptées aux nouveaux problèmes qui se posaient et remettre à plus tard la coordination, l'harmonisation ou l'unification des politiques économiques nationales. Devant l'urgence du premier choc pétrolier et d'une crise économique, qui s'est développé à partir de l'automne 1973, il y eu un mouvement de repli des économies nationales et des politiques économiques nationales sur les données propres à chaque pays, c'est-à-dire un mouvement qui allait exactement à l'inverse de la coordination ou de l'unification des politiques économiques nationales.

Les années 70 et les années 80 ont été à cet égard très significatives en démontrant les limites de la coordination des politiques économiques nationales dans un contexte conjoncturel, défavorable pour chaque Etat membre comme pour l'ensemble des Etats membres regroupés dans la Communauté Européenne.

Après deux décennies de blocage, le Traité sur l'Union Européenne (1992) présente des dispositions qui sont tout à fait nouvelles et importantes pour la coordination des politiques économiques. Il indique que les Etats membres s'engagent à une étroite coordination de leurs politiques économiques. Il ne s'agit pas d'une simple déclaration d'intention – puisque cette étroite coordination des politiques économiques n'est pas simplement annoncée, mais organisée autour de nouveaux instruments techniques – qui s'appellent les Grandes Orientations de Politique Économique. Ces Grandes Orientations de Politique Économique sont élaborées et adoptées par le Conseil et elles sont gérées par le Conseil et la Commission. Elles sont considérées comme des questions d'intérêt commun. Il ne s'agit donc pas d'agglomérer ou d'additionner des préoccupations nationales, il faut définir des orientations européennes de politique économique. Ces Grandes Orientations de Politique Économique font l'objet d'une surveillance multilatérale, la Commission et le Conseil – examinant périodiquement les orientations données à chaque politique économique nationale et la convergence qu'elles doivent réaliser avec les objectifs européens. On prévoit donc un suivi très précis pour la mise en place de ces orientations.

Le troisième pilier du Traité de Maastricht, après les grandes orientations de politique économique et la surveillance multilatérale, concerne la surveillance budgétaire. Il est précisé que les Etats doivent éviter les déficits excessifs. On affirme que les déficits budgétaires et les endettements publics doivent être limités de façon précise, à la décimale près. Ils ne doivent pas dépasser 3% du produit intérieur brut pour le déficit budgétaire – et 60% du produit intérieur brut pour l'endettement. C'est une forme de coordination contraignante, qui est assortie de sanctions. Il semblerait donc que le Traité sur l'Union européenne réalise un pas important dans la mise en place et la gestion de la coordination des politiques économiques.

Cinq années après le Traité de Maastricht, le pacte de stabilité et de croissance reprend les dispositions contraignantes de la surveillance budgétaire et de la surveillance de l'endettement public qui étaient énoncées par le Traité de Maastricht. Il les étend à tous les Etats membres de l'Union et il les prolonge dans le temps. Les critères de Maastricht ne sont pas simplement des critères d'entrée dans la zone euro, ce sont des critères qui doivent être respectés – même après l'admission dans la zone euro. Le pacte de stabilité et de croissance organise avec un luxe de détail, toutes les procédures de suivi, toutes les procédures d'instruction, toutes les procédures de sanction contre les Etats qui ne respecteraient pas la discipline budgétaire prévue par le Traité de Maastricht et le Pacte de stabilité.

Il semblerait donc que l'on soit là à un stade très avancé de la coordination des politiques économiques. La réalité est un peu différente. Elle est différente parce que les cinq premières années du XXIème siècle ont montré que l'application de sanctions prévues par le pacte de stabilité et de croissance était quasiment impossible et ce pour toute une série de raisons. La coordination coercitive prévue par le pacte de stabilité et de croissance n'a pas pu être concrétisée. Tout d'abord, parce qu'elle ne tenait pas compte des facteurs économiques conjoncturels, qui peuvent justifier en partie des dérapages en matière budgétaire ou en matière d'endettement public – selon la nature des financements qui sont opérés, notamment pour les investissements. On retombe dans le débat entre keynésiens et monétaristes sur ce point. Les sanctions coercitives n'ont pas été possibles parce que l'organe de décision pour prononcer les sanctions est le Conseil des Ministres qui est avant tout un organe politique. L'histoire récente a montré que, lorsque de grandes pays, notamment les deux principaux pays de la zone euro, l'Allemagne et la France, ne respectaient pas les règles limitant le déficit budgétaire, la décision qui aurait dû s'appliquer et qui était demandée par la Commission, a été refusée par le Conseil, lequel a trouvé des excuses, des raisons économiques affichées et des raisons politiques non affichées, pour finalement ne pas donner suite aux procédures de déficit excessif demandées par la Commission. La Commission a très mal pris la chose, a parlé de trahison de la lettre et de l'esprit du Traité et a cru devoir engager un contentieux devant la Cour de Justice des Communautés Européennes sur ce refus du Conseil d'édicter les sanctions prévues par le pacte de stabilité. L'arrêt de la Cour, rendu en urgence, le 13 juillet 2004, a largement donné raison au Conseil. Si, sur certains points de procédure, la Cour rappelle les responsabilités de la Commission et son droit d'initiative, elle a dû constater que la décision de poursuivre une procédure de déficit excessif résultait d'une majorité qualifiée au sein du Conseil et que, si cette majorité qualifiée n'était pas atteinte, la procédure ne pouvait pas être poursuivie. L'arrêt marque donc incontestablement un rappel des limites d'une coordination coercitive à l'égard des politiques budgétaires et des politiques financières nationales[1].

Faut-il s'affliger d'une telle situation? Le réalisme conduit à constater que dans toutes les formes de coordination (coordination incitative ou coordination coercitive), la coordination des politiques économiques ne peut être obtenue sans un véritable engagement politique des Etats membres. Cette situation conduit à réfléchir sur le véritable objectif de cette coordination des politiques économiques nationales. Il ne s'agit pas de mettre sous tutelle les différents Etats membres. L'objectif est d'assurer une continuité, une cohérence dans la gestion économique entre le niveau des Etats membres et le niveau communautaire. Pour arriver à cela, il n'y a peut-être pas nécessité d'utiliser des sanctions automatiques, comme certains protagonistes du pacte de stabilité le souhaitaient à l'origine. Le plus important est d'obtenir un véritable engagement politique des Etats membres – sans lequel, que la coordination soit incitative ou coercitive, la nature des évolutions ne changera pas. C'est tout au moins l'analyse que l'on peut établir au regard des efforts qui ont été développés au cours des dix dernières années.

---

[1] Cf. sur ces différents points, notre commentaire de l'arrêt C27/04 CJCE du 13 juillet 2004 – Revue des Affaires européennes, 4/2004.

Le projet de Traité Constitutionnel était d'une grande discrétion sur la coordination des politiques économiques. Son article 1.15 précisait simplement que les Etats membres coordonnaient leurs politiques économiques au sein de l'Union, sans aucune précision sur la nature de la coordination et sur les moyens pour améliorer et augmenter le degré de coordination. On peut s'étonner de la discrétion de cet article 1.15 dans la perspective générale du Traité qui visait un renforcement de l'intégration.

II – La coordination des politiques économiques, contrainte spécifique de la zone euro

Le projet de Traité Constitutionnel précisait qu'en matière de coordination des politiques économiques, des dispositions spécifiques seraient organisées pour les Etats membres dont la monnaie est l'euro. Il s'agit, pour les Etats membres de la zone euro, de rechercher une articulation entre les politiques économiques nationales et la politique monétaire unifiée gérée par la seule Banque Centrale européenne, totalement indépendante des Etats membres, des institutions européennes, des marchés, des pouvoirs financiers et de tous les opérateurs économiques, ayant pour mission principale le maintien de la stabilité des prix. Or, cette Banque Centrale européenne totalement indépendante, disposant de tous les leviers techniques de la politique monétaire (émission, gestion des paiements, surveillance de la politique de change, etc) ne trouve pas d'interlocuteur en charge de la centralisation des politiques économiques.

Il faudrait donc, pour pallier partiellement ce vide institutionnel, pouvoir compter sur des dispositions spécifiques en matière de coordination des politiques économiques. C'est la condition *sine qua non* pour pouvoir envisager une amorce de «policy mix» au niveau communautaire.

La solitude institutionnelle actuelle de la BCE renforce la fonction traditionnelle de bouc émissaire qui, selon les spécialistes, est, explicitement ou implicitement, dévolue à toute banque centrale. Dans le contexte institutionnel actuel, la BCE, seul organe de type fédéral dans l'Union économique et monétaire européenne, va être rendue responsable de toutes les difficultés économiques, sociales, politiques, sectorielles, internationales, qui peuvent venir contrarier l'évolution économique dans chacun des Etats membres ou dans l'ensemble de l'Union Européenne. Si les choses ne vont pas bien dans l'Union Européenne, si la croissance n'est pas assez forte, si le chômage persiste, la Banque Centrale Européenne sera mise en cause. Henri Bourguinat[2] parle, à cet égard, de procès en sorcellerie fait à la Banque Centrale Européenne. En réalité, la BCE peut avoir certaines responsabilités, mais ce n'est ne pas simplement la variation de quelques dixièmes de point des taux d'intérêt de base qui peut ajuster le marché du travail, restaurer la compétitivité, remplacer les réformes structurelles, dynamiser tel secteur ou tel ensemble de secteurs, dans un monde globalisé où la concurrence émane de toutes parts, d'Amérique du Nord, d'Amérique du Sud, des nouveaux adhérents de l'Union Européenne d'Europe Centrale et Orientale, des pays émergents, etc.

Pour éviter ce genre de situation et ce genre de dilemme, il faudrait, à l'intérieur de la zone euro, arriver à "organiser un "policy mix", c'est--à-dire une articulation technique entre la politique monétaire définie par la seule Banque Centrale Européenne et les autres volets des politiques economiques, qui restent du domaine des Etats membres: la politique budgétaire, la politique conjoncturelle, la politique sociale, la politique salariale, etc. Depuis bientôt dix ans que la zone euro a été créée – et depuis sept ans qu'elle fonctionne, personne n'arrive à trouver une solution dans ces structures non organisées: une Banque Centrale totalement indépendante et toute puissante en matière monétaire et des politiques économiques nationales qui ne sont pas suffisamment coordonnées. On a cru résoudre ce problème en évoquant le concept de gouvernance économique. C'est par une gouvernance économique de la zone euro que l'on pourrait contrebalancer le pouvoir de la Banque Centrale Européenne et que l'on arriverait à construire ensuite un "policy mix" européen. Le concept de gouvernance peut avoir un certain sens en science politique mais dans le domaine économique c'est un concept qui demeure imprécis, qui ne prend pas parti entre deux approches de base de la gouvernance économique. Par gouvernance, évoque-t-on simplement un degré supérieur dans la coordination des politiques économiques, c'est--à-dire une intensité plus grande de la coordination? Ou, envisage-t-on une fusion des politiques économiques en une seule politique européenne qui serait la politique économique de la zone euro? Il y a là, une option essentielle que l'invocation de la gouvernance ne précise pas. Par ailleurs,

---

[2] *Les intégrismes économiques*, Dalloz, 2006, p. 140.

certains Etats craignent que le concept même de gouvernance – ou l'objectif de gouvernance – de la zone euro ne soit dirigiste impliquant un degré de centralisation qui fausserait la structure et le fonctionnement de l'union économique et monétaire et, notamment, le fonctionnement du marché intérieur.

Dans la situation actuelle de la zone euro caractérisée par l'incertitude et l'absence de structures permettant d'assurer une amorce de gouvernance économique de la zone, il faut donc se limiter à souligner le caractère impératif d'un renforcement de la coordination des politiques économiques. Ce renforcement est réclamé, à chaque occasion, par M. Juncker, Président de l'Eurogroupe, qui y voit l'amorce d'un «gouvernement économique» de la zone et le préalable à toute amélioration de la cohérence entre politiques économiques et politique monétaire au sens de l'Union économique et monétaire européenne. La Commission européenne, de son côté, ne cesse de déplorer le manque d'ambition et de discipline des Etats en ce domaine. Le Commissaire en charge des questions monétaires, J. Almunia, déclarait récemment, «je me demande si les Etats membres de la zone euro ont bien intégré au niveau de leurs politiques nationales les implications d'une appartenance à une union monétaire». De fait, les Etats membres de la zone, dessaisis de toutes leurs prérogatives monétaires et d'une grande partie de leurs prérogatives budgétaires (contraintes du Pacte de stabilité et de croissance, surveillance multilatérale des finances publiques) semblent peu pressés d'abandonner les autres leviers de la politique économique.

Le projet de traité modifiant le Traité sur l'Union européenne et le traité instituant la Communauté européenne adopté en octobre 2007 à Lisbonne se limite à réaffirmer la nécessité d'un renforcement de la coordination des politiques économiques au sein de la zone euro sans proposer de nouveaux moyens à cette fin. Il prévoit dans le cadre du nouvel article 114 que le Conseil doit adopter des mesures concernant les Etats membres dont la monnaie est l'euro pour contribuer au bon fonctionnement de l'union économique et monétaire. Ces mesures consistent à:

> « *a*) renforcer la coordination et la surveillance de leur discipline budgétaire;
>
> *b*) élaborer, en ce qui les concerne, les orientations de politique économique, en veillant à ce qu'elles soient compatibles avec celles qui sont adoptées pour l'ensemble de l'Union, et en assurer la surveillance».

En dépit des succès techniques et de l'extension progressive de la zone euro, on aura sans doute encore de multiples occasions pour disserter ... sur la coordination des politiques économiques.

Ne s'agirait-il pas d'une sorte de serpent de mer toujours présent au fil des décennies de construction de l'Union économique et monétaire européenne?

THE RATIFICATION OF EUROPEAN TREATIES
– LEGAL AND CONSTITUTIONAL BASIS
OF A EUROPEAN REFERENDUM

MARTIN SEIDEL[*]

I. REFERENDA – HURDLES TO THE PROCESS OF EUROPEAN INTEGRATION?

1. Lessons from the recent national referenda

The referenda which took place within some Member States of the European Union on the occasion of the ratification of European Treaties are not seldomly regarded as hurdles or troublemakers or obstacles to the process of European Integration. The Treaty of Maastricht from 1993, by which the European Union was founded and its first pillar, the European Community, has been restructured to an Economic and Monetary Union was threatened to nearly failing during the process of its ratification within the 15 Member States because of the result of the referenda in France and in Ireland and above all because of the result of the referendum in Denmark. As far as France and Ireland were concerned, in both countries only a very short majority of the people approved the Treaty, in Denmark the people had to be asked for its consent a second time after a negative result of the first referendum. The Treaty of Nice has only been adopted in Ireland after a second refrendum which had contrary to

---

[*] University of Bonn.

the first one a positive result. The Treaty "establishing a Constitution for Europe"which had been adopted nearly unanimously by the European Convention and, in accordance with this has been approved by the governments of all Member States did not get the consent of the French and the Dutch people. Both people were involved in the rarification processes by referenda which were arranged in these two countries in accordance with their constitutional procedures governing the inclusion of European Treaties. As far as the United Kingdom of Great Britain and Ireland, Sweden, Denmark, Poland and Czech Republic are concerned, even European-minded optimists in these countries and in the European Union reckon on disapprovals by the people of each of these countries in the case that referenda on the said Constitution Treaty during the ratification processes should take place.

This beeing so, the course of the European Integration process during the last decades very strongly gives advise to academic scholars as well as to politicians to reflect on the role and function and, above all, on a possible new constitutional placing of national referenda within the ratification procedure of European Treaties. Especially such reflexions seem to be necessary in the context of the highly urgent need to negotiate among the meanwhile counting 27 Member States – as envisaged and dicussed – a minimised new European Treaty by which the said monstrous Treaty on a Constitution for Europe could and should be substituted. Without a new Treaty, as envisaged, minimised and properly dressed which as heir of worthy work of the European Convention would have to be a getting out of the constitutional dilemma and a breakthrough at any case, the failed Constitution Treaty could probably not be saved from totally being condemned and impolitely being buried.

Some people occasionally classify or even blame national referenda which take place within Member States in accordance with their constitutional law as "hurdles" or as "troublemakers" or even as "obstacles" to the process of European Integration, especially in the case that they have negative results. Often these people are of the opinion that national referenda have to be contained or even to be completely eliminated. All these peope do not do enough justice to the referenda as institutions of public life being legitimated not only under national constitutional law but also under the constitutional law philosophy of the European Union.

Using such phraseology and blaming the referenda in the described way reveals ignorance of those people or even their disregard if not even disrespect vis-à-vis a basic democratic institution. The basic understanding of democracy is that public power emanates from the people and that the people as sovereign do not exclusively have to exercise its sovereignty by a group of elected delegates constituting the representative institution, called Parliament or National Assembly. The sovereign is not blocked by delegating its powers to its representation to exercise the sovereignty "on its own". Directly acting in the sense that political issues are decided by simple acclamation or by the taking place of referenda is not a lower ranking principle of democracy, i.e. of the "governing of the people". Therefore, as far as debates and discussions on the role of referenda in the ratification processes of European Treaties are concerned, the decisive question is not whether the existing national referenda could and should be eliminated or at least restricted. Legitimated only is the asking for the feet on which referenda should be installed in the ratifiction processes and, above all, in which way they should reasonably be arranged and properly be placed. Should they be reasonably and more adequately restructured and still be placed within the constitutional framework of the Member States or instead of this within the constitutional framework of the European Union and be arranged by the Member States under the supervision of the European Union´s organs. If politicians, for escaping out of the dilemma, should argue as they have done that one could and should go to the people and repeat the referenda as many times as necessary until the "right" answers are given they would not pay respect to the sovereign. Furthermore, "to treatise" the people in such an unworthy way of handling the "affaire" – by no means spleeny but an actual idea – would simply ignore that arranging further referenda which are not completely redressed and restructured, i. e. consisting of the same questions and objects, arranged to the purpose of overruling "unwished" results of the "failing" of a former referendum are regarded as unconstitutional according either by expressively written or, at least by unwritten national constitutional law.

2. The monstrous dressing of the referenda as hurdles to their proper functioning

Instead of criticising referenda as hurdles, troublemakers or even as obstacles to the process of European Integration the eyes should be strictly put on the volume, the object, the content, and the dressing of all national referenda which took place in the past during the various processes of the ratification of European Treaties. It simply seems necessary to ask wether not the way referenda are traditionally arranged and dressed as far as their volume, content and object are concerned should be approached as the "villain", i.e. the hurdle or the troublemaker or the outstanding obstacle to European integration. The number of problematic questions which the European Treaty on the constitution for Europe raises is far from being few and even more far from simply being solved. The complexity and the legislative implications of a Treaty like the Treaty establishing a Constitution for Europe can hardly be understood and decided by the people without broadly commentating article by article. The complexity of the Constitution Treaty surmounts the compexity and implications of nearly every normal legislative undertaking. The Treaty contains nearly 200 pages written text and consists of more than 400 hundred articles, it is, as its text is concerned, hardly readable and probably non understandable although it is, for the people more important than any other proposal for legislation. The Treaty, using the description of its content as a Constitution for Europe, ascription which normally refers to the fundamental law of a state, does not clarify that the European Union will not be established as a "European Superstate". A Treaty like the European Constitution Treaty simply is not suited for asking millions of men and women, living within 27 countries, speaking different languages and being embedded within different political cultures for their opinion. Under the given circumstances a clear and cut workable decision on whether this Treaty should be adopted as fundamental law of the European Union cannot be considered and taken by the people, at least not under the conditions as they exist that there are not enough facilities for an effective, i.e. an integrated political dispute shaped by an integrated European public opinion, especially no facilities enough for the offsetting of opinions across the boarders within the European Union which would have to be administered by an integrated media and news paper systems as well as other institutions capable for shaping public opinion. Even experts who are trained in constitutional law and in European law are likely not generally capable to the complete understanding and to a correctly assessing of the implications of such a voluminous and complicated set of rules and norms which the Treaty on the Constitution for Europe consists of.

Arranging referenda within the Member States in a way as described, has to take into account that not only Europe´s appropriate constitutional structure but its development as such, and above all the fate of Europe is at stake. Therefore, an uncountable number of questions, which are interlocked one with the other in different ways, sinply cannot reasonably and responsibly be presented to the people for giving decisive answers. National or European referenda which are dressed in this way are games the outcome of which are always uncertain, they are anything else than a reasonable contribution to the process of European integration. If for example, the question would have been presented to the French and the Dutch people for their approval of the proposed new prescription that the President of the European Commission should be elected in the future under the condition that European Parliament be more involved in than in the past such a reduced referendum would have probably had a positive result in both countries. The specific prescription has been incidentally rejected in France and in the Netherlands by the total disapproval of the Treaty. It is worth to ask how many Frenchmen and Dutchmen at all have been aware of this special provision of the Treaty. The said prescription which has been incidentally rejected does not only improve the procedure for the election of the President of the Commission but strengthens the democratic legitimation of the European Commission as such.

The primary concern to deal with is not the referendum as such but are the manner and the bulk the questions which are presented to the people to be decided by them. It is necessary that the object, i.e. the questions of the referendum, have to be not too numerous and have to be absolutely understandable to the common man. For properly fulfilling its function the referendum has to be dressed and structured in the way that the questions could serve as basis for reflections and discussions.

The Governments and not the people are primarily responsible for constitutionalising Europe. The dressing of referenda in a way that the referenda fulfil their functions is an important task of the governments in the context of properly constitutionalising Europe. Governments could be approached for any failure of managing their task. They should be approached in the future if they do not correctly assess the decision capacity of their people and, especially, should be approached if their referenda are not structured in a way that the people could porperly and responsibly exercise their role in the process of ratification of European

Treaties. The Constitution Treaty, meanwhile set aside is an example of a rarely readable and rarely understandable volume of articles, legal norms and rules, declarations and protocols. It is an example of a reasonably structured object neither for a national referundum nor for an European referendum. It should not have been presented to the people as such, at least not without primarily putting concrete and understandable single questions.

II. REPLACING THE REFERENDA AS INSTITUTION OF DEMOCRACY WITHIN THE PROCESSES OF RATIFICATION OF EUROPEAN TREATIES

Apart of the necessity to redress the referenda as described above it seems to be worthwhile to examine whether the existing national referendum as a democratic institution could be replaced or substituted within the processes of ratification of European Treaties.

1. Repealing national referenda

It is not questionable that Member States could abstain from referenda by autonomous decisions if they want to facilitate the processes of ratification of European Treaties or if they want to prevent the eventual failing of European Treaties following from disapproval by their people. But the question is whether they can be obligated to do so by a legal act of the European Union.

Member States whose constitutional law does not strictly prescribe a referendum in cases of European Treaties but gives discretional power to the President like in France or to the government or to Parliament to arrange a referendum do not have the same dfficulties to abstain from a referendum than those countries the constitutional law or a established custom of which, strictly provides for referenda. But, even in cases where referenda are not strictly prescribed public opinion and the political circumstances can constitute stringent guidelines and instructions which might set boarders to the government, to the head of the state or to the goverment for an envisaged abstaining from a referendum.

The abstention from referenda creates nearly insurmountable difficulties in those countries in which the referenda are prescribed by constitutional law. In these states abstaining from referenda requires a formal change of the constitution which presupposes a long during and complicated political and legislative process. In these Member States any changing of the constitution for the said purpose would hardly be taken into consideration if among the people the rate of consent to the process of European integration is traditionally low or, as in Germany, has considerably decreased in the recent past. Critical situations are more or less the case in nearly all Member States.

Abstainig from national referenda on the basis of an obliging legal act of the European Union seems to be no solution. As far as the existing law of the European Union or, respectivly of the European Community is concerned none of the organs of the European Union is authorised and, further more, not legitimated to adopt a legal act which obligates the Member States to abstain from referenda, if necessary by changing their constitutional law. The existing law of the European Union does not even include an authorisation and sufficient legitimation of the European Parliament, of the European Council or of the Commission to recommend the Member States the changing of their referenda legislation and practice. The national constitutional law which way it might be shaped forms part of the national identity of the Member State which according to the law of the European Union has to be strictly respected by the European Union (article 6 EU-Treaty). National referenda reflect the principle of democracy which according to the law of the Euroepan Union has also to be strictly respected by the European Union. Respecting the principle of democracy is a condition for membership within the European Union for the countries admission and their further staying within the European Union. To make it clear, all special authorisations and competences to harmonise national law and legislation which actually are provided for by the constituional system of the European Union and its legal order, the prescriptions of the Treaty on a constitution for Europe included, do not authorise to harmonise national constutional law, even not in the case that the authorisations would be broadly and extensively interpreted. The articles 94 and 95 of the EC-Treaty which entitle the European legislator to harmonise national law for the purpose of creating and the proper functionning of the Common Market and article 308 EC-Treaty (former article 235 EC-Treaty) which authorises the European Union to harmonise national legislation under special conditions cannot be applied.

If the European Union should like to obligate the Member States to abstain from referenda in the ratification process on European Treaties a new authorisation for the adoption of such an appropriate legal act of harmonisation in this field of national constitutional law would have to be created by altering the Treaty of Maastricht by a new Treaty to be concluded by the Member States. Such a Treaty the content of which would have been the creation of a special authorisation to harmonise national constitutional law for the purpose of abstaining from referenda had to be adopted by the national Parliaments and, respectively, by their second Chambers and had to be presented to the people for approval within those Member States in which referenda are provided for. Within these countries the people would probably not give their approval to a European Treaty changing the national constitution and depriving them from their right to approve or to disapprove European Treaties.

2. Arranging national referenda at the same date

Arranging national referenda within the Member States concerned at the same date does not seem to be in discussion. But it is worthwhile not to abstain from reflecting on this idea. Here too, adopting a legal act by the European Union which would oblige the Member States concerned to arrange the agenda this way that they take place on the same day would touch national constitutional law and presuppose an authorisation of the European Unions´legislator. The authorisation would have to be created before and this could only be done by altering the Treaty of Maastricht as prescribed before.

The question is whether, at least, the European Union, could adopt a recommendation asking for national referenda at the same date under the existing European law. The prevailing theory of European Law says that the European Union can only adopt recommendations in fields in which it is authorised by a specil prescription to act either by policy measures or as legislator. A recommendation of the European Union that a referendum should take place on a special date and this together with the taking pace of referenda in other Member States would evidently touch the right of the national governments based on the national constitution to freely choose the appropriate date. But Member States are obliged to refrain from actions which are running against the interests of the European Union or as the Treaty on the Constitution for Europe more precisely states they are even obliged "to facilitate the achievements of the European Union´s tasks and to refrain from any measure which could jeopardise the attainment of the objectives" of the European law.

Since the result of a national referendum, especially if it is a negative one, could influence in whatever way and in whatever direction the people in other countries where the referenda take place at later dates, arranging national referenda at the same dates clearly lies within the interests of the European Union. Elections or referenda within Member States which do not take place simultaneously in all parts of their territory are regarded as hardly being in accordance with the principle of democracy and are not usual. The European Union should be regarded as authorised by an unwritten authorisation of European law to recommend the Member State that in the European Union´s and their own interests their referenda have to take place at the same date.

But one has to be aware that the election to the European Parliament do not take place at the same date in all Member States, nonetheless the possible "cataract and domino effect" of this proceeding.

3. The European Referendum

The arrangement of a so-called European Referendum would comply with the principle of democracy and would make national referenda as superfluous. Due to the possible abandonment of national referenda the European Referendum is the most dicussed idea and proposal in the context of replacing and restructuring the national referenda in a way that the process of European integration is not harmed more than necessary.

Theoretically, two different structures of organising the European Referendum are thinkable. The referendum could be structured this way that the votes of the European citizens are counted separately in each Member State and that the result of the national voting within each Member State is decisive which means that a majority of the people in all Member States would have to approve the European Treaty (national counting system). This structure of the referendum would extend the referenda which are taken place in some Member States to all the other Member States. Whether the "national counting system" would facilitate European integration even if the referenda would take place at the same date is highly questionable. But the idea "Europe for the Citizens" would certainly be honoured and be strengthened. Secondly, the referendum could be organised this way that regardless the voting by the people in the Member States the votes of the European citizens are counted within the European Union across the national borders and the union wide counted voting alone would be decisive for the appoval of the European Treaty (unified union wide counting system).

In the first case the voting proecedure on the level of the people and the voting procedure on the Parliamentary level do not raise questions. Since the people of all Member States would have to agree the normal and usual procedure of the voting via referenda could and should be applied, namely that the majority of the votes are decisive (simple majority). On the Parliamentary level the question whether unanimity or a two third majority should be decisive does not arrive. Since the electorates of all Member States would have to give their approval the national Parliaments would also have to give their approval by unanimity. Since Parliaments respect the vote of their electorates the voting results of their people whether they are approving or disapproving the European Treaty need not to be binding to Parliaments.

The second type of a European Referendum, i.e. the referendum which is institutionalised the way that the votes of the European Citizens are counted across the national borders raises questions and creates implications which are crucial. An answer has firstly to be given to the question whether the – simple – majority of the votes of the European Citizenry or a qualified majority, i.e. a two third majority of the votes should govern the voting procedure. Than the by far most crucial question nessessitates an answer whether on the Parliamentary level unanimity should be required for the adoption of the European Treaty or whether two thirds of the national Parliaments – the second chambers included – would be sufficient for its adoption.

The voting procedure on the level of the citizens evidently creates a problem because of the different growth of the population of the Member States. Even the "qualified majority solution", but more the "simple majority solution" would not exclude the feeling of the people of the less larger and smaller Member States, that they might be "governed" by the people of the larger Member States. Since the new 12 Member States mostly are less larger and smaller Member States the vote of the people of the older Member States would be decisive in most of the cases.

Probably all Member States would have a preference for the qualified majority voting solution. This solution would be absolute necessity in the case that on the Parliamentary level not unanimity but a two third majority desion would be sufficient for the setting into force of the European Treaties. Indeed, the decisive question which this type of a European Referendum raises is whether on the Parlamentary level unanimity as the actual rule of procedure should persist or whether already a two third majority vote – a simple majority vote is absolutely out of question – should be sufficient for the approval of an European Treaty.

Traditionally, majority ruling is far from governing the process of setting European Treaties into force. According to European law European Treaties have to be approved and ratified by the Parliaments – in additon by existing second chambers – of all Member States. The requirement of unanimity might not correspond to the national procedure as povided for in the case of changing national constitutions but it would be in accordance with the constitutional law as it exists within the European Union. The requirement of unanimity on the parliamentary level would certainly not facilitate the process of integration. Parliaments which would not be backed by the votes of their population would feel be bound by the opinion of their electorates and would probably hesitate to give their approval to a European Treaty even more than they did in the past. If the people in Germany where for the time being referenda do not take place would not approve a European Treaty the Bundestag and the Bundesrat would probably pay full respect to the opinion of the people and would not overrule its disapproval. All those, politicians and scholars, who are favouring European referenda argue that a European referendum would not make any real sense if the existing ruling procedure on the Parliamentary level would not be changed and the requirement of unanimity would not be abandoned in favour of a two third majority solution. Instead of facilitating the process of European integration one should not put further burden it.

But transgressing to the two third majority solution, as charming and wishfull it may be, a clear answer has to given to the question whether those Member States which were overruled should be bound to the decision possibly and are probably suffering from the feeling that they are now "forced Members" of the European Union or whether they should have the right to withdraw from their membership of or even be forced to leave the European Union. For the time being Europen law does provide neither for the withdrawal from Membership nor for a forced expulsion in cases where Member States are overruled in normal legislative processes of the European Union. All deliberations going into the direction of an exemption for the process of constitutionalising Europe do not sufficiently take into account the basic aims and the philosophy which underlines the process of European integration. This process guaranteeing freedom, security and growing wealth, aims at the irrevocational inclusion of all European national states and the further staying of them within the European Union. The European Union ist not constitutionalised comparable to classical international organisations the statutes of which provide for free withdrawal at any time. From a material point of view unanimity is the basic ruling procedure within the European Union. The majority ruling has to step back in cases in which its so-called external costs exceed the inner costs and benefits of a decision. The expulsion of a Member State who has been overruled or the withdrawal from membership are regarded as external costs and would exceed the benefit of a legislative measure or of a European Treaty being a more or less substantial step towards European integration. The European Union would collapse if the overruling of Member States and their voluntary or forced withdrawal from membership would become normalcy. Therefore, the two third voting procedure does not seem to be the preferable solution.

a. The necessary authorisation for arranging European Referenda

A European Referendum which should be arranged by the European Union requires that the European Parliament and the Council as common legislator of the European Union are authorised to adopt a legal act which obligates the Member States to organise referenda. The necessary authorisation of the European Parliament and the Council cannot be deduced from the present legal and constitutional order of the European Union. It would have to be introduced into the legal and constitutional order of the European Union by changing the Treaty of Maastrich in its version of the Treaties of Amsterdam and Nice. The necessary amendment to the Treaty of Maastricht would have to be arranged before the start of any legislative activity of the European Commission, of the European Parliament and of the Council.

This being so, the European Referendum presupposes that the Member States have to initiate a European Treaty which simply has as its content the recreation of the needed authorisation of the European legislator to arrange European referenda and the obligation of the Member States to abstain from their traditional national referenda. Since unanimity among the Member States is a requirement for negotiating and adopting European Treaties it would be a requirement in the case of the "Authorisation Treaty", too. If the Member States should reach unanimity on a "Authorisation Treaty" which probably would not be an easy undertaking all national Parliaments – and the second chambers – would have to give their consent to the authorisation in question as well as to the elimination of national referenda. In those Member States in which the ratification of European Treaties require a referendum the creation of an authorisation of the European Parliament and the Council to arrange a European Referendum and to obligate Member States to abstain from their traditional national referenda the people have to be asked for their approval of the Treaty. People would have to consent that the traditional national referendum will disappear and that they will be deprived of an existing right without having the absolute assurance that the European Union would compensate their loss by granting equal possibilities of taking part in the process of constitutionalising Europe.

During the negotiations on the "Authorisation Treaty" probably all basic questions which have been elaborated, the necessary "dressing" of the referenda included, would have to be discussed and would have to be solved by the governments of the Member States by unanimity. Without giving detailed instructions and guidelines to the European legislator for the dressing of a European Referendum the national governments, especially those in the countries of which like in France, in the Netherlands, in the UK and in some other countries referenda in the context of European Treaties take place, would hardly be willing to give the envisaged authorisation to the European legislator.

The most crucial aspect of constitutionalising Europe the way, that a European referendum takes place, namely the different weight of the population of the larger Member States in relation to the weight of the less larger or even smaller Member States would probably be the main issue of dispute if not even cause for the failing of the conference. The less larger and the smaller Member States would probably not accept that the results of the voting within the larger Member States, under certain constellations, could be decisive or at least of relative greater importance for the adoption or the rejection of European Treaties than the voices of their people. The less larger Member States and the smaller Member States would certainly stress the solution that all national Parliaments would have to approve the European Treaty if they would not even make their consent dependent on this solution or even torpedo the whole undertaking.

b. The "nation building aspect" – A European Referendum organised according to the principle of union-wide counting of the votes of the European Citizens and the principle of counting the Member States'parlamentary voting on the basis of qualified majority

The European Referendum, if it is organised according to the pinciple of union-wide counting of the votes of the people, raises a further aspect and a constitutional problem which until now does not seem to be sufficiently seen, at least not enough discussed. The said aspect being primarily of academic interest could work as "powder pleg" when the European Referendum of the described type should become the issue of a controversial political discussion among the Member States. Despite of its complexity, this aspect can be shortly described: A European Referendum, structured by union-wide counting of the voting, simply implies that the 27 nations of the European Union are bound together in a way that they are regarded as an integrated European people or an integrated European citizenry. As such the 27 national citizenry or nations, unlike as in all other cases, are functionning like an integrated European Nation or an integrated European Citizenry, i.e. as an institution which is not provided for by the constitutional system of the European Union. The fictitiously setting up of a "European Nation" or of a "European Citizenry" or a "European Electorate" can hardly be brought in compliance with the prevailing philosophy of constitutionalising Europe and the status of actual deliberations on progressing towards the end of Europe´s unification process. The European Referendum of the type in question has a "nation building aspect" since it implies that a simple or qualified majority of the citizens of all Member States, artificially being bound together and constitutionalised as an integrated European Citizenry has to approve or disapprove a European Treaty i.e. has to make a binding decision as one of several partners of the process of constitutionalising the European Union. The fictitious European Citizenry is not only authorised to take part on the process of constitutionalising Europe but makes its decisions which decisively contribute to the constitutionalisation of Europe, regardless of the nationality of their members, on the basis of equal voting rights.

Restructuring the people of the Member States of the European Union in the way that they build up an integrated "European Nation" or a "European Citizenry" or at least, like the Swiss people, build up a "community of common will and fate" might be a theoretical vision but means subordination of the actual 27 national citizenries being the sovereigns of the European Union to a suparnationally structured European institution. Besides this, equal rights of voting cannot be deduced from the constitutional law and from the prevailing philosophy of constitutionalising Europe. The two idealistic structural elements are deduced from the constitution and structure of a federal typed central state and do not fit into the constitutional system and theory of the European Union. In times they have been in discussions these two structural elements have been regarded as an utopian vision and have always been proved as unacceptable to the Member States.

Under the constitutional system national citizens as "European citizens" do not have equal voting rights. About this, a European Citizenry based on the principle of equal voting rights and artificially created – a European Nation is out of question – would properly not function as "supreme sovereign" if not before the political and the societal system of the European Union would have been basically reversed and properly restructured.

In the case of elections for the European Parliament the deputies of which are directly elected since 1979 equal voting rights of the European Citizens are not provided for. Equal voting rights does not mean that the election takes place in all Member States according to the same procedure of voting but means that the Members of European Parliament are elected according to the principle "one man – one vote". As well known, the seats in the European Parliament are apportioned to the Member States and this in a way that although the larger Member States have more parliamentarians than the smaller Member States the latter are over represented of the size of their electorates. The consequence of this is that the basic democratic principle of equal right of voting in the sense that every man´s vote has equal value in counting is not guaranteed in the European Union – at least not as far the election to European Parliament is concerned. Equal rights of voting cannot be granted by the European constitutional legislator to the people as long as the existing system of proportioning the number of seats has not been abandoned. Even under the Treaty on the Constitution for Europe the votes of electors in the larger Member States would count for considerably less than those of electors in the smaller Member States. Depending on where Union citizens choose to reside, they could increase the weight of their vote by two, three or maybe even eleven times.

The Members of the European Parliament are according to the special disribution of their seats elected by the national people, not by a single European people in the sense that the national people are brought and bound together within the European Union. The Members of the European Parliament elected on the basis of national elections are representatives of the national people. They are not representatives of a – non existing and non thinkable – "European Nation" or of an "European Citizenry" or of a "community of men and women having a common will and destiny". The European Parliament may appear to represent a genuine authority but in terms of its structure, the European Parliament more or less reflects the confederal nature of the European Union and, respectively of the European Community as an association of states. The European Parliament as the European Union as such does not exercise rights and competences the authorisation of which derives from a single electorate as the souvereign. Its authority derives from the Member States and their various electorates in terms of both its origin and its legitimation. The legal entities bearing responsibility for the European Unions´s and the European Community's competences and authority are the Member States. The citizens of the European Union do not enjoy protection from the European Union nor do they owe it substantial obedience. The Member States are ultimately accountable to the people for all decisions and acts that emanate from the European Union.

If the European Union should derive its authority from the European citizenry, the European Union itself would have to be restructured from a confederation to a federation and as a first step before, the European Parliament staying within the centre of the constitutional system and representing the citizenry would have to be reorganised and restructured as a representation of the European Citizenry on the basis of equal voting rights.

The lack of voting equality is due to the fact that the European Parliament, in origin, has been an assembly of representatives of – equal – Member States. Like the constitution of the European Union itself the structure of the European Paliament is still – to a less extent – based on the principle in international law that each state in an association or conferation has an equal right to share in the exercise of their common sovereignty. The "Parliament" of such an association does not have to abide by the principle that each citizen should share equally in the exercise of that sovereignty. The constitutional principle that all citizens should take an equal part in the exercise of state authority is the essential foundation of a federal union, but not necessarily of a confederal union of states.

There are no signs and indications that in the future, at least in the near future, the European Union would be restructured from a confederation to a real federation, from "United Nations of Europe" to "United Europe". Member States are evidently not willing to transfer more sovereignty to the European Union than they did in the past. Amomg other reasons they have the feeling that a federalised Europe as a federally structured central state would degrade and considerably subordinate them as Member States to subordinated organisations. And there are no indications and signs to assume that the European Parliament might take up the flag for a constitutional breakthrough, as far as its part is concerned.

There are other substantial reasons that the creation of a federally typed European State within which decisions are taken by a Parliament elected by an European Citizenry on the basis of equal voting rights is not a realistic vision. The parliamentary system of a European Union restructured as described would probably not function as well as expected and in way the national parliamentary systems do. The European Union itself would likely not be governable under a parliamentary system. Its failing would partly be due to the fact that despite of the existence of a newly created "European Citizenry" a federalised European Union will continue to consist of separate nations even if they were theorethically and legally "subordinated" to the "European Citizenry" for a long time to come. A properly functioning parliamentary system requires much more than just the formal restructuration of the European Parliament into a representation of the European Citizenry as the new sovereign, especially requires much mor than the introduction of voting equality. For the well and adequately functioning of a parliamentary system at the level of the European Union some kind of centralised political filtering system to serve as an infrastructure of the parliamentary system would have to be in existence as a precondition. With regard to the size of the European Union, this political filtering system would have to be highly centralised. For the effectively operating of this system, beneath the European Parliament, an institutional framework would have to be established on the level of the society, centrally structured, to weigh up and balance all communications relevant to policy in a proper and efficient manner. This new famework would have to replace the existing national communications frameworks which are encrusted in national attitudes, and for the time being probably would have different influences on the European development. The key players in shaping public opinion, in particular the mass media, would have to be organised and, above all, would have to operate along central lines. All these preconditions would generate a centralised political culture oriented towards the European Parliament. A properly functioning parliamentary system therefore implies to some extent a rejection of the call for multiculturalism and regionalism in the European Union. The European Union would have to reconsider the demand for multiculturalism and regionalism in the context of extending the role of the European Parliament to that of a genuine representation of the citizens of the European Union.

The functional prerequisites for a European parliamentary system of government cannot be imposed by a fiat of the European Union. They can only develop of their own accord as the result of a process of social and political integration. The task of the European Union, however, would be to remove the obstacles and barriers to their emergence, in particular to the growth of an integrated filtering system in the shape of political parties and social groupings.

Under the exisiting constitutional law of the European Union, i.e. the Treaties of Rome and Maastricht in the version of the Treaties of Amsterdam and Nice, the basic polical aim of the European Union is the creation of an "ever closer Union" of its Member States and of their people, but not to unify the Member States and their people. The European constitutional law, and so does the Treaty on the Constitution for Europe, very clearly abstains from a more far reaching aim, ie. the setting up of an federalised central European State.

Unifying the citizens of the Member States to an "European Citizenry" as the European Referendum of the discussed type does and endowing this fictitious "European Citizenry" with the power to make binding decisions is not only not in compliance with the constitutional system of the European Union but even overreaches the aim of the integration process as far as its aims are consented among all Member States.

The assessment might be another one in the case of a European Referendum which is organised on the principle that the votes of the European Citizen are not counted union-wide but on the national basis. A European Referendum which is structured this way respects the structure of the constitutional and the societal situation as they are existing and could be brought in compliance with the aim of th European Union.

III. FINAL REMARKS

As far as forseeable European Referenda on European Treaties, typed in the way that the votes of the cititizens are counted within the national frameworks might be consistent with the aims of the European Union and its constitutional system but would only extent the national referenda practised in some countries to all of them, it would by no means facilitate neither the process of ratification of European Treaties nor of the European integation process as such.

As far as the federal type of a European Referendum is concerned, considerable doubts are justified whether their setting up would be accepted by the Member States, not because of their constitutional implications, but simply by political reasons. This type of a European Referendum would surely not be acceptable to all Member States if it should provide for the double vote in that way, that the approval on the national parliamentary level does not require unanimity but a two third majority might be sufficient for approval.

Those who would be involved in the process of negotiating as politicians or their advisors would be very soon aware of a "substantial disparity" which would rule the elections if the referendum would be introduced within the voting systems in the case of a European Treaty. They could convincingly argue that in the process of approving the European Treaties people participate by voting according to the principle of equal voting rights whereas in the forgoing process of shaping the European Treaty, which are much more important than the latter and which indirectly implies the participation of the people, the said principle be not applied. A qualified majority of the people can approve a European Treaty which when being shaped has been indirecty disapproved by their majority. For the time being the European Parliament is only involved in the process of shaping a European Treaty this way that it is consulted, but probably in the future as proposed and foreseen within the Treaty of a Constitution for Europe by its consent. Its members are not elected on the basis of equal rights the consequence of which means different participation of the European Citizens in this process. As far as the negotiating and adopting of the Treaty by the national governments is concerned, the status of indirect participation of the people is strongly different, too. The picture of non coherency and of a schizophrenic participation system might become the basic arguement not to accept the federal typed European Referendum and by doing so to reject a new possible breakthrough of the European integration process.

The requirement of unanimity on the parliamental level instead of the crucial requirement of a two third majority does not facilitate the process neither of the raticification of Europan Treaties nor of the European integation process as such. This type of a European Referendum would probably not be acceptable to those Member States and their people who are more in favour of the strengthening of European integration and are favouring steps towards "United Europe" whenever such steps are possible.

In the near future, not European Referenda will govern the scene but the national referenda will prevail. But the national referendum, as far as its structuring and the putting of questions is concerned has to be redressed in a way that it functions in accordance with its philosophy. Clear and cut formulated questions which are understandable at least for a big majority of the people have to be presented, they should not be interlocked in a confusing way and their number has to be limited. This new dressing of the national referendum should be regarded as a stringent obligation of the Member States´ governments. If the process of integration of Europe, as it has been the case in the past, should no even become more burdened and suffering from a deceasing rate of consent of the people within nearly all Member States and the referenda should not be restructured as proposed not only the European Treaty as the basic instrument of the gradual progression of Europe´s integration but Europe´s integration as such would be at stake, if not even be jeorpardised. The national governments, the organs of the European Union and all the other institutions like the conventions and like the media participating in the process of Europe´s building up are faced with the described task resulting from the dilemma which the national referenda have created in their traditional dressing. If they would not assume responsibility and succeed in solving the dilemma they would be responsible for and could be blamed for a further stagnation of the process of European integration if not even of its slowing down. Correctly organised, referenda are not hurdles, troublemakers or obstacles to the process of European integration but are contributing to its legitimation and acceptance among the European Citizenry.

A UNIÃO EUROPEIA
E OUTROS SISTEMAS DE INTEGRAÇÃO

Luiz Olavo Baptista[*]

Bom dia a todos. Eu agradeço à Universidade Clássica de Lisboa o honroso convite para participar deste colóquio.

Achei muito interessante este colóquio sobre processos de integração ser realizado no auditório de um museu. Museu este que exibe obras antigas, modernas e contemporâneas, e esta num belo prédio de arquitectura moderna, no meio de um parque antigo, num bairro antigo de Lisboa. É como se estivéssemos numa encruzilhada entre a cultura, diferentes épocas históricas, diversas visões político-institucionais, e preocupados com o futuro.

Ao mesmo tempo, os que aqui se manifestaram falaram sobre aspectos econômicos e sobre uma questão política interessante que é o referendo europeu, sem descuidar do aspecto jurídico.

Percebi que, sutilmente, o Professor Paulo de Pitta e Cunha, quando determinou o objeto de minha palestra, mostrava que seu interesse era que eu refletisse ou dirigisse meu olhar sobre as integrações sob o prisma da cultura.

O Direito, como sabemos, é parte da cultura. Cultura é um termo polissémico que na sua acepção mais corrente denota o produto de um grupo, ou de uma sociedade de seres inteligentes, nos domínios da tecnologia, da arte, das ciências, sistemas morais, incluindo características de

---

[*] Presidente do Órgão de Apelação da OMC.
Universidade de São Paulo.

conduta e hábitos. Então, a cultura caracteriza e distingue um grupo determinado. Se eu falar, por exemplo, de Nação, eu vou-me referir à sua cultura, mas se eu falar dos amantes do golfe ou do pólo, também estarei me referindo à cultura desses grupos. Mas, aqui nós estamos cuidando da cultura num âmbito mais amplo, daquela de determinados Estados e Nações que entenderam que podiam proceder à sua integração política.

Evidentemente, como o Direito é parte dessa cultura, ele não só resulta de um trajeto histórico, como de maneiras de encarar o mundo e de escolhas diante das alternativas que o tempo foi colocando à frente dos atores da sua elaboração.

Cabe recordar que Jacques Le Goff, escrevendo sobre as raízes mundiais da Europa, lembrava-nos que "a Europa hoje é ainda algo a ser feito ou pensado, o passado propõe, mas não dispõe, o presente é determinado tanto pelo acaso, como pelo livre arbítrio, quanto é pela herança do passado". Ao apontar as possibilidades de escolha que a Europa tinha para se construir, o historiador estava justamente apontando para nós aquilo que acontece em relação ao Direito. Mas o raciocínio que desenvolveu aplica-se também a outros continentes ou Nações.

Por isto, proponho que voltemos nosso olhar para três modelos diferentes de integração, situados em três continentes diferentes: na América do Norte, na América do Sul e na Europa. Na Europa, evidentemente, é para a União Européia que olharemos; na América do Norte, para o NAFTA; e, na América do Sul, para dois modelos aparentemente completamente diferentes, mas que têm uma raiz comum, e que são o Pacto Andino e o Mercosul.

Devemos levar em conta outra questão importante ligado à cultura que é o facto de que a economia e as instituições estão intimamente ligadas e interagem afetando uma à outra e vice versa, para que nós possamos completar a trama do painel que examinaremos.

O facto de que a economia e as instituições estão ligadas uma à outra é ressaltado por recentemente o Prêmio Nobel da Economia ter sido atribuído ao Professor Douglas North por sua obra sobre esse tema da interação entre a economia e as instituições. Pois bem, tenho a impressão de que North, quando escreveu sobre a integração da economia e das instituições, estava traduzindo em termos teóricos aquilo que aprendemos a fazer com a idade, ou seja, a integrar os nossos conhecimentos todos num corpo único para bem utilizá-los. Normalmente, nosso aprendizado se faz aprendendo por bocados, como uma mãe que ensina a criança a

A União Europeia e Outros Sistemas de Integração 239

comer dando-lhe comidinhas diferentes e separadas para que ela vá desenvolvendo o paladar e depois passa a dar-lhe as misturas. A criança vai integrando a memória dos sabores e tem como apreciar os mais complexos. Assim também no ensino; nós começamos por lecionar disciplinas que não abrangem o universo jurídico, mas apenas uma pequena parte deste, segundo o pensamento de Descartes de que as coisas complexas devem se dividir em coisas menores para torná-las mais simples e compreensíveis.

Pois bem, considerando que todos aqui já atingiram a idade adulta, (alguns até a mais provecta, como é o meu caso), minha idéia é a de examinar, integradamente, o desenho ou, se preferirem, a morfologia dos movimentos de integração e o ambiente cultural em que frutificaram. História, antropologia, etnologia, economia, e outros setores do conhecimento organizado nos darão seu apoio. Forçosamente, este exame integrado, com a prática e o hábito que se tem de separar, não virá tão harmônico e organizado, será antes uma apresentação, quiçá cubista, mas não será uma apresentação clássica.

Dito isto, vamos tentar compreender, nesta visão cubista, o que é que caracteriza cada um dos movimentos de integração a que antes me referi.

Comecemos pela União Europeia.

A União Europeia, historicamente, não nasceu, como apontam alguns, apenas de uma necessidade da Europa se abrigar do risco em que se via, quando da criação das primeiras Comunidades, de ser absorvida pelo bloco soviético; tão pouco nasceu só da necessidade de reconstrução econômica do segundo pós-guerra. Estes fatores, freqüentemente lembrados, foram importantes no seu tempo.

Mas a Europa nasceu, também, de uma tradição, de um pensamento que vem de muito longe. Há quem lembre, por exemplo, de uma famosa carta de Victor Hugo, que está na sua casa-museu, na Place des Vosges, onde ele escreve que gostaria de ver um dia formados os Estados Unidos da Europa. Outros se recordam do pensamento do escritor italiano Benedetto Croce que, escrevendo sobre a Europa do século XIX, em 1932, teve uma frase interessante: – "já em toda a parte da Europa se assiste ao germinar de uma nova consciência, uma nova nacionalidade, porque as nações não são dados naturais, mas estados de consciência e formação histórica, de tal modo que já passam setenta anos um napolitano do antigo reino piemontês ou do reino subalpino se fizera italiano não renegando o seu ser anterior, mas elevando-o e resolvendo-o naquele seu novo ser, assim como franceses, alemães, italianos e todos os outros se alçarão europeus e seus pensamentos se endereçarão à Europa e seus corações baterão por ela, como antes batiam pelas pátrias menores, não esquecidas, mas melhor amadas. Este processo de União Europeia, que é directamente oposto às condições dos nacionalismos, está contra esses e um dia poderá liberar de facto a Europa e tende a liberar ao mesmo tempo de toda a psicologia que conjuga os nacionalismos, sustenta e cria modos, hábitos e acções afins e isto acontecendo, ou quando acontecerá, a liberdade ideal será restaurada plena nas almas e tomará esse domínio." É essa uma frase ao mesmo tempo romântica e profética, porque quando foi escrita, em 1932, não se pensava na União Europeia, expressão que nela aparece. Croce descreve aquilo que se vê hoje quando as pessoas hoje mostram o seu passaporte europeu, ou colocam nos seus carros a bandeirinha estrelada da Europa no lugar daquela do seu próprio país, mas não deixam de ser aquilo que eram no seu próprio país. Os países, culturalmente vão se tornando províncias da Europa.

Mas, a frase de Croce não é tão profética como parece – e aí vem a História a explicar o porquê. Todos os países europeus que resultaram de uma integração de diferentes principados, regiões ou o que seja, sabem o que é isso. A Alemanha se integrou já faz bastante tempo, depois das guerras napoleônicas, e a França por meio de uma construção que vem desde os tempos medievais, em torno do poder crescente dos Reis. A Itália se integrou mais recentemente, graças a Cavour, Garibaldi e muitos outros. Essas Nações tiveram um processo de coalescência que, certamente ficou no inconsciente coletivo, elas continuaram esse mesmo progresso de integração para chegar à Europa.

Isto quer dizer que a União Europeia nasce não só da circunstância, isto é, do acaso, como dizia LeGoff, mas também do livre arbítrio da escolha que se fez naquele momento de tentar construir dentro da Europa uma realidade diferente que assegurasse a paz e fizesse tudo isso. Mas, isto se fez por que havia uma herança de um passado comum. Nesta herança do passado comum, nós vamos encontrar o quê? Nós vamos encontrar uma tradição jurídica comum, dos países europeus, como nós vamos encontrar a mesma tradição jurídica comum dentro dos países que formam o NAFTA ou na América do Sul.

Essa tradição jurídica comum tem que ver com vários aspectos. Em primeiro lugar, com a herança representada pelo Direito Romano. No desenho do que é a Europa cultural, não a Europa das fronteiras

A *União Europeia e Outros Sistemas de Integração* 241

geográficas, nós vamos encontrar a presença do Império Romano, que se vai repetir depois no Império Romano-Germânico, e depois no predomínio da igreja católica sobre as estruturas políticas, e mais tarde na tentativa napoleônica de formar um império único e em várias outras tentativas. Isto é, há uma força centrípeta forte dentro da Europa que faz parte da sua própria história e cultura. Ela não é percebida claramente pelas pessoas porque ela fica no inconsciente de cada um. Ela é mais forte do que a força centrifuga.

E é tão forte que atrai até Nações que, por terem vivido separadas, apegaram-se a uma cultura que aparentemente diverge no campo jurídico. A cultura anglo-saxónica da "common law", face à cultura da *civil law* parecem-nos diferentes. Mas as diferenças não são tão grandes como se imagina, porque elas refletem duas fases históricas diferentes do Direito Romano. A "common law" nasceu numa Nação que fora ocupada por Roma durante alguns séculos quando ainda predominava o Direito Romano do fim da República, do começo do Império. Era um direito pretoriano e não codificado, cuja característica era que precisava-se de ter uma "actio" para ter um "jus", como o ilustra a história da carroça que se desgoverna na ausência do carroceiro e causa danos, dando causa à responsabilidade do dono pelo facto da coisa. Além disto, a existência do *jus gentium* permitia absorver os direitos dos sucessivos invasores que se sucederam aos romanos – anglos, saxões, normandos, – e aplicar os princípios do direito romano como se fora o direito comum a todos, daí a "common law". Por sua vez, na Europa continental a presença romana persiste por muitos séculos mais, e o direito evolui a partir das primeiras codificações do Direito do Império tardio, e em parte da Europa do direito do Império Bizantino.

Então esta evolução histórica faz com que haja uma ênfase diferente na maneira de ver o direito, não só o privado, mas também o *jus publicum*, a organização do Estado e a administração da justiça. A idéia de República, de direito do cidadão, o julgamento por júri eram todos elementos típicos do direito romano da era republicana. A idéia de poder centralizado, administração burocrática e permanente, julgamento por funcionários designados pelo soberano, e outras têm que ver com o pensamento político, e, portanto, o direito do Império tardio. Isto influenciou o modo como os Estados se organizaram e as pessoas se relacionaram com os soberanos. Não cabe no tempo de que dispomos examinar mais a fundo este tema, mas podemos estar certos de que ele vai-se refletir nos modelos de integração.

Quando na União Europeia, se constrói a estrutura que representa a maneira prática de incorporar esta tendência à força centrípeta que leva à unificação, o que acontece? A estrutura jurídica que se erige tende a criar instituições supranacionais, uma forma centralizada de produção legislativa que vai penetrar as outras instituições pouco a pouco, de uma maneira ou de outra, seja pela unificação, seja pela harmonização, mas também pelo estabelecimento de uma área cultural comum. Ao mesmo tempo, isto significa que estas instituições se organizam em forma piramidal e hierárquica, umas sobre as outras, e que se privilegia também um sistema judiciário de solução de disputas que depende da própria estrutura, que está ligado à central de poder representada por aquilo que é a instituição, que pode ser o Estado ou pode ser a União Européia. Mas a tendência centralizadora do poder (ainda que seja organizado democraticamente) é obrigada a chegar a um consenso com a visão descentralizadora da tradição da "common law".

Finalmente, a idéia que estava por trás da criação das Comunidades era a de se chegar a União Européia, o que é revelado, entre outras coisas, pela construção simétrica das mesmas, que facilitou a unificação.

Do outro lado, do Atlântico, o modelo jurídico que vamos encontrar privilegia o resguardo das soberanias e das diferenças jurídicas dos Estados nos EUA, e das Províncias no Canadá. A estrutura judiciária funciona num processo descentralizado, onde há o predomínio do júri sobre o juiz togado. Isto está ligado a uma visão de democracia como exercício ativo da cidadania. Isto ecoa a lição deixada pelos romanos, que os "clerks" foram recordar para esboçar a carta dos direitos que os barões ingleses impuseram ao Rei João Sem-Terra, e persistiu na disputa do rei com Tomas Moore, e em muitos outros episódios da história inglesa. Essa visão do mundo é a que inspirou os criadores das primeiras colônias britânicas na América do Norte.

Aqueles que leram Tocqueville vêm a admiração que tinha pelo facto de que a democracia americana é pulverizada, e é exercida em todas as coisas. O papel que as associações de cidadãos interessados por algum tema desempenham nessa democracia é o papel de encaminhar, delegar e organizar a vontade popular, que é exercida pelo cidadão a cada momento, e também formalmente em cada eleição – para "xerife", promotor de justiça, prefeito, congressista estadual ou federal, presidente, etc.

O que assistimos freqüentemente em Nova Iorque, pessoas que desfilam na frente de uma loja protestando contra determinada acção do dono da loja, nós não veremos acontecendo na Europa, ou, se ocorrer, será muito raramente.

Quando nós vemos cidadãos se reunirem na frente da Casa Branca para exigir que o Governo mude a sua conduta, por dias ou meses, logo nos lembramos de alguma passeata duma tarde que pára o trânsito em Paris. O fenômeno é a certeza do cidadão de que passando meses andando em frente à Casa Branca com cartazes para dizer "Bush, saia do Afeganistão", ou "saia do Iraque", ou como disseram antes ao Johnson: "saia do Vietname", ou, como fizeram os movimentos dos descendentes africanos buscando a igualdade, é isto: uma militância constante, uma manifestação de vontade constante, que obriga o Estado a responder a cada momento à vontade do cidadão. A própria Constituição, quando estabelece que os mandatos dos deputados são mais curtos, renovando-se a cada dois anos, permite que o deputado seja constantemente plebiscitado pelo seu distrito, isto é, lá não há necessidade do referendo, porque ele se faz pela renovação dos delegados que decidem, e pelo facto de que eles decidem tudo. Por outro lado, é um tipo de estrutura que favorece e faz crescer o individualismo. É uma estrutura que não deixa de ter algumas raízes do lado mais anárquico da governança. Então, deste tipo, desta maneira de exercer a democracia, nasce uma escolha de um modelo de integração diferente.

Se nós olharmos, por exemplo, de um lado a existência do Tribunal Europeu, a existência da Corte de Justiça, o papel que os judiciários nacionais desempenham dentro de tudo isso, formando uma cadeia única que vai terminar lá na Corte Europeia que diz o que é e o que não é o Direito europeu, tal como a corte constitucional diz o que é e o que não é o Direito local de cada país, vamos ver também que no NAFTA não é isso que acontece.

São painéis arbitrais "ad hoc", ou são juízes isolados, federais, dos países participantes que decidem as questões descentralizadamente. Não há uma corte suprema do NAFTA. Podem ocorrer painéis do NAFTA que se opõem um ao outro.

Ao examinar o NAFTA, constatamos que na sua estrutura há três acordos, dos quais o acordo de livre comércio é o mais importante, o acordo sobre cooperação do meio ambiente e o acordo sobre cooperação em matéria de trabalho são seus acólitos. Estes acordos definem a estrutura do NAFTA. Não há nenhuma instituição, sequer um secretariado.

Isto é interessante, porque se nós recordarmos a atuação dos Estados Unidos, que são o motor do NAFTA e que promoveram, junto com o

Canadá (que concordam em muitas coisas com esta visão do mundo), na sua política externa, veremos que no pós-guerra, a criação do GATT e sua evolução tiveram papel de relevo, tão importante quanto as questões relativas à guerra fria. Ao ser levada à aprovação, a que seria a Carta de Havana, os norte-americanos não quiseram a criação de uma organização única para o comércio, por ela prevista e boicotaram-na, só deixando subsistir um capítulo sobre tarifas e prática aduaneiras, que veio a ser o GATT. A OMC veio nascer quarenta anos depois, porque na visão deles não era necessária uma instituição para assegurar o comércio.

E afirmavam que tanto isso é verdade que ao nascerem os Estados Unidos como Nação independente, as treze colônias iniciais que foram formadas por dissidentes religiosos vindos da Inglaterra e que atravessaram o oceano para escapar ao domínio da coroa inglesa, com o pensamento de que "a distância dá a independência que precisamos, já que não podemos assegurá-la por outra forma", se auto-organizaram e criaram seu próprio governo local, sem que a coroa interferisse, e fundaram instituições adaptadas aos seus ideais, em que o individualismo era fundamental. Ao se tornarem independentes, unidos para proteger a liberdade recém adquirida, eles resolvem colocar na Constituição uma cláusula, que é muito importante para a criação efetiva dos EUA como Estado. É a cláusula de comércio, que está no artigo 1º, sessão 8, cláusula 3, da Constituição Americana, e diz que "o congresso terá o poder de regular o comércio com as nações estrangeiras, entre os Estados e com as tribos indígenas". Vejam que coisa interessante, "entre os Estados", então não é só o comércio com as Nações estrangeiras e com as tribos indígenas (que são Nações), é entre os Estados também, o que mostra que os Estados estavam para esse e muito outros efeitos em pé de igualdade com as Nações estrangeiras. Mas, a cláusula deixava claro também que se haviam submetido a uma posição especial diferente das dos outros.

Alguns autores falaram em cláusula de comércio exterior, outros falavam de cláusula de comércio interestadual e outros de cláusula de comércio dos índios. Mas, a doutrina e a jurisprudência que se seguem à cláusula de comércio nos Estados Unidos levaram a que ela, na verdade, fosse o mecanismo que permitiu progressivamente à Suprema Corte norte-americana ir integrando, pouco a pouco, passo a passo, o país e criando uma legislação federal. A legislação federal se funda, ao fim e ao cabo, na cláusula de comércio e nenhuma outra razão.

Então, recordando a importância que esta cláusula teve na história dos EUA, compreendemos porque que nos acordos bilaterais que os

A União Europeia e Outros Sistemas de Integração 245

Estados Unidos passam, na sua política externa e também na criação do NAFTA, o que se buscou foi criar um mecanismo similar ao da cláusula de comércio. Isto porque, como é um mecanismo que funcionou historicamente, acreditam que possa funcionar em outras situações.

Existe outro aspecto da cláusula de comércio, que é a chamada cláusula de comércio negativa, que completa a anterior, pois ela tem implicações que permitem ao Congresso proibir qualquer legislação dos Estados que impeça a liberdade de comércio entre eles. Esta cláusula de comércio negativa vai dar origem depois, na história do direito norte--americano, à formação de mecanismos contra distorções ou obstáculos ao comércio, que vão aparecer no plano internacional. Finalmente, se na Europa havia uma tendência centrípeta, integradora, na América do Norte a tendência cultural era centrifuga. Mas, economicamente, o peso do comércio e da economia dos EUA tinha uma atração gravitacional forte que obrigou seus vizinhos a sentarem-se, um depois do outro, à mesa de negociação. Aí o modelo descentralizado veio a facilitar as coisas.

Então, por essas razões que não são de natureza jurídica, mas informaram a elaboração do modelo institucional, o NAFTA difere, fundamentalmente, do que adotou-se na União Européia.

Finalmente passamos aos modelos da América do Sul.

Eles se baseiam e tem sua origem num sector do pensamento da cultura da Europa, a experiência ibérica. As matrizes do pensamento latino americano estão no pensamento ibérico. Eu emprego a expressão "ibérica" propositalmente, porque como todo o descendente de portugueses, que eu sou e que a maioria dos brasileiros também é, nós sabemos que houve um período em que portugueses e espanhóis formaram uma Nação só, um período de sessenta ou setenta anos, sob os Habsburgos. Houve um único rei e nós vivemos um período importante do ponto de vista do direito. Nesse período alguns eventos de grande importância se passaram e talvez o mais relevante de todos, que não chama a atenção do geral dos historiadores, mas chama a minha, porque eu sou alguém vinculado ao direito, foram as Ordenações Filipinas.

Elas foram uma grande codificação que teve efeitos em todos os aspectos da vida e que repercutiram em toda a história da América Latina, até aos nossos dias. Foi só depois da independência dos países latino-americanos que outra corrente do pensamento europeu, principalmente o pensamento republicano vindo da revolução francesa, passou a influenciar, sem que, contudo, rompesse a tradição patrimonialista, mercantilista e autoritária dos tempos colônias. Os novos Estados foram buscar os códigos civil e comercial franceses, e, depois, o alemão, visto na época como mais moderno que o código napoleônico, para as relações privadas. Mas a democracia até nossos dias ainda não se exerce plenamente em todos os países da região. Em muitos ela é vitima de tradições burocráticas, da desigualdade econômica, e da ignorância das camadas mais pobres da população.

Mas, na construção do Direito é importante mencionar que na América Latina o elemento constitucional de facto, importante, foi o código civil. Os códigos civis latino-americanos têm disposições regulatórias do direito de propriedade, dos direitos humanos, que são importantes e que asseguraram, com todas as mudanças constitucionais e com todos os problemas políticos, a persistência de uma estrutura de um Estado de Direito que deveria ser assegurado por uma Constituição. Esta vaiou ao sabor dos golpes de Estado, das revoluções das ditaduras. Eu diria que a verdadeira Constituição dos países latino-americanos ainda são os seus códigos civis. Pois bem, o que é que esses códigos civis reflectem?

De um lado uma visão de um Estado patrimonialista, onde o chefe de Estado tem, ainda, uma função de soberano, e só muito recentemente o "pater familias" perde o seu poder. Todavia, mesmo as reformas legislativas – o Brasil reformou o código de Bevilacqua, em 1962, para assegurar igualdade de direitos às mulheres, – mas a lei permaneceu letra morta, sufocada pelo peso da tradição. Esta vem dos tempos pré-independência, da Monarquia absoluta, o que a linguagem das pessoas dirigindo-se aos juízes ou funcionários e o comportamento destes dirigindo-se ao povo leva a este tipo de coisa: – ninguém pede ao juiz algo porque seja seu direito, nem exige o seu direito, pede e espera receber mercê, como pedia e esperava receber mercê do rei.

O cidadão latino-americano comum – não falo dos intelectuais esclarecidos – ainda é, na sua alma, um súbdito, apesar da lei dizer que ele é um cidadão, pensa como súbdito e espera ser tratado por um Estado paternalista como um bom filho é tratado por um bom pai. Isto levou a que primeiro: O Estado fosse visto como algo que é preciso preservar, ninguém troca de pai freqüentemente não é? Todos querem ter um único pai, então o Estado tem que ser aquele único detentor do poder do "pater familias", daí por que, em todo o curso da história da América Latina moderna, valoriza-se extremamente a independência e a autonomia do Estado, em especial nas relações internacionais. Não é por acaso que é

A União Europeia e Outros Sistemas de Integração

na América latina que aparece a doutrina Drago ou a cláusula Calvo e outras construções da mesma natureza.

Então, o modelo do Mercosul nasceu como um modelo interestadual, isto é, os Estados pensam "contrataremos certas regras comuns para promover o comércio que vamos editar para uso interno." O Mercosul repete o mesmo mecanismo de direito internacional que foi usado no Benelux, e isto foi feito sem que os diplomatas argentinos, brasileiros, paraguaios ou uruguaios soubessem o que era o Benelux, ou se lembrassem de que existia. Eu conversei com todos os que trabalharam na criação do Mercosul e constatei que ninguém sabia o que era. Isto ocorreu, porque se buscou um mecanismo clássico do Direito Internacional, o tratado; então, como o ensino clássico do Direito Internacional é fortemente influenciado pelo que chamamos de pensamento ocidental, usaram o mecanismo que tinha prestado serviços a outros em caso similar, a partir do mesmo raciocínio – preservar a autonomia do Estado tanto quanto possível, sacrificando ou compartilhando o mínimo de soberania.

E o mecanismo de disputas adotado é aquele clássico consolidado nas convenções de paz do fim do século XIX, começo do século XX, as Convenções da Haia, que diziam que os Estados resolverão as suas disputas por negociações diplomáticas, se não forem eficazes, eles recorrerão à arbitragem.

É o que vemos na origem do Mercosul: há negociações diplomáticas, e depois, arbitragem. Esta criação recente do Protocolo de Olivos, que é a criação de um Tribunal de revisão, foi um facto político criado para tentar dar um pouco de oxigénio a um organismo que estava um pouco anoréxico, e quase desaparecendo, o mecanismo político do Mercosul.

No Pacto Andino, a proposta já foi diferente: "Por que nós não vamos copiar a experiência Européia que deu certo? As estruturas da União Europeia são copiadas pelo Pacto Andino, onde existe uma comissão, existe um tribunal, existe um parlamento.

Mas o que aconteceu com estas experiências Latino Americanas que as tornam diferentes da experiência europeia e da experiência da América do Norte?

É que a experiência europeia e a experiência da América do Norte não só nasciam de sua história e eram compreendidas aceitas pela maioria do povo, como, também, estavam ancoradas em realidades económicas, na história, em aspirações populares, ao passo que as duas criações latino-americanas foram criadas por uma elite dirigente, de cima para baixo, vendo a integração como uma necessidade; é um pouco como acontece hoje, com as novas gerações que querem usar determinadas marcas norte-americanas e para parecerem modernas resolveram enveredar por esse caminho. Mas a decisão foi política, e mudanças na economia ou na visão dos dirigentes colocaram as instituições em crise. As crises não levavam a resultados positivos, porque faltava o apoio que uma vivência realmente democrática teria proporcionado. Hoje, o Mercosul sofre uma crise política muito grande, ele só sobrevive porque convém para as empresas, que comerciam – a realidade econômica predomina –, mas corre riscos com a eventual mudança da conduta dos dirigentes dos Estados Membros que cada vez mais o ignoram de facto, embora no discurso o valorizem.

No Pacto Andino nós vimos a crise econômica esvaziá-lo, mas as estruturas políticas estão lá, o tribunal funcionando, a comissão funcionando, as normas sendo editadas, mas a prática do comércio não existe ou é tão pequena que, pouco a pouco, os Estados Membros vão partindo com o cansaço de quem acha que a festa está terminando.

Então é interessante ver nestas duas experiências que a falta da sua ligação com a realidade, a ausência de uma construção realmente democrática, amparada por práticas de cidadania ativa – isto é, por fatores culturais – as estruturas jurídicas não conseguem manter o momento evolutivo.

Nas outras duas experiências, a da NAFTA e a da União Europeia, as estruturas jurídicas estão vivas e fortes, porque são ancoradas numa cultura própria, o que é importante, mas, sobretudo, porque são suportadas pela população democraticamente.

Eu espero ter trazido alguma contribuição original e se não lhes despertei a curiosidade, tê-los distraído um pouco nestes vinte minutos.

Muito obrigado.

THE STABILITY AND GROWTH PACT AND ITS REVISION[*]

VITO TANZI[**]

I. SOME BACKGROUND

1. A basic question in fiscal policy is whether it should be guided by rules or by discretion.

2. For at least two thousand years the fiscal behavior of governments had been guided by a rule. This rule was described concisely by Cicero in the year 63 B.C.

He wrote:

"The budget should be balanced; the treasury should be refilled; public debt should be reduced".

3. Seventeen centuries later, David Hume, the famous British economist and philosopher, wrote:

"The practice...of contracting debt will almost infallibly be abused in every government. Therefore, "... consequences...must indeed be one of...two events: either the nation must destroy public credit, or public credit will destroy the nation."

4. George Washington believed that "There is no practice more dangerous [for a government] than that of borrowing money."

---

[*] Revised version of a paper presented at "European Integration for the 21st Century – Lisbon International Conference, 27-28, June 2007. Comments received from Ludge Schuknecht were much appreciated.

[**] University of George Washington.

5. The view that the budget should be balanced did not imply an *annual* balancing. That is a modern and accounting-based interpretation of the balanced-budget rule that has made it easy to criticize it. It was always recognized that particular events (wars, pandemics, catastrophes) could lead to borrowing. But

(a) borrowing should be temporary,

(b) it should be caused by extraordinary events, and

(c) it should be repaid as soon as possible.

6. The "Keynesian revolution" was a frontal attack on the traditional balanced-budget rule a rule that in recent decades came to be seen as an almost barbaric relic of the past. After the Keynesian revolution, discretion replaced the rule, and a new orthodoxy replaced the past one. It came to be believed that wise and unbiased policymakers, with good and immediate information, would be able to use fiscal tools (spending and taxes) to maintain aggregate demand at a level consistent with "full" employment and "potential" output.

7. In theory, countercyclical fiscal policy would produce deficits during economic slowdowns and surpluses during upswings. Thus, well behaved economic cycles and wise and powerful policymakers would prevent public debt from accumulating over time. Borrowing during recessions would be repaid during booms and public debt would stay close to zero. This was the nirvana promised or recommended by Keynesian economics.

8. Unfortunately, in reality things did not work out as hoped and debt started accumulating, not just in exceptional periods but also in fairly normal periods without extraordinary events that would justify borrowing. For example the countries that make up the EU 12 saw their combined public debt grow from 31 percent of GDP in 1977 to 75.4 percent of GDP in 1996-97. Clearly for these countries, discretion was not working the way it had been assumed to work.

9. Many theories, or reasons, have been advanced by economists to explain this fiscal behavior. These include: (a) electoral cycles; (b) common pool problems; (c) role of bureaucracies; (d) political bias toward current generations; (3) bias toward large governments; (f) asymmetrical behavior of policymakers over the cycle; (g) inability of financial markets to send the right signals to monitor the behavior of policymakers and so on. Whatever the reasons, it is clear that discretion often does not work as well as hoped.

10. It could be argued that responsible governments do not need rules to guide their behavior. And that rules may not be sufficient to make irresponsible governments behave responsibly. Thus, rules would not help for governments in these polar positions. However, most governments are not fully responsible or fully irresponsible. They tend to fall in between. Therefore, they may find easier to follow good policies when they have the support of a good rule especially when the rule includes the real possibility of being penalized for not abiding by it.

11. Much has been written in recent years about fiscal rules and the characteristics that good fiscal rules must have. This is a new area that has attracted a lot of attention especially in the past decade. Following Kopits and Symansky (1998) a good fiscal rule must be: (a) well defined; (b) transparent; (c) adequate; (d) simple; (e) flexible; (f) consistent; (g) enforceable; and (h) efficient.

It is difficult to identify a fiscal rule that meets all of these criteria. Such a rule probably does not exist. Often more than one rule may be needed to achieve particular objectives. This must be kept in mind when assessing the Stability and Growth Pact. In time it may have to develop in a direction that will require multiple rules.

II. THE MAASTRICHT TREATY AND THE STABILITY AND GROWTH PACT

12. When the discussions that led to the signing of the Maastricht Treaty in 1992 took place, they took place at a time when the economic conditions of the relevant countries were widely different. These differences involved inflation rates, exchange rates, interest rates, levels and structures of public spending and revenue, levels of fiscal deficits and public debt and so on. The reputations of the countries' policymakers were also different, having been shaped by their past performances.

13. Some of these differences could be ignored. Some could be assumed to disappear automatically once the European Monetary Union (EMU) came into existence. Some would be reduced gradually by market forces. But some were seen as a danger for the functioning of the EMU. Among these were the countries' fiscal situations. The sizes of the fiscal deficits and public debts were especially different.

14. There are several reasons why a monetary union needs some fiscal coordination. First, an effective monetary policy that aims at price stability cannot tolerate major fiscal disequilibria. Second, the existence of large fiscal deficits and public debts almost always leads to pressures by finance ministers on the central banks to keep the discount rates low to make the servicing of the public debt easier. These pressures, if successful, can compromise the objective of price stability. Third, by creating a union-wide financial market, a monetary union makes it easier for a member country to finance larger fiscal deficits. At the same time the monetary union creates negative externalities for the other countries that experience an increase in *their* interest rates because of the fiscal deficit in one of the union's member. Finally, if large fiscal disequilibria persist, it would be more difficult for the union's currency (the Euro) to establish itself as an international currency.

15. For the above and other reasons, the 1992 Maastricht Treaty, while it could not require the countries to immediately eliminate their fiscal deficits and high debts, it introduced various injunctions on countries aimed at promoting better fiscal behavior on their part. First, it prohibited the financing of fiscal deficits by central banks. Thus, inflationary finance was out. Second, it introduced a no-bailout clause for countries that ran into financial difficulties. Third, it required member countries to avoid "excessive" fiscal deficits or debts. These were defined as deficits above 3 percent of GDP and debts above 60 percent of GDP. Because several countries (Italy, Belgium, Greece) had debts *much* above 60 percent of GDP and others had debt somewhat above 60 percent of GDP, the 60 percent debt limit was seen as a target to be reached within a reasonable time and not immediately. Thus, the rule established by the Treaty was apparently transparent, well defined, and simple.

16. Considerable progress (some more apparent than real) was made in reducing fiscal deficits in the period when countries were still candidates to become member of the EMU. However, a classic time consistency problem developed once they became full members of the Union. Once they achieved that objective, their fiscal policy became more lax, perhaps before some of the skeletons that had been pushed into the closets started to reemerge; or, perhaps, because of genuine adjustment fatigue.

17. The formal agreement on the conduct of fiscal policy among the European Union member states was adopted in a resolution of June 1997

of the European Council. The agreement went under the name of "Stability and Growth Pact" (SGP). The SGP was amended in 2005 after a lively debate that lasted several years. We shall discuss, first, the original SGP and then describe and comment on the revisions made in 2005.

18. The SGP operates through two arms: (a) a preventive arm and (b) a corrective (or deterrent) arm. It is guided by the rule that the countries' general governments' deficits, defined according to criteria established by Eurostat, in any particular year should stay below 3 percent of their gross domestic product (GDP), and their public debts should be under 60 percent of GDP or should move towards that objective at an acceptable speed. Thus, in some way the SGP removed at least *some* discretion over fiscal policy from the countries' policymakers. However, the discretion remained vis-à-vis the speed at which the public debt would be reduced toward the 60 percent target.

19. Under the preventive arm of the SGP each member state submits annually a "stability program" which provides detailed information on the economic and fiscal policies that the country plans to implement. These programs must specify the medium-term objectives (MTOs) of the country's fiscal policy. The original intention of the Pact was that the MTOs should aim for close to balance deficits for all countries and for small surpluses for countries with larger debts or with long-term spending commitments (because of ageing or other reasons) or with the need to make major investments, or to reduce taxes.

20. A country that actually reached a balance or a small surplus in its fiscal accounts would be able to pursue, if it wished, a strong discretionary countercyclical policy during recession years without breaking the three percent ceiling. Starting from a balanced budget, it would take a large fall in GDP to bring the fiscal deficit to the three percent limit. However, several countries did not aim their fiscal policy toward a "close to balance or small surplus" or if they did it, they did it will one off or cosmetic measures. Their policymakers assumed that virtue consisted in keeping their deficit under three percent of GDP and not in balance. This deprived them of their important countercyclical tool and led to their complaint that the Pact was impeding their use of countercyclical fiscal policy when the economies slowed down. Also the debt objective was demoted to a secondary objective (and limited attention was devoted to it). In several countries it remained very high and in some others it went over the 60 percent of GDP limit.

21. An important point to make is that in the original SGP the *long-term consequences of current fiscal policy,* defined in terms of promises to citizens implied in their current laws and not in terms of current statistical outcomes, received less attention than they should have. Countries with similar *current* fiscal outcomes can have very different future implicit liabilities because of the different impact that the ageing of the population will have on spending. Therefore, *the long-term* objectives of fiscal policy should also be important, in addition to the current outcomes and the *medium-term* objectives. Current surpluses should be seen as more desirable in a world where rapid ageing is a reality. Current surpluses can reduce public debts and lead to the accumulation of assets by the government that in the future can be used to meet growing public obligations.

22. Another long-term implication ignored by the Pact is the impact that the size of public spending and revenue can have on the economy over the long run. The Pact was and still is indifferent between a country that meets the 3 percent deficit ceiling with 20 percent of GDP in revenue and 23 percent of GDP in public spending and one that meets the ceiling with 50 percent of GDP in revenue and 53 percent in public spending. These percentages are assumed to reflect the countries' political choices. However, ceteris paribus, *over the long run* the policymakers of the first country will have a much easier time with their fiscal policy than those of the second. Theoretical and empirical evidence suggests that the first country will grow more rapidly than the second over the long run. Furthermore, countries with high tax burdens may face increasing difficulties in maintaining their high tax levels in the face of increasing tax competition from low tax countries such as China, India, Mexico and others.

23. The stability programs submitted annually by the countries are assessed by the European Commission and examined by the ECOFIN Council that, if necessary, can issue a warning to the country. This is the soft or preventive side of the SGP. Here the focus is largely on the short run and, in the original version of the Pact, the "quality" of the fiscal measures that produced, or would produce, the fiscal outcome received relatively little attention. The attention was on the short run "quantitative" results. The revised Pact would increase the focus on the quality of the measures and would pay more attention to developments over the longer run.

24. When we move from the preventive to the corrective arm of the Pact, we enter the area where, at least in principle, the fiscal rule of the SGP becomes more rigid and constraining. When the reference value of 3 percent of GDP for the fiscal deficit is reached, the Excessive Deficit Procedure (EDP) comes, or should come, into play. For members of the EMU this could potentially lead to financial sanctions. In past years, six EMU countries were judged to have exceeded the fiscal deficit limit. These were Portugal (2001 and 2005), Germany and France (2002), Netherlands and France (2003), and Italy (2004).

25. Several issues have been or can be raised in connection with the Excessive Deficit Procedure. First, is the fact that the penalties would be applied by the Council of Ministers upon the recommendation of the European Commission. Although punitive proceedings were started against Portugal (2002) and Greece (2005) the penalties were never applied. Second, the decisions would be based on *preliminary* statistics that, later, might be subjected to large revisions. There have been uncomfortably large statistical revisions for some countries that have changed the initially determined positions. These revisions have been in the direction of increasing the deficits raising the question of whether they were based on innocent mistakes. These statistics are produced by national offices and may be massaged or even manipulated especially when the deficit is approaching the danger point. (See Gordo Mora and Nogueira Martins, 2007). Third, being a political and not technical body, the Council of Ministers is more likely to be tough with small countries (Portugal and Greece) and less tough with large countries (Germany, France, and Italy). Thus, the principle of equal treatment may be violated. Some observers believe that the Council lost the courage to go after big countries, such as Germany and France, in 2002 and Italy in 2004 when it should have. Fourth, that the Procedure may be too mechanistic and that "particular circumstances" may occasionally explain or even justify the breaking of the ceiling by some countries in particular moments. The unification of Germany may have been one such circumstance because it forced that country to sharply increase public spending for some years.

26. A particular problem was created for the SGP in 2001 and the following years when the rate of growth of several European countries slowed down even though technically they were not in a recession. Some policymakers and economists started to argue that, given the slowdown,

fiscal policy should be used to promote growth. Some believed that a fiscal stimulus (i.e. a larger fiscal deficit) could help bring the actual GDP closer to the presumably higher potential. Some even believed that the longer run growth rate could be raised with enough fiscal stimulus. These views led to strong attacks on the SGP that was accused of promoting too much stability and to little growth.

27. Some policymakers and economists argued that more public spending for public investment, research and development, education, and so on, was needed and that this spending should not be counted in the calculation of the deficit relevant for the SGP. Blanchard and Giavazzi (2004) made this argument especially for the treatment of net public investment. The British "golden rule "was often mentioned as a relevant application of this view forgetting that that rule applies only when public debt is below 40 percent of GDP. Others argued that some structural reforms, that required more current spending, but that could improve the fiscal accounts in the future, were being prevented by the limits imposed by the SGP. The stage was set for a revision of the SGP.

III. THE REVISED STABILITY AND GROWTH PACT

28. Before discussing the main changes to the Pact agreed in 2005, it might be worthwhile to provide a concise but more complete summary of the main criticisms made against the original Pact. Some of these criticisms played a role in the revision. This summary is largely taken from a recent paper issued by the European Central Bank. See paper by Morris, Ongena, and Schuknecht, June. 2006.

29. The most important criticisms against the SGP were the following:

(d) The SGP took little account of the *current* economic circumstances in enforcing its rules;

(e) It stressed formal quantitative compliance over substantial compliance;

(c) It ignored longer run considerations, such as fiscal sustainability, public investment needs, and the impact of public investment on growth;

(d) It ignored the need for and the short-run budgetary costs of structural reforms;

(e) It applied similar quantitative rules to countries that were in widely different circumstances with respect to public debt, growth rate, size of public sector and so on;

(f) When the corrective decisions were made, the SGP required immediate correction regardless of the prevailing cyclical circumstances;

(g) It ignored the "quality" of the fiscal corrections made to the fiscal accounts by the countries;

(h) More specifically, it gave the same weight to corrections that have durable and long-term consequences and to ad hoc or *una tantum* policy changes with little long term impact on the fiscal accounts, such as tax amnesty, sale of public assets, or various maneuvers of financial engineering. These maneuvers might even be encouraged by the need to comply with the fiscal rule.

30. The European Commission was bombarded by literally hundreds of proposals for the reform of the Pact. It attempted to react to at least some of them. In the process some of the original simplicity of the fiscal rule would inevitably be compromised.

31. Many of the specific proposals can be arranged in various categories. We identify here the most important. Some have been already mentioned.

32. Some economists and policymakers argued that particular expenditures – gross or net public investment, expenditure for R & D, some spending arising from pension reforms, some spending connected with structural reforms, etc. – should be subtracted from total public spending in order to calculate the fiscal deficit that should interest the Pact. The argument here was that this spending would raise the growth rate and make it easier to service the larger public debt.

33. Some argued that one-off measures should be excluded from the revenue side because they often do not have a permanent impact on the fiscal accounts. Some countries were making large use of these measures. See Koen and van den Noord (2006).

34. Some would apply the fiscal rule only to cyclically-adjusted revenue and expenditures so that only *structural* deficits and debts and *potential* incomes became relevant. However, structural deficits and potential incomes are virtual and not real concepts. Their calculations require highly controversial assumptions. See Tanzi (2007).

35. Some would give more weight to the share of public debt into GDP and less to the cyclically-adjusted or unadjusted fiscal deficit. See especially Pisani-Ferry (2002).

36. Some would focus on so-called sustainability measures, such as, for example, the "net worth of the public sector." See Buiter and Grafe (2002) In this context the realization that demographic changes would soon lead to large increases in public spending, under current programs, has raised the question of how much weight should be assigned to the implicit debt associated with unfunded public commitments to pensioners and to the users of public health services. This debt often overwhelms the formal debt that is the subject of the SGP.

37. Finally, there was an increased focus on the fact that institutions that help determine budgetary outcomes also deserve attention. See Persson and Tabellini (2002) and Wyplosz (2005).

38. The suggested proposals ranged from the very simple and practical to the very complex and impractical. At the same time some observers continued to believe that, in spite of its obvious shortcomings, the current rule of the SGS was a reasonable one especially if it were applied to fiscal positions that were close to equilibrium. In such a situation the three percent deficit limit would allow countries ample scope to pursue countercyclical fiscal policy especially through built-in stabilizers when needed. For these people the main problem was one of enforcement of the SGP in the face of opportunistic behavior on the part of the policymakers of some countries.

39. The prolonged discussion on the need to reform the Pact probably created uncertainty for policymakers and for economic agents and may have contributed to the fiscal relaxation and the economic slowdown that took place between 2001 and 2005.

40. The 2005 reform of the SGP made several significant changes but left in place the quantitative ceilings of three percent of GDP, for the fiscal deficit, and 60 percent of GDP, for the public debt. However, important changes were introduced in both the Preventive and the Corrective Arms of the Pact. See Almunia (2006) and Morris, Ongena, and Schuknecht (2006) for more details.

41. The main features of the reformed Pact can be reported citing a paper by Almunia (2006). They are the following:

42. "The preventive dimension of the Pact has been strengthened by a stronger and more differentiated medium-term orientation of the rules".

In the future "the medium-term budgetary objective of a country will be defined on the basis of its current debt ratio and *potential* growth... [C]ountries with a combination of low debt and high *potential* growth will be able to run a small deficit *over the medium run*, whereas a balanced budget or a surplus will be required for countries with ... high debt and low *potential* growth". Highlights added.

43. "...major structural reforms that have direct long-term cost-saving effects and verifiably improve fiscal sustainability over the long-term will be considered". This is supposed to make the Pact more consistent with the Lisbon agenda.

44. "...the new interpretation of the rules allows expanding the one-year deadline for the correction of an excessive deficit [i.e. one over three percent of GDP] by an additional year in case a correction in the year following the identification of an excessive deficit makes little economic sense."

"The SGP refers now to the "relevant-factors" that the Commission and the Council take into account for those decision [concerning excessive deficit]... These factors include, inter alia, "developments in potential growth and prevailing cyclical conditions, alongside considerations with respect to debt sustainability, the implementation of policies geared toward meeting the objectives of the Lisbon agenda or the record of fiscal consolidation in good time."

45. In addition to the above, in reforming the Pact the Council also made some suggestions with respect to (a) the role that national institutions and parliaments should play in domestic budgetary surveillance; (b) the "quality, reliability and timeliness" of government accounts statistics; and (c) improved communication between governments and the Commission and the public.

46. The revised Pact has tried to go a considerable way toward meeting some of the criticisms that had been advanced against the original version of the Pact. It has attempted to pay more attention to current and future economic developments. It has tried to differentiate more between countries. It has tried to reduce the role of one-off measures in its assessment of fiscal situations. It has increased its assessment of policy changes that might raise current spending, and thus the size of the deficit, but reduce future spending. It has aimed at increasing the closeness of the dialogue between the Commission and the representatives

of the national governments. It has also attempted to pay more attention to institutional arrangements, statistical issues, and the communication between the governments, the Commission, and the public.

47. These are important changes. Whether the new version of the Pact will prove more or less useful in promoting sound and sustainable fiscal polices, only time will be able to tell. We shall conclude with a few comments.

V. CONCLUDING REMARKS

48. We started this paper with the question of whether fiscal policy should be guided by some "rule" or by full "discretion." We mentioned that the Keynesian Revolution had created a presumption for many economists in favor of discretion. If policymakers were saints, had the wisdom of Solòmon and the accumulated knowledge contained in Google, they would deserve to have full discretion and the freedom to choose for us without any limitations to that freedom. Unfortunately, most policymakers are not saints, do not have the wisdom of Solomon and the knowledge of Google. They are essentially like the rest of us with biases, virtues, and defects. Historical evidence indicates that when they have full discretion, they are perfectly capable of making big mistakes. Unfortunately, the survivability of the EMU cannot tolerate big mistakes in fiscal policy.

49. With all its shortcomings, the original SGP provided clear rules for the conduct of fiscal policy. If followed, they would have provided a clear and useful compass to policymakers. However, the SGP never satisfied convinced Keynesians and was not welcomed by policymaker who saw their freedom of action curtailed.

50. The revised version of the Pact has attempted to meet the critics and to correct some legitimate defects by bringing more flexibility in the use of the rule. The real test will be how much of the greater flexibility will be used wisely and how much it will be abused. The danger is that the SGP might become an "SGP lite",

51. More flexibility has been introduced in the Pact in order to increase its ownership by the national authorities. Objective and real concepts such as actual deficits, actual GDPs, actual rates of growth and so on will be replaced to a large extent by "virtual" concepts, concepts

that do not exist in reality but that must be fabricated on the bases of often highly questionable assumptions. "Cyclically adjusted incomes", "potential outputs", "cyclically adjusted revenue", "cyclically adjusted debt", "acceptable structural reforms" and so on are not objective concepts or variables. Thus they may lend themselves to abuse. See Tanzi (2007).

REFERENCES

ALMUNIA, Joaqin (2006), "Fiscal Discipline and the Reform of the Stability and Growth Pact," in National Bank of Poland, *Fiscal Policy and the Road to the Euro* (Warsaw, 2006)

BALASSONE, F., D. FRANCO and S. ZOTTERI (2006), "EMU Fiscal Indicators: A Misleading Compass?" *Empirica*, 3 (2)

BLANCHARD, O. J. and F. GIAVAZZI (2004). "Improving the SGP Through a Proper Accounting of Public Investment," *CEPR Discussion Paper* No. 4220

BUITER, W. and C. GRAFE (2002), "Patching Up the Pact: Some Suggestions for Enhancing Fiscal Sustainability and Macroeconomic Stability in an Enlarged European Union," *CEPR Discussion Paper* No. 3496

BUTI, M. (2006), "Will the New Stability and Growth Pact Succeed? An Economic and Political Perspective," *European Commission Economic Papers*, No. 241

COEURE, B. and PISANI-FERRY (2005), "Fiscal Policy in EMU: Towards a Sustainability and Growth Pact," *Bruegel Working Paper* No. 2005/01

DETKEN, K., V. GASPAR and B. WINKLER (2004), "On Prosperity and Posterity: The Need for Fiscal Discipline in a Monetary Union," *ECB Working Paper* No. 420

European Commission (2006), *European Economy: Public Finances in EMU*, No. 3

GORDO MORA, Luis and Joao NOGUEIRA MARTINS (2007), "How Reliable are the Statistics for the Stability and Growth Pact?," *European Economy Economic Papers*, No. 273, February 2007

KOEN, V and P. VAN DEN NOORD (2006), "Fiscal Gimmickry in Europe: One--off Measures and Creative Accounting" in Wierts et al. (eds) (2006)

KOPITS, G. and S. SYMANSKY (1998), "Fiscal Policy Rules," *IMF Occasional Paper* 162

MORRIS, R., H., ONGENA and L. SCHUKNECHT (2006)m "The Reform and Implementation of the Stability and Growth Pact," *European Central Bank, Occasional Paper* Series, No. 47 (June)

PERSSON, T. and G. TABELLINI (2002), *The Economic Effects of Constitutions: What Do the Data Say?* Cambridge, MA (MIT Press)

TANZI, Vito (2004), "The Stability and Growth Pact: Its Role and Future," *Cato Journal*, vol. 24, No. 1-2 (Spring/Summer)

_____ (2006), "Fiscal Policy: When Theory Collides with Reality," *CEPS Working Document*, No. 256 (June)

_____ (2007), "Fiscal Policy and Fiscal Rules in the European Union," *Europe After Enlargement*, edited by Anders Aslund and Marek Dabronski (Cambridge University Press, 2007)

WIERTS, P. Deroose, E. FLORES and A. TURRINI (eds) (2006), *Fiscal Policy Surveillance in Europe*, Palgrave Macmillan.

WYPLOSZ, Charles (2005), "Fiscal Policy: Institutions versus Rules", *National Institute Economic Review*, January.

A UNIÃO EUROPEIA:
A CAMINHO DE UM ORÇAMENTO FEDERAL

J. SILVA LOPES[*]

1. Factores económico e políticos na determinação do orçamento da União europeia

Para responder à pergunta "A União Europeia: a caminho de um orçamento federal?" será necessário considerar critérios de eficiência económica, de redistribuição e de preferências políticas relativas ao binómio nacionalismo/federalismo. A força dos grupos de pressão é também um factor a ter em conta.

Os critérios de eficiência económica basear-se-ão em análises de alocação de recursos, de estabilização económica e de dinamismo no crescimento económico.

Os critérios de redistribuição dependem fundamentalmente de opções políticas, embora a análise da eficiência económica também os deva influenciar.

As preferências quanto ao doseamento de nacionalismo e de federalismo são também fundamentalmente ditadas por posições políticas. É indispensável todavia que nelas não se ignore a análise económica, até porque a maior integração orçamental na União Europeia não corresponde a jogos de soma nula.

Finalmente, a pressão dos grupos de interesse têm grande peso nas escolhas políticas, principalmente quando a análise económica mostra

---

[*] Presidente do Montepio Geral.

que algumas dessas escolhas devem ser excluídas por terem efeitos globais de sinal negativo. O peso que os gastos com a Política Agrícola Comum (PAC) têm no orçamento da UE, claramente não justificado na base de razões económicas, é bem demonstrativo do poder que os grupos de interesse podem ter na determinação do conteúdo e características desse orçamento.

O presente texto procura analisar o problema do Orçamento Europeu na base de um enfoque fundamentalmente económico. Atende por isso sobretudo a considerações sobre a eficiência na alocação de recursos, sobre o crescimento económico, sobre a estabilização conjuntural e sobre as políticas redistributivas.

Os aspectos políticos não podem todavia ser ignorados. Não vale a pena perder tempo com hipóteses economicamente desejáveis, mas que sejam obviamente irrealistas do ponto de vista político (em face nomeadamente das preferências das maiorias dos cidadãos e dos governos em matéria de soberania nacional).

As análises económicas, mesmo as que procuram ser mais objectivas, são sempre influenciadas por preferências ideológicas. Por isso, até em estudos que pretendam ser fundamentalmente técnicos, as conclusões relativas à dimensão e à composição do orçamento da União Europeia, são sempre influenciadas pelas opções dos seus autores entre liberalismo económico e intervencionismo e entre nacionalismo e federalismo. Constata-se que em geral os que se inclinam mais para o liberalismo económico são dos que mais se opõem ao federalismo e aos poderes supranacionais e que, inversamente, os que mais defendem o federalismo tendem em, com frequência, advogar níveis significativos de intervenção pública no funcionamento dos mercados.

Nestes termos a análise aqui apresentada, embora procure ser orientada por considerações objectivas de técnica económica, está fortemente influenciada pelas preferências ideológicas do seu autor. Essas preferências devem por isso ser aqui enunciadas: elas não são a favor nem do liberalismo económico avançado, nem do nacionalismo arreigado; elas inclinam-se para intervenções públicas significativas que corrijam falhas do mercado, incluindo as que têm a ver com a redistribuição, e para metas relativamente ambiciosas de integração económica e política na União Europeia.

2. Não há sinais de que o orçamento da UE esteja a caminho de se tornar federal

Desde 1995 até 2006 o orçamento da União Europeia cresceu apenas 8,2% em termos reais, enquanto os orçamentos nacionais dos Estados membros da União aumentaram cerca de 23%. O peso das despesas do orçamento europeu em relação ao Rendimento Nacional Bruto da UE foi de 1,13% em 1993 e de aproximadamente 1% em anos recentes.

O contexto político actual não permite prever que as tendências dos últimos 10 anos se alterem substancialmente nos próximos 10. Pode deste modo afirmar-se com toda a segurança que *não há sinais de que a União Europeia esteja a caminho de um orçamento federal.*

A extrema exiguidade dos traços federalistas no Orçamento UE é posta em evidência pelas comparações com os orçamentos federais de Estados organizados como federações. O Gráfico 1 apresenta uma comparação desse tipo. Ele mostra que o peso do orçamento da UE em relação ao PIB fica a léguas de distância dos dos Estados Federais existentes: 1% na UE contra mais de 20% nas Federações com menos peso do Estado nas suas economias e mais de 30% nas Federações em que o intervencionismo estatal na economia é maior (tal como sucede na maioria dos países da UE, incluindo os que não são Federações).

Até mesmo as propostas do Relatório McDougall (MacDougall: *The Role of Public Finance in European Integration*, European Commission, Brussels, 1977) que recomendam um orçamento Europeu da ordem de 5% a 7% do PIB, numa fase federal com intervenção pública modesta, ficaram de longe muito abaixo dos níveis observados em Estados Federados. Isso não impediu que essas propostas tenham sido postas totalmente de lado, por ter sido considerado que elas estabeleciam metas excessivas de federalismo orçamental.

Gráfico 1

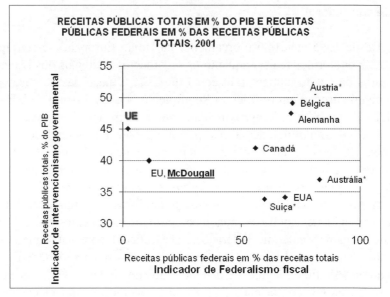

Nos países com * os valores do eixo das abcissas referem-se às % entre as receitas fiscais federais e a totalidade das receitas fiscais
Fonte: OECD Economic Outlook 2007; Joumard e Kongsrud, 2003

3. Perspectivas de Reforma do Orçamento Europeu propor

As instituições europeias estão comprometidas a efectuar, no decurso dos anos de 2008 e 2009, a revisão das actuais perspectivas Financeiras, que estão em vigor para o período de 2007-2013.

De acordo as com orientações anunciadas, nessa revisão atribuir--se-á especial prioridade à discussão das despesas com a Política Agrícola Comum (PAC) e ao problema do reembolso ao Reino Unido.

Em geral não se esperara que o exercício de discussão da reforma orçamental venha a trazer transformações radicais. O mais provável é que ele recomende apenas ajustamentos menores nas Perspectivas Financeiras actuais (2007-2013). Em princípio, tais ajustamentos deveriam recair sobretudo sobre as despesas do PAC e sobre o reembolso ao Reino Unido, mas mesmo isso é bastante duvidoso. O principal resultado do exercício da Revisão de Perspectivas Financeiras 2007-2013 será presumivelmente o de iniciar uma reflexão sobre as orientações a estabelecer para os

A *União Europeia: A Caminho de um Orçamento Federal* 267

orçamentos da União relativos aos anos posteriores a 2013. Tudo leva a crer que é no quadro dessa reflexão que poderá começar a ser debatida a reforma profunda do Orçamento, tão necessária para definir o futuro da União Europeia.

4. Grandes questões a considerar numa Reforma profunda do Orçamento Europeu

Entre as principais questões a considerar na Reforma profunda do Orçamento Europeu avultam:
- o financiamento da PAC;
- o princípio do "juste retour";
- o fornecimento de mais bens públicos;
- a alteração do sistema de recursos próprios;
- a função redistributiva ;
- o papel do Orçamento na estabilização económica;
- a votação dos recursos e das perspectivas orçamentais por maioria qualificada.

Apresentam-se a seguir comentários breves sobre cada um destes pontos

4.1. *O Financiamento da PAC* – O montante dos dispêndios do Orçamento da UE com a PAC é vigorosamente criticado por quase todos os economistas.

É apontado que tais dispêndios:
- introduzem distorções não justificáveis do ponto de vista económico na alocação de recursos e resultam por isso em perdas de eficiência produtiva.
- têm consequências adversas sobre a equidade, na medida em que se traduzem por redistribuições de rendimentos frequentemente de tipo regressivo;
- são a causa principal das desigualdades das contribuições líquidas dos Estados Membros para o Orçamento da UE e estão portanto na origem das discussões sobre o "juste retour";
- absorvem recursos orçamentais que poderiam ser aproveitados no financiamento de outras despesas com maiores benefícios para a UE.

A explicação para a manutenção das despesas da PAC a níveis tão elevados como os que ainda subsistem está na força dos grupos de interesse, nomeadamente os dos países que ganham com a PAC à custa dos demais.

Por todas estas razões, é indiscutível para a esmagadora maioria das opiniões informadas que uma das principais prioridades da reforma do Orçamento da UE terá de ser a redução drástica das despesas com a PAC.

4.2. *O princípio do "juste retour"* – Nas discussões sobre o Orçamento Europeu tem sido dada grande ênfase às comparações entre as contribuições líquidas dos diferentes Estados (isto é às diferenças entre o que cada Estado paga para o Orçamento e o que dele directamente recebe). Com base nessas comparações tem sido frequentemente reclamada a aplicação do princípio do "juste retour" (isto é a redução das disparidades no peso proporcional daquelas contribuições líquidas suportado pelos vários países) .

Os cálculos do "juste retour" são em regra de validade altamente duvidosa. Eles não levam em conta que a participação na UE não envolve apenas custos e benefícios orçamentais. Estes são de fraquíssima importância relativa em relação aos benefícios económicos mais gerais da livre circulação de bens e serviços e de factores produtivos, da adopção de regulamentações comuns ou harmonizadas, da política comercial comum em relação a terceiros países, etc. Não faz sentido procurar equilibrar os custos e benefícios orçamentais (que aliás são extremamente difíceis de estimar), sem olhar ao mesmo tempo para todos os outros custos e benefícios da participação na UE.

A insistência no princípio do "juste retour" torna o orçamento comunitário mais complexo, menos transparente, menos eficiente e por vezes até menos equitativo

Os exemplos de distorções introduzidas no orçamento da UE pelo princípio do "juste retour" são múltiplos: é estranho que os países mais pobres estejam a contribuir para o reembolso recebido por um país rico como o Reino Unido; alguns países beneficiam artificialmente de reduções na taxa do IVA e das contribuições sobre o PNB que têm de entregar ao Orçamento da UE, para dessa forma se evitar que suportem contribuições líquidas muito superiores às de outros Estados Membros; com o mesmo acesso objectivo, há reembolsos dos encargos de cobrança de direitos aduaneiros sobre mercadorias importadas de países terceiros que

A União Europeia: A Caminho de um Orçamento Federal   269

são de longe superiores ao custo efectivo desses encargos; e há também transferências de Fundos Comunitários de apoio às regiões mais pobres que são encaminhadas para países ricos, em prejuízo de regiões bem mais carenciadas de países pobres (sendo nomeadamente de assinalar que 40% dos recursos dos fundos estruturais atribuídos ao objectivo 1 vão para países ricos).

Por todas estas razões, um dos objectivos fundamentais da reforma do orçamento da UE deve ser o de eliminar a influência do princípio do "juste retour" orçamental. É necessário dar mais força aos princípios da solidariedade e da equidade. A haver apreciações sobre os custos e benefícios que cada país suporta e obtém com a sua participação na UE, essa apreciação (que aliás será praticamente impossível quantificar adequadamente) teria que abranger todos os aspectos daquela participação e não apenas os que têm a ver com o Orçamento.

Não podemos todavia deixar de reconhecer que haverá sempre boas razões para defesa do princípio do "juste retour" enquanto permanecer a irracionalidade das despesas da PAC. A redução drástica dessas despesas é por isso condição indispensável para que o princípio do "juste retour" seja afastado das discussões relativas ao Orçamento Europeu. A ampliação dos gastos orçamentais da UE com o fornecimento de bens públicos e a introdução de verdadeiros impostos europeus contribuiriam também poderosamente para que o princípio do "juste retour" deixasse de ter relevância que desde há um certo número de anos lhe vem sendo atribuída.

4.3. *O Financiamento de bens públicos* – A estrutura das despesas do Orçamento Europeu para 2006 apresentou a seguinte composição percentual:

PAC e desenvolvimento rural	46,2%
Coesão	32,8%
Outras Políticas (bens públicos e administração)	21,0%
	100,0%

As despesas da PAC e desenvolvimento rural e as da Coesão também envolveram fornecimentos de bens públicos, mas devem ser classificadas essencialmente como despesas redistributivas.

As despesas com bens públicos dificilmente podem deixar de ser consideradas como demasiado exíguas pelos que ambicionam uma Europa mais forte e com maior coesão. São justificados mais financiamentos europeus de políticas comuns em domínios em que actualmente há apenas regulamentos e coordenação e só há financiamentos nacionais. A necessidade de ampliar as despesas do Orçamento Europeu com o fornecimento de bens públicos assenta em pelo menos duas razões:

- o aproveitamento de economias de escala em actividades que actualmente são desenvolvidas a nível dos Estados Membros com maiores custos e menos eficiência.

- o aproveitamento de economias externas transfronteiriças, ou seja, o financiamento pela União de despesas que, embora realizadas num Estado Membro, trazem benefícios para outros (por exemplo, algumas despesas de protecção do ambiente, despesas em infra-estruturas de transportes que sirvam outros países, etc).

Entre os bens públicos onde é mais aparente a necessidade de maiores financiamentos comunitários são de apontar:

a) Várias actividades relacionadas com a concretização de estratégias de Lisboa, nomeadamente as que têm a ver com infra-estruturas europeias, a formação avançada e o apoio a grandes projectos de inovação tecnológica europeia. Os apoios a actividades destes tipos podem, por vezes, envolver conflitos com objectivos de equidade. Os objectivos de eficiência não devem porém ser sacrificados: se eles implicarem conflitos significativos com objectivos de equidade entre Estados Membros, o que será necessário é desenvolver em paralelo acções separadas compensatórias dirigidas para objectivos de redistribuição e equidade.

b) Políticas do ambiente de alcance transnacional, como por exemplo políticas de combate ao aquecimento global e à poluição transfronteiriça. O financiamento europeu de políticas dc ambiente poderá nalguns casos ser combinado com despesas relativas ao desenvolvimento rural.

c) Imigração – O controlo da imigração e o policiamento das fronteiras do Espaço Schengen são obviamente actividades de interesse comunitário. É por isso absurdo esperar que os países mais expostos aos fluxos de imigração ilegal tenham de suportar por si só os custos com o controlo desses fluxos. É fundamental que tais custos passem a constituir encargo do Orçamento Europeu.

d) Segurança interna – Há cada vez mais redes de crime e de terrorismo organizadas à escala internacional. Não é eficiente, nem é equitativo, que a luta contra essas redes seja financiada apenas por orçamentos nacionais. Não bastam formas de cooperação entre os Estados Membros como as que existem hoje. É necessária uma política europeia de segurança interna com órgãos próprios (Procurador Europeu, Centro Europeu de Coordenação Judicial e Policial, etc) e com recursos financeiros fornecidos pelo Orçamento Europeu.

e) Defesa – É duvidoso que o reforço do poder militar unificado à escala europeia possa ser, na fase actual, um dos objectivos fundamentais da União Europeia. Compreende-se que as questões de defesa estão no cerne das soberanias nacionais e são por isso das que por agora menos se prestam a iniciativas de integração europeia. Mesmo assim, vale a pena olhar para os ganhos de eficiência em termos económicos, na defesa da paz à escala mundial, que poderão resultar da colaboração mais estreita e de acções comuns à escala europeia no domínio da defesa. Para suportar tal colaboração mais estreita poderão justificar-se financiamentos (em escala moderada) suportados pelo Orçamento Europeu.

O fornecimento de mais serviços públicos pela União Europeia nem sempre terá de ser integralmente financiado através de verbas inscritas no Orçamento Europeu. Em muitos casos, poderão adoptar-se competências partilhadas (orçamentos do tipo pigouviano que envolvessem co-financiamentos da União e nacionais, incentivos suportados pelo Orçamento Europeu e penalizações financeiras por este recebidas).

4.4. *Recursos próprios do Orçamento Europeu* – O actual sistema de recursos que alimentam o Orçamento Europeu deixa muito a desejar do ponto de vista da racionalidade, da eficiência, e da equidade. Para o tornar mais adequado deveriam ser de encarar reformas como as seguintes:

a) fusão da contribuição baseada no IVA com a contribuição baseada do PNB, passando esta a absorver aquela;

b) progressividade nas contribuições baseadas no PNB, estabelecida em função do PNB per capita;

c) criação de impostos europeus para financiar uma boa parte das despesas com bens públicos. Entre os possíveis impostos europeus a considerar merecem referência: impostos sobre as emissões de CO^2, imposto sobre sociedades, imposto sobre transacções no mercado de capitais, imposto Tobin, a inscrição como receita do Orçamento Europeu do imposto de senhoriagem arrecadado pelo Banco Central Europeu.

4.5. *A Função redistributiva do Orçamento Europeu* – Actualmente, o Orçamento Europeu alimenta duas políticas redistributivas importantes: a política de coesão económica e social, financiada pelos Fundos Estruturais, que absorvem cerca de um terço da despesa total; e a PAC, incluindo o desenvolvimento rural, que absorve cerca de 46% da mesma despesa.

Essas políticas redistributivas são altamente discutíveis. A redistribuição pela PAC tem pouco a ver com objectivos de equidade, e muitas vezes tem efeitos inegavelmente regressivos, como já atrás foi referido.

As despesas de coesão económica e social alimentadas pelos Fundos Estruturais produzem no conjunto redistribuições que melhoram a equidade, além de promoverem a eficiência económica, mas são muitos os casos em que assim não acontece. Elas têm financiado muitos projectos de eficiência duvidosa, bastantes dos quais envolvendo desperdícios e fraudes. Há também exemplos importantes de efeitos negativos sobre a equidade horizontal e sobre a equidade vertical (bastas vezes, resultantes da interferência do princípio do "juste retour") A função redistributiva do orçamento Europeu deveria ser mais transparente e principalmente atender mais ao princípio da equidade e aos conflitos que possam ser criados com o princípio da eficiência.

Para se melhorar a efectividade da função redistributiva do Orçamento Europeu, haverá que olhar para reformas como as seguintes:

a) Reformas do lado da receita: sistema de recursos próprios mais orientado para a equidade horizontal, combinado com progressividade nas contribuições baseadas no PNB;

b) Reformas do lado da despesa: predomínio do critério da eficiência na alocação das dotações orçamentais para bens públicos, a financiar sobretudo por impostos europeus; redução drástica das despesas da PAC já atrás apontada; reforma das políticas de desenvolvimento regional por forma a melhorar a sua eficiência e a sua equidade e libertá-las da influência do princípio do "juste retour", devendo nessa reforma reconhecer-se que os países ricos têm mais recursos que os países pobres para apoiar as regiões e os sectores económicos com mais dificuldades ou mais problemas de atraso; aumento dos recursos do Orçamento Europeu consagrados ao combate à pobreza e à marginalidade dos cidadãos, que deveria passar a ser um objectivo de coesão muito mais importante do que até aqui.

As dificuldades da concretização destas orientações são porém consideráveis. Não se pode por enquanto contar muito com solidariedade substancial entre os países da União. As posições nacionalistas e a insistência nas reclamações de "juste retour", inviabilizarão por certo progressos substanciais na melhoria da equidade orçamental.

4.6. *O Orçamento Europeu e a estabilização económica* – Ao contrário do que acontece com os orçamentos nacionais, o Orçamento Europeu não tem qualquer papel de estabilização económica anti-cíclica. A sua dimensão exígua (1% do PNB) não permite acções significativas nesse domínio. As funções de estabilização macro-económica também são impedidas pela proibição de a União Europeia emitir dívida para financiar o seu Orçamento.

Tem-se discutido porém se o Orçamento Europeu deveria ou não apoiar os países membros atingidos por fortes choques assimétricos. As Uniões Monetárias dos Estados Federais podem contar com contribuições orçamentais para a estabilização económica, assentes essencialmente em estabilizadores automáticos e também muitas vezes em políticas discricionárias que reduzem a severidade de choques assimétricos. Esses exemplos têm sido apontados como justificação para que na União Económica e Monetária Europeia funcionem esquemas semelhantes. Mas a falta de solidariedade, os nacionalismos e a força das posições de liberalismo económico têm impedido que isso aconteça.

Um dos objectivos da Reforma do Orçamento Europeu deveria ser o de ultrapassar a situação existente, estabelecendo um Fundo de Apoio à reconversão económica dos sectores económicos ou regiões gravemente atingidos por choques externos assimétricos, incluindo os choques na procura ou na oferta, os choques tecnológicos e os choques da globalização. Poderá argumentar-se que alguns apoios distribuídos pelos Fundos Estruturais da UE se dirigem a essas finalidades. O montante dos recursos movimentados e as directivas para a sua utilização estão contudo muito longe de satisfazer adequadamente as necessidades que se têm sentido e continuarão a aparecer no futuro.

4.7. *A necessidade de maioria qualificada nas decisões do Orçamento* – As decisões do Conselho Europeu sobre o Orçamento exigem unanimidade. Com essa exigência é muito pouco provável que alguma vez se venham a conseguir as reformas orçamentais de que a União precisa para progredir.

Os países que querem evitar o acréscimo de poderes da União, poderão bloquear sempre com o seu veto a ampliação das dimensões do Orçamento Europeu. Opor-se-ão por essa via ao maior fornecimento de bens públicos pela União e a qualquer reforço das funções redistributivas e de estabilização económica. Impedirão a criação de impostos Europeus e serão intransigentes na defesa da sua total soberania fiscal, mesmo quando estejam a criar concorrência fiscal prejudicial para os restantes Estados Membros. Aliás, a concorrência fiscal prejudicial cria já hoje problemas de extrema gravidade. Ela cria distorções difíceis de aceitar no funcionamento do mercado interno e obriga os Estados Membros mais atingidos a sacrificarem a sua própria soberania fiscal. É que esses outros Estados Membros vêm-se forçados a adoptar as suas políticas tributárias e de despesas públicas, às condições impostas pelos que desenvolvem aquela concorrência ao abrigo da soberania absoluta que reivindicam para si, ainda que obrigando os outros a sacrificarem a sua.

Para quem aspira a uma União Europeia com mais eficiência, com mais equidade e com maior projecção no Mundo, uma das maiores falhas do Tratado de Lisboa de Dezembro de 2007, foi a de não ter conseguido substituir a regra da unanimidade pela da maioria qualificada em decisões sobre o Orçamento Europeu e sobre mínimos de harmonização fiscal entre os Estados Membros.

5. Conclusão

Os resultados das múltiplas propostas que têm sido formuladas relativamente à reforma do Orçamento Europeu podem ser sintetizados, em cenários numéricos. Um dos cenários recomendados, que merece ser aqui mencionado, é o que foi apresentado no Relatório Sapir (*An Agenda for a Growing Europe, The Sapir Report*, European Commission, 2003).

Nesse cenário, assume-se que não deve haver aumento do peso do Orçamento Europeu em relação ao PNB, que se devem reduzir drasticamente os gastos com a Política Agrícola Comum e que se deverão aumentar bastante os apoios à Investigação e Desenvolvimento, à educação e formação e às infra-estruturas e energia.

A União Europeia: A Caminho de um Orçamento Federal

Quadro 1
COMPOSIÇÃO DO ORÇAMENTO DA UE

	Em % do total			Em % do PNB		
	Orçamento 2006	Relatório Sapir	Hipótese após 2013	P. Financ. 2007-2013	Relatório Sapir	Hipótese após 2013
Bens públicos e crescimento	**23,60**	**50,00**	**59,00**	**0,24**	**0,50**	**0,89**
Investigação*	4,45	25,00	16,67	0,05	0,25	0,25
Educação, formação	0,58	7,50	5,00	0,01	0,08	0,08
Infra-estruturas, energia	0,91	12,50	8,33	0,01	0,13	0,13
Desenvolvimento rural e ambiente	9,90		6,67	0,10		0,10
Reestruturação e choques assimétricos		5,00	3,33		0,05	0,05
Política Externa	6,85		5,00	0,07		0,08
Cidadania, segurança e justiça	0,91		8,67	0,01		0,13
Defesa			5,33			0,08
Redistribuição	**69,02**	**50,00**	**36,33**	**0,70**	**0,50**	**0,55**
Fundos estruturais e convergência	32,80	35,00	24,33	0,33	0,35	0,37
Pobreza e exclusão			5,33			0,08
Secção garantia da PAC e pescas	36,22	15,00	6,67	0,37	0,15	0,10
Administração e diversos	**7,38**		**4,67**	**0,09**		**0,07**
Total	**100,00**	**100,00**	**100,00**	**1,03**	**1,00**	**1,50**

* - Investigação e desenvolvimento: inclui sociedade do conhecimento

Os comentários acima expostos significam que o Orçamento Europeu deverá ter maior peso do que o recomendado pela Comissão Sapir. O cenário aqui apresentado (Hipótese após 2013) propõe que aquele peso suba do nível actual de 1% do PNB da União Europeia para 1,5%.

Mas, mesmo com uma tal subida, o Orçamento Europeu para 1,5% do PNB, ele continuaria a ser insignificante em comparação com os Orçamentos Federais dos Estado estruturados em federações. Ficaria até muito abaixo dos níveis modestos recomendados pelo relatório MacDougall, de 1977: dimensão da ordem de 2 a 2,5% do PIB numa fase pré-federal da integração europeia e 5 a 7% numa fase federal com pequeno sector público.

O cenário aqui apresentado, ao apontar para um orçamento maior do que os que têm estado em vigor e do que a Comissão Sapir recomenda, permitiria que a União Europeia tivesse um papel bastantes mais activo no fornecimento de bens públicos pan-europeus, não só nos domínios que aquela Comissão menciona (Investigação e Desenvolvimento, Educação e Desenvolvimento, Infra-estruturas e Energia), mas também em bens públicos e funções redistributivas de tipo transfronteiriço a que a mesma

Comissão não atribui relevo (ambiente, combate aos efeitos de choques assimétricos, segurança interna e justiça, defesa, apoio ao combate contra a pobreza).

O cenário aqui exposto representaria um avanço fraco no caminho para um orçamento federal. Mas mesmo assim ele é certamente irrealista em face as opiniões hostis à maior integração europeia que são actualmente dominantes em boa parte dos países da União. A conclusão com que se termina este texto é desse modo, a de que *a Europa não está a caminho de um Orçamento Federal, nem se vislumbram quaisquer indícios relevantes de que a médio prazo se venha iniciar esse tal caminho.*

INTELLECTUAL PROPERTY RIGHTS
ARE BECOMING UNBALANCED
IN THE UNITED STATES

DOUGLAS E. ROSENTHAL[*]

The idea deserves challenge that a technologically advanced society needs sweeping intellectual property laws – that intellectual property is the keystone of political and economic development in the modern age. This idea was strong during the last half of the 19th Century. It lost ground during the first half of the 20th Century. It is now back, stronger than ever, becoming virtually a sectarian dogma in the past 30 years.

In 1776 the Declaration of Independence asserted that the three core values of proper government are the protection of "life, liberty, and the pursuit of happiness." The pursuit of happiness, many of us understand to mean equality of opportunity – the right to be free of such impediments to self-fulfillment as discriminatory application of law, and to succeed by merit, unencumbered by distinctions of birth and heredity.

---

[*] Mr. Rosenthal is a partner in the Washington DC Office of The Law Firm Constantine Cannon LLP

A Former Chief of the Foreign Commerce Section of the Antitrust Division of the U.S. Department Justice, he has written three books and some four dozen articles about legal topics, with a special emphasis on international and antitrust law and policy.

For related considerations about the interface between antitrust and intellectual property, see his article: Do Intellectual Property Laws Promote Competition and Innovation? The Sedona Conference Journal, 145 (2006). ©The Sedona Conference 2006. A copy may be found at http://www.constantinecannon.com/speeches/speeches.html

In 1787, The U.S. Constitution, in its Fifth Amendment, dropped the pursuit of happiness and, in its place, elevated the right to own and keep property.

I think it is no accident that nowhere in the Declaration is the word "property" to be found. Though a man of property, Thomas Jefferson valued equality of opportunity more highly. The Constitution reflects the more conservative, Federalist view of a man's almost paramount right to protect the property he amasses or inherits. It also reflects the view of John Locke that democracy is best practiced by men of property. The populist response has been that equality of opportunity, the right to a fair choice to lift oneself from poverty and exploitation, requires access to knowledge and education as a critical path to self-improvement, and that clearing this path often requires restrictions on the freedom of those with property and great power.

The right to equality of opportunity during these two centuries was seized as a rallying point by "nations" of ethnic, religious and racial minorities.

Armenians, Jews, Scots, Sicilians, Czechs, and hundreds of other communities all had common languages, shared traditions and customs and a sense of self, inextricably connected with membership in an unofficial nation. They understood life, liberty and equality to support and justify their right to self-determination – to nationhood. This powerful push to be part of a community which could protect its members, and give them self esteem is, like property vs. opportunity, a constant political issue of the 19th and 20th Centuries. As Isaiah Berlin has reminded us, nationalism started as a positive force. But we have seen its dark side in the intervening 200 years. Frequently, nations have built community by making war on their enemies – real or perceived – and the dark side of nationalism threatens democracy today, not unlike 70 years ago.

There is considerable agreement as we begin the 21st Century that life, liberty, property and equality of opportunity remain core values in civilized societies. The failure of communism and the sad experience of Weimar Germany teach that property also needs protecting to promote well-being. However, the success of any law or policy should be judged by how well it promotes a balance of these core values. Unbalanced pursuit of one or two of the four diminishes the rest.

Competition law and policy are supported because they promote freedom of economic choice in the market and protect property acquired by honest effort. Competition can do harm; it can exploit the weak and the poor, pollute our environment and undermine trust and well-being by encouraging greed, selfishness and insecurity.

The exercise of property rights can promote innovation – enhancing productivity and raising the prosperity of most of the people, their sense of freedom, security, well-being and opportunity. But property can be abused. Its concentration among a small number can add to the burdens of the poor and disadvantaged, and can choke off equality of opportunity, freedom, and even life itself – for example, where expensive medicines that can save lives are not deployed to the poor in need. The way intellectual property in the United States today is protected may be doing more harm than good.

IP is expanding dramatically in the United States. According to an article in *The Economist*, about 75 percent of the value of publicly traded companies is comprised of intangible assets (essentially derived from intellectual property) as compared to 40 percent 20 years ago.[1]

In important ways, intellectual property is very different from these more concrete property forms. While rights to tangible property change over time by law and custom, the degree of change is not so great as when new IP laws are adopted. Issues of ownership as to tangible property are not usually so difficult to determine – except in periods of mass theft, like the Holocaust, or the Japanese Internment in the Western United States and Canada, after the bombing of Pearl Harbor, because of the ownership right of a holder in due course. IP is a matter of more subjective judgment, with fewer clean boundaries. Reasonable people differ greatly about what is new, creative and worthwhile. Different governments at different times have had very different ideas about how broad and deep intellectual property rights need to be to promote innovation and consumer welfare while assuring inventors some reward for their inventiveness. This is not the case with respect to owning tangible property – once slaves were freed and women were emancipated.

Thomas Jefferson as Secretary of State in 1790 became the first official in the U.S. government responsible for reviewing patent applications. Although a prolific innovator himself, like his friend Benjamin

---

[1] Kenneth Cukier – *A Market for Ideas: A Survey of Patents and Technology*. The Economist (Special Issue) October 22, 2005 at 3.

Franklin, Jefferson never sought or received a patent. He had strong reservations about the "whole idea of patents." See Bedini and Martin in Bridget McLaughlin's The Patent System. As McLaughlin has observed, among Jefferson's problems with patents, were that as:

> "a strong proponent of equality among all people, he was not sure if it was fair or even constitutional to grant what was essentially a monopoly to an inventor who would then be able to grant the use of his idea only to those who could afford it. Inventors could keep useful tools and machines from the common people of whom Jefferson was such a protector. He often referred to patents as "embarrassments to the public," meaning that someone being given exclusive rights to something by the government for some defined period of time was somewhat of an awkward concept (Martin 42). Jefferson himself paid royalties of his own accord on an idea for a mill to a man who would never be granted a patent for his plan "as a voluntary tribute to a person whose talents are constantly employed in endeavors to be useful to mankind" (quoted in Martin 43). He thought that monopolies could also "withhold technological progress from other inventors" by keeping new technology that could spark ideas in others out of reach of those without a lot of money (Bedini 207)... He did however, think that inventors should have exclusive rights to their inventions to an extent, stating that "an inventor ought to be allowed a right to the benefit of his invention for some certain time" (quoted in Martin 42). However, he believed that it was "equally certain it ought not to be perpetual; for to embarrass society with monopolies for every utensil existing, and in all the details of life, would be more injurious to them than had the supposed inventors never existed" (The Jeffersonian Cyclopedia, 679).

The first patent act was far more limited in scope and duration than today's successor laws. As an OP-ED article published recently in The *New York Times* points out, Microsoft accomplished its monopoly in operating system software at a time when Microsoft opposed the patentability of software. At that time an internal memorandum from Bill Gates to senior staff is reported to have stated "if people had understood how patents would be granted when most of today's ideas would be invented, and had taken out patents, the [software] industry would be at a complete

Intellectual Property Rights are Becoming Unbalanced in the United States 281

standstill today."[2] Like Jefferson, Gates worried that "some large company would patent some obvious thing" and use the patent to "take as much of our profits as they want."

It is surprising how little empirical evidence there is to challenge the notions that Jefferson and the younger Bill Gates had that patents were often abused, often retarded innovation and often made the rich richer at the expense of the more productive and the less well off. Today Microsoft, now an established monopolist based on unlawful conduct in operating system and office productivity software, which has still not been corrected, holds more than 6,000 patents and is seeking several thousand new patents each year. Periodically, Microsoft threatens patent enforcement war on open-source software. Microsoft asserts that it owns 235 patents which are infringed by free and open source software. Parloff, R. (2007). ("Microsoft Takes on the Free World," *Fortune Magazine*, June 14, 2007.)

OSS promotes product interoperability, lower cost software for consumers and has helped make low cost computers more widely available for education and general use in developing countries. It provides Microsoft with the only significant competition left in the operating system software market. If Microsoft were to seek to enforce these patents against the OSS Movement, it would fortunately, probably trigger massive retaliation by the friends of OSS. These friends include IBM, Oracle and several large financial, industrial and telecommunications customers who use OSS in their computer networks. IBM holds even more software and related patents than Microsoft. thus, in today's environment of bloated intellectual property rights, it is the threat of mutually assured destruction that prevents the adverse economic effects of a total patent wave. That is not a healthy dependency for modern society.

Microsoft has used the excuse of a property-taking of the software intellectual property rights it once eschewed, as the justification for non-compliance with both the watered-down U.S. Government antitrust consent decree entered 6 years ago and the European Commission's order of mandatory licensing imposed 3 years ago. According to the EC Commissioner for Competition Policy, Neelie Kroes, this is the first time

---

[2] Timothy B. Lee, Adjunct Scholar, The Cato Institute, "A Patent Lie," *New York Times* OP-ED, June 9, 2007 at A-29.

in 50 years that the Commission has faced such non-compliance by a respondent. (Remarks to the Antitrust Section of the American Bar Association, Washington, D.C., April 20, 2007.)

There is an important difference between U.S. and EC law with respect to a monopolist like Microsoft, which unilaterally refuses to share its code with competitors where it dominates an essential point of access between customers and suppliers. In the United States, as a result of dictum in the important Supreme Court case, *Verizon Communications v. Trinko*, 540 U.S. 298 (2004). such a monopolist may not be required to provide interoperability by sharing patented information with competitors. This is so even if its monopoly is maintained and extended for anticompetitive purposes. In certain circumstances in Europe interoperability must be facilitated by the monopolist through required disclosure of information. The European rule is an important social protection against monopoly abuse and overbroad patent claims. In September 2007, the European Court of First Instance upheld the European rule and enforcing the Commission's Order against Microsoft. This is a welcome and important development in better balancing competition and intellectual property.

One of the problems for antitrust in the 21st Century is that the legal issues involving high-tech products and services are becoming so complex and costly to analyze, let alone litigate, that enforcement agencies and courts find it increasingly difficult to get and to use the resources needed to do their job. Nowhere is this more true than in the interface between intellectual property claims and contrary antitrust claims.

One way to address this problem is to encourage the innovation and entrepreneurship of private antitrust claims, including class action claims. Skilled plaintiffs' lawyers are often willing to invest the resources and several have the expertise to bring cases seeking to stop the competitively suspect exercise of overbroad intellectual property rights. Over the past 80 years at least as much antitrust law generally has been made in private litigation as has been made by U.S. government enforcement. Regrettably, recent U.S. judicial decisions have severely restricted the rights and opportunities for private antitrust actions. This does not promote consumer welfare or effective law enforcement.

A further problem is that a company like Microsoft which, for years has been earning net profits from its software monopoly of $1 billion a month, may quite simply have more political power to resist the antitrust enforcement of governments than the governments have to require compliance. The very ability of governments effectively to enforce national law against aggressive monopolists in global markets is put in question.

A third way in which intellectual property differs from tangible property is that patent rights when legally challenged often prove invalid. In many litigations, asserted patents are either obvious, plagiarize or not useful. At some points in our history, almost half of the U.S. patents judicially challenged have been invalidated. The uncertainty of the validity of patent claims frequently deters small and medium-sized inventors and customers. I personally have known of individuals and companies with innovative ideas, some of which they patented, for which they were unable to obtain venture capital or other investment financing because the technology they were pursuing might lead to products that would compete with giant companies like Microsoft or Phillips. The investors were afraid. Intellectual property rights can and do deter innovation.

Because we know so little about: (1) how short should be the term of monopolies granted to a patent holder to, on balance, promote innovation; (2) how broad the categories of patentable knowledge should be to, on balance, promote innovation; and (3) how broad or narrow the concept of obviousness used in granting patents should be to, on balance, promote innovation, we should not assume that the current system of broad patents accumulated by large companies in an orgy of applications and acquisitions is the optimum patent system. It is irresistible, being given the pleasurable opportunity to speak here in beautiful Lisbon, to remind people that Dr. Pangloss in Candide, who believes that all is for the best in the best of all possible worlds, was the creative product of Voltaire's indignation at the human tragedy of the Lisbon Earthquake in 1755. Many devout people of the day saw little reason to alleviate the suffering of the earthquake victims since, after all, the human disaster must have been the result of God's will. Analogously, the current elevation of intellectual property to hitherto unknown heights should not be ascribed to God's will in a best of all possible worlds.

The conservative Ninth Circuit Judge Alex Kozinski has said it well. Overprotecting intellectual property is as harmful as under protecting it. Creativity is impossible without a rich public domain. Nothing today, likely nothing since we tamed fire, is genuinely new. Culture, like science and technology, grows by accretion, each new creator building on the works of those who came before. Overprotection stifles the very creative forces it's supposed to nurture.[3]

Systems of title recordation for real estate, for registration of motor vehicles and for other personal property, arrangements for marking them and possessing them in a way which leads to a heavy presumption of ownership, create much less uncertainly about the ownership of real and personal property and make these traditional forms of property quite different from IP. Small property holders are always at a disadvantage in a legal system which favors the deep pocket litigant. Still, the chances of successfully litigating most tangible property disputes seems greater than the chances of the medium-size company with patents successfully litigating against the patent infringement claims of a giant corporation.

There are now more than 160 governments entitled to define their own patent law and policy – within the parameters of the World Trade Organization TRIPS Treaty. Why should many of these countries adopt the view of intellectual property ascendant in the United States, rather than the Jeffersonian or young Bill Gates view? Other than the TRIPS Treaty, which many WTO members now repent adhering to, there is no international law or policy fixing the scope or terms of global patent protection. If we are going to move in the direction of harmonization and balance, we will need more empirical evidence of what IP policy works best to promote the values we care about. The distinguished American economist, F. M. Scherer, has assembled some of the empirical evidence on how well intellectual property rights promote innovation as against market competition.[4] He finds, for example, that AT&T and Microsoft were most innovative when faced with competition. Innovation declined when their rivals were foreclosed.

It has been decided by the United States Court of Appeals for the Federal Circuit, and appears to be the current view of the Antitrust Division of the U.S. Department of Justice, that lawfully obtaining a patent or suite of patents implies a virtual presumption that refusing to

---

[3] White v. Samsung, 989 F.2d 1512, 1513 (9th Cir. 1993).

[4] See the chapter by F.M. Scherer entitled "Technological Innovation and Monopolization" in a forthcoming volume on antitrust law edited by Dale Collins, Issues in Competition Law and Policy. ABA Section of Antitrust Law (2007).

license or even licensing with broad provisions that may restrict the ability of potential competitors to develop alternative technologies, is a lawful exercise of the monopoly patent grant. Increasingly, there is little effective balancing between the consumer welfare values promoted by competition against those promoted by monopolists exercising intellectual property rights and insisting upon restrictive licenses to customers and potential competitors.

One of the many factors that has increased the power of intellectual property rights as against competition concerns is that many of the judges on The Federal Circuit Court of Appeals believe in the paramountcy of intellectual property laws. By statute, they have exclusive jurisdiction over patent appeals. This creates a special court with an institutional bias, very rare in the United States federal court system. Except perhaps for the U.S. Tax Court, the federal system is broadly committed to courts exercising general jurisdiction over the full range of justifiable disputes. By self-assertion of judicial prerogatives, this Court has given itself the right to decide conflicting claims between antitrust and intellectual property. Mostly, it legitimates broad restrictive patent licenses and, in difficult cases, reaches facile results in which IP trumps competition concerns. This arrogation of power has stacked the deck against sensible antitrust judicial decisions in this area. Within the past half year, a few cases have been decided by the Federal Circuit that do a better job of balancing intellectual property protections with other important values.[5]

Nonetheless, it remains true that restrictive licenses are given too little enforcement scrutiny. A balance should be restored between IP and antitrust concerns. We must stop denying that those concerns may, and sometimes do conflict. While it is not favored today, the reasoning of the Ninth Circuit Court of Appeals in Image Technical Services v. Eastman Kodak is sound. It promotes such a proper and nuanced balance.

We started with the four core values of life, liberty, equality and property. Neither intellectual property nor competition law should value property or the market over human life. I have heard of respected antitrust lawyers saying that regulation of health care markets to save the poor who suffer from curable disease undermines competitive markets.

---

[5] "Patent Pushback: The Federal Circuit gets the message, may be loosening patent protections." *ABA Journal*, December, 2007 at 14.

Such casualness about human life should be unacceptable in the 21st Century. We have all heard about a corporation that learned from Amazon Tribes about traditional herbs with healing properties. The corporation then patented chemicals within those herbs without telling those who taught them, or sharing with them their royalties. This may be apocryphal, rather than a true story, but it shows how intellectual property can be used to take from people their right freely to use and enjoy their work – especially as Jefferson worried about, their work that is innovative.

The concept of markets in competition, when combined with intellectual property rights, may be used to justify restrictions on the dissemination of copyrighted information where people are unable to pay the price for it. However, if we are to promote greater equality of opportunity globally in the 21st Century, we may need to restrict markets and restrict the rights of holders of intellectual property to challenge the interoperability of technologies so as to make data more generally accessible to global consumers – and at lower costs. We may need to restrict intellectual property rights to promote the use of the World Wide Web and modern telecommunications, to make civilization's knowledge more accessible to all who crave access, and to facilitate their communication with each other to aid new understandings.

In the United States, national cultural protection laws are widely viewed as an unjustified departure from freer international trade. I disagree. They often are a justified departure. Laws in countries like France and Canada which seek to preserve and promote the culture, language and traditions of a national community are not, primarily, a matter of economic protectionism. If we are to combat successfully the dark and vicious side of nationalism, the terror, violence, alienation and fear that one's heritage is being destroyed, we must learn to respect, to value, and to help nurture the positive side of distinctive national cultures. As Claude Levi-Strauss taught us in <u>Tristes Tropiques</u>, the extinction of a language or a culture, and extinctions occur frequently, is a blow to our humanity and the richness and variety of our world.

A brilliant and award-winning production of a play (actually a trilogy) by the greatest living playwright in the English language, Tom Stoppard, recently closed on Broadway. It's title is The Coast of Utopia. It was inspired by, in Stoppard's words, the "presiding spirit" of Isaiah Berlin. The play focuses on leading Russian thinkers of the 19th Century – mostly liberal, some conservative, one an anarchist. The central figure is a somewhat tragic hero of Berlin's, Alexander Herzen. Some of them, but not Herzen, nor Ivan Turgenev, who also appears, believed in utopias. The utopians thought that freedom, equality or human happiness could be absolute obtainable goals of political action. Herzen and Turgenev were wealthy men. Like Jefferson, they respected property. But they were appalled by the idea that property rights should be put above life, liberty and equality. During the first time period covered in the two plays eighty percent of the people of Russia were themselves property, were serfs. Herzen and Turgenev did as much as anybody by their writings to persuade Tsar Alexander to free the serfs.

Neither Herzen nor Turgenev thought that utopias were obtainable. The coast of utopia might be a vision in the distance, but you could never reach or land on a utopia, nor should you want to. Utopias would disappoint everyone. Those who got their unilateral wishes would find them insufficient. Those whose wishes were overridden by the one great idea (Berlin's hedgehog) would feel oppressed. Herzen and Turgenev were "more human less doctrinaire" than the utopians that followed – like Lenin. They were losers in the sweep of history over Russia, but were more admirable then those who succeeded them and who established the Soviet Union.

In the 21st Century, we should learn the lesson that Isaiah Berlin taught. There are no utopias. Rampant intellectual property protection is no utopia. Unbridled competition is no utopia. Economic and political nationalism is no utopia. Neither life, liberty nor equality alone is a utopia. If we are to advance, globally, the vision that the Founding Fathers of the American nation inscribed 200 years ago, that was affirmed 50 years ago by the founders of the European Union, we must balance these four core values and related legal doctrines like the general goal of "free and undistorted markets" with a focus on practical human welfare rather than ideological absolutism.

Thank you.

THE REDISTRIBUTION FUNCTION
OF THE EUROPEAN UNION

WILLEM MOLLE[*]

Thank you very much, Mr. Chairman. Ladies and gentlemen, I want to start with a very warm word of thanks to those who have invited me to this very interesting conference. I have worked with many of them in the past and it is really a pleasure to be here among you.

The main subject of this conference is: what are the challenges of the XXIst century? The organisers have invited me to discuss notably the challenges in terms of internal EU redistribution. The second subject of the conference is the role of the Portuguese Presidency. I have some suggestions about the answers to the challenges before us that I would like to submit to the Portuguese Presidency.

In the first part of my presentation the question what challenges for Europe is central. To answer that question I use the idea of the policy cycle. It distinguishes several stages. These are subsequently the assessing of problems, the design of an intervention system, the specification of objectives, the implementation of actions, the check on effectiveness and, finally, the drawing of lessons.

Now, the first stage consists of course in the assessment of the problems.

These consist of the huge disparities in income that exist between different areas in the EU. We are not certain neither theoretically nor

---

[*] University Erasmus of Rotterdam.

empirically, whether the system by itself aggravates the problem (that is creates divergence) or, from time to time contributes to its solution (that is produces convergence). So, there is a need for policy intervention. So, the conclusion here is that redistribution is necessary for cohesion. The definition of cohesion is a very fuzzy one. In practice the improvement of cohesion is assumed to be there in case disparities decrease.

In the second stage we ask the question: What sort of basic intervention system do you need in order to improve cohesion? The EU constitution doesn't answer this question. One thing is clear however, there is a need for an EU system. The application of the subsidiarity principle shows that there is really a need for a European solution. The improvement of the equilibrium between European regions and between European member States is something which cannot be solved by intergovernmental cooperation.

The European Union has made two very important decisions in terms of the basic system.

1. The first one is that it does not want to become involved in interpersonal redistribution. In Europe we do not sufficiently satisfy all the necessary conditions to make such a system feasible.
2. The second one is that there will be no redistribution via the income side of the EU budget. I know that there is some blurring of that basic choice (e.g. in the form of the British rebate). However the basic principle is upheld, which means that the whole burden of redistribution fall on the expenditure side.

The system installed by the EU and gradually adapted to its new needs responds to several of the specific aspects of the cohesion problem. The problems are of a very long standing structural nature and hence solutions need to be of a structural nature as well. As a consequence the policy framework needs to provide multi-annual predictability in order that different actors can act on a long term basis. So there are Multi-annual funds. These funds are not just handed out to the poor. The risk of these funds being abused would be very large. For that reason the European Union has set up a system of specific purposes grants. The EU regulates very specifically the type of use beneficiaries can make of it. They have to contribute to a structural improvement of the economy and thereby to enhance competitiveness.

So, to conclude on this stage of the cycle one may say that the fundamentals of the European system are adequately adapted to the EU needs.

The third stage is about the specification of the objectives. All of you probably know that the new regulations specify three of them: convergence, competitiveness/ employment and territorial cooperation. In the past, albeit under different headings, the same objectives have been pursued.

One need to recognise though that cohesion policy has in the past also served as support for the movement into higher stages of integration on two scores:

1. Deepening. When the internal market was created, cohesion policy has served to ease the whole situation. It has done the same for the EMU; at the moment that number of countries had difficulties of coming up to the criteria, cohesion policy has made money available to ease their adaptation.
2. Widening. Spain, Portugal have been afraid of the consequences of the widening of the European Union with Eastern Europe. For that reason cohesion funds have been given to them to facilitate adaptation.

A third objective is support to other policies, such as R&D, environment and transport. The European budgetary authorities have refused to vote significant amounts of money for these policies. So, under a cohesion label a lot of work is actually done for R&D, transport and so on.

Now, some observers have said that these two side objectives are actually distorting cohesion. Others have said that such side objectives are fine as long as they also serve the purpose of bringing the regions and countries into line with the rest of the European average.

The fourth stage is about the delivery of the policy; about its actual implementation. Most of you are familiar with it. In view of the time constraint I skip the analysis and present immediately the conclusion of this part of the analysis. It states that the European Union has put a delivery system in place that is adequate for the job that needs to be done.

The fifth stage is about evaluation. In other words, has the EU policy brought the effects that it said it would? The primary question is then: Has the money that we have made available resulted in the reaching of the prime objective. In other words has it delivered structural improvement and a decrease of disparities? We, as academics, have tried our best with all sorts of methods to give firm answers to these questions. I have reviewed all the literature that came to my knowledge and on that basis one can conclude that it is plausible that there is a positive effect, but there is no scientific proof for it. In the fourth cohesion report the European Commission draws a much less careful conclusion. It actually tells an enthusiastic story about what the benefits have been of the European cohesion policy in the past and how likely it is that this will be continuing in the future. I want to be a little more careful by saying that the effectiveness is not really the problem. The problem is in the lack of efficiency. The European system is extremely heavy and costly; it requires a lot of resources in terms of preparation, lobbying, administration auditing and so on.

Now the EU cohesion policy also served other objectives besides less disparity, in particular to facilitate the movement into higher stages of integration. Again, as academic, I have to say there is no proof. But again all the evidence suggests that it is very plausible.

Finally cohesion policy was supposed to contribute to the reaching of the objectives of other EU policies. Has it done that? The evidence for the past is mixed. For the present however the result is positive. The structural funds have been instrumentalised for Lisbon objectives. This means that the different countries have put forward programs that are aligned to the objectives of the Lisbon strategy.

I now get to the question whether all these considerations and conclusions lead to some suggestions for the Portuguese Presidency?

I would say yes. The main task is to keep the cohesion policy geared to its stated objectives. The policy has just been recast and the new forms have been established for the coming six years.

In the past, cohesion has often been used as, I have explained, to palliate inadequacies in several other policy areas. We have just heard in one of the previous contributions to this conference about the negative sides of the common agriculture policy. What we can learn from the experience of the CAP is that a policy area monopolised by a specific set of political actors (namely agricultural interest groups) is diverted from original purposes and creates great distortions. Now, something like that could happen for cohesion policy as well. And my suggestion, then, to the Portuguese Presidency is that they have to think very clearly about where the main objectives are, where the principles of intervention are, and how you avoid the sort of slippage that has made the CAP a monster impossible to tame.

Mr. Chairman, for those of you who thought it was too short, I have just finished a book, which is called European Cohesion Policy[1], those of you who are interested in it, can read the details there. Thank you very much.

---

[1] Willem Molle (2007) *European Cohesion Policy*, Routledge, Abigdon/London

THE U.S. PERCEPTION AND ATTITUDE TOWARDS THE EU: TRENDS ON FOREIGN POLICY AND THE FAILURE OF THE CONSTITUTION*

WHAT IS BAD (OR GOOD) FOR THE EU IS GOOD FOR THE UNITED STATES?

JOAQUÍN ROY**

The relationship between the United States and Europe will heavily depend on the political ambition will exercised by the leadership at both

---

* Paper presented at the International Conference on "Europe and the Challenges of the 21st Century" held in Lisbon on June 27-29, 2007, in the occasion of Portuguese Presidency of the EU. An advanced version of this paper was originally presented in a different format in the panel on "The Constitutionalization of the EU Common Foreign and Defense Policy" at the biannual meeting of the European Union Studies Association held in Austin, Texas, on March 30-April 2, 2005, and at the "EU-NATO Think Tank Summit", organized by the Center for Strategic and International Studies, Washington D.C., held at the Wye Plantation on April 17-19, 2005. An updated version was also presented as a lecture at the Visiting Guest Speakers program of the European Commission, Brussels, on July 15, 2005. My gratitude is extended to Wolfgang Wessels, Simon Serfaty, Pierre Debaty, and the organizers of the University of Lisbon's Law School, for the invitations, to Eloïsa Vladescu for reorganizing the bibliographical sources, to Aimee Kanner for editing portions of the manuscript, to Ambler Moss for some reading and content suggestions, and to Leonardo Capobianco for additional bibliographical transcribing.

** JOAQUÍN ROY (Lic. Law, University of Barcelona, 1996; Ph.D, Georgetown University, 1973), is Jean Monnet Professor of European Integration, Director of University of Miami European Union Center and Co-Director of the Miami European Union Center. He has published over 200 academic articles and reviews, and he is the author, editor, or co-editor of 25 books, among them *The Reconstruction of Central America: the Role of the European Community* (North-South Center, 1991), *The Ibero-American Space/ El* sides of the Atlantic to correct the excessive disagreement exposed after September 11. It will also continue to suffer the impact of a permanent endemic dimensions affecting mutual perceptions. In essence, as the popular saying goes, it takes two to tango. Experts and influential scholars agree that this task is of the outmost importance.[1]

However, based on the assessment made by experts regarding the consolidation of the hegemonic superiority of the United States, this is the irreplaceable actor. Much depends of its behavior to shape future nature of the corresponding relationship. An interesting angle to observe the evolution of European perception of the United States, and most especially the profile of U.S. perception of the EU experiment, is the context of the presidential travels to the European continent made by George W. Bush since coming to office in 2000 and especially after his reelection in 2004. No other trip[2] has raised more expectations and set more consequences that the one taken in early 2005[3] to the heart of the EU institutions, as if signaling a change of course of U.S. presidential attitude.

Keen observers would not miss the detail that subsequent trips, mostly taken in the setting of meetings of the G-8 group, would heavily prime the "new Europe" (Latvia, Poland, the Czech Republic, Bulgaria, Slovakia, even Albania) with few anchors (Netherlands, Italy) in the "old",[4] avoiding conflictive scenarios and sidelining leaders difficult to deal (Chirac) with or countries perceived as unfriendly (Spain).[5] Although official declarations would avoid signs of satisfaction, the underlying perception would not be able to mask the relieve of certain circles in Washington and U.S. media over the difficulties experienced by the EU

Espacio Iberoamericano (U.Miami/University of Barcelona, 1996), *Cuba, the U.S. and the Helms-Burton Doctrine: International Reactions* (University of Florida Press, 2000), *Las relaciones exteriores de la Unión Europea* (México: UNAM, 2001), Retos de la integración regional: Europa y América (México: UNAM, 2003), and *La Unión Europea y el TLCAN* (México: UNAM, 2004). He has also published over 1,200 columns and essays in newspapers and magazines. Among his awards is the Encomienda of the Order of Merit bestowed by King Juan Carlos of Spain.

[1] See Serfaty 2007.

[2] For the subsequent 2005 trip, see U.S. Department of State information.

[3] For context, see La Franchi.

[4] As sample of media reflection on the 2007 trip: Pasquier, Love, AP, Stearns, Fletcher, Ward, Stolberg, and Ottolenghi.

[5] For the 2006 trip: Hunt and Gardiner.

in ratifying the constitutional project. The main thrust of this perception was the potential scuttling of an autonomous EU foreign and defense policy, independent of the U.S.-dominated NATO.

After the disaster of the French and Dutch referendums

Uncorking the champagne and speeding up the 4th of July fireworks started early in the White House in celebration of the "no" vote on the EU Constitution given by the French and Dutch electorates. Since President Bush's first election, and most especially after the invasion of Iraq, any factor that contributes to the weakening of the European integration process and the development of an independent foreign and defense policy has been mostly welcome in certain government power centers of Washington.

In the aftermath of the terrorist attacks of September 11, 2001, once the honeymoon of sympathy and support was over, Bush had enough with the Franco-German axis. Secretary of Defense Donald Rumsfeld slapped them with the term "Old Europe". All rules were valid to debilitate the European coalition. They included the use of new EU members as Trojan horses, pressure to get Turkey into the EU quickly, and slamming down the brakes on an autonomous defense policy under the argument that it weakens NATO.

After Bush's reelection, however, troubles in Iraq and the sinking of the US image in the world pressured him to make the reparations of U.S. – European relations a top priority. To make peace with the unruly European, he elected to use a diplomatic strategy delegated to Condoleezza Rice. However, the latent sentiment of distrust and fear towards Europe was waiting for an opportunity to resurface. Liberation came with the one-two punch executed by the French and Dutch. The smile in the White House was evident. The Europeans (called "euros" in some offices), according to some conservatives, did not and still don't know where they are headed. The United States would, again and again, divide and conquer them.

This temporary satisfaction, however, may turn to preoccupation when considering the sources of the "no" vote and the consequences of potential EU disintegration. Believing that a marooned Europe would be friendlier to U.S. interests is an illusory calculation from a political and strategic angle. It is also damaging for the national security of the United States. The last thing Bush and any of his successors need now is a debilitated and introspected Europe.[6]

In the first place, the negative vote may give the impression that it is actually a rejection of a regulatory EU that wants to control the market, and that is acting as a support for the welfare state, and consequently is an enemy of foreign investors. On the contrary, a notable part of the "no" vote (mostly from the left, but also from a populist right) believed that the design proposed in the Constitution was too business-oriented. As a consequence, the EU leadership would receive the heat to side with the people.

On the other hand, an important sector on the right rejected the project for nationalistic reasons, in good company with the radical left. It is fearful of immigration and opposed to EU enlargement, especially to Turkey. This sector could capture, at any moment, once again, the anti-US sentiment, with a more damaging impact than the one emanating from the left. This racist and ultra nationalist band would extend to the United States the accusation o for causing the alleged loss of national identity.

Whatever their actual numbers, the fact is that the ranks of the opposition to the Constitution are very vocal, are able to pull all the populist triggers, and can control public demonstrations. In sum, they can afford to be intransigent and intolerant to guarantee, for example, the rigidity of the markets, not exactly in the best interest of U.S. investment.

Within this panorama, the moderate sectors that form the grand coalition (social democrats and centrist conservatives) that has made the current EU possible still feel intimidated. They would at any time elect to back national interests, not always coinciding with the United States. From Airbus subsidies, support in Iraq, ideological battles such as the International Criminal Court, dispute clashes at the WTO, and cultural confrontation, all may become a weapon in times of confrontation.

Although it is too fuzzy for safe predictions, it is nonetheless certain that the pressure to leap forward will be strong for the formation of a series of European "reinforced cooperation" schemes (in foreign policy and defense especially), because they will respond to the nationalist pressure from the electorate. This is what happened when the time for crucial decisions was approaching in the eve of the closing of the German

---

[6] See columns by Eizenstat and Drodziak ("European self-absorption")

presidency of the EU in late June 2007. Ironically, this panorama is not exactly what the White House was expecting, waiting for a slow and consensual process, installed in a constitutional text that would take time to be fully implemented.

To paraphrase President Eisenhower Defense Secretary and former CEO of General Motors Charley Wilson, the ones who believe that what is bad (or good) for Europe is good for America may get a shock. In sum, President Bush in a way lost the referendum, too. He is still loosing while the EU difficulties survive, but he does not realize this diagnosis.

A new strategy?

Optimistic observers and diplomats on both sides of the Atlantic expressed at the time their satisfaction for the reassuring results achieved by the debut of Secretary of State Condoleezza Rice during her heavily choreographed ten-stop trip to the Middle East and Europe in early February 2005. This was simply in preparation for the even more important visit by President Bush (right after his second inauguration) to the symbolic cities of Brussels, Mainz and Bratislava. Right at the beginning of the UK presidency of the EU in the second semester of 2005, Bush would travel to Europe four times since his reelection (of a total of eighteen since his first election). While in mathematical statistics this was a remarkable record, in substance the improvement is dramatic. In contrast to the president's previous approach to refrain from making any references to the European Union in speeches since September 11, 2001 – with the exception of one isolated remark made in his second inaugural address –, Rice mentioned the EU three times in her lecture in Paris. It was a fitting prelude for her endorsement of a more united Europe in her visit to Brussels where she met with the "who is who" of the EU. New Secretary of Commerce Carlos Gutiérrez also made his first international trip to Brussels. As a consequence, high expectations were set for Bush's historical trip to Europe and the first ever of a U.S. president to the EU institutions. However, as it is a well-known fact, the background circumstances of U.S.-European relations were a little cloudier and left much room for improvement.[7]

---

[7] See commentaries by Dowd, Hollinger, Sciolino, Strobel, Weisman and Wright, as well as notes by Financial Times.

Still, the immediate results of the trip were translated into high hopes of a meeting of the minds. On the one hand, the overtures made by President Bush and his calls for cooperation in the sensitive areas that caused the divorce between the United States and Europe were politely answered by European leaders eager to diminish the tensions. On the other hand, closer cooperation based on a mutual attitude would enhance the chances of a stronger and more assertive foreign and security policy run by the Europeans. The optimistic resulting scenario is that this new context would benefit both sides.[8] This positive atmosphere was later confirmed by a comprehensive world cooperation to contribute to the consolidation of the new Iraq regime, in an effort to consider the European-United States clash as a chapter of history.

However, once the novelty of the summits cyclically disappears, reality sets in with considerable tenacity. It usually outlines the background of a well-entrenched posture of an influential political and media leadership of the United States towards an autonomous EU foreign and security mechanism. Eventually, it also surfaces with satisfaction when the EU experiences difficulties, as it is the case with the debacle of the ratification process of the European Constitution.

Significantly, this critical U.S. perception of a stronger EU capability is not exclusive to the entourage of President George W. Bush. Neither is it solely identified with the political developments derived from the attacks of September 11, 2001. In fact, U.S. apprehension and opposition to the EU's autonomous foreign profile has been forming for decades; it became prominent after the Cold War, and has been reinforced by the drastic turn of events of the last three years.

Trends and findings

Enough available evidence contributes to an assessment of a negative, critical, adversarial U.S. attitude towards a more assertive, strong, integrated Europe. In consequence, it reflects a barely hidden welcome

---

[8] See comments and reports by Bosworth, Bumiller, Dempsey, Dombey, Freedman, Froomkin, Harding, Hunt, Hutcheson, Munchau, Peel, and Stephens, the special column by Donald Rumsfeld, and the two commentaries of *The Financial Times* on February 15 and 22.

sign when a legal consolidation of a cohesive policy eventually ran into trouble. Factual proof shows that the influential political and economic establishment that controls the most sensitive decision-making mechanisms in the United States today (Congress, the White House, the Departments of Defense and State) considers the move towards a deeper and supranational, and explicitly "constitutionalized" EU foreign policy, as erroneous, shaky, costly, and even threatening. These centers of power also judge that this project is implemented not only in competition with the interests of the United States but also in a directly disloyal hostility.[9] This attitude dramatically surfaces during the last stages of the German presidency of the EU in June 2007 when the UK, led for the last time by Tony Blair, insisted in reducing the role of the proposed position of Minister of Foreign Affairs, opposing its upgrade from High Representative. Same can be said for resistance to decide my majority vote on sensitive measures.

With a minimum of recent historical perspective, there is enough evidence of a mild déjà vu. An influential sector of the U.S. leadership, confirmed after the November 2004 reelection of George W. Bush, has been experiencing nowadays the same feeling as at the beginning of the deepening process of the EU that led to the implementation of the Maastricht Treaty and the adoption of the euro as the common currency of twelve countries. This symptom became obvious during the trips made by Secretary of State Condoleezza Rice and President Bush to Europe in February of 2005.

At the beginning of the 90s, Washington did not take these EU trends and movements too seriously. It was believed that both (transforming the EC into the EU, and the adoption of the euro) would fail. The most that the U.S. establishment was ready to accept was that the European experiment would be at least as slow as the painful evolution of the Common Market from the late 50s to the mid 80s. The Europeans would be incapable of getting their act together, was the prediction made.

Once the reality of the cohesiveness of the still imperfect three pillars (apparently a British invention, destined to officially vanish with the now failed approval of the new Constitution) and the efficacy of the euro became evident, this leading sector in the United States proceeded in a fast forward motion to catch up with evolving events. The analysts and

---

[9] See articles by Cimbalo and Savodnik.

observers that warned much earlier in the 90s about the seriousness of the European process were vindicated. "I told you so", was the common expression, although few voices dared to violate diplomatic protocol.

September 11 caught Washington flatfooted in many dimensions, particularly military and intelligence matters. However, it did not surprise the White House and the Pentagon in their ideological perspectives. In spite of what could be expected, the new design, as expressed in successive declarations of President Bush and his advisers, was solidly grounded on a U.S. cohesive fundamental doctrine that can be traced back not only to the Kennan memorandum of 1947 but also to the Monroe Doctrine of 1823, the founding perspective of a global strategy. By a combination of factors and beliefs, the rise of the European process and its deepening, simultaneously with its unstoppable widening, the EU began to be the target of uneasiness first, then of preoccupation and animosity, and finally of fear.

The euro ceased to be the object of badly-intentioned op-ed pieces and think tank analysis as a potential source for the resurgence of European confrontations and even wars. Then it became a well-identified enemy, labeled as the cause of the fall of the value of the dollar. The fact that the exchange rate trend has not reflected an alleged strength of the European economy and an alleged weakness of the U.S. performance has not stopped pundits and casual observers from blaming Europe.

Paradoxically, the U.S. pressure of past decades for burden sharing in defense spending has given way to a protest call for what appears to be a serious theoretical design of a real common foreign and security policy. Europeans are humorously confused: for years Americans insisted on the Kissinger question for the telephone of Europe. The EU first responded with the creation of the position of High Representative of the Common Foreign and Security Policy, a post entrusted to Javier Solana, who was drafted out of his job as NATO's Secretary General. Subsequently, the EU seemed to be posed for an ambitious serious development of a foreign policy, not limited to a phone line. It was to be legally processed through the constitutional treaty. Washington was not happy then and later it experienced a sign of relieve.

Deepening into a more historical perspective, the contrast with today's U.S. attitude and the satisfaction[10] of being present at the creation

---

[10] However, concern was initially expressed in power circles in Washington, fearing the formation of a cartel. See paper by Armitage.

of the European Community is starkly different. The initial encouragement of U.S. leaders in the 50s and 60s (such as Eisenhower and Kennedy) for the process of European integration, as a mechanism complementary to NATO, has been transformed today into an erratic, contradictory, and aggressive policy of what was called almost officially "disaggregation".

The historical opportunity of ending the artificial European division caused by the reapportionment of War World II by proceeding to execute an act of political justice with the ambitious and costly enlargement of the EU, was turned upside down by Washington. It has been used and manipulated by the U.S. leadership, most significantly since September 11 and especially since the split of European attitudes towards the Iraqi adventure. The "new Europe" invented by Donald Rumsfeld has been labeled as a sort of dissidence movement opposed to Brussels, following the cues of the White House.

The highly sensitive issue of the future membership of Turkey was erratically and undiplomatically converted into a weapon of pressure brandished by the Departments of Defense and State at the worst time. Not only was the issue raised at the height of the Iraq war controversy, but also during the last leg of the final months of the evaluations of the credentials of Turkey for EU membership. The wrong timing and the lack of diplomacy met the stern reply of Brussels and some key European capitals. Commentaries included comparative references to a potential membership of Cuba in NAFTA. The mildest of the responses were reduced to remind Washington that the United States was not a member of the European Union.

Significantly, a pattern of insistence on recommending membership in the EU reappeared in late 2004 when the Ukraine went through convulsion caused by the fraudulent presidential elections. From a status of obscurity, condemned to a long existence between Russia and the European Union borders, Ukrainian membership in the EU was energetically advocated by U.S. officials. Commentaries in Brussels and other European power circles were this time more restrained, among other reasons because the U.S. peddling was in a way a recognition of the usefulness of the security and economic advantages of EU belonging.

In the months before, the scandalous lack of any reference to the EU in any fundamental declarations or speeches by President Bush since September 11 was only a confirmation of the fundamental distrust not only of multilateral schemes of integration and cooperation, but especially of treaties and organizations to which the United States does not belong. This does not mean, however, that President Bush demonstrated ease in settings such as the United Nations or even the World Trade Organization. This ambivalence was amply demonstrated by his early disdain to NATO when he disregarded the urgent and unconditional support on September 13 after its historical activation of Art. 5, although the organization was later used to stabilize the situation in Afghanistan.

This fact contrasts with the energetic admonition against an autonomous foreign and defense policy for the EU, reacting to the suggestion made by German Chancellor Schroeder in looking for additional forums to deal with European security. Bush insisted then that NATO is the only valid setting.

The insertion of the NATO issue in discussing the development of an autonomous EU foreign and defense policy contributes a concrete anchoring for the negative assessment of the European design. Far from vague declarations and covering domestic interests of dominance, when opposing "constitutionalization", a victim is seen as unnecessary collateral damage: NATO. All the historical background and accomplishments of the organization, in addition to its current capabilities, are used in rationalizing against the development of an independent defense and security mechanism for Europe. As we will see later on in this paper, this strategy misses several historical points and sanitizes the rather pragmatic principles of the Alliance, some of them not only respond to innate modes and patterns of U.S. foreign policy, but also reflect important chapters of foreign policy practices.

In essence, before and after Bush's "historic" trip in 2005, the reality is that too many dimensions of the new EU, before and after the constitutional crisis, seem to be considered detrimental for U.S. national interests. The attitude sometimes looks as an adoption of a perennial zero sum calculation. If the EU wins something and makes some progress, this must be at the cost of a U.S. vital interest. In popular terms, the rephrasing of Calvin Coolidge's statement has received a new shape and tone: "What is good for the EU, is not good for the United States."[11]

---

[11] See my column "Leaders must side with the people".

Among the potential explanations for this composite assessment is the reinforcement of the perennial exceptionalism[12] doctrine that has propelled the United States to world dominance and self-assurance, as well as justification for actions that objectively should be contrary to some well-founded beliefs of the Republic.[13]

This fundamental feeling leads to the obsessive resistance to any kind of supranational entity that is above the solid grounds of the institutional framework of the United States. What is a quasi-divine belief and inspiration that can be easily understood in domestic terms is apparently usually transferred to experiments implemented beyond its borders. This influential political and military leadership seems to be unable to consider submitting to a commonly pooled sovereignty of even small portions of the economy. This denial makes processes such as the FTAA or even an enhanced NAFTA (called now NAFTA-plus) impossibility or a very imperfect arrangement. It also leads to transfer the same logic to organizations and pacts to which the United States does not belong, a behavior that, as a result, irritates foreign dignitaries.

The complexity of entities such as the EU and the whole European fabric in terms of history, politics, economics, intellectual evolution and societal intricacies, is often reduced to oversimplification that makes the prospect of cooperation and a true alliance a doubtful success. It is a rather ironic twist, but the current scene reveals odd dimensions. From paradigms in which Americans were liberal and democratic, while Europeans were religious fundamentalists and intolerants, we have been confronted today with one-liners depicting Europeans descending from Venus and Americans from Mars.

Nonetheless, serious consideration is given to the notion that the rift and the gap across the Atlantic are not only permanent, but are even wider in terms of distance between the two parts, and deeper with respect to fundamental issues. This diagnosis has been shared by a growing number of observers and scholars, in spite of the self-evident common roots and values shared by the United States and Europe, and the surviving

---

[12] See Pfaff 2007.

[13] As a sample of U.S. alarming analysis on this historical trend, see comment by Moss.

validity of the concept of the West, an idea that has led conspicuous observers to ask if it really exists anymore.[14]

Among the signals that confirm a trend that seems to be chronic has been paradoxical fact of the continued stream of commentaries in the main media and think-tank publications recommending leaders to take urgent action on both sides of the Atlantic Ocean.[15] Most interesting is the persistent campaign of alarming warnings made by keen American observers to the extent that the apparent divorce between an important part of Europe and the United States is actually detrimental to U.S. interests. Polite silence seems to be a consensus in non-elite circles.

Popular wisdom is that the United States has not caused the damage. Applying this logic to the specific issue of the role and purposes of the EU, the stark reality is that for the U.S. public outside the Washington beltway and the scholarly community, the EU is either an unknown entity or it is plainly seen as an adversary. This feeling makes congressional attitudes very difficult and risky, depending on feelings coming from the voters. In consequence, a populist tactic applied at a given moment (free trade, subsidies, tariffs, sanctions) is the outcome most expected.

Disagreements on concrete and specific issues in trade, subsidies, and legal controversies are seen simply as the limited tip of the iceberg of a more profound divorce regarding a basic stance towards a handful of themes that acquire a more defined profile when codified in the text of the Constitution or any of its "light" transformations in the alternative treaty to be entertained in the last part of 2007. Kyoto, China arms sales, Boeing-Airbus government aid, Microsoft, extraterritorial laws, bananas, etc., are, in comparison, minute. In fact, they only represent a small percentage (not even 10%) of economic links in which Europe and the United States have disagreements. Bilateral trade is $1.5 billion per day. It is dispute-free. In most of the other 90% of economic issues, the United States and Europe are in full synchronization.[16]

---

[14] For a selection of works on the trans-Atlantic relationship and recommendations to improve it, see: Albright, Burghardt, Chalmers, Daalder, Drozdiak, Cohen, Judt, Kennedy, Lambert, Markovits, Moïsi, Moravsik, Roger, and Voigt.

[15] As an example of think tanks analysis, see works by the Center for Strategic and International Studies researchers Balis, Niblet, and Serfaty.

[16] See report by Eurofocus, "Europe and America".

The rift is, therefore, more philosophical and, let's say it, ideological. Even the frequent joint declarations (sometimes co-signed by important political figures at the highest levels) claiming a basic agreement on a global strategy against the scourge of terrorism seem to reflect a sense of a shaky alliance ready to break.[17]

The blunt language sometimes used by specialists, as well as the refusal of U.S. government officials to correct misinterpretations or soften statements in a more diplomatic mode, plus the fact that envoys do not seem to restrain themselves from making negative remarks about the fundamental concepts of the European Union; all indicate a reflection of a mood that is entrenched at the high levels of officialdom. In reverse, frequent declarations of EU officials in Washington in expressing contrary views to the U.S. policy in Iraq, have been a new trend that contrasts with the usual bland discourse used by the opaque EU institutions.

Media phenomena that usually could simply be attributed to carelessness or lack of information seem to be part of the overall scenario. Too many in number and too often placed in key times, a dripping of inaccurate and plainly aggressive informative articles appear regularly on issues of the European Union. This only contributes to confuse the general public, leaving scholars that form a well-prepared minority in U.S. universities and think tanks bewildered and consumed by a sense of damage-control.[18]

As mentioned above in general terms, behind the resistance, ignorance, or episodic information about EU foreign policy is an acute popular black hole about its fundamental nature. Obsession with the notion of free trade as a means and as an objective of the original process of European integration is still a formidable ballast that places an obstacle for the true comprehension of the EU. "To make war unthinkable and materially impossible" is a thought that never crosses the minds of educated Americans when polled about the aims of the EU. Admittedly, this shortcoming is shared by younger generations in Europe for which the memory of war is only a distant historical reference. This fact discourages leaders from explaining realities that are far away from the minds of voters for whom the experience of wars are reduced to historical accounts

---

[17] See collective declaration headed by Giscard and the column signed by the duet formed by Powell and Solana.

[18] Analyses by Asmus, Howorth and Wolf.

spanning in the distance of a century and a half, mostly expeditionary actions, and the recent new trends of terrorists attacks reduced to the events of September 11. This perturbing factor became evident in the context of the French and Dutch referendums that derailed the EU constitutional ratification process. Perceived as a European negative attitude towards its own deepening integration process, U.S. observers received a reinforcement for their guarded attitude towards the EU. When free from total ignorance, Americans only seem to comprehend the EU as a mechanism to compete with the United States in an adversarial manner. Even the most aware leadership would not find it convenient and electorally profitable to counteract this notion.

Means to oppose

Once this assessment is set, observers should ask about what ways the present U.S. leadership and allies usually elect to zap the process of a deeper EU integration and more especially its project of an autonomous foreign and security policy. There are many and varied in scope and mechanisms. Some are blunt and open; others are covert and discreet.

The usual procedure is the perennial Roman maxim of divide and conquer. It was used heavily during the months leading to the war on Iraq, and it was helped by a cadre of European governments and individuals who expressed publicly their support for Bush, making any cohesive European front an impossibility, or at least a very difficult task. This sector coincides in identity with the governments of countries that showed a deeper reluctance to accept the reformed voting system in the Council, from a weighted vote in the Treaty of Nice to the double majority (55% of countries and 65% of the population) combination in the Constitution project. Even today, some protagonists of the pro-Bush camp in the dangerous months that led to the Iraq war who subsequently lost power are still executing a campaign that has as a limited result the endemic division of the European front.[19]

---

[19] The most obvious is the former Prime Minister of Spain José María Aznar. See my paper entitled "Spain's Return to 'Old Europe' ".

Partially as a reward for the lack of support in the Iraq war, reinforced by the easily detectable inclination to Kerry in the election, the Bush forces had initially intended to retaliate against the notoriously critical colleagues. Sidelining any real or potential EU lineup, Condoleezza Rice, while still acting as National Security adviser to President Bush, was widely quoted as allegedly recommending to "ignore Germany, forgive Russia, and punish France". Under the pressure to obtain the necessary backing for a refreshed policy during the second presidential term, Bush apparently decided to retract. Preliminary circumstantial evidence derived from the trip to Belgium, Germany and Slovakia leads to think that Bush had decided to give due attention to Germany, half way forgive France, warn Russia, and... punish Spain.

There was much speculation to see how far this strategy would be implemented by Condoleezza Rice, once she would completely settle in Foggy Bottom. However, the subsequent events as a result of the congressional defeat revealed a more prudent approach. What remains in place is the philosophical principle of avoiding entanglement in multilevel negotiations and maneuvering through intricacies of supranationality even of a modest scale.

Rigorous scholarship will show anytime that picking favorite agents to undermine the efforts of a common strategy has been a trademark of U.S. foreign policy in the past, not limited to a geographical area. History reveals that Washington likes to work with anchors in which to set the regional tone and allows the subsidiary country to become an axis for the rest of the countries in a given region. In the trans-Atlantic scene, this pivotal role has always had a permanent member: the United Kingdom. The special relationship between the United States and Britain has made it very easy for Washington to justify a natural alliance, something that only conveniences of modern times have made possible to enter into agreements with other odd countries. After the constitutional debacle, with some key European governments in trouble (Germany and France, especially), the United Kingdom (the key Bush ally) came out damage-free, reinforced in its claim to EU rebate funding and a reduction of the agricultural subsidies.

This new shaky European scene has uncovered the myths of the historical involvement of allies of the United States. For example, Germany has been an adversary in two world wars. France has been a historical competitor for dominance, although it has been a claimant for the role of a perennial ally, even though the fact that the real motivation has been competition with Britain. Smaller actors also fit this picture, such as the case of Spain, an adversary in the Spanish-American War of 1898, a neutral in World War I, an initial backer of Hitler and Mussolini (while ruled by Franco), and finally an ally in exchange for consolidating the Southern flank during the Cold War, and at the price of extending the dictatorship until the end of the life of the Generalissimo.

Those observers expressing critical views on the constitutional process for an autonomous defense policy of the EU seemed to enjoy concentrating on the low record of approval of certain deepening measures of the EU, the flat rejection in referendums, or the prediction that if put to a vote, they would be rejected, an ominous thought that was confirmed.

Media inclined to support the Republican interests, led by The Wall Street Journal in the print sector and by FOX News in television, will usually find a way to critique the project of a common autonomous defense on grounds that it is duplication that lacks effective means. Moreover, commentaries will stress the aloofness of individual critical governments such as France and Germany, identifying the loyalty of the UK, in stark contrast with others belonging to "Old Europe".

When reporting or venturing opinion, either in short op-ed pieces or in rather more elaborate and longer essays published in the well-established leading foreign policy magazines, American observers too often misrepresent European intentions and legal realities or offer a distorted profile of mechanisms and purposes. This assessment has caught the eye of notable U.S. commentators who have acted as firefighters, denouncing the danger of a self-inflicted wound making trend.

The U.S. government increased its insistence on Turkish membership in the European Union and started its "campaign" for a closer cooperation between the EU and the Ukraine, aiming at full membership some day. Ironically, the explicit basic argument for both campaigns is shared by the European leadership, including the sectors that are opposed to the entrance of Ankara, on grounds of differences in culture and geography. All seem to agree that membership in the EU consolidates democracy and the rule of law, and in both cases the inclusion of both countries will avoid their drifting to the murky waters of the Middle East and the nostalgia of a Russian-dominated Soviet Union.

However, the cost of the success of what is called the unmatched "power of injunction" of the EU is the eventual distraction of the energies of the entity in facing the costly enlargement. An autonomous EU defense will have to come at the expense of other areas of the EU assistance, either in the "neighborhood" or in distant regions. Prospects of membership of Turkey and Ukraine, in addition to the unstoppable but slow inclusion some day of the former Yugoslavia republics, will definitely take a toll on the plans for a common autonomous defense. This perspective received new strength after the negative constitutional referendums and the collapse of the budget talks.

The Nato Syndrome

In an example of utterly double standards, the logic of "coalition of the willing" seems not to be easily accepted by Washington when it is applied by the Europeans when forming entities such as the Eurocorps (a very useful mechanism that could have been used more often to contribute to peace making and maintenance). The project of forging mini-alliances within the framework of the Constitution project (or alternatively as a reinforced cooperation crafted by some members) often touched a nerve in the White House and Pentagon circles, under the pretense that NATO would be undermined because the same units belong to the two twin sets of military mechanisms. Ironically, the project to develop an autonomous EU foreign and defense policy is seen simultaneously as an enhancement of NATO, a threat to the organization, or simply irrelevant. It is obvious that it cannot be the three at the same time.[20]

Most American observers beyond the elite circles paid less attention to a coincidence that had significant political importance. While President Bush's Air Force One was flying on February 20 to Europe, the Iberian Peninsula was executing a significant one-two movement. Spain was leading the rest of the EU with the first referendum to ratify the European Constitution. Simultaneously, the Portuguese elected the new Social Democratic government, with a first absolute majority since the rebirth of Portugal's democracy in 1974, as a result of the Carnation Revolution.

---

[20] See comment by Howorth.

In addition to the improvement of President Bush's comprehension of the institutional framework of the EU, it is significant his insistence on reminding his European counterparts of the historical record of NATO given to European "democracy and liberty". In consequence, he insisted on the necessity of continuing the pivotal role of NATO as a forum for the security relationship between the United States and Europe. German Chancellor Schroeder had earlier reminded him of the existence of other mechanisms, notably the EU. That view is not much different than the one espoused by Merkel.

On the one hand, Bush should know very well that European members of NATO behave differently in the setting of the EU. Without the protection of the veto power or the overbearing presence of the United States, the need to obtain unanimity in the Council when dealing with pillar II and III items is softened by the calculation of qualified majorities when administering the fully pooled sovereignty.

On the other hand, historical rigor advises prudence when systematically mentioning NATO as a protector of European democracy. NATO was basically founded "to keep the Germans down, the Americans in, and the Russians out," a triple thought that many U.S. observers think it should be maintained in its essence. During the Cold War it fulfilled its mission. With Germany reformed, it stopped Soviet expansion without firing a missile. Truman's interpretation of Kennan's containment worked.

But NATO also consolidated the dictatorship of Oliveira Salazar in Portugal (a founding member of the Alliance in 1949). It never raised an eyebrow when Turkey (a member along with Greece in 1952) was under the influence of its military. And it never moved a finger when Athens fell under "the dictatorship of the Colonels". The oddity of the status of Cyprus is still the apparently perennial collateral damage of the Greek military policy at that time, replicated by the Turkish reaction. This is only one of the many pending issues facing Turkey for an eventual membership in the EU.

When Spain survived the coup of February 23, 1981, the government pressed for membership in NATO. De facto, Spain was already a partner thanks to the agreements made by Eisenhower and Franco in 1953, with the result of consolidating the dictatorship. After the rebirth of Spanish democracy in 1975, the Left sent a bill to Washington, expressing a sentiment that is frequently reinforced by the recent U.S. unilateralist policy.

In stark contrast to the "flexible" membership requirements in NATO (a sort of a "coalition of the willing"), Greece, Portugal and Spain had to wait to enjoy impeccable democratic credentials to enter the European Union. This shows the clear difference in membership conditions, reflecting a deeper philosophical aim. Double standards do not work in Brussels.

Positive signs

In spite of the difficulties and endemic U.S. resistance to an autonomous EU foreign policy, certain positive and hopeful signs can be detected as a base for a mutually beneficial compromise:

- The speeches by Rice and Bush set in 2005 a model for friendlier U.S. discourse with the potential of a positive European response.
- Naming of a security attaché in the US mission in Brussels signals a reinforcement of the attention of the U.S. government for the reinvigorated role of the EU institutional framework
- Calls by U.S. columnists and experts have been stressing the need to pay more attention to an assertive role of the EU.
- Influential European scholars and journalists publishing in Europe's newspapers and magazines with a wide circulation in the United States, or even with special editions that seem to have the U.S. reader very much in mind (which is the case of The Financial Times, and to a lesser extend The Economist) have insisted with similar recommendations. This trend was replicated in the aftermath of the referendums troubles
- The U.S. government and independent analysts have admitted the logistical limitations of the United States in meeting the demands of the consolidation of democracy in Iraq, at the same time as addressing other threats.
- Mild personal conversions in attitudes point out to a reformatting of the U.S. policy and stubborn resistance to EU autonomy.
- During the second term of President Bush, there was fear that there would be less restraint for counteracting what was perceived as a wrong policy emanating from Europe. With no pressure for reelection, priorities would have been defined in an even more narrow sense. However, these negative predictions were not confirmed.

Darker signals

On the negative side, ominous signs keep acting to reinforce the resistance towards recognizing the validity of an autonomous EU foreign policy. Among the signs and evidence are the following:

- U.S. public opinion and government circles are under the frequent influence of what we may call "doomsday papers". These are documents produced by think tanks and self-appointed commissions, offering a predictable scenario in 10 or 20 years. With no way to back assertions made, these papers present a picture of a consolidated EU in economic terms and as a total failure in terms of political integration. This trend received new energy with the referendum collapse.
- Deep personal convictions (bordering divine revelation) dominating the minds of the central U.S. leadership continues to exert considerable influence in formatting the official attitude towards the EU. Perceived EU weakness in meeting the demands of the war on terrorism is translated into adamant intolerance and consequently opposition for schemes that are perceived as repetitious and ineffective.
- Consistent anti-EU campaign performed in part of the influential media (especially <u>The Wall Street Journal</u>) have showed no signs of moderation. After the referendum failure, signs of satisfaction became salient, confirming the trends outlined above.
- Alternating negative assessments of the EU's external policy and defense capabilities in the elite foreign affairs publications with counter arguments will continue to reinforce doubts and will invite second thoughts in the Washington political and strategic establishment.
- Deep in the heart of America, ignorance and then apprehension for the EU have continued fee arguments to members of Congress weary of the sentiments of their constituencies. Resistance to free trade (not only related to agreements with Latin America) is frequently identified with an image of the EU as protectionist and an economic competitor of the United States. An autonomous foreign policy only contributes to reinforce this stereotype.
- The persistent behavior of certain EU member states (notoriously Poland, but also the UK and others) opposing measures of an

autonomous foreign and defense policy, acting apparently as agents of the U.S. administration. This assessment can be extended to the controversial project of placing an anti-missile system in Eastern Europe.

Conclusion

The U.S. perception of an autonomous foreign, security and defense policy has been oscillating towards the end of a downward move in a perennial roller coaster cycle. From an enthusiastic beginning of encouraging European integration and backing it with military guarantees, the United States descended to a deep sense of disinterest, disdain and then economic concern for what appeared to be the building of "Fortress Europe" in the early 90s. Washington met this challenge with a loyal competitive fashion and contributed to the construction of other free trade mechanisms designed to protect some spheres of influence in Latin America and the Pacific. The cloudy atmosphere inaugurating the new century has given way to a more aggressive attitude to the EU integration process and especially to the design of a European autonomous defense and security policy. September 11 and its consequences have exacerbated the self-propelled U.S. mission of dominating the world after the end of the Cold War.

However, especially since the legislative disaster of 2006, the U.S. leadership seemed to be poised to execute a mild correction to this trend, forced by the limitations of military and economic power, as well as by the erosion of world soft power and influence, if not its absolute disappearance. By recognizing the useful alliance with a stronger EU, the gap over the Atlantic has been expected to shrink considerably. Nonetheless, it will all depend on the depth and substance of the recognition of an autonomous EU foreign policy awarded by the U.S. leadership, and the nature of the coordinated missions to be implemented, in substitution for the existing unilateral strategy of its variance conformed as a coalition of the willing. The recent past and the idiosyncrasies of the U.S. political culture do not seem to predict a too ambitious outcome.

Nonetheless, the pressure for an understanding comes from the overwhelming EU-US trade that flows at all times and with a normal pace without problems, in spite of disputes and threats of sanctions. At the end of the day, an agreement is found, among other reasons because a notable two-way investment helps a lot and ends up imposing its own logic. The two regions are each other's most important partners in trade and investment, making the economic interests the most significant dimension of the transatlantic relationship.

A different story is the fact that other remaining issues are not that easy for an agreement. This is most especially the case of the theme of this paper, foreign and security policy. Both sides, then, simply have to accept that they have to learn to "agree to disagree". Both will have to come to terms with the evidence that that this trend and solution may not be temporary –they will be permanent. The contrast with past times is that during the Cold War there was a basic agreement regarding the threat and some of the methods to face it. Now, the situation is different.

While observers at both sides of the Atlantic may disagree on the economic models to follow or the ideal shape of the world in a multipolar or unipolar fashion, the truth is that Washington and Europe at large seem not to be in synch regarding the best way to fight terrorism. The quagmire of Iraq serves as an argument to demonstrate the dimension of the gap in opinion. While European diplomats and most leaders do not say it loud, U.S. policies are a source of destabilization, generating terrorism and conflict instead.[21] All this evidence causes an uncomfortable feeling. But that sensation should mean that it is catastrophic. In Spanish popular terms, the commentary should be a relative comparative: "más se perdió en Cuba".

Still, in the event that a successful and pragmatic meeting of the minds is developed between the U.S. and European leaderships, observers may be tempted to believe that the concept of West is still a reality. However, if the electorates at both sides of the Atlantic continue to exert pressure to favor, on the one hand, an even unilateralist U.S. policy, distrustful of European initiatives, while on the other hand European votes back a hardening of defense and security policies, following a more autonomous path, one may come to the conclusion that the West is not as cohesive as it once was believed to be. The gap might be as wide as a split of a civilization in two distinct branches that makes automatic cooperation a dubious enterprise. It all depends not only of the evolution of popular attitudes, but of effective leadership, political and intellectual, some commodities that seem today to be short supply.

---

[21] See column by Pfaff.

References

ALBRIGHT, Madeleine, et. al. "Joint Declaration: Renewing the Transatlantic Partnership," Center for Strategic and International Studies, May 14, 2003.

AP. "Bush opens Europe trip on jarring note". *USA Today*, June 3, 2007.

ASMUS, Ronald D., Blinken, Antony J. and Gordon, Philip H. "Nothing to Fear". *Foreign Affairs*. January-February 2005.

BALIS, Christina and Collett, Elizabeth. "Europe's Constitutional Contentions". *Euro-Focus*, vol. 9, no.4. April 16, 2003.

BALIS, Christina V. and Serfaty, Simon (editors). *Visions of America and Europe: September 11, Iraq, and Transatlantic Relations*. Washington, D.C.: Center for Strategic and International Studies Press, 2004.

BARBÉ, Esther (ed.). *¿Existe una brecha transatlántica?: Estados Unidos y la Unión Europea tras la crisis de Irak*. Madrid: La Catarata, 2005

BARBER, Lionel. "Diplomatic mission for a heavy-hitter". *Financial Times*. December 31, 2004 – January 1-2, 2005.

BOSWORTH, Stephen and Abramowitz, Morton. "The Six Parties should act together". *Financial Times*. February 22, 2005.

BUMILLER, Elizabeth. "Bush Is Expected to Express Support for a 'Strong Europe' Today". *The New York Times*. February 21, 2005.

BUMILLER, Elizabeth. "Delicate Diplomacy for This Guest List". *The New York Times*. February 21, 2005.

BURGHARDT, Günther. "A Transatlantic Agenda for 2010". *Transatlantic Internationale Politik*, 2/2000, pp. 31-34.

Center for Strategic and International Studies. "Bush Trip to Europe: President Must Build Personal Relationships to Manage Policy Rifts". February 17, 2005.

Center for Strategic and International Studies. "Transforming Transatlantic Relations: Former U.S., European Officials Cite Iran, Ukraine, Terrorism, Trade for Joint Action". February 23, 2005.

CHALMERS, Malcolm, "The Atlantic burden-sharing debate – widening or fragmenting?" *International Affairs,* 77, 3 (2001), pp., 569-585.

CHUNG, Joanna and Alden, Edward. "US to send security attaché to EU". *Financial Times*. January 13, 2005.

CIMBALO, Jeffrey. "Saving NATO from Europe". *Foreign Affairs*. November-December 2004.

DAALDER, Ivo. "Are the United States and Europe heading for divorce?" *International Affairs,* 77, 3 (2001), pp. 553-567.

DEMPSEY, Judy. "An E.U. Voice of Caution". *The International Herald Tribune*. February 21, 2005.

DOMBEY, Daniel and DINMORE, Guy. "US and Europe say they want closer ties. Can they overcome their differences?" *Financial Times*. November 15, 2004.

DOMBEY, Daniel and Jansson, Eric. "Changing of the guard: the EU seeks to show the US it is serious about defence". *Financial Times*. December 2, 2004.

DOMBEY, Daniel. "Leader sees political role for NATO". *Financial Times*. November 16, 2004.

DOMBEY, Daniel. "NATO chief eyes broader political role". *Financial Times*. February 21, 2005.

DOWD, Maureen. "Condi's French Twist". *The New York Times*. February 10, 2005.

DROZDIAK, William. "European self-absorption is a problem for America", *Financial Times*, June 20, 2005.

DROZDIAK, William. "The North Atlantic Drift," *Foreign Affairs*, January-February, 2005, pp. 88-98.

EISENSTAT, Stuart. "European discord can harm America's interests", *Financial Times* June 15, 2005.

European Union. European Commission. *Eurofocus*. "Europe and America: An Economic Union" July 2005.

Financial Times. "Blunt Schröder has a point". February 15, 2005.

Financial Times. "Bush hails strong Europe as partner". February 22, 2005.

Financial Times. "Rice reaches out to Europe". February 9, 2005.

Financial Times. "Rice's mission to reassure". February 4, 2005.

Fletcher, Michael A. "European concerns face Bush in Europe". *Boston.Com*, June 5, 2007.

FREEDMAN, Lawrence. "Europe must focus on more than America's weaknesses". *Financial Times*. February 22, 2005.

FROOMKIN, Dan. "Same Old Bush". *Washington Post*. February 22, 2005.

FRUM, David. "The end of the transatlantic affair". *Financial Times*. January 31, 2005.

GARDINER, Nile. "President Bush in Europe: Shaping U.S. Policy Toward Germany". *The Heritage Foundation*, July 12, 2006.

GISCARD D'ESTAING, Valéry, AMATO, Giuliano and DAHRENDROF, Ralf. "Carta al presidente Bush". *El País*. November 28, 2004.

HARDING, James and Williamson, Hugh. "Bush in nod to Europe on diplomatic Iran strategy". *Financial Times*. February 24, 2005.

HARDING, James. "Back in the EU: Bush now travels as a diplomat to bear his message of change". *Financial Times*. February 18, 2005.

HOLLINGER, Peggy and Dinmore, Guy. "Rice holds out olive branch to Europe". *Financial Times*. February 9, 2005.

HOWORTH, Jolyon. "Letters to the Editor". *Foreign Affairs*. January-February 2005.

HUNT, Terence. "Bush Travel to Europe to Shore Up Ties". *FoxNews.Com*, June 20, 2006.

HUNT, Terence. "Bush, in Belgium, calls for new unity". *The Miami Herald*. February 21, 2005.

HUNTER, Robert E. "A Forward-Looking Partnership: NATO and the Future of Alliances". *Foreign Affairs*. September-October 2004.

HUTCHESON, Ron. "For allies, tough times ahead". *The Miami Herald*. February 25, 2005.

JAUVERT, Vincent. "Chirac-Bush: The Cordial Mistrust". *Le Nouvel Observateur*. February 17, 2005.

JUDT, Tony. "Europe vs. America". *The New York Review of Books*. February 10, 2005.

KENNEDY, Craig, and Marshall M. Bouton, "The Real Trans-Atlantic Gap," *Foreign Policy*, November-December 2002, pp. 66-74.

KIRK, Lisbeth. "NATO to be marginalized by the EU". *EU Observer*. January 17, 2005.

KUPCHAN, Charles A. "The Travails of Union: The American Experience and its Implications for Europe". *Survival*, vol. 46, no. 4, pp. 103-120. Winter 2004-05.

LAFRANCHI, Howard. "Bush visits a Europe ever further away". *The Christian Science Monitor*, February 18, 2005.

LAMBERT, Richard. "Misunderstanding each other". *Foreign Affairs*, 82, no. 2, March-April 2001, pp. 62-74.

LANDAY, Jonathatn S. "Globalization, terrorism forecast to spread". *The Miami Herald*. January 14, 2005.

LAQUEUR, Walter. "Washington y la crisis europea", *La Vanguardia*, 18 junio 2005.

LIEVEN, Anatol. "Partial visions of an ugly spectacle". *Financial Times*. February 19-20, 2005.

LOVEN, Jennifer. "Bush Takes a Kinder Face to Europe". *Philly.Com*, June 3, 2007.

MARKOVITS, A. *On Antiamericanism in West Germany*, Cambridge, MA: Harvard University Press, 1985.

MOISI, Dominique. "Lessons from the Bismarck model of diplomacy". *Financial Times*. January 21, 2005.

MOÏSI, Dominique. "The Real Crisis Over the Atlantic," *Foreign Affairs*, Vol. 80, No. 4, July-August 2001, pp. 149-153.

MORAVSIK, Andrew. "Striking a new Transatlantic Bargain," *Foreign Affairs*, Vol. 82, no. 4, July/August 2003, pp. 74-89.

MOSS, Ambler. "Stumped by Bush brand of foreign policy", *The Miami Herald*, January 16, 2005.

MUNCHAU, Wolfgang. "America should focus on Europe as an entity". *Financial Times*. February 21, 2005.

MUNCHAU, Wolfgang. "Time for a political patch-up for Europe and the US". *Financial Times*. January 24, 2005.

Niblett, Robin and Mix, Derek. "Europe in 2005: A Distracted Partner". *Euro-Focus*, vol. 11, no. 1. January 31, 2005.

OTTOLENGHI, Emanuele. "Middle Eastern Agenda for President Bush". *The Washington Institute*, June 5, 2007.

PASQUIER, Sylvaine and Chevelkina, Alla. "Lexinton Against anti-Euro-peanism". *The Economist*, 28 de Abril al 4 de Mayo de 2007.

PEEL, Quentin. "An alliance of conflicting priorities". *Financial Times*. February 17, 2005.

PEEL, Quentin. "Euroscepticism spreads west". *Financial Times*. December 2, 2004.

PEEL, Quentin. "Why Europe needs a foreign minister". *Financial Times*. February 24, 2005.

PFAFF, William. "El destino manifiesto de EE UU: ideología y política exterior". *Política Exterior*, núm. 117. Mayo/Junio 2007.

PFAFF, William. "The Atlantic just got wider", *The International Herald Tribune*, June 8, 2005.

POWELL, Colin and Solana, Javier. "Building stronger bridges across the Atlantic". *Financial Times*. June 25, 2004.

RAMOS ALBA, Alfredo. "Estrechar el eje atlántico", Cambio16, 6 junio 2005.

ROGER, Philippe. *L'ennemi américain: Généalogie de l'antiaméricanisme français*. Paris: Seuil, 2002.

ROY, Joaquín, "Leaders must follow the people," *The Miami Herald*, June 23, 2005.

Roy, Joaquín. "Otan y UE: diferencias y semejanzas", *El Nuevo Herald*, NH 050304

Roy, Joaquín. "Spain's Return to "Old Europe": Background and Consequences of the March 11 and 14, 2004 Terrorist Attacks and Elections". Miami European Union Center/Jean Monnet Chair. Vol. 5, No. 6, March 2005. www.miami.edu/eucenter/royaznarfinal.pdf

Roy, Joaquín. "U.S. and Europe: Rift remains, but Bush trip may improve alliance", *The Miami Herald*, Feb. 21, 2005.

Rumsfeld, Donald. "U.S. and Europe share common interests, goals". *The Miami Herald*. February 20, 2005.

Savodnik, Peter. "Hill anger grows at perfidious Europe". *The Hill*. February 14, 2005.

Sciolino, Elaine. "French Struggle Now With How to Coexist With Bush". *The New York Times*. February 8, 2005.

Serfaty, Simon. "Purpose and Commitment". *Euro-Focus*, vol. 10, no. 2. June 1, 2004.

Serfaty, Simon. "Terms of Enlargement: The Euro-Atlantic Partnership at Sixty". *CSIS Euro-Focus*, March 15, 2007.

Serfaty, Simon. "Vital Partnership: Half After Bush". *Center for Strategic and International Studies*. November 3, 2004.

Serfaty, Simon. *The United States, the European Union, and NATO: after the Cold War and Beyond Iraq*. Washington, D.C. Center for Strategic and International Studies, 2005.

Stearns, Scott. "Bush Visits Europe". *VOA News*, June 4, 2007.

Stephens, Philip. "An American map of the future Bush cannot ignore". *Financial Times*. January 21, 2005.

Stephens, Philip. "It is time for old Europe to turn back towards liberty". *Financial Times*. February 25, 2005.

Stephens, Philip. "Second term, second chance for Bush's foreign policy". *Financial Times*. January 14, 2005.

Stolberg, Sheryl Gay. "Bush in Europe was a man on the run". *Herald Tribune*, June 11, 2007.

Strobel, Warren P. "Rice seizes opportunity to mend rift with Europe". *The Miami Herald*. February 9, 2005.

The Miami Herald. "Chance to rebuild alliance with Europe". February 20, 2005.

The New York Times. "Bush's Speech in Brussels". February 21, 2005.

The New York Times. "The Americans Are Coming". February 21, 2005.

The White House News Releases. "President and French President Chirac Discuss Common Values, Vision". February 21, 2005.

The White House News Releases. "President and Secretary General de Hoop Scheffer Discuss NATO Meeting". February 22, 2005.

TUCKER, Robert W. and Hendrickson, David C. "The Sources of American Legitimacy". *Foreign Affairs*. November-December 2004.

U.S. Department of State. "President Bush's Travel to Europe". May 7, 2005.

U.S. Department of State. "Travel to Europe". May 6, 2005 to May 10, 2005.

VOIGT, Karsten. "The Labor Pains of New Atlanticism," *Transatlantic Internationale Politik*, 2/2000, pp. 3-10.

WARD, Andrew. "Travels through Europe with President Bush". *Financial Times*, June 13, 2007.

WEISMAN, Steven R. "Europe United Is Good, Isn't It?" *The New York Times*. February 20, 2005.

WEISMAN, Steven R. "Rice Calls on Europe to Join in Building a Safer World". *The New York Times*. February 9, 2005.

WEISMAN, Steven R. "Rice Gets Pledge From Schröder to Do More to Help Iraq". *The New York Times*. February 5, 2005.

WOLF, Martin. "The transatlantic divide must not be allowed to widen". *Financial Times*. June 23, 2004.

WRIGHT, Robin and Richburg, Keith B. "Rice Reaches Out to Europe". *Washington Post*. February 9, 2005.

A FUNÇÃO REGULADORA E AS ESTRUTURAS DE REGULAÇÃO NA UNIÃO EUROPEIA

Luís D. Silva Morais[1]

1. Introdução e Razão de Ordem

1.1. O tema que nos propomos tratar, de algum modo, faz a síntese do espírito subjacente à presente publicação (e à Conferência

---

[1] *Doutor em Direito – Faculdade de Direito da Universidade de Lisboa (FDL); Pro-fessor da FDL. Advogado.*

O presente texto tem por base a intervenção efectuada na Conferência Internacional A Integração Europeia: Desafios do Século XXI – No Limiar da Presidência Portuguesa da UE, que decorreu em Lisboa entre 27 e 29 de Junho de 2007 – promovida pelo Instituto Europeu e de que o autor foi co-organizador com o Prof. Doutor Paulo de Pitta e Cunha. Aproveitamos, de resto, este ensejo para lhe prestar aqui homenagem, repetindo aquela que publicamente lhe fizemos aquando da nossa intervenção na Conferência, pelo seu papel fundamental no desenvolvimento dos estudos científicos sobre a integração europeia, quer introduzindo de forma pioneira esses estudos em Portugal, quer trilhando novos caminhos críticos nas mais recentes e controvertidas fases do processo de integração comunitária. A Conferência de Junho de 2007, que origina a presente publicação – da qual tivemos o significativo privilégio de ser co-organizadores – reflecte, ainda e sempre, esse papel fundamental nos estudos de integração em Portugal e no contexto europeu.

Como é natural, **o texto reflecte largamente essa origem, tendo-se intencionalmente limitado os aspectos de adaptação e desenvolvimento face ao teor da originária intervenção verbal na Conferência e reflectindo-se assim, em contrapartida, elementos de carácter mais coloquial associados às circunstâncias concretas dessa intervenção.** Importa também referir que, como é natural, atendendo à data em foi realizada a intervenção em causa, não são feitas referências a desenvolvimentos ulteriores, que culminaram com a aprovação do Tratado de Lisboa, em Dezembro de 2008 (também neste ponto de forma intencional, o presente texto não comporta uma actualização relativa

Internacional que esteve na sua origem). Trata-se de uma reflexão crítica sobre o estado da integração europeia e de processos de integração que implicam novas estruturas institucionais e políticas. Reportamo-nos aqui, quer a novas formas de 'experimentação' estadual, quer a formas de 'experimentação' em novas estruturas políticas de tipo não estadual. Para além disso, essa reflexão sobre os processos de integração – assim entrevistos de forma muito lata – é feita com base na perspectiva que se possa ter dos dois lados do Atlântico[2] (relativa aos EUA e à UE).[3]

A ideia de criação de um Estado regulador e de desenvolvimento de estruturas de regulação da economia na Europa comunitária é um tema largamente tratado nos últimos anos, sobretudo a partir da matriz conceptual proposta por autores como GIANDOMENICO MAJONE, BURKARD EBERLEIN ou EDGAR GRANDE.[4] MAJONE, de resto, praticamente cunhou essa expressão

---

a esses desenvolvimentos mais recentes). Tal não prejudica que o conteúdo dessa intervenção seja retomado noutras publicações futuras, com base numa investigação mais extensa e numa enumeração mais desenvolvida de fontes e referências doutrinárias consultadas, bem como tomando-se em consideração as actualizações decorrentes do carácter especialmente dinâmico do processo de integração europeia.

[2] Interessa aqui trazer à colação – neste contexto – os projectos de investigação e construção doutrinária que se têm proposto analisar os processos de construção jurídica em que podem assentar formas diversas de integração económica e políticas, convocando a experiência federal norte-americana e a experiência original comunitária. Pensamos em especial na obra *Integration Through Law – Europe and the American Federal Experience*, Edited by MAURO CAPPELLETTI, MONICA SECCOMBE, JOSEPH WEILER, Walter de Gruyter – Berlin – New York, 1986.

[3] Sobre o desenvolvimento de modelos de regulação numa perspectiva transnacional, tomando em consideração a experiência norte-americana e a experiência europeia cfr., em geral, MARIE-ALURE DJELIC, KERSTIN SAHLIN-ANDERSSON (Editors), *Transnational Governance: Institutional Dynamics of Regulation*, Cambridge University Press, 2006. Para uma visão global do fenómeno da regulação, numa análise já clássica e de referência sobre a matéria, cfr. ALFRED KAHN, *The Economics of Regulation – Principles and Institutions*, The MIT Press, 1998. Ainda numa perspectiva global do fenómeno da regulação da economia, cfr. ROBERT BALDWIN, MARTIN LOVE, *Understanding Eegulation – Theory, Strategy and Practice*, Oxford, 1999.

[4] Sobre essa matriz conceptual cfr. as obras fundamentais de GIANDOMENICO MAJONE, *The Rise of the Regulatory State in Europe*, in *The State in Western Europe: Retreat or Redefinition?*, WOLFGANG C. MÜLLER, VINCENT WRIGHT (Editors), Ilford. Frank Kass, 1994, pp. 77-101; "From the Positive to the Regulatory State. Causes and Consequences of Changes in the Modes of Governance", in Journal of Public Policy, 1997, 17 (2), pp. 139 ss.; "The Regulatory State and Its Legitimacy Problems", in West European Politics, 1999, 22, pp. 1 ss.; "The Credibility Crisis of Community Regulation", in Journal of Common

A *Função Reguladora e as Estruturas de Regulação na União Europeia*   325

paradigmática, que fez escola, de *Estado regulador* (*"regulatory state"*), aplicando-a, em especial, à construção comunitária (embora se possa questionar aqui a utilização da ideia de *"Estado regulador"* a propósito da construção comunitária, atendendo aos contornos específicos que esta apresenta num nível supranacional que não corresponde ainda a uma dimensão estadual *proprio sensu*[5]). O certo é que se expandiu e consolidou a ideia da União Europeia (UE) como um Estado regulador ou uma estrutura de regulação por excelência, embora este *nominalismo jurídico* ou estas qualificações nem sempre correspondam a uma sedimentação de aspectos substantivos subjacentes a esta qualificação.

O que se justifica salientar *ab initio* sobre os aspectos da *função reguladora e das estruturas de regulação na UE* que nos propomos equacionar criticamente é que a intersecção entre os **(i)** processos de regulação jurídica da economia, por um lado, e o **(ii)** processo de construção jurídica da integração comunitária, por outro, cria um dos espaços políticos e institucionais que maior problematização e questões mais interessantes tem gerado do ponto de vista da teoria institucional da organização política (suscitando no presente uma das mais interessantes discussões neste domínio).[6]

Tem já sido preconizado, de resto, que o programa do mercado único corresponde ao projecto regulador da economia de maior alcance e mais

---

market Studies, 2000, 38, pp. 273 ss. Cfr., ainda, sobre esta material BURKARD EBERLEIN, *Formal and Informal Governance in Single Market Regulation*, in T. CHRISTIANSEN, S. PIATTONI, (Edts.), *Informal Governance in the EU*, Cheltenham. Edward Elgar, 2003, pp. 150 ss.; BURKARD EBERLEIN/EDGAR GRANDE, *Die Europäische Union als Regulierungsstaat*, in MARKUS JACHTENFUCHS/BEATE KOHLER-KOCH (Edts.), *Europäische Integration*, 2. Auflage. Opladen.Leske Budrich, 2003, pp. 417 ss.

[5] Sobre os contornos *sui generis* da construção, de base jurídica, do processo da integração europeia, bem como sobre os contornos específicos da dimensão supranacional subjacente a tal integração, cfr., *inter alia*, DEIRDRE CURTIN, *European Legal Integration: Paradise Lost?*, in *European Integration and the Law*, Antwerp:Intersentia, 2006, p1-54. Como aí se refere, *"The ultimate goal of the EU (previously the EC) may always have been political (ever closing union among the peoples of Europe), its immediate objectives economic and social, but the means and techniques used to achieve it have traditionally been 'legal': the application and progressive development of common rules and enforcement procedures (...)"* (*op. cit.*, p. 1).

[6] Sobre esse tipo de problematização no tempo actual, cfr. C. KNILL, A. LENSHOW, *Modes of Regulation in the Governance of the European Union*, in JORDANA, LEVI-FAUR (Editors), *The Politics of Regulation in the Age of Governance*, Cheltenham. Edward Elgar, 2004.

ambicioso em todo o mundo. A este propósito, autores como Jacint Jordana e LEVI FAUR sustentaram, em obra de referência, que dificilmente se poderá incorrer em exagero ao enfatizar o grau ou a intensidade das grandes transformações na forma como o governo da economia, através da regulação económica, é exercido.[7]

Face a esta constatação, importa contrapor, ao iniciarmos a nossa análise da matéria que existem muitos exageros, bem como confusões analíticas, não sobre esta mudança de paradigma de governo económico, mas sobre as próprias ideias centrais de *regulação* e de *desregulação* ('*regulation*' e '*deregulation*'). Estas confusões são de, algum modo, representadas pela ideia de *Estado pós-regulador*. Referimo-nos aqui à ideia, crescentemente difundida, de advento de um '*post regulatory state*', que se teria desenvolvido nos últimos anos.[8] Este conceito corresponde, porventura, a uma boa fórmula para, em termos sincréticos e algo difusos, denominar realidades novas que não sabemos ainda enquadrar ou caracterizar.

1.2. Para chegarmos ao âmago de alguns dos principais tópicos jurídico-económicos que nos propomos equacionar, importa, em primeiro lugar, explicitar o que se encontra verdadeiramente em causa na ideia de desenvolvimento do *Estado regulador* e da União Europeia como um *Estado ou uma estrutura de regulação por excelência* (*infra*, ponto **2.1.**).

Em segundo lugar, neste nosso roteiro de análise, impõe-se propor – face à controvérsia existente sobre a própria caracterização técnico-jurídica de regulação da economia – um *conceito geral de regulação* e identificar, a partir desse conceito nuclear, *algumas das principais modalidades sistemáticas de regulação da economia*, pois regulação não corresponde a um fenómeno uniforme (*infra*, ponto **2.2.2.**).

A partir desses dois pilares procuraremos, então, identificar e problematizar criticamente algumas das principais questões em aberto

---

[7] Cfr., em geral, JACINT JORDANA, LEVI FAUR, *The Politics of Regulation in the Age of Governance*, cit..

[8] O conceito de '*post regulatory state*' foi delineado por autores como, *inter alia*, COLIN SCOTT. Cfr. deste A., *Regulation in the Age of Governance: The Rise of the Post--Regulatory State*, in JORDANA, LEVI-FAUR (Editors), *The Politics of Regulation in the Age of Governance*, cit.. A perspectiva subjacente a este denominado '*post regulatory state*' assenta numa diluição da distinção entre agentes públicos e privados da regulação da economia, fazendo avultar no processo de regulação elementos não directamente associados com a autoridade estadual ou pública e com os poderes de imposição e coercivos inerentes à mesma.

suscitadas por várias dimensões do cruzamento – inicialmente referido – entre o desenvolvimento de processos de regulação económica e o desenvolvimento do processos de construção jurídica supranacional da integração comunitária (*infra*, ponto **3.**).

2. Conceito e Modalidades de Regulação da Economia e o Seu Desenvolvimento na UE

2.1. O desenvolvimento do denominado *Estado regulador* corresponde a uma mudança de paradigma, uma verdadeira mudança de paradigma no quadro da qual a um chamado *Estado positivo* – de feição keynesiana – em que prevaleciam funções de redistribuição da riqueza e de estabilização macroeconómica, sucede um novo modelo de organização das funções públicas de intervenção na economia. Neste novo modelo, a função de regulação da economia, ganha proeminência sobre aquelas funções tradicionais de redistribuição e de estabilização macroeconómica.[9] Sucede que, neste contexto, *o processo de construção comunitária apresenta atributos que favorecem especialmente esta reordenação das funções públicas de intervenção na economia e que estimularam a acima referida alteração de paradigma de governo económico* (cristalizada na fórmula, por nós inicialmente referida, de desenvolvimento do Estado regulador e da União Europeia como um Estado ou uma estrutura reguladora por excelência).

Muito sinteticamente, *brevitatis causae*, poderemos referir a esse propósito, entre outros, três atributos essenciais da construção comu-nitária:

(i) Em primeiro lugar, avulta o facto de a Comunidade Europeia e depois a União Europeia, como estruturas supranacionais com características *sui generis* terem sempre assumido poderes muito limitados no plano da redistribuição e da estabilização macroeconómica (ou não terem de todo poderes nestes domínios quanto a certas matérias). Este facto, por si só, fez avultar,

---

[9] Sobre essa transição de funções tradicionais de redistribuição e de estabilização macroeconómica para funções de regulação cfr., por todos, G. Majone, *Regulating Europe*, London, Routledge, 1996, e do mesmo A. "From the Positive to the Regulatory State. Causes and Consequences of Changes in the Modes of Governance", cit., pp. 139 ss..

no quadro da construção comunitária, a dimensão de regulação como uma *intervenção indirecta na economia*, que procuraremos de seguida procurar caracterizar. Em súmula, poder-se-á afirmar neste contexto que a Comunidade Europeia e a União Europeia foram construídas e ganharam consistência, como um conjunto complexo de *estruturas de regulação*.

(ii) Em segundo lugar, justifica-se destacar o facto de na CE a dimensão de regulação da economia corresponder a uma dimensão reflexa dos processos de liberalização – *maxime* dos processos de liberalização mediante desmantelamento de anteriores monopólios públicos, sobretudo nos sectores tradicionalmente conhecidos como '*utilities*', tendo como base normativa uma das disposições mais complexas do Tratado CE (o artigo 86.º do Tratado CE). Compreenderemos, de resto, melhor essa dimensão específica e o seu alcance ao analisamos, de seguida, as principais modalidades sistemáticas de regulação.

(iii) Um terceiro facto ou elemento pode ainda justificar que a construção comunitária tenha contribuído para esta mudança de paradigma, pelo menos no quadro europeu. Referimo-nos aqui ao facto de as políticas e os processos de regulação – processos normativos de intervenção indirecta na economia, nos termos que já caracterizaremos – estarem globalmente menos dependentes de condicionamentos orçamentais. Ora, nesse contexto, sendo o orçamento comunitário pequeno e rígido comparado com o dos Estados-Membros, e não dispondo, a CE de poder tributário próprio, compreende-se que, ao contemplar-se um crescimento das actuações e dos poderes de intervenção da CE – designadamente, no plano institucional, através da Comissão Europeia – esse crescimento tenha ocorrido predominantemente através do aumento da actividade reguladora (em si mesma menos tributária, que é menos dependente de meios orçamentais, que faltam, em larga medida à CE.

O último argumento financeiro supra enunciado (**iii**), explicativo da dinâmica de regulação e da sua expansão no processo de edificação da UE, é, de resto, muito enfatizado, por autores como MAJONE.[10] Contudo,

---

[10] Cfr. a esse propósito G. MAJONE, "From the Positive to the Regulatory State. Causes and Consequences of Changes in the Modes of Governance", cit., pp. 150.

A *Função Reguladora e as Estruturas de Regulação na União Europeia*   329

pela nossa parte, opor-lhe-íamos algumas reservas ou, pelo menos, não o sobrevalorizaríamos tanto.

Na realidade, consideramos que nesta influência da construção comunitária sobre o desenvolvimento dos processos de regulação da economia não estão apenas em causa condicionamentos financeiros, mas uma verdadeira *preferência implícita* – em termos de modelo subjacente ao que já corresponde no presente a uma constituição económica comunitária em sentido material –[11] *pela intervenção reguladora sobre outros tipos de intervenção pública na economia.*

2.2.1. – Tendo enunciado esta mutação de paradigma do que denominámos como **Estado positivo** para um **Estado regulador** e tendo identificado factores específicos que contribuíram para que o processo de construção comunitária favorecesse tal mutação, importa agora passar a equacionar – conquanto de modo muito sintético – o *conceito geral de regulação da economia* que propomos. A partir dessa clarificação conceptual procuramos identificar *modalidades distintas de regulação de economia* – numa perspectiva sistemática – pois a regulação jurídica da economia não é um fenómeno uniforme.

2.2.2. – A propósito dessa primeira e decisiva clarificação conceptual, pensamos que se impõe separar noções muito amplas de regulação da economia – e que, por isso, não têm uma função analítica relevante ou significativa – de noções técnico-jurídicas precisas de regulação. Importa reconhecer, como primeiro ponto, que existe uma considerável controvérsia doutrinal neste domínio. Existem mesmo posições doutrinárias que põem em causa a base para a identificação de um conceito geral – de referência – de regulação da economia (que enquadre satisfatoriamente os vários processos regulatórios distintos da actividade económica). De acordo com tais orientações, existiriam múltiplas formas de regulação da economia, sendo impossível enquadrar o fenómeno de uma forma unitária e enunciar um conceito geral de regulação da economia que consubstancie de forma válida ou rigorosa os vários processos de

---

[11] Sobre a ideia de uma *constituição económica comunitária em sentido material* cfr., por todos, Julio Baquero Cruz, *Between Competition and Free Movement – The Economic Constitutional Law of the European Community*, Hart Publishing, 2002.

regulação, que se desenvolvem em termos de intervenção pública na actividade económica.[12]

Pela nossa parte discordamos dessas orientações e consideramos possível a fixação de um conceito geral de regulação da economia, a partir de uma compreensão crítica e sistemática da transposição dos modelos de regulação jurídica da economia norte-americanos para a Europa comunitária e dos modelos desenvolvidos na Europa (na verdade, apesar da inegável origem desses modelos no ordenamento norte-americano, teremos ensejo de observar adiante que existem, no presente, influências recíprocas entre os dois lados do Atlântico).

Assim, em termos extremamente sucintos, podemos fixar os contornos essenciais de um *conceito geral de regulação da economia* como correspondendo ao desenvolvimento de *processos de intervenção jurídica indirecta na actividade económica* – indirecta, no sentido da exclusão da participação pública directa na actividade económica produtiva – *incorporando algum condicionamento ou alguma coordenação da actividade económica e das condições básicas para o seu exercício, visando garantir o funcionamento equilibrado dessa actividade económica em função de determinados objectivos públicos precisos.*

Na actual fase evolutiva do fenómeno da regulação da economia – sobretudo na Europa comunitária – avultam com especial dinamismo os objectivos públicos de garantia preventiva de abertura de certos mercados e de permanente funcionamento aberto desses mercados (na sequência dos processos acima referidos de desmantelamento de monopólios públicos, *ex vi* do artigo 86.º do Tratado CE). Refere-se, a esse propósito, a existência de processos de regulação da economia como formas intervenção indirecta *ex ante* na actividade económica – intervenção preventiva frequentemente contraposta àquela que decorre das normas de concorrência como normas de intervenção *ex-post*, ou seja, normas que pressupõem a verificação prévia de certos comportamentos, sobretudo comportamentos por parte das empresas.[13] Assim, no domínio da

---

[12] Sobre essas visões que consideram a ideia de regulação da economia como refractária a uma conceptualização geral, cfr., por todos, G. J. STIGLER, *Comment*, in *Studies in Public Regulation*, (edited by G. FROMM), Cambridge, the MIT Press, 1981.

[13] Quanto a este tipo de contraposições cfr. MARIA MANUEL LEITÃO MARQUES, JOÃO PAULO SIMÕES DE ALMEIDA, ANDRÉ MATOS FORTE, *Concorrência e Regulação – A Relação entre a Autoridade da Concorrência e as Autoridades de Regulação Sectorial*, Coimbra

regulação visa-se estabelecer à partida – *ex-ante* – condições padronizadas para o exercício das actividades económicas e supervisiona-se a adequada observância dessas condições.

Aprofundando esta caracterização e procurando, sobretudo, a partir da mesma uma compreensão sistemática de diferentes modalidades de regulação, pensamos que se justifica distinguir dois corpos essenciais, distintos, de regulação da economia:

- Em primeiro lugar, um corpo nuclear de regulação, orientada no sentido da promoção de valores de mercado e de abertura de sectores económicos à concorrência, o qual corresponde presentemente na Europa comunitária ao corpo mais dinâmico e em expansão de regulação (associado aos processos de liberalização e desmantelamento de monopólios públicos, com base no artigo 86.º do Tratado CE).

- Em segundo lugar, um corpo distinto de regulação – porventura menos dinâmico no presente – através do qual se pretende garantir equilíbrios entre valores de mercado e outros valores correspondentes a interesses públicos diversificados, acolhidos nas constituições económicas (interesses públicos como, *v.g.*, a salvaguarda da pluralidade da informação, defesa e salvaguarda da poupança dos cidadãos etc.).

Sinteticamente, podemos, deste modo, identificar um corpo de regulação visando a criação de novos mercados ou a manutenção de condições para a sua abertura continuada à concorrência (*"market creating"* ou *"market making regulation"*, que tende a ser actualmente dominante na CE), e um segundo corpo de regulação visando a correcção do funcionamento dos mercados em função de interesses públicos específicos que extravasam a tutela do livre funcionamento desses mercados (*"market correcting regulation"*, o qual pode, de resto, envolver

---

Editora, 2005, esp. pp. 38 ss.. Para uma sugestiva contraposição no domínio da regulação das comunicações electrónicas que, desde 2002, assimilou múltiplos conceitos e categorias do direito da concorrência, tornando a vários títulos mais densa e porventura complexa a linha de delimitação da intervenção ex ante reguladora e da intervenção ex post jusconcorrencial, cfr. ALEXANDRE DE STREEL, *Remedies in the Electronic Communications Sector*, in *Remedies in Network Industries: EC Competition Law vs. Sector-Specific Regulation*, Intersentia, Antwerp, Oxford, 2004, pp. 67 ss..

objectivos predominantemente socio-económicos).[14] A propósito destas últimas realidades, devemos, em qualquer caso, referir a nossa discordância em relação às posições de autores que, em Portugal, preconizam a ideia de um *regulação social*, supostamente contraposta à *regulação económica* (posições sustentadas por autores como VITAL MOREIRA[15]). Pela nossa parte, consideramos muito artificial essa contraposição e admitimos que a mesma pode conduzir a resultados práticos indesejáveis. Referir-nos-emos, pois, no quadro deste segundo corpo de regulação económica de correcção do funcionamento dos mercados ao peso especial, em certos domínios de regulação de determinados objectivos socio-económicos sem que tal se traduza na autonomização *proprio sensu* de uma dimensão de regulação social contraposta à regulação económica.[16]

3. A Intersecção entre a Construção Supranacional da UE e a Regulação Económica – Problemas em Aberto

3.1. A partir das bases conceptuais cobertas pelos pontos anteriores, propomo-nos num terceiro ponto do roteiro analítico que traçámos enunciar e equacionar criticamente alguns *topoi* jurídico-económicos em aberto, que são especialmente suscitados pelo **cruzamento** – a que já

---

[14] Sobre a contraposição da *"market making regulation"* e da *"market correcting regulation"*, cfr., por todos, BURKARD EBERLEIN/EDGAR GRANDE, *Die Europäische Union als Regulierungsstaat*, in MARKUS JACHTENFUCHS/BEATE KOHLER-KOCH (Edts.), *Europäische Integration*, cit., pp. 417 ss. e EDGAR GRANDE, *Vom produzierenden zum regulierenden Staat: Möglichkeiten und Grenzen von Regulierung bei Privatisierung*, in KLAUS KONIG, ANGELIKA BENZ Editors, *Privatisierung und staatliche Regulierung*, Baden-Baden, Nomos, 1997, pp. 576 ss..

[15] VITAL MOREIRA preconiza na sua obra *Auto-Regulação Profissional e Administração Pública*, Almedina, Coimbra, 1997, tal contraposição da regulação económica propriamente dita com o que denomina como regulação social, a qual apresentaria, segundo este autor, *"finalidades exteriores à actividade económica"* (cfr. A. cit., op. cit., pp. 39 ss.).

[16] Não temos aqui, contudo, manifestamente espaço para desenvolver este ponto de análise e caracterização sistemática (que nos propomos retomar noutros estudos). De qualquer modo, sobre o problema da contraposição entre regulação económica e um suposto domínio de regulação social, cfr. VITAL MOREIRA, *Auto-Regulação Profissional e Administração Pública*, cit, pp. 39 ss. e A. I. OGUS, *Regulation*, Oxford, Clarendon Press, 1994, pp. 4 ss..

A Função Reguladora e as Estruturas de Regulação na União Europeia   333

aludimos – **entre o desenvolvimento, paralelo no tempo, dos processos de regulação da economia na Europa comunitária e do próprio processo de construção das integração europeia nas suas bases jurídicas e institucionais**. Tal cruzamento no tempo destes dois processos tem, na realidade, suscitado questões específicas, muitas das quais não resolvidas satisfatoriamente, que nos limitaremos – no essencial – a enunciar, sob a forma de quatro tópicos teóricos de discussão (*infra*, pontos **3.2.** a **3.4.**).

3.2. O primeiro tópico relevante traduz-se na tentativa de perceber *como é que os poderes de regulação da economia – as competências regulatórias – foram criados e organizados (institucionalizados) num sistema europeu de governo a vários níveis e com uma dimensão supranacional, ("multi-level governance", que corresponde de facto a um quadro específico europeu)*

Neste domínio importa reconhecer que existem significativos limites quanto à transferência de poderes regulatórios explícitos, dos Estados para o plano da CE. Existem, desde logo, limites normativos que decorrem do artigo 7.º do Tratado CE e têm sido configurados limites que resultam de orientações tradicionais sobre a matéria, *maxime* a que resulta da denominada doutrina *Meroni* (que aqui não temos espaço para aprofundar do ponto de vista teórico).[17]

Pela nossa parte não chegaremos ao ponto de afirmar, como alguns fazem autores,[18] que as competências regulatórias ou de regulação da UE são apenas indirectas ou implícitas. Contudo, pensamos que existem limites significativos a esta transferência de poderes de regulação dos Estados para a Comunidade Europeia e, para além disso, nas várias áreas sectoriais da economia há graus muito variáveis, de '*transnacionalização*' dos poderes de regulação. Ora, face a estes limites ou condicionamentos

---

[17] Sobre essa teorização e – designadamente sobre a denominada doutrina *Meroni* – e as limitações resultantes da mesma em termos de desenvolvimento de poderes de regulação no plano comunitário, cfr. MAJONE, "Delegation of Regulatory Powers in a Mixed Polity", in European Law Review, 2002, pp. 319 ss.. Cfr. ainda sobre a mesma matéria e do mesmo autor, *Functional Interests: European Agencies*, in J. PATERSON, M SHACKLETON (Editors), *The Institutions of the European Union*, Oxford University Press, 2002, pp. 292 ss..

[18] Parece ser essa, designadamente, a posição de EDGAR GRANDE. Cfr., a esse propósito, A. cit., *The Regulatory State in the European System of Multi-Level Governance*, Munich Ludwig-Maximilians University, 2005.

quanto à atribuição expressa de competências regulatórias ou de poderes de regulação à UE, verificou-se a tendência no espaço comunitário, – e em larga medida por impulso da Comissão Europeia – para encontrar alguns 'atalhos' que suportassem determinadas transferências de actividades regulatórias para o plano da União. Tal foi assegurado, designadamente, através da criação de redes de reguladores nacionais – concebidas como estruturas algo sui generis e atípicas de redes de autoridades reguladoras nacionais, articulados com a Comissão Europeia ou com outros organismos comunitários, e funcionando com um elevado grau de informalidade.

Trata-se de redes de reguladores nacionais articulados com a Comissão Europeia ou com outros organismos comunitários, em que os intervenientes, podem estar ligados por relações que tipicamente assumirão uma tripla natureza: (**a**) *relações de controlo*; (**b**) *relações de coordenação*; ou (**c**) *relações de cooperação*. Nesse contexto, admitimos que tenda a prevalecer a dimensão de *coordenação* ou, quanto muito, a dimensão de *cooperação*.[19]

3.2. O segundo tópico relevante está naturalmente ligado ao primeiro. Assim, os modelos modernos de regulação da economia, designadamente através da criação de autoridades reguladoras independentes (ou autoridades reguladoras autónomas, designação que preferimos[20]) – largamente importado do ordenamento norte-americano – criam problemas

---

[19] Sobre esta matéria cfr. igualmente de EDGAR GRANDE, *The Regulatory State in the European System of Multi-Level Governance*, cit. e D. KELEMEN, "The Structure and Dynamic of EU Federalism", in Comparative Political Studies, 2003, pp. 184 ss..

[20] A razão para essa preferência resulta de considerarmos falaciosa a qualificação de autoridades reguladoras *independentes*, apensar de muito difundida nos ordenamentos continentais de Estados-Membros da EU. Em nosso entender, a não sujeição a poderes de superintendência e o grau muito limitado de poderes governamentais de intervenção nas áreas estatutárias de actuação dessas autoridades públicas de regulação, tipicamente detentoras de extensos poderes de regulamentação, de supervisão e sancionatórios que quase reproduzem numa esfera própria a tríade de poderes tradicional (legislativo, executivo e judicial), só em termos falaciosos e com menor rigor técnico-jurídico pode ser globalmente qualificada como um estatuto de independência (o que, para além disso, apresenta a desvantagem suplementar de relativizar os necessários mecanismos de escrutínio das autoridades de regulação por entidades democraticamente eleitas). Consideramos, pois, mais rigoroso referir um grau reforçado de autonomia de um conjunto significativo de autoridades de regulação.

A *Função Reguladora e as Estruturas de Regulação na União Europeia*   335

de legitimidade democrática (*"accountability"* democrática), pelo facto de envolverem delegações de poderes muito extensos em organismos não eleitos. Tende-se, pois, neste plano, a contrapor uma denominada ***legitimidade processual*** das autoridades reguladoras independentes (ou autónomas), sob a forma de uma base normativa clara para a criação dessas autoridades reguladoras e de mecanismos *ad hoc*, de escrutínio, em graus e intensidades variáveis (*"accountability"*), dessas autoridades face a organismos eleitos, à ***legitimidade democrática*** destes últimos organismos.[21] *Ora, essa legitimidade processual, se já se mostra complicada de justificar e balizar em Estados unitários ou em Estados que representam estruturas federais consolidadas, como sucede com os Estados Unidos, é exponencialmente muito mais complicada no plano comunitário face aos necessários equilíbrios e balanços institucionais da UE, implicando a resolução de problemas que estão associados a a sucessivas delegações ou transferências de poderes para organismos não previstos nos Tratados.*

O complexo quadro institucional da UE agrava, pois, a natureza do problema da *legitimidade democrática* das autoridades reguladores independentes (ou autónomas) – só parcialmente resolvido através da chamada *legitimidade processual* nos Estados unitários ou com estruturas federais consolidadas, mostrando-se essa solução – em si mesma precária – muito mais difícil de estabelecer no plano comunitário.

3.3. Num terceiro tópico relevante importa trazer à colação uma fundamental tendência evolutiva da mutação dos modernos modelos de regulação da economia. Na realidade, face à tendência para o desenvolvimento institucional de processos de regulação envolvendo interacções entre Estados e estruturas supranacionais – largamente consubstanciada no plano comunitário na criação de redes de reguladores nacionais sujeitos a poderes de coordenação (ou, pelo menos, de cooperação) a partir de

---

[21] Sobre as necessidades de escrutínio dessas autoridades reguladoras independentes (ou com grau reforçado de autonomia, na designação que preferimos) cfr., *inter alia*, M Thatcher, "Delegation to Independent Regulatory Authorities: Pressures, Functions and Contextual Mediation", in West European Politics, 2002, pp. 125 ss.. e, do mesmo A., "Regulation after Delegation: Independent Regulatory Agencies in Europe", in Journal of European Public Policy, 2002, pp. 954 ss. e "The Third Force? Independent Regulatory Agencies and Elected Politicians in Europe", in Governance, 2005, pp. 347 ss..

um pólo comunitário – verifica-se ainda, noutra dimensão paralela, uma evolução para um patamar superior de complexidade dos modelos de regulação. Trata-se da criação de verdadeiras *'constelações'* variáveis de regulação, congregando de forma paradigmática dois planos:

(i) um plano que implica a interacção entre os Estados e estruturas supranacionais; no caso comunitário, a interacção entre o nível estadual e o nível comunitário;

(ii) um segundo plano, que envolve complementarmente a interacção entre uma esfera pública e uma esfera privada de intervenção reguladora na actividade económica – interacção que resulta de associações ou da *'parcerias'* com entidades privadas que são chamadas a colaborar no desenvolvimento da função reguladora.[22] Referimo-nos aqui a múltiplas entidades – compreendendo *inter alia* associações profissionais, organizações empresariais, grupos de peritos – que são convocadas para uma verdadeira parceria de regulação, contribuindo para criar estas *constelações complexas de regulação* em que os poderes se distribuem, por um lado, entre os Estados e o nível comunitário e, por outro lado, entre o sector público e o sector privado.

A este propósito, diversos autores referem a formação de um **Estado pós regulador** ("*post regulatory state*") –[23] expressão que consideramos,

---

[22] A propósito deste tipo de *'parcerias'* entre entidades públicas e privadas para o desenvolvimento de funções de regulação, gerando que alguns denominam como constelações complexas de regulação, cfr., inter alia, JULIA BLACK, "Decentring Regulation: The Role of Regulation and Self-Regulation in a Post-Regulatory World", in Current Legal Problems, 2001, pp. 103 ss.; YVES DEZALAY, *Between the State, Law and the Market: The Social and Professional Stakes in the Construction and Definition of a Regulatory Arena*, in WILLIAM W. BRATTON, JOSEPH MCCAHERY, SOL PICCIOTTO, COLIN SCOTT (Editors), *International Regulatory Competition and Coordination*, Oxford University Press, 1996.; PETER GRABOSKY, "Using Non-Governmental Resources to Foster Regulation Compliance", in Governance, 1995, pp. 527 ss..

[23] Sobre esta ideia de um "*post regulatory state*", que consideramos, contudo, ambígua quanto ao seu real alcance e sgnificado substantivo, cfr., *inter alia*, COLIN SCOTT, *Regulation in the Age of Governance: The Rise of the Post-Regulatory State*, National Europe Centre Paper N.º 100, June 2003, Australian National University. Autores como MICHAEL MORAN criticaram o conceito de "*regulatory state*" como excessivamente orientado para um papel central do Estado e de organismos públicos na regulação da economia, o que já não corresponderia à realidade mais recente, supostamente assente numa diluição

A *Função Reguladora e as Estruturas de Regulação na União Europeia*   337

contudo, ambígua e desprovida de alcance substantivo específico (como sucede frequentemente com este tipo de qualificações genéricas). Independentemente de qualificações gerais deste tipo de fenómenos complexos em curso – que serão sempre redutoras apesar de na aparência sugestivas – a questão substantiva de fundo que deve merecer reflexão sistemática traduz-se no seguinte: *Neste quadro de desenvolvimento de estruturas complexas de regulação envolvendo os dois níveis acima enunciados* [**3.3.**, **(i)** e **(ii)**], *cabe indagar a que nível se devem colocar os limites para a expansão de tais constelações complexas de regulação.*

Pela nossa parte, consideramos que um enquadramento global, coerente e necessariamente limitativo deste processo implicará em boa parte a concepção do papel dos agentes privados – apesar do carácter por vezes impressivo do seu envolvimento em impulsos de regulação da actividade económica – como um papel, no essencial, subordinado ou sujeito a poderes públicos de coordenação dos processos de regulação globalmente considerados. *Impõe-se, contudo, uma reflexão sistemática que possa identificar neste domínio sensível os necessários equilíbrios para as 'parcerias' de regulação entre entes públicos e privados* (movendo-nos aqui, tão só, o propósito de identificar esta questão e suscitar a sua discussão, que nos propomos retomar noutras sedes de análise[24]).

3.4. Finalmente, num quarto tópico – algo mais provocatório para os nossos interlocutores norte-americanos (no quadro da Conferência

---

das linhas divisórias entre a intervenção de entes públicos ou privados e numa visão *descentrada* da regulação muito menos tributária do exercício de poderes coercivos de origem pública. Cfr. A. cit., "Not Steering but Drowning: Policy Catastrophes and the Regulatory State", in Political Quarterly, 2001, pp. 414 ss. e "Review Article: Understanding the Regulatory State", in British Journal of Political Science, 2002, pp. 391 ss..

[24] Encontra-se em causa uma reflexão global sobre os novos modelos de regulação menos tributários de poderes coercivos públicos (poderes tradicionalmente associados à denominada '*command and control regulation*') e preferencialmente assentes em feixes de cooperação entre agentes públicos e privados (muitas vezes baseados em sistemas de compromissos negociados e estabelecidos com as entidades económicas reguladas). Trata-se de tema conceptualmente denso, que justifica uma análise ex professo, que nos propomos desenvolver autonomamente em trabalhos ulteriores. Para além de identificarmos aqui este problema essencial, move-nos aqui também o propósito de afirmar uma ideia de necessária limitação do papel dos agentes privados no quadro de modelos de regulação mais descentralizados, mas no âmbito dos quais fenómenos de cooperação devem ser articulados com poderes de coordenação (exercício de coordenação que é compatível com sistemas relativamente *descentrados* de regulação).

Internacional que origina a presente publicação) – justifica-se uma última e porventura algo inesperada nota comparativa entre o modelo de regulação económica norte-americano e o correspondente modelo comunitário.

Como já referimos, existe uma convicção generalizada sobre a influência essencial do modelo de regulação norte-americano, designadamente através da criação de autoridades reguladoras independentes (ou autónomas), em relação aos modelos de regulação desenvolvidos na Europa comunitária. Estes teriam assimilado elementos primaciais do modelo norte-americano de intervenção predominantemente indirecta na actividade económica produtiva.

Contudo, se essa ideia é em larga medida justificada, justifica-se contrapor, que existe, em contrapartida, uma forte originalidade da arquitectura institucional da regulação económica na UE. Assim, nos EUA – pelo menos num plano de poderes exercidos ao nível da federação – tende a existir uma regulação da economia mais institucionalmente concentrada (existe uma superior concentração institucional no exercício dos poderes de regulação). Ora, a Europa comunitária, pelo facto de ter 'vivido' em simultâneo os dois processos de modernização que vimos caracterizando – o desenvolvimento de uma integração supranacional crescente e um processo paralelo de transição para o Estado *regulador* ou para um modelo de estruturas híbridas – originou uma arquitectura institucional *sui generis* dos processos de regulação. Trata-se de uma **arquitectura institucional de regulação mais complexa com uma grande *fragmentação horizontal* e uma grande *fragmentação vertical*** (à luz do que fomos expondo supra, nos pontos anteriores sobre os seus vários níveis).

Todavia, em muitos casos, esta arquitectura de regulação mais complexa da Europa comunitária apresenta uma eficácia considerável que pode ser comparada, em termos para esta muito favoráveis, com a eficácia das estruturas de regulação nos EUA. Admitimos, mesmo, que essa superior eficácia comparada de tais estruturas de regulação comunitárias, possa resultar precisamente da *fragmentação horizontal e vertical* que as mesmas apresentam. Perguntar-se-á qual a razão desse aparente paradoxo?

Em nosso entender, tal resultará do facto de esses fenómenos de *fragmentação horizontal vertical* das estruturas de regulação tornarem muito mais difíceis os processos conhecidos – e precisamente teorizados por autores norte-americanos – como processos de *captura dos reguladores pelos interesses regulados.*[25] Esta captura dos reguladores pelos interesses regulados, que é um problema fundamental da regulação económica através de *autoridades reguladores independentes* (ou com *grau reforçado de autonomia*, na qualificação que consideramos preferível), poderá, na realidade, desenvolver-se com maior facilidade ou probabilidade em estruturas regulatórias federais mais concentradas, como tende a suceder nos EUA. Em contrapartida, esse fenómeno poderá não se desenvolver com a mesma intensidade nas estruturas muito fragmentadas de regulação da Europa comunitária.

Numa altura em que proliferam as tentações de criação de *agências reguladoras comunitárias* em domínios económicos fundamentais (como, *v.g.*, a energia ou as comunicações electrónicas), com poderes reforçados de *coordenação* ou até – em certas áreas delimitadas – poderes de *direcção* da esfera de actuação de autoridades reguladoras nacionais dos Estados-Membros, *justificar-se-á aprofundare esgotar todas as virtualidades do modelo de regulação progressivamente desenvolvido na UE, assente em níveis vários de estruturas complexas de regulação.*[26]

Essa superior complexidade e aparente fragmentação podem, como observámos, funcionar com eficácia e melhores garantias de defesa dos interesses públicos, representando também o produto paradigmático do cruzamento dos processos de regulação da economia com os processos de

---

[25] Não havendo aqui espaço (*brevitatis causae*) para referências directas e desenvolvidas sobre esta matéria, cfr. por todos, para uma referência extensa à doutrina norte-americana, designadamente a autores ligados à Escola de Chicago, como STIGLER, PELTZMAN ou BECKER, que referem um risco especialmente elevado de *captura das autoridades reguladoras pelos produtores* – sendo esse risco em contrapartida menor no que respeita aos consumidores – M. THATCHER, "Regulation after Delegation: Independent Regulatory Agencies in Europe", in Journal of European Public Policy, 2002, pp. 954 ss..

[26] Elementos positivos de reflexão neste domínio, num sentido de afastar modelos de excessiva uniformização pareciam encontrar-se em documentos de análise recentes da Comissão, como a Comunicação *"Action Plan – Simplifying and Improving the Regulatory Environment"* [Brussels, 5.6.2002 – COM(2002) 278 final] ou na Comunicação *"The operating framework for the European Regulatory Agencies"* [Brussels, 11.12.2002 COM(2002) 718 final]. Seria importante o aprofundamento dessa reflexão, na senda dessas comunicações, sem opções porventura precipitadas por modelos de rápida expansão de agências reguladoras europeias em detrimento dos modelos de funcionamento em rede, congregando autoridades reguladoras nacionais, que se possam coadunar com o exercício de certos núcleos de poderes de coordenação a partir do plano comunitário.

desenvolvimento de arquitecturas institucionais complexas e originais no quadro da integração europeia.

É também matéria a que nos propomos regressar num espaço de análise teórica mais alargado, deixando aqui apenas esse '*leitmotif*' de reflexão, que convoca a diversidade e o carácter *sui generis* e criativo dos processos de construção jurídica e institucional na UE, em detrimento dos modelos tendentes a maior uniformização. Afigura-se-nos ser esta, de resto, uma nota apropriada para encerrar esta nossa contribuição na Conferência Internacional na origem da presente publicação, através da qual se procurou ensaiar um balanço crítico global do estado da integração europeia e, em larga medida, uma comparação sistemática com o modelo historicamente distinto de integração norte-americano.

A UNIÃO EUROPEIA NAS NEGOCIAÇÕES COMERCIAIS INTERNACIONAIS

TERESA MOREIRA[*]

Começo por dirigir um breve mas muito sincero agradecimento ao Professor Doutor Paulo de Pitta e Cunha e ao Professor Doutor Luís Morais, na qualidade de organizadores desta conferência, pelo facto de me terem dado a oportunidade de intervir num evento deste relevo. É para mim um privilégio participar numa conferência com tão ilustres oradores e, mais concretamente, num painel com as personalidades que me rodeiam.

Vou abordar um tema que é muito amplo e que poderá parecer demasiado genérico, em contraposição com as intervenções que se vão seguir à minha: está em causa a participação da União Europeia (designação utilizada apenas por maior facilidade de discurso, dado que, em rigor, é da Comunidade Europeia e dos Estados-Membros da União que se trata) nas negociações comerciais internacionais, isto é, no quadro da Organização Mundial do Comércio (OMC).

Recordo sumariamente que, na base desta participação, está algo que é único, que é o facto da Comunidade Europeia ou das Comunidades Europeias, na época (isto é, em 1994, aquando da assinatura dos Acordos

---

[*] Nota prévia: Esta intervenção seguiu, de certa forma, o sentido do texto intitulado "A União Europeia e a Organização Mundial do Comércio" da presente autora, publicado na Revista de Estudos Europeus, Ano I – N.º 1, Almedina, Coimbra, 2007, não obstante a actualização relativa aos desenvolvimentos do Tratado que estabelece uma Constituição para a Europa, do Tratado de Lisboa e ainda a referência a alguns contributos académicos sobre o futuro do sistema multilateral.

[*] Mestre em Direito, Instituto Europeu da Faculdade de Direito de Lisboa.

de Marraquexe que concluíram as negociações do ciclo do Uruguai e criaram a Organização Mundial do Comércio) serem membros fundadores da OMC, a par dos Estados-Membros da União, sendo a OMC a organização multilateral de âmbito económico mais recente, encontrando-se em funções desde o início de 1995.

Neste domínio, deparamo-nos, pois, perante uma situação pouco habitual: tanto a Comunidade Europeia como os seus Estados-Membros são membros de pleno direito da OMC, sendo, contudo, supostos manifestar-se a uma só voz, uma vez que o número de votos atribuídos à Comunidade mais aos seus Estados-Membros[1] (que eu vou passar a designar por União Europeia para simplificar) é o número de votos correspondente apenas ao número global de votos atribuídos aos Estados--Membros[2]. Resulta destas regras o pressuposto de que a União Europeia vai actuar em bloco no quadro da OMC, o que tem presente o facto de a participação da União Europeia na OMC resultar da primeira verdadeira e única política comum da Comunidade Europeia, que é a política comercial comum.

Este processo iniciou-se com a construção do mercado interno (então designado mercado comum), tendo-se começado pela instituição de uma união aduaneira, dotada de uma pauta aduaneira comum e à qual foi associada uma política comercial comum. Esta primeira etapa da integração económica europeia implicou a transferência das competências dos Estados-Membros nessa esfera para a Comunidade Europeia, desde então impedidos de actuar autonomamente naquela matéria.

Recorde-se, no entanto, que os parâmetros da política comercial comum e, em consequência, os termos que definem a participação da União Europeia no plano comercial multilateral, são estabelecidos através de um sistema de *checks and balances* que envolve a Comissão Europeia, o Conselho e, de forma crescente, o Parlamento Europeu[3]: assim, a Comissão

---

[1] O artigo XI, n.º 1 do Acordo que institui a Organização Mundial do Comércio reconhece as Comunidades Europeias como "membros originais da OMC". Segundo o disposto no artigo IX, n.º 1, segundo período do mesmo Acordo, a cada membro da OMC é atribuído um voto, seguindo, aliás, o estabelecido na vigência do Acordo Geral sobre Pautas Aduaneiras e o Comércio (Acordo *GATT*), de 1947 (artigo XXV, n.º 3), que consubstanciou o sistema comercial multilateral durante quase 50 anos,

[2] Artigo XI, n.º 1, terceiro período do Acordo que institui a Organização Mundial do Comércio

[3] Veja-se o disposto no artigo 133.º, n.os 2 a 4 do Tratado que institui a Comunidade Europeia, quando confrontado com o previsto no artigo 300.º, n.os 1 a 3 relativo à celebração

A *União Europeia nas Negociações Comerciais Internacionais*   343

Europeia é a negociadora por excelência no plano comercial externo, sendo certo que actua na base de um mandato que lhe é conferido pelo Conselho por maioria qualificada, pelo menos em termos formais.

Na prática, os mandatos para efeitos das negociações comerciais multilaterais têm sempre sido estabelecidos por consenso, a que não é alheio o facto de algumas das matérias em discussão não terem sido (ainda) transferidas para a Comunidade, permanecendo, assim, na esfera de competências dos Estados-Membros.[4] Neste quadro, a definição consensual da posição da Comunidade Europeia e dos seus Estados-Membros reforça, sem dúvida, a sua coesão e a sua consistência. Mas não há dúvida que esta é, de facto, uma primeira característica duma verdadeira política comum, o facto de o Tratado que institui a Comunidade Europeia prever que o Conselho delibera nesta matéria por maioria qualificada.

Desde 1958, a política comercial comum foi sempre considerada como tendo uma natureza evolutiva. Tal resultou consideravelmente da postura assumida pela Comissão neste domínio, a qual, plenamente consciente, como se esperaria, do seu papel de guardiã dos tratados e por força do seu interesse activo numa matéria objecto de uma política *comum*, foi, de alguma forma, forçando, no sentido positivo do termo, a expansão das competências comunitárias no domínio comercial.

Nesta perspectiva, a Comissão foi muito apoiada pelo Tribunal de Justiça, sobretudo até meados dos anos 80, que subscreveu, de forma constante, a visão evolutiva da política comercial comum, com base no princípio das competências implícitas da Comunidade Europeia, do princípio do paralelismo de competências e tendo presente a própria realização do mercado interno.

Curiosamente, é quando a OMC é instituída pelos Acordos de Marraquexe de 1994, depois de ter sido criada uma União Europeia pelo Tratado de Maastricht[5], que o Tribunal de Justiça é chamado a pronunciar-se sobre a repartição de competências entre a Comunidade e os Estados-Membros, justamente porque a OMC, e o sistema comercial multilateral

---

de acordos externos com Estados terceiros ou organizações internacionais, no que toca às competências do Parlamento Europeu.

[4] Apesar do âmbito evolutivo da política comercial comum, é esse hoje o caso do investimento directo do exterior, tal como no passado foi o caso dos serviços e da propriedade intelectual, ainda que não na íntegra.

[5] Artigo 1.º do Tratado da União Europeia.

344   *Teresa Moreira*

passaria daí a abranger, para além das mercadorias (produtos agrícolas e produtos não agrícolas), também o comércio de serviços e os aspectos comerciais da propriedade intelectual, para além de um pequeno conjunto de outras matérias relacionadas com o comércio. E porque a política comercial comum, estabelecida no início do processo de construção europeia, tinha sido concebida e delimitada numa época em que o comércio de mercadorias é que constituía o grosso do comércio internacional.

Nesta sequência, com o parecer n.º 1/94, emitido a solicitação da Comissão[6], o Tribunal de Justiça veio pronunciar-se sobre o âmbito da política comercial comum, tendo como pano de fundo a nova dimensão do sistema comercial multilateral, logo, em face de desenvolvimentos relevantes e muito recentes. Com este parecer, o Tribunal defraudou um pouco as expectativas da Comissão Europeia ao considerar que, em matéria de política comercial comum, só alguns dos aspectos das novas matérias – comércio de serviços e aspectos comerciais da propriedade intelectual – só umas franjas muito específicas é que faziam parte da competência exclusiva comunitária, concluindo, em relação às restantes, que eram objecto de competências partilhadas entre a Comunidade Europeia e os Estados-Membros.

Ao contrário do que se poderia esperar, perante o alargamento do próprio sistema comercial multilateral, o Tribunal não quis reconhecer a expansão da política comercial comum em detrimento das competências dos Estados-Membros e, igualmente, não pareceu ter extraído ilações da qualidade de membro da OMC assumida *ex novo* pelas Comunidades Europeias nem tão pouco da nova dimensão do sistema multilateral de comércio.

Ora, será evidente que, se a Comunidade e os Estados-Membros participam ambos como membros de pleno direito no OMC, mas se nem todas as competências no domínio comercial (entenda-se, abrangidas pelos acordos da OMC) foram transferidas para a Comunidade Europeia, é indispensável e inevitável uma articulação entre todas as partes e uma ponderação de interesses, nem sempre coincidentes, que tem corrido razoavelmente bem, mas que não é objecto de enquadramento formal.

---

[6] Parecer do Tribunal de Justiça de 15 de Novembro de 1994 sobre a competência da Comunidade para concluir acordos internacionais em matéria de serviços e de protecção da propriedade intelectual, publicado na Colectânea de Jurisprudência 1994, página I-0526.

A *União Europeia nas Negociações Comerciais Internacionais* 345

Posteriormente, o Tratado de Nice introduziu uma alteração nas normas relativas à política comercial comum[7], procedendo ao alargamento das competências comunitárias exclusivas nesta sede e o Tratado que estabelece uma Constituição para a Europa, no domínio da política comercial, vinha sistematizar adequadamente esta matéria, afirmando finalmente, de forma clara e transparente, as competências da União Europeia no domínio da política comercial[8], aliás, enquadrando esta matéria no domínio mais amplo da acção externa da União, agora orientada por um conjunto coerente de princípios e objectivos.[9]

O Tratado Constitucional, hoje ultrapassado, contribuiu para reiterar a natureza comunitária da política comercial comum, e alargava claramente o seu campo de aplicação já não só a alguns domínios dos serviços que antes tinham sido objecto de reservas por parte dos Estados-Membros, mas também a uma matéria fundamental no plano do relacionamento económico externo que é o investimento directo do exterior.

Ao mesmo tempo, pela primeira vez, o Tratado Constitucional associara formalmente o Parlamento Europeu ao domínio da política comercial. Parlamento Europeu esse que, dentro das principais instituições comunitárias, era como que o grande ausente nesta matéria, o que, ademais, contrastava manifestamente com o papel crescente que lhe tem vindo a

---

[7] Veja-se o aditamento dos números 5 a 7 do artigo 133.º. O Tratado de Amesterdão viera unicamente a acrescentar um novo número 5, entretanto revogado, a esta norma, que apenas estabelecia a possibilidade de "comunitarização" do comércio de serviços e dos aspectos comerciais da propriedade intelectual mediante uma deliberação por unanimidade do Conselho, o que representava uma excepção única à regra geral prevista para as deliberações do Conselho neste domínio, a maioria qualificada (n.º 4 do artigo 133.º). Com esta alteração, alguma doutrina questionara a justificação de se abrir, desta forma, a porta a uma possível revisão do Tratado CE à revelia do procedimento próprio legalmente estabelecido para tal.

[8] Depois de inserir a política comercial comum no campo das competências exclusivas da União Europeia, no artigo I-13.º, n.º 1, alínea e), esta matéria era apenas objecto de duas disposições, os artigos III-314.º e III-315.º, mas tendo o último dispositivo sido revisto e sistematizado, de forma a clarificar a extensão do âmbito da política comercial comum, não obstante exigisse a deliberação do Conselho por unanimidade, a título excepcional nesta sede, em áreas sensíveis para os Estados-Membros no quadro dos serviços (artigo III-315.º, n.º 4, alíneas a e b).

[9] O artigo III-292.º, encabeçando as disposições de aplicação geral da acção externa da União, era especialmente elucidativo, desenvolvendo o disposto no artigo I-3.º, n.º 4, relativo aos objectivos da União, cuja redacção se iniciava com "Nas suas relações com o resto do mundo, a União afirma e promove os seus valores e interesses".

ser reconhecido no processo decisório comunitário, desde o início da construção europeia, a ponto de deter um poder equivalente ao do Conselho num conjunto de matérias relevantes.

O recente Tratado de Lisboa, assinado em 13 de Dezembro de 2007, retomou o essencial das disposições relativas à política comercial comum previstas no Tratado Constitucional, mantendo igualmente o destaque atribuído ao Parlamento Europeu nesta sede, não obstante a negociação e a decisão de acordos comerciais permanecer cometida à Comissão e ao Conselho.[10]

Com a entrada em vigor do Tratado de Lisboa e, no futuro, a tendência será sempre no sentido de uma política comercial comum mais abrangente, reflectindo o aprofundamento do processo de integração europeia, por um lado, e, por outro, os desenvolvimentos expectáveis do âmbito do sistema comercial multilateral.

Porque é que esta matéria é tão importante? Segundo dados da própria OMC relativos a 2006/2007[11], a União Europeia é o primeiro

---

[10] Artigo 188.º-C, n.ᵒˢ 1 e 4 quanto às matérias abrangidas na política comercial comum e à excepcional deliberação por unanimidade prevista para casos em que se verifique o paralelismo das regras de votação para a adopção das normas internas (n.º 4, segundo parágrafo – corpo) e quando estejam em causa os serviços culturais e audiovisuais, os serviços sociais, educativos e de saúde (n.º 4, segundo parágrafo – alíneas *a* e *b*). O n.º 6 deste dispositivo vem, por sua vez, proceder a uma reafirmação dos limites das competências comunitárias, afastando a possibilidade de "comunitarização" implícita por via do eventual exercício de competências previsto neste dispositivo. Os n.ᵒˢ 2 e 3 deste artigo, terceiro parágrafo referem-se, expressamente, ao papel do Parlamento Europeu neste domínio.

[11] Fonte: *Trade Profiles 2007* da Organização Mundial do Comércio, e o 8.º *Trade Policy Review* das Comunidades Europeias realizado pelo Orgão de Revisão da Política Comercial da OMC no final de Fevereiro de 2007, ambos disponíveis em www.wto.org. De acordo com os dados avançados no Relatório do Secretariado da OMC relativo ao Exame da Política Comercial das Comunidades Europeias, a CE (25 Estados-Membros) detinha, em 2004, 18% do comércio mundial de mercadorias, sendo igualmente o líder do comércio mundial de serviços com 27,8% das exportações globais de serviços e 24,5% das importações globais de serviços. Era ainda o maior destino e o principal fornecedor de investimento directo do exterior, representando, em 2004, 45,2% do *stock global* "inward" e 53,3% do *stock* global "outward". Os elementos informativos que constam do *Trade Profiles* 2007 relativos à União Europeia atribuem-lhe, em 2006, o primeiro lugar no comércio de mercadorias (excluindo intra-UE), com 16,4% no total das exportações mundiais e 18,14% no total das importações mundiais e também nos serviços comerciais (excluindo intra-UE), detendo 27,3% das exportações mundiais e 24,3% das importações mundiais. É ainda o principal doador de ajuda pública ao desenvolvimento.

exportador mundial de mercadorias, o segundo importador mundial de mercadorias, o líder do comércio internacional de serviços e o maior anfitrião e fornecedor de investimento directo estrangeiro, sendo um investidor líquido no exterior.

Em face destes elementos, sem prejuízo de a União Europeia assumir, inevitavelmente, um papel importante em várias vertentes no plano internacional, designadamente no domínio da defesa e segurança externas[12], verifica-se que o contributo da política comercial comum e do relacionamento económico externo para a afirmação da União Europeia no mundo é frequentemente ignorado ou indevidamente valorizado. E esta constatação é imerecida e até injusta porque, nestas matérias, a União Europeia há muito ultrapassou a lógica mercantilista que terá presidido ao Tratado CE, uma vez que, por força dos valores e dos princípios gerais perfilhados pela União Europeia, as relações económicas externas da União Europeia têm prosseguido valores caros à UE tais como a liberdade, a democracia, o Estado de Direito, os direitos do Homem, o desenvolvimento sustentável e têm integrado incentivos adicionais para o cumprimento dos princípios internacionais relativos aos direitos fundamentais do trabalho, à defesa do ambiente, à boa governação[13]. Neste domínio, a força integradora do projecto europeu, do ponto de vista económico, e o potencial que ele tem no domínio das relações externas e, sobretudo, na própria afirmação da União Europeia no mundo como um grande actor internacional tem sido negligenciado, o que se afigura

---

[12] Matérias que, contudo, mais não dispõem do que uma cooperação reforçada no quadro da União, conforme os artigos 11.º a 28.º do Tratado da União Europeia.

[13] De acordo com informação disponibilizada pela Direcção-Geral do Comércio da Comissão Europeia (www.ec.europa.eu/trade), a 1 de Abril de 2007 a Comunidade Europeia tinha concluído 23 acordos comerciais regionais (preferenciais), que se encontram em vigor, que incluem 3 uniões aduaneiras (com a Turquia, Andorra e San Marino), 5 acordos de comércio livre com países europeus (entre os quais a Suiça, a Macedónia, a Croácia e a Albânia), 9 acordos de associação com os países mediterrânicos, os acordos de associação, parceria económica, cooperação e desenvolvimento com o Chile, o México, a África do Sul, o Acordo do Espaço Económico Europeu (com a Islândia, Liechtenstein e Noruega) e o Acordo de Cotonou celebrado com os 77 países ACP (África, Caraíbas e Pacífico), que serve de quadro para a conclusão de acordos de parceria económica individuais, visando a criação de zonas de comércio livre. A estes acordos terá de se juntar o Sistema de Preferências Generalizadas da CE, cujos destinatários são países em desenvolvimento fora dos parceiros do relacionamento comercial preferencial referido, e iniciativas dispersas dirigidas aos países menos avançados.

lamentável perante o significado desta realização, no plano interno da União e a título de exemplo no plano externo.

Neste momento está em curso o primeiro ciclo de negociações comerciais lançado pela Organização Mundial do Comércio cujo programa de trabalhos se intitula "A Agenda de Desenvolvimento de Doha"[14]. Muito se tem falado destas negociações, cuja agenda foi aprovada em Novembro de 2001, e que, falhado o prazo inicial de 2005, por diversas vezes, se esperou pudessem ter sido entretanto concluídas. Tal não foi ainda possível por um conjunto de razões que, desde logo, incluem, pela primeira vez, a extensão da agenda negocial – cobrindo o acesso aos mercados dos produtos não agrícolas, a agricultura, o comércio de serviços, a revisão de regras existentes (instrumentos de defesa comercial, por exemplo) e ainda novas matérias, tais como a relação entre comércio e ambiente –, e o elevado número de participantes – os actuais 151 membros da OMC, três quartos dos quais são países em desenvolvimento, onde se têm vindo a destacar algumas economias emergentes como o Brasil, a Índia, a China, que hoje são dos principais protagonistas das relações económicas internacionais –, ofuscando a União Europeia, os EUA, o Japão, o Canadá e, inevitavelmente, estando na origem de diferentes alianças e a coligações de interesses que variam com as matérias tratadas e não facilitam a obtenção do consenso necessário à conclusão das negociações.

Justificar-se-à tanta expectativa em relação a este ciclo negocial? Como explicar as críticas e os comentários acesos relativamente ao percurso da Agenda de Desenvolvimento de Doha desde 2002?

É inquestionável que, a par da análise dos temas da agenda, das posições dos membros da OMC e dos progressos ou do impasse dos

---

[14] A Decisão Ministerial de Doha, que aprovou o programa do ciclo negocial designado como a "Agenda de Desenvolvimento de Doha" em 14 de Novembro de 2001, (documento WT/MIN(01)/DEC/1), está disponível no sítio da OMC na internet em www.wto.org/english/thewto e/minist e/min01 e/mindecl e.htm, devendo ser vista à luz das revisões que lhe foram introduzidas pela 5.ª Conferência Ministerial de Cancún em 2003, pela decisão adoptada na reunião do Conselho Geral da OMC de Julho de 2004 ("pacote de Julho" 2004) e pela 6.ª Conferência Ministerial de Hong Kong, em Dezembro de 2005. As negociações, suspensas no final de Julho de 2006 pelo Conselho Geral da OMC em face dos impasses registados, foram retomadas no início de 2007, tendo conhecidos progressos em diferentes áreas desde Julho de 2007 (visíveis na circulação e discussão de novos textos negociais, segundo as notícias do sítio *web* da OMC – www.wto.org), que apontam para uma possível conclusão positiva do ciclo em 2008.

A União Europeia nas Negociações Comerciais Internacionais   349

trabalhos, se deverá, paralelamente, reflectir sobre a actualidade do enquadramento do sistema multilateral perante as necessidades e desafios hoje enfrentados e encarar seriamente a possibilidade de revisão, se justificada.

As críticas ao funcionamento da OMC, assumindo especial destaque quando da realização da 3.ª Conferência Ministerial, realizada em Seattle, nos EUA, no final de 1999, conduziriam ao reconhecimento pela própria organização da necessidade de melhorar a transparência no plano interno, assegurando uma participação mais efectiva de todos os membros nos trabalhos, e ainda a transparência no plano externo, propiciando um maior acesso da sociedade civil aos documentos e também à actividade corrente desenvolvida pela OMC.

Em Dezembro de 2004, foi publicado o relatório do Conselho Consultivo do então Director-Geral da OMC, Supachai Panitchpadki, presidido por Peter Sutherland e composto por sete especialistas em comércio internacional sobre o futuro da OMC[15], que se debruçou sobre diferentes temas[16], antes de formular algumas recomendações com vista a melhorar a organização, relativas aos assuntos de fundo considerados, tais como o controlo acrescido dos acordos comerciais preferenciais pela OMC, a reconsideração de abordagens plurilaterais nas negociações comerciais ou a possibilidade de as compensações atribuídas no quadro da resolução de litígios assumirem forma monetária, mas também a aspectos organizativos, respeitantes ao mandato do Director-Geral e ao papel do Secretariado, ao diálogo com a sociedade civil e à revisão de alguns procedimentos da resolução de litígios.

Mas a pressão do termo das negociações da Agenda de Desenvolvimento de Doha até à 6.ª Conferência Ministerial de Hong Kong, em Dezembro de 2005, não permitiu ainda uma verdadeira discussão entre os membros sobre a extensão e os contornos de uma eventual reforma da OMC, ainda que iniciativas anualmente promovidas por esta organização,

---

[15] "The Future of the WTO – Addressing institutional challenges in the new millennium", disponível em www.wto.org.

[16] A globalização e a OMC; A erosão da não discriminação; Soberania; Coerência e coordenação com organizações intergovernamentais; Transparência e diálogo com a sociedade civil; O sistema de resolução de litígios da OMC; Uma instituição *results-oriented*: processo decisório e geometria variável; Uma instituição *results-oriented*: reforço político e processo eficiente; O papel do Director-Geral e Secretariado (tradução nossa).

intituladas "WTO Public Symposium/Forum", que juntam especialistas académicos, representantes de empresas e de associações empresariais, organizações não governamentais e elementos dos *media* tenham, desde 2005, comentado as conclusões do relatório supra citado, designado como *relatório Sutherland*.[17].

Este relatório, mais não pretendendo do que contribuir, de forma construtiva e em termos não exaustivos, para a reflexão em curso, fica talvez algo aquém do que seria esperado de um texto relativo ao futuro da OMC, na medida em que não propõe medidas radicais nem modificações inesperadas, até defendendo a manutenção de aspectos habitualmente criticados, como seja a regra de deliberação por consenso (positivo)[18], por permitir preservar o equilíbrio desde cedo consagrado entre os membros desta organização, tipicamente Estados-Nação.

Assim, poder-se-à concluir que não só é urgente a conclusão das negociações do ciclo de Doha com vista a incentivar o comércio mundial, numa época marcada pelo espectro da recessão económica de alguns países desenvolvidos, como rever as pedras basilares do sistema multilateral, começando desde logo pelos objectivos prosseguidos pela OMC e pelo papel que lhe caberá desempenhar hoje.

Também neste ponto julgo que a União Europeia pode desempenhar um papel fundamental.

A OMC, sendo recente – tem treze anos de funcionamento – é herdeira do Acordo *GATT*, de 1947, muito inspirado pela filosofia neo-liberal que presidiu à ordem internacional económica instituída na sequência da II.ª Guerra Mundial. A questão que neste momento se deve colocar é se, no século XXI, poderá ainda o quadro regulador das relações económicas internacionais ser adequadamente assegurado por organizações que reflictam uma inspiração algo datada, sobretudo, quando há hoje tantos novos intervenientes e actores activos nas relações económicas internacionais, concretamente no campo do comércio internacional.

---

[17] Veja-se em www.wto.org. a documentação relativa ao *WTO Public Symposium* de 2005 – "WTO After 10 Years: Global Problems and Multilateral Solutions", ao *WTO Public Forum* de 2006 – "What WTO for the first XXIst century?" e ao *WTO Public Forum* de 2007 – "How can the WTO help harness globalization?".

[18] Muito enraizada numa organização de natureza intergovernamental, cuja iniciativa tem sido, desde sempre, ditada pela vontade dos membros, apesar de o consenso positivo facilitar a adopção de deliberações e de o relatório Sutherland sustentar a exclusão de alguns temas, processuais, destas regras.

A *União Europeia nas Negociações Comerciais Internacionais* 351

As reacções suscitadas pelo Tratado que estabelece uma Constituição para a Europa, a subsequente tentativa de acordar um "Tratado simplificado" e os trabalhos que culminaram no Tratado de Lisboa obrigam-nos a reflectir sobre o futuro da União Europeia, sobre o sentido do projecto europeu e, claro, sobre os valores e os princípios que deve prosseguir e disseminar. Estas questões repercutem-se, inevitavelmente, na responsabilidade que a União Europeia tem no contexto internacional, designadamente no plano externo, e, em termos mais precisos, no domínio do relacionamento económico externo.

E neste âmbito, tem a União Europeia vindo a adoptar medidas muito oportunas, desde 2006, com o reconhecimento pela Comissão Europeia, com o apoio do Conselho, do papel do comércio na estratégia de prossecução de uma maior competitividade europeia, a Estratégia de Lisboa renovada, que, como sabem, é o referencial das reformas económicas, sociais e ambientais da União Europeia, que visa transformá-la numa economia baseada no conhecimento e no espaço mais competitivo até 2010. Nesta iniciativa foi acentuada a importância de a União Europeia assumir grande activismo no exterior, atribuindo grande prioridade do multilateralismo e à OMC, com a implícita rejeição de princípio do proteccionismo interno[19]. Apesar das posições de conteúdo diferente, pontualmente defendidas por alguns Governos dos Estados-Membros perante uma conjuntura económica adversa e receando uma recessão económica mundial, esta postura de princípio da UE tem sido constante ao longo do tempo, obrigando-a a actuar em conformidade.

Assim, mesmo depois de passos muito positivos no sentido da assunção dessa responsabilidade, a União Europeia não se pode apenas contentar com uma conclusão positiva da Agenda de Desenvolvimento de Doha, que tem vindo a registar progressos negociais mesmo em temas sensíveis como a agricultura mas cujo desfecho não depende unicamente da UE, como será óbvio: espera-se, pois, da União um papel bastante mais activo na reforma e na revisão da OMC, à medida da sua responsabilidade e à luz da sua dimensão política e económica no mundo, contribuindo para uma verdadeira transformação do quadro regulador das

---

[19] Veja-se a Comunicação da Comissão ao Conselho, ao Parlamento Europeu, ao Comité Económico e Social e ao Comité das Regiões, de 4 de Outubro de 2006 (COM (2006)567 final), intitulada "Europa Global: Competindo no Mundo – uma contribuição para a Estratégia de Crescimento e Emprego da União Europeia".

relações económicas internacionais, cada vez mais necessário neste contexto de globalização crescente.

Foi a própria União Europeia que estabeleceu um nível elevado de ambição no domínio externo, elegendo um conjunto de princípios que correspondem a valores políticos muito mais importantes do que meras escolhas comerciais, mas como tal foi a União que colocou a si própria uma exigência considerável. Espera-se, agora, que actue de forma a poder atingir essa ambição, podendo conseguir que o seu papel no mundo seja devidamente reconhecido, pela via do relacionamento económico externo, cuja relevância assim sobressairia.

Citando, de cor, o Professor Loukas Tsoukalis, que referiu que a União tinha uma obrigação de defesa de bens públicos globais, como a energia e o ambiente, e que deveria ter uma aspiração ou a obrigação de influenciar e modelar a globalização através de uma acção colectiva, permitia-me dizer que é tempo de uma actuação consistente com este nível de ambição. Só faço votos é que a próxima presidência da União Europeia, a Presidência Portuguesa, possa contribuir para a sua realização.

Muito obrigada.

Nota final: No início de 2008, continuando a decorrer as negociações comerciais da Agenda de Doha no sentido da sua possível conclusão ainda este ano, subsistem as interrogações sobre o futuro do sistema multilateral do comércio, as quais continuam a merecer a atenção de centros de reflexão académicos, de "think tanks" vários e de organizações não governamentais activas em temas como o comércio e o desenvolvimento, como decorre da diversidade dos participantes nos *fora* anuais da OMC.

Entre outras contribuições, merece destaque o recente relatório da primeira *Warwick Commission*, intitulado "The Multilateral Trade Regime: which way forward?", publicado pela Universidade de Warwick em Dezembro de 2007[20]. Presidida por Pierre Pettigrew, ex-Ministro do Comércio do Canadá, o trabalho da Comissão beneficiou do concurso de diversos académicos e especialistas nestas matérias, abordando cinco desafios que se colocam hoje ao sistema multilateral: a ascensão e a queda do apoio

---

[20] Disponível em www2.warwick.ac.uk/research/warwickcommission, *website* da Comissão *Warwick*.

A *União Europeia nas Negociações Comerciais Internacionais*   353

à abertura (dos mercados); a gestão da governação económica global multipolar; a definição dos contestados limites da OMC; a OMC trabalhando para todos os seus membros – questões de justiça e equidade e desenvolvimento; a multilateralização dos acordos comerciais preferenciais.[21]

Este documento, a par de outros contributos, oferece uma análise crítica mas construtiva e soluções objectivas, isentas de interesses nacionais ou sectoriais, sob a forma de recomendações[22] (tal como o relatório Sutherland) para a questão em aberto – qual o papel da Organização Mundial do Comércio e qual o sentido do sistema comercial multilateral?[23]

---

[21] (tradução nossa).

[22] Começara por identificar 5 desafios a enfrentar para que o sistema multilateral tenha sucesso no início do século XXI – a crescente oposição a uma liberalização comercial acrescida nos países industrializados; a emergência de uma alternativa multipolar ao tradicional regime bipolar assente nos EUA e na Europa Ocidental; a necessidade de um (novo) acordo abrangente sobre os objectivos e funções da OMC, que permita a redefinição dos seus limites; o enfoque na relação entre regras comerciais, equidade, justiça e desenvolvimento, para que o sistema da OMC beneficie os seus membros mais fracos; o aproveitamento possível da proliferação dos acordos comerciais preferenciais para o progresso dos princípios da não discriminação e transparência do comércio internacional.

[23] A primeira recomendação refere-se a "afirmações em vez de recomendações", relativa à responsabilidade colectiva dos membros de apoiar a OMC e de explicar os benefícios do sistema multilateral à sociedade civil, associando-os a esta causa, sem descurar os interesses dos membros mais pequenos e mais fracos da organização. A segunda respeita a uma maior flexibilidade das regras de funcionamento da OMC, no que toca à escolha da agenda negocial, sugerindo que seja explorada a abordagem plurilateral, que se melhore a transparência e a eficácia da resolução de litígios, atendendo em especial à posição dos países menos avançados (sugerindo a criação de um provedor nesta sede e a possibilidade destes países receberem compensações monetárias). A terceira dirige-se à matéria do Tratamento Especial e Diferenciado, defendendo a sua revisão para melhor adequação às necessidades do desenvolvimento, e apoiando as iniciativas de assistência técnica e de capacitação institucional (por exemplo, quanto à facilitação do comércio, o único "tema de Singapura" ainda na agenda negocial), sobretudo a da Ajuda ao Comércio ("Aid for Trade"), apelando às responsabilidades dos membros doadores e destinatários, *a latere* das negociações. Quanto aos acordos comerciais preferenciais, a quinta recomendação aponta para a clarificação e o melhoramento das regras e procedimentos da OMC nesta matéria, sugerindo que os países industrializados renunciem a concluir acordos deste tipo entre si, aplaudindo o recente Mecanismo de Transparência instituído e o reforço da fiscalização colectiva nesta área, com o estabelecimento de um código de boas práticas. A última recomendação refere-se ao lançamento de um processo

Não contendo recomendações totalmente inovadoras, como será difícil esperar de qualquer contributo com este objecto, tal como se apontou ao relatório Sutherland, esta reflexão toca muitos aspectos que dependem apenas da iniciativa dos membros da OMC e da sua mobilização, ainda que possam muito beneficiar da adesão e do empenho de elementos chave da estrutura desta organização, como é o caso do Director-Geral.

A par do renovado compromisso e do esforço constante no progresso das negociações comerciais, não será já tempo de os membros da Organização Mundial do Comércio, em especial aqueles que podem e devem ser os catalisadores das reformas, tal como a União Europeia, se debruçarem concretamente sobre as questões pendentes e de começarem a construir o futuro?

Alguma bibliografia

Quanto à participação da Comunidade Europeia e dos Estados-Membros da União Europeia na Organização Mundial do Comércio:

– Gstöhl, Sieglinde – "Political Dimensions of an Externalization of the EU's Internal Market", *EU Diplomacy Papers, 3/2007, EU International Relations and Diplomacy Studies, College of Europe, Bruges, Belgium*;

– Hoffmeister, Frank – "Outsider or Frontrunner? Recent Developments under International and European Law on the Status of the European Union in International Organizations and Treaty Bodies" *in Common Market Law Review, volume 44, 2007*, págs. 41-68;

– Petite, Michel – "Current Legal Issues in the External Relations of the European Union", *EUI Working Papers, Law No. 2006/38, European University Institute, Department of Law, Badia Fiesolana, Italy*;

– Steinberger, Eva – "The WTO Treaty as a Mixed Agreement: Problems with the EC's and the EC Member States' Membership of the WTO" *in European Journal of International Law, Volume 17 (2006), No. 4*, págs. 837-874.

---

de reflexão na OMC, liderado pelo Presidente do Conselho Geral e/ou o Director-Geral, que analise os desafios e oportunidades que se colocam à OMC e delineie um plano de acção para os abordar.

Quanto ao Relatório sobre o Futuro da OMC e aos desafios do sistema multilateral:

– Autores vários – "Mini-Symposium on the Consultative Board's Report on the Future of the WTO" *in Journal of International Economic Law, Volume 8, Number 2, June 2005*, págs. 287-346 e *Number 3, September 2005*, págs. 591-690;

– Jackson, John H. – "International Economic Law: Complexity and Puzzles" *in Journal of International Economic Law, Volume 10, Number 1, March 2007*, págs. 3-13.

THE EUROPEAN REACTION
TO CLIMATE CHANGES

DIMITRI ZENGHELIS[*]

Thank you very much and thanks very much the organisers for inviting me here.

My name is Dimitri Zenghelis. My name, some of you will recognize, is Greek and people keep asking me, am I English or am I Greek, and I think in Portugal is best probably to be English on account that the Portuguese national football team regularly make mince meat out of the English football team but, if memory serves, with the Greeks they recently had a little bit more complications, so I am English today, for sure.

The Stern review, for those who don't know, was published in the autumn of last year and its remit was to develop an understanding of the evidence behind climate changes and trend, trend I think of some policy principles and frameworks that will encourage action to resolve the problem. It was commissioned by the Chancellor, who is now the Prime Minister and the then Prime Minister reporting back to them and that displays a realisation at the heart of UK government. This was a project, that has the potential to cut across all walks of economic life tense. This was an economic review, an independent review, but it was based at the Finance Ministry, it was not a narrow environmental issue and I think that is quite important.

Now, ordinarily, I would talk it trough the science and the way we went about evaluating the impact and how we came to the conclusion that the costs of action are significantly smaller than the costs of inaction.

---

[*] Member of the Stern Commission.

But, as we only have 20, 25 minutes and I want to put an European context, I am going to skip over that, but take it from me, the costs of inaction really are significantly lower than the costs of action and maybe one or two charts will give you a summary indication of the nature of the problem.

This chart shows the degree of commitment to warming in average degree Celsius relative to pre-industrial levels, that is the horizontal axis. I hope you can see that is a bit, but it goes from nought to five. And the science of climate changes very much probabilistic, there is a lot that we do not know with certainty but there is enough that the science can tell us that we can explicitly deal with the probabilities. So, those who will tell you there is a lot we do not know are not exaggerating. However, those that then say there is a lot we don't know, so we know that this is not happening and we know that it is not caused by human beings are being nothing other than logically incoherent. There is a lot we do not know, but we know enough about the distribution, and these red lines show 90% probability bounds of temperature changes relative to a variety of greenhouse gas concentrations. That is what these p.p.m. numbers you see here represent. It is the stock of greenhouse gases in the atmosphere that causes the problem, not the annual emissions into that stock.

The red lines, are 90% confidence intervals based on two reports, the IPCC third assessment report of 2001, the Hadley Center report of 2004. IPCC because is internationally recognised, Hadley because it is more recent and has a more explicit treatment of probabilities. We basically talked to the same scientists as the recent IPCC report, the fourth assessment, so we came up with the same scenarios. We did not do a new science, we had scientists on the team, but our expertise concerned the evaluation on the economics.

So, we are already at around for 420 parts for millions CO2 equivalent, if we stabilise at 450 parts for millions of CO2 equivalent that is a quintet, fifty-fifty change of the temperature increase of two degrees. That is the European Union's target, a stated target. 550. That is about fifty-fifty change of three degrees. If we do not do anything, we will get to and beyond 650, by the end of the century, and then beyond 700, 750 and so on, by the next century. Note the doted grey lines are abroad eleven studies, scientific studies, so we took a rather optimistic view of the impact of the science and we have been criticised for being a little bit optimistic on our view of the science, in particular by scientists if not by economists, but we are happy with that, because the case for action is still very strong, even on this optimistic scenario.

But, we are at 430, we are adding about two to two and half parts for million per year. If we carry on as we are, we will get to 550 really within the next 20, 30 years or so. 550 parts for million, and I am going to talk as a potential area for stabilisation. It is not a very nice place to be. We would expect up to a million more people to be at risk from hunger, significant increases in diseases, in conflict, in migration and in particular in water stress and drought. There are also significant increases in the probabilities of these non linea events, these uncertain events of which climate changes are replete. To give you a few examples, at certain temperatures, we know that the thunder is going to start to melt and release methane. Methane is a very potent greenhouse gas and it will accelerate the process of global warming. At certain temperatures, the Amazons is going to start dying and the Amazons is a great store of carbon dioxide. Once that happen, the process accelerates. Once ice sheets, such the west Antarctica ice sheet and the Greenland ice sheet start to melt, it is very difficult to stop them. Sea levels will then jump in a non-linear manner. There are many other uncertainties, some of which do not have probabilities distribution.

These risks and uncertainties begin to emerge particularly at about 3 or so degrees. They become very provable at 5 degrees, which is the kind of temperature we would reach if we carried on the business as usual. So that is a sort of snapshot, but I do not really have a chance here to talk through the precise damages. But, what I do want to talk about is the kind of emissions pathways that would be required in order to limit some of those damages.

I am switching here, you probably can't see this unfortunately, because it is too dark, but let me then read out what the axis are. The vertical axis is annual emissions into the stock of greenhouse gases, the flow into the stock. At the bottom is time and what we see at the blue line that heads north is business as usual. If we do nothing, emissions which are currently around 45 gigotons of CO_2 equivalent every year will double to around 80 by the middle of this century. In order to stabilise as within any stock flow system inputs have to equal outputs and that is widely recognise to be around 5 to 10 gigotons of CO_2 every year. We are at 45, we are going to 80. We need to get down to 5, to 10. That is the nature of the challenge. How can we do that? Well, depending on what temperature you want to stabilise, you can do that with varying degrees of difficulty. The bottom line, the brown line shows stabilisation at 450 parts per millions CO2 equivalent, costing your minds back to the previous chart that gives you a fifty-fifty chance of a two degree temperature change. It would require emissions to peek, as you can see by that dark line, pretty much tomorrow and then decline by about 6 to 10% thereafter. That would require scraping perfectly workable capital, it will require taking on technologies well before they have matured and at rather high costs. Bottom line, we have already missed the chance really to meet the EU's target of a two degree temperature rise with any confidence. If we had started 10 years ago, of course, the level of greenhouse gases in the stock would have been well below 4.30 and we might have had a fighting chance of achieving that target.

What about 5.50 parts for millions CO2 equivalent? I said that is roughly equivalent to a fifty-fifty chance of a three degree temperature rise. That is the yellow line you see above. Much more relaxed profile for emissions. Emissions can actually peek by 20-20 and then decline at a rate to 1 to 2,5% per year thereafter. That we can do. It is still affordable to do that. You can work with the investment cycle and you can wait for the expensive technologies to mature while taking action on the very cheap technologies, for example in electricity generation whether renewal technologies are already viable, in energy efficiency – energy efficiency by definition is free, you got no greenhouse gases and you save resources –, and in the things like deforestation which are a very efficient way of reducing emissions, whilst investing in the technologies that will bring the reductions later on. 5.50, three degrees. If we wait another ten years, because of the nature of the stock flow system, the stock will be much higher, we will have a profile for 5.50 that looks like the dark plan at the bottom. 5.50 will become too expensive. So, time is very important, we are probably already too late to meet the EU target.

What about the cost, then, of meeting the 550 stabilisation target? I will not talk in detail about how we went about this, but primarily we summarised a lot of literature and we did our own resource cost investigation, including commissioned research from Dennis Anderson – is a professor at Imperial College, in London –, and all the evidences pointed very strongly towards a cost of about 1% of GDP by the middle of the century to do a way, with risks and uncertainties, that depending on evaluation are variable between 5 and 20% of GDP. As a kind of insurance premium, we would all be prepared to pay to go away with the problem of climate change, something that can be higher, something that can be lower. I will not go in details on that, but since the publication of the Review, we have become ever more confident that those numbers, if anything, are underestimated. So, 1% to save you, perhaps, up to 20% of GDP sounds like a good deal.

I am going to talk a little bit about competitiveness here, because I think this is important to the European context. The main object of any action on climate changes got to be to change the relative price of greenhouse gas, related activities, production and consumption. If it is not changing behaviour, it is not working. So, there has got to be a little bit of an impact. The main challenge will be to manage the transition to low greenhouse gas production. In the UK, and in many other industrialised countries, total fuel energy cost account rounds 3% of variable costs in production. If you apply the kind of carbon costing that we are suggesting, that are consistent with the top range of the European emissions trading price, somewhere between 20 and 30 euros, up a ton of CO2 equivalent, ignore this pounds numbers here, 30 euros per ton of CO2 equivalent. The Stern review, I should say, was very much internationally minded and all the principles and points are based at a global level. This is one study we did at UK level, because we had UK production data, and we used this as an example. In the UK, if energy costs are about 3% of GDP, total energy cost from the kind of carbon price we are talking about would increase by about 20%, the total cost of the UK economy, in terms of variable cost, will be about 1% of GDP. Interesting, it backs up the numbers that we saw before on the 1% of GDP.

What about if we work, think of this 70 pounds again, numbers equivalent around 20 to 30, closer to 30 euros per ton of CO2. This is carbon, it is effectively the cost we thought would be appropriate to meet the stabilisation target of 550 and it is also at the operendum of the European emissions trading scheme price. What does that mean in terms of the impact? We look at the UK data and we used input-output tables, which take costs all the way trough the entire UK economy, trough all the production processes, to intermediate production right out to producer and consumer prices. And, immediately, this chart lists the top industries that will see variable costs increase as the result of greenhouse gas pricing, of the kind we think are necessary. Yellow is gas, brown is coal, blue is oil – obviously they have different carbon intensity, so you will see different cost increases in the component – and this show contributions to these price changes. Immediately, you see that petroleum, gas and electricity production are the only sources of production where costs rise by significant amount, because the main users, of course, of electricity and cement are the main users of coal. The main users of electricity include the electricity sector itself and, of course, refining has very large petrol, oil component. But, is also includes sectors such as agriculture, forestry, fishing and chemicals. For the UK as a whole, total variable cost account for only 3% of GDP, so total cost in the UK rise by no more than about 1% of GDP. Out of 123 pro-ductions sectors, only 19 saw price increases of more than 2%. Moreover, these are amongst the slower growing components and they account for less than 4% of UK total output, so very narrow sector of the economy, which is sensitive to changes in carbon costing of the kind that we recommend. When you look at consumer prices, it is equivalent to one of increasing total consumer car prices of around 1% of GDP.

How does this compare with the kind of price changing's we have seen anyway? We will just look at one market oil, again, where the key thing to note is the kind of fluctuation. The purple line is the US oil price, the brand spot, brand crude spot price historically up upon until about 2006, when we published. The point I want to show is the kind of change in the price of oil that would be required from the carbon price. What we are talking about is around 70 pounds per ton of carbon. That is about that much, however you want to show it. In other words, it is tiny compared to the kinds of fluctuations you see in energy prices in the world anyway. Tiny, also, compared to the kind of fluctuation you see in exchange rates. So, we are not talking about something without precedent, we are talking about a small change in energy prices, which would bring about the ne-cessary behaviour reaction to bring about a reduction in greenhouse gas emissions. Why is it so small? Partly, because energy, electricity generation is just one sector. Larger than transport, for example, is land use, which includes deforestation or separately agriculture. Action needs to be taken in those sectors, as well. Action also needs to be taken on energy efficiency.

So, one of the benefits of this stories, you can do an awful lot of small things across the nature of the production system that we would not really notice, which is why the impact amount only 1%, in gross terms, by the way. 1% by the middle of the century is nearly negligible in terms of growth, and represents very small changes required to bring about the necessary reduction in emissions, which we would not otherwise have.

I run out of time. So, I will just summarise this chart by saying, those sectors that had high changes in prices as a result of carbon costing are also the sectors that are least tradable. That is what the vertical axis shows. So, to the extend that some carbon intensive sectors will see price increases, these numbers, these sectors are very non tradable. So, susceptibility to loss of competitiveness and relocation is very small. At the UK level, if we look at it in terms of only trade outside the European Union, it falls by 5%. So, most of the UK trade, in the energy intensive sector, is with Europe, very little of it goes on outside Europe.

I think I have run out of time. I will wrap it up then and thanks very much.

Annex

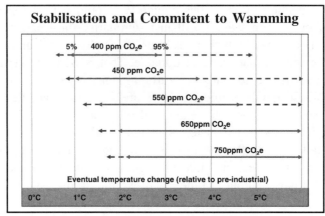

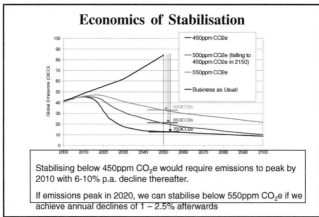

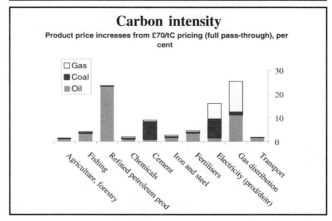

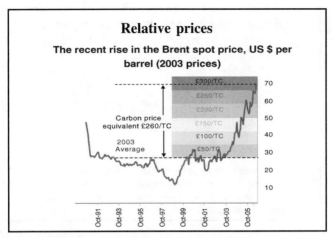

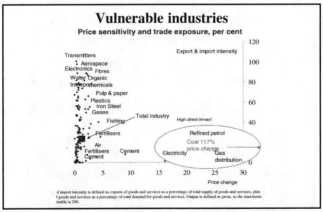

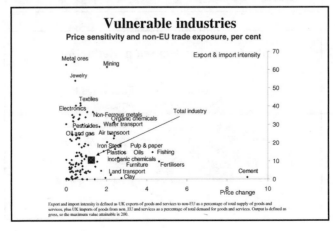

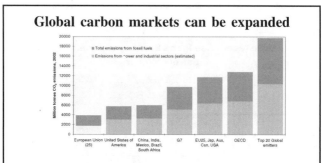

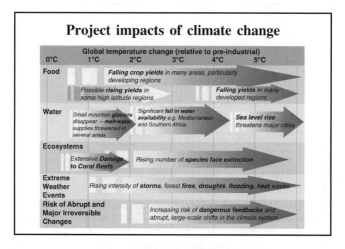

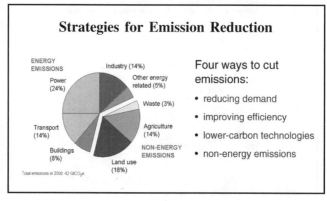

The European Reaction to Climate Changes

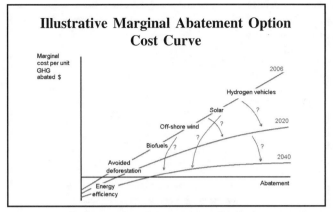

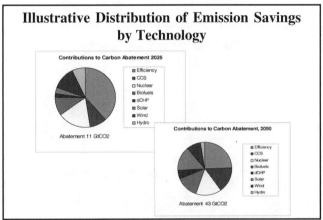

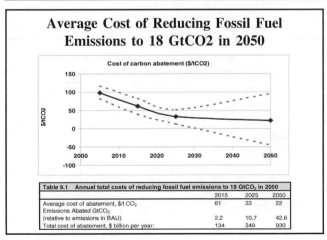

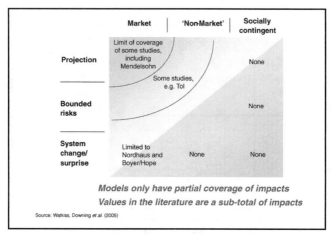

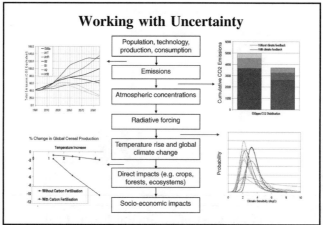

Aggregate Impacts Matrix

- Essential to take account of **risk and uncertainty**
- Models do **not** provide **precise** forecasts
- Assumptions on **discounting, risk aversion and equity** affect the results

	Market impacts	Broad impacts
Baseline climate	5% (0-12%)	11% (2-27%)
High climate	7% (1-17%)	14% (3-32%)

Rough estimate of equity weighting: 20%

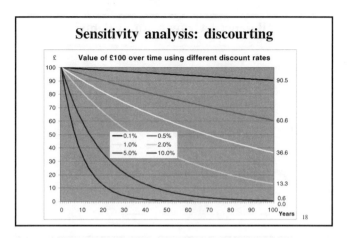

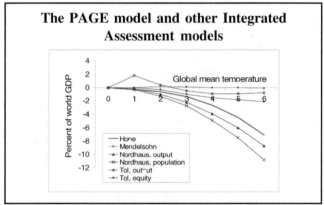

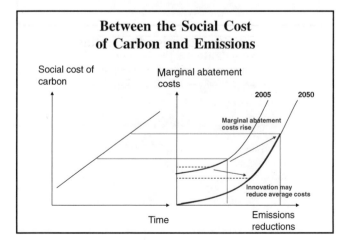

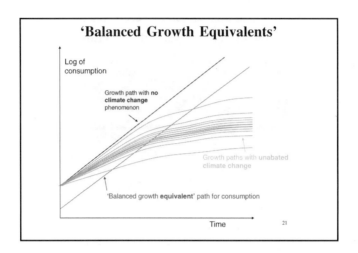

Discounting

Pure time discount rate (%) δ	Probability of human race surviving 100 years
0.1	0.905
0.5	0.607
1.0	0.368
1.5	0.223

Discount Rate: η × GDP growth rate + δ

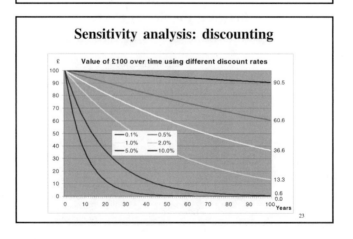

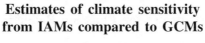

Estimates of climate sensitivity from IAMs compared to GCMs

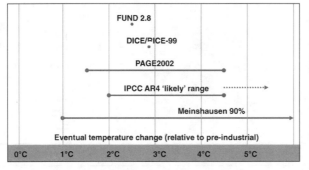

Sensitivity analysis of cost estimates – model structure

	Variation	Change in % consumption damages (BGE)
Emissions scenario (population)	40% lower	-4
Increasing the damage function exponent	**Stochastic - 3**	**+20**
Growth	1% higher	+
Terminal conditions	Continued growth past 2200 or decline	High Sensitivity ++
Incorporating further risk and uncertainty	More parameter and baseline uncertainty	+3
Aversion to irreversibilities		+
Rise in price of environmental goods relative to consumption goods	Equivalent loss in consumption	++

Bold – direct calculation (others are from other studies or 'back of the envelope')

Sensitivity analysis of cost estimates – value judgements

	Variation	Change in % consumption damages (BGE)
Increasing the elasticity of marginal utility of consumption (inequality and risk aversion)	**1-2**	**-7**
Increasing the pure rate of time preference	**0.1-1.5%**	**-8**
Intra-generational income distribution/regional equity weighting	Regional distribution	+6

Bold – direct calculation (others are from other studies or 'back of the envelope')

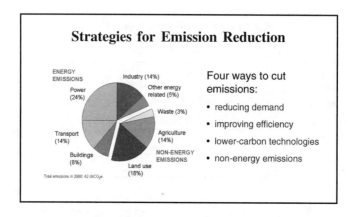

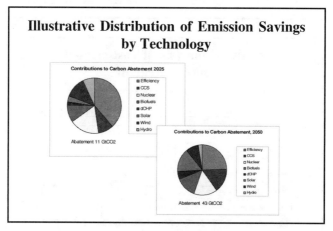

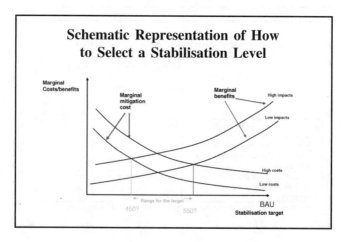

Technology needs more than a carbon price

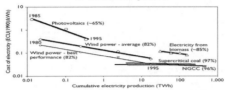

Carbon price alone not enough to bring forward the technologies we need

One way of doing this is through global public funding for technologies:
- R&D funding should double, to around $20 bn
- Deployment incentives should increase 2 to 5 times, from current level of $34 bn

Adaptation

- Development increases resilience
- Adaptation will put strong pressure on developing country budgets and ODA: essential to meet 2010 and 2015 commitments
- International action also has a key role in supporting global public goods for adaptation
    - Disaster response
    - Crop varieties and technology
    - Forecasting climate and weather

Sensitivity analysis: discounting

Damage function exponent	Utility discount rate	Baseline climate; market impacts + risk of catastrophe	Base climate; market impacts + risk of catastrophe + non-market impacts	High climate; market impacts + risk of catastrophe + non-market impacts
Low range	0.1	5.0	10.9	14.4
	0.5	3.6	8.1	10.6
	1.0	2.3	5.2	6.7
	1.5	1.4	3.3	4.2
High range	0.1	6.0	14.2	21.9
	0.5	4.3	10.2	15.8
	1.0	2.7	6.4	9.8
	1.5	1.7	4.0	5.9

Sensitivity analysis: damage function and elasticity of marginal utility of consumption

Damage function exponent	Elasticity of marginal utility of consumption	Baseline climate; market impacts + risk of catastrophe	Baseline climate; market impacts + risk of catastrophe + non-market impacts	High climate; market impacts + risk of catastrophe + non-market impacts
		Mean (5th percentile, 95th percentile)	Mean (5%, 95%)	Mean (5%, 95%)
Low range	1.0	5.0 (0.6-12.4)	10.9 (2.2-27.4)	14.4 (2.7-32.6)
	1.25	3.8 (0.6-9.6)	8.7 (2.2-21.7)	12.1 (2.7-26.0)
	1.5	2.9 (0.5-7.1)	6.5 (1.7-16.5)	10.2 (2.0-20.0)
High range	1.0	6.0 (0.8-15.5)	14.2 (2.8-32.2)	21.9 (3.7-51.6)
	1.25	4.6 (1.8-12.0)	11.3 (2.6-25.2)	16.2 (3.8-41.9)
	1.5	3.4 (0.3-9.0)	8.7 (1.8-19.2)	15.3 (2.8-33.1)

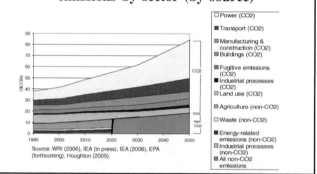

Historical and projected GHG emissions by sector (by source)

Source: WRI (2006), IEA (in press), IEA (2006), EPA (forthcoming), Houghton (2005).

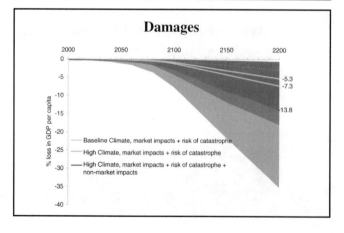

Damages

'Output gap' between the '550ppm CO_2e and 1% GWP mitigation cost' scenario and BAU scenario, mean and 5tth –95th percentile range

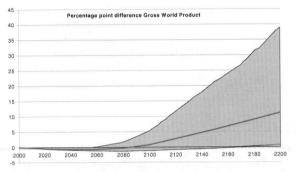

The are more than enough proven reserves to get to 1000ppm CO_2

Peak oil is not the answer... Non-conventional sources of oil (tar sands, coal liquefaction etc) are far more carbon intensive than conventional oil deposits

Large reserves of coal available for cheap and reliable energy in many large and fast-growing economies

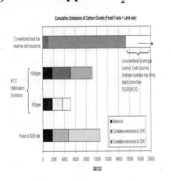

Source: Lenton et al (2006), IPCC

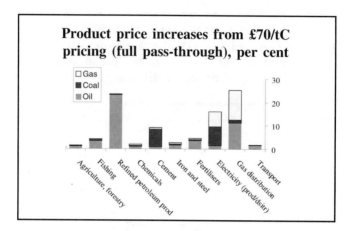

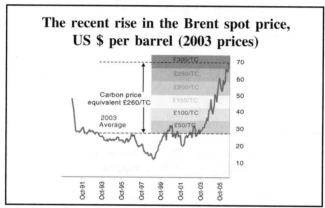

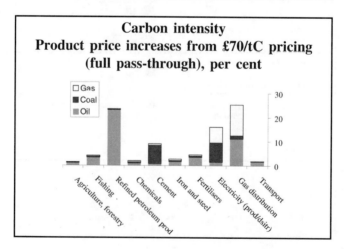

Avoiding deforestation

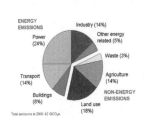

- Curbing deforestation is highly cost-effective, and significant
- Forest management should be shaped and led by nation where the forest stands
- Large-scale pilot schemes could help explore alternative approaches to provide effective international support

Has energy policy risen to meet the climate change challenge?

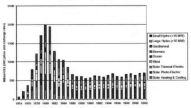

Figure 11 Renewable Energy Technology RD&D (IEA, 2004)

Energy RD&D more generally shows a similar pattern

Renewable energy RD&D remains at around 8% of total energy RD&D

Vulnerable Industries
Price sensitivity and trade exposure, per cent

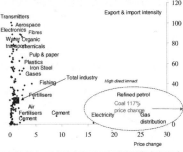

Export and import intensity is defined as exports of goods and services as a percentage of total supply of goods and services, plus imports of goods and services as a percentage of total demand for goods and services. Output is defined as gross, so the maximum value attainable is 200.

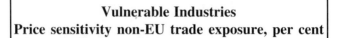

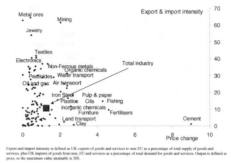

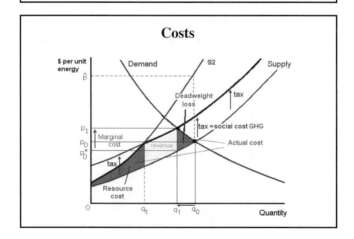

The European Reaction to Climate Changes

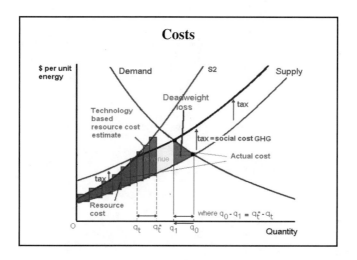

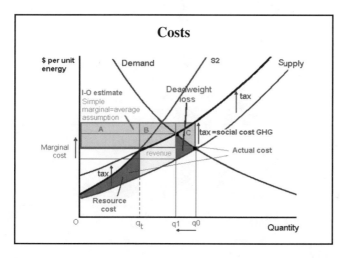

HOW TO TACKLE EU'S ENERGY DEPENDENCY?

P. J. SLOT[*] and N. TEZCAN

Introduction

This article deals with EU's energy dependency and the ways to minimize this dependency. After a brief account of the legal framework within which energy policy developed, the current situation as well as future projections concerning EU's energy dependency are laid out. The focus of this paper is on the question: "How to tackle EU's import dependency and ensure security of supply?". The main suggestions to that effect are diversifying energy sources (the prospects of nuclear energy, renewables and coal are discussed); ensuring energy efficiency (managing demand); improving external relations with EU's energy partners; and developing/ completing the internal energy market.

1. The Past of EU Energy Policy

In the 1950s the European energy sector was viewed as an area requiring urgent development of common policies and coordinated actions.[1] In a way, this was also reflected by the two treaties establishing supranational communities concerning certain aspects of the energy sector, i.e. The Treaty of Paris (1951) establishing the European Coal and Steel Community (ECSC) for a fifty-year period, and one of the Treaties of Rome (1957)

---

[*] Professor of European and Economic Law, Europa Institute, Leiden University.
[1] See, 'The Spaak Report', Brussels, 1956.

establishing the European Atomic Energy Community (EAEC) for an unlimited period. However, the more general of these communities established in 1957, the European Economic Community (EEC) did not contain a word on energy policy.

The absence of provisions on energy in the EEC Treaty hindered the development of an effective common policy for energy between 1958 and 1972. The response of the Member States to the 1973 oil crises was to protect their national interests on their own. It was only after the crises that attention was paid to reducing external dependency. Directives based on the old Article 103(4) EEC established a crisis mechanism.[2] The second oil crisis led to an extension of these measures[3] and also to measures concerned with energy saving.[4]

The Single European Act (SEA) amended each of the treaties for the three communities. However, the most important of these changes were the ones made to the EEC Treaty. Article 8a (now 14 EC) established the objective of an 'internal market' by the end of 1992, and Article 100a (now Article 95 EC) established a legal basis for the adoption of related legislation. The Commission used these provisions as the legal basis for its broad legislative initiatives in the electricity and gas sectors. The Treaty on European Union (1992) was also significant as it listed measures in the 'spheres of energy, civil protection and tourism' among the various activities of the Community (Article 3(u) EC), and added Article 129b (now Article 154 EC) on promotion of trans-European networks (TENs) in the areas of transport, telecommunications and energy infrastructures.

The unratified Constitutional Treaty for Europe also added a long--sought Treaty section on energy policy. Article III-256 stated the Community's basic energy policy objectives and indicated the respective competences. Together with other provisions of the Constitutional Treaty

---

[2] Dir. 73/238, OJ 1973 L 228/1 was preceded by Dir. 68/414, OJ 1968, L 308, on minimum stocks of crude oil and/or petroleum products.

[3] The crisis measures implemented the International Energy Agency's rules (Dir. 73/238, OJ 1973, L 228/1). They are supplemented by an agreement between the major oil companies, which was the subject of exemption under Art. 81(3) EC (Dec. 83/671 OJ 1983 L 376/30 *International Energy Agency*, renewed by Dec. 94/153 OJ 1994 L 68/35).

[4] See further: Cross, Delvaux, Hancher, Slot, Van Calster, and Vandenberghe, "EU Energy Law", in Roggenkamp, Redgwell, Ronne, del Guayo (eds.), *Energy Law in Europe – National, EU and International Law and Institutions*, OUP, 2nd edition, 2008.

(eg. Article I-14, Article III-234, and Declaration 22 annexed to the Final Act), the special status of energy policy was recognized, and it was indicated as one of the many areas of shared competences between the Community and the Member States.[5] These provisions are now contained in the Lisbon Treaty.[6]

The situation in the energy market now is that – with the exception of nuclear energy – the general provisions of the EC Treaty apply, which means that for that part of the energy market there is in principle no other regulatory regime than the liberal market regime of the Treaty itself.[7]

2. The Present Situation

The adoption of the directives on the internal market for electricity and natural gas[8] gave a concrete shape to the Community energy policy. These directives were amended in 2003 in an effort to step up the liberalization effort[9] and tackle the unexpected challenges in the process. Yet, one of the challenges looms ever larger on the Union: the security of energy supplies. The EU's growing dependence on external energy sources prompted the Commission in 2000 to publish a Green Paper named "Towards A European Strategy for the Security of Energy Supply"[10] to be followed by another one in 2006 entitled "A European Strategy for Sustainable, Competitive and Secure Energy".[11] The reason for concern

---

[5] Ibid.

[6] Article III-256 of the Constitutional Treaty corresponds to Article 194 of the Treaty on the Functionning of the European Union (TFEU); Article I-14 corresponds to Article 4 TFEU; and Article III-234 corresponds to Article 192 TFEU.

[7] Kapteyn – VerLoren van Themaat, *Het recht van de Europese Unie en van de Europese Gemeenschappen*, Kluwer – Deventer, 2003, pp. 1045-1046.

[8] Dir. 96/92 concerning common rules for the internal market in electricity, OJ 1997, L 27/20 (also referred to as the electricity directive); and Dir. 98/30, concerning common rules for the internal market in natural gas, OJ 1998, L 204/1 (also referred to as the natural gas directive).

[9] Dir. 2003/54 concerning common rules for the internal market in electricity, repealing Dir. 96/92, OJ 2003, L 176/37. Dir. 2003/55 concerning common rules for the internal market in natural gas, repealing Dir. 98/30 OJ 2003, L 176/57.

[10] COM (2000) 769 final.

[11] COM (2006) 105 final.

is the current dependency of the EU on external supplies of energy and future projections predicting the exacerbation of that dependency.

Total EU-25 energy consumption in 2004 amounted to an estimated 1745 million tones of oil equivalent (mtoe). Oil is the most important fuel in the EU's total energy consumption, to be followed by natural gas, coal, nuclear power and renewables. EU's total energy consumption by fuel in 2004 was as follows:[12]

Figure 1 – Total energy consumption by fuel 2004

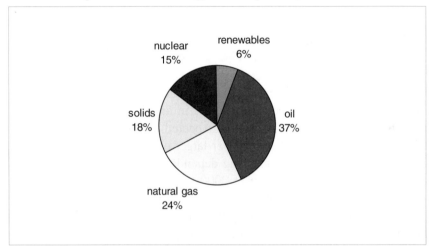

Currently, about half of EU energy consumption is produced within the EU while the other half is imported. Import dependency is the highest for oil. Net oil imports account for %81 of oil consumption. More than the half (%54) of gas consumption comes from outside the EU. Import dependency on solid fuels amounts to only %38, as lignite is produced exclusively within the EU and large quantities of coal are still mined within the Union. Nuclear and renewables are treated as indigenous fuels so that their dependency is zero in Eurostat statistical conventions.[13]

---

[12] Annex to the Green Paper, COM (2006) 105 final, p. 8.

[13] Ibid, p. 9. Nuclear fuels can be stocked covering the needs for a long period of time. However, uranium is imported into the EU and many Russian type reactors in the new Member States are using Russian fuel.

3. Future Projections

Europe's heavy dependence on fossil fuels is predicted to continue for the foreseeable future. The baseline scenario developed by the Commission represents the trends and policies as implemented in the 25 Member States of the EU up to the end of 2004 (i.e. Bulgaria and Romania have not been included).[14]

Figure 2 – Share of energy sources in total energy consumption (in %)[15]

	1990	2000	2010	2020	2030
Solid fuels	27.8	18.5	15.8	13.8	15.5
Oil	38.3	38.4	36.9	35.5	33.8
Gas	16.7	22.8	25.5	28.1	27.3
Nuclear	12.7	14.4	13.7	12.1	11.1
Renewables	4.4	5.8	7.9	10.4	12.2

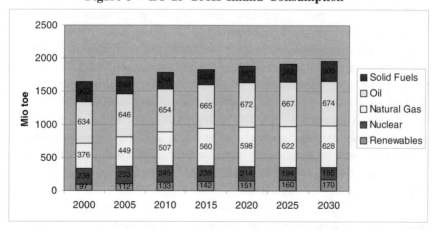

Figure 3 – EU 25 Gross Inland Consumption[16]

---

[14] For more details on how the baseline modelling was developed see, Annex to the Green Paper, COM (2006) 105 final, p. 9-10.
[15] Ibid, p. 11.
[16] European Commission, Scenarios on Key Drivers, Brussels, Sept. 2004

According to the baseline scenario, total EU-25 energy consumption will continue to increase till 2030. In 2030, total energy consumption is projected to be %15 higher than it was in 2000. The growth rates of energy become smaller over time with consumption virtually stabilizing post 2020. This will be due to stagnating population and consequently lower economic growth.[16]

The energy consumption increase is expected to be met by natural gas and renewables, which are the only energy sources that increase their market shares. Oil remains the most important fuel, despite slow growth over the next 10 to 15 years and expected decline afterwards, which would mean that oil consumption in 2030, would not exceed the current level. Demand for natural gas is expected to increase considerably by 140 mtoe from 2000 to 2030 after a substantial increase already seen in the 1990s. Solid fuels are projected first to decrease by 2020 and to come back to the current level in 2030.[18]

While energy consumption is expected to increases at a rather low pace through to 2030, external dependency is to increase at a higher pace. This is mainly due to a steep decline in indigenous production, in particular of hydrocarbons, solid fuels and nuclear (current revival of discussions on nuclear puts a question mark on the projections on nuclear). Only renewables production is expected to increase. In 2030, Commission's baseline projections as of 2004, have oil production declining by %73, gas production by %59 and solid fuel production by %41. Nuclear projection might decrease by %11. All together, total indigenous production in 2030 would be %25 lower than it was in 2000.[19]

Import dependency in 2030 is approximately %15 higher than the level of 2004. Import dependency for oil is still the highest at %94 in 2030. Gas import dependency rises substantially from around %50 at present to %84 in 2030. Similarly, solid fuel supplies will be based on imports reaching %59 in 2030.[20]

Projected import growth for natural gas is largely caused by depletion of internal European reserves, such as the UK North Sea, the

---

[17] Annex to the Green Paper, COM (2006) 105 final, p. 10.

[18] Ibid.

[19] Ibid, p. 11.

[20] Ibid.

Netherlands Groningen field[21] (to some extent) and the expansion of the Union to the non-producing countries of Eastern Europe.[22] The other three producers with some significance in the EU: Germany, Italy, and Denmark, are also expected to witness decrease in their production within this decade.[23]

Figure 4 – Natural Gas Demand and Supply outlook 2001-2020

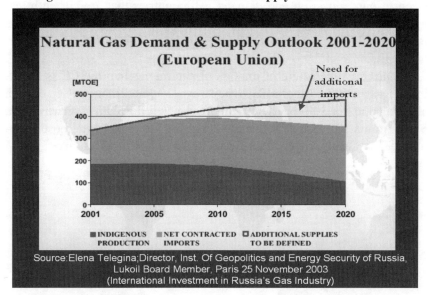

If the 20th century was the century of 'oil', the 21st century is the century of 'natural gas'. Global consumption of natural gas is expected to increase more in absolute terms than that of any other primary energy

---

[21] While some believe that Dutch gas production will also decline (see, Widdershoven, 22 below), others (CIEP, note 23 below) argue that for some more years to come Dutch production will remain at the level it was in the previous decade, i.e. 70-80 bcm.

[22] Widdershoven, "Energy Security and Liquefied Natural Gas", available online at: http://www.iags.org/n0929034.htm

[23] Production in the year 2000 has been in the following amounts: Germany 22 bcm, Italy 16 bcm and Denmark 8bcm. See Clingandael International Energy Programme (CIEP), "Natural Gas Supply for the EU in the Short to Medium Term", March 2004, p. 12. Available online at: http://www.clingendael.nl/publications/2004/20040300_ciep_paper.pdf

source. Natural gas has inherent environmental advantages over other fossil fuels, including lower carbon content and fewer emissions of noxious gases. Demand is expected to grow at an average annual rate of 2.3%, and most of the increase is anticipated to come from the power generation sector.[24]

According to IEA forecast, inter-regional trade will more than triple over the projection period, as a result of the geographical mismatch between resource location and demand. All countries that are currently net importers of gas will see their imports rise, both in volume and as a share in their total gas consumption. The biggest increase in volumes will occur in the EU.[25]

Currently, the origin of imports of natural gas into the EU is as follows: Russia 50%, Algeria 23%, Norway 22%, and others 5%[26]. Russia also accounts for 30% of EU oil imports, to be followed by Norway 18%, Saudi Arabia 10%, Libya 8% and others 34%. Relations with those countries will be analyzed in more detail in the following section.

Figure 5 – The Origin of Natural Gas and Oil Imports into the EU 25

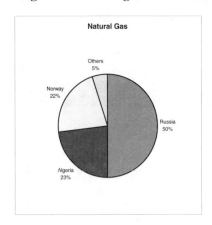
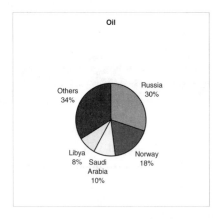

---

[24] IEA, *World Energy Outlook 2004*, pp. 130-132.

[25] Ibid, p. 140.

[26] We need to note that some those imports in the form of LNG, come mainly from Algeria and Nigeria. Portugal (2%), Greece (2%), Belgium (9%), Italy (16%), France (28%) and Spain (43%) have the respective shares of LNG imports in 2003. See, Wood and Pyke, "Crating an Effective Gas Supply Network to Europe", *Petroleum Review*, January 2005. Available online at: http://www.dwasolutions.com/images/JAN2005PetRevDWWPPt2.pdf

4. How to tackle EU's import dependency and ensure security of energy supply?

In its Green Paper[27] to be able to balance sustainable development, competitiveness and ensure security of supply, the Commission identified six priority areas for action. These priority areas, some of which will be analyzed below, are as follows: completing the internal energy market, solidarity between Member States, diversification of the energy mix, external policy, innovation and an integrated approach to tackling climate change.

4.1. *Towards a more sustainable and diverse energy mix*

In principle it is up to each Member Sate to choose its own energy mix. However, choices made by one Member State inevitably have an impact on the energy security of its neighbours, on the Community as a whole, as well as on competitiveness and the environment.[28] Diversifying energy sources, countries of import, transit routes etc. are ways to increase security of supply for individual States. Diversifying the energy mix by substituting imported energy sources by indigenous ones where possible, such as renewables, nuclear and solid fuels, is a way to tackle energy dependency.

4.1.1. *Nuclear Energy*

Although the nuclear option seemed to be fading away few years ago, nowadays it is again one of the hotly debated issues in many Member States. It is for each Member State to decide whether or not to use nuclear power. However, the Commission must ensure the existing installations have a high level of security and that both radioactive waste and the fuels are managed safely and without damaging the environment.[29]

---

[27] Green Paper, A European Strategy for Sustainable, Competitive and Secure Energy, COM (2006) 105 final, Brussels, 8.3.2006.

[28] Ibid., p. 9.

[29] DG TREN, Report on the Green Paper on Energy – Four years of European Initiatives, European Communities, 2005, p. 10.

Recently France and Finland decided to construct new nuclear reactors. Other EU countries, including the Netherlands, Poland, Sweden, Czech Republic, Lithuania, Estonia, Latvia, Slovakia and the United Kingdom have re-launched debates on their nuclear policies. With 152 reactors spread over EU-27, nuclear power contributes %30 to Europe's electricity today. To meet the growing energy demand and reduce European dependency on imports, decisions could be made on new investments or on the life extension of some plants.[30]

Figure 6 – Share in Electricity Generation in EU-25[31]

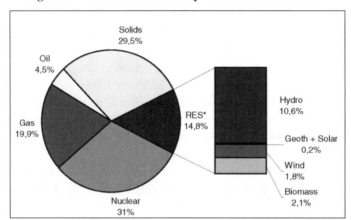

---

[30] Communication from the Commission to the Council and the European Parliament – Nuclear Illustrative Programme Presented under Article 40 of the Euratom Treaty for the opinion of the European Economic and Social Committee, COM (2006) 844 final, 10.1.2007.

[31] Annex to the Communication from the Commission to the Council and the European Parliament – Nuclear Illustrative Programme Presented under Article 40 of the Euratom Treaty for the opinion of the European Economic and Social Committee, Annex 1 for the Draft Nuclear Illustrative Programme, SEC (2006) 1717, Brussels, 10.1.2007, p. 2.

Figure 7 – Share in Energy Consumption in the EU-25[32]

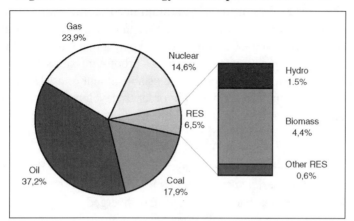

In the UK for instance, the government's White Paper published in early 2003 left the door open to nuclear power "if circumstances required". Moreover, the country's energy minister announced that the government's plans for developing green energy might turn out to be too expensive, and that more nuclear power plants might need to be built instead.[33] A Consultation Document on "The Future of Nuclear Power" published in May 2007 elaborates extensively on the issue and attempts to answer the question "Why we need to consider the future of nuclear power now".[34] In Germany the power utilities (EoN, RWE, EnBW and Vattenfall) are relentlessly lobbying the government to reverse its decision to phase out the country's nuclear capacity.[35]

Similarly, a recent Commission Communication on the Nuclear Illustrative Programme, argues that nuclear energy can contribute to diversification and long-term security of energy supply for the following reasons: nuclear fuel constitutes only %10 to 15 of the total cost of generating

---

[32] Ibid, p. 3.

[33] *MarketWatch: Energy*, February 2004, p. 4.

[34] Department of Trade and Industry, The Future of Nuclear Power – The role of nuclear power in a low carbon UK economy, Consultation Document, May 2007, available online at: http://www.dti.gov.uk/files/file39197.pdf See also, Meeting the Energy Challenge – A White Paper on Energy, May 2007, available online at: http://www.dti.gov.uk/files/file39387.pdf

[35] *MarketWatch: Energy*, February 2004, p. 4.

electricity, it is easy to stockpile uranium, which is also found in stable parts of the world (%45 of the EU uranium needs come from Canada and Australia). Furthermore, reinforcing nuclear power generation could also be an option for reducing CO_2 emissions and play a major role in addressing global climate change (nuclear power is carbon-emissions free).[36]

The Commission has proposed the establishment of a EU High Level Group of national nuclear regulators in order to develop a common understanding and European rules in the field of nuclear safety and security. This area is governed by the rules of the Euratom Treaty, however, thoughts of nuclear installations safety and radioactive waste did not have priority in the minds of the authors of the Treaty. It was not until 1975 that the Community realized the seriousness of the issue. By that time, nuclear programmes in Member States had progressed and diverged along very different routes. Not only were the installations very different, but also the national systems regulating them were very different. These differences hindered the establishment of common rules to be applied across the Community till 1970s. As a result of cooperation between the main actors since the 1970s, a "non-binding acquis" built on fundamental common principles emerged over time. These formed the basis of all the EU national nuclear safety regulations. However, enlargement brought the prospect of Soviet-designed nuclear reactors' location within the Community, which raised the question "What are western standards on nuclear safety?". As Commissioner Palacio then (in 2002) commented, it was difficult to understand how the EU could adopt detailed standards for the quality of water in rivers and lakes but not have a common approach on nuclear safety.[37] The issue of nuclear safety is high on the agenda and the Commission is aiming at harmonizing the nuclear rules of liability within the Community. An impact assessment will be carried out to this end in 2007.[38]

---

[36] Nuclear Illustrative Programme, note 31 above, p. 9-16.

[37] Fernando De Esteban, Deputy Director-General DG TREN, "The future of nuclear energy in the European Union", Background paper for a speech made to a group of representatives from nuclear utilities in the context of a "European Strategic Exchange", Brussels, 23rd May 2002.

[38] Nuclear Illustrative Programme, note 30 above, p. 17.

4.1.2. *Renewable Energy Sources*

Given the three objectives of EU energy policy: environmental sustainability, security of supply and competitiveness, the development of renewable energy sources has been seen as an important pillar potentially contributing to all of these three objectives. As part of its Energy Policy for Europe, the Commission put forward in January a proposal for a long--term Renewable Energy Road Map[39]. The proposal includes an overall binding %20 renewable energy target and a binding minimum target of %10 for transport biofuels for the EU by 2020, as well as a pathway to bring renewable energies in the fields of electricity, heating and cooling and transport to the economic and political mainstream.

In 2001 the EU had already set a target so that %21 of electricity generated in the Union would come from renewable energy sources by 2010.[40] A Commission report issued in January revealed that the EU is almost on track in reaching its 2010 renewable electricity target, reaching %19 by 2010.[41]

Wind energy has been a clear success, with a growth in wind capacity of %150 since 2001. The EU is the established leader in the field and has %60 share of the global market. However, in half of the EU, wind power is not sufficiently harnessed. Solar energy is also promising. Total installed photovoltaic capacity in the Union has been growing at an annual average rate of %70 over the last five years, with Germany taking the lead. Electricity production from geothermal sources are mainly used in Italy, Portugal and France, with Italy possessing over %95 of all installed capacity in the EU.[42]

Biofuels are very important, since they are considered to be the only source of renewable energy that could potentially take the place of petroleum in the road transport sector. Accordingly, the EU adopted a

---

[39] SEC (2006) 1719, Brussels, 10.1.2007.

[40] The EU also adopted an important Directive in September 2001 to create a framework for a significant increase in green electricity in the medium term. See, Directive 2001/77/EC of the European Parliament and of the Council of 27 September 2001 on the promotion of electricity produced from renewable energy sources on the internal electricity market, OJ L 283, 27.10.2001, p. 33-40.

[41] "EU almost on track in reaching its 2010 renewable electricity target", MEMO/ /07/12, Brussels, 10.1.2007.

[42] Ibid.

Directive on the promotion of the use of biofuels for transport in May 2003.[43] The Directive stipulates that biofuels should account for %5.75 of that market by the end of 2010. As mentioned above, the Renewable Energy Road Map envisages the increase of biofuels for transport to %10 by 2020.

4.1.3. *Revamping Coal*

Since the adoption of the climate convention the success of coal in the energy sector has been fading away. This is unfortunate, given the fact that coal, contrary to other fossil fuels is found across the globe and is sold on the international market at a relatively stable and low price. In other words, coal could make a very useful contribution to enhancing security of supply in the EU, the main obstacle being the CO_2 emissions released by coal.[44]

The Commission has acted on two fronts. First of all, it has supported technical progress through its research fund for coal. Research programmes looking into how to capture and isolate carbon, if successful, could help reduce the emissions produced by burning of coal. Secondly, the Commission is focusing on maintaining coal as an optional energy source. Due to high costs of mining in some Member States, after the expiry of the ECSC Treaty on 23 July 2002, the EU decided to adopt a regulation aimed at gradually decreasing State aid to the coal industry.[45] In February 2002, Member States decided to transfer the assets of the ECSC to the European Community and to set up a common research fund to be managed by the Commission.

---

[43] Directive 2003/30/EC of the European Parliament and of the Council of 8 May 2003 on the promotion of the use of biofuels or other renewable fuels for transport, OJ L 123, 17.5.2003, p. 42-46.

[44] DG TREN, Report on the Green Paper on Energy – Four years of European Initiatives, European Communities, 2005, p. 11.

[45] Council Regulation (EC) No 1407/2002 of 23 July 2002 on State aid to the coal industry, OJ L 205, 2.8.2002, p. 1-8.

4.2. *Energy Efficiency/ Managing Demand*

Prior to the Green Paper, the EU had already drawn a plan for action for energy efficiency.[46] The Green Paper gave a fresh boost to the implementation of that plan. Many proposals were drafted and introduced. Some of these are as follows: a directive on the energy performance of buildings[47], which account for %40 of total energy consumption across the EU. This directive sets minimum requirements concerning the integrated energy performance of buildings and binds the Member States to inspect all heating and air conditioning installations.

The Union has also adopted a series of regulations with respect to the labeling of household appliances: air conditioners[48], electric ovens[49], refrigerators and freezers[50]. The Union and the US have signed an agreement concerning the coordination of energy efficiency labeling programmes for office equipment ('Energy Star').[51] These developments are not insignificant. It has been proven that the labeling system introduced by the Commission in 1994 resulted in an increase of more than %30 in the energy yield index for new refrigerators and freezers between 1996.

In October 2006, the Commission proposed a new Energy Efficiency Action Plan. The Plan contains a package of priority measures covering a wide range of cost-effective energy efficiency initiatives. Stringent new efficiency standards, promotion of energy services, specific

---

[46] Communication from the Commission to the Council, the European Parliament, the Economic and Social Committee and the Committee of the Regions – Action plan to improve energy efficiency in the European Community, COM (2000) 247.

[47] Directive 2002/91/EC of the European Parliament and of the Council of 16 December 2002 on the energy performance of buildings, OJ L 1, 4.1.2003, p. 65-67.

[48] Commission Directive 2002/31/EC of 22 March 2002 implementing Council Directive 92/75/EEC with regard to energy labelling household air-conditioners, OJ L 86, 3.4.2002, p. 33-39.

[49] Commission Directive 2002/40/EC of 8 May 2002 implementing Council Directive 92/75/EEC with regard to energy labelling household electric ovens, OJ L 128, 15.5.2002, p. 45-46.

[50] Commission Directive 2003/66/EC of 3 July 2003 amending Directive 94/2/EC implementing Council Directive 92/75/EEC with regard to energy labelling household electric refrigerators, freezers and their combinations, OJ L 170, 9.7.2003, p. 10-14.

[51] Regulation (EC) No 2422/2001 of the European Parliament and of the Council of 6 November 2001 on a Community energy efficiency labelling programme for office equipment, OJ L 332, 15.12.2001, p. 1-6.

financing mechanisms to support more energy efficient products are proposed. Altogether 75 measures are set forth. If successful, this would mean that by 2020, the EU would use approximately %13 less energy than today, saving € 100 billion and around 780 million tones of CO2 each year.[52]

4.3. *External Relations with EU's Energy Partners*

As seen above, half of the Union's energy comes from imports and this trend is set to grow further, so strengthening ties with EU's energy partners should become a priority. EU has a complex web of relations with these countries: bilateral energy dialogues, regional energy dialogues, various other policy frameworks such as the European Neighbourhood Policy, or the Mediterranean Partnerships are used as frameworks to discuss energy issues.

4.3.1. *Relations with Russia*

For Europe Russia is "the key" to energy security. Russia accounts for %50 of natural gas and %30 of oil imports into the Union. Dependency on Russian energy in particular, differs from one Member State to another reaching its highest points in the new Member States. The most extreme example is Slovakia, which has 97% dependency on Russian gas, and 98% on Russian oil.[53] To take Germany as another example, in 2003, Germany satisfied 24% of its own demand with domestic production, received 44% of its natural gas imports from Russia, 31% from Norway, and 20% from the Netherlands.[54]

Yet, this is a mutual dependence. EU imports a large percentage of the gas it needs from Russia, which means that the Russian gas industry is to a great extent maintained by its revenues from exports to Europe.

---

[52] "Saving 20% by 2020: European Commission unveils its Action Plan on Energy Efficiency", MEMO/07/6, 10.1.2007.

[53] Monaghan, and Montanaro-Jankovski, "EU-Russia energy relations: the need for active engagement ", EPC Issue Paper No. 45, March 2006, p. 16. Available online at: http://www.theepc.be/TEWN/pdf/89495137_EPC%20Issue%20Paper%2045%20EU-Russia%20energy%20relations.pdf

[54] http://www.eia.doe.gov/emeu/cabs/Germany/NaturalGas.html

The fact that Russia accounts only few percentage points of EU global trade, while the Union accounts for half of Russia's foreign trade is another factor cementing the EU-Russian interdependence.

The EU's existing institutional architecture with respect to Russia reflects the centrality of energy matters in relations between the two actors. The centerpieces of the Union's approach can be found in the Energy Charter Treaty (ECT), the EU-Russia Energy Dialogue, and the more broadly construed Four Spaces Policy. These initiatives are built on the legal foundations of the EU-Russia Partnership and Co-operation Agreement (PCA) of 1994, which is to be renegotiated in 2007.

Russian President Putin recently repeated that there will be no change in his country's position regarding the ECT. Moscow considers the charter to be skewed in favour of energy importers. Russian ratification of the ECT would mean the opening of Russian pipelines and deposits to both European companies and to gas exports from Central Asia, which would be a development that Gazprom's current policy is designed to prevent. As a result landlocked Central Asian States, which have no other pipeline connections other than those through Russia, end up selling their gas very cheaply to Russia, which doubles the price and forwards those supplies to Europe.

After hopes on Russian ratification of the ECT faded, the idea of establishing an Energy Dialogue was put forward. The aim of the Energy Dialogue agreed at the Paris summit of 2000, was to institutionalize energy discussions with Russia. This has contributed to helping solve a number of important misunderstandings and problems between the EU and Russia, such as "underlining the importance of long term gas contracts, resolving the question of destination clauses which existed in some long term gas supply contracts, confirming the absence of any EU limit of 30% on imports of fossil fuels from a single external source, addressing certain energy trade issues in the context of the negotiations for Russia's future membership...etc".[55] The decision to increase the capacity of the Yamal-Europe gas pipeline and the agreement in principle on the realization of the North European gas pipeline project are other important developments taking place within the framework of the Energy Dialogue.[56]

---

[55] EU-Russia Energy Dialogue, Sixth Report, Moscow/Brussels October 2005, p. 2
[56] Ibid, p. 6.

The dialogue has provided a forum to deal with key disputes on long-term contracts and destination clauses. One of the most important deals in the area of abolishing territorial sales restrictions was achieved between Gazprom and its Italian counterpart ENI. In this case, the Commission did not initiate a formal procedure, but allowed ENI and Gazprom to find a commercial solution to the problem identified by the Commission. The two companies reached an agreement to delete the territorial restriction clauses in their existing gas supply contracts. This enables ENI to resell the gas that it buys wherever it likes. The settlement also frees Gazprom to sell to other customers in Italy without having to ask for ENI's prior consent.[57]

ENI was the first European importer to achieve an agreement with Gazprom, and others followed. One of the most recent cases, which has been settled, is between Gazprom and the Austrian oil and gas company OMV. The Commission decided in February 2005 to close its investigation into the contracts at issue after the parties agreed to remove the clauses that infringed Article 81 EC. The other important case was between Gazprom and the German Ruhrgas (part of E.ON Group of companies), which is one of Gazprom's most important customers. The two companies agreed to delete the territorial sales restrictions from the contracts under investigation. These were important steps towards creating a com-petitive and integrated European gas market.[58]

The formal basis of the Russia-EU relationship is the Partnership and Cooperation Agreement (PCA) signed in 1994, and in force since December 1997 for an initial duration of 10 years. PCA is primarily an ambitious normative framework, designed to bring Russia closer to EU legislative, economic and trading standards. Yet, there has been little progress in implementing the agreement, due to domestic reasons (mainly due to political and economic crises, and lack of commitment to effective structural and economic reform). The recent EU-Russia summit at Samara passed in a tense atmosphere, and "[n]o substantial progress was made on the opening of negotiations on a new partnership agreement, which is still in suspense, due – in part – to the embargo on Polish agricultural products."[59]

---

[57] IP/03/1345 of 6 October 2003, "European Commission reaches breakthrough with Gazprom and ENI on territorial restriction clauses."

[58] See, Commission Press Releases, IP/05/195 of 17 February 2005, and IP/05/710 of 10 June 2005.

[59] Bulletin Quotidien Europe No. 9429, 22.5.2007, p.5.

Many commentators agree that the fault of the EU lies in its not being able to present itself as a single entity when dealing with Russia and not speaking with a single voice. Unity is not easy to achieve, as the interests of Member States do not always converge. Moscow plays on these differences and seeks to discuss and negotiate separately with one or the other of the Member States depending on the subjects or circumstances in question.[60]

Germany is the primary example of a Member State thwarting the EU approach. Germany has pulled away from the community approach, developing bilateral relations with Russia to such an extent as to have in effect a "special relationship". This relationship is multi-faceted, complex and deep, possessing both personal and formal components. The Baltic Pipeline, "bypassing the eastern European Member-States, provides a core physical link, and the Gazprom-Ruhrgas relationship is cemented in shares and contracts."[61] Furthermore, Gazprom is an explicit critic of the Commission's plans on ownership unbundling, making Ruhrgas's case for it, and on top of that, key politicians are directly involved.[62]

Being pipeline-dependent Russia's approach towards the EU has been twofold. First, to build its relationship with Germany as the pipeline and contracting hub; and secondly, to squeeze the alternative supplies from the Caspian, using the Soviet strategy of routing its export via Russia, while frustrating alternative (non-Russian) routes via for instance, Georgia.

Gazprom is quite successful in its divide-and-rule strategy. A month ago Hungry signed an agreement with Russia to extend the Blue Stream pipeline to Hungary, and declared that its involvement in this project meant its withdrawal from the Nabucco project. Nabucco was one of the projects in the "Priority Interconnection Plan", which would provide Europe with a 'fourth corridor'[63], bringing alternative gas from Central Asia, the Caspian region and the Middle East.

To the objection that this would mean the collapse of EU energy policy, the Hungarian Prime Minister (Ferenc Gyurcsany) is reported to have replied that "you can't make something that doesn't exist collapse."

---

[60] Bulletin Quotidien Europe No. 9431, 24.5.2007, p.3.

[61] Helm, "Russia, Germany and European energy policy", 14.12.2006. Available online at: http://www.opendemocracy.net/globalization-institutions_government/energy_policy_4186.jsp

[62] Gerhard Schröder is chairman of the North European Gas Pipeline project.

[63] The other three are the corridors from Russia, Norway and North Africa.

According to experts, "Gazprom has allegedly promised to make Hungry a crucial distribution center for Russian gas in Europe, building storage, management and distribution infrastructure there."[64]

Abandoning Nabucco would mean that Russia would fully control gas supplies to the EU from the countries from the former USSR. In other words, running after their own national interests, Member States compromise EU energy objectives of diversifying sources and routes. If EU ever wants to see the realization of its energy policy plans, it needs to learn to speak and act as a single unit.

4.3.2. Relations with Norway

Norway is a member of the European Economic Area (EEA) and applies most of the EU *acquis* including legislation on the internal energy market, competition, environment etc. Bilaterally, the EU-Norway Energy Dialogue aims at coordinating energy policies in a wider sense, including research and technological development in the energy sector and relations with other energy producing countries.[65]

4.3.3. Relations with Algeria

Algeria is one of Europe's Mediterranean partners. The main framework for relations is the Euro-Mediterranean Agreement establishing an Association between the Community and Algeria, which foresees a reinforced cooperation in the energy and mining sectors.[66] According to BP's Statistical Review of World Energy, Algeria was the largest MENA (Middle East and North Africa) supplier of gas to Europe in 2004, with 35bn cu metres supplied by pipeline and 19.1bn cu metres of LNG.[67]

Algeria is currently linked to Europe by two pipelines, one to Italy (via Tunisia) and the other to Spain (via Morocco). The capacity of these lines is being expanded and two more pipelines are to be constructed for Algerian gas – Medgaz to Spain and Galsi to northern Italy via Sardinia.

---

[64] Bulletin Quotidien Europe No. 9425, 12.5.2007, p.3.

[65] Annex to the Green Paper, SEC (2006) 317/2, p. 38.

[66] OJ L 265, 10.10.2005.

[67] "Europe's Supply Lines", *Business Middle East*, January 16th-31st 2006, p. 2.

Bilateral discussions with Algeria have already resolved some of the issues about the conformity of long-term contracts with European legislation.

4.3.4. *Relations with the Countries of the Gulf-Cooperation Council (GCC)*

The six countries of the GCC (United Arab Emirates, Bahrain, Saudi Arabia, Oman, Qatar and Kuwait) and the European Community have drawn a cooperation agreement aimed at strengthening their relations in contractual and institutional form.[68] The importance of the EU-GCC relationship lies in the parties' extensive interdependence in terms of energy, trade and investment. The EU needs energy supplies from the GCC countries and imports refined petroleum products, petrochemical products and aluminium. The EU is also one of the largest investors in the GCC.

Qatar and Oman supplied 5bn cu metres of LNG to the Union in 2004. Qatar is gearing up to rival Algeria as the chief supplier of LNG to Europe. The Qatargas 2 project, which is to be operational by 2008, aims at supplying around 21.5bn cu metres/y to the UK through a new terminal being built in Milford Have, Wales.[69]

4.3.5. *Relations with Iran*

Iran is the world's 4th largest oil exporter. It has the second largest reserves in the world for both oil and gas. It is also at the cross-roads of a major transit route: half of the world's traded oil is transported via the Straits of Hormuz. Negotiations for a EU-Iran Trade and Cooperation Agreement started in 2002 and comprised a section on energy. However, since the crisis (due to Iran's wish to develop nuclear capabilities) erupted in August 2005, the EC has frozen the TCA talks and the energy dialogue with Iran is on hold.[70]

---

[68] Council Decision 89/147/EEC, OJ L 54, 25.02.1989.
[69] "Europe's Supply Lines", *Business Middle East*, January 16th-31st 2006, p. 2.
[70] Annex to the Green Paper, SEC (2006) 317/2, p. 38-39.

4.3.6. *Relations with Iraq*

Iraq is important not only for its oil supplies, but also as a potential gas supplier to the EU. The 2004 Commission Communication[71] on Iraq proposed, among other things, the establishment of joint experts' working group on energy issues. However, to date, the Commission has not been successful in launching its planned actions due to the lack of a functioning administration on the Iraqi side. The recently proposed TCA mandate includes energy as one of the potential areas of cooperation.[72]

4.3.7. *Relations with Egypt*

Egypt is a rapidly expanding natural gas producer and it has started exporting gas to the EU. Egypt has a strategic role to play also due to the Suez Canal and the Sumed (Suez-Mediterranean) pipeline, the Arab Natural Gas Pipeline and by construction of LNG export facilities plus gas interconnections with Libya. Egypt is a Euro-Mediterranean partner and is also included in the European Neighbourhood Policy (ENP). On 6 March 2007 the 3rd EU-Egypt Association Council adopted the EU-Egypt Action Plan under the ENP. The Action Plan contains a chapter on energy cooperation.[73]

4.3.8. *Relations with Libya*

The EU has no relations with Libya, a major gas producer. It is neither a Euro-Mediterranean partner nor included in the ENP[74] (due to UN Security Council sanctions). Italy, Germany, Spain, France, and Greece are Libya's top five export markets absorbing %78 of its manufactured goods, energy, food products and raw materials.[75]

---

[71] Communication from the Commission to the Council and the European Parliament of 9 June 2004: "the European Union and Iraq, a framework for engagement", COM (2004) 417 final, not published in the Official Journal.

[72] Annex to the Green Paper, SEC (2006) 317/2, p. 39.

[73] "EU-Egypt: European Neighbourhood Policy Action Plan adopted', IP/07/284, 6.3.2007.

[74] It is included as an observer in the ENP.

[75] See, http://ec.europa.eu/external_relations/libya/intro/index.htm

4.3.9. Relations with Neighbours (the European Neighbourhood Policy (ENP))

Enhancing the energy partnership with the neigbouring countries is a strategic clement of the ENP. Twelve Action Plans are already in force: Armenia, Azerbaijan, Egypt, Georgia, Israel, Jordan, Lebanon, Moldova, Morocco, the Palestinian Authority, Tunisia and Ukraine.

The energy sections of the ENP Action Plans include broad areas of cooperation: energy dialogues, convergence of energy policies and legal/ regulatory frameworks, energy networks, energy efficiency, nuclear safety and (sub) regional cooperation.[76]

4.4. Development of the Internal Electricity and Gas Market

Greater security of energy supply also means having an effective, correctly regulated market, which will enable avoiding potential crises. The problem of physical congestion in networks for gas and electricity must be solved and more must be done to link these networks together. As energy networks become more and more connected, it should become easier to balance supply and demand across the EU.

The recent Energy Sector Inquiry[77] showed the achievements as well as the shortcomings existing in the internal gas and electricity markets. Major problems inherited from monopolistic times such as high concentration levels, lack of liquidity on the wholesale markets, vertical foreclosure, lack of transparency... etc., still exist and give the impression that there is still a long way to go to achieve the objective of a single European energy market. That being the case, a look back at the earlier times (early 1990s) shows us that most of the reforms seen as far-reaching and controversial at the time, for example, account and legal unbundling, have been more than achieved, although proved to be insufficient.

The discussions in the Energy Sector Inquiry, clearly illustrate that new legislation/ strengthened regulatory framework is needed if the

---

[76] Annex to the Green Paper, SEC (2006) 317/2, p. 37. For more details on the ENP, see, http://ec.europa.eu/world/enp/index_en.htm

[77] European Competition, DG Competition Report on Energy Sector Inquiry – 10 January 2007, SEC (2006) 1724, Brussels, 10.01.2007, p. 4.

completion of energy market liberalization is to be achieved in the EU. To be effective, this regulatory framework will need to function hand in hand with EU competition law. Greater powers are needed for national competition and regulatory authorities, whose cooperation is indispensable for the Commission to be able to lead and coordinate the efforts on the way to full liberalization.

5. Conclusion

Another important development towards an Energy Policy for Europe (EPE) has been the adoption in the 2007 May European Council of a comprehensive energy Action Plan for the period 2007-2009 (Annex I), based on the Commission's Communication "An Energy Policy for Europe". Paragraph 37 of the Presidency conclusions summarizes not only the content and objectives of the Action Plan, but also the issues raised in this article, and serves as a useful indicator for the steps forward. It reads as follows:

The Action Plan sets out the way in which significant progress in the efficient operation and completion of the EU's internal market for gas and electricity and a more interconnected and integrated market can be achieved. It envisages the nomination of EU coordinators for four priority projects of European interest. It also addresses the crucial issue of security of energy supply and the response to potential crises. As regards security of supply the European Council stresses the importance of making full use of the instruments available to improve the EU's bilateral cooperation with all suppliers and ensure reliable energy flows into the Union. It develops clear orientations for an effective European international energy policy speaking with a common voice. It fixes highly ambitious quantified targets on energy efficiency, renewable energies and the use of biofuels and call for a European Strategic Energy Technology plan, including environmentally safe Carbon Capture and Sequestration, to be examined at the Spring 2008 European Council meeting.

AS DIFERENTES VISÕES
DA INTEGRAÇÃO EUROPEIA

PAULO DE PITTA E CUNHA[*]

1. Sendo o fenómeno da integração europeia marcadamente dinâmico, não surpreende que as teorias explicativas procurem ajustar-se às variações observadas no processo. Persiste, porém, a antinomia entre as visões neo-funcionais, que constituem uma forma incremental de construção da federação, e as teses intergovernamentais, que propendem a defender o "statu quo", ou, até, a fazer retroceder o processo.

As teorias referidas concentram-se no fenómeno da soberania, que a primeira pretende ver assumida pela estrutura federal preconizada, e que para a segunda é o marco indelével da subsistência dos Estados no coração do movimento.

À dicotomia supranacionalismo/intergovernamentalismo têm-se oposto outras soluções, como a da governação em diferentes níveis, para explicar a hibridez do fenómeno da integração da Europa e, de certo modo, ladeando as questões do destino último do poder soberano, pela consideração de que a União Europeia não pretende assumir a forma típica de um Estado, mas corresponde a um estilo diferente de governação.

2. Novas tensões se produzem no decorrer da integração, afastando-se dos pressupostos em que assenta a dicotomia clássica.

Para além das visões da integração em que o movimento opera por igual para todos os Estados (recusando-se globalmente a abdicação dos poderes nacionais, ou, no outro extremo, preconizando-se que se

---

[*] Professor jubilado da Faculdade de Direito da Universidade de Lisboa; Presidente da Direcção do Instituto Europeu da Faculdade de Direito de Lisboa.

arranque de modo homogéneo para a federação), tende a assumir crescente importância a perspectiva da decomposição daquele fenómeno, sob a forma de integração diferenciada.

São conhecidas as diferentes intensidades da diferenciação, desde as várias velocidades à geometria variável e, no limite, as modalidades "à la carte". Essa perspectiva ganha vigor à medida que os limites geográficos da União se vão alargando, atenta a crescente heterogeneidade que o alargamento implica. Não foi por acaso que a regulação do instituto da cooperação reforçada no direito originário coincidiu com a perspectiva de quase duplicação do número de membros da União (Tratado de Amesterdão).

Mas o fenómeno de diferenciação entre países não se limita às preferências manifestadas por determinados grupos por formas mais intensas de actuação. Nele também se comportam as situações de tratamento desigual dos Estados membros ligadas ao factor dimensão – é este o quadro da oposição entre os países grandes e os países médios e pequenos, oposição que durante muitos anos esteve apenas latente, mas que surgiu a plena luz quando, a partir de Nice, os primeiros procuraram assegurar-se de maior fatia de poder no processo de tomada de decisões no Conselho.

Esta linha foi fortalecida pela solução do Tratado constitucional, ligando o peso do voto, em pleno, ao elemento demográfico.

3. Mas a questão do equilíbrio entre os Estados membros não se põe apenas no plano político-institucional, pois subjacente a ela está a ideia da formação de uma espécie de directório em que pontifiquem os grandes. Manifestações do fenómeno foram, no fundo, as iniciativas franco-germânicas do passado.

Mas o bloco com vocação directorial não está presentemente definido, embora, por exemplo, os esforços diplomáticos em relação ao Irão por parte do Reino Unido, da Alemanha e da França, a propósito do programa nuclear daquele país, estejam na linha da superioridade dos grandes. A composição de um núcleo dirigente é mutável, podendo completar-se com a mobilização de alguns dos médios e dos pequenos países gravitando em torno dos grandes.

O projecto de Constituição comportava aspectos de protofederalismo, num fundo de afirmação da desigualdade entre os Estados

As Diferentes Visões da Integração Europeia 407

membros, expressa no peso demográfico. Vinha, nessa medida, ao encontro das pretensões hegemónicas contidas nas propostas em que a intensificação da integração é confiada a uma vanguarda ou a um grupo pioneiro.

Na fase actual de recuperação parcial daquele projecto, torna-se difícil prever o futuro da integração europeia. O objectivo último do processo continua indefinido, salvo quando encarado numa óptica federalista extrema. O alargamento da União descaracteriza-a. O avanço da construção por mecanismos de cooperação reforçada traz sérios riscos de pulverização do processo.

Neste contexto de incerteza, não se compreende a ânsia que se vai afirmando pela precipitada revisão dos Tratados, por via da substituição dos vigentes por um outro em que se procurem salvar as disposições institucionais da malograda Constituição.

4. Para além dos modelos políticos (Europa federal ou Europa intergovernamental), importa considerar a posição que se desenha quanto aos modelos económicos da integração.

Trata-se aqui do choque da perspectiva do mercado aberto e da plena concorrência, que constitui a actual fase de integração introduzida pela CEE e continuada através do mercado único, e a abordagem intervencionista do fenómeno, como afirmação dos objectivos de política económica nacional, designadamente em termos da realização do chamado "modelo social". Torna-se difícil fundir as duas correntes, sendo certo que, na sua lógica extensão, o intervencionismo não deixa de se mostrar contrário ao próprio desígnio da integração. Até agora, o esforço de compatibilização tem sido empreendido por instrumentos flexíveis de "soft law", como é o caso da Estratégia de Lisboa.

5. A União Europeia, impulsionada pelos alargamentos, excede amplamente os Estados Unidos da América em nível demográfico (a sua população é 50% superior), e aproxima-se muito deste país em termos de produto e de comércio externo. No entanto, continua a ser aquilo que foi qualificado como "uma curiosa espécie de união" – basicamente, uma entidade política de essência confederal com traços de federação.

6. Cabe reconhecer que, tal como hoje se apresenta, a União Europeia se parece cada vez mais com um Estado.

Na verdade:

a) A arquitectura institucional é semelhante à de uma federação.

b) Existe uma cidadania própria da União.

c) O Parlamento Europeu, orgão supranacional, assume crescente influência no processo de criação legislativa.

d) Existe um orgão executivo também de índole supranacional, a Comissão, independente dos Governos dos Estados membros.

e) Há um orgão jurisdicional que pode sancionar o incumprimento por parte dos Estados membros e anular os actos dos outros orgãos da União.

f) As instituições da União têm poder de criação legislativa, em termos de supremacia do respectivo ordenamento sobre os ordenamentos nacionais.

g) Para os países que entraram para a união económica e monetária, existe uma moeda comum e uma política monetária comum.

h) Aplica-se um sistema de recursos próprios ao orçamento da União.

i) Os Estados membros são sujeitos a sanções em situações de incumprimento e de défice orçamental excessivo.

7. Outros elementos, porém, não tornam possível classificar a União Europeia como um Estado.

Assim:

a) Baseia-se em Tratados internacionais, que só podem ser revistos por unanimidade dos Estados participantes.

b) A União só actua nos domínios que lhe são atribuídos pelos Tratados.

c) O orgão impulsor da integração é o Conselho Europeu, de carácter intergovernamental.

d) A União não detém o poder coercitivo das decisões que adopta.

e) O Conselho, orgão intergovernamental, mantém papel primordial no processo de criação normativa, havendo campos em que as suas decisões são tomadas por unanimidade.

f) A cidadania da União é apenas complementar das cidadanias nacionais.

g) Os campos da política externa e da defesa permanecem adstritos aos Estados membros, apenas sendo abordados nas formas clássicas de cooperação.

As Diferentes Visões da Integração Europeia

h) Não existem impostos criados e geridos pela União.

i) O orçamento da União é diminuto e não incorpora as funções próprias de um Estado, quer no aspecto da afectação de recursos, quer, substancialmente, no da redistribuição, quer no da estabilização.

j) A vertente económica da UEM está apenas esboçada, cabendo as decisões fundamentalmente aos Estados membros.

8. O Tratado constitucional (rejeitado nos referendos francês e holandês)não iria alterar substancialmente as características híbridas que ficam referidas. A União continuaria a estar longe de poder considerar--se como um Estado. Mas o Tratado continha aspectos que apontavam nitidamente no sentido federal. Era definida uma separação de competências entre a União e os Estados Membros, em termos favoráveis àquela. O presidente da Comissão passaria a ser eleito pelo Parlamento Europeu. Eram criadas figuras novas: Presidente (fixo) do Conselho Europeu, Ministro dos Negócios Estrangeiros da União. Alargava-se a área das votações por maioria qualificada. O Parlamento dava mais um passo em frente no processo legislativo. Os regulamentos e as directivas receberiam a denominação de leis e leis-quadro. Muitas destas alterações são aparentemente formais, mas a verdade é que poderiam funcionar como catalisador de uma evolução no sentido federal. A adopção do termo "Constituição" reforçava fortemente esta tendência – até por que atrás dele vinham os símbolos – o hino, o lema, e mesmo o dia "nacional".

Ora, o arranjo a que se chegou na recentíssima reunião do Conselho Europeu, marcado pela contestação da Polónia ao sistema de votação em base demográfica e pela insistência nas excepções britânicas, veio eliminar alguns dos símbolos do superEstado, mas a verdade é que, na substância, retomou as disposições institucionais do Tratado constitucional.

O novo documento é concebido como Tratado simplificado, ou Tratado renovador, o que constituiu uma forma de tornear os embaraços representados pelos referendos. A Europa institucional prossegue, assim, em passos furtivos, deixando para o futuro a resolução dos problemas reais.

9. No momento presente, talvez a distinção mais relevante em termos de visões da integração seja a que opõe a perspectiva das propostas radicais, de grande ressonância (como foi o caso da Constituição europeia) à óptica instrumentalista dirigida às políticas que visem resolver as questões concretas que preocupam os europeus (a segurança energética, a prossecução do emprego, o combate às alterações climáticas, a repressão do crime internacional, a baixa demográfica, o problema da imigração). São deste tipo as questões pelas quais se pode apreciar a medida de satisfação dos cidadãos europeus pela forma como a integração está a ser conduzida e avaliar o grau de reconhecimento dos benefícios que esperam ver resultar do processo.

Junho de 2007

THE DIFFERENT PERSPECTIVES
OF EUROPEAN INTEGRATION

PAULO DE PITTA E CUNHA[*]

1. Considering the fact that the phenomenon of European integration is markedly dynamic, it is not surprising that the explanatory theories do try to adapt themselves to any variance that may occur along this process. However, the antinomy persists between neo-functional views, which constitute an incremental form for the creation of a federation, and the intergovernmental theses, which tend to favour the "statu quo", or even to make the process to move back.

These theories are all focused on the sovereignty phenomenon, that the former wishes to see assumed by the advocated federal structure, and to the latter is the indelible landmark of subsistence of the power of the States in the heart of this movement.

Other solutions (such as governance at different levels) have been urged against the dichotomy supranationalism/intergovernmentalism to explain the hybridism of the European integration phenomenon and, in a given way, circumventing the issues concerning the ultimate purpose of the sovereign power, by considering that the European Union is not meant to assume the typical form of a State, but rather corresponds to a different style of governance.

2. New tensions are arising along the integration process, deviating from the preconditions on which the traditional dichotomy is anchored.

---

[*] Professor at the Faculty of Law of the University of Lisbon; President of the Board of the European Institute of Faculty of Law of Lisbon.

Beyond those perspectives of integration according to which the movement operates equally for every State involved (globally refusing the surrender of national powers or, in the opposite stance, advocating a homogenous launching towards a federation), the perspective of decomposition of such phenomenon under the form of a differentiated integration tends to assume an ever increasing relevance.

The different degrees of intenseness for such a differentiation are well-known, from two or more speeds to the variable geometry and, ultimately, the so-called à la carte modalities. This perspective is getting further force insofar as the geographic boundaries of the Union are expanding, due regard being had to the increasing heterogeneity that such enlargement implies. It was not by chance that the regulation of enhanced cooperation in the primary law did coincide with the perspective of an almost duplication of the number of Union members (Amsterdam Treaty).

However, the phenomenon of differentiation among countries is not limited to preferences shown by certain groups through more intensive ways of action. It also includes those situations of unequal treatment of Member States in connection with the dimension factor – this is the context of the opposition between big countries and medium/small size countries, an opposition that for many years was only latent, but came fully to light when, since Nice, the big countries are trying to procure themselves a bigger slice of power in the Council decision-making process.

This line was reinforced by the solution adopted by the Treaty establishing a Constitution for Europe to the extent that it fully links the weight of voting to the demographic element.

3. Nevertheless, the question of balance among Member States does not arise just at the political-institutional level, insofar as the underlying idea of forming a sort of directoire where the big countries may pontificate does exist. In the past the manifestations of this phenomenon were, usually, Franco-German initiatives.

The bloc with a directorial vocation is not yet clearly defined, although (for instance) the diplomatic efforts in relation to Iran on the part of the United Kingdom, Germany and France, in connection with the nuclear programme of this country, are in line with the command of the big ones. The composition of a ruling nucleus is quite changeable and may be completed by the mobilization of some medium and small countries which orbit the big countries.

The draft Constitution comprised some aspects of protofederalism against a background of assertion of inequality among Member States, as expressed in the demographic weight. To that extent, it kept in line with the hegemonic claims comprised in the proposals under which the reinforcement of integration is committed with a forefront or a pioneer group.

At the present stage of partial retrieve of such project, it is difficult to anticipate the future of the European integration. The ultimate goal of the process is still to be defined, unless if envisaged from an extreme federalist viewpoint. The enlargement of the Union deprives it of its main features. The furtherance of the construction by way of enhanced cooperation mechanisms brings with it serious risks of pulverization of the process.

In this context of uncertainty, it is not easy to understand the reiterated eagerness in doing a hasty revision of Treaties by way of the replacement of those in force with another one, under which the institutional provisions of the unsuccessful Constitution are meant to be rescued.

4. Beyond the political models (a federal Europe or an intergovernmental Europe), it is important to discuss the stance that is being outlined in respect of the economic models of integration.

What is at stake here is the clash of the open arm's length market viewpoint that constitutes the current stage of integration first introduced by the EEC and thereafter carried on by the single market, and the interventionist approach of this phenomenon as an assertion of domestic economic policy goals, particularly in terms of achievement of the so-called "social model". It would appear difficult to merge both currents, bearing in mind that interventionism, in its logical spreading, is not without proving itself contrary to the own purpose of integration. Until now, the compatibilization effort has been achieved through some flexible "soft law" instruments, such as the Lisbon Strategy.

5. The European Union, on the spur of its enlargement, exceeds by far the United States of America at the demographic level (its population is 50 per cent higher) and is quite close of this country in terms of product and external trade. Nevertheless, it continues to be what has been qualified as "a curious kind of Union" – basically a political entity of confederal nature with some features of a federation.

6. It must be recognized that the European Union, in its present form, bears more and more a greater resemblance to a State.

As a matter of fact:

a) The institutional architecture is similar to that of a federation;

b) The Union has its own citizenship;

c) The European Parliament, a supranational body, assumes an increasing influence in the process of law-making activities;

d) There is an executive body also of a supranational nature, the Commission, independent from the governments of the Member States;

e) There is a jurisdictional body endowed with powers to impose sanctions on non-compliance by Member States and to make null and void acts performed by other Union bodies;

f) Union institutions are assigned legislative powers in terms of precedence of their own legal system over national ones;

g) For those countries having accessed to the economic and monetary Union, there is a common currency and a common monetary policy,

h) A system of own resources is applicable to the Union budget;

i) Member States are liable to penalties in case of non-compliance and excessive budgetary deficit.

7. Other elements, however, make it impossible to qualify the European Union as a State.

Thus:

a) It is rooted in international Treaties, which may only be reviewed by unanimous voting of the participating States;

b) The Union only acts and operates in those domains assigned to it under Treaty provisions;

c) The driving body for integration is the European Council of an intergovernmental nature;

d) No coercive powers are conferred upon the Union for any decisions adopted;

e) The Council, an intergovernmental body, maintains a leading role in the process of normative activity, with some areas in which its decisions are taken by unanimous vote;

f) The Union citizenship is only complementary to national citizenships;

g) The domains of foreign policy and defence are kept assigned to Member States, being addressed under the classical forms of cooperation;

h) There are no taxes established and managed by the Union;

i) The Union budget is quite reduced and does not incorporate those functions which are proper of a State both in what concerns the allocation of resources and, substantially, in what concerns reallocation or stabilization;

j) The economic aspect of the EMU is barely outlined, and decisions are essentially incumbent upon Member States.

8. The Constitutional Treaty (rejected in the French and Dutch referendums) would not change substantially the above-mentioned hybrid characteristics. The Union would be all the same far from being perceived as a State. Notwithstanding this, the Treaty contained some aspects which clearly pointed out towards a federal solution. A separation of competences between the Union and Member States was therein set out in terms favourable to the Union. The president of the Commission would be elected by the European Parliament. New figures would be created: a (permanent) President of the European Council, a Minister for Foreign Affairs for the Union. The area of qualified majority voting would be extended. The Parliament would take a further step forward in the legislative process. Regulations and directives would be given a new designation as laws and framework-laws. A number of these changes are apparently formal, but the truth is that they could function as a catalyst for a development towards a federal goal. The adoption of the word "Constitution" came to strongly strengthen this trend – so much so because of all the symbols behind it: the anthem, the motto and even the "national" day.

The arrangement reached at the quite June meeting of the European Council, that was marked by the Polish objection against the demography-based voting system, and the insistence on British exceptions, happened to eliminate some of the super-State symbols, but the fact is that the project resumed, in substance, the institutional provisions of the Constitutional Treaty.

The document is construed as a simplified Treaty, or a renovating Treaty, what seems to be a way of coping with the hindrances caused by the referenda. The institutional Europe is creeping along with stealthy steps, leaving the real problems unsolved.

9. The Reform Treaty, whose formulation was defined at the informal European Council of 22 June 2007, was aimed at maintaining the substance of the frustrated Constitutional Treaty with a number of symbolic terminological changes. The most substantial features were almost fully kept with just some slight mitigation of the centralising guidance underlying the Constitution.

The Reform Treaty – that stands as quite a perfect "Ersatz" to the European Constitution – is thus the direct follower (and, to a large extent, the "resuscitator") of the European Constitution under a hardly innocuous cover. However, if the intention is, as it appears to be, to try to avoid the ratification process by way of national referendums, evoking the narrower scope of the new Treaty to justify the fact that ratification is made by Parliamentary decision, such an assertion is not deemed acceptable.

In plain language, what is subjacent to the artfully ingenious proposal made by the Reform Treaty is the intention to obviate the risky obstacle of an electorate voting by way of a comfortable approval at the Parliamentary level; it means that, all along the European integration, the stealthy method of approval of essential changes behind the citizen's back has been retrieved. In this case, it is still more consequential since this procedure is adopted following the refusal of the Constitutional Treaty by the electorate of two countries, moreover EEC founders, this representing a serious depreciation of the democratic value of the voting then made.

10. After the "Community" has been merged into the single concept of a Union, it will be the modified Treaty of the European Union that will fully enshrine the Union objectives.

The no less artful dilution of the reference to the principle of an "open market economy with free competition" (art. 4 of the European Community Treaty currently in force), as opposed to the emphasis given to the formula "social market economy, aiming at full employment and social progress" contained in art. 3 of the proposed new version of the European Union Treaty, is probably designed to mitigate criticism from those sectors unfavourable to the neo-liberal integration bases.

11. Since the Draft Constitutional Treaty became known, a number of serious reserves on its contents have been formulated: emphasized prevalence of the larger States; negative implications of a fixed presidency – a particularly sensitive aspect for Portugal, at a moment on which this country was benefiting from the visibility that resulted from the half-yearly rotation; lack of financial solidarity mechanisms among Member States; federalist drive of the European integration process, eventually leading one day to the loss of the "State status" for the countries involved in a European federal structure(*). As it happens to be, all these features are contained in the proposed Reform Treaty.

12. It is to be regretted that non-big countries (at least the six medium countries ranked between 10 and 15 million inhabitants, particularly un-favoured in terms of individual voting power at the Council and number of deputies at the European Parliament) have not taken advantage from the extended "period for reflection" to assume a common position in respect of the changes to the text of the Constitutional Treaty which better matched their own interests.

Basically, there were only two disagreeing voices and both of them in countries with about 40 million (or more) inhabitants: that of the United Kingdom, urging quite a number of exceptions, and that of Poland against the voting system on a mere demographic basis. Unfortunately, there seems to have been no sensitive reticences formulated by medium States, either jointly or individually – namely by Portugal.

13. Following its approval by the Governments, the new Treaty should be submitted to the referendum approval procedure, if anything in those Member States where there was a political commitment – as is the case of Portugal – to have recourse to such procedure in regard to the European Constitution (not to mention, obviously, those countries that, with different success, have already held referendums around this same Constitution). Otherwise, the democratic legitimacy of the "resuscitation" of the European construction will be seriously damaged, given the undervaluation of the meaning of direct voting by the citizens as compared to that of their representatives.

14. At the present moment, the most relevant distinction in terms of perspectives of integration is perhaps the one opposing the perspective of

---

(*) See the study "Reservas à Constituição Europeia", Coimbra, 2005, p. 87 ff.

radical proposals which had a considerable echo (as is the case of the European Constitution) and the instrumentalist point of view addressed to those policies designed to solve some particular issues of concern for the Europeans (energetic safety, unemployment and social exclusion, climatic changes, combat of international crime, demographic decline, the immigration problem). It is in the solution this kind of issues that one can appreciate the satisfaction of the European citizens on how integration is being conducted and the assessment of the degree of recognition of benefits expected from this process.

June 2007

PORTUGAL E A EUROPA – O PASSADO[*]

EDUARDO VERA-CRUZ PINTO[**]

Muito bom dia. Começo por agradecer ao Senhor Professor Paulo de Pitta e Cunha o convite para aqui estar e dizer da muita honra que tenho em estar num círculo de Conferências com este nível realizado em Lisboa.

O tema que me coube foi Portugal e o passado, atendendo sobretudo à forma como Portugal deve estar no futuro na União Europeia.

Ora o passado, sobretudo de um país que é um Estado-Nação dos mais antigos da Europa, pelo menos com mais estabilidade nas suas fronteiras, nos 25 minutos que o Senhor Professor Jorge Miranda me deu, não deixa de ser uma aventura. Seleccionei então cinco dos elementos principais da nossa História relacionados com a Europa para fazer depois uma síntese, que seja, pelo menos prospectiva relativamente à forma como o século XXI pode ser vivido num Portugal europeu.

Começaria por um episódio em que Portugal foi pioneiro, e seleccionei quatro ou cinco episódios em que Portugal e os portugueses foram pioneiros na maneira de pensar ou na maneira de fazer, porque, compulsando os livros de História da Europa ou de História do Direito Europeu, raramente encontramos referências a Portugal ou aos portugueses que fizeram a História de Europa. Por isso, já que a Conferência é em Lisboa e já que se trata de uma Conferência dada por um português, eu seleccionei estes episódios que me parecem sintomáticos.

Começo com o período pré-nacional, antes da fundação da nacionalidade um dos episódios mais marcantes da presença romana em Portugal

---

[*] Texto não revisto pelo Autor e publicado com o seu consentimento.
[**] Faculdade de Direito da Universidade de Lisboa.

foi a do governador Sérvio Sulpício Galba, um episódio esquecido, por vezes aparece referido nos livros da pré-história, naquelas enciclopédias do Círculo dos Leitores lá vem uma referência mais desenvolvida porque aquilo são muitas páginas e convém desenvolver mais os episódios. O que aconteceu foi o seguinte: os lusitanos estavam a fazer uma forte resistência aos romanos (não queria estar a falar muito da ligação entre os lusitanos e os portugueses porque isso levou a uma querela e a desafios para duelo, no século XIX, entre o Herculano, Oliveira Martins. Houve aí uma grande pega, mas, sem agora fazer a relação entre os lusitanos e os portugueses num espaço geográfico que hoje é Portugal, embora também alguma historiografia espanhola considere que os lusitanos são oriundos da Andaluzia e não propriamente de Portugal ou da Serra da Estrela, mas, enfim, se levantar as polémicas todas da historiografia, depois, meto-me em demasiados atalhos para depois poder voltar à auto-estrada, de forma que vou continuar aqui pelo caminho largo). Houve um massacre, Viriato tinha 14 anos, e os romanos mandaram para cá um senador que já tinha sido pretor. Havia o *cursus honorum* em Roma, e este senador decidiu acabar com a resistência dos lusitanos assinando um pacto: "Vamos assinar um pacto, vamos fazer a paz! Vocês ficam com umas terras..." etc. já então, tinha escrito um historiador romano, que vivia aqui na ponta da Europa, um povo que nem se governava nem se deixava governar. Não sei se isto é sintomático para o futuro, o certo é que Galba fez um pacto com os lusitanos, chamou-os para as comemorações do pacto e depois num Vale, o Vale de Ossoa, ocorreu o massacre. Os massacres naquele tempo levavam vários dias, não havia a tecnologia de hoje e, por isso, os lusitanos foram passados pela espada. Morreram milhares de lusitanos, segundo rezam as crónicas, e muitos foram feitos escravos e levados para fora da Península.

Galba ficou ilustre, tinha vencido a resistência dos lusitanos. Quando chegou a Roma encontrou um velho de noventa e tal anos, já na altura, Catão, que disse: "Não vale tudo! O Direito deve ser cumprido. Roma tem regras e, por isso, conseguir vencer o inimigo violando a palavra do povo romano, isso tem que ser aferido da responsabilidade!". E Galba foi julgado por iniciativa do Senado. Pela primeira vez, por causa do massacre dos lusitanos, introduziu-se no Processo Penal Romano a ideia de que num julgamento não devem estar apenas em causa os factos ocorridos, mas também a vida da pessoa que está a ser julgada. Galba disse: "Eu servi Roma, tenho esta idade, não tenho

Portugal e a Europa – O passado   421

nenhuma nódoa no meu curriculum, estive sempre ao serviço do povo de Roma. Fiz uma coisa para poupar vidas de romanos, acabei com um povo longínquo, um povo bárbaro lá da Lusitânia e agora julgam-me em Roma por causa disso?! Então tomem a minha mulher e os meus filhos, criem--nos, que eu morro em nome de Roma." Foi uma grande comoção, o tribuno da plebe apareceu em defesa, porque estes demagogos romanos normalmente arrastavam as multidões, dizendo "Parece incrível, com um homem que está ao serviço de Roma, apesar de matar os lusitanos lá longe, o que é que isso faz? Ninguém sabe quem eles são, ninguém os conhece! E nós conhecemos Galba e o seu percurso, portanto em vez de condenar Galba à morte, vamos absolvê-lo ou, pelo menos, dar-lhe uma pena mais ténue." E assim foi.

Logo, um episódio ocorrido aqui no território que hoje é Portugal levou a uma mudança profunda na forma como a jurisprudência romana – não estou a falar da jurisprudência no sentido actual das sentenças dos tribunais, mas dos jurisprudentes romanos – alterou um pouco o curso do processo penal, e passou-se a considerar este elemento subjectivo na objectividade da prova.

Este episódio serve também para explicar que grande parte da população portuguesa do final da antiguidade clássica não tem muito a ver com os povos pré-históricos, ou aqueles povos, os tordetanos, os tartésios etc. Tem pouco a ver com isso, porquê? Porque os Romanos esvaziaram a Península e trouxeram gente nova, grande parte da população são colonos vindos da Itália. Não posso desenvolver muito o tema, mas há uma ruptura na continuidade antropológica com a invasão romana.

Segundo episódio já ligado à independência de Portugal. Portugal estava num processo de separação do reino de Leão, o panorama na Península era muito complicado, porque o ambiente era de reconquista e havia uma verdadeira revolução mental. Já devem ter ouvido falar do Renascimento do Século XII. O século XII mexeu com tudo, mas mexeu sobretudo no plano eclesiástico, a reforma canónica, a reforma gregoriana, a forma como se entendia que o Papa devia intervir nas questões políticas, as guerras entre o papado e o império. E foi neste ambiente assim muito tumultuado que Afonso Henriques começa o processo de autonomização e depois de independência relativamente ao reino de Leão.

Em Portugal, sobretudo na zona do Douro para cima, havia o problema da luta entre a facção francesa e a facção moçárabe, enfim, peço vénia aqui ao Professor Manuel Porto, mas Coimbra foi o centro desta polémica e desta confusão, se me permite dizer assim, porque Afonso Henriques cedo mudou a capital, se é que podemos falar assim de mudar a capital naquela altura, mas mudou o centro de decisão política de Guimarães para Coimbra, e juntou alguns clérigos muito cosmopolitas[1].

Afonso Henriques juntou em Coimbra uma série de clérigos cosmopolitas, muito ligados à Europa, muito ligados a Cluny, muito ligados a Roma. Telho, Teotónio, João Peculiar eram homens que peregrinavam à Terra Santa, tinham relações com os grandes abades, os grandes mosteiros da altura. Foram estes homens europeus, verdadeiramente europeus, que deram a Portugal uma dimensão logo no início importante, porque retirou Portugal da prisão centrípeta de Madrid. Ainda hoje sabemos a força atractiva da centralidade Ibérica. E assim sendo, estes homens conseguiram passar os Pirinéus, ir a França, a Cluny, meter-se nos movimentos de ideias políticas e de renovação canónica e trazer para Portugal, com grande pioneirismo, estas ideias e estas ordens, por exemplo, os templários que chegaram a Portugal, ainda antes de serem reconhecidos pelo Papa, e os movimentos canónicos que em Coimbra afastaram a ideia Moçárabe, a liturgia moçárabe, a bíblia traduzida para Árabe, num ambiente de crispação da reconquista, lutas religiosas, lutas políticas etc. Portugal nasce através de um contributo fortíssimo dos portugueses que saíram da Hispânia e foram à Europa buscar ideias, buscar instituições, que depois marcaram o século XII português e foram determinantes no reconhecimento pelo Papa na *bula manifestus probatum* da soberania – isto agora também é um anacronismo –, mas da soberania portuguesa.

---

[1] *Cosmopolis* tem pouco a ver com a *civitas maxima* e, portanto, falar de juristas, mesmo que sejam eclesiásticos cosmopolitas, não deixa de ser uma certa heresia e um anacronismo. Todos sabemos que os gregos tinham muito a ideia da cidade do *cosmos*, e aí temos as obras gregas. Os romanos pelo contrário tinham a ideia da *civitas*. Esta diferença é muito importante, até para compreendermos algumas destas influências actuais do Direito Europeu, gregos, Atenas, Jerusalém e Roma. Muitos ensaios que têm saído agora sobre a ideia da Europa trazem-nos esta tripla influência. Claro que, como professor de Direito Romano, não posso deixar de dizer que Roma é determinante e que Jerusalém e Atenas são assim uma espécie de subsidiárias na ideia de Europa, porque os gregos tinham uma ideia de nacionalidade, e de pertença muito ligada ao sangue, muito ligada à nacionalidade e os romanos muito ligada ao estatuto jurídico. Era romano quem por Direito pudesse ser romano, interessava pouco a sua origem étnica, religiosa, geográfica ou outra.

Avanço na História, e vou para a crise de 1383-85. Aí, outra vez, a Europa presente na forma como Portugal sobrevive. Já a Universidade de Bolonha tinha dado os seus frutos, já Portugal beneficiava desse movimento de releitura do *Corpus Iuris Civilis* e, nessa altura, dá-se uma crise que todos conhecem. O rei morre, não tem herdeiros, o herdeiro é uma senhora que, em virtude de uma aventura política e militar de D. Fernando onde é celebrado um Tratado, a herdeira do trono de Portugal casará com o herdeiro do trono de Espanha e desta união nascerá depois uma união política mais efectiva. Ora, este Tratado e esta ideia que alicerçou no povo a ideia do "nem bom vento, nem bom casamento" vindo de Espanha, porque os casamentos continuavam a continuidade dinástica, e a continuidade dinástica, era o certificado de idoneidade e de independência de Portugal. O casamento da beltraneja Dona Joana com o D. João I de Castela colocou um problema seríssimo. O Tratado foi negociado de forma que alguns anos permitissem a Portugal arranjar uma solução qualquer, mas a independência estava comprometida. A revolta da Casa dos Vinte e Quatro, das doze corporações de Lisboa, episódios que bem conhecem da revolução, levaram a que o ainda não rei, o Mestre de Avis, D. João I, combinasse um casamento com a filha do Duque de Lencastre. Ora, a filha do Duque veio para Lisboa e ficou cá para conhecer o noivo e aguardar o casamento. Neste entretém está D. João I, o Mestre de Avis, a aguardar a dispensa papal, porque era Mestre de uma ordem militar, tinha voto de celibato. Tendo voto de celibato não podia casar, estava à espera da dispensa papal. Ora, o Duque de Lencastre viajando para Espanha, reorganizou a vida dele e combinou com o rei de Castela dar-lhe a mesma filha para casar com ele. Não sei se espiões, ou talvez a velha intriguinha nacional trouxeram aos ouvidos de D. João I que a duquesa ia embora, que o pai já tinha combinado tudo com o rei de Castela e que iam retirá-la de noite para uma nau que estava aqui em Lisboa e que iria para Espanha. Ele convocou o Conselho, alarmado, e o Conselho tinha um homem, plebeu, que era conhecido por João das Regras, todos nós já ouvimos falar de João das Regras – tem aliás uma estátua na Faculdade de Direito, não é uma estátua, é um arbusto. Ora, João das Regras colocado perante este facto "Vamos perder a independência porque um casamento feito fora da Hispânia não pode acontecer", disse a D. João I através da leitura que fazia dos textos, que o seu voto de celibato se mantinha se ele consumasse o casamento antes dele ser consumado, porque não tinha voto de castidade, porque era membro de uma ordem militar. Ora, esta solução jurídica, que eu não sei se ocorreu, mas que houve casamento creio que sim. D. João das Regras arranjou uma forma de permitir que D. João I, dentro da lei, efectivasse uma das alianças mais importantes para o futuro de Portugal. Logo, o Direito Romano, os juristas, e neste caso muito daquilo que é ligar Portugal à Inglaterra foi determinante para manter a independência do Reino. Aproveito para dizer que todos sabemos, todos creio eu, em termos de geopolítica que Portugal, para se manter independente, não apenas no plano político e económico, mas em todos os planos, no todo hispânico, precisa de uma fronteira marítima diversa da fronteira terrestre. Se tivermos a fronteira terrestre fechada pela mesma potência que nos fecha a fronteira terrestre nunca seremos independentes.

Ora, esta ideia de D. João I de ter uma fronteira marítima aberta, de ter o estuário do Tejo aberto a uma das armadas que se estava a fazer, e que foi uma das mais importantes armadas que depois sustentou o império britânico, a aliança de Portugal e de Inglaterra é determinante para manter a diversidade das fronteiras e, assim, a independência de Portugal.

Não tenho possibilidade de falar dos Descobrimentos, porque os Descobrimentos foram um momento de grande afirmação nacional, no sentido de que Portugal consegue através das Descobertas dar à Europa uma ideia de unidade, que já existia de alguma forma mas que, pela primeira vez, se confronta, se é que é verdade, às ideias de Charles Smith, daquele tópico de análise de Ciência Política – Amigo/Inimigo – que a identidade só se constrói em contraste com outros. Então, a identidade europeia, que já conhecia os homens negros da África, que já conhecia os homens amarelos da Ásia, não conhecia os homens da América. É uma descoberta estes homens diferentes, estes homens que são dóceis no trato, mas que são muito ariscos à escravatura, não se submetem, preferem morrer, que não têm propriamente religiões, sobretudo os ianomanios, os tapajós, as tribos com que os portugueses começaram por contactar no Brasil, e assim sendo, o Direito das Descobertas, a construção da Segunda Escolástica, Francisco Suaréz, Luís de Molina, Spúlveda, não é nosso mas eram todos mestres em Évora, todos estes homens ajudaram a construir um Direito novo para uma situação nova e para homens completamente novos, que os europeus conheceram por causa das Descobertas.

Gostava de vos falar do Padre António Vieira e da importância que a construção do Padre António Vieira, sobretudo no Quinto Império, no império do Espírito Santo, teve numa espécie de desmaterialização dos

Portugal e a Europa – O passado　　　425

impérios. A Europa ainda vivia a ideia da *Translactio Imperi* e logo todas as cidades com sete colinas mereciam ser capitais de império, Roma tinha sete colinas, Constantinopla tinha sete colinas, Moscovo tinha sete colinas, Lisboa tinha sete colinas e o Rio de Janeiro... Bom.... Então a ideia de sete colinas, da *translactio imperi*, a ideia de que Portugal podia ser a cabeça de um império de homens, de armas para expandir a fé encontrou na *Clavis Profectarum, A História do Futuro*, escrita pelo Padre António Vieira, uma ideia completamente diversa, e tão ameaçadora para Portugal que, como se sabe, o Padre António Vieira foi muito incomodado pela Inquisição, como já tinham sido muitos humanistas portugueses antes, e só a intervenção do Papa permitiu ao Padre António Vieira continuar a escrever, apesar daquele processo complicado que também conhecemos os pormenores.

Sem tempo para abordar isto, eu entraria directamente no Iluminismo e dizer da importância, da novidade, que foi a intervenção do Marquês de Pombal na Universidade de Coimbra. Não queria estar agora a pôr adjectivos no comportamento político do Marquês, parece que foi brutal e que a intervenção do Marquês na História ainda hoje desperta paixões. Ora, não é altura de grandes paixões, seja como for, a intervenção do Marquês na Universidade de Coimbra através de um estrangeirado que foi Luís António Verney, através dos livros, O *Verdadeiro Método de Estudar, A Obrigação dos Compêndios* etc. juntar-se a isto a forma como foi desmantelada a ideia pedagógica dos jesuítas de um ensino escolástico, de um ensino muito baseado na História e muito pouco baseado naquilo que era a lei da altura, foi uma revolução de mentalidades. Se me permitem uma opinião pessoal, foi uma revolução para pior, o Marquês obrigou os universitários a fazer exegese legislativa, ora a palavra exegese já diz tudo. Exegese é para o texto bíblico, nós só fazemos exegese de textos sagrados, ainda hoje às vezes os jurisconsultos falam de exegese. A exegese é uma palavra muito complicada.

Ora, em vez de se ensinar Direito nas Universidades, e sobretudo nas Faculdades de Direito, aqui a de Coimbra era a única, começou-se a ensinar as Ordenações. Todos percebemos o fim disto, ainda hoje grande parte do ensino superior do Direito, e peço vénia aos Mestres que aqui estão, se faz através de textos legislativos. O poder político ganhou importância, uma importância visível porque o Direito passou a ser a expressão política da vontade do legislador. Ora, esta confusão entre Direito e lei, que ainda hoje está muito por aí, basta ver os caloiros de

Direito com o Código Civil empinado nos autocarros a caminho da Cidade Universitária, "Estou a estudar Direito! Tenho um Código!" Confundir um código com a totalidade do Direito tem sido mau. Ora isto começou, o movimento na Europa já era grande, mas foi a Universidade de Coimbra pioneira nesta maneira de fazer do curso de Direito e do *curriculum* importo pelo governante a sua vontade expressa na lei. Deixou-se de ensinar Direito Natural, deixou-se de ensinar Direito Canónico, deixou-se de ensinar todas as fontes de Direito que não eram controladas pelo poder político local. Este Iluminismo na versão pombalina preparou depois o totalitarismo positivista da lei que a revolução liberal instaurou.

Logo, em que é que a História de Portugal passa pela Europa? Passa porque foram buscar estrangeirados para fazer a reforma da Universidade e, ao mesmo tempo, a reforma da Universidade feita cá; um professor de Coimbra, o Professor Figueiredo Marcos, fez esse estudo – muito influenciou o resto da Europa e as reformas feitas na universidade europeia.

Último episódio, como o Senhor Professor Manuel Porto vai abordar os aspectos históricos da integração europeia, deixarei o Século XX íntegro para o senhor Professor Manuel Porto, porque todos entendemos que num país assim já com nove séculos de História, o século XX é quase actualidade jornalística. O século XIX foi um século também muito importante na relação de Portugal com a Europa porque as invasões francesas trouxeram a Portugal a ideia de que a revolução também se exporta e exporta-se na ponta da baioneta. As ideias francesas entraram em Portugal muito através do movimento militar. A divisão entre o partido francês e o partido inglês era óbvia. A presença de portugueses em Londres era de tal forma que havia mais de trinta e tal títulos de periódicos a circular entre a comunidade exilada em Inglaterra.

Logo, as ideias de uma reforma política, que aliás arranca na Inglaterra muito da Revolução do Crommwel em 1648, a Revolução francesa com todo o esteio de nacionalistas que ali está, a Universidade portuguesa que estava um pouco parada, mesmo durante o século XIX – quem não conhece o aniversário da sebenta celebrado pelos vencidos da vida Antero, Teófilo e outros, que tanto criticavam os mestres que não se actualizavam, que iam a banhos à Figueira quando eles precisavam dos professores para tirar dúvidas na Universidade –, os professores que deixaram o ensino do Direito muito desactualizados, esquecendo-se completamente da ideia do compêndio instituído pelos estatutos da Universidade de Coimbra, os estatutos pombalinos. Por isso, o século XIX traz-nos um contacto com a Europa que vem desta clivagem entre uma

Portugal e a Europa – O passado

reforma feita através de processos internos, à inglesa, e uma reforma feita através de uma imposição de fora, que é a Revolução Francesa. Também aqui, o contributo da Europa para Portugal e de Portugal para a Europa é um contributo dialéctico.

Para concluir, queria tentar coser estes episódios e falar um pouco daquilo que é o tema deste ciclo de Conferências. Eu escolhi, sem grande critério como repararam, episódios em que Portugal esteve presente na vida da Europa e em que deu um contributo para aquilo que se passou na Europa. Creio, no entanto, que o maior contributo que Portugal pode ter dado está num episódio histórico muito esquecido que é a batalha de Alcácer Quibir. Em Alcácer Quibir o que estava em causa era a invasão turca, islâmica, da Europa, porque havia uma disputa dinástica em Marrocos. Um dos herdeiros ao trono, dos pretendentes era apoiado pelo império turco Otomano e o outro candidato não tinha apoiante. A corte de D. Sebastião percebeu que era importante apoiar o outro candidato e, se repararmos bem no pouco relato histórico que existe da preparação da batalha de Alcácer Quibir, aquilo que é dado como justificação dogmática, é que era muito importante travar o turco ainda em África, que o turco não entrasse pela meseta ibérica e falava-se de Aníbal, do episódio dos elefantes de Aníbal a avançar etc.. Havia, portanto, aquele trauma da meseta ibérica, da entrada na Europa – claro, não vinha referida a barreira dos Pirinéus –, de que poderia haver uma outra invasão islâmica da Europa a partir da meseta ibérica, e os portugueses entenderam que deviam travar esta batalha. Houve uma grande quantidade de cartas, de emissários que seguiram para a Europa, para a França, para a Inglaterra, a dizer "Atenção venham connosco! Há ali uma batalha determinante para o futuro de Europa, é importante que venham tropas da Europa para fazer isto!". Todos sabemos da tropa europeia que veio ajudar Afonso Henriques, depois do discurso de Pedro Pitões no Porto, incitando os cruzados a matar mouros porque a cruzada começava aqui na Hispânia. Não era preciso ir a Jerusalém, a ideia de ganhar Jerusalém celeste através da Jerusalém terrestre era uma ideia antiga, mas Pedro Pitões dizia "Combatam-nos primeiro aqui, depois nós vamos com vocês lá". Ora, se foi assim, se houve este contributo europeu para a conquista de Lisboa, D. Sebastião dizia "Venham outra vez ajudar-me mas agora nas terras de África tentando travar a invasão islâmica lá". Ninguém veio. Portugal ficou vazio. D. Sebastião levantou tropas e foi para o Norte de África. A derrota é conhecida e os efeitos da derrota também, até na literatura, nas profecias de Bandarras, essas coisas todas que falam do

Encoberto. Mas foi uma batalha perdida, que teve um significado único. Os turcos não entraram pela meseta ibérica, os turcos não desembarcaram nas costas de Gibraltar, os turcos não vieram por aqui invadir a Europa, e porquê? Porque em termos idiossincráticos, de mentalidade ficou ali expressa uma forte determinação da defesa da Europa. Creio que isto é um exagero, aqueles que lá morreram não tinham tanto, nem quereriam tanto, mas o significado que se retira, no futuro, da batalha de Alcácer Quibir é que esta foi a primeira barreira que, em termos mentais, foi de uma importância única para dizer "Aqui há quem defenda a Europa deste tipo de invasões políticas!".

Ora, numa altura em que existe tanta crispação à volta desta ideia, existe a islamofobia, existe a ideia do terrorismo islâmico, existe a problemática do confronto de civilizações, a ideia do choque das civilizações e, depois, do fim da história e do último homem, é preciso dizer que em vários episódios da História portuguesa relacionada com a Europa, os portugueses têm um passado que deve ser dito no presente para garantir que Portugal está na Europa por direito próprio, independentemente do número de habitantes, independentemente do número de kilometros, mesmo que tenha um PIB muito baixo, os portugueses continuam a ser um importante pilar da construção da União Europeia porque têm esta História, porque têm esta vontade e porque nunca discutiram a sua europeidade, mesmo quando optaram pelo Atlântico.

Muito obrigado.

ASPECTOS HISTÓRICOS DA INTEGRAÇÃO DE PORTUGAL NA EUROPA COMUNITÁRIA

MANUEL LOPES PORTO[*]

Muito obrigado.

Muito agradeço o convite do Professor Paulo de Pitta e Cunha, na sequência de convites com que me honra todos os anos para vir cá ao Instituto; tendo eu ainda a sorte e o benefício de haver reciprocidade, com a colaboração que aceita prestar à Associação de Estudos Europeus de Coimbra. Daqui a quinze dias lá o terei no Seminário de Verão da Faculdade de Direito da Universidade de Coimbra, com mais uma concretização da ligação tão estreita que tem existido sempre entre as nossas duas Faculdades.

Quero dirigir igualmente uma palavra especial ao Professor Jorge Miranda, meu amigo do coração, numa amizade longa que não é preciso estar a recordar neste momento, bem como ao Professor Eduardo Vera Cruz Pinto, naturalmente com uma ligação mais recente.

É um gosto enorme estar aqui também com todos os demais presentes, designadamente com pessoas que conheço de longa data e tenho assim a oportunidade de reencontrar.

Gostei muito de assistir à apresentação anterior, do Professor Eduardo Vera Cruz, tendo tirado duas notas que não resisto a referir.

Uma delas sobre D. Afonso Henriques, nosso primeiro Rei, fundador da nacionalidade, devidamente mencionado. É pessoa que também admiro, sem limites, admiro designadamente a visão que teve na

---

[*] Faculdade de Direito da Universidade de Coimbra.

expansão do território para sul. Mas quase 900 anos depois não posso deixar de lamentar, admitindo responsabilidades suas na ampliação do palácio real, o edifício onde está instalada a Faculdade de Direito de Coimbra, com paredes tão largas que em alguns espaços é difícil a captação dos telemóveis. Há pois a este propósito uma falha de D. Afonso Henriques, não tendo tido a previsão devida, pela qual lhe "rogo pragas" todos os dias...

Quanto à referência que o Prof. Vera Cruz fez no fim, a que depois de em épocas passadas termos pedido tropas à Europa passámos a pedir dinheiro, além de sublinhar que se trata de algo a que temos direito e no interesse do todo comunitário (mesmo dos mais ricos, beneficiados com uma Europa mais equilibrada e com um mercado maior), sublinharei que o mais importante da integração de Portugal nas Comunidades não tem sido nem poderá ser o recebimento de fundos. Embora não sendo quantificáveis, são de maior relevo os benefícios de ordem política e social (com a garantia da democracia e dos direitos ligados à cidadania), e mesmo no plano económico sobreleva a exigência de eficácia e competitividade a que somos obrigados com a integração na Europa.

Agradeço ao Senhor Presidente ter-me dado o tema dos aspectos históricos da integração de Portugal na Europa Comunitária, obrigando-me a lembrar elementos que fui coligindo em ocasiões anteriores, alguns deles em meras conversas, e a fazer uma nova reflexão, actualizada, sobre a evolução que se foi verificando: com lições para o futuro, face às perspectivas que agora se abrem.

Têm sem dúvida o maior interesse investigações históricas que não permitam tirar ilações com essa utilidade. Mas sempre que a história proporcione ensinamentos em relação ao futuro é bom, é mesmo indispensável, que os tenhamos presentes nas políticas a seguir.

1. A tradição de abertura da economia portuguesa

A primeira nota que tinha para partilhar convosco é a de que Portugal é, tradicionalmente, um país de abertura comercial (e económica em geral).

Tratando-se sem dúvida apenas de uma ilustração a este propósito, é curioso lembrar que o exemplo de Ricardo, da teoria da vantagem comparativa, é com a Inglaterra e Portugal: com a Inglaterra especializada na

Aspectos Históricos da Integração de Portugal na Europa Comunitária 431

produção de têxteis, que exportava para cá, e Portugal especializado na produção de vinho, que exportava para lá. É o exemplo que continua a ser referido na generalidade dos livros de comércio internacional.

Podendo haver outra razão para tal, é sintomático que Ricardo se tenha lembrado do nosso país para ilustrar uma teoria de tanto relevo.

2. A evolução verificada antes e a partir dos anos 50 do século XX

Embora o tema que me foi atribuído seja "Aspectos Históricos da Integração de Portugal na Europa Comunitária", vou começar alguns anos antes de poder pensa-se sequer em tal integração, mesmo antes dos anos 50.

2.1. Pode constatar-se que, desde sempre, Portugal foi um país de grande abertura económica. Não vou encharcá-los com números, recordando apenas alguns.

A taxa de abertura comercial foi sempre grande, aumentando ao longo dos anos. Medindo o relevo das exportações e das importações em relação ao PIB, tinhamos em 1938 uma taxa de abertura de 11,7%, razoável então em termos mundiais, mesmo razoável quando comparada com a de países avançados da actualidade. E depois foi aumentando, sendo de 15,4% em 1948 e de 18,8% em 1958.

A quem não esteja dentro destes números, posso assegurar que é uma taxa de abertura grande, havendo países muito importantes da actualidade, por exemplo os Estados Unidos e o Japão, em 2005 com 12,7 e 11,9 %, respectivamente ("pesando" sem dúvida o facto de, sendo grandes, poderem ter um grande mercado interno).

2.2. Em termos de distribuição geográfica, ainda antes do Tratado de Estocolmo, antes de 1959, era já grande a nossa ligação a países que vieram a estar connosco na EFTA, principalmente o Reino Unido. A nossa tradição histórica era basicamente de comércio com este país.

O comércio com os seis países fundadores das Comunidades Europeias representava então 23% do total, com os Estados Unidos 12% e com as antigas "províncias ultramarinas" – ou "colónias", como se queira chamar – 25%.

Nos anos 50 era pois muito grande o relevo do nosso "velho império".

2.3. Quanto à composição, sendo em grande medida inter-sectorial, nas exportações era um comércio muito baseada em produtos primários.

Temos todos a imagem dos pesos da cortiça e do vinho, que continuam a relevar, mas hoje em dia representam muitíssimo menos em termos percentuais. Exportávamos basicamente produtos primários, embora começassem então a ter relevo alguns produtos manufacturados, designadamente no sector têxtil e das confecções, com um *boom* já nos anos 60.

3. A adesão aos movimentos em que podíamos integrar-nos

Será interessante recordar agora os passos que foram sendo dados em relação aos vários movimentos de abertura e integração, em termos que talvez não fossem de esperar.

Muito em particular, será de recordar primeiro uma carta do Presidente do Conselho na altura, Oliveira Salazar, enviada em 1953 aos Embaixadores portugueses no mundo: carta altamente confidencial, agora publicada pelo Instituto Nacional de Administração (INA), mas que tive a possibilidade de ler antes, facultada pelo Embaixador Rui Teixeira Guerra, numa conversa (de boa parte de uma tarde, não o conhecendo antes e tendo-lhe solicitado cinco minutos...) quando preparava um relatório para o Banco Mundial (com os Professores Jorge Braga de Macedo e Cristina Corado), num projecto sobre os processos de liberalização do comércio (*The Timing and Sequencing of a Trade Liberalization Policy*).

A orientação de Salazar era de que a vocação portuguesa não era de integração europeia, mas sim de ligação aos espaços ultramarinos (v.g. transatlântica), numa carta em que punha aliás em dúvida a viabilidade do projecto europeu, com países diferentes, designadamente nos seus regimes políticos, tendo alguns repúblicas e outros monarquias (circunstância a que se dá agora pouco relevo, tal como pôde ser "sentido" pelo autor destas linhas, tendo vivido em diferentes anos em monarquias, no Reino Unido e na Bélgica, e numa república, em Portugal...).

Havendo tal dúvida e a orientação mencionada, é interessante que Portugal se tenha integrado contudo, na maior parte dos casos como membro fundador, nos vários movimentos de abertura e integração de que podia fazer parte; com grande relevo para o papel desempenhado então pelo Ministro José Correia de Oliveira.

Aspectos Históricos da Integração de Portugal na Europa Comunitária 433

3.1. Começou por ser interessante a adesão inicial à OECE, como membro fundador, em 1950, tal como se concretizou, protagonizada pelo Embaixador Teixeira Guerra. Tendo tido a responsabilidade de representar Portugal nas negociações, soube já em Paris que Salazar não queria que tivéssemos a ajuda Marshal (não tínhamos entrado na Guerra e tínhamos balança comercial superavitária...). Não tivemos por isso apoio financeiro do Plano Marshal nos dois primeiros anos, mas fizemos parte desde o início da organização, da OECE, tendo estado na primeira linha do cumprimento do compromisso de desarmamento alfandegário a que ficámos obrigados. E dois anos depois, já com défice comercial, viemos a beneficiar de alguma ajuda financeira.

3.2. Foi também muito interessante a entrada na EFTA, em 1960, igualmente aqui como membro fundador.

Não entrámos nas Comunidades, designadamente na Comunidade Económica Europeia, não só porque não nos aceitavam lá, não tendo um regime democrático, como porque não era aceitável para nós: sendo a CEE uma união aduaneira, deixaríamos obviamente de poder ter um regime alfandegário preferencial para os territórios ultramarinos, Angola, Moçambique, Guiné e todos os demais. Não poderia haver pois um "espaço económico português".

Tendo aparecido então a iniciativa da organização da EFTA, por parte de um conjunto de países que não queriam fazer parte das Comunidades, Portugal apareceu na primeira linha, segundo sabemos de novo devido em boa medida à intervenção do Embaixador Teixeira Guerra. Fomos pois parceiros fundadores, a par de países ricos (dos mais ricos...) do norte e do centro da Europa, de um "clube" de que não fizeram parte por exemplo a Espanha e a Grécia.

Era uma área de comércio livre que abrangia apenas produtos industriais e em que havia um regime especial para Portugal, no Anexo G, com alguma capacidade temporária de proteccionismo, tendo em conta que Portugal era claramente o país menos desenvolvido dos sete que formaram a EFTA (nas negociações do acordo participou um dos oradores de ontem, o Dr. José Silva Lopes).

3.3. Seguiram-se a integração no GATT, em 1962, e dez anos depois o primeiro acordo comercial celebrado com as Comunidades Europeias, renegociado depois do 25 de Abril, em 1976: considerando todavia também apenas produtos industriais.

3.4. Tratou-se de acordos e integrações com inegável relevo, num período histórico com grandes alterações na economia portuguesa, determinadas naturalmente também por outras circunstâncias, internas e externas, económicas, sociais e políticas.

a) Curiosamente, apesar de terem sido muito importantes os efeitos da adesão à EFTA (referiremos alguns adiante), nos anos 60 não houve um grande aumento do grau de abertura da economia, que aumentou apenas dos referidos 18,8% em 1958 para 19,5% em 1968. Foi já maior nos anos 70, apesar da mudança política e das dificuldades económicas verificadas nesta década, na sequência da crise petrolífera de 1973: o grau de abertura subiu para 26,2 % em 1978 (e para 33,0 % 1988, quando estavam ainda muito no início os efeitos da adesão às Comunidades; tendo-se verificado depois alguma baixa, sendo de 31,8 % em 2005).

O pequeno aumento do grau de abertura nos anos 60 terá estado ligado a uma circunstância curiosa que tive ocasião de apurar quando elaborei uma das teses da minha carreira académica. Apesar de ter diminuído então naturalmente a média dos impostos alfandegários (a "protecção" nominal), de 18,2% em 1964 para 14,4% em 1970, como consequência designadamente do "efeito EFTA" e ainda da adesão ao GATT, no início dos anos 60, houve um aumento geral da protecção efectiva, de 48,4 para 50,7%. Assim terá acontecido como consequência da diminuição da tributação de *inputs* (matérias-primas e bens inter-mediários) importados para sectores de maior influência nas decisões políticas. Só depois, no início dos anos 70, se verificou uma diminuição geral do proteccionismo, com a média dos impostos alfandegários (dos valores nominais) a descer de 14,4 para 7,7% e da protecção efectiva de 50,7 para 31,5% (cfr. a minha *Teoria da Integração e Políticas Comuni-tárias*, 3ª ed., 2001, pp. 132-5. Depois, com a alteração política e a crise económica ocorridas em meados dos anos 70, seguiu-se, como se sabe, algum ressurgimento proteccionista, com a subida para o dobro, em 1976, de muitas das taxas específicas da pauta alfandegária portuguesa (só em 1980-82 passou a ser ad valorem) e a aplicação de uma sobretaxa entre 1976 e 1979.

b) Quanto à distribuição geográfica, houve claramente um "efeito--EFTA", estudado por vários autores, designadamente por Valentim Xavier Pintado. Para o ilustrar, poderei recordar que nos anos que segui-ram ao seu início o comércio com os países da EFTA teve um cresci-mento anual de 17%, quando nos anos anteriores havia sido de 4%. Houve pois, como seria de esperar, uma aproximação aos países dessa área.

c) Houve também uma alteração sensível em termos sectoriais, com um grande *boom*, conhecido de todos, nas industrias têxtil, do vestuário, do calçado ou ainda da pasta de papel, com as unidades fabris então instaladas.

d) Embora não houvesse ainda naturalmente circulação livre das pessoas, v.g. dos trabalhadores, sendo em muitos casos mesmo ilegal e dificultada, os anos que medearam entre 1960 e 1975 foram caracterizados por um movimento emigratório de muito maior dimensão e diferente do anterior.

Não pode deixar de impressionar que entre esses anos, em 16 anos, tenham emigrado cerca de um milhão e quinhentos mil portugueses, de um país com menos de dez milhões de habitantes. Numa "piada" de mau gosto, poderá dizer-se que foi muito grande quando era proibida, passando a ser pequena, tal como acontece agora, quando é permitida; sendo talvez nula se fosse "obrigatória"...

Houve por seu turno uma mudança sensível no destino preferencial dos emigrantes, que deixou de ser as Américas (Brasil, Venezuela ou Estados Unidos) e a África (os territórios portugueses ou a África do Sul), para passar a ser a Europa.

Tratou-se de um movimento que teve duas consequências importantíssimas. A primeira foi de aliviar ou evitar mesmo problemas de desemprego, permitindo que tivéssemos tido então em Portugal, nos anos 60 (nos nossos *golden sixties*) um crescimento enorme, sem inflação e ainda sem desemprego. O grande "desemprego oculto" que havia antes, em especial com muita população activa na agricultura, foi absorvido na industrialização portuguesa e para além disso pela emigração, evitando-se problemas sociais. A outra consequência de grande relevo foi a chegada das avultadíssimas remessas dos nossos trabalhadores no estrangeiro, contribuindo para a situação favorável da balança dos pagamentos e para animação do mercado no conjunto do território português (designadamente para a animação do mercado imobiliário, em todo o território, embora nem sempre da forma mais aconselhável...).

e) Também neste caso sem ligação, ou apenas com uma ligação ténue, ao movimento de integração (embora beneficiado com a prosperidade que se foi verificando), há que referir nessa época o aumento enorme do turismo em Portugal: designadamente com a atracção de zonas antes muito menos procuradas, como era o caso do Algarve.

f) Um outro elemento a referir será o começo do aumento do relevo do comércio intra-sectorial (*intra-industry trade*, IIT, na designação em inglês), acentuado mais tarde, como veremos adiante. Sendo de 15% em relação à generalidade dos países em 1964 (quando era de 17% em Espanha, de 6% na Grécia ou por exemplo de 45% na Alemanha), em 1970 passou a ser de 19 e em 1980 de 39% (com subidas também sensíveis nos outros países do sul).

Quando antes por exemplo importávamos automóveis e exportávamos produtos primários, passámos a exportar também muito desse primeiro sector, não só os produtos finais (v.g. com a montagem dos carros), também bens intermediários (componentes).

Como sublinharei adiante, foi basicamente assim com os demais países da Europa, com uma aproximação sensível da estrutura da economia portuguesa, já não por exemplo com países da África.

4. A integração nas Comunidades Europeias

A entrada nas Comunidades, em 1986, teve naturalmente consequências em diferentes domínios.

4.1. *Uma aproximação geral*

Os primeiros anos, designadamente 1987, 1988 e 1989, foram anos "de glória", de que nos lembramos com saudade: anos em que crescemos muito, na casa dos 5% ou mais, em que o investimento aumentou na casa dos 10% e em que o investimento directo estrangeiro em Portugal mais do que duplicou em cada ano. Deu-se então assim um contributo assinalável para a convergência real da economia portuguesa em relação ao conjunto europeu verificada ao longo do século XX, com um crescimento médio de 4,5 % ao ano, o maior da Europa, depois de ter perdido terreno durante o século XIX, conforme é bem ilustrado por Abel Mateus no seu livro sobre *A Economia Portuguesa*, considerando o *Crescimento no contexto internacional*, 1910-2006.

Tendo 59% do PIB *per capita* quando entrámos nas Comunidades, passados 16 anos estávamos com 72%, ou seja, tínhamos recuperado 13% em relação à média; havendo infelizmente algum recuo na época actual.

4.2. **Uma desilusão em relação ao equilíbrio do país**

Tendo havido uma recuperação geral em relação à Europa, não pode dizer-se o mesmo em relação às diferentes regiões, com especial relevo para o interior.

É uma desilusão em relação ao que seria de desejar e de esperar, tendo em conta designadamente o que será referido no número seguinte: uma grande aproximação à Espanha, quando as ligações terrestres assumem naturalmente um relevo cada vez maior.

Em vários textos que ao longo dos anos fui escrevendo, designadamente em documentos da Comissão de Coordenação da Região Centro, fui afirmando a convicção de que passariamos a ter no interior a atractividade e a dinâmica que ao longo dos séculos tivemos no litoral. É por isso uma enorme desilusão constatar o esvasiamento do interior, que continua a acentuar-se.

Trata-se de desilusão, mesmo de "revolta", por ser bem claro que assim acontece por "vontade dos homens", não porque seja uma consequência inevitável, ou aceitável porque seria do interesse do país (da maioria das pessoas) apostar-se apenas em Lisboa ou talvez também no Porto (a par de uma ou outra área).

Poderia julgar-se talvez que o futuro estaria apenas nos litorais, devendo perder-se a esperança em relação às áreas continentais, e nas grandes concentrações urbanas.

O retrato da Europa e do mundo não é todavia este, não aponta (pelo menos necessariamente) neste sentido. De facto, mais de 65% do PIB da Europa está na chamada "banana de ouro", que começa em Roterdão, mas depois vem pela Alemanha até à Suíça, por uma zona não marítima, bem do interior; sendo de sublinhar ainda que se trata de um território equilibrado, "bem ordenado", sem nenhuma cidade do tamanho de Lisboa ou mesmo do Porto (com um mapa esclarecedor, bem como com outras ilustrações dos maus resultados da macrocefalia da França, vale a pena ver *L'Aménagement du Territoire*, de Jérôme Monod e Philippe de Castelbajac, 12ª ed, 2004, em particular pp. 19 e 109). Nos Estados Unidos da América ou no Brasil algumas das zonas mais dinâmicas não são do litoral nem têm grandes urbes. Por fim, podemos dar um exemplo que está muito na moda, o exemplo de Bangalore, com um enorme peso mundial nas novas tecnologias, mesmo liderante: uma cidade bem do interior da Índia (sem as "vantagens" de uma cidade portuária, como Bombaim, ou de ser a capital do país, como acontece com Nova Delli).

Estando até agora o centro económico da Península Ibérica no litoral, designadamente no litoral português, a aproximação deste litoral a Espanha e ao centro da Europa, com uma muito maior utilização do transporte terrestre, teria levado naturalmente ao desenvolvimento do interior: necessariamente atravessado e servido nas melhores condições, não se levantando pois os delicados problemas de opção que se põem por exemplo nos países nórdicos, em relação ao serviço às áreas excêntricas da Lapónia.

4.3. *Um novo quadro geográfico para o comércio externo*

Com a entrada nas Comunidade houve naturalmente uma alteração muito sensível na repartição geográfica do nosso comércio externo.

. *a*) Em 1985, portanto um ano antes da entrada, tínhamos com a Europa Comunitária 58% do nosso comércio, percentagem que subiu para 81% em 1995; mantendo-se desde então aproximadamente neste valor. Há aliás sempre uma pequena diferença, que bem se compreende, entre as exportações e as importações, sendo maior a nossa dependência da UE nas exportações do que nas importações, como consequência de termos de importar petróleo (bem como outros produtos, matérias-primas e mesmo produtos agrícolas, apesar do proteccionismo da PAC) de países terceiros.

b) Além desta aproximação geral, é impressionante a aproximação com a Espanha Custa a acreditar, mas em 1960 o nosso comércio com a Espanha representava menos de 1% do total (estando ainda por começar o *boom* desse país, produzindo produtos mais cotados, ao longo dos anos 60). Mas mesmo em 1985, no ano anterior à adesão, exportámos para Espanha apenas 4% das nossas exportações e importámos de lá apenas 7% das nossas importações.

Entre Portugal e a Espanha não se "beneficiou" da abertura que teria resultado de a Espanha ter feito parte dos mesmos espaços de integração: v.g. não foi fundadora nem membro da OECE e da EFTA, vindo apenas a ter alguma influência a circunstância de ter celebrado também um acordo comercial com as Comunidades, já nos anos 70. Chegou-se assim à situação de em 1985 a média dos direitos nominais sobre as importações de Espanha ser de 19% e a média dos direitos nominais da Espanha sobre as nossas exportações ser de 22% (sendo naturalmente muito mais

Aspectos Históricos da Integração de Portugal na Europa Comunitária 439

elevados os níveis de protecção efectiva). Havia, para além disso, outras formas bem conhecidas de proteccionismo, algumas delas com grande referência na imprensa da época: do lado espanhol os impedimentos à importação de determinados garfos e a autocarros da Marcopolo, com a alegação de riscos para a saúde e defeitos inexistentes; podendo referir--se do lado português demoras selectivas na concessão dos Boletins de Registo de Importações, os BRI´s...).

Tratava-se de intervenções que naturalmente as autoridades Comunitárias não consentiram a partir do momento em que ambos os países passaram a ser membros da CEE.

O afastamento de todos os tipos de barreiras, a par das dinâmicas das economias, levou à rápida progressão dos números, passando a Espanha a ser de longe o nosso principal parceiro comercial, na casa dos vinte e muitos por cento. Valerá aliás a pena sublinhar que temos um grande défice comercial, com a cobertura apenas de cerca de metade das nossas importações pelas nossas exportações (para a Espanha o comércio com Portugal representa mais do que o comércio com toda a América Latina...), mas que pelo contrário temos mais investimento em Espanha do que a Espanha cá.

Nem tudo é mau, pois, a menos que, com o nosso "pessimismo crónico", consideremos mau o investimento espanhol cá, porque estão a "dominar-nos", e simultaneamente mau o nosso investimento lá, porque não estamos a criar empregos portugueses com os nossos aforros...

É por seu turno inquestionável o benefício enorme que temos com o turismo do país vizinho: são espanhóis a maior parte dos turistas que nos visitam, não se concentram apenas nas épocas (ou na época) mais favoráveis, vindo ao longo de todo o ano, mesmo no Inverno e nos fins de semana, vêm a todo o território, designadamente ao interior raiano e mais desfavorecido, e têm bom gosto, apreciando a boa comida e as boas instalações (diferentemente do que se passa com os turistas de outros países, que procuram apenas o que é mais barato...).

4.4. *A evolução sectorial*

Por fim, há a registar uma evolução sensível na composição sectorial do nosso comércio, designadamente na composição das nossas exportações: com perda de relevo de sectores tradicionais, não tanto nos valores absolutos, que em vários casos felizmente se mantêm, mas sim nos valores percentuais (com o ganho de relevo de outros produtos).

Assim, comparando os dados de 1983/84 com os dados de 2000/03, constatamos que o relevo dos produtos agro-alimentares baixou de 12,4 para 7,6%, continuando todavia a ser significativo, com grande competitividade mundial (por exemplo a produção e a exportação de vinho, tendo é de ser de boa qualidade, face a novas concorrências...); a madeira e a pasta de papel aumentaram em termos absolutos e diminuíram apenas ligeiramente em termos percentuais, de 13,9 para 13,6%; tendo sido naturalmente mais acentuada a descida do têxtil e das confecções, de 19,6 para 16,3%.

Há por seu turno dois aumentos muito significativos: das máquinas, cujo peso nas exportações subiu de 12,1 para 19,4% da percentagem total, e do material de transporte, com um peso que, apesar de termos deixado de fazer produtos finais em alguns casos (de ter a montagem dos carros de algumas marcas), subiu de 4,3 para 16,4% do total, uma subida de 12,1 pontos percentuais, sendo actualmente a primeira rubrica das exportações portuguesas.

Trata-se de evoluções que se traduziram na acentuação da evolução, já iniciada, no sentido de também em Portugal (no quadro europeu) se acentuar o relevo do comércio intra-sectorial: todavia com uma diferença sensível consoante a comparação é feita com outros países europeus ou com terceiros países, tal como se constatou num estudo por que fomos responsável, neste caso para a Comissão Europeia, também aqui com a colaboração indispensável de Fernanda Costa (cfr. loc. cit., pp. 72-84, bem como Marius Brülhart e Robert Hine, ed., *Intra-Industry Trade and Adjustment. The European Experience*, 1999).

Apurámos aliás uma evolução muito curiosa, sendo até 1977 o comércio intra-sectorial de Portugal com países da União Europeia menor do que com países terceiros; mas desde então, com uma aproximação rápida das economias, passou a ser muito mais importante o papel dos países da EU: sendo em 1991 de 41,8% em relação a estes países e de 26,1% em relação aos países terceiros (sendo bem expressivas as figuras apuradas, mostrando também, como seria de esperar, valores maiores no sector secundário do que no sector primário).

A integração na UE tem sido pois um factor claro de aproximação da estrutura da nossa economia em relação às dos demais países.

Aspectos Históricos da Integração de Portugal na Europa Comunitária   441

5. Os desafios a que há que dar resposta. Implicações para Portugal

Embora o convite formulado tenha sido para considerar os aspectos históricos da integração de Portugal nas Comunidades, não deixo de mencionar, a concluir, os desafios principais que agora se levantam; procurando basicamente ver se, na linha referida atrás, a história nos dá alguma indicação no que respeita à resposta a dar, pela Europa e mais particularmente por Portugal.

5.1. *O desafio dos alargamentos e de outras aproximações*

Sendo difícil ou mesmo impossível dizer quais deverão ser ou serão as fronteiras últimas da União Europeia, trata-se de desafio a que tem de ser dada resposta.

Aliás, mesmo ficando-se pelas fronteiras actuais, com 27 países, não deixaria de haver uma maior aproximação dos demais países europeus e vizinhos: de acordo com o modelo do Espaço Económico Europeu, da Nova Política de Boa Vizinhança ou, independentemente de qualquer acordo, na lógica da dinâmica das economias.

É pois inevitável uma concorrência acrescida com o nosso país, da parte de países que, a par de outros atributos, têm em muitos casos uma posição mais vantajosa no seio da Europa, mais perto dos mercados principais, e pessoas com níveis mais elevados de qualificação.

5.2. *O desafio da globalização*

Não se justifica que utilizemos muitas linhas, num texto que já vai longo, para lembrar que os desafios de Portugal, de modo crescente, não se confinam ao espaço europeu e talvez à sua vizinhança; tendo de estar preparados, no século XXI, para uma concorrência global e muito difícil.

Não deixará de haver a concorrência dos outros dois espaços já mais industrializados e também de grande dimensão, os Estados Unidos e o Japão, que connosco compunham a "tríade" em grande parte do século XX. E a concorrência vem agora igualmente, talvez em maior medida, de outros espaços, alguns dos quais deixaram de concorrer basicamente com matérias-primas, produtos alimentares ou produtos industriais menos sofisticados, numa linha de comércio inter-sectorial: cada vez mais concorrem com produtos industriais e mesmo serviços com a maior sofisticação.

Nesta preocupação estamos naturalmente a pensar em grande medida na China e na Índia. Não é aliás fácil perceber por que é que estes dois países perderam terreno durante os últimos séculos, em maior medida nos últimos dois séculos (em 1820 tinham 42% da produção mundial, quando a Europa tinha 20% e os EUA estavam ainda pelos 1,9%...). Com civilizações antiquíssimas e populações cada vez melhor preparadas para os desafios do mundo moderno, não pode haver dúvidas acerca da sua capacidade concorrencial.

6. A estratégia a seguir

Para a Europa e muito em particular para Portugal não pode haver alternativa em relação a uma política de promoção dos nossos recursos.

Trata-se de política com implicações em diversos domínios, que procurei sintetizar recentemente, num artigo elaborado para o livro de homenagem aos Doutores António Ferrer Correia (antigo presidente desta Fundação), Orlando de Carvalho e Vasco Xavier e num artigo para o CEDOUA, sobre o PNPOT.

Face às experiências do século XX, experiências tão esclarecedoras, positivas e negativas, temos de caminhar para:

a) quadros desburocratizados, com Estados leves e eficientes, orientados em grande medidas para funções de regulação;

b) sociedades fortes, em que contributos de menor e maior relevo sejam dados por todas as pessoas, individualmente ou através de entidades com as mais variadas características;

c) o desenvolvimento de um modelo (ou modelos) socia(ais) realista(s), preocupado(s), prioritariamente com a criação de emprego;

d) a máxima formação das pessoas, sendo inquestionável que dependerá basicamente da sua qualificação (v.g. ao longo da vida) a possibilidade de se dar resposta aos desafios que se avizinham (que temos mesmo já no presente);

e) ocupações correctas dos territórios, evitando-se as ineficiências dos grandes aglomerados e racionalizando-se os tecidos existentes,

Aspectos Históricos da Integração de Portugal na Europa Comunitária   443

designadamente com a implantação adequada das infra-estruturas de transportes (sendo infelizmente exemplos muito maus,
em Portugal, o traçado da rede do TGV de ligação a Espanha e
a localização do futuro aeroporto de Lisboa, não servindo bem a
população e a actividade que deveriam ser servidas).

Promovendo as potencialidades de que se dispõe e ganhando-se
escala indispensável no quadro mundial, é de desejar que continue a
contribuir-se para o reforço do "mercado único" europeu, onde por seu
turno Portugal terá de se afirmar.

São estas as vias a seguir, com a história a ensinar-nos bem que não
poderá pensar-se em seguir a via proteccionista, admitindo que fosse
possível. Sem querer de forma alguma o mal das suas populações, pelo
contrário, regozijando-me com os progressos e o bem-estar actuais, constatamos aliás que Portugal progrediu em maior medida nas décadas do
século XX em que havia no centro da Europa e na China regimes politica
e economicamente fechados. "Beneficiámos", pois, com a ausência então
da sua concorrência, tendo sido de grande altruísmo os portugueses com
crença que rezaram então (em particular em Fátima) para que mudasse
o sistema aí implantado...

Não podendo desejar-se ou de qualquer modo esperar-se que esses
países voltem atrás, importa é que com realismo afirmemos as nossas
capacidades, com especial relevo para a qualificação das pessoas, onde é
especialmente sensível o atraso no nosso país.

Não há de facto alternativa à abertura, não podendo Portugal e a
Europa (onde não podemos deixar de estar integrados...) cometer no
século XXI os erros que a China e a Índia cometeram ao longo de
séculos, com consequências tão dolorosas.

Foram consequências magnificamente retratadas numa obra de referência de há 40 anos, quando eu era estudante de post-graduação, aluno
do Professor Teixeira Ribeiro na cadeira de Teoria do Desenvolvimento:
o *Asian Drama*, de Gunner Myrdal, de 1968, quando eram especialmente
chocantes os "dramas" da China e da Índia, com o sofrimento e mesmo
a morte de milhões de pessoas. São países que inquestionavelmente
devem o progresso actual, um progresso sustentado, à abertura externa e
interna das suas economias.

Se a Europa seguisse o seu mau exemplo, fugindo à globalização,
teria seguramente no terceiro milénio da nossa era a "evolução" (mais
rigorosamente, a regressão) que a China e a Índia tiveram na segunda

metade do segundo milénio. Depois de termos tido um *Asian Drama* teríamos um *European Drama*, com consequências especialmente negativas para Portugal; país que, como vimos atrás, sempre beneficiou com a abertura comercial e económica em geral, com os seus agentes, designadamente os seus empresários, a responder aos desafios que lhes eram lançados.

Muito obrigado.

O EURO E A ECONOMIA PORTUGUESA

JOÃO FERREIRA DO AMARAL[*]

1. O Euro, ou a aliança do federalismo com o neoliberalismo

O tema que vou abordar tem a ver com o Euro e a Economia portuguesa. É claro que era um tema que tinha mais interesse quando havia uma economia portuguesa pujante. Desde que a economia portuguesa tem definhado, dificilmente se poderá deixar de atribuir ao Euro uma elevada dose de responsabilidade nesse definhamento. Por isso, vou abordar a questão fundamentalmente do ponto de vista político. O Euro sempre foi um projecto político. A criação de uma moeda única teve muito pouco a ver com a economia, e muito mais com a política. Aliás, do meu ponto de vista, não todas, mas uma boa parte das dificuldades actuais da economia portuguesa estão associadas à adesão ao Euro. Mas esse é um debate em que tenho participado desde há muito tempo e que não vou reproduzir aqui. Vou, antes, como disse, olhar para os aspectos de natureza política.

Visto em perspectiva, a minha opinião é que o Euro é filho de um casamento ou de uma aliança contra-natura: a aliança entre as concepções federalistas europeias e as concepções da chamada *nova economia clássica*, que é um dos pilares daquilo que normalmente se chama neoliberalismo. Embora – saliente-se – o termo *neoliberalismo* tenha caído um pouco já na banalidade, tal como, por exemplo o termo *fascismo*, que muitas vezes significa tudo aquilo de que não gostamos numa situação política.

---

[*] Instituto Superior de Economia e Gestão.

Mas a nova economia clássica é um conceito bem definido. Tem um conjunto de teses conhecidas, nomeadamente quanto à forma de fazer a política económica – que deve ser feita por regras fixas e não de forma discricionária – na forma de encarar o desemprego – que considera que é um problema do funcionamento do mercado de trabalho e não um problema macroeconómico – e por aí fora.

Pois bem, do casamento dessas duas concepções – federalista europeia e nova economia clássica – nasceu o Euro. Nasceu o Euro que é fundamentalmente uma aliança negativa, pois, no fundo, as duas concepções o que têm em comum é a vontade de abater o poder do Estado--Nação, já ele próprio debilitado pelo processo de globalização. Dessa aliança nasceu a triste criatura que foi o Tratado de Maastricht e o estabelecimento da moeda única. Aliás – ainda agora ouvimos na intervenção muito interessante que acabou de fazer o Dr. Poiares Maduro – as concepções do próprio Tribunal de Justiça vão no sentido de uma jurisprudência neoliberal, baseada mais no conceito de abertura de mercados do que de não discriminação entre nacionais, como deveria ser se estivesse ainda vigente a concepção da integração europeia tal como a conhecíamos há décadas.

É muito interessante verificar que esta concepção, esta convergência de posições tem, na base, a ideia de que o espaço europeu é algo de homogéneo e que esta coisa de culturas e histórias é muito bom para pôr no Tratado como respeito pela diversidade mas na prática não tem, de facto, aplicação. O que interessa pura e simplesmente é fazer regras comuns que todos têm que aplicar sem respeito pela sua geografia, história, ou tradições.

Vou dar dois exemplos.

Não sei se tiveram oportunidade de ver o debate no *Prós e Contras* quando esteve cá o presidente da Comissão, Durão Barroso, há poucos dias atrás. A certa altura no debate um dos intervenientes, o Dr. Carlos Carvalhas, dizia que o Euro, nomeadamente o facto de o Euro ser uma moeda forte, estava a prejudicar as actividades económicas portuguesas. Não vou discutir se isto é verdade ou não (embora em minha opinião seja de facto verdade). O que é interessante é a resposta do Presidente da Comissão. Qual foi a resposta do Presidente da Comissão? "Não, isso não é verdade. Não é verdade porque a Alemanha é o maior país exportador do Mundo e continua a funcionar muito bem com o Euro". O que é que está na base desta concepção? É que a Alemanha e Portugal são iguais do ponto de vista económico e portanto se o Euro é bom para a

O Euro e a Economia Portuguesa

Alemanha, é com certeza bom para Portugal. Se não é bom é porque somos um povo de incompetentes que não sabe funcionar com o Euro.

Segundo facto interessante: Cada vez que o Banco Central Europeu altera a taxa de juro – nos últimos tempos tem sido na subida, mas o efeito, embora contrário, também seria verificável na descida – os efeitos na economia portuguesa são muito mais amplos que noutras economias da zona Euro. E porquê? Porque o nosso nível de endividamento das famílias e das empresas é extraordinariamente elevado: Essa circunstância amplifica extraordinariamente também os resultados da política monetária. Logo, a política monetária única não tem efeitos únicos, tem efeitos muito diferenciados consoante a situação de cada país. E isso prova que tentar aplicar o mesmo tipo de regras a espaços económicos, sociais, culturais e históricos muito diferenciados dá sempre mau resultado. Aliás a História demonstra isso vezes sem conta.

Federalismo e neoliberalismo, ou se quiserem nova economia clássica, entenderam-se em Maastricht. Simplesmente sucedeu aquilo que já se temia. É que as ideias federalistas e o projecto federalista – que é um projecto estimável, embora não seja o meu – foram-se degradando, um pouco à semelhança daquilo que sucedia com os regimes ideais que Aristóteles identificava na sua *Política*. O federalismo degradou-se. Degradou-se em quê? Numa coisa que à falta dum nome eu chamaria um *dirigismo com fachada federalista*, ou seja, a adopção da fraseologia e, eventualmente de uma ou outra disposição mais federal, para dar cobertura ao aumento de poder dos Estados de maior dimensão. E o resultado disso foi o Tratado Constitucional, o suposto Tratado Constitucional que, adoptando embora a fraseologia, alguns símbolos como a bandeira, o hino etc. de índole mais federal, apontava de facto para uma extraordinária redistribuição de poder dos pequenos países para os países maiores.

Ora, essa degradação foi chumbada, como sabemos. Chumbada não só por um país considerado pequeno como a Holanda, mas até por um país grande como a França e provavelmente até teria sido chumbada por outro país grande como é o Reino Unido. No entanto, a prova de que este processo não foi por acaso é que ele está de novo aí. De facto, no Conselho de Bruxelas o que se fez foi retomar exactamente naquilo que era fundamental e tirando alguma cosmética para tornar mais passável esta trapaça. O Dr. João Salgueiro chamou-lhe vigarice, eu prefiro chamar-lhe trapaça que é um pouco mais reles, porque é de facto bastante reles. A verdade é que aparece aí de novo com a máscara de tratado reformador!

O novo (velho) tratado reformador, o que fará se for ratificado, é proceder a uma quase anulação do peso dos pequenos países na cena mundial.

2. A anulação dos pequenos países e a vergonhosa revisão constitucional de 2004

Vamos olhar, por exemplo, para o caso português. Portugal não é dos países mais pequenos, até se poderia considerar um país médio dentro da União Europeia. Há um conjunto de coisas que, se foram para diante, significarão uma redução drástica do peso do Estado português nas relações internacionais e também dentro da União Europeia. E antes de enumerar esses aspectos, eu queria chamar a atenção para algo de muito importante.

Parece que agora a teoria entre os europeístas é que Portugal só se poderá desenvolver se evoluir sem autonomia política, como se fosse uma mera região administrativa no espaço europeu. Isto é algo de profundamente errado. São raríssimas as experiências históricas de uma região diferenciada culturalmente e com localização periférica, se conseguir desenvolver e progredir em termos económicos e mundiais sem autonomia política. O progresso que houve nessas regiões foi sempre baseado numa autonomia política e num estatuto internacional reconhecido pelos outros. Mesmo no caso da Irlanda que é uma região periférica da União Europeia e que teve um desenvolvimento extraordinário nos últimos tempos, este só foi possível porque a Irlanda quando tomou as medidas necessárias ainda não existia o Euro, e pode, portanto desvalorizar a moeda, implantando um sistema fiscal discriminador positivamente para o investimento na Irlanda. Hoje provavelmente já não seria possível.

Portanto a autonomia política e o estatuto internacional de uma região são fundamentais para o desenvolvimento. Pensar-se que Portugal se vai desenvolver diluindo o seu poder na União Europeia, deixando de ter autonomia de decisão e deixando de ter um estatuto internacional capaz, é uma miragem que iremos pagar, com certeza, muito caro.

Quais são os aspectos em que a nossa posição – nossa e dos outros países naturalmente – se vai drasticamente reduzir se o Tratado vier a ser ratificado? Em primeiro lugar, o fim das presidências rotativas. É claro que se pode dizer "Mas com vinte e sete países só de quatorze em quatorze anos, é que um país tem a presidência. Já não é tão importante". É, continua a ser. Mesmo de quatorze em quatorze anos continua a ser importante que um país tenha pelo menos seis meses para poder, de alguma forma, usar a presidência para fazer avançar os seus interesses, na medida em que isso, evidentemente, é possível.

Em segundo lugar, o alargamento do número das votações por maioria qualificada, é, do meu ponto de vista, inaceitável. A ideia de que para haver eficiência na decisão comunitária é preciso passar quase tudo para decisões por maioria qualificada, é uma ideia tecnocrática. É uma ideia que restringe, de facto, o poder de negociação de muitos países pequenos. Quem tem o poder de iniciativa é a Comissão. Obviamente que a Comissão vai deixar de negociar as suas propostas com os pequenos países. Para quê? Não vale a pena! Para quê negociar com Portugal isto ou aquilo se não vai ser o voto de Portugal que vai decidir? Isto decorre da ideia, que na base é uma ideia federal, que um país pode ser prejudicado para beneficiar os outros, ao mesmo tempo (é o tal dirigismo de que há pouco falei) que os países grandes ficam privilegiados na maioria qualificada..

Sou contra o processo de integração que vá nessa via e por isso é que sou anti-federalista e anti-dirigismo de fachada liberal. Julgo que justamente o facto de os Estados serem entidades histórico-culturais bem definidas, devia impedir que o sistema de decisão levasse um Estado a ser prejudicado em benefício dos outros. Com a decisão por maioria qualificada, isso pode suceder nos domínios mais diversos, pelo que poderemos ter de aplicar em Portugal normas – que inclusivamente passarão por cima da nossa Constituição depois de assim ter sido estipulado pela vergonhosa revisão constitucional de 2004 – com as quais nós não concordamos nada, mas que somos obrigados a assumir.

Em terceiro lugar, o ministro dos negócios estrangeiros, agora rebaptizado de alto representante para a política externa, ou qualquer coisa do género, com o seu serviço diplomático que se chama serviço de acção exterior – mas que é um serviço diplomático, quer se queira, quer não – vai reduzir drasticamente o peso das diplomacias dos pequenos países. Não é o peso jurídico-formal. Esse continuará a existir, mas mesmo assim, mais tarde, provavelmente, até ele desaparecerá. A Baviera, quando se formou o Império alemão, manteve o seu serviço diplomático próprio. Onde é que ele já está neste momento! Porquê? Porque deixou de ser útil a certa altura uma vez que tudo passava pelo governo imperial alemão e os países terceiros deixaram de se interessar em usar esses canais diplomáticos para negociar. E o mesmo vai suceder aos pequenos países da União Europeia. Só se manterão efectivas as diplomacias dos grandes países, a Alemanha porque é o maior e o que tem maior peso na União Europeia, e a França e a Inglaterra porque têm os seus respectivos lugares de membros permanentes do Conselho de Segurança. A própria Itália, sendo um país de grande dimensão, provavelmente verá a sua acção diplomática muito reduzida.

Depois, temos também o fim do comissário nacional, cargo que era considerado muito importante e agora de repente deixou de ser. Parece que é uma coisa de somenos, mas era também de uma enorme importância e não se pode dizer que aqui estejam em causa questões de eficiência. É perfeitamente possível, sem prejuízo da eficiência, garantir sempre uma representaçao adequada dos interesses nacionais na Comissão. Já se sabe que os comissários devem defender os interesses da União e não os interesses nacionais, mas todos nós sabemos também que, no fundo, o que eles fazem é um misto das duas coisas e esse misto seria importante que continuasse a existir.

Julgo que é inegável e não há forma de esconder isto, que, se o tratado que resultar deste mandato for para a frente, significará uma redução do estatuto internacional do nosso país como dos outros países de pequena dimensão ou média dimensão na União Europeia. Poderá não ser no imediato – essas coisas evoluem muitas vezes de forma gradual – mas será efectivo. Creio que isto é intencional, e bem-vindo nas elites europeístas portuguesas, porque como disse, há quem considere que isso é desejável. É desejável que Portugal se dilua no espaço da União Europeia, porque assim é que se vai desenvolver. A experiência histórica mostra justamente o contrário.

3. A necessidade de um referendo

Em resumo, do meu ponto de vista, quer o Tratado Constitucional, quer este – que tem um ou outro aspecto, é também justo dizer, que apesar de tudo melhora algumas coisas do Tratado Constitucional, quanto mais não seja o fim dos símbolos federais – são, a meu ver inaceitáveis. Mais: cria-se um ambiente completamente diferente, para pior, à posição externa de Portugal e ao seu papel na comunidade internacional, e portanto a sua ratificação deve ser sujeita a referendo.

Pode-se dizer "Mas os Parlamentos têm plena legitimidade para proceder à ratificação!" Não é verdade! Os Parlamentos recebem um mandato dos eleitores, para exercerem o poder em seu nome, não recebem o mandato para entregar o poder a outros. Portanto é o tipo de decisão que, sem qualquer dúvida, deve ser sujeita a referendo. Do meu ponto de vista pessoal interessa-me que haja referendo, não só para haver debate sobre as questões europeias, mas para o eleitorado poder votar "Não".

Julgo que haveria boas perspectivas para isso se as pessoas fossem confrontadas com aquilo que este Tratado irá significar.

O ENVOLVIMENTO NA INTEGRAÇÃO ECONÓMICA E NA INTEGRAÇÃO POLÍTICA

João Salgueiro[*]

1. O envolvimento de Portugal nos processos de integração implica a avaliação rigorosa das realidades europeias, em particular das profundas forças de mudança que actualmente alteram a sua configuração.

Vivem-se hoje em pleno as consequências da queda do muro de Berlim em 1989. Antes de mais, o alargamento da U.E. ao centro e leste da Europa mas também uma quebra da coesão política que resultava da ameaça externa e de um quadro geo-estratégico de confrontação – com evidentes consequências quanto à menor solidariedade financeira e aos renascidos esforços para hierarquização das nações europeias.

Também ao nível mundial, como é bem conhecido, vivemos todos os desafios que resultam da globalização, do comércio, da concorrência dos países emergentes, da deslocalização dos investimentos e do agravamento dos custos das matérias-primas e energia – sem esquecer as novas ameaças do terrorismo e das tendência demográficas.

Uma participação activa e positiva de Portugal não autoriza que se mantenham ilusões sobre as novas regras de jogo. Ou, o que é o mesmo, não permite extrapolar as experiências do passado para responder aos desafios do futuro. Nem extrapolar para Portugal os benefícios da primeira década na União Europeia – como se torna já tão aparente com a persistente divergência que se regista no PIB e nos níveis de desemprego. Outros países compreenderam antes e melhor do que nós que as regras de jogo exigem que contemos antes de mais com nós próprios e com estratégias competitivas de afirmação.

---

[*] Presidente da Associação Portuguesa de Bancos.

Desenvolver estratégias próprias – como a Espanha e outros países asseguraram em tempo – é indispensável para o futuro dos países mas também, paradoxalmente, para o sucesso do projecto da U.E no novo quadro mundial, pelo aproveitamento de especificidades de relacionamento intercontinental de diferentes nações europeias. Importa combater as tendência de centralização regulamentar de Bruxelas – em geral ainda agravadas em Portugal, submetido a complexos de bom aluno – que, na prática, contribuem para consolidação de um sistema de concorrência monopolística, limitam o potencial de criatividade de um modelo diversificado e pluralista e reduzem a capacidade de adaptação a novos desafios.

De igual modo, é essencial assegurar soluções institucionais que traduzam o princípio da igualdade dos Estados e que reforcem o princípio da coesão económica ·e social. Trata-se de exigências que traduzem a necessidade de compensar os custos sociais das políticas comuns, do reforço da livre concorrência e da perda de soberania, através de progressos na consolidação do federalismo fiscal.

O projecto do novo Tratado e o processo que tem conduzido à sua negociação e aprovação, constituem uma boa demonstração da distância existente entre as boas intenções e o peso das realidades, e oferece também um panorama actualizado dos desafios reais que defrontaremos na integração europeia.

São estes os temas que, sumariamente, me proponho abordar.

2. Estamos no início da presidência portuguesa que é reconhecidamente um momento alto da vida política nacional. Assim aconteceu nas duas bem sucedidas anteriores presidências. Em geral, tem sido reconhecido na Europa que as presidências rotativas são um avanço substancial na criação de uma cultura comum e na melhor percepção das realidades europeias. Raramente se fala tanto da Europa como durante as presidências nacionais. Só me ocorre outra alteração institucional com tanto impacto na alteração de mentalidades: a criação do ERASMUS. Tenho constatado através dos alunos que participam no programa progressos sensíveis na compreensão dos desafios europeus. Considero que as presidências rotativas e o ERASMUS têm feito mais para criar um sentimento europeu do que todos os arranjos institucionais com que sucessivamente nos brindam, com as correspondentes polémicas e redefinições.

Manifestando o meu apreço pela presidência portuguesa, parece-me necessário sublinhar que esta ganharia em ter um horizonte mais alargado

O *Envolvimento na Integração Económica e na Integração Política* 455

do que parece provável vir a acontecer. Na prática, temos um guião que nos é fornecido pela presidência alemã. Lembro-me que em Novembro do ano passado, portanto, antes da presidência alemã, teve lugar em Berlim uma reunião do Conselho da Federação Bancária Europeia. É nor-mal os representantes do Governo do país anfitrião dirigirem-se ao Conselho e, assim, o Ministro de Estado alemão teve ocasião de explicar como seria a presidência alemã: "Nós vamos fazer um processo de consulta (o que aliás se verificou...), um processo de consulta a nível diplomático e a nível ministerial, definiremos o modelo para a Europa e depois Portugal resolve o resto". Pareceu-me uma posição simpática para a presidência portuguesa, resolver o que tinha sido decidido na presidência anterior, mas se calhar traduz o peso das realidades.

Não podemos esquecer que os problemas fundamentais da Europa e da integração europeia não têm sido suficientemente analisados, desprezando excelentes oportunidades de aprofundamento. Por outro lado, importa aproveitar a possibilidade de encontrar respostas efectivas para os novos desafios que a integração europeia hoje consubstancia.

3. O povo português e os nossos agentes económicos, têm sido chamados episodicamente a mudar de comportamento. Por exemplo, quando da introdução da moeda única, assim aconteceu. Também quando das negociações da adesão de Portugal à União Europeia – organizaram-se quase duas dezenas de dossiers, que implicavam alterações importantes no comportamento dos agentes e na organização da sociedade portuguesa: a introdução do IVA, a eliminação dos monopólios do Estado, diferentes regras de concorrência, a política agrícola e das pescas... áreas muito diversificadas em que tivemos que assegurar mudanças efectivas.

Paradoxalmente, são muito raras as mudanças de nossa própria iniciativa, para responder aos novos desafios e oportunidades que tendem em regra a ser esquecidos ou adiados. Parece que somos muito mais eficazes a corresponder aos desafios vindos do exterior do que àqueles que resultam do nosso próprio interesse. Se pudesse fazer algum voto, seria de que a nossa presidência contribuísse para pensar os problemas da Europa de forma mais estratégica – prospectiva e consistente – mas também para pensar os problemas de Portugal no espaço europeu e no espaço internacional.

A Europa defronta, necessariamente, problemas muito graves que resultam das mudanças em curso na vida mundial. Claramente o mundo já não é o mesmo. Não há maneira de defender um futuro melhor pela simples extrapolação dos resultados do passado. Temos que encontrar melhores respostas para os novos desafios.

Se virmos como hoje se justificam os méritos da continuação de Portugal na União Europeia, encontraremos alegações de que Portugal ganhou muito por ter entrado na União Europeia e acedido aos fundos comunitários. São resultados que se podem registar e discutir, mas não tem nada a ver com o que vai ganhar no futuro, que dependerá de respostas face aos novos desafios e não das soluções do passado. Tendemos demasiadamente a extrapolar: "os fundos estruturais foram uma grande ajuda para Portugal". Mas continuarão a ser? Provavelmente não, até porque estão em declínio. "Portugal teve grandes desafios e mudou muita coisa!". Mudou no que resultava do Tratado de Adesão ou da convergência para a moeda única. Mas quais são agora os desafios para Portugal?

É estranho que face aos novos desafios da globalização haja tão pouca reflexão europeia, excepto talvez a propósito da Estratégia de Lisboa. Mas a Estratégia de Lisboa – tornar a Europa a economia mais avançada e mais competitiva – tem tido escassos resultados. É necessário ir mais longe e com mais realismo, na perspectiva dos desafios não previstos criados pelas economias emergentes.

4. As reformas institucionais têm concentrado o essencial das atenções e dos debates na União Europeia. Se olharmos para o que se tem passado nos últimos quatro anos, poderíamos, querendo ser simpáticos ou antipáticos, definir o que tem acontecido ao nível da classe dirigente europeia como uma trapalhada ou como uma vigarice. Ou o que se tem passado é uma improvisação que não tem conseguido resolver as questões pendentes, ou é opção intencional e trata-se de uma vigarice. A menos que se trate conscientemente de limitar as decisões a círculos políticos restritos evitando consultas alargadas.

O que parece ter presidido a todas as alterações institucionais é, antes de mais, a busca de novos arranjos de poder. Em rigor, a luta pelo poder já existia, mas os arranjos têm agora de ser diferentes para conseguir o mesmo resultado. Por outro lado, parece que importa impedir os povos de tomarem decisões, fazendo o necessário para que o eleitores não se possam pronunciar. Para tanto importa repetir as informações politicamente correctas, e depois rapidamente considerar aprovado o que não foi suficientemente analisado nas suas consequências.

Um artigo lúcido e demolidor do Dr. Pacheco Pereira no Público do dia 23, analisa a campanha maciça, organizada com fundos da União Europeia, para fazer passar a versão correcta dos acontecimentos. O orçamento é pesado: no Parlamento Europeu, nas suas Delegações, nas Delegações da Comissão, eventos para jornalistas, publicações e inquéritos de opinião. Repetiu-se incansavelmente que o Tratado Constitucional Europeu não tinha vingado apenas porque os problemas internos da França e da Holanda – leia-se políticas partidárias dos dois países – tinham vetado a Constituição necessária para a Europa. Ninguém procurou saber se a União Europeia tinha posto a debate a ideia que o Tratado Constitucional não tinha passado porque não era o que alguns povos europeus queriam naquele momento. E, no entanto, um representante do Governo alemão disse "Se houvesse um referendo na Alemanha também perdia porque os alemães não votavam este Tratado".

Esta orientação é hoje também evidente, sendo agora proibido falar de Tratado Constitucional quando meses atrás o mesmo era indispensável e urgente: "Agora trata-se de um Tratado diferente, um Tratado minimalista proposto para ratificação". Mas até que ponto é diferente? Podemos recear que a trapalhada – ou a vigarice, ou uma estratégia elitista continuem – se virmos as diferentes interpretações a que tem sido sujeito. Nos países que ratificaram o Tratado Constitucional o novo texto é apresentado como essencialmente o mesmo. Os deputados dos grupos parlamentares do Partido Popular e do Partido Socialista no Parlamento dizem que é idêntico, só formalmente diferente, mas no fundo o mesmo Tratado. É essa opinião que se veicula para concluir que não é preciso novo referendo. Mas nos países que o recusaram ou ainda não referendaram, como Portugal ou o Reino Unido ou a França, diz-se que "Não, este Tratado é substancialmente diferente e não justifica um referendo". Muitos desconfiarão de que é apenas uma trapalhada outros pensarão que se trata de uma estratégia pouco transparente em relação aos eleitorados.

5. Falemos agora do dito Tratado minimalista no quadro dos desafios internacionais, dos desafios nacionais e do momento que vivemos. Tanto quanto vejo, como referi, o que há de claro neste Tratado, como em todos os episódios anteriores, é uma estratégia de poder.

Perdeu-se uma oportunidade magistral de pensar o futuro da União quando da Convenção Europeia por não se ter cumprido o Mandato de Laeken. O Mandato de Laeken, deveria orientar os trabalhos da

Convenção e, consequentemente, o relatório a apresentar à conferência intergo-vernamental. O Mandato impunha orientações que não foram respeitadas. Mandava fazer uma reflexão aprofundada sobre os desafios da Europa, que não foi feita. Também mandava que quando houvesse dúvidas sobre as soluções institucionais, fossem apresentadas alternativas, o que não aconteceu. E mandava, ainda, fazer um exercício de subsidiariedade para responder ao mal-estar resultante do excesso de intervencionismo da Comissão Europeia, de modo a deixar aos Estados a liberdade de tentar caminhos diferentes, sem definir burocraticamente opções à partida. Nenhuma destas orientações foi cumprida, aliás sob influência directa de Giscard d'Estaing – mas provavelmente assim aconteceu por corresponder a interesses mais generalizados. Foi apresentado como um Tratado acabado, com auto-elogios no preâmbulo aos membros da Convenção, emulando os trabalhos de Filadélfia dois séculos atrás, para a Constituição de uma Nação Continental. Assim se chegou a um Tratado Constitucional para uma nova nação, o que não havia sido solicitado.

Esse projecto foi apresentado ao Conselho de Ministros sob chantagem: se não fosse aprovado sem alterações, tal e qual e imediatamente, a Europa desabava porque era ingovernável. Felizmente isso não aconteceu. Mesmo antes dos resultados dos referendos na França e na Holanda, o próprio Conselho introduziu algumas alterações. A ameaça de que a Europa era ingovernável sem um novo Tratado evidentemente não tinha fundamento, como se provou. A União Europeia continua e não está nem pior nem melhor do que estava antes.

Este clima de forçar a mão à classe dirigente que, por sua vez, força a mão aos povos, parece ser a regra geral. Mas será isto um exercício de autoritarismo ou de maquiavelismo? Penso que não. Parece sim que a classe dirigente europeia está a interpretar as realidades de forma que não me parece positiva, apenas superficialmente coincidente com os seus interesses.

Ou de outro modo: podemos dizer que existe um deficit democrático essencial na Europa. Não pela ausência dos jornalistas nas reuniões do Conselho ou por falta de mais informação politicamente correcta. Não é esse o deficit democrático mais essencial da U.E.. Resulta sim do facto de as instituições não traduzirem opções genuinamente europeias, mas apenas agregados de opções nacionais.

O órgão máximo que decidirá o novo Tratado a ratificar pelos países-membros será o Conselho Europeu. O Conselho Europeu é composto pelas

O Envolvimento na Integração Económica e na Integração Política 459

primeiras figuras dos diferentes países-membros – os Primeiros-Ministros e o Presidente da França. Na prática não votam enquanto europeus. Votam, antes de mais, à luz das realidades nacionais dos seus países. O senhor Sarkozy fará em relação a este Tratado o que achar que interessa à lógica da política interna da França; o senhor Blair procurou ajudar a aceitação do Tratado em Inglaterra, impondo excepções substanciais ao Acordo maioritário.

Assim tem sido sempre. Cada governante nos Conselhos – e nos trabalhos preparatórios – define as suas posições em função de lógicas políticas – ou partidárias – nos seus países. Provavelmente numa situação de emergência actuariam como europeus; perante uma ameaça inverosímil de invasão por extraterrestres ou pelos Turcos ou pelos Tártaros, seriam inspirados por um sentimento comum europeu. Mas em circunstâncias normais são inspirados pela dinâmica política do seu País, porque, como é lógico, aí terão de prestar contas quando forem reeleitos ou não nas próximas eleições, e o desempenho dos dirigentes no quadro europeu será provavelmente uma das componentes importantes para as próximas eleições nacionais.

Mas não teria que ser necessariamente sempre assim? Não necessariamente. Depende em larga medida das opções institucionais. Não é assim, por exemplo, nos EUA, na Suíça ou na Alemanha. Nos EUA os presidentes sabem que podem ser eleitos ou reeleitos pela diferença de votos em qualquer Estado. Para o presidente Bush foram os resultados da Florida que fizeram a diferença. Em todas as eleições pode haver um ou dois ou três Estados que decidem da sorte da eleição ou reeleição.

Na Europa isso não é possível. Os resultados são feitos pela ponderação dos votos dos representantes dos Governos nacionais, não pela opinião dos eleitores. Nos EUA o presidente é eleito directamente pelos povos. Está agora prevista a figura de um presidente do Conselho Europeu, mas não eleito directamente. O voto directo não vai contar, vai apenas contar o voto dos Governos, com ponderadores muito diferentes, permitindo que meia dúzia de países determinem o resultado, tornando os restantes irrelevantes.

6. Pode-se perguntar se algo mudou recentemente. Mudou, desde logo, em consequência do alargamento. Anos atrás, em mais de uma intervenção, tive oportunidade de sublinhar a ligeireza com que se procedeu ao alargamento da União Europeia, depois da queda do muro de

Berlim. Na altura referi que, no dia seguinte à queda do muro de Berlim, a União Europeia deveria ter proposto imediatamente um apoio concreto aos países que se libertavam de um contexto esmagador, proporcionando--lhes a entrada numa zona de comércio livre; a adesão à NATO e um programa de auxílio – como o Plano Marshall – para reconfiguração das suas economias. Com estes três pilares aqueles países estariam já em melhor situação do que estão hoje. Adesões seriam negociadas depois, sem pressões de risco político e após os ajustamentos institucionais da U.E. que, de qualquer modo, os sucessivos alargamentos já justificavam.

O imediatismo mal ponderado e a falta de imaginação para encontrar novas soluções conduziu a generalizados processos de adesão, com os problemas que isso cria à União Europeia e com problemas para os próprios países. É evidente que alguns países – como a República Checa, ou a Hungria ou a Polónia – poderiam eventualmente pedir a adesão, mas pediriam com base no mérito próprio, como aconteceu com a nossa negociação, exigindo o tempo que fosse necessário. Não se assistiria à entrada acelerada de doze países e provavelmente de mais sete Estados dos Balcãs. O precedente que se criou torna difícil dizer que a Croácia ou a Sérvia não vão entrar, ou a Bósnia ou a Macedónia, ou o Montenegro ou a Albânia e, porventura, o Kosovo, ou a Moldávia ou a Geórgia. A prazo uma decisão impensada conduziu a sucessivas fugas para a frente. Vale a pena reflectir sobre este passado recente porque ainda permanece a lógica que o tornou possível.

7. O peso relativo do alargamento recente levou naturalmente a adoptar contra-medidas por parte dos países que na prática entendem governar a União Europeia, – a Alemanha e a França antes de mais, e com distintos objectivos o Reino Unido, e por vezes a Itália ou a Espanha – para salvaguarda das suas posições relativas. Assim, entenderam que seria preciso criar uma nova lógica que os pusesse ao abrigo da influência da multidão de países irrelevantes agora membros da União. Evitar Presidências organizadas por Malta ou pelo Chipre, Estónia ou Letónia. Rever os ponderadores de voto que atribuiriam a maioria a estes países. Nomear um Ministro dos Negócios Estrangeiros que diga com ponderação o que a Europa pensa, evitando que todos os países opinem sobre a política das relações externas da União. Importa igualmente reduzir o risco das presidências rotativas, e escolher um presidente mais estável, que pode ser reeleito, se merecer aprovação.

O Envolvimento na Integração Económica e na Integração Política 461

Trata-se, de facto, de alterações institucionais que no seu conjunto reconfiguram o anterior modelo da U.E. que conhecíamos, desde a fundação, modelo que visava reforçar a coesão e evitar reforço de lideranças nacionais. Pelo contrário, caminha-se agora para um Directório de alguns Estados com estatuto de protectorado para os restantes.

Justificar-se-ia submeter a Referendo todas estas alterações? Justificaria certamente um alerta explícito porque vamos entrar num novo quadro de soberania limitada face aos principais países europeus. Paradoxalmente, admito que não fosse indispensável um referendo em Portugal quando do Tratado de Maastricht porque, basicamente, o que se alterou foi a introdução do Euro e era fácil perceber o contorno da moeda única, à qual, na prática, poderíamos aderir ou não, conforme quiséssemos: bastava que não cumpríssemos os critérios de convergência, ou até podíamos cumprir e não aderir como aconteceu à Suécia, que cumpre e não adere. Não se impunha uma alteração ao próprio modelo da União Europeia. Não é hoje o caso quando se alteram tão significativamente as regras internas de funcionamento e o poder relativo dos vários Estados.

Sem interpretações de oportunidade, importa tomar inteira consciência das alterações. As mesmas pessoas que nos dizem que é muito importante a presidência portuguesa, dizem-nos que é irrelevante deixar de haver presidências rotativas; as mesmas pessoas que nos dizem que é importante ter um comissário permanente em Bruxelas, dizem que não é importante que agora passe a ser rotativo; as mesmas pessoas que nos diziam que poderíamos aderir ao Banco Central Europeu porque teríamos sempre um representante, aceitam que possa deixar de ser permanente, prevendo-se um mecanismo de rotação.

Considera-se também que não faz diferença a existência do novo "Ministro dos Negócios Estrangeiros". Talvez a França ou a Inglaterra tenham poder próprio para continuar a manter a sua política externa, mas no caso português, por exemplo nas relações com o Brasil, Angola ou Moçambique, se os nossos interesses não coincidirem com os da maioria da U.E. o ponderador da importância não jogará a nosso favor. As posições portuguesas tenderão de facto e de direito a ser mais irrelevantes.

8. Por outro lado, este Tratado contém algumas explicitações que contribuem também para a hierarquização dos países membros. A política externa passa a ser comum, mas acrescenta-se uma adenda sobre manutenção de privilégios em política externa. Vai-se até ao ponto de pré-determinar o futuro dizendo que se manterão os lugares no Conselho de Segurança das Nações Unidas. Esta explicitação tem destinatários conhecidos. Mas aparentemente aqueles lugares cativos não se justificarão no novo contexto europeu e mundial. Em 1945, os membros permanentes do Conselho de Segurança, eram os cinco impérios mundiais existentes: a China, a União Soviética e os Estados Unidos pela sua própria dimensão; o Reino Unido e a França porque governavam centenas de milhões de cidadãos em diferentes Continentes. Por outro lado, não havia a realidade da União Europeia, para a qual se pretende agora uma voz única. No mesmo documento que diz que a Europa deve ter uma voz única, salvaguardam-se duas vozes no Conselho de Segurança, que se entenderão, ou não, e que representam ou não o sentimento europeu – e vimos na crise do Iraque que nem sempre a unanimidade existe. Para ser coerente e transparente seria lógico que a U.E. tivesse um representante permanente no Conselho de Segurança com uma política aberta ao futuro. Mas não é esse na realidade o espírito do Tratado. Parece que há uns mais iguais que outros, tratando alguns de conservar o poder que têm, mas reduzindo-o aos que aceitam maior subalternização.

Sabemos que neste momento a afirmação de poder se exerce antes de mais no domínio económico, traduzindo-se na prática pela aceitação de dois pesos e duas medidas nas relações entre os Estados. Temos tido várias provas ao longo das últimas décadas envolvendo a França, a Alemanha e a própria Espanha. É evidente que neste momento não está ameaçada a nossa independência política, inconcebível no espaço da U.E.. Mas, em grande parte por nossa inibição, tem sido a Espanha a definir os traçados do TGV e a orientação das nossas ligações à Europa. Na prática, e ao contrário do que acontecia no Séc. XIX, a interligação exigiria agora a passagem por Madrid.

A conjugação de cláusulas de concorrência no mercado interno com a defesa dos interesses nacionais têm diferentes ponderações consoante os Estados envolvidos. Recordamos ainda as objecções que Espanha pôs à compra por uma empresa italiana de uma fábrica de refinação de azeite, porque se tratava de uma produção estratégia para a Espanha. Mesmo quando as questões vão a tribunal e se arrastam por anos, sobressai a diversa influência dos governos interessados. Caso flagrante foi o que resultou da oferta de compra da Endesa, mal recebida pelas autoridades do País vizinho e a forma como acabou, porque entretanto houve tempo para ir reorganizando sucessivamente as trincheiras que inviabilizavam a operação.

O Envolvimento na Integração Económica e na Integração Política   463

No novo Tratado foram incluídas cláusulas que permitem interpretação discricionárias em matéria de concorrência, autorizando a invocação de interesses nacionais, regionais ou locais em relação a diferentes actividades industriais e infra-estruturas. Estas cláusulas foram, em larga medida, introduzidas por iniciativa da França, que não disfarçou os seus objectivos. Mas também a Inglaterra, como habitualmente, se auto--excluiu em relação a diversas políticas que considera sensíveis – o que se traduz numa lista de opting-ins mais do que de opting-outs – mantendo-se alheada de políticas comuns em que só participará se e quando entender.

Por outro lado, parece lamentável que não se tenha feito qualquer exercício sério para reforçar áreas de subsidiariedade e reduzir excessos de centralismo e normalização. Seria de esperar que a Convenção tivesse avançado nesse domínio. Sabemos, no entanto, que são profundas as razões para o alargamento das intervenções comunitárias. Cada Comissário em Bruxelas superintende em uma ou mais direcções-gerais e os diferentes departamentos encontram justificação para a sua existência no alargamento e aprofundamento das políticas comuns. Mais tarde ou mais cedo teremos políticas comuns contra o ruído ou a obesidade. Serão essas políticas comuns essenciais para o funcionamento da U.E.? Em muitos domínios existe mais normalização na Europa do que nos EUA, que ao fim de mais de dois séculos de unidade política, mantêm profundas diferenças e autonomias estaduais, até ao ponto de existirem distintos regimes quanto aos direitos cívicos, à pena de morte, ao porte de arma ou à eutanásia, que continuam a ser competência própria dos diferentes Estados.

9. Para assegurar um quadro estável e realista, teria sido desejável que o Tratado tivesse sido precedido de uma análise de diferentes modelos institucionais e de uma reflexão sobre a posição da Europa no novo quadro da economia global. A governabilidade da União Europeia não pode ser baseada no modelo do Mercado Único a seis, que tem vindo a ser estendido tanto quanto possível, e já resiste mal. Para responder às questões institucionais que defrontamos deveríamos considerar outros modelos e comparar o mérito de soluções alternativas desenvolvidas em outros países. Por exemplo, como é que se salvaguarda a igualdade entre os Estados? Na RFA, na Suiça e nos Estados Unidos, existe uma segunda câmara. Essa hipótese chegou a ser discutida, foi rejeitada por ser federalista. Mas como podemos aceitar que numa confederação ou federação os seus Estados sejam tratados com mais dignidade do que países independentes no caso da União Europeia? Na União Europeia, países soberanos aceitam ponderadores de voto, quando em federações e confederações se assegura igualdade entre Estados de diferentes dimensões.

O modelo da U.E. faz muito pouco sentido e por isso não tem sido discutido. A situação é ainda mais inexplicável porque é normal, como nos Estados Unidos, que o acesso aos fundos federais constitua um direito. Mas na U.E. tem que ser negociada a boa-vontade da Comissão e de alguns Estados-membros para atribuição dos fundos estruturais, cujo desaparecimento tem sido mesmo já anunciado. Aceitam-se assim as consequências de políticas comuns – como a concorrência, o comércio, externo, a agricultura ou as pescas – sem o respaldo da garantia do reforço de mecanismos de solidariedade. É injustificado aceitar reduções de competências próprias sem a definição de um quadro estabilizado de co-res-ponsabilização orçamental.

10. O segundo aspecto essencial que deveria ser analisado, e ficou esquecido, é o da nova posição da Europa no Mundo. A realidade global é diferente desde 1989 com a queda do muro de Berlim. Antes não teria sido possível o alargamento, como é evidente; e também não teria sido possível a globalização das economias, nem a entrada da China e do Vietname no mercado mundial. Até 1989, mantinha-se efectiva concorrência entre dois sistemas económicos – a economia de mercado e a economia planificada –, sistemas de economia mista no terceiro mundo e forte auto-regulação da economia de mercado. A Constituição alemã definia bem esta realidade, assumindo-se como uma economia social de mercado, com o predomínio da lógica social assente nos resultados da livre concorrência e no mercado.

Hoje os sistemas são de total abertura à livre concorrência internacional, tornando a importância da regulação do mercado interno europeu muito menos relevante. Neste momento, a importância do mercado interno, também para Portugal é muito menor do que quando aderimos. Cada vez mais é o mercado mundial, que, directa ou indirectamente, condiciona as actividades económicas em Portugal como nos países europeus.

E, no entanto, a União Europeia continua a alimentar a lógica de mercado interno, e tem-se esforçado por criar campeões europeus, com uma política que não é neutra em relação à dimensão das empresas. Prefere encorajar as empresas de maior dimensão, na indústria como na banca, estimulando as práticas de fusões e aquisições, aparentemente por

O Envolvimento na Integração Económica e na Integração Política   465

considerar que assim reforça a unidade do espaço europeu. Em outras economias, pelo contrário, confere-se particular atenção ao estímulo de empresas de menor dimensão, – como nos EUA, na Suíça, ou mesmo na Alemanha ou na Espanha, onde por exemplo bancos locais ainda dispõem de enquadramento mais favorável do que bancos de maior dimensão.

Esta orientação da U.E., ao contrário dos seus objectivos, não contribui para difundir comportamentos competitivos e aumenta a dimensão dos riscos em períodos de crise económica. Tivemos recentemente exemplos destas consequências no novo quadro mundial: fizeram-se campeões europeus ao nível da indústria do aço, mas as duas maiores empresas – uma que resultava da fusão das siderurgias francesa, espanhola e luxemburguesa e outra das siderurgias inglesa e holandesa – foram compradas por empresários indianos com intervalos de poucos meses. A orientação de criar campeões europeus como a melhor resposta para assegurar a afirmação europeia, é uma opção que sempre me pareceu controversa, mas sobrevalorizar hoje a importância do mercado interno é não perceber que estamos a viver num mercado de concorrência mundial, contribuindo para não equacionar os seus desafios em toda a dimensão. Nada prova que um sistema mais diversificado com empresas de variada dimensão e estratégias diversificadas não possa ser mais eficaz na resposta aos desafios da nova economia global.

11. Importa ainda anotar a incapacidade crescente de Portugal na resposta aos novos desafios. Podemos dizer que até 89 a nossa participação na União Europeia constituiu um estímulo, conduzindo a importantes reformas, decorrentes do Tratado de Adesão e do caminho para a moeda única. Posteriormente, tem vindo cada vez mais a constituir um álibi para nos dispensar de estratégias eficientes. Achamos que a Europa decide por nós e não precisamos de ter objectivos próprios, ao contrário do que se passa em outros Estados-membros. Mesmo quando se diz e repete que os nossos agricultores são idosos, analfabetos, sem espírito de inovação e traumatizados pela reforma agrária, considera-se dispensável uma política de investigação e extensão agrícola, o que não acontece por exemplo na Holanda, na França ou nos EUA. Também entendemos que não precisamos de uma política de pescas, ignorando que ao mesmo tempo que desmantelávamos grande parte da nossa frota a Espanha construía a segunda frota da Europa.

Podemos interrogarmo-nos sobre se interessa aos portugueses ter um futuro melhor no seu próprio País. Se não interessa, a emigração permite oportunidades imediatas de emprego. Mas se queremos conciliar opções próprias com um futuro melhor, é indispensável promover activamente o desenvolvimento da nossa economia. Temos que perder alguns complexos dentro da Europa, aceitar plenamente os desafios políticos e económicos e assumir as nossas próprias opções. No novo quadro, é indispensável ter consciência de que o futuro depende antes de mais de nós próprios.

Faz sentido, por exemplo, fixarmos como desígnio fundamental o Mar e desenvolver trabalhos para alargar a plataforma marítima e, ao mesmo tempo, aceitar que a competência exclusiva em relação aos recursos biológicos marinhos é da União Europeia? Competência exclusiva? Nem ao menos participada. Como é que Governos portugueses podem aceitar esta orientação, que vai mesmo contra resoluções das Nações Unidas sobre protecção dos recursos naturais no mar. E nem sequer tem lógica, porque é difícil imaginar as competências da Áustria. República Checa ou Hungria sobre as políticas da pesca.

Trata-se sem dúvida de um sector que exige políticas concertadas entre alguns países-membros da U.E. mas também com vizinhos não membros. Será possível fazer uma política de pescas integrada no mediterrâneo sem intervirem os países da margem sul? Ou no Báltico sem a Rússia ser ouvida? Ou no Mar do Norte sem a participação da Noruega e da Islândia? Trata-se de um caso claro em que a coordenação de políticas, que é fundamental, não coincide com o espaço comunitário. Acresce que Portugal sempre conseguiu melhores resultados em negociações directas com a Noruega, a Islândia ou os países da costa de África. Portugal é também o maior consumidor e o maior importador de peixe per capita, e tem uma muito extensa zona exclusiva. É difícil ignorar o nosso interesse fundamental neste domínio e prescindir de competências próprias.

De igual modo, não podemos ignorar as relações especiais que decorrem de uma história de séculos com países como o Brasil ou os PALOPs. A nossa língua é a terceira mais falada na União Europeia, mais que o francês e o alemão, e merece também uma estratégia de afirmação, não sendo aceitável a subalternização que tende a decorrer por equiparação aos idiomas de alguns dos novos países-membros.

12. Permitam-me que a finalizar, e como exemplo, registe o contraste entre Portugal e alguns países europeus de menor ou igual dimensão,

O Envolvimento na Integração Económica e na Integração Política

corrigindo a ideia de que os pequenos países não podem ser afirmativos. Foi agora publicado o Eurobarómetro de Abril, e face a uma das perguntas "Como é que aprecia a sua situação económica?". Em Portugal 88% das pessoas classificavam-na como má ou muito má; na Dinamarca 99% das pessoas consideravam que era boa ou muito boa. São os dois extremos. A seguir à Dinamarca vem a Suécia e a Irlanda, tudo países de dimensão reduzida, e Portugal aparece como o segundo pior, apenas um pouco menos mal que a Hungria. Mas a Dinamarca tem políticas próprias. Quando entrou em conflito por causa das pescas excluiu as Feroé e a Groenlândia do espaço comunitário. Também não aderiu à política externa de defesa, nem faz parte da agência europeia de defesa, porque entende manter a sua autonomia de negociação com outros países. Mantém a sua própria moeda e políticas exigentes para a agricultura e indústria da pesca.

Nem em todos os domínios estas opções constituiriam exemplo para Portugal, mas devem contribuir para eliminar a convicção, que temos mantido, de que as competências europeias exigem a eliminação das competências nacionais. E também as experiências da Áustria, da Irlanda, da Holanda ou da Suécia convidam a uma reflexão. Não podemos ignorar a exigência de objectivos e competência próprias e o elevado custo que o seu esquecimento tem representado.

Sem perdermos complexos de dependência, de que um país pequeno não pode escolher o seu futuro, não seremos capazes de uma integração saudável e sustentável na Europa. Nem sequer contribuiremos plenamente para que a União Europeia assuma um posicionamento correcto na nova economia global e no novo relacionamento mundial, por não potenciarmos as nossas afinidades nas relações intercontinentais.

Referimos já como alguns outros Estados-membros – mas também a Finlândia ou os países do alargamento – participam na União com o desígnio de reforçar as capacidade próprias de afirmação. No caso português, seis anos de divergência em relação ao desempenho comunitário confirmam que sem uma mudança da nossa capacidade para construir o próprio futuro não será fácil encontrar resposta para as aspirações dos portugueses: de auto-confiança, de qualidade de vida e de empregos qualificados. A crescente dependência não é, como se tem provado, a melhor resposta para uma saudável integração económica e política. Importa, pelo contrário, potenciar a nossa capacidade de afirmação dentro e fora da U.E. assumindo com independência e auto-confiança os desafios que a tornam possível.

EUROPEAN CONSTITUTIONALISM
AND THREE MODELS OF SOCIAL EUROPE

MIGUEL POIARES MADURO[*]

In this paper I review three models of the relationship between the constitutionalization of the project of European integration and social values. This analysis is also linked to different conceptions of the role of private law in the context of European integration. Finally, I also review the connection between the forms of European constitutionalization and these alternative models of Social Europe. It must be stressed that, as always, these models are heuristic devices rather than 'real-life' representations. Elements of all are to be found, to a greater or lesser extent, in the European Union.

The first model arises from the constitutionalization of market integration. Market integration rules constituted the basis for the initial process of constitutionalization of the project of European integration and they shaped the impact of that process on the European social model (referring both to the social model of the European States and that of the European Union itself). It is a model where both the impact of EU law on national social values and the development of European social values are linked to the logic of market integration and its focus on negative integration (the development of economic integration by deregulation at the national level). This is a model where the legitimacy of European constitutionalism derives from the functional development of the rules on

---

[*] Advocate-General at the Court of Justice of the European Communities.

This paper was originally published in M. W. Hesselink (ed.), *The Politics of European Civil Code*, 125-141 e 2006 Klumer Law International. Printed in the Netherlands.

market integration coupled with a constitutional ideology centered on the rights of individuals and the maximization of their private autonomy.

The second model has grown out of the policies of social harmonization. It is a model which understands the European social model as a set of basic social values and rules which are promoted or set by the European Union but are mainly to be guaranteed and protected by the States. It either aims at guaranteeing a level playing field in the social sphere so as prevent social deregulation at the State level or, in certain States, attempts to promote further social regulation by shifting the level of decision-making of national social policies to what is perceived to be a more social-friendly political sphere. This model can be pursued either as a technocratic exercise (what is instrumental to the good functioning of the internal market) or as a comparative exercise (comparing national social values). These two methodologies are also clearly visible in the alternative dominant strategies for an emerging common European contract law[1]. The legitimacy of the model is two-fold: on the one hand, it is perceived as a further instrument for the effective operation of the internal market; on the other hand, it is presented as an attempt to introduce social values into the logic of market integration, balancing the 'economic bias' of a European Constitution which has been promoted mainly by free movement and competition rules.

The third and final model assumes that the European social model must entail both a definition of genuinely European social values and mechanisms of distributive justice at the European level. The underlying idea is that the European Union needs a political identity and that the latter requires a European definition of a core set of social values (including, in this respect, some core aspects of private law). It can also be argued that the increased redistributive consequences of some EU policies and its increased majoritarian character require a criterion and policies of distributive justice so as to legitimize and compensate for those redistributive consequences and to guarantee the necessary political loyalty of those in the minority. This model would require harmonization policies not as instruments of market integration (to guarantee a level

---

[1] See M.W. Hesselink, 'The European Commission's Action Plan: Towards a More Coherent European Contract Law' (2004) 4 *European Review of Private Law* 397, 402 ff.

playing field) but as instruments of a set of European social values that the Union ought to pursue. It would also require further instruments of distributive justice at the EU level (including taxation mechanisms). Again, this model also appears in the discussions on a common European contract law. Hesselink has argued that such a project should depart from a genuine debate on a set of common European values and should be detached from the project of the internal market.[2]

These models do not simply represent different understandings of the role and place that social values ought to have in the project of European integration. They embody different processes of decision-making with respect to social values in the European Union and these processes offer, in turn, different degrees of participation to different social groups. Much of this is of general interest to the current strategies on the drafting of a common European contract law. In reality, I would argue that these models of approaching a social Europe also correspond to different ways of approaching the development of European contract law.

I will assess the extent to which these three models have been adopted by the European Union, their connection with European constitutionalism and their possible consequences. In this light, I would also take into account the possible impact of the recent constitutional developments (including the Charter, the Nice Treaty and the now in doubt Draft Constitutional Treaty).

I. MODEL 1: ECONOMIC FREEDOM AND SOCIAL NON-DISCRIMINATION: CONSTITUTIONALIZING PRIVATE AUTONOMY

A. Negative integration and Private Autonomy

It is well known that the initial process of constitutionalization of the project of European integration was supported by the rules of market

---

[2] Ibid and M.W. Hesselink, 'The Politics of a European Civil Code' (2004) vol. 10 *European Law Journal* 675.

integration. These rules are at the core of the founding Treaties and provided the basis for the conception of those Treaties as individual rights oriented. This, in turn, required a uniform and effective application of EU law to be guaranteed by the conferral of direct effect and supremacy to its rules. This constituted a claim of independent normative authority, legitimated by the need to protect those individual rights, and attributed to those norms a supervisory role over large bodies of national law.

Such europeanization of national policies through market integration can, in the first place, be seen in the way in which the Court of Justice and, to a lesser extent, the Commission have controlled the exercise of many national competences through the application of the rules of market integration. A good example regards the interpretation of the free movement rules. The Court interpreted the scope of application of these rules larger than the scope normally attributed to trade rules and has used the free movement rules to review almost any area of national legislation that impacts on the market. The extensive interpretation of the free movement rules led to a spill-over of EU law and its rationale of market integration into political and social spheres at the national level. National legislation intervening in the market became subject to review under EU law and assessed under criteria of necessity and proportionality, independently of any intended protectionism. This meant that EU law would often second-guess the reasonableness of national mesures in areas such as social, consumer, environmnental and health policies. Another example can be detected in the use by the Commission of its discretionary power to authorize State aids to *de facto* impose certain elements of a Community industrial policy on the Member States, including some aspects of social policy (in particular, regarding restructuring processes).

This impact on national social policies is further reinforced by the mechanism of regulatory competition among States generated by the internal market and the mobility it entails. The 'forum shopping' of companies, consumers and tax-payers allowed by economic integration and market competition challenges the autonomy of States even in the realm of policies shaping their criteria of distributive justice.

The traditional core of the European Constitution therefore lies in market integration. It was mainly with this legitimacy and through the rules provided in the Treaties that the Court has developed the notion itself of a European Constitution. Though the Treaty of Rome also contains social provisions (notably, free movement of workers and Articles 136 ff) the core of market integration are the free movement provisions promoting market access to the different national markets. The Court has defined these free movement provisions as 'fundamental freedoms'. The fundamental rights character granted to the free movement provisions and the widening of their scope of application in order to extend European supervision over national regulation and support the constitutionalization of Community law, have led to a spill-over of market integration rules into virtually all areas of national law and has led some to argue that they should be conceived of as fundamental economic freedoms limiting public power and safeguarding competition in the free market. This dynamic has been reinforced by the patterns of litigation in European law with emphasis on the fundamental rights discourse of the European Court of Justice. Most cases on fundamental rights decided by the Court of Justice under the doctrine now enshrined in Article 6° n. 2 addressed economic rights and freedoms such as the right to property and freedom of economic activity.

This, in turn, has been presented by others as giving rise to a social deficit. Negative integration (promoting economic integration by deregulation at the national level) was the preferred tool of economic integration. That was not mainly due to an ideological preference for economic deregulation but more to the difficulties inherent in the decision-making process of the European Communities which hindered the mechanisms of positive integration (the promotion of economic integration through regulatory harmonization at the European level). Nevertheless, the promotion of economic integration through negative integration has been presented as creating a bias in favour of economic deregulation in the process of European integration. The institutional constraints may indeed have shaped the regulatory model of the European Union.

B. The Legitimacy of the Constitutionalization of Negative Integration: The Role of Private Autonomy

The emerging European constitutionalism promoted the authority of the Communities in encroaching upon the sovereign spheres of the States but was legitimated either through the degree of voice of the States in the process of deliberation or through the conception of that encroachment as protecting freedom and individual rights. It is notable, with respect to the latter, that the areas where the Community started to evolve towards more majoritarian decision-making, were those directly related to the internal market. These were easier to legitimize both by the functional construction of the Communities and the link to a limited conception of constitutionalism as a limit to power and as protecting private autonomy.

In the early constitutionzation of the project of European integration, constitutionalism was linked to two different visions of the legitimacy of the process of European integration. The first is that embodied in a functional and technocratic conception of the European Union as an efficiency – oriented and problem-solving entity to whom States delegate the resolution of collective action problems they can no longer address individually.[3] The second, is that which follows the tradition of limited government and conceives the process of European integration as a new constitutional constraint on public power, protecting freedom and private autonomy.[4] Functional legitimacy fitted well with the nature of the process of decision-making and its intergovernmental deliberation. Limited goals that were instrumental or complimentary to the State, did not have redistributive effects, and were furthermore legitimized by a form of deliberation centred on the aggregation and conciliation of State interests (dominated by unanimity). Where the Union encroached upon State's sovereignty, that construction of legitimacy was supplemented by an appeal to the protection of freedom and private autonomy. The European common good was either a product of an agreement between States or conceived of as the protection of private autonomy and freedom enshrined in the logic of market integration.

---

[3] G. Majone, 'The regulatory state and its legitimacy problems' (1999) *West European Politics* 22 (1) 1-24.

[4] See ordo-liberals, like Hayek, *Law Legislation and Liberty*, vol. 1 (London: Routledge and Keagan, 1973); Petersmann 'Constitutional Principles Governing the EEC's Commercial Policy', in M. Maresceau (ed), *The European Community's Commercial Policy after 1992: The Legal Dimension* (Kluwer 1993) 21.

C. The Emergence of a European Social Status Through Negative Integration

This model based on negative integration is not, however, absent from the promotion of certain elements of a social Europe. These elements are also a product of the logic of market integration, particularly mobility, the prevention of distortion of competition and the prohibition of discrimination [s1] [s2]. Most initial developments in the area of social rights were closely linked to the objectives of a well-functioning common market.[5] It is well known that such was the origin of the principle of equal pay between men and women which is protected by Community law since the original version of the Treaty of Rome (Article 141 EC, previously 119 EC). This principle was enshrined in the Treaty to prevent the distortion of competition between companies that could be subject to different legislation in this regard.

Perhaps the most important developments, however, have arisen out of the connection the Court of Justice has established between free movement of persons, non-discrimination and citizenship. The coordinated interpretation of these rules has, indeed, reinforced the social status of European citizens in three different ways:

a) Free movement and fundamental social rights. In the same way that free movement provisions have been used to promote economic freedom they can also be used to promote certain social rights which can be presented as instrumental to those free movement provisions. In particular, the broader interpretation which has been granted to the provisions on the free movement of persons by the Court since the 90's allows for a broader set of social rights to be claimed on the basis of those provisions. The *Bosman* decision is a paradigmatic example, supporting a right to work and the freedom of workers to choose their work and employment.[6] This decision prohibited rules that, albeit not discriminating against workers of other Member States, reduced their fine movement by imposing limits on their freedom to leave their employer and to

---

[5] See Maduro, 'Striking the Elusive Balance Between Economic Freedom and Social Rights', in Alston (ed), *The European Union and Human Rights* (Oxford: Oxford University Press, 1999).

[6] Case C-415/93 Bosman [1995] ECR I-4921 (ECJ).

choose among different employment contracts. The consequence of the recent expansion of the free movement of persons provisions beyond the simple prohibition of discrimination on the basis of nationality[7] may be the recognition of a set of European social rights linked to a broader protection of the free movement of persons. Developments in this sense will depend heavily on the sophistication and capacity of social actors to raise litigation combining Community law arguments with fundamental social rights.[8] In this respect, what many perceive as a bias in the application of internal market rules may be more a consequence of the different use of litigation by different social actors.

b) Social mobility and meta-citizenship. In a different set of cases in which the Court of Justice has addressed the consequences of the general right to reside in another member State (Article 18 EC) together with the prohibition of discrimination on the basis of nationality (Article 12 EC), the Court has gradually recognized an important social dimension in the concept of European citizenship. There is now a general right to choose the Member State where one wants to reside subject only to restrictions conforming to the principle of proportionality. [Case C-413/99, *Baumbast v. R and Secretary of State for the Home Department* [2002] ECR I-7091.] Furthermore, this right is complemented by the right to have the same social status as that of the citizens of the State of residence so long as an effective link with that State can be established. [C-138/02, *Brian Francis Collins* v. *Secretary of State for Work and Pensions* [2004] I-2733.]

These cases extend the social content of the different national citizenships to European citizens who establish a stable link with the Member State in which they have chosen to reside. It is the emergence of a kind of meta-citizenship: European citizenship includes the right to choose among different national political communities and, so long as there is an effective commitment to that national political community, to benefit from the same social status as the original citizens of that national political community.

---

[7] That I try to explain below.

[8] That has not been the case up to now. In this sense, see E. Szysczak, 'future Directions in European Union Social Policy Law'(1995) *ILJ* 19, at 31.

c) Solidarity among national social services. The third social dimension arising out of the interpretation and application of free movement provisions has to do with the choice which is increasingly given to European citizens with respect to national social services. This is the case with education but also, most notably and recently, with health services. The need to protect the cross-border provision of health services has led the Court to recognize, in several circumstances, the rights of patients to choose the Member State where they wish to be treated. This allows citizens to choose from a broader array of treatments and also to benefit from a faster and better treatment than that which may be available in their country of residence. Some critics have pointed out, however, that this may impose too great a burden on the financial foundations of national health systems. So far, the Court has been careful in this regard but one must recognize that such a system involves a certain degree of cross-subsidization. That such forms of solidarity are inherent in the logic of an internal market which includes a dimension of citizenship appears obvious. The remaining question is how such solidarity should be organized.

II. MODEL 2: PROTECTING THE SOCIAL MODEL OF THE MEMBER STATES

As stated above, European economic integration (in parallel with global economic integration) has generated pressures towards de-regulation and challenged national social standards and welfare. It is easier to promote integration by reducing state legislation interfering with economic activities (negative integration) than by creating common standards and regulatory frameworks for economic agents (positive integration). The latter requires an agreement on social policies and rights normally expressed in the form of legislation, and is difficult to achieve in the EU context characterized by different national interests and ideological stand points. The argument in favour of a European social policy attempts to reintroduce such political control over the economic sphere at the European Union level. The European Union would become the relevant level for the establishment and protection of social policies since both negative integration and its associated regulatory competition among the States challenge the capacity of States to protect certain social values. Negative integration at the State level should be followed by positive integration at the Union level.

This model has slowly emerged in the European Union with the development of its capacity to intervene in the social sphere. Today there are enhanced and facilitated legislative competences for the Union to intervene in the social sphere.[9] At the same time, incentives have been created for social partners to shift their social dialogue into the European arena.[10] These developments have, however, remained prisoners of the logic of market integration whereby they secure equal conditions of competition while imposing common social standards which are to be secured and guaranteed by the different Member States.

Even social lawyers tend to argue for EU social rights in the light of the need to guarantee a common level playing field that will prevent a race to the bottom of national social rights and policies.[11] EU social rights are not conceived as rights corresponding to social entitlements that EU citizens can claim with regard to the European polity. They are conceived, instead, either as an instrument of undistorted competition or as a guarantee that such competition will not affect the level of social rights protection afforded by the States.

This emerging social policy is not one in which the Union takes on the burden of guaranteeing a minimum safety net and social protection for all European citizens. Instead, it is a social policy in which the European Union requires its member States to comply with some social standards in order to fully benefit from their membership of the internal market. This is why Europe's social policy is built upon the joint-efforts of two different forces: European States with an interest in promoting higher social standards to secure their competitive position; and national social actors who use European social policy as an alternative political process to promote national social rights. However, the alliance between these two forces is only possible with regard to social rights which can be construed as preventing unfair competition in the internal market. Rights which could promote redistribution in European terms and would require a commitment of the Union to distributive justice are excluded from European social policy. Moreover, even the social rights which are

---

[9] See, notably, Art. 137 of the EC Treaty.

[10] See Arts 138 and 139 EC Treaty.

[11] I develop this point in M. Poiares Maduro, 'Europe's Social Self: 'The Sickness Unto Death', in J. Shaw (ed), *Social Law and and Policy in an Evolving European Union* (Oxford: Hart Publishing, 2000).

enacted as part of that social policy are, as a consequence of the limits under which such social policy is conceived, the result not of a genuine deliberation on what European social values ought to be but instead the product of bargaining dominated by the different interests of the Member States in projecting their national rules on the playing field of the European market. In other words, the European social values emerging from this model are not elements of a genuine European political identity.

Bob Hepple, for example, argues that 'until such time as European social policy is explicitly based on general principles which reflect common social values, there will be no rational basis for Community legislation and judicial interpretation in the social field'.[12] But even Hepple appears to concentrate on the protection of a common set of social values (which he derives from the different Member States) from the intrusion of market integration and efficiency-enhancing policies and not on the establishment of European policies which would promote a European dimension of that common set of social values.[13] The social constitution of Europe to which this author refers will serve as a yardstick for the protection of social rights at the national level and by Community norms but would not, in and of itself, promote forms of redistribution and social allocation at the European level. It will therefore preserve the idea of Europe's social policy as establishing a common set of social values to be achieved and safeguarded by the different Member States and not as promoting a European ideal of distributive justice expressed as independent political and social goals. In other words, that the social constitution of Europe will guarantee a level playing field within Europe and impose on all States a core set of social values to be respected by all but would not entrust to the Union the promotion of a genuine social Europe to be achieved in accordance with a European criterion of distributive justice. The social perspective underlying this limited conception of Europe's social identity is that which merges the interests of those who want to guarantee a level playing field in the internal market with regard to social standards with the interests of those who want to use Europe to promote more social rights at the national level. This limited version of the European social self does not really

---

[12] 'Social Values in European Law', *Current Legal Problems* (1995) 39, at 40.
[13] Ibid, mainly at 40 44. 52 ff and 60.

recognize a right for Europe legitimately to establish and exercise an independent redistributive function.

In this context, the social values which emerge from this model are, to a large extent, depoliticized and presented as the product of both a technical exercise (determining what social policies are necessary to the well functioning of the internal market and preventing distortion of competition) and an exercise in comparative law (comparing and bringing together the different social legislations of the Member States). As said above, this logic also permeates much of the usual strategy for the development of a common European contracts law.

At the same time, this conception spills-over to the broader constitutional debate on the relationship between social values and the European Union. A good example is the discussion on the Charter of Fundamental Rights.

A. The Role of the Charter: Protecting the Social Model of the States

As mentioned above, the economic integration status quo has had two main consequences: first, social rights have had a lower impact on the fundamental rights discourse developed by the Court of Justice; second, many national social rights and policies have been challenged under the free movement provisions since the balance between economic freedom and social rights in the European Constitution was largely defined by the balance between market integration and national social rights.

The Charter of Fundamental Rights attempts to correct this social deficit in Europe's consitutional discourse by eliminating the uncertainty regarding the status and catalogue of fundamental social rights in the EU legal order. Social rights are given an important role in the context of the Charter and they are systematically placed in an equivalent position to other economic rights. Some of the social rights affirmed by the Charter are immediately effective and judicially enforceable while others are rights of a programmatic character expressing goals which are to be attained on a gradual basis. The qualification of social rights as 'real rights' (enforceable in courts) or goals will, no doubt, be an issue of contention in the interpretation of the Charter, reinforced by the distinction it makes between rights and principles that, in turn, are not really identified or defined.[14] That is, however, nothing particular to the European Charter and has constituted a topic of heated debate surrounding national constitutions for a long time.

In any event, the Charter may promote a more active judicial review of EU acts in the light of fundamental social rights. Rights of a programmatic character may both strengthen the position of social values in EU law and allow for such social rights to be used as possible exceptions to free movement rules and their possible deregulatory impact on national social policies.[15] [C-112/00, *Schmidberg* v. *Austria* [2003]ECR I-5659; Case C-36/02, *Omega Spielhallen- und Automatenaufstellungs-GmbH* v. *Oberbütgermeisterin der Bundesstadt Bonn,* Judgment of 14 October 2004, nyr.]

Still the Charter also poses some clear limits on the potential use of these rights. Notably, it would be difficult for European citizens to claim new social entitlements from the European Union. This is so because none of these rights may give rise to a new competence or power of the EU (Article II-111 n.2). In this respect, the social content of the Charter appears to fit closely with the intentions of this second model of social Europe. The limits imposed on the nature of the rights recognized therein and, mostly, on the potential for new competences arising from its social rights, appear to correspond to a conception of the Charter aimed simply at guaranteeing that EU rules will not affect the social values of the Member States and not promote an independent EU social policy reflecting a European criterion of social justice.

In the light of this conception of the Charter, its set of rights will serve (directly, if and when they are given legally binding status or indirectly, as criteria to determine the common constitutional traditions of the Member States that guide the Court in its fundamental rights

---

[14] von Bogdandy, 'The European Union as a human rights organization? Human rights and the core of the European Union' (2000) CMLR 37, 1307 and F. Rubio Llorente, 'Una carta de dudosa utilidad', in A.A.V.V. (Dir. Francisco Javier Matia Portilla), *La protección de los Derechos Fundamentales en la Unión Europea* (Madrid, 2002) 171-172.

[15] The ECJ has admitted that fundamental rights can, in some circumstances, justify restrictions on free movement rules. See notably Case C-368/95. *Vereinigte Familiapress Zeitungsverlag- und vertriebs GmbH* v. *Heinrich Bauer Verlag* [1997] ECR I-3689.

jurisprudence) either to guarantee that Community legislation does not reduce the level of social protection normally afforded by the Member States or to allow derogations from Community rules (in particular, market integration rules) justified by the need to protect the social values of the States recognized in the Charter.

III. MODEL 3: THE SOCIAL MODEL OF THE EUROPEAN UNION

If one looks at Marshall's well known description of the three waves of fundamental rights associated with citizenship one is bound to notice that, while political rights have emerged in the European Union, social rights continue to be the main gap in the process of constructing European citizenship. As we have just seen, however, even the arguments in favour of European social rights tend to focus on the need to create a set of rights in relation to which the European Union is to ensure State compliance. The debate on social values at the level of the European Union is not guided by a debate on what the common European social values are or ought to be but, instead, on which of these values are affected by European economic integration and require appropriate mechanisms of protection. It is a debate instrumental to economic integration and which is, therefore, guided by its perceived technocratic ideology and comparative methodology. The idea of European social rights as a product of a genuine debate about social values[16] and the possibility of European social entitlements arising from a criterion of distributive justice agreed among all citizens of the Europe Union is rarely, if ever, discussed.

The recognition of a set of social rights accorded to all European citizens both with regard to the different national demos and the emerging European demos would instead follow from a notion of citizenship that can no longer be exclusive of those which can more easily make use of the free movement provisions. Otherwise, many Europeans will feel like strangers with regard to European citizenship.[17] But this would require European social rights to be complemented by effective EU

---

[16] For a similar analysis in the context of private law see Hesselink, *op. cit.*
[17] Ibid.

policies promoting those rights and not simply to constitute elements of a social harmonization necessary to the pursuit of market integration. This would in turn, have to be founded on a new form of political discourse on social values at the level of the European Union.

However, this will not be an uncontroversial issue. Debates on efficiency *versus* distributive justice have never been so and will be much more controversial in the context of a 'contested' European political community whose degree of cohesion and solidarity is, at best, weak. The problem is that decisions on those issues are already being taken at the European level. In the absence of an agreed European social contract, those decisions simply flow from the functional ideology of market integration. Moreover, European integration has reached a point where its emerging European demos and its redistributive and majoritarian elements can no longer be socially accepted and legitimized without an underlying social contract and a criterion of distributive justice.

A major constitutional challenge brought by European integration relates to the underlying conditions for the performance of certain functions of governance. In this respect, the promotion of legislative harmonization at the social level between States may not be enough. Europe's economic integration has limited the capacity of States to pursue traditional functions of governance, in particular those relating to market regulation and distributive policies. Internal market rules, for example, have impacted on national regulatory policies well beyond trade considerations, in effect constraining national policies in areas as different as social, environmental and consumer policies. Moreover, in some cases, increased mobility and economic regulatory competition also affected national redistributive policies. These limits on the pursuit of these functions of governance at the national level are not compensated by a degree of EU intervention to secure those functions. The Union as yet does not fulfil the conditions nor has it the capacity to perform those functions of governance. Fritz Scharpf has presented this as a result of the gap between negative integration (economic integration through national market deregulation) and positive integration (economic integration through Community wide re-regulation).[18] The consequence is that

---

[18] 'Negative and Positive Integration in the Political Economy of Welfare States', in Marks, Scharpf, Schmitter and Streeck (eds.), *Governance in the European Union*, Sage, London, 1996.

the process of European integration is seen not simply as challenging the capacity of States to perform those functions of governance but, more broadly, as challenging those functions of governance themselves. For some, the process of European integration challenges the conception of the Welfare State that has supported the subsistence of national political communities and moulded our conception of public power. Others, notably Jürgen Habermas, perceive that challenge as resulting from broader global processes and, instead, conceive the European Union as an opportunity to rise to that challenge and protect the values of the Welfare State required for the subsistence of political communities and civic solidarity.[19] In this case what would be required from the current constitutional process is the adoption of a social contract clarifying the foms of civic solidarity on which the European polity ought to be based. This would in turn require important and very controversial reforms on the nature of its policies, the nature of its deliberation and even its budgetary regime.

This debate on a European social contract is nevertheless promoted by an additional constitutional challenge faced by European integration. It regards the increased redistributive consequences of its policies. The assumption of economic integration was increased growth without interference in the distributive function of markets. But a viable and sustainable integration is only workable if economic growth is fairly distributed. The issue of redistribution is therefore present from the outset in any project of economic integration. It is well known in economic theory that, although all may gain from economic integration and trade liberalization, it is to be expected that richer and more competitive countries may gain more than less developed countries.[20] Still the focus of the project of European economic integration has been on enhancing efficiency and maximizing wealth. The economic growth to be expected from market integration was beneficial to all albeit not in equal shares. Moreover, the degree of economic and social cohesion of the starting members of the European project also reassured all that redistributive effects would not impose an undue burden on any of the members. For the most part, as in most economic integration agreements, States make

---

[19] See *The Postnational Constellation* (London: Polity Press, 2001).

[20] See Mestre and Petit, 'La cohesion économique et sociale après le Traité sur l'Union européenne' (1995) *RTD eur.* 31(2) 207, at 241.

their cost/benefit analysis at the time of signing an international agreement and if necessary, obtain specific compensations in agreeing to certain areas of economic integration. The fact that redistributive effects have taken place as a consequence of the developments in other policies of the Union could also be legitimized in the light of the adoption of unanimous voting for decision-making in the European Community. In this case, States could either prevent policies which could have adverse redistributive effects for their own welfare or could subject their agreement to the condition of receiving some form of compensation in other areas of European policy (something referred to as issue linkage).[21] It is this which determined the pattern of both goals determination and institutional development of the European Communities. In the absence of a common belief in some kind of European ideal or political concept of European integration, integration could only proceed if the overall net of decisions, even in an increased majoritarian context, satisfied all States. This could be achieved either by guaranteeing that all would have to agree to a specific decision (institutional rule promoting Pareto efficiency) or by agreeing on mechanisms of compensating those who would be worst off by virtue of a certain decision (subordinating institutional and substantive developments to a form of Kaldor-Hicks efficiency). The 'fairness'of the decisions was measured by the degree to which the overall set of decisions obtained a consensus among Member States.

However, the development of European integration has strained this form of relation between the model and degree of integration and its ideals. The degree of integration, the expansion of the scope of action of the European Union and its institutional changes are producing redistributive effects which can no longer be either traced back to an original agreement of the States or be predictable as part of ad hoc political bargaining that may legitimize them through appropriate forms of compensation. Instead, the degree of majoritarian decision-making, the scope of European policies and the open and undetermined character of

---

[21] According to Shlomo Weber and Hans Wiesmeth, 'an international regime (...) provides a political environment that naturally promotes issue linkage: by affecting 'transaction costs', the costs associated with acts of non-co-operative behaviour, it makes it casier to link particular issues and to negotiate side-payments that allow some actors to cxtract positive gains on one issue in return for the favours expected on another', 'Issue Linkage in the European Community' (1991). *JCMS* 255, at 258.

political action produce increased redistributive effects. The institutional shift majoritarian decision-making (both through the extension of majority voting and Parliamentary intervention) and the growth of the EU's competences tend to make the EU have a redistributive impact larger than what could be functionally legitimized.

There is a broader problem arising from the emergence of majoritarianism and the growth of EU competences in a context where deliberation is predominantly inter-governmental. Many EU policies are still the result of inter-State bargaining and legitimized as such. As a consequence, many are simply drafted along State lines (national quotas and some aspects of the structural funds for example) or are drafted in such a way as to reproduce that inter-State bargaining. Under this logic, it is not important to assess if such policies treat all citizens alike or not but, instead, to determine if they have achieved a consensus among States or are the product of a legitimate balance among those States' interests. Since, however, these policies directly affect individuals, they often perceive them as discriminatory and arbitrary. In other words why should it be legitimate for a group of citizens from State A to bear certain costs from a particular EU policy to which State A has agreed in exchange for benefits accruing for another group of its citizens from a different EU policy? From an international law and intergovernmental perspective this is the natural and legitimate consequence of the fact that it is States that aggregate their citizens interests in the international arena. But is this legitimate and sustainable in the context of the EU? Is the fact that different treatment is given to different EU citizens depending on the bargaining of their respective Member States with respect to their interests acceptable under an understanding of the EU as a novel political community subject to a constitutional regime?

Whatever the adopted perspective it is now clear that we must link European social expectations to principles of social justice[22] and that this requires a debate ou Europe's social contract.

---

[22] See S. Sciarra, 'European Social Policy and Labour Law – Challenges and Perspectives' Collected Courses of the Academy of European Law vol. IV, Book I, 301, at 310.

A. Europe's Constitutional Project and Social Europe

The Nice Treaty and the Draft Constitutional project are, independently of the final outcome of the latter, two important landmarks in a constitutional project for Europe. One of the key elements of this project is the growing majoritarian character of the EU political system. However, such a system needs a political community that guarantees the legitimacy of the system and secures the necessary safeguards to prevent risks. Securing political loyalty, changing the character of political deliberation and universalizing its policies, ought to be the priorities of any constitutional reform of the European Union that takes seriously its democratic rhetoric and the need for social legitimacy. This has important consequences regarding what ought to be the dominant conception of a Social Europe.

What can be done to secure the loyalty of European citizens towards a project of European integration with an increased majoritarian nature and redistributive impacts? In this paper, I cannot go into details regarding a broader project of constitutional legitimacy for the Union but I want to note two aspects which relate to the nature of the EU social model and its policies.

The first relates to the character of deliberation of these policies and the impact on its framing. Intergovernmental aspects have dominated the conception of EU policies. As stated, many continue to be framed largely as policies that distribute between States and not as policies based on the individual status of EU citizens independent of their nationality. This exacerbates the risks of malfunction in the majoritarian political process given that such policies can easily mirror the power of the majority in concentrating the benefits on some States. It also makes it much more difficult to both legitimize the current redistributive effects of EU policies and to develop genuine redistributive policies.

Deliberative constitutionalism would require EU policies to move into a framework of universalisability, satisfying substantive, and not simply formal, conditions of generality and abstraction and where their redistributive impact is determined by the individual conditions of EU citizens. One must replace bargaining with principles as the basis for EU policies. Only policies supported and conforming to universal principles can be understood and supported by the citizens. Otherwise, in popular terms, the questions will increasingly be along the lines of: Why should poor citizens of state A be made to pay for both poor and richer citizens of state B? Or why should some citizens of State A receive less than citizens in a similar situation in State B simply because State A agreed to this in exchange for benefits for a different group of its citizens?

The second issue regards how to generate political loyalty in a context of an increasingly majoritarian polity. In my view, this requires two things: granting a basic social status to all citizens of the polity and developing a common political identity by engaging in a truly European discourse on, among others, its social values. It is easy to perceive how difficult it will be to achieve these two requirements in the European Union.

The Charter of Fundamental Rights and the important place granted to social rights in the Charter could be seen as promoting both of these aspects. But that sounds utterly optimistic. I believe it is important to distinguish between two different set of rights that a Charter of Fundamental Rights could promote in the European Union. Rights that European citizens may have to protect themselves from EU institutions and rights that they can claim from the European polity. This does not correspond to the traditional distinction between negative and positive rights since the rights that European citizens can claim from the European polity may relate to their protection *vis-à-vis* the powers of national institutions. The first set of rights simply guarantees that European citizens will not see their sphere of personal autonomy (in civic, political but also social and economic terms) diminished by the powers granted to EU institutions. It guarantees the status quo of fundamental rights protection. The second set of rights, on the other hand, incorporates any new rights that European citizens may claim from European institutions or from Nation States through EU law. They may include the expansion of the scope of political and civic rights with regard to Nation States (for example, electoral rights, non-discrimination on the basis of nationality or, in some respects, the free movement of persons) or even new instruments for their protection (EU review of national acts with regard to fundamental rights). However, they also include new social, cultural and economic entitlements that European citizens may claim from European institutions (for example, free movement rules and their link to economic freedom or emerging social rights such as those regarding working conditions and possibly in the future even distributive justice in Europe).

The relevance of distinguishing between these two sets of rights lies in their relation to the development of a political community in the EU.

Rights given to EU citizens to protect them from EU institutions are aimed at providing regime legitimacy.[23] They guarantee that the sphere of individual political and social autonomy is not diminished by the powers granted to the EU. EU institutions will act in accordance with the fundamental rights that are inherent to any constitutionally democratic system. Further, the recognition of economic and social rights, in this context, is simply aimed at preserving the social and economic freedom and protection that citizens are granted by their States. It mainly enhances the protection of States' social policies linked to fundamental rights from the disintegrative fears promoted by European integration. Such a set of rights, however, will not have a substantial effect in terms of polity building. They do not justify the need for a new polity. They, simply assure that such a new polity will not threaten the fundamental rights linked to the States.

The building of polity legitimacy requires the second type of rights: new rights derived from the European polity. It is in these new rights that citizens can find the added value of European integration with regard to their national polities. In this respect, however, that the Charter is more disappointing. This second dimension would require the discussion of much more contentious issues regarding what ought to be the fundamental rights policy of the EU. It would require a different kind of discourse on fundamental rights at the EU level. It would also require the recognition in the Charter of those rights to be complemented by a discussion on how the Union could promote such social rights (including in budgetary terms).

To sum up, the polity building power of European social rights would require them to be linked to much more ambitious and contested dimensions of fundamental rights protection and discourse in the European Union. To define what other roles an EU fundamental rights strategy should assume beyond guaranteeing EU compliance with traditional national fundamental rights standards, we must first agree on the political goals of the project of European integration. We need to promote a genuine discourse on European values to provide for the polity legitimacy necessary to support the current developments in its regime. The

---

[23] See N. Walker (2001) The White Paper in Constitutional Context. Florence: European University Institute. www.jeanmmonnetprogram.org/papers/01/011001.html

problem is that we have not yet found any appropriate system for such a discourse in the current context where the need for the discourse is itself contested. For those who oppose a European political community any debate on European values is unacceptable. The problem is that this may not be enough to rise to the real challenge of legitimacy faced by the European Union: how to legitimize the claim of an independent political power assumed by an emerging European polity of a majoritarian type. The way in which we will attempt to answer this question will determine the extent to which the Union develops the different models of Social Europe.

PORTUGAL NA EUROPA E NO MUNDO

RUI MACHETE[*]

Desejo, naturalmente, em primeiro lugar, agradecer o convite que me foi formulado para intervir nesta conferência, da qual, infelizmente, pude beneficiar relativamente pouco; mas o pouco que ouvi evidenciou claramente que se trata de uma conferência de invulgar importância para, justamente, dilucidar os aspectos da Europa e os desafios do século XXI.

E, por isso, peço-vos desculpa de, aquilo que vou dizer, porventura, não estar em absoluta concordância com muito do que já anteriormente foi referido, pela própria dificuldade de interpretar o tema que me foi dado: Portugal na Europa e no Mundo, numa perspectiva da integração europeia e dentro do âmbito mais largo dos desafios do século XXI no limiar da presidência portuguesa. Podemos interpretar este tema numa perspectiva internacional e fundamentalmente acentuando o aspecto cultural olhá-lo, fundamentalmente, como a projecção de Portugal no mundo. Todavia, isso parece-me ser empobrecedor das potencialidades do tema e de resto alguns aspectos já foram anteriormente brilhantemente tratados já pelo Doutor Rui Vilar, no âmbito da questão mais vasta de que se ocupou. Prefiro adoptar a óptica das relações internacionais, não seguindo a análise tradicional baseada nos Estados como sujeitos únicos ou principais das relações internacionais, mas numa perspectiva diversa. Numa orientação que privilegia as pessoas, os grupos, as entidades, que fazendo parte da sociedade civil, ou mesmo integrando a administração pública, se diferenciam, contudo, do Estado, considerado este como pessoa colectiva de direito público e dotada de uma certa impermeabilidade, como diziam

---

[*] Presidente da Fundação Luso-Americana para o Desenvolvimento.

os juristas clássicos. Deste modo, pode melhor aperceber-se o papel das empresas, dos sindicatos, das universidades, das associações e instituições culturais, das fundações, etc., o qual não é tido em conta se nos limitarmos às relações interestaduais ou relações abrangendo, para além dos Estados, as organizações internacionais de que estes fazem parte e que são também sujeitos tradicionais de direito internacional. É a óptica perfilhada pelos escritores que utilizam o conceito de softpower, desenvolvido nos anos 90 por Joseph Nye no seu célebre livro "Bound to Lead" e pelos que utilizam o "conceito de rede", o qual representa uma outra forma de concretização desta nova perspectiva.

No caso da exposição presente e dada a especificidade do obejcto desta conferência e a clara distinção feita, no tema que me foi dado, entre a Europa e o resto do mundo, o qual inclui os Estados Unidos e os países da Comunidade dos Países de Língua Portuguesa (CPLP), justifica-se dar prevalência ao Estado, quando a nossa atenção incide sobre o espaço europeu, e dar maior importância à perspectiva mais ampla do hardpower/softpower, quando nos debruçamos sobre o resto do mundo, tendo, todavia, em consideração que as relações económicas tem igual importância numa e noutra perspectiva.

Restrições de tempo obrigam-nos a ser muito sucintos.

Quanto à Europa, se usarmos a chamada "teoria da diferença", tão conhecida dos juristas que a utilizam no campo da responsabilidade civil, poderemos fazer a comparação entre a situação actual de Portugal como entidade política global com a situação hipotética que existiria se o nosso país não tivesse entrado no, então, Mercado Comum em 1986. O resultado do cotejo entre uma e outra é, estou seguro, claramente favorável às vantagens do ingresso.

Fazendo rapidamente o cômputo destas últimas poderemos dizer:

No domínio político, garantimos a estabilidade do regime democrático e pluralista e consolidámos o Estado de Direito. Esta foi, aliás, a principal razão que determinou, no momento em que foi feita, a opção europeia. Permitiu-nos também recuperar do trauma político-cultural da perda do império, da perda das colónias, e da construção mítico-justificativa da missão civilizadora e do destino agregador dos portugueses. Este desígnio imperial, é bom lembrá-lo, não constituía apenas um sonho e uma ideologia da direita portuguesa, mas um sentimento bastante generalizado, embora com matizes diversos, em muitos sectores da vida política e cultural portuguesa.

Ainda do ponto de vista político, mas agora já institucional, deu-nos acesso à participação em centros de decisão política internacionalmente muito relevantes, os órgãos da União Europeia: o Conselho Europeu, o Conselho de Ministros, a Comissão, o Parlamento Europeu, e ainda o exercício das presidências portuguesas, como aquela que agora se anuncia. A possibilidade de portugueses terem acesso, em termos pessoais, a areópagos importantes constituiu igualmente uma vantagem significativa para o nosso País. Ganhámos também uma outra forma de realizar o equilíbrio na balança de poderes europeia que o multissecular Tratado entre Portugal e a Grã-Bretanha já não permitia assegurar no mesmo modo do passado e, mesmo fora da Europa, a nossa autonomia aumentou, designadamente em relação aos Estados Unidos.

No plano da economia, o facto de sermos membros da União Europeia deu-nos acesso a mercados e fontes de financiamento de que não gozaríamos se permanecêssemos no exterior desta. Os fundos estruturais permitiram-nos aumentar os investimentos públicos por forma relevante, designadamente no que concerne às infra-estruturas físicas; o euro deu-nos maior credibilidade nos mercados financeiros; as empresas modernizaram-se num grau relativamente importante graças, em parte, à inovação que incorporaram, embora tivesse sido uma inovação sob a espécie de importação e de imitação.

No campo da cultura, da educação e da investigação científica estabeleceram-se novas relações, alargaram-se os contactos e intensificaram-se os intercâmbios.

Em conclusão, o sistema político democrático estabilizou-se, a economia experimentou um processo apreciável de sofisticação e desenvolvimento, a cultura e a sociedade tornaram-se mais abertas. O saldo, em termos de comparação com o que aconteceria se ficássemos à margem é, assim, largamente positivo.

Mas, uma coisa é compararmo-nos com uma situação hipotética de não participação e ostracismo, outra é apreciar o que não foi feito e onde claudicámos. Há, assim, um "mas", porventura um grande "mas", a ser examinado. É que as dificuldades actuais com as quais nos defrontamos são bastantes. Por um lado, numa observação simples que qualquer um pode fazer, prevalece uma situação prolongada de estagnação económica e de défice financeiro; instalou-se um cepticismo algo generalizado quanto à ultrapassagem da crise. Tal resulta, em parte, de um conjunto de circunstâncias que há que mencionar para termos uma ideia da gravidade da situação e das possibilidades de a superarmos. Há, desde logo, que constatar que permanece a herança de alguns excessos revolucionários, como é o caso do grande peso do Estado, devido, em parte, às nacionalizações. A grande amplitude e o pormenor da regulamentação jurídica, o número exagerado de funcionários públicos com um estatuto privilegiado, designadamente em matéria de segurança social, em relação aos restantes trabalhadores; os benefícios que os trabalhadores com contratos sem prazo têm em relação aos que têm contrato a prazo ou não dispõem de emprego e a falta de formação da força de trabalho, tudo são factores que dificultam a recuperação do nosso atraso. Por outro lado, o descontrolo e o despesismo das finanças públicas, estaduais e também nas autarquias, tem sido um factor que não tem ajudado. A esta conjunção acresce a crise europeia que também se instalou originada por motivos vários, mas que numa parte substancial resulta do chamado modelo social europeu, tal como tem sido configurado e prevalecido, sobretudo nos países da Europa continental, visto que Grã-Bretanha e Irlanda de algum modo evitaram os excessos desse modelo. Por seu turno a globalização obriga a uma dura competitividade entre as economias nacionais e até entre as sociedades no seu todo. A competitividade e a concorrência estendem-se, inclusivamente, aos próprios sistemas jurídicos que podem passar a ser escolhidos voluntariamente em função daquilo que é mais favorável aos seus potenciais destinatários, fenómeno particularmente evidente no campo da economia e da fiscalidade.

A soma entre as especificidades da história recente portuguesa e as dificuldades do modelo europeu conduzem, assim, a problemas acrescidos; importa naturalmente conhecer em que medida é possível resolvê--los. A sua solução requer duas respostas que convirjam: uma primeira relativa ao esforço nacional c, uma segunda tem a ver com a contribuição que a própria Europa possa dar.

Em resumo e de um modo muito sumário, importa encontrar fórmulas de diminuir o peso do Estado e de dar maior importância ao mercado sem cair nos excessos do neo-liberalismo mas permitindo que a concorrência e a inovação funcionem eficazmente.

Para dar um exemplo muito concreto no plano nacional, os mecanismos de constituição e, particularmente, de extinção de empresas, por falência, é marcadamente no nosso País um sistema obsoleto bem como ineficientes são e burocratizados os programas de ajuda à inovação e à modernização das empresas.

Também no plano fiscal assistimos a um aumento disfarçado da carga tributária a propósito das pseudo taxas pagas como taxas moderadoras pelos utentes dos serviços públicos, ou pelos destinatários da regulação instituída em certos sectores. A verdade é que esses dinheiros aumentam os ingressos no erário público mas normalmente não levam à diminuição dos tributos clássicos.

Os modelos anglo-saxónicos e certas experiências escandinavas apontam-nos alguns caminhos, mas esses caminhos não são apenas indicações para Portugal. É importante que, na Europa, outros Estados membros da União diminuam o peso da intervenção do Estado e da sua tributação de modo a tornarem-se mais competitivos.

É interessante verificar que a crise da constituição europeia e as recentes decisões tomadas no último Conselho Europeu levam a pensar que, efectivamente, a Europa começa a arrepiar caminho e a deixar de sonhar pouco realisticamente com certos aspectos demasiado federalistas que estavam traduzidos no chamado Tratado Europeu.

Põe-se aliás a questão de saber se regressamos à ideia original que informou o mercado comum, isto é, fazer primeiro funcionar a economia duma maneira eficaz para permitir outros planos e outros sonhos e não proceder ao contrário, negligenciando o mercado e a sua eficácia e ao claudicar aí destruir a base que tornará viável o terceiro pilar e a política externa europeia e uma política de defesa minimamente autónoma.

Nestes termos, do ponto de vista da projecção de Portugal em relação à Europa, os problemas que enfrentamos são, prevalecentemente problemas económicos que acentuam a necessidade de Portugal e da União Europeia em geral aceitarem desenvolver um modelo social que permita maior competitividade face à concorrência global.

Quanto ao resto do mundo gostaria apenas de sublinhar alguns aspectos onde o softpower português tem maiores oportunidades e importância: a relevância da língua portuguesa como instrumento político e económico, matéria que é habitualmente esquecida ou mencionada como puro "lipservice" de homenagem à língua de Camões, mas sem atender a aspectos funcionais decisivos; a importância da diáspora portuguesa, e o seu papel do ponto de vista político, económico e cultural, em que também aqui, *mutatis mutandis*, pode reproduzir-se a mesma crítica de há pouco; a falta de uma política coerente de defesa e expansão da cultura portuguesa e da cultura da língua portuguesa em que participem os países da CPLP.

Na zona que conheço melhor no momento presente, os Estados Unidos da América, têm vindo a registar-se alguns progressos, mas partiu-se de uma situação de grande inferioridade. O português é, como provavelmente saberão, em termos de número de falantes, a terceira língua mais difundida do Ocidente, depois do inglês e do espanhol. Mas não tem um estatuto que nem de perto nem de longe corresponda a essa sua posição. Isto impõe esforços conjuntos e articulados dos países da CPLP, particularmente do Brasil e de Portugal par mudar este estado de coisas. Estamos aí, infelizmente, num grau ainda muito inicial.

A questão das relações bilaterais entre Portugal e os Estados Unidos e entre Portugal e os países da CPLP assume um papel verdadeiramente decisivo na projecção de Portugal no mundo. Essa relevância tem também implicações no nosso *bargaining power* na construção europeia, reforçando a nossa capacidade negocial.

Por razões de tempo omitirei a matéria relativa à nossa participação em organismos internacionais de vocação mundial e mesmo em relação à NATO. Trata-se de matérias relativamente conhecidas.

Limitar-me-ei, para concluir, a insistir na importância da opção metodológica que já referi.

Nos tempos de hoje, os Estados, as realidades políticas que habitualmente são referidas com o termo Estado, não podem ser compreendidas apenas em termos de pessoas colectivas de direito público e como os principais sujeitos das relações internacionais. Essa é a visão clássica. Há, pelo contrário, que atender à comunidade política, ao povo, se quiserem, à nação, e às comunidades intermédias, seja de base territorial seja institucional, e aos próprios cidadãos. Em suma, à sociedade civil.

É aliás interessante verificar que, mesmo na União Europeia, que é fundamentalmente uma união de Estados, o conceito de cidadania começa a desempenhar um papel relevante, não apenas em termos de elemento integrante de um órgão político, mas na sua dimensão cultural e associativa. Nós, portugueses, devemos fazer um esforço grande para aproveitar as potencialidades que há pouco mencionei, da língua, da diáspora, das entidades resultantes do direito de associação livremente exercido. Poderemos assim, à nossa dimensão, participar activamente na vida internacional, ajudando a construir um futuro para a Europa e para o mundo.

A cultura em sentido amplo assume assim um papel fundamental na preservação da nossa identidade e da nossa autonomia, não em termos defensivos mas de participação activa na estruturação das novas realidades da vida internacional.

A POLÍTICA CULTURAL EUROPEIA

EMÍLIO RUI VILAR*

1. Uma leitura da Comunicação da Comissão Europeia sobre uma nova agenda europeia para a cultura[1], de 10 de Maio de 2007, cujas epígrafes são eruditas citações de Denis de Rougemont, Yehudi Menuhim, Francesco Alberoni, Octavio Paz e Gao Xingjian, confirma uma suspeita: a dificuldade que todos experimentamos de, ao falar sobre cultura, e em especial sobre cultura europeia, não recorrermos a aforismos. O discurso sobre "cultura" na Europa surge normalmente entrelaçado numa imensidão de evocações que podem porventura desviar-nos do essencial. Não porque o seu conteúdo não seja importante mas, pelo contrário, porque a cultura europeia é o resultado sedimentar de muitos e importantes contributos. O desafio parece-me, então, iniciar esta minha intervenção sem citar qualquer um dos inumeráveis autores que, desde ainda antes de a Europa ser Europa, formam o nosso património cultural comum e ao qual não podemos renunciar no projecto de construção europeia.

2. Mas como estamos num seminário organizado pelo Instituto Europeu da Faculdade de Direito, devo recordar o artigo 151.º do Tratado, que estabelece as bases para a intervenção da União Europeia no domínio da cultura.

Este artigo 151.º, introduzido apenas em 1992 pelo Tratado de Maastricht (inicialmente artigo 128.º), diz-nos que:

"1. A Comunidade contribuirá para o desenvolvimento das culturas dos Estados-Membros, respeitando a sua diversidade nacional

---

* Presidente da Fundação Calouste Gulbenkian.

[1] *Comunicação sobre uma agenda europeia para a cultura num mundo globalizado*, COM (2007) 242 final, Bruxelas, 10.05.2007

e regional, e pondo simultaneamente em evidência o património cultural comum.

2. *A acção da Comunidade tem por objectivo incentivar a cooperação entre Estados-Membros e, se necessário, apoiar e completar a sua acção nos seguintes domínios:*
   – *melhoria do conhecimento e da divulgação da cultura e da história dos povos europeus,*
   – *conservação e salvaguarda do património cultural de importância europeia,*
   – *intercâmbios culturais não comerciais,*
   – *criação artística e literária, incluindo o sector audiovisual.*

3. *A Comunidade e os Estados-Membros incentivarão a cooperação com os países terceiros e as organizações internacionais competentes no domínio da cultura, em especial com o Conselho da Europa."*

O Tratado de Amesterdão, em 1997, adicionou um número 4 ao artigo, relativo à diversidade cultural: *"Na sua acção ao abrigo de outras disposições do presente Tratado, a Comunidade terá em conta os aspectos culturais, a fim de, nomeadamente, respeitar e promover a diversidade das suas culturas.[2]"*

Estas normas evidenciam-nos, no entanto, que essencialmente, a cultura continuará a ser um assunto nacional ou local e que a acção da União a este nível, sobretudo para protecção do já referido património cultural comum, deverá sempre respeitar o princípio da subsidiariedade, numa lógica de possível complementaridade das acções dos Estados--membros[3].

3. Temos, então e pelo menos, duas culturas à partida: a cultura de cada Estado-membro e uma cultura europeia, o que facilmente definimos

---

[2] Esta disposição é reproduzida no Tratado de Lisboa, com ligeiras alterações: onde está *Comunidade* passará a estar *União* e será actualizada a parte respeitante aos processos decisórios. No artigo 2.º do Tratado da União, introduz-se um parágrafo ao número 3 que dispõe que a União respeitará a riqueza da sua diversidade cultural e linguística e velará pela salvaguarda e pelo desenvolvimento do património cultural europeu.

[3] O Tratado de Lisboa introduz um artigo 2.º-E ao Tratado da União, segundo o qual a União passará a dispor de competência para desenvolver acções destinadas a apoiar, coordenar ou completar a acção dos Estados-Membros no domínio da cultura.

A *Política Cultural Europeia*

pela síntese "unidade na diversidade", por oposição às outras grandes culturas, ou na fórmula "na Europa sou português, na América sou europeu".

Mas a facilidade é aparente: o conceito de cultura é complexo. Desde logo, e transversal às anteriores, temos a distinção entre a cultura enquanto identidade, independente de quaisquer circunscrições geográficas, e a cultura enquanto produção cultural. São estas duas "culturas" que nos interessam para compreendermos e projectarmos as políticas da União nesta área.

3. Importa por isso começar por explorar o conceito polissémico do termo "cultura". Aproveitando a proposição de T.S. Eliot (*hélas*, não consegui resistir às citações!), da "cultura enquanto desenvolvimento de um *indivíduo*, de um *grupo* ou *classe*, ou da *sociedade como um todo*"[4] podemos assinalar três sentidos à palavra cultura: a cultura enquanto formação ou educação, "bildung", a cultura enquanto identidade de um grupo ou civilização, "kultur", e, finalmente, a cultura enquanto conjunto dos produtos e serviços do tríptico Artes/Humanidades/Ciência.

No primeiro sentido assinalado, "cultura" supõe uma característica do indivíduo, a formação ou a educação, a "Paideia" grega, tudo aquilo que envolve a formação da mente ou do intelecto.

No segundo sentido, a expressão ou palavra cultura é utilizada num quadro antropológico ou sociológico para descrever um conjunto de atitudes, crenças, costumes, valores e práticas que são comuns ou são partilhados por um determinado grupo. O grupo pode ser definido em termos políticos, geográficos, religiosos, étnicos ou outros e as características que o definem e podem ser materializadas em signos, símbolos, textos, linguagem, artefactos, tradição oral ou escrita, ou outros meios. A função crítica destas manifestações da cultura do grupo consiste em estabelecer ou contribuir para estabelecer a identidade distintiva do grupo, deste modo proporcionando os instrumentos ou os meios através dos quais os membros do grupo conseguem ou "sentem" distinguir-se dos membros de outros grupos[5].

No terceiro sentido, a expressão "cultura" revela uma noção sobretudo funcional, traduzindo determinadas actividades relacionadas com os

---

[4] Ts Eliot, *Notes towards the definition of culture*, 1962, pág. 21.
[5] David Throsby, Economics and Culture, 2001, pág. 4.

500   *Emílio Rui Vilar*

aspectos intelectuais ou artísticos da vida humana, como a criatividade, bem como os produtos e serviços decorrentes e resultantes dessas actividades (a literatura, as artes plásticas, o cinema, etc., etc.)

4. Quando mencionamos o património cultural comum da Europa estamos a referirmo-nos à cultura no segundo sentido que assinalei. Pelo contrário, quando utilizamos a expressão "indústrias da cultura", ou encaramos a cultura como uma realidade económica estamos a pensar no último sentido. A este nível, quer a produção quer o consumo de bens culturais podem ser situados dentro de um quadro ou lógica industrial e/ou comercial. Os produtos e os serviços culturais, assim, podem ser considerados como bens transaccionáveis praticamente nos mesmos termos que outros bens produzidos no sistema económico, ressalvados aspectos específicos como o que diz respeito aos direitos autorais[6].

Se até Outubro de 2006, data da publicação de um estudo encomendado pela Comissão, designado "A Economia da Cultura na Europa"[7], a importância estatística da cultura enquanto realidade económica tinha meramente uma base opinativa e/ou estimada, depois deste estudo já não a podemos ignorar.

Este estudo assumiu-se como a primeira tentativa de capturar o impacto socio-económico, directo e indirecto, do sector cultural na Europa. Os resultados quantitativos apurados revelam os seguintes indicadores: um rendimento de 654 biliões de euros em 2003; uma contribuição de 2.6% para o PIB europeu em 2003; um crescimento de 19.7% no período de 1999-2003, o que significa um crescimento 12.3% superior ao da média da economia em geral; 5.8 milhões de pessoas a trabalhar no sector em 2004, o que representa 3,1% da população activa da União Europeia.

5. Foram precisamente estes números, ou aquilo que traduzem, que conduziu a Comissão a apontar recentemente "a promoção da cultura como catalizador da criatividade no âmbito da Estratégia de Lisboa para

---

[6] EMÍLIO RUI VILAR, *Sobre a Economia da Cultura*, in Comunicação & Cultura, n.º 3, 2007, Faculdade de Ciências Humanas da Universidade Católica Portuguesa, pág. 131 e segs..

[7] Comissão Europeia, *A Economia da Cultura* (Direcção-Geral para a Educação e a Cultura), Outubro de 2006, http://ec.europa.eu/culture/eac/sources_info/studies/economy_en.html

o crescimento e o emprego"[8] entre os objectivos da uma nova agenda Europeia para a Cultura num mundo globalizado. Com efeito, a cultura, como expressão da criação e da criatividade, pode impulsionar a inovação e a competitividade.

De acordo com o próprio texto desta Comunicação, a nova agenda deverá apoiar-se em três grandes objectivos inter-relacionados. Para além do já referido objectivo de crescimento e emprego, a Comissão aponta a promoção da diversidade e do diálogo intercultural; e a promoção da cultura europeia como elemento vital nas relações internacionais da União e na sua afirmação no mundo. Designadamente na defesa dos seus valores que são os direitos invioláveis e inalienáveis da pessoa humana, a liberdade, a democracia, a igualdade e o primado da lei; ou em maior exigência no domínio do Ambiente.

A cultura é assim posicionada em diferentes perspectivas ou dimensões da construção europeia. Como factor de integração de uma Europa, onde convivem cada vez mais culturas. Como factor de desenvolvimento económico de uma Europa que se pretende cada vez mais baseada na criatividade e no conhecimento. E, finalmente, como factor de cooperação nas relações externas de uma Europa que pretende desempenhar um novo papel no contexto internacional.

6. Acrescentaria apenas uma dimensão muito importante pela qual a cultura pode também desempenhar um papel fundamental, ou seja, na revitalização da relação entre os cidadãos europeus e as instituições europeias. Não nos podemos esquecer da dupla legitimidade da União Europeia: uma união de Estados soberanos, mas também uma união de pessoas que partilham uma cidadania supranacional. Na procura do equilíbrio entre estas duas dimensões da integração europeia, a dimensão cultural pode emergir como um elemento catalítico. Na maior parte da história de sucesso da União, a dimensão económica tem sido o mecanismo mais visível de promoção do desenvolvimento e de superação das diferenças entre os Estados. Os desafios externos actuais e as expectativas dos cidadãos europeus reclamam, no entanto, uma aproximação mais política e sobretudo cultural.

---

[8] *Comunicação sobre uma agenda europeia para a cultura num mundo globalizado*, COM (2007) 242 final, Bruxelas, 10.05.2007

7. Gostaria de apresentar algumas propostas concretas para uma política cultural europeia, que as instituições Europeias poderiam promover a curto prazo e que se podem enquadrar na nova agenda apresentada pela Comissão:

a) Promoção efectiva da mobilidade de autores e artistas dentro da União Europeia e países vizinhos. Análogo ao bem sucedido programa ERASMUS de intercâmbio de estudantes, sugeri no ano passado, na Conferência de Berlim e aproveitando os 250 anos do nascimento do grande compositor de Salzburg, a criação de um programa MOZART para a mobilidade e intercâmbio de artistas (MO para mobilidade, Z para Este-Oeste e Norte-Sul, ART para artistas).

b) Criação de condições para a circulação do património cultural móvel que integra o imaginário Europeu, com a constituição de uma espécie de "espaço cultural Schengen".

c) Financiamento e apoio à tradução cruzada de literatura Europeia, em especial das línguas europeias minoritárias.

d) Promoção da arte imaterial, do cinema, do audiovisual e do multimédia, com a utilização das novas tecnologias de comunicação, reforçando a produção de conteúdos, como contraponto aos grandes produtores (os Estados Unidos, em breve a Índia e a China).

e) Facilitação da aprendizagem de línguas não-europeias (Árabe, Turco, Mandarim, Persa, Hindu), como um factor de abertura e de integração de imigrantes.

8. A Europa é, como espaço de acolhimento de milhões de imigrantes, e sê-lo-á cada vez mais, uma realidade intercultural e a interculturalidade vai passar a ocupar um papel central na política cultural europeia. Também por este motivo, a União designou 2008 como Ano Europeu do Diálogo Intercultural. Tal como a biodiversidade é essencial para a nossa sobrevivência e desenvolvimento, deveríamos igualmente utilizar a diversidade cultural para benefício do projecto Europeu.

São dolorosamente evidentes os falhanços de políticas de integração que pareciam ser casos de sucesso, quer segundo modelos multiculturais, quer baseadas no conceito da cidadania laica e republicana. Modelos e conceitos que, no entanto, tanto agradam à nossa própria tradição cultural e civilizacional.

Mas a realidade pós-colonial é mais complexa, multifacetada e conflitual. Esta(s) realidade(s) e a acrescida mobilidade do processo de globalização implicam abordagens específicas baseadas em conhecimento mais aprofundado e não em arquétipos simplificados ou em "clichés" redutores ou caricaturais. É todo um vasto campo de acção de "advocacy" (no sentido da defesa de valores), de investigação (aumento e disseminação do conhecimento) e de intervenções no terreno, com a virtude (e a virtualidade) dos efeitos concretos e de serem replicáveis.

As organizações da sociedade civil podem assumir uma importância fundamental no que diz respeito ao diálogo intercultural, interétnico e inter-religioso, apoiando, por exemplo, a adopção das melhores práticas na promoção da compreensão do fenómeno das migrações e da integração das culturas minoritárias.

As fundações, em particular, enquanto instituições independentes, têm capacidade para desenvolver a sua missão sem limites geográficos, de língua ou de fé religiosa. As fundações podem, deste modo, fomentar o conhecimento mútuo através de uma cooperação especializada, em rede, aumentando a exposição a experiências transfronteiriças e fortalecendo o diálogo intercultural.

Como referi em Washington DC, na abertura da exposição sobre os descobrimentos portugueses, "Encompassing the Globe", organizada pela Arthur M. Sackler Gallery em parceria com o National Museum of African Art, em Junho de 2007: "Ao apoiar esta iniciativa, a Fundação Gulbenkian não está apenas a contribuir para um melhor entendimento do nosso passado comum. Está a lançar novos caminhos para um melhor conhecimento do "outro", do que é "diferente". Nos tempos que correm, a compreensão das diferentes culturas é a melhor forma de combater os crescentes surtos irracionais de fanatismo e radicalismo. É urgente desenvolver um forte sentimento de que há um só mundo onde todos temos de viver. E ter consciência disso é o primeiro passo para começar a amar e a cuidar."

O PROGRAMA DA PRESIDÊNCIA PORTUGESA DE 2007

LUÍS AMADO[*]

Muito obrigado, Doutor Jorge Sampaio. Muito Obrigado, Doutor Rui Machete. Doutor Rui Vilar, peço a sua condescendência; não só não tive o prazer de ouvir a sua comunicação, por ter chegado atrasado, como tenho o desprazer de ter de o forçar a ouvir uma segunda intervenção minha na mesma semana, o que é algo muito agressivo, penso eu. Vou tentar não me repetir. É a vantagem, também, de não termos um texto escrito. É que não direi seguramente o que disse aqui, exactamente nos mesmos termos, há dois ou três dias atrás, só para não o maçar tanto ouvindo-me. De qualquer modo, não posso, naturalmente, fugir ao guião. Pediram-me que falasse das prioridades da presidência portuguesa e não posso deixar de começar por evidenciar quais são as circunstâncias que, de alguma forma, justificam o programa que ainda ontem foi apresentado publicamente e que reflecte as orientações que o Governo português pretende transmitir ao exercício da sua presidência durante os próximos meses.

Tenha-se em consideração, como tive oportunidade de sublinhar, a circunstância de pela primeira vez o programa da presidência a seis meses não ser um exercício autónomo da presidência, mas ser um exercício que decorre de uma concertação prévia entre os Governos da Alemanha, de Portugal e da Eslovénia. Pela primeira vez, no âmbito do exercício das presidências da União Europeia, avançou-se para uma experiência nova de transmitir ao programa alguma estabilidade, permitindo justamente a elaboração de um programa a dezoito meses. Os exercícios

---

[*] Ministro dos Negócios Estrangeiros.

das presidências semestrais têm de assumir a responsabilidade de desenvolver a sua parte desse programa.

Não é um exercício irrelevante. No caso, do meu ponto de vista, foi um exercício bastante interessante. A circunstância de termos, no trabalho de preparação desse programa, que decorreu durante seis a oito meses, um país fundador com o peso político na Europa que é a Alemanha; a circunstância de termos um país com a dimensão de Portugal que faz parte da Europa desde os anos oitenta e um país de pequena dimensão como a Eslovénia, recente membro da União, permitiu um exercício que, de alguma forma, permite desenvolver esse princípio fundador da própria construção europeia: a diversidade, a unidade na diversidade. E essa diversidade projectou-se bastante, quer nas inquietações que os diferentes Governos transmitiram na discussão do programa relativamente à forma como olham o mundo e as relações da União Europeia com o mundo, quer, naturalmente, em relação às questões que querem colocar na agenda mais actual da Europa nos diferentes sectores e que decorrem, como não pode deixar de ser, dos seus interesses. Não deixou, por outro lado, de evidenciar as dificuldades com que a União se confronta, numa fase que, como todos nós sabemos, é difícil, crítica mesmo, e que de alguma forma ficou bastante bem reflectida na forma como o trabalho de preparação desse programa se desenvolveu.

A presidência portuguesa vai, por isso, desenvolver um programa que, em boa medida, é o resultante dessa condição: a de ser um programa elaborado em conjunto com a presidência alemã e com a presidência eslovena e, portanto, ter de reflectir um equilíbrio de visões e de expectativas diferentes, dos três Estados. Mas, simultaneamente, também projectando a realidade que é hoje bem diferente da realidade que nós tínhamos no ano 2000. E quando confrontamos a nossa presidência com as presidências anteriores é bom ter consciência de que o que muda não é, muitas vezes, o que é referido e que tem apenas um aspecto muito marginal ou periférico o facto de ser no segundo semestre, o facto de serem vinte e sete Estados, o facto de termos um presidente da Comissão que é da mesma nacionalidade. Esses aspectos são, sem dúvida, de considerar, mas não são os aspectos determinantes. Do meu ponto de vista, o aspecto fundamental, sem dúvida, prende-se com a natureza da União. Não podemos pensar que estamos a lidar com a mesma realidade com que lidávamos há meia dúzia de anos atrás. Depois do alargamento, a organização que tutela hoje os destinos da Europa tem uma configuração

O Programa da Presidência Portuguesa de 2007

diferente que é, em boa medida, o resultado de ter feito um alargamento muito rápido – passou de quinze a vinte e sete Estados muito depressa – e, sobretudo, não é o número de Estados que, de alguma forma, influencia a realidade da União; é, sobretudo, a natureza da experiência histórica dos Estados que a constituem. Hoje – e eu tive a experiência também de estar no Conselho Europeu em 2000 e de tomar o pulso político e ideológico do desenvolvimento do projecto europeu nos finais dos anos noventa, início deste século –, é bem diferente a realidade com que nos confrontamos, e temos de ter a noção política de que a Europa que agora temos, a União Europeia que hoje temos, tem uma natureza e uma configuração diferente.

A cultura histórica dos países do leste europeu que aderiram muito rapidamente à Europa, num processo talvez excessivamente rápido, é bem diferente da cultura dos países que fundaram a União, das Comunidades de então, e dos que se lhe foram associando, com a experiência da Europa ocidental e de uma cultura histórica europeia que era depositária de um conjunto de referências geopolíticas, estratégicas, históricas, diferentes daqueloutras e que se projectam, naturalmente, no imaginário político e na acção política dos dirigentes em causa. Todos nós temos em mente um conjunto de Estados que têm delineado nos últimos meses, em particular, um conjunto de referências que estão, logicamente, muito identificadas com esse património de vivência histórica colectiva que essa região da Europa viveu no último século. E, por isso, a União é hoje, de facto, uma entidade com uma natureza diferente e temos de ter uma boa dose de realismo quando pretendemos trabalhar sobre essa realidade e, sobretudo, quando pretendemos fazer com que essa realidade se mova e evolua num sentido construtivo, capaz de realizar objectivos que são os objectivos que nos guiam – paz, estabilidade, desenvolvimento crescimento, na Europa –; é esse o *leitmotiv* da construção europeia desde o seu início, e é sobre essa realidade que nós temos de trabalhar e, por isso, de alguma forma a discussão que tivemos no último Conselho foi muito reveladora da distância entre o voluntarismo de algumas propostas, que todos nós tínhamos sobre a mesa, e a necessidade prática de lidar com uma realidade que não comporta movimentos tão amplos como os que esse voluntarismo projecta, do ponto de vista político e do ponto de vista ideológico. Nessa perspectiva, creio que o mandato que foi aprovado no último Conselho Europeu, como já tive oportunidade de sublinhar, é um mandato equilibrado que procede a um reajustamento do projecto europeu na perspectiva desta nova realidade que hoje enforma a Europa e que, de alguma forma, também permite, sobretudo, manter uma linha de continuidade na afirmação do projecto europeu como projecto capaz de responder às inquietações com que a Europa se confronta hoje no cotejo das suas posições com as posições do mundo envolvente. Creio que é essa outra realidade, a da pressão do exterior, a da pressão da agenda externa com que a União Europeia se confronta, que de alguma forma também condicionou a dinâmica de negociação que levou a um resultado positivo.

Acredito ainda que todos os responsáveis políticos europeus, e tenho-o sentido no último ano, em que participo nas reuniões do Conselho, têm a noção muito delicada do caminho estreito que existe entre o sucesso e o fracasso deste projecto. E, por isso, tem havido em momentos difíceis – lembro-me que entrei na semana anterior a decisões sobre a participação no Líbano, e essa mesma consciência se projectou nas decisões que tiveram que ser tomadas então –, a aguda consciência de que a realidade exterior é hoje de tal forma pressionante sobre o desenvolvimento da agenda interna da União Europeia que o fracasso na frente interna condiciona de forma definitiva, do meu ponto de vista, o papel relevante que a União Europeia pode ainda ter no sistema internacional, como força de equilíbrio, como força moderadora, como força de estabilização do sistema internacional. No momento em que o sistema se confronta com uma das situações mais críticas depois do fim da Guerra Fria, se analisarmos bem o desenvolvimento dos conflitos que estão perante nós, está longe o tempo de uma leitura tão optimista e tão positiva como a que fazíamos ainda no final da década de noventa sobre o desenvolvimento do sistema internacional. Estamos hoje confrontados com uma situação de crise de grande complexidade, de grande dificuldade, no seu controlo e na sua regulação.

Creio que há um ciclo que se abriu com o fim da Guerra Fria, um ciclo estratégico que a Europa e os Estados Unidos souberam gerir com muita inteligência estratégica, com grande capacidade de liderança, com grande ambição e motivação, quando o colapso do império soviético abriu essa perspectiva de grande instabilidade em toda a região do império soviético. Apesar de tudo, a Europa reagiu e o sistema Euro-Atlântico soube adaptar-se a essa nova condicionante estratégica com pleno êxito. O trabalho de integração, de alargamento da União Europeia, de reunificação na Alemanha, de reposicionamento da Europa na relação com a

O Programa da Presidência Portuguesa de 2007

Rússia, foi sem dúvida um dos trabalhos mais bem conseguidos nas últimas décadas pelos responsáveis políticos europeus. De alguma forma, esse ciclo estratégico que se abre com a queda do muro de Berlim está, em boa medida, realizado. Nós temos uma situação de relativa estabilidade na fronteira leste da Europa.

Há, ainda, problemas no relacionamento estratégico com a Rússia, dadas as condicionantes que esse país hoje projecta face à nova situação interna que presentemente conhece. Há problemas, ainda, de política de vizinhança na relação com alguns países. Especificamente quanto à Ucrânia, teremos com a mesma uma cimeira que será problemática, justamente porque a situação interna da Ucrânia está ainda longe de se clarificar; a situação com a Bielorússia, com a Geórgia, sem contar com os problemas de relacionamento com a Ásia central e com os países do Mar Negro e do Cáucaso, onde a disputa grande pelas reservas energéticas muito significativas que alguns desses Estados têm é hoje um factor de grande importância do ponto de vista geopolítico e onde se confrontam interesses dos Estados Unidos, da China, da Rússia e da União Europeia. Há aí um conjunto de problemas muito sérios ainda por resolver, sem dúvida. Há que encontrar uma solução definitiva para o Kosovo e, portanto, para a estabilização definitiva dos Balcãs ocidentais, situação que será seguramente um dos maiores desafios com que nos vamos confrontar nos próximos meses. É difícil admitir que se possa prolongar por muito mais tempo a situação de indefinição e de indecisão da parte da União Europeia relativamente a essa questão.

Mas, sem dúvida, como dizia, parece-me que de alguma forma esse ciclo estratégico está já num período de resolução. Mas, ainda assim, está sobreposto a um novo ciclo estratégico que se abriu com os acontecimentos do 11 de Setembro e com todos os acontecimentos que se lhe seguiram e que, de alguma forma, abriram perspectivas completamente diferentes para a evolução do sistema internacional, e perspectivas diferentes também para a relação, sobretudo, de vizinhança da União Europeia com todo o seu flanco sul, e para a recomposição inadiável da relação entre a União Europeia e os Estados Unidos no quadro do sistema de segurança transatlântico.

Há, por isso, um momento de sobreposição de dois ciclos, que torna ainda mais complexo, do meu ponto de vista, a gestão do sistema internacional e, em particular, a gestão das relações externas da União Europeia durante os próximos anos.

Temos um problema interno que está longe de estar ultrapassado. Penso que se se conseguir negociar, nos termos do mandato aprovado no último Conselho Europeu, um novo tratado, poderemos ter estabilidade por mais uma ou duas décadas no sistema de poder da Europa que temos a vinte e sete. Admito que se for possível fechar um acordo até ao final do ano, iniciar um processo de ratificação que seja bem sucedido antes das eleições de 2009, a Europa possa ter, em boa medida, encontrado uma forma para estabilizar o seu sistema de poder durante mais uma ou duas décadas, mas é absolutamente inadiável que o faça, sob pena de nós não conseguirmos durante muito mais tempo dar continuidade, do ponto de vista da gestão corrente da União, aos desafios com que nos confrontamos.

Basta sentarmo-nos na mesa do Conselho e acompanharmos os trabalhos de um ou dois Conselhos sobre temas muito diferentes, para percebermos onde estão as fragilidades do sistema de poder e a necessidade de um novo equilíbrio que nos permita, do ponto de vista institucional, dar resposta aos desafios com que nos confrontamos. Mas, se o fizermos, admito que a União Europeia pode assumir um papel de relevo, então, como força de estabilidade do sistema internacional, desde que, do meu ponto de vista, seja capaz de, com clarividência, contribuir para a renovação da relação transatlântica. É essa a alavanca de sustentação do seu poder na relação com o mundo; e pensar que se pode potenciar o poder da União Europeia na relação com o mundo sem solução para o seu sistema de segurança e defesa é, do meu ponto de vista, uma visão ingénua, pelo que eu reputo da maior importância um papel activo da União Europeia em conjunto, naturalmente, com os Estados Unidos e com o Canadá para a renovação da agenda transatlântica, absolutamente inadiável, do meu ponto de vista, na perspectiva das novas ameaças com que o sistema internacional se confronta depois dos acontecimentos do 11 de Setembro e de toda uma mudança de cenários estratégicos com que estamos confrontados.

Todos estes factores a par (não o referi previamente) de uma dinâmica de globalização económica que faz emergir muito rapidamente, no horizonte de uma década, ou menos do que isso, pólos de poder económico e financeiro absolutamente extraordinários – a China, a Índia, o Brasil, a Rússia – aliás, países com os quais, durante o segundo semestre, teremos cimeiras de alto nível onde, naturalmente, estas questões estarão na ordem do dia. Mas, como sublinhava, do meu ponto de vista, é

O *Programa da Presidência Portuguesa de 2007*

absolutamente impossível a União Europeia desenhar qualquer projecto de liderança no sistema internacional se não for capaz de, com clarividência, preparar a renovação da agenda transatlântica em função, naturalmente, das perspectivas que pode e deve transmitir nesse exercício de renovação da agenda, que me parece absolutamente inadiável.

Na leitura que faço, a agenda da aliança atlântica está ainda muito condicionada pelo ciclo a que fiz referência, o ciclo pós-soviético, no seu movimento de alargamento da NATO, na forma como projecta o papel interventor da aliança no mundo, na forma tímida com que tem encarado, por exemplo, o desenvolvimento de instrumentos como o do diálogo do Mediterrâneo ou da iniciativa de Istambul, para não referir, por exemplo, a forma absolutamente incipiente como tem tratado as questões da segurança colectiva no continente africano ou no Atlântico Sul. Há um conjunto de temas de renovação para a agenda transatlântica que entendo ser obrigação da Europa liderar no debate com os Estados Unidos e com os diferentes aliados e, naturalmente, também com a Rússia, no quadro da parceria muito especial que a NATO desenvolveu no Conselho (a NATO – Rússia). Do meu ponto de vista, essa acção é absolutamente fundamental e é um exercício no qual a União Europeia, no desenrolar da sua acção externa quotidiana, estará presente, e a que, também durante a presidência portuguesa, será dada, naturalmente, atenção.

Segundo vector estratégico: O processo de consolidação da estabilização da fronteira leste da Europa, o que passa, naturalmente, por encarar de forma mais responsável a situação dos Balcãs ocidentais. Continuamos a abordar a situação do Kosovo, nos conselhos europeus, de uma forma um tanto ou quanto leviana; o problema está criado, tem havido uma enorme indefinição da parte da União Europeia, falta de capacidade de decisão e falta de iniciativa política, mas o problema está lá; estamos reféns do veto russo ou duma declaração unilateral americana. Não há, de facto, uma acção política pensada e amadurecida estrategicamente em função dos interesses europeus para essa região e penso que é absolutamente inadiável que essa questão seja colocada sobre a mesa.

O diálogo com a Rússia vai ter também como ponto importante e esse processo de estabilização da fronteira com o leste. Teremos uma cimeira com a Rússia. Será, provavelmente, um dos momentos mais mediáticos da nossa presidência, embora não se fale muito nele. Mas é natural que o desenvolvimento de alguma tensão com a Rússia, que tem vindo a ocorrer nos últimos meses, não deixe de se projectar na agenda da cimeira e nos resultados dessa cimeira. Achamos, contudo, que todo esse trabalho de relação com a fronteira leste acaba por ter influência na forma como lidamos estrategicamente com a Rússia e com definimos os contornos para um novo mandato, porque é disso que se trata. Gostaríamos de ter condições políticas para poder aprovar o mandato para o novo acordo de parceria estratégica com a Rússia, durante a nossa presidência, mas sabemos que essa era a prioridade das prioridades da presidência finlandesa e era a prioridade também da presidência alemã, pelo que temos de ser realistas, perceber que a dinâmica destes acontecimentos muitas vezes ultrapassa o poder dos Estados-Membros e, em particular, o poder de um pequeno Estado como Portugal. Mas não deixaremos de dar ênfase particular à questão, dada a acutilância estratégica que, do nosso ponto de vista, tem a estabilização da relação com a Rússia, para nos confrontarmos com um conjunto de problemas muito mais sérios no sistema internacional. Não deixaremos de dar a maior das atenções a esse projecto, da mesma forma que daremos continuidade ao trabalho que a presidência alemã, de uma forma pioneira, começou a desenvolver na relação com os países da Ásia central. Haverá uma tróica, durante a nossa presidência, com esse grupo de países que constitui hoje um grupo com a maior importância para a segurança energética da Europa nas próximas décadas.

Terceira prioridade: as relações com o Mediterrâneo e com o flanco sul da Europa. A escalada de tensões que se desenvolve entre o mundo islâmico e o mundo europeu e ocidental tem de ser contida, sob pena de nós nos confrontarmos, nas próximas décadas, com problemas muito difíceis de gerir. Não apenas na relação com essa parte do mundo, mas dentro das nossas próprias sociedades, há um radicalismo ideológico que se tem vindo a expandir no mundo islâmico, em particular no mundo árabe, no âmbito de uma guerra civil que atravessa o mundo árabe e islâmico e que torna ainda mais complexa a gestão dessa relação. Mas ela deve ser tratada do ponto de vista estratégico e não pode ser encarada pela Europa com os instrumentos que eram os instrumentos que a Europa desenhou para a relação com o mundo Mediterrâneo há vinte anos atrás e há quinze anos atrás. Depois do 11 de Setembro e depois dos acontecimentos que se verificam em toda a região, a escalada de tensões que se desenvolve, a fragilização dos regimes moderados, que eram os principais interlocutores do mundo europeu e ocidental durante as últimas décadas, toda essa nova dinâmica de instabilidade que se instalou na

O *Programa da Presidência Portuguesa de 2007*

nossa fronteira sul tem de ser encarada do ponto de vista estratégico pela Europa com uma motivação bem diferente daquela que havia quando o processo de Barcelona se iniciou e quando se lançaram um conjunto de iniciativas que já não têm capacidade de resposta, do nosso ponto de vista, à natureza dos problemas que entretanto se agravaram e se multiplicaram nessa relação. É por isso, crê-se, absolutamente indispensável dar outra atenção a essa relação. A presidência francesa, com particular instinto, mas também condicionada, naturalmente, pela forma como encara a perspectiva de alargamento à Turquia, colocou sobre a mesa a ideia de uma união mediterrânica. É apenas uma ideia, ainda, para um debate que se vai desenvolver nos próximos meses e nos próximos anos, com o peso que a França pode trazer a um debate desta natureza. Mas hoje há a percepção de que na relação da Europa com o seu flanco sul, com a fronteira mediterrânica, árabe e islâmica, há um trabalho a desenvolver com uma forte densidade estratégica e política e que a Europa tem que assumir como prioridade, do ponto de vista da sua acção externa. Essa é também uma das prioridades que assumimos e, no âmbito de algumas reuniões euro-ministeriais mediterrânicas, teremos oportunidade de desbravar caminho para esse debate nos próximos meses.

Por último, acho que a Europa pode e deve, no contexto de uma relação de reestruturação da aliança atlântica, marcar mais a agenda global, a agenda das questões globais, a agenda das questões que todos nós hoje reconhecemos. Não sendo abordada no plano internacional pelos principais actores que têm peso geopolítico que possa contribuir para a sua evolução, serão problemas sem solução a segurança energética, as alterações climáticas, a segurança alimentar, a segurança no domínio da saúde, as migrações, o desarmamento e não proliferação, o comércio internacional ... É um conjunto de questões que hoje são denominadas como questões globais. Percebe-se que nenhum Estado, nem a super potência, nem as potências europeias, tem condições de, por si só, gerir as questões globais no plano internacional. Só uma abordagem multilateral pode promover soluções compatíveis com objectivos tão ambiciosos. E, nessa perspectiva, a Europa, no quadro da relação transatlântica que tem, no quadro de uma relação de parceria estratégica com a Rússia, com a Índia, com a China – agora com o Brasil, a partir da nossa presidência –, tem alavancas políticas suficientes para colocar na agenda essas relações. Não apenas as relações de interesse bilateral, mas também as relações que se prendem com o equilíbrio do sistema internacional e com a regulação de grandes e importantes questões para o desenvolvimento económico e para o equilíbrio ambiental do planeta. Nessa perspectiva, também durante a nossa presidência procuraremos marcar vivamente, dentro das nossas possibilidades, essa função liderante que a Europa pode assumir, que já assumiu, por exemplo, no Conselho Europeu de Março em relação a objectivos na área da segurança energética e das alterações climáticas, e que pode relativamente a outras das questões que mencionei ter iniciativa, capacidade de decisão e capacidade de influência por essa via da dinâmica do próprio sistema internacional.

São estas algumas das ideias que marcam a nossa perspectiva para a presidência portuguesa.

Não poderemos deixar de acompanhar com particular atenção o desenvolvimento de algumas situações de crise e de conflito em que a Europa está directa ou indirectamente envolvida. Já referi o Kosovo e a estabilização dos Balcãs ocidentais. Não poderemos de deixar de dar a maior das atenções às novas iniciativas que se desenham para o processo de paz do Médio Oriente. Estaremos, no âmbito do quarteto, no centro do panorama hoje mais propício à abordagem desse conflito, tão complexo e tão difícil de enquadrar do ponto de vista político. Teremos de dar atenção a outras crises, designadamente humanitárias. A França tem posto particular atenção no acompanhamento da crise do Darfur nos últimos tempos. O desenvolvimento das crises no Afeganistão e no Iraque seguramente continuarão na agenda da União Europeia ainda por muito tempo.

São estes os desafios com que nos confrontamos. A nossa motivação é grande, a nossa ambição também, na medida das nossas possibilidades. Eram estas as ideias que vos queria transmitir, agradecendo a paciência e a atenção que tiveram e que me dispensaram. Muito obrigada.

A PRESIDÊNCIA PORTUGUESA DAS COMUNIDADES EUROPEIAS EM 2007 E A SITUAÇÃO DA UNIÃO EUROPEIA

MESA REDONDA

MARCELO REBELO DE SOUSA[*]

Muito boa tarde. Professor Paz Ferreira muito obrigado pelas suas palavras. Queria começar por saudar um ausente, mas que foi a alma desta reunião, o professor Pitta e Cunha, ele não está aqui por razões familiares, mas foi ele o grande entusiasta desta reunião, organizou-a em nome do Instituto Europeu da Faculdade de Direito da Universidade de Lisboa, e foi um grande sucesso.

Queria ainda a título pessoal, e enquanto presidente do Conselho Científico da casa, saudá-lo, agradecer-lhe por este contributo para um debate que foi dos melhores contributos no plano interno e no plano internacional, tirando obviamente a minha participação, dos últimos tempos.

Sou testemunha do europeísmo, embora de um europeísmo crítico quando necessário, do professor Pitta e Cunha. Quando era difícil ser-se europeísta, esteve na primeira delegação de professores universitários portugueses a Bruxelas num contexto muito difícil, coincidiu com a aprovação da lei da unicidade sindical, portanto, vejam há quanto tempo isto foi. E lembro-me ainda que metade ou mais de metade dessa delegação era contra a adesão de Portugal às Comunidades Europeias, era

---

[*] Texto não revisto pelo Autor e publicado como seu consentimento.
Professor Catedrático da Faculdade de Direito da Universidade de Lisboa.

então presidente da Comissão o político de origem francesa François-
-Xavier Ortoli, como se afrontaram falando em nome da delegação
portuguesa duas visões no jantar final. Uma visão de um professor, aliás
ilustre, do Porto, totalmente anti-europeu que disse "Estamos aqui, mas
nunca quereremos entrar na Europa, somos contra a Europa e, portanto,
é uma grande maçada estarmos aqui estes dias, embora a convite vosso",
e depois, de facto, o professor Pitta e Cunha que teve uma intervenção
numa altura particularmente complexa, em plena revolução, no sentido da
adesão de Portugal às Comunidades Europeias.

Feito este cumprimento que penso que é justíssimo, mau grado
a sua ausência, vou tomar cinco minutos, vamos lá ver se não os
ultrapasso, com o enquadramento – pena que não esteja cá o Dr.
Pacheco Pereira –, e outros cinco minutos, não muito mais do que
isso, com a presidência portuguesa durante estes seis meses.

Enquadramento. Também penso que a Europa nasceu de determinados ideais e esses ideais eram ideais de solidariedade, de tendencial
igualdade dos Estados-membros, de atlântismo (de ligação aos EUA), de
construção pela via pragmática – uma vez que a via política falhou,
como sabem, houve quem a tentasse mas falhou em França, económica
e com consequências sociais, a que se seguiria a integração política por
pequenos passos. Tudo acompanhado de um espírito europeísta entu-
siástico. E a Europa avançou sempre que teve líderes com esse espírito
europeísta, e a Europa tem grandes europeístas: o chanceler Kohl e o
presidente François Mitterrand, entre outros – estou a falar dos mais
liderantes.

E colocou-se essa questão, chegou até a falar-se numa confederação
europeia como forma de antecâmara ou como forma de integração que
não pusesse em causa aquilo que era o modelo pensado, como disse o
Dr. Pacheco Pereira, para uma tendencial unidade dos Estados-membros.
Era uma opção difícil e que tinha um preço, qualquer que fosse a
escolha. A escolha era "não integramos" – um preço elevadíssimo –
apesar de, e bem, a aliança atlântica ter tratado de se alargar e começar
a discutir o seu alargamento para servir de antecâmara e de apoio a essa
nova realidade político-estratégica; segunda hipótese "integramos", isso
significava o fim de muito do projecto inicial europeu, tinha de ser outro
projecto, era um projecto europeu noutros termos, porque eram estádios
de desenvolvimento económico e social diferentes, com problemas
muito específicos que colocavam nesse virtual alargamento, problemas

que não tinham comparação com os alargamentos a economias ricas como aconteceu com o alargamento subsequente à entrada de Portugal, da Grécia e da Espanha.

A opção foi: alargamos. Há razões geopolíticas, e os EUA bem fizeram os impossíveis para isso, sabia-se que isso ia custar, por exemplo, a integração das cooperações reforçadas, isto é, várias velocidades, isso ia custar geometrias variáveis, isso ia custar o reabrir do debate sobre a Europa do directório, que era uma coisa diferente da Europa solidária e tendencialmente da igualdade.

Portanto, não há bela sem senão! É evidente que é fácil e é justo dirigir muitas críticas a essa escolha. Foi uma escolha entre dois caminhos possíveis e, portanto, é em Maastricht que começa, não é nem em Amesterdão, nem em Nice, nem é hoje que começa a corporização em termos de Tratado desta escolha. E não é por acaso que o Presidente Mário Soares, eu modestamente, e muitos outros... o Dr. Pacheco Pereira, o Dr. Medeiros Ferreira, defendemos o referendo na altura do Tratado de Maastricht, porque era um salto qualitativo que não tinha nada a ver com o Acto Único Europeu e muito menos com tudo o que tinha ficado para trás, e não era apenas por causa do Euro, era no plano político, porque havia uma escolha que se fazia. Essa escolha implicava sacrifícios, isto é, sacrifício das decisões por unanimidade, aumentadas por maioria; debate sobre a ponderação de votos e revisão da ponderação de votos; cooperações reforçadas, o que significa, embora sejam cooperações abertas, uns estão, outros não o que é um factor de dissemelhança. Este é o primeiro apontamento que queria deixar.

O segundo apontamento é que se sabia que, nesses países que iam entrar, havia países mais complicados e outros menos complicados, e que a Polónia era dos mais complicados. Lembro-me sempre, porque era líder do PSD na altura e promovi uma Conferência no Centro Cultural de Belém para discutir os efeitos e os custos do alargamento, onde foram convidados governantes dos países virtualmente aderentes, de se debater um estudo feito por economistas portugueses que demonstrava que a economia que mais pagava o custo do alargamento era a economia portuguesa. Os húngaros, por maioria de razão os búlgaros e os romenos, e todos os outros não foram recalcitrantes. O único governante que foi verdadeiramente recalcitrante, ao ponto de se criar uma situação de conflito muito desagradável, foi um sub-secretário de Estado polaco que dizia "Desculpe, mas é que isto é uma visão nacionalista vossa, isso é uma visão inaceitável, essa ideia dos custos... Há outras realidades e não estão a olhar para a nossa realidade, e a realidade polaca, e a realidade polaca, e a realidade polaca..." Na altura lembro-me de ter pensado para comigo mesmo se há no quadro da actual União Europeia potências imperiais, que o são assumidamente, a Polónia, trucidada por vários vizinhos com vocação imperial, quis-se pelo menos o sub-imperialismo sempre, e foi muitas vezes injustiçada, portanto era um caso complicado. Sabia-se que era um caso complicado antes mesmo de haver a orientação política hoje dominante, continua um caso complicado e continuará um caso complicado, mesmo que o vizinho não fosse a Alemanha, mesmo que não houvesse os agravos que há, mesmo que a História não tivesse sido o que foi, mesmo que a realidade política não fosse aquela que é.

Isto portanto para dizer que é verdade que, hoje, se colocam novamente problemas, como se colocaram no Tratado da Constituição Europeia ou Tratado Constitucional Europeu, de escolhas que têm consequências no plano político em relação ao modelo inicial, ao projecto inicial da Europa. Mas é assim desde Maastricht, não é novo, se se quiser é mais acentuado e mais claro, é mais claro o tro-pismo para o directório, é mais claro o *forcing* alemão, é mais claro a deslocação do centro da Europa de Bruxelas para Berlim com o alargamento, tudo isso é cada vez mais claro. Agora não é uma realidade nova e não é uma realidade em que porventura possamos dizer que há soluções óptimas alternativas. Todas as soluções, isso viu-se logo em Maastricht, têm um preço.

Está-se a pagar o preço da integração acelerada por razões geopolíticas, de economias e de sociedades na sequência da implosão da União Soviética, porque isso tinha um preço na correlação de forças, na afirmação do peso da Alemanha, no reequacionar do eixo Paris-Berlim e por aí em diante. Se somarmos a isto que desde a liderança Kohl--Miterrand, isto é, a decisão sobre o alargamento, a reunificação, o alargamento e o euro, com raras excepções, não tem havido lideranças europeístas na Europa, isto é, não há alma na Europa e alma não significa substituir as almas nacionais, que essas existem e nunca morrerão, como houve nos fundadores. Há então o quê? Oportunismo de gestão europeia em muitos casos com raras e honrosas excepções. É evidente que o panorama é mais complicado, e o que se pode agora discutir é se a Senhora Angela Merkel é finalmente um exemplo dessa alma europeia, desse reviver europeu... Pode ser que sim, não o tinha sido na sua vida... Chirac foi ou não foi? Sarkozy não era, mas pode vir a ser. Portanto, às

A Presidência Portuguesa das Comunidades Europeias em 2007 e a Situação da UE   519

tantas, a Europa que avança na base daqueles que tinham tido as maiores das críticas em relação à própria realidade europeia é quase uma impossibilidade porque avança na base de acordos ou de consensos pontuais de gestão da conjuntura. Mas, esse é um problema que sobretudo os mais europeístas vêem com preocupação, que existe e temos a noção disso mesmo.

O que será a nova realidade europeia? Que o novo ciclo se inicia, que se vai iniciar nos EUA, mesmo com a vitória republicana, parece-me inquestionável, que se inicia na Europa quando temos em vez do Senhor Blair o Senhor Gordon Brown, mas que tem como Ministro dos Negócios Estrangeiros David Miliband, que é de um europeísmo diverso e mais intenso do que é habitual na administração pública britânica. O que é que o Senhor Sarkozy quer ser e até onde é que vai em termos europeus – naturalmente pensando no interesse francês, como é legítimo que faça? Até onde vai a Senhora Angela Merkel? Ninguém sabe. Agora, que é uma realidade de liderança diferente, e é um círculo político diferente que se inicia.

Neste quadro, a presidência portuguesa é uma presidência, e já foi tudo dito, que vai acabar com as presidências, portanto tendencialmente será das últimas presidências. Não ponhamos o carro à frente dos bois, terá de haver a ratificação do Tratado ou dos Tratados. Ocorre num contexto que já aqui foi descrito – muito programado – e em termos de Tratado, também tinha a mesma convicção do Presidente Mário Soares de que o mandato era um mandato claro, preciso, rigoroso, mas não com vírgulas. Hoje, tenho a convicção de que é com vírgulas, pontos e pontos e vírgulas, mas só tenho essa convicção porque nos últimos dias amigos do Secretariado do Conselho ou parlamentares europeus, porque estão muito metidos, pois, terão uma função liderante na CIG, me transmitiram essa noção, que já aqui vi mais ou menos confirmada pelo Doutor Goucha Soares. Nas questões fundamentais os artigos estão feitos, todos feitos até ao pormenor, estão escritos, e, portanto, não se trata de dizer esta é a solução pouco mais ou menos. Não, os artigos estão escritos, e o Doutor Goucha Soares, embora com a sua modéstia académica, até já disse mais ou menos em que termos é que são, isto é, tudo o que podia cheirar a forma de Constituição, de Estado ou referência a Tratado Constitucional desaparece, tudo o que é de substancial no Tratado Constitucional permanece, ou arrumado como estava ou rearrumado de outra maneira. Ele foi simpático disse 80%, eu diria 87,5%, mas podíamos discutir se é 80% se é 87,5%, isto é, o aumento de decisões por maioria, diminuição de decisões por unanimidade, a ponderação de votos – porque é evidente a Polónia ganhou x anos, mas está lá, se entrar em vigor automaticamente, decorridos os anos, passa a ser adoptado –, o Ministro dos Negócios Estrangeiros que se chama outra coisa, o Presidente que se chama a mesma coisa, a estrutura diplomática que se chama a mesma coisa, a redução da Comissão, os poderes do Parlamento, o relacionamento com os parlamentos nacionais... milhentos aspectos! Podemos discutir se é 90%, se é 87%, se é 85%, se é 80%, mas uma maioria esmagadora está lá. Tem uma coisa que foi chamada à atenção pelo Doutor Goucha Soares e a mim me preocupa, como jurista, mas sobretudo politicamente: fica mais confuso. O Tratado da Constituição Europeia, uns gostando, outros não gostando aqui nesta mesa, ou gostando mais ou gostando menos, visava clarificar um direito que é muito pouco claro, muito confuso e muito complicado, como quem conhece o direito comunitário sabe, fica mais complicado um pouco pelas remissões – não se mete a Carta dos Direitos Fundamentais, remete-se para... tem o mesmo valor, mas não está lá, é uma subtileza de jurista, mas vale o mesmo! Não está neste Tratado, está num Tratado de Funcionamento, mas está lá. Sem a ironia e o talento irónico do Doutor Medeiros Ferreira, é, de facto, um maná para os professores de Direito Comunitário em termos de interpretação e de aplicação do direito, mas é evidente que é um factor de complicação adicional. Obviamente, além de todos aqueles que já foram referidos por vários interventores, o domínio da política externa vai ser o ponto dominante e que vai sobressair da presidência portuguesa.

É evidente que a Cimeira com o Brasil, a Cimeira com a África, a Cimeira Mediterrânica, a Cimeira com a Rússia, tudo isso são grandes momentos de fotografia, e provavelmente também grandes momentos políticos, pelo menos de perspectivas futuras, mas a CIG, não tenhamos ilusões, vai ruir três vezes porque os artigos estão feitos. Reúnem-se à volta da mesa, reúnem-se três vezes para não ser escandaloso não reunirem e está pronta em Outubro, e é porque se mete Agosto pelo meio, como é evidente, porque senão, estava pronto antes, porque quem sabe o que é a feitura de diplomas, sabe que quando está tudo pronto... Dir--se-á, "Mas a Polónia pode pensar e voltar atrás, pode haver umas extensões". Pode haver até para consumo interno. Da óptica polaca isso seria mau porventura se eles não dessem a sensação internamente de algum atrito institucional e de alguma expectativa. Agora está lá.

A Presidência Portuguesa das Comunidades Europeias em 2007 e a Situação da UE   521

Portanto, não tenho dúvidas de que a CIG vai decorrer rapidamente, vai ser aprovado e o processo de ratificação vai iniciar-se. E é porque penso isso que tenho entendido sempre que não se pode pôr o carro à frente dos bois e, portanto, a questão do referendo ocorre depois. Parece--me uma evidência que, desde já, temos elementos para perceber que há todas as razões para referendar este novo Tratado, porque se ele tem 85% ou 80% do que tinha o Tratado Constitucional aqueles que, mais europeístas ou menos europeístas, mais favoráveis ou mais desfavoráveis, entendiam que devia haver referendo, entendem na mesma que deve haver referendo. Não é o problema de a bandeira não estar lá, continua hasteada por todos os sítios; o dia não está lá, continua a existir; o hino não está lá, mas continua a ser tocado nas cerimónias.

Portanto, de facto, vamos à substância porque a substância é essa. Pertencendo aos mais europeístas, e, portanto, não fanáticos, no quadro que expliquei, pragmaticamente aceitando, dentro de certos limites, equilíbrios que têm que se estabelecer, gostando menos de uns, mais de outros e tendo a noção exacta de que há cedência à Europa do directório – que o ideal era não ter existido –, há uma coisa de que não prescindo que é a intervenção dos povos, gostem ou não gostem. E é uma ilusão o Senhor Sarkozy estar convencido que evita o referendo. Acho que ele não vai evitar, porque para evitar o referendo tem de ter 3/5 nas duas Câmaras do Parlamento em reunião conjunta. Basta o partido socialista francês permanecer na exigência do referendo que vai ser muito difícil obter os 3/5, e, portanto, terá que se fazer o referendo. E o que digo da França, digo da Holanda. É evidente que à partida a ideia é não haver, mas basta haver uma corrente da opinião pública forte para existir.

Na Irlanda já sabemos que tem de existir. No Reino Unido alguém se convence de que se o Partido Conservador fizer grande finca-pé com a ala esquerda do Partido Trabalhista que o Senhor Gordon Brown con-segue até 2009, com eleições em 2009, recusar o referendo? Vai ser muito difícil. Portanto, devo dizer que nem percebo porque é que da parte dos defensores destes passos no quadro europeu, para uns bons, para outros maus, mas para aqueles que defendem que são bons, ou pelo menos inevitáveis, há medo do referendo? Porque é que há uma coisa que o Professor Adriano Moreira uma vez qualificou e bem, de Europa confidencial. Eles não percebem que isso só aumenta os eurocépticos, o medo do referendo da parte daqueles que são defensores, mais ou menos entusiásticos, de certas modificações só avoluma de passo para passo os protestos populares, as exigências legítimas de transparência, a contestação em relação àquilo que é feito a portas fechadas... e por isso é que eu não percebo.

É evidente que faz parte da lógica das sucessivas presidências para se valorizarem, por uma questão de não elevarem as expectativas – o que eu compreendo que seja bem feito –, ir deferindo esse problema, ir empurrando com a barriga para a frente. Mas há um momento em que ele tem que ser assumido sem medo, e isto de as principais formações políticas e partidárias estruturantes de uma democracia como a portuguesa terem medo do referendo, como terem medo da pedagogia europeia, como terem medo do debate europeu, nesse ponto penso que estamos de acordo o Presidente Mário Soares, o Dr. Pacheco Pereira e eu, e por isso esta iniciativa é tão importante. Consegue passar-se, da óptica de alguns tecnoburocratas nacionais ou europeus, uma presidência inteira sem discutir nada de substancial. Primeiro, porque não sabem ainda, portanto como não sabem, ainda não está definido, porque o mandato e tal... Depois começa a saber-se; quando se começar a saber está-se em Outubro, fim da presidência portuguesa. Começa a saber-se, mas é prematuro aí estar a trocar impressões porque ainda pode haver uns retoques. Quando se começar a saber terminou a presidência portuguesa, já se está a querer a mata-cavalos fazer a ratificação, e isso acho que é uma derrota para a Europa, não é uma vitória para a Europa.

Portanto vai ser, juízo meu em relação à presidência portuguesa, dizia o Professor Medeiros Ferreira "Mas falta originalidade, rasgo". Mas também não sei em quem é que ele estava a pensar para essa originalidade e esse rasgo. Estamos, portanto, no quadro em que nos estamos a mover com os líderes que existem, com a Europa que existe e com o país que existe, e portanto o Doutor Medeiros Ferreira como veio a viajar dos Açores... Portanto, há expectativas que são as expectativas mais surpreendentes, porque as coisas são como são, a última Cimeira foi como foi, a realidade é o que é, no quadro em que é, e, portanto, aí não seria tão pessimista quanto ele foi e tão exigente quanto ele foi. Se houver aquilo que se avizinha em termos de política externa, se houver a capacidade para gerir o imponderável (que nenhum de nós falou aqui no imponderável, mas há imponderável), o Senhor Tony Blair está mandatado para ir para a Palestina, eu não diria que é a figura mais adequada para o efeito, embora eu seja um defensor do senhor Tony Blair e ache que ele foi num momento vazio de liderança europeia dos europeístas mais

A Presidência Portuguesa das Comunidades Europeias em 2007 e a Situação da UE 523

inesperados, porque vinha de uma realidade insular e era mais europeísta do que os continentais. É uma coisa verdadeiramente espantosa, mas é verdade. Sempre o elogiei, sempre gostei dele, não sei se é exactamente o mais adequado para aquela missão, mas enfim, pode acontecer que sim.

Há problemas que se vão colocar obviamente noutras áreas do globo e que se podem colocar a todo o momento. Hoje mesmo, no Reino Unido, para celebrar a passagem de poder regressou a intervenção terrorista para medir o pulso, ou que não se sabe se é, pode ser ou não ser. Mas sem querer maximizar isso, uma coisa é certa, há imponderáveis. No quadro dos imponderáveis diria que as perspectivas são razoavelmente favoráveis. Serão efectivamente favoráveis se houver a coragem de assumir os passos que são dados, e uma das formas de assumir é não ter medo de discutir a Europa com os portugueses, de fazer pedagogia sobre a Europa, outra é não ter medo do referendo. É tudo.

A PRESIDÊNCIA PORTUGUESA DAS COMUNIDADES EUROPEIAS EM 2007 E A SITUAÇÃO DA UNIÃO EUROPEIA

MESA REDONDA

O Mandato da Conferência Intergovernamental de 2007

ANTÓNIO GOUCHA SOARES[*]

Muito obrigado, Senhor Presidente. Queria começar por agradecer ao Professor Pitta e Cunha, bem como aos Professores Paz Ferreira e Luís Morais, a gentileza do convite para participar nesta Conferência sobre a Europa e os desafios do novo Século.

Antes de iniciar a minha intervenção, gostaria de fazer uma breve declaração de interesses: fui defensor da Constituição europeia, pelo que tenho uma perspectiva necessariamente contrastante com a visão que o Dr. Pacheco Pereira acabou de expor. Atendendo ao tema do presente painel, vou concentrar-me na Presidência portuguesa e, em especial, no que o Primeiro-Ministro anunciou como prioridade absoluta da Presidência: a Conferência intergovernamental (CIG), em resultado do Conselho Europeu de Junho de 2007.

O Presidente Mário Soares manifestou algumas reservas em relação ao mandato confiado à Presidência portuguesa. Aproveitaria a intervenção do Presidente Mário Soares para falar sobre o mandato outorgado à Presidência portuguesa na Cimeira de Bruxelas. Desde logo, diria que a Conferência intergovernamental de 2007 tem um mandato inédito.

---

[*] Instituto Superior de Economia e Gestão.

Inédito quer pela sua extensão, quer pelo seu conteúdo, quer ainda pelo seu detalhe.

Tivemos 5 conferências intergovernamentais nos últimos 20 anos, ou seja, desde que somos membros da União Europeia. Do Acto Único até ao Tratado Constitucional, nenhuma se iniciou com um mandato tão detalhado quanto a CIG de 2007. Nalguns casos, o mandato chega a ponto de redigir o conteúdo de cláusulas que integrarão o próximo Tratado. Pelo que estamos num cenário de negociação diferente, quando comparado com as anteriores conferências intergovernamentais.

Quais as razões para o Conselho Europeu ter aprovado um mandato com semelhante nível de detalhe? Penso que na origem desta situação está a actual crise europeia, materializada no chamado impasse constitucional, provocada pelos referendos em França e na Holanda. A que acresce o facto de o período de reflexão sobre o devir da Constituição, iniciado em 2005, se ter revelado bastante inconclusivo.

Este ano havia uma série de circunstâncias que jogavam em favor de uma solução para a crise constitucional. Por um lado, a Presidência alemã e o crescente protagonismo da Senhora Merkel, que se tem vindo a revelar como uma estadista europeia de grande visão, comparável à geração de líderes europeus do Presidente Mário Soares, os quais revelaram um compromisso inabalável para com a construção europeia. Tal comprometimento tem escasseado na Europa, na última década. Por isso, o Conselho Europeu soube reconhecer a posição única da Senhora Merkel para ser mediadora de um acordo político com estas características.

Por outro lado, a conjuntura política nos dois outros principais países (para além da Alemanha) da União Europeia, com a anunciada mudança das chefias de governo em França e no Reino Unido. O novo Presidente francês já havia enunciado uma solução para o impasse constitucional, que passaria pela adopção de um mini-Tratado. Bem como o termo do consulado do Primeiro-Ministro britânico mais europeísta dos últimos 20 anos. Pelo que, de alguma forma se tinha de aproveitar o aludido europeísmo do Primeiro-Ministro Blair para obter uma solução que pudesse também englobar o Reino Unido.

Penso que o acordo que resultou da Cimeira da semana passada reflecte, de facto, o papel primordial que a Senhora Merkel conseguiu alcançar na cena política europeia, e a posição única em que se encontrava para obter um consenso que permitisse superar o impasse constitucional.

Contextualizando um pouco o acordo alcançado no Conselho Europeu, recordaria que no início da Presidência alemã ainda se pensava que seria possível salvar a Constituição europeia. Não a Constituição europeia no formato em que foi apresentada nos referendos de 2005, mas uma versão que seria objecto de uma espécie de cosmética jurídica que permitisse salvar a Constituição, através do seu desdobramento em dois novos Tratados. Um Tratado base, que resultaria da chamada Parte I da Constituição, a qual foi fruto dos trabalhos da Convenção Europeia, dirigida pelo Presidente Giscard d'Estaing; E um segundo Tratado, baseado na Parte III da Constituição europeia, a qual, na verdade, constituía um *remake* do Tratado da Comunidade Europeia.

Em meados da Presidência alemã – nos meses de Março, Abril – começou a ser evidente que esta solução já não teria possibilidade de obter o consenso dos 27 Estados-Membros, tendo aparecido no debate europeu a chamada solução do mini-Tratado.

A solução do mini-Tratado consistia em salvar o essencial. Pretendia-se recuperar o acervo da Constituição europeia, o valor acrescentado produzido pelo Tratado Constitucional. Ou seja, resgatar o conjunto de alterações que os Estados-membros tinham acordado em 2004, e que introduziam uma melhoria no funcionamento da União Europeia. Portanto, a solução mini-Tratado consistia nos Estados-membros adoptarem um Tratado que fosse o mais próximo possível da Parte I da Constituição europeia, abdicando da chamada Parte III do Tratado Constitucional, ou seja, o *remake* do Tratado de Roma.

Diga-se que o *remake* do Tratado de Roma era importante porque conferia à União Europeia uma lógica de cidadania. A Comunidade Europeia repousa ainda na integração económica, sendo caracterizada por uma lógica acentuadamente mercantil. A União do século XXI pretende ser uma união de Estados, mas também de cidadãos, que se revê mais num Tratado inspirado por uma lógica de cidadania, do que num acordo regido por uma lógica mercantil. Embora a alteração da lógica subjacente, promovida pela Parte III, fosse interessante, a meio da Presidência alemã já se havia abandonado o cenário que permitiria recuperar na íntegra essa Parte do Tratado Constitucional.

Na segunda metade da Presidência alemã ficou claro que não seria possível salvar toda a Constituição europeia, tendo emergido a ideia de adoptar um tratado simplificado, solução apoiada pela França do Presidente Sarkozy. O Conselho Europeu de Junho de 2007 adoptou uma solução que os franceses apelidam "Tratado modificador", ou Tratado Reformador, na versão portuguesa. No desfecho da crise constitucional da União é, todavia, forçoso sublinhar o contributo essencial dado pela Alemanha.

Qual o balanço geral que se poderá fazer do mandato para o chamado Tratado Reformador? O Tratado que resultará da concretização deste mandato mantém os actuais Tratados em vigor. Nesse aspecto, dissocia-se formalmente do Tratado Constitucional, que os substituía. Mas ao mesmo tempo que enterra a Constituição europeia, o novo Tratado recupera todo o acervo da mesma Constituição. Portanto, realiza um compromisso entre duas visões aparentemente contrastantes sobre o Tratado Constitucional.

Em termos de dissemelhanças temos, portanto, uma diferença formal que consiste no abandono da Constituição europeia e na manutenção dos Tratados vigentes. Recordo que se fez um Tratado Constitucional porque se queria simplificar os Tratados, para melhorar a relação dos cidadãos com as instituições europeias e com o processo de integração, melhorando a legibilidade dos Tratados para que a União Europeia não fosse uma entidade destinada apenas aos burocratas de Bruxelas – de que fala o Dr. Pacheco Pereira – e a alguns iluminados, como tem sido nos últimos 50 anos.

Obviamente que os Tratados são pouco legíveis, pelo que tem havido problemas a nível referendário, sobretudo quando os cidadãos lêem os Tratado de forma voluntária, revelando dificuldade em apreender o respectivo conteúdo. Nesse aspecto a solução encontrada não foi a ideal, pelo que é de lamentar que não se tenha podido recuperar a melhoria de legibilidade que a Constituição introduzia.

Contudo, em termos de simplificação creio que a solução que decorre do mandato tem aspectos positivos. Por um lado, acaba-se com uma situação anacrónica que existe nos actuais Tratados que é o sistema de pilares – que foi uma invenção da Cimeira de Maastricht, por sugestão do Ministro dos Negócios Estrangeiros britânico de então. É uma situação absurda e difícil de explicar aos cidadãos europeus, ou a quaisquer outros que pretendam entender os motivos por que a União Europeia repousa sobre três pilares distintos.

Com o novo Tratado a Comunidade Europeia será absorvida pela União Europeia, pondo-se termo à separação existente entre União e Comunidade. Em virtude do desaparecimento da Comunidade Europeia, que tem personalidade jurídica, o Tratado Reformador conferirá personalidade jurídica à União Europeia, de forma a assegurar a continuidade dos seus compromissos no plano internacional. Pelo que a atribuição de personalidade jurídica à União Europeia não implica um desenvolvimento de

A *Presidência Portuguesa das Comunidades Europeias em 2007 e a Situação da UE* 529

tipo federal, sendo antes consequência do desaparecimento da Comunidade Europeia.

No que se refere aos motivos que constituíam a razão de ser da arquitectura em pilares, conseguiu-se uma solução que atende às preocupações de alguns Estados-Membros. A Política Externa e de Segurança Comum, que é a parte mais sensível da União, porque directamente relacionada com o conceito de soberania nacional, mantém-se como uma área que se rege por um modelo de funcionamento estritamente intergovernamental, tendo sido incluída na estrutura do Tratado da União Europeia.

Em termos de conteúdo, o mandato para a negociação do novo Tratado procurou eliminar todos os aspectos que pudessem ser associáveis à ideia de Estado no Tratado Constitucional, tendo operado uma limpeza cirúrgica dessas mesmas disposições. O mandato enfatiza que não se trata de realizar um Tratado Constitucional, embora os Tratados sejam há muito considerados como carta constitucional pelo Tribunal de Justiça. São suprimidas as disposições relativas aos símbolos da União, tais como o hino, a bandeira e o dia. É abandonada a expressão Ministro dos Negócios Estrangeiros da União, mas mantida a mesma função na figura do Alto Representante, sendo que o conteúdo é mais relevante que a designação. Houve também a preocupação de acabar com as categorias formais de lei europeia e de lei-quadro europeia (não sei se os Estados-membros adversários da Constituição preferiam as designações regulamento e directiva, mas são questões de gosto). O mandato retirou do conteúdo do futuro Tratado uma norma que também causava apreensão em certas correntes de pensamento, por referir que o Direito europeu prevalece sobre o Direito nacional; na verdade, vai continuar a prevalecer – já prevalece desde 1964, por efeito da jurisprudência do Tribunal de Justiça – só que não fica escrito no texto do Tratado, mantendo-se a opacidade do princípio do primado. Se considerarmos que a democracia se funda na transparência, seria preferível que o primado do direito da União decorresse dos Tratados. Assim, mantém-se uma solução cujo conhecimento se encontra apenas ao alcance dos iniciados.

Em relação à estrutura do Tratado Reformador, creio que se verifica algum progresso. Embora se mantenham os dois Tratados vigentes, o Tratado da União Europeia recebe importantes alterações em termos de estrutura. Em particular, são introduzidos dois novos Títulos, um relativo aos princípios democráticos, que enumera os valores políticos da União Europeia – democracia representativa, democracia participativa, cidadania, iniciativa legislativa popular – tal como sucedia na Constituição europeia. O Tratado da União passará também a incluir um Título dedicado às Instituições. De certo modo, pode afirmar-se que a futura estrutura do Tratado da União se inspira naquela que orientava a Parte I da Constituição, aproximando-o do formato de um Tratado base.

Por outro lado, o outro fundamento específico da intergovernamentalidade – o famoso terceiro pilar, relativo à cooperação policial e judiciária em matéria penal – é retirado do Tratado base, ou seja, do Tratado da União Europeia, sendo remetido para o Tratado da Comunidade Europeia, que se passará a designar Tratado sobre o funcionamento da União. É curioso notar que este Tratado terá uma designação próxima da epígrafe da Parte III do Tratado Constitucional, intitulada Políticas e Funcionamento da União. Com o Tratado Reformador passará a ser referido como Tratado sobre o funcionamento da União, mas as políticas estão todas incluídas neste Tratado, com excepção da política externa.

Outro desenvolvimento interessante para a União Europeia – que tem um forte compromisso na tutela dos direitos humanos – é relativo à Carta dos Direitos Fundamentais (que é uma espécie de declaração de direitos dos cidadãos no confronto das instituições da União, e dos demais poderes públicos que apliquem o direito comunitário), a qual passará a ter força jurídica. Embora não seja incorporada no texto dos Tratados, como sucedia na Constituição europeia, o Tratado da União conterá uma disposição que lhe atribui natureza vinculativa.

Por outro lado, há também um reforço da posição dos Parlamentos nacionais no processo político da União. Creio que é um aspecto interessante porque a União Europeia sofre de uma crise de legitimidade política, sendo que os Parlamentos nacionais são tidos como órgãos políticos dotados de maior legitimidade que as instituições europeias. Portanto, se os Parlamentos nacionais estiverem mais envolvidos no processo político europeu é de esperar que tal possa constituir um contributo para melhorar a qualidade da democracia europeia. Comparativamente ao Tratado Constitucional o Tratado Reformador prevê, inclusive, um reforço do papel dos Parlamentos nacionais.

O chamado pacote institucional estabelecido pela Constituição europeia mantém-se na íntegra, ou seja, o Conselho Europeu é reconhecido como instituição e terá uma Presidência própria; o Conselho de Ministros adoptará o sistema de votação por maioria qualificada definido pelo Tratado Constitucional, bem como as alterações ao funcionamento das

A *Presidência Portuguesa das Comunidades Europeias em 2007 e a Situação da UE* 531

Presidências rotativas; a Comissão verá a sua composição reduzida; o Parlamento Europeu conhecerá um incremento dos seus poderes legislativo e orçamental; foi suprimida a designação Ministro dos Negócios Estrangeiros, mas é prevista a existência de um Alto Representante para os Negócios Estrangeiros, com as mesmas funções.

De notar, ainda, que é introduzida uma norma nos Tratados – proveniente da Constituição europeia – visando tranquilizar eventuais receios de que a União Europeia venha a assumir natureza estadual, prevendo expressamente que qualquer Estado-membro possa decidir abandonar a União, consagrando o direito de saída voluntária.

Relativamente ao Tratado sobre o funcionamento da União Europeia, poderia existir dificuldade em perceber como se compatibilizará com o Tratado da União, mas o mandato para a Conferência intergovernamental refere que são dois Tratados com idêntica força jurídica. Portanto, embora o Tratado sobre o funcionamento da União possa ser considerado como um Tratado de aplicação do Tratado base, certo é que têm o mesmo valor jurídico, ou seja, a sua validade não decorre das disposições do Tratado da União.

Em síntese, e porque estou no limite de tempo da minha intervenção, vou enunciar brevemente o que o Tratado sobre o funcionamento da União irá conter. Receberá um Título sobre a delimitação de competências (a que os alemães eram particularmente apegados) ou seja, será este Tratado que regulará a questão de saber "quem faz o quê". A divisão de competências entre a União Europeia e os Estados-membros foi um tema muito discutido na Convenção europeia – a qual permitiu uma significativa clarificação na matéria – sendo que essas normas serão agora recuperadas pelo Tratado sobre o funcionamento da União.

Do mesmo modo, o Tratado sobre o funcionamento da União incluirá as disposições da Constituição europeia sobre a votação por maioria qualificada; a distinção entre actos legislativos e actos não legislativos, fazendo a ligação no processo legislativo entre as categorias dos actos jurídicos e o procedimento relativo à sua adopção; as normas relativas ao espaço de liberdade, segurança e justiça, que englobam as disposições do actual terceiro pilar.

Prevê-se ainda que a União possa aderir à Convenção Europeia dos Direitos do Homem, o que é também um desenvolvimento em prol da democracia europeia, porque os Estados-membros são fiscalizados pelo sistema desta Convenção, sendo que a mesma supervisão externa não se verifica no caso do direito da União.

Em conclusão, diria que o mandato para a conferência intergovernamental mantém o acervo da Constituição europeia, embora não pareça poder gerar a aprovação de um Tratado simplificado. À primeira vista parecerá mesmo um Tratado complicado, porque será um Tratado com uma filigrana de normas muito mais complexa que o Tratado Constitucional.

Ficaria por aqui. Muito obrigado.

A PRESIDÊNCIA PORTUGUESA DAS COMUNIDADES EUROPEIAS EM 2007 E A SITUAÇÃO DA UNIÃO EUROPEIA

MESA REDONDA

CARLOS BLANCO DE MORAIS[*]

Muito obrigado Senhor Professor Paz Ferreira, a quem felicito, juntamente com o Professor Pitta e Cunha, pelo êxito deste Congresso e dos presentes trabalhos.

Falarei apenas sobre a temática do Tratado dito "Reformador", desacoplada de enquadramento político, dado que o mesmo foi feito pelos oradores que me precederam.

1. Começarei pelas perspectivas que aguardam a presidência portuguesa. Em face do acordo conseguido no último Conselho Europeu em Bruxelas, julgo que o sucesso ou insucesso da presidência portuguesa, sem prejuízo dos seus demais propósitos ambiciosos, ficará irremediavelmente ligada à adopção, ou não adopção, do Tratado reformador, seja por mérito próprio, seja por mérito alheio. Isto, não só porque o Tratado foi considerado como o mais importante objectivo da presidência portuguesa, mas porque foi no último Conselho que, graças à hábil e paciente diplomacia alemã, foram criados os pressupostos para poder ter lugar a realização de uma CIG (Conferência Inter-Governamental), emergindo, por conseguinte, fortes expectativas relativamente à adopção do Tratado reformador.

---

[*] Professor de Direito Constitucional e Direito Internacional Público da Faculdade de Direito de Lisboa.

Penso, apesar de tudo, que a presidência portuguesa se irá defrontar quer com obstáculos, quer com algumas facilidades instrumentais. As dificuldades, por exemplo, poderão radicar na aptidão ou não dos negociadores da presidência portuguesa em se desembaraçarem de algum lastro relativo às posições pro-constitucionalistas que assumiram antes do Conselho de Junho bem como na sua capacidade discutível para se adaptarem a uma nova realidade ditada por exigências de pragmatismo que não admitem mais, enfim, qualquer espécie mítica neo-federal, impondo-se ao invés a necessidade de ajustamento a difíceis equilíbrios no âmbito de uma política realista. Será um regresso a uma certa *realpolitik* ditada pelas circunstâncias que rodearam precisamente o último Conselho.

Em segundo lugar, outro aspecto que poderá dificultar a presidência portuguesa dirá respeito ao peso muito relativo de Portugal, que será um dos Estados-membros que mais debilitado sairá com o sistema de votação que de alguma forma irá ser consagrado. E esse peso específico, como pólo de condução negocial, irá defrontar-se com os imponderáveis de que falou o professor Marcelo Rebelo de Sousa e dificuldades que irão surgir necessariamente. Hoje já surgiram notícias sobre uma Polónia que repensa compromissos assumidos, fazendo antever factores de perturbação que poderão eventualmente manifestar-se nos últimos momentos da CIG.

Finalmente, importa destacar que ficará à prova a capacidade ou não da presidência portuguesa em reunir um conjunto de especialistas de Direito Comunitário, bem como de juristas e de redactores hábeis que, em articulação com juristas da União e dos Estados que contam sobretudo neste processo, consigam conferir o mínimo de coerência no texto normativo que se prepara; tal como aqui foi dito o articulado é muito complexo, sendo certo que é nas palavras que se esconde muitas vezes o diabo. Muitos compromissos estão já efectivamente formalizados num mandato, mas é efectivamente muitas vezes na redacção sobre pontos delicados que podem surgir grandes impasses, quer em conceitos indeterminados, quer em normas excessivamente determinadas. Portanto, terá de haver alguma habilidade e autonomia própria da presidência no seu contributo para a redacção.

Quanto às vantagens oferecidas à presidência portuguesa, entendo que os efeitos recentes do triunfo de Nicolas Sarkozy nas eleições francesas tiveram o mérito de sepultar a emergência de uma "Constituição Europeia" e gerar uma nova dinâmica em torno de um Tratado mais pragmático e mais ajustado aos paradigmas tradicionais que marcaram a construção europeia, e menos afeiçoado a uma versão soldada a um quimérico conceito constituinte que suscitaria objecções em diversos Estados e dificultaria ao extremo, o trabalho do Governo de Lisboa.

Em segundo lugar, e aqui parece-me uma questão importante, o eventual sucesso dependerá também do mandato preciso e pormenorizado que saiu do Conselho Europeu, o qual, não dará grande margem de actuação ao Estados, já que terá todos os preceitos, não direi previamente redigidos, mas suficientemente densificados quanto ao seu sentido e objectivos. Acho que esse relativo acabamento, que constitui um mérito da Presidência alemã, resulta ser positivo na medida em que, se o mandato português fosse excessivamente amplo... eu não quero ser céptico, mas tenho as mais sérias dúvidas que, alguma vez, dele saísse qualquer espécie de Tratado que viesse a merecer um consenso alargado. Por outro lado, o facto de a presidência portuguesa poder contar com a colaboração estreita de um português como presidente da Comissão Europeia (o qual, sobretudo nos últimos tempos, reforçou o seu peso institucional junto de alguns Estados que contam para a existência de um Tratado institucional), não deixa de ser um factor importante para o trabalho do Governo. Finalmente, algum consenso institucional entre os principais órgãos de soberania e dos grandes partidos portugueses sobre a nova configuração do Tratado, configura um factor de fluidez interna que ajudará o processo negocial.

Direi, nestes termos, que há aspectos positivos e negativos que aguardam a presidência portuguesa mas, sem ser meteorologista, vislumbra-se talvez mais sol do que nuvens.

2. Outra questão que está ligada ao Tratado e que se dirige à da ordem interna portuguesa (sem prejuízo de poder afectar outros Estados e, como tal, a existência do tratado) será a da convocação ou não de um referendo nacional. Trata-se de uma matéria interessantíssima, mas que se arrisca a envenenar desnecessariamente a presidência portuguesa, sendo prematuro promover no momento presente a mesma discussão. E é prematuro porque nem tudo o que será o futuro Tratado se encontra necessariamente pré-determinado e fixado em detalhe, pelo que, enquanto não se conhecer efectivamente o teor concreto das normas dessa convenção, considero que não existirão razões convincentes e oportunas para discutir a convocação de um acto referendário. É que, se efectivamente não se colocarem questões fundamentais de soberania que o anterior Tratado transportava (como a da transição para a futura criação de um Estado europeu de recorte federal, a qual tinha no art.º I-6º, uma regra lapidar), não haverá razão para submeter a nova Convenção a referendo, tal como não houve relativamente a algumas Convenções anteriores. Isto, apesar da perda real de poder que irá inevitavelmente atingir Portugal e outros pequenos e médios Estados relativamente ao sistema de votação inerente às decisões no Parlamento e Conselho europeus.

É óbvio que podem surgir, e repito as minhas palavras de há pouco, problemas críticos na redacção das normas do Tratado, e o Dr. Pacheco Pereira sublinhou-o cabalmente. Existe, efectivamente, o risco de a propósito do póstumo art.º I-6.º, que implicava uma cláusula de prevalência total do Direito da União Europeia sobre o direito nacional (nele compreendidas as Constituições dos Estados), se defraudar a intenção já expressa de o remover, através da formulação de declarações interpretativas no mesmo sentido. Resta, pois, saber se a declaração que irá constar sobre essa matéria, com remissão para a jurisprudência do Tratado de Justiça das Comunidades terá ou não valor jurídico. A ser uma declaração política parece inequívoco que não terá força imperativa. Só que cenários ambíguos presos à natureza dessa declaração, que impliquem a existência de mecanismos ou institutos federais dissimulados por detrás de redacções foscas, podem muito justamente justificar a convocação de um referendo. Dir-se-á, portanto, que a questão referendária é, para já, prematura, e se lançada antes da redacção final do tratado pode prejudicar a estratégia de toda a presidência portuguesa.

Já agora, sobre esta problemática das cláusulas de prevalência de direito europeu, gostaria de formular uma amiga discordância com o professor Goucha Soares e que é a seguinte: não está efectivamente consagrado no âmbito do direito positivo da União Europeia em vigor, nenhuma cláusula de prevalência das normas comunitárias sobre as Constituições dos Estados. Existe uma jurisprudência do Tribunal de Justiça das Comunidades que defende esse primado e que considera que já vigora uma "Carta Constitucional" que compreende todo o "acquis" comunitário. Só que esse entendimento faz parte do *obiter dicta* da jurisprudência do mesmo Tribunal europeu que não é fonte de direito interno. Ora, eu quero advertir para o facto (e isso é muito importante porque se trata de uma questão jurídica que emergiu sobretudo nos últimos anos), que a jurisprudência do Tribunal das Comunidades Europeias foi directamente enfrentada por diversos Tribunais Constitucionais que dizem (e

A Presidência Portuguesa das Comunidades Europeias em 2007 e a Situação da UE 537

foco essencialmente o Tribunal Constitucional alemão, o Conselho Constitucional francês e o Tribunal Constitucional italiano) que, efectivamente, o direito Comunitário (vide tratados, regulamentos e decisões) prevalece inclusivamente sobre alguns aspectos da Constituição dos Estados, menos sobre os princípios e as normas estruturantes dessas Constituições, fórmula que é um pouco diferente da dos princípios fundamentais do Estado de Direito democrático que a nossa Constituição consagrou na revisão de 2004.

Ora, existe um braço de ferro entre os órgãos de justiça constitucional dos Estados e o Tribunal de Justiça das Comunidades e, como se sabe, pela primeira vez, o Tribunal Constitucional alemão declarou muito recentemente a inconstitucionalidade de uma decisão-quadro comunitária, assim como fez o Tribunal Constitucional polaco e o Supremo Tribunal do Chipre. Portanto, não há consenso jurisprudencial sobre esta matéria do alcance do primado do direito europeu sobre normas constitucionais dado que a jurisprudência de alguns Tribunais Constitucionais contesta efectivamente esse primado em áreas estruturantes das Constituições. Portanto este não é um problema fechado, e é importante, senão mesmo vital, que a disposição do art.º I-6.º tenha desaparecido do Tratado Reformador fazendo toda esta questão, tão pouco discutida no plano jurídico e político, uma importante diferença entre os dois tratados.

Portanto, quanto ao referendo a recomendação será a de um *wait and see*, e esperar para ver qual o conteúdo final das normas do Tratado. Convocar um referendo quando nomeadamente muitos soberanistas moderados que se opunham ao Tratado Constitucional, como sucedia com professores universitários e líderes empresariais e sindicais (os quais apresentaram uma petição para o controlo de constitucionalidade da revisão constitucional de 2004, que alterou o art.º 8.º da CRP, no sentido de o ajustar ao nado-morto art.º I-6.º do Tratado Constitucional) poderão não ter razões para se oporem ao novo texto equivalerá a referendar um Tratado sem virtual oposição (a qual se reduziria a pequenos partidos marxistas). E será também promover um referendo sem a hipótese de um debate consistente e relevante, correndo-se o risco de uma abstenção esmagadora que poderá eventualmente deslegitimar, por via referendária, algo que se pretendia legitimar nas urnas.

3. Finalmente, num apontamento muito breve e puramente politológico, entendo que o desastrado processo pseudo-constituinte europeu que agora se exauriu no último Conselho tornou patente, na Europa, um duelo de legitimidades políticas, a saber: a legitimidade legal-racional dos parlamentos nacionais que pretendiam dotar a Europa de uma Constituição e a legitimidade de uma democracia referendária nacional que foi processada em dois Estados-membros, e que matou literalmente a Constituição europeia. Eventualmente terá sido um único desses Estados, a França, a fazê-lo, constituindo a posterior vitória eleitoral do Presidente Sarkozy o golpe de misericórdia no processo, na medida em que abandonou a ideia de Constituição em favor de um Tratado reformador dito abreviado, tendo sido esta ideia de uma convenção podada dos elementos federais que acabou por passar no último Conselho europeu.

Portanto, o impedimento ao nascimento do Tratado Constitucional europeu decorreu necessariamente de referendos nacionais. E nestes, o "não" francês foi um "não" dotado de um peso totalmente diferente do "não" holandês ao mesmo tratado, e do "não" irlandês e dinamarquês a outros Tratados. É que, em relação aos pequenos Estados que recusaram Tratados institucionais, a União poderia sempre forçá-los a realizar tantos referendos, quanto os necessários até à obtenção de um "sim". Já quanto à França foi consensualizado que tal não era possível tendo-se chegado a um impasse, na medida em que não era exequível avançar para uma Constituição ou para uma construção política da Europa, à margem de um dos Estados fundadores que compõe o chamado motor da União.

A conclusão portanto quanto a este aspecto é que não só a democracia representativa foi posta em causa por uma democracia referendária nacional, mas também de que na construção europeia, todos os referendos são iguais, mas haverá seguramente alguns mais iguais do que outros.

Terminaria com uma brevíssima nota pós-federal. Foi dito aqui, e é em parte verdade, que os dois novos Tratados de alguma forma absorvem cerca de 80 a 90% daquilo que era o texto da Constituição Europeia. Só que aquilo que opôs, nomeadamente em Portugal, um sector da elite da sociedade civil à Constituição Europeia, não foi apenas o sistema de votação (o qual é particularmente importante dado que reforça uns Estados em detrimento de outros, e Portugal é daqueles que pior sai deste processo) nem outras questões não menos relevantes como a gestão europeia dos recursos marinhos na Zona Económica Exclusiva (e que não estão ainda resolvidas). Foi sim, a imposição pretoriana de um conjunto de regras de claro recorte federal que marcavam aquilo que se pode chamar uma ideia de Constituição, um conceito de Constituição, um

A *Presidência Portuguesa das Comunidades Europeias em 2007 e a Situação da UE* 539

processo constituinte europeu. Ora, são esses elementos que desapareceram (a começar com o art.º I-6.º e a acabar na conversão das directivas, regulamentos e decisões em normas típicas de um Estado, como seriam as leis-quadro, leis e actos administrativos).

Quanto a outros elementos eliminados, embora se possa dizer que serão "apenas" elementos mitológicos, ou simbólicos (ideia de Constituição, incorporação da carta de direitos no texto constitucional, o hino, a bandeira e o ministros dos negócios estrangeiros europeu), não deixam os mesmos de assumir, nessa qualidade, uma incontornável relevância que ultrapassa o formalismo jurídico. E porquê? Porque são aqueles elementos os que traduzem a ideia de um momento constituinte inerente à formação de um novo Estado, que era o que se queria construir à revelia dos povos da Europa. Não há, na realidade, uma Constituição sem uma mítica e um processo constituinte e, a este propósito veja-se a patética tentativa do "Presidium" da Convenção giscardiana em reviver Filadélfia, sem que houvesse, contudo, uma alma constituinte radicada e legitimada na vontade livre dos povos da Europa. Ora, essa alma, como reconheceu o dr. Mário Soares em intervenção anterior, está ausente ou desapareceu no Tratado reformador, e esse é talvez o aspecto mais interessante e positivo do processo de adopção do mesmo tratado. Não se trata de matar o espírito europeu, mas sim matar uma determinada concepção, a meu ver perigosa, de construção europeia.

Em suma, aquilo que ocorreu foi talvez o nascimento de uma Europa mais realista e mais pragmática, onde emerge uma nova geração política, e o eventual ocaso de uma velha geração de construtores bem como de um outro conceito mítico de Europa, apostado em erigir uma Constituição federal em sobre uma instável Torre de Babel. Ora, será melhor ter um Tratado, mesmo juridicamente inextricável, que faça funcionar 27 Estados, do que eventualmente uma Europa proto-federal assente em pés de barro e pronta a desmoronar-se à primeira crise.

E com isto terminaria a minha intervenção um pouco em contra--corrente com as anteriores. Muito obrigado.

ÍNDICE

Apresentação 5

Programa 7

Introdução – Paulo de Pitta e Cunha 11

Introduction – Paulo de Pitta e Cunha 13

50 ans d'intégration européenne: Du Plan Schuman à la période de réflexion sur la Constitution européenne – Etienne Cerexhe 15

European integration as a realistic utopia – Glyn Morgan 23

The European integration in a global world – Loukas Tsoukalis 45

The evolution of the judicial system of the European Union – Koen Lenaerts 51

O modelo social europeu e a Estratégia de Lisboa – António Vitorino .. 85

Les élargissements et les limites de l'Union Européenne – Jean-Claude Gautron 97

Democracy and European integration: A legacy of tensions, a re-conceptualisation and recent true conflicts – Christian Joerges 111

Les referenda dans le processus de ratification des Traités européens – Philippe Moreau Defarges 151

A cooperação externa da União Europeia – Eduardo Paz Ferreira 159

Will the Constitution make EU decision-making easier? – Simon Hix 169

542 *A Europa e os Desafios do Século XXI*

The Constitution of Europe: Resquiecat in pacem – Joseph Weiler 179

Constituição Europeia e Constituição da República Portuguesa – Rui Manuel Moura Ramos 185

As Presidências portuguesas de 1992 e 2000 – Fernando Neves 195

L'évolution de la coordination des politiques économiques nationales aux différents stades de l'intégration européenne – Jacques Bourrinet 205

The ratification of European Treaties – Legal and constitutional basis of a European referendum – Martin Seidel 215

A União Europeia e outros sistemas de integração – Luiz Olavo Baptista .. 237

The stability and growth pact and its revision – Vito Tanzi 249

A União Europeia: A caminho de um Orçamento Federal – J. Silva Lopes . 263

Intellectual property rights are becoming unbalanced in the United States – Douglas E. Rosenthal 277

The redistribution function of the European Union – Willem Molle 289

The U.S. perception and attitude towards the EU: Trends on foreign policy and the failure of the Constitution – Joaquín Roy 295

A função reguladora e as estruturas de regulação na União Europeia – Luís D. Silva Morais 323

A União Europeia nas negociações comerciais internacionais – Teresa Moreira 341

The European reaction to climate changes – Dimitri Zenghelis 357

How to tackle EU's energy dependency? – P. J. Slot and N. Tezcan 381

As diferentes visões da integração europeia – Paulo de Pitta e Cunha .. 405

The different perspectives of European integration – Paulo de Pitta e Cunha 411

A Europa e os Desafios do Século XXI

Portugal e a Europa – O passado – Eduardo Vera-Cruz Pinto 419

Aspectos históricos da integração de portugal na Europa comunitária –
Manuel Lopes Porto 429

O euro e a economia portuguesa – João Ferreira do Amaral 445

O envolvimento na integração económica e na integração política – João
Salgueiro 453

European constitutionalism and three models of social Europe – Miguel
Poiares Maduro 469

Portugal na Europa e no mundo – Rui Machete 491

A política cultural europeia – Emílio Rui Vilar 497

O programa da presidência portugesa de 2007 – Luís Amado 505

A Presidência portuguesa das Comunidades Europeias em 2007 e a situação
da União Europeia – Mesa Redonda
Marcelo Rebelo de Sousa 515
António Goucha Soares 525
Carlos Blanco de Morais 533